JOHN WITHERSPOON'S
AMERICAN REVOLUTION

JOHN WITHERSPOON'S

AMERICAN REVOLUTION

Gideon Mailer

Published for the

OMOHUNDRO INSTITUTE OF

EARLY AMERICAN HISTORY AND CULTURE,

Williamsburg, Virginia,

by the

UNIVERSITY OF NORTH CAROLINA PRESS,

Chapel Hill

The Omohundro Institute of Early American History and Culture
is sponsored by the College of William and Mary. On November 15, 1996,
the Institute adopted the present name in honor of a bequest
from Malvern H. Omohundro, Jr.

© 2017 The University of North Carolina Press

Manufactured in the United States of America

The University of North Carolina Press has been a member
of the Green Press Initiative since 2003.

Cover images: Jonathan Fisher, *Nassau Hall, a North West Prospect,* 1807, oil on canvas, after engraving ca. 1764. Princeton University Art Museum / Art Resource, NY. *Inset:* Rembrandt Peale after Charles Willson Peale, *John Witherspoon,* 1794, oil on canvas. National Portrait Gallery, Smithsonian Institution; partial gift of Mrs. Samuel Matthews.

Parts of this book draw on previously published work: "Nehemias (Scotus) Americanus: Enlightenment and Religion between Scotland and America," *Historical Journal,* LIV (2011), 241–264; "Europe, the American Crisis, and Scottish Evangelism: The Primacy of Foreign Policy in the Kirk?" in William Mulligan and Brendan Simms, eds., *The Primacy of Foreign Policy in British History, 1660–2000* (Basingstoke, U.K., 2010), 119–136; "Anglo-Scottish Union and John Witherspoon's American Revolution," *William and Mary Quarterly,* 3d Ser., LXVII (2010), 709–746.

Library of Congress Cataloging-in-Publication Data
Names: Mailer, Gideon, author. | Omohundro Institute of Early American History & Culture.
Title: John Witherspoon's American Revolution / Gideon Mailer.
Description: Chapel Hill : University of North Carolina Press, [2016] | "Published for the Omohundro Institute of Early American History and Culture, Williamsburg, Virginia." | Includes bibliographical references and index.
Identifiers: LCCN 2016024829| ISBN 9781469628189 (cloth : alk. paper) | ISBN 9781469628196 (ebook)
Subjects: LCSH: Witherspoon, John, 1723-1794. | Presbyterian Church—United States— Clergy—Biography. | United States. Declaration of Independence—Signers—Biography. | Statesmen—United States—Biography. | United States. Continental Congress— History. | United States—History—Revolution, 1775-1783. | United States—Politics and government—1775-1783. | Church and state—United States—History. | Princeton University—History—18th century.
Classification: LCC E302.6.W7 M35 2016 | DDC 973.3029 [B] —dc23
LC record available at https://lccn.loc.gov/2016024829

For my parents, and for Betty Wood

ACKNOWLEDGMENTS

I owe so much to Betty Wood, who first supervised me in early American history for Part I of the Cambridge Tripos, before mentoring me through graduate work and beyond. We are the closest of friends. Betty's influence continues in the British Group of Early American Historians, which has supported and inspired me over the years. I offer particular thanks to Simon Middleton.

I am grateful for the path-defining work of the Eighteenth-Century Scottish Studies Society, especially Richard Sher, Roger Fechner, and Ned Landsman. Without Ned's work as a reviewer, mentor, and inspiration in the field, this project would be greatly diminished.

At the University of Cambridge, I am obliged to my early Director of Studies at Peterhouse, Scott Mandelbrote, for supervision in eighteenth-century history, and to the late Michael O'Brien for his razor-sharp thoughts and critiques. I thank the Faculty of History at Cambridge, particularly the American history subject group.

The U.K. Arts and Humanities Research Council provided financial support, and I appreciate as well the financial and intellectual support of the Master and Fellows of St. John's College, Cambridge, during my four-year postdoctoral Title A Fellowship. At St. John's, Sylvana Tomaselli became a special friend and mentor, always keen to discuss eighteenth-century intellectual thought, always guiding my professional path.

In Scotland, Ireland, England, and the United States, I am grateful for support, advice, and inspiration from scholars David Abulafia, Alexander Broadie, Frank Cogliano, Karen Collis, Sylvia Frey, Mark Goldie, Nancy Hewitt, Colin Kidd, James Kloppenberg, Tim Lockley, Michael Ledger Lomas, Ian McBride, the late Susan Manning, Peter Messer, Mary Beth Norton, Andrew Preston, Tom Rodgers, Sophia Rosenfeld, Steve Sarson, Brendan Simms, Tom Stammers, Hilary Stroh, Simon Szreter, William Harrison Taylor, and Peter Thompson.

At the University of Minnesota, Duluth, the College of Liberal Arts and, especially, Dean Susan Maher provided financial support as well as an environment of humanistic rigor. I thank my colleagues in the Department of History, led by Steve Matthews, for bringing me to the shores of Lake Superior and for mentoring me since I arrived in 2012. All my students, both in Cambridge and in Duluth, have helped me to refine my ideas. Thanks, in particular, to Garet Anderson-Lind. I sincerely appreciate the generosity of Mary Ellen Klemer and Andrew Klemer for looking after me and providing a home in my first months in Minnesota.

Invaluable to my work have been the librarians and research assistants at Cambridge in the University Library, St. John's College Library, the Seeley Historical Library, and Westminster College; at the Bodleian Library, University of Oxford; at the National Archives of Scotland and the National Library of Scotland, Edinburgh; at the British Library, London; at the Manuscripts and Archives Division in the New York Public Library; at the Seeley G. Mudd Manuscript Library at Princeton University; at the New Jersey Historical Society, Newark; in the University of Minnesota library system; and at the Rare Books and Special Collections Division in the Library of Congress, Washington, D.C. I would like to offer special thanks to Eric Frazier at the Library of Congress for all his help locating material.

I owe an extraordinary debt of gratitude to the Omohundro Institute of Early American History and Culture. Christopher Grasso and the editors and reviewers at the *William and Mary Quarterly* helped me to refine important concepts and offered priceless care and attention. And it was an honor and a privilege to work with the Book Publications team at the Institute and at the University of North Carolina Press. I thank the anonymous reviewers of this book for their lengthy and tremendously incisive comments. Fredrika J. Teute offered all the rigor, precision, and flair I had heard so much about from other scholars. Over the years, she steered my project in ways that enabled me to incorporate many different historiographies and analytical traditions. Nadine Zimmerli also refined my arguments and guided the chapters with a laser focus. Her editorial work clarified some important concepts that I had always struggled to explain in ways that were not byzantine. Her suggestions allowed me to broaden the scope of this study. Virginia Montijo Chew offered one further layer of penetrating analysis, both conceptual and stylistic. Her comments on language, structure of argument, and scholarly method have changed this project. To all three scholars and to the team of editorial apprentices who worked under their guidance and training: you have provided a model that will inspire me forever.

Finally, thank you to my friends and family, who have supported me during the many, many years of this project: Avril, Clifford, Gregory, Nicholas, Leanna, Victoria, Judy, Jessica, Nicola, Moss, Karen, Peter, Olivia, Felicity, Mike, Linda, Martin, Terence, Bethan, and my grandmother Sarah, who once asked me about this book project: "What more can anyone say about these people?"

CONTENTS

ILLUSTRATIONS

❧❧

JOHN WITHERSPOON'S
AMERICAN REVOLUTION

*"She thinks she's Providence, thought Sandy, she thinks
she is the God of Calvin, she sees the beginning and the end."*
"Where there is no vision, Miss Brodie had assured them, the people perish."
MURIEL SPARK, *The Prime of Miss Jean Brodie*

INTRODUCTION

Enlightenment and Religion between Scotland and America

How deeply affecting is it that those who were often the same in complexion, in blood, in language, and in religion should, notwithstanding, have butchered one another with unrelenting rage and gloried in the deed? In the two centuries since British subjects and American Revolutionaries stabbed, clubbed, maimed, shot, and tortured one another, further butchery, often internecine, has taken place through and beyond the Atlantic world. Nonetheless, it remains startling to recall the violent exchange between cousins and even brothers and sisters during the final decades of the eighteenth century, as British America became something called the United States.

A few weeks before he became the only clergyman to sign the American Declaration of Independence, John Witherspoon surveyed the earliest skirmishes of the imperial crisis, asked similar rhetorical questions, and made similarly bleak observations. In his sermon, *The Dominion of Providence over the Passions of Men,* he found evidence of the "Wrath of Man" in the quick transformation of imperial subjects into warring enemies. Six months later, most of his personal library would burn to ashes, set alight by British soldiers and Hessian mercenaries. In the fire there would be books by Augustine and John Calvin, pamphlets written by Scottish Enlightenment thinkers and by their Scottish evangelical foes, works in Greek and Latin, and manuscripts on the colonization of North America. Witherspoon's son would be buried in a grave that had been dug for fallen patriots. A few years later, another son would be captured and imprisoned by British forces.[1]

1. John Witherspoon, *The Dominion of Providence over the Passions of Men* . . . , in [Ashbel Green, ed.], *The Works of the Rev. John Witherspoon, D.D.L.L.D. Late President of the College at Princeton, New-Jersey* . . . , 2d ed., rev., 4 vols. (Philadelphia, 1802), III, 17, 37. There are two American editions of Witherspoon's *Works,* which were first printed in 1800–1801 and in 1802. Both were published by William Woodward in Philadelphia and edited by Witherspoon's former student, the Reverend Ashbel Green (1762–1848). Green graduated from the College of New Jersey in 1783 and served as president of the College between 1812 and 1822. In his own account of the life of Witherspoon, contained in a manuscript written between 1830 and 1835, Green explains that only Witherspoon's "Lectures on Moral Philosophy" and "Lectures on Eloquence" were complete as printed in his *Works.* See Ashbel Green, *The Life of the Revd John Witherspoon, D.D., LL. D.: With a Brief Review of His Writings and a Summary Estimate of His Character*

There was a poignant irony in the suffering of Witherspoon's offspring at the hands of the British army and its German proxies. Three decades earlier, as a young evangelical minister, Witherspoon had fought for the Protestant cause of a Hanoverian king and a British union. In early 1746, "for the support of our religion and liberty," he collected £88 15s. to help the military effort against Charles Edward Stuart, the "Young Pretender" to the British throne. Witherspoon commanded nearly 150 Scottish soldiers against men who viewed the Hanoverian royal line as an illegitimate usurper of the religious and political legacy of the Stuart dynasty. In 1746, he sat in a stone chamber, temporarily imprisoned by Jacobite rebels for supporting the British Empire's status quo, "our religion and liberty." Thirty years later, having moved from Scotland to New Jersey, he would laud "American religion." Though he noted the problem of "wrath" and "pride" on both sides of the Revolutionary conflict, he also alluded to America's "Spirit of Liberty" from Westminster. As the president of the College of New Jersey (later known as Princeton University), he became a mentor to U.S. constitutional architect James Madison. As a member of the nascent American Congress, he would recommend "that a plan of union should be laid down for all the colonies" to resist injustices in British policy: "The Congress is, properly speaking, the representative of the great body of the people of North America."[2]

---

and Talents, ed. Henry Lyttleton Savage (Princeton, N.J., 1973), 127-128, 183-185. In the "Advertisement" that prefaced the revised second edition of Witherspoon's works, Green suggested that chronology of content was less important than its thematic order; see Greene, "Advertisement to the Second American Edition," in [Green, ed.], *Works of Witherspoon,* 1. There were two Scottish editions of Witherspoon's *Works,* which were published in Edinburgh in 1804-1805 and 1815. The contents of all four editions are the same except for additional maxims that Witherspoon added to his *Ecclesiastical Characteristics* (1753) that were published in his American editions. The Scottish editions of the *Works* contain more misprints and errors than the American editions. Thus, the second Philadelphia edition, published in 1802, is here used. For the Scottish editions, see *The Works of John Witherspoon . . . D.D. . . . ,* 9 vols. (Edinburgh, 1804), and the subsequent 1815 Edinburgh edition. On the death of Witherspoon's son at the Battle of Germantown, see [Rufus W. Griswold], *Washington and the Generals of the American Revolution* (Philadelphia, 1856), 328. On the capture and subsequent release of Witherspoon's other son, see Committee for Foreign Affairs to Benjamin Franklin, May 9, 1781, in Leonard W. Labaree et al., eds., *The Papers of Benjamin Franklin,* 41 vols. to date (New Haven, Conn., 1959-), XXXV, 48; Green, *Life of the Revd John Witherspoon,* ed. Savage, 206-207. On the burning of the library in Nassau Hall after the Battle of Princeton, see Thomas Sullivan, "The Battle of Princeton" (January 1777), *Pennsylvania Magazine of History and Biography,* XXXII (1908), 54; Thomas Nelson to Thomas Jefferson, Jan. 2, 1777, in Julian P. Boyd et al., eds., *The Papers of Thomas Jefferson,* II (Princeton, N.J., 1950), 4.

2. The description of "religion and liberty" is attributed to Witherspoon, accompanied by his

Adam Ferguson, a professor of moral philosophy at the University of Edinburgh and a British commissioner to the colonies, wrote the following of "Johnny Witherspoons" in a 1779 letter to Alexander Carlyle: "We have 1200 miles of Territory in Length occupied by about 3,000,000 People of which there are about 1,500,000 with Johnny Witherspoons at their head against us. . . . I tremble at the thoughts of their Cunning and determination opposed to us." Like Ferguson, Carlyle had studied with "Johnny" at Edinburgh during the late 1730s and early 1740s before rising through the educated ranks of the Church of Scotland. All three men had positioned themselves in support of the new British state in opposition to Jacobites in 1745 and 1746. Yet Witherspoon soon became known for his public opposition to their civic, religious, and philosophical stance. In the two decades before his 1768 departure for America, Witherspoon became estranged from his friends, a member of an opposing theological and philosophical faction in the Kirk.[3]

Those who opposed Witherspoon formulated a religious and intellectual stance that scholars have since defined as central to the eighteenth-century Scottish Enlightenment. Yet Ferguson and Carlyle would have been surprised to learn from later historians that "the Scottish Enlightenment Was Useful" to American founders, including Witherspoon, and that such an axiom would come to be loved by political scientists, popular historians, and Scottish diplomats visiting Washington D.C. Examining the wider meaning of Witherspoon's move from the Kirk to the American Congress, this book will question such a scholarly assumption. In emphasizing the civic necessity of personal religious conversion, Witherspoon and other Scottish evangelical ministers perceived their distinction from Scottish churchmen and moral philosophers who linked societal coherence to the innate ethical awareness of all people. When he highlighted "wrath" and "pride" on both sides of the Revolutionary conflict, Witherspoon deliberately exposed a continuing moral and philosophical tension between the chaos, the uncertainty, and the depravity of the imperial crisis and the enlightened association of common moral sensibility and civic cohesion. Witherspoon was painfully aware that former members of the same imperial union fought and died in the name

signature and a receipt for funds collected for the anti-Jacobite campaign; see Varnum Lansing Collins, *President Witherspoon: A Biography*, 2 vols. (Princeton, N.J., 1925), I, 22. See also James Dennistoun, ed., *The Cochrane Correspondence regarding the Affairs of Glasgow, 1745–6* (Glasgow, 1836), 120. For Witherspoon's statements, see John Witherspoon, *Address to the Inhabitants of Jamaica, and Other West-India Islands, in Behalf of the College of New Jersey*, in [Green, ed.], *Works of Witherspoon*, IV, 190; Witherspoon, "Thoughts on American Liberty," ibid., 297, 300.

3. For this often-quoted statement, see Adam Ferguson to Alexander Carlyle, Feb. 9, 1779, in Vincenzo Merolle, ed., *The Correspondence of Adam Ferguson*, 2 vols. (London, 1995), I, 201–202.

of ostensibly similar political and philosophical theories. He continued to doubt the innateness of moral benevolence through the American Revolutionary era, irrespective of political and national ideology. He incorporated the resulting philosophical tension in his teaching, in his religious proclamations, and in his developing political theory.[4]

The philosophical tension that Witherspoon brought to the American founding was rooted in early modern Anglo-Scottish debates about the relationship between piety, moral philosophy, and political unionism. Those debates provide a lens to integrate the often overlooked political and religious influences of the 1707 Act of Union between England and Scotland on the subsequent history and ideology of the American Revolution.

Since the 1730s, political patronage had allowed London politicians to place Scottish religious elites — churchmen as well as university professors — under their constitutional authority. Some clergyman and educators were able to circumvent local parish election procedures, having already been planted in or near communities in which local peers, their patrons, resided. Those Scottish peers exercised a significant power of prerogative thanks in part to their perceived backing from the Westminster political establishment and the royal court. Through the 1740s, Witherspoon became increasingly wary of these worldly political connections, worrying that the civic realm would impose barriers to the Kirk's encouragement of spiritual salvation. By the early 1750s, he became widely known as a controversial leader of the minority evangelical Popular party faction of the Kirk, in opposition to the dominant Moderate establishment. In his eyes, the Moderate debt to patronage squandered the Kirk's institutional autonomy, which Presbyterians had negotiated as a part of British constitutionalism following the 1707 Act of Union between the Scottish and English Parliaments. The Kirk had seemingly lost its freedom to promote Presbyterian revivalism in Britain and its wider Empire.[5]

4. Daniel Walker Howe, "Why the Scottish Enlightenment Was Useful to the Framers of the American Constitution," *Comparative Studies in Society and History*, XXXI (1989), 572–587. For a study of common moral sensibility during the American Revolution, including its influence through Scottish Enlightenment writings, see Sarah Knott, *Sensibility and the American Revolution* (Chapel Hill, N.C., 2009), 8–10. For studies that suggest Witherspoon's specific influence through Scottish common sense philosophy, see Scott Philip Segrest, *America and the Political Philosophy of Common Sense* (Columbia, Mo., 2010), 64–100; Daniel W. Howe, "John Witherspoon and the Transatlantic Enlightenment," in Susan Manning and Francis D. Cogliano, eds., *The Atlantic Enlightenment* (Aldershot, U.K., 2008), 61–79; M. E. Phelps, "John Witherspoon and the Transmission of Common Sense Philosophy from Scotland to America" (D.Phil. thesis, Oxford University, 2001).

5. On the growing distinction between "Moderate" and evangelical "Popular party" Presby-

According to Maxim VI of Witherspoon's *Ecclesiastical Characteristics,* a 1753 satire, Moderate ministers such as Carlyle and Ferguson believed in the "perpetual duration of Mr. H——n's works, notwithstanding their present tendency to oblivion. Amen." Witherspoon was referring to Francis Hutcheson's posthumous impact on the Church of Scotland. After his death in 1746, the so-called father of the Scottish Enlightenment influenced the thought of clergyman, educators, and writers such as Carlyle, Ferguson, Lord Kames, John Millar, William Robertson, William Smellie, and even Adam Smith. They were less inclined than evangelicals to examine the tension between the conception of a universal ethical sense and the Calvinist doctrine of natural depravity, or between the reliance on regenerating divine grace and the assumption that human efforts could improve society. In advanced political unions, according to their natural law reasoning, individuals were freer to harness their inborn moral perception. Thus, Moderates were less likely than evangelical Presbyterians to describe the necessity of a full salvation experience for objective ethical understanding, even while they claimed that innate morality served to corroborate ethical ideas that could be found in scripture.

---

terians in the Kirk, see John R. McIntosh, *Church and Theology in Enlightenment Scotland: The Popular Party, 1740–1800* (East Lothian, U.K., 1998), 19–40. On Witherspoon's orthodox evangelicalism in the development of Popular party ideology, see ibid., 19, 37, 43-47, 79–81, 85–89, 117–118, 128–131, 158–160. On the division between Moderate and Popular church culture, see Jonathan M. Yeager, *Enlightened Evangelicalism: The Life and Thought of John Erskine* (Oxford, 2011), 5–6. On the Moderates as a dominant group, see Richard B. Sher's seminal study, *Church and University in the Scottish Enlightenment: The Moderate Literati of Edinburgh* (Princeton, N.J., 1985); Ian D. L. Clark, "From Protest to Reaction: The Moderate Regime in the Church of Scotland, 1752-1805," in N. Phillipson and Rosalind Mitchison, eds., *Scotland in the Age of Improvement: Essays on Scottish History in the Eighteenth Century* (Edinburgh, 1970), 200–224; Andrew Drummond and James Bulloch, *The Scottish Church, 1688–1843: The Age of the Moderates* (Edinburgh, 1973); Peter Jones, "The Polite Academy and the Presbyterians, 1720-1770," and John Dwyer, "The Heavenly City of the Eighteenth-Century Moderate Divines," in Dwyer, Roger A. Mason, and Alexander Murdoch, eds., *New Perspectives on the Politics and Culture of Early Modern Scotland* (Edinburgh, 1982), 156–176, 291–315. Luke Brekke summarizes the Moderate stance: "Some churchmen eschewed the traditional dogmatism of the Church of Scotland for a polite Christianity compatible with the new sensibilities of Georgian Britain, focusing less on sin and redemption by Christ and more on the importance of virtue and the benevolence of the Deity." See Brekke, "Heretics in the Pulpit, Inquisitors in the Pews: The Long Reformation and the Scottish Enlightenment," *Eighteenth-Century Studies,* XLIV (2010), 79. In the eyes of evangelical Popular party members, Moderate thinkers were given a social niche, and even an opportunity for social mobility, at the expense of evangelically inclined ministers. See John Dwyer, *Virtuous Discourse: Sensibility and Community in Late Eighteenth Century Scotland* (Edinburgh, 1987), 74.

Secure in their clerical standing through patronage, Witherspoon asserted, Moderates diluted the unambiguous stress on the need for salvation in the Westminster Confession of Faith, the definitive standard of Scottish Presbyterian piety since 1647. In 1763, Witherspoon recalled the reception of his satirical publications among Scotland's Moderate establishment: the "most opprobrious names were bestowed upon the concealed author, and the most dreadful threatenings uttered."[6]

By the 1770s, now residing in New Jersey, Witherspoon and his sons came to suffer at the hands of the British military. The military's actions in North America were supported by his former college classmates, Moderate ministers who had become the most prominent members of the Scottish Presbyterian Church. One of Witherspoon's earliest American congressional proclamations asked the new United States "to implore of Almighty God the forgiveness of the many sins prevailing among all ranks" through "the exercise of repentance and reformation." Such a statement, which addressed the immorality of all ranks, suggests that Witherspoon's evangelical faith was translated to American public discourse, notwithstanding his change in po-

6. John Witherspoon, *Ecclesiastical Characteristics . . .* , in [Green, ed.], *Works of Witherspoon,* III, 233, 234; Witherspoon, *A Serious Apology for the Ecclesiastical Characteristics,* ibid., 269–270. For Ferguson on commercial and social development in the American colonies, see Lisa Hill, *The Passionate Society: The Social, Political, and Moral Thought of Adam Ferguson* (Dordrecht, U.K., 2006), 223–224. Ironically, conventional historiography of the "Arminian" Scottish Enlightenment has drawn much of its language from evangelical critiques during the 1740s and 1750s. J. G. A. Pocock has thus explored the extent to which Scottish "Moderatism" constituted "a regional and late variant of the 'Arminian Enlightenment,' in which criticism of the Calvinist absolute decrees developed into an erastian politics, a pursuit of polite culture, and a reputation not always undeserved for anti-Trinitarian theology." See Pocock, *Barbarism and Religion,* II, *Narratives of Civil Government* (Cambridge, 1999), 270, and *Barbarism and Religion,* V, *Religion: The First Triumph* (Cambridge, 2010), 14; Pocock, "Cambridge Paradigms and Scotch Philosophers: A Study of the Relations between the Civic Humanist and the Civil Jurisprudential Interpretation of Eighteenth-Century Social Thought," in Istvan Hont and Michael Ignatieff, eds., *Wealth and Virtue: The Shaping of Political Economy in the Scottish Enlightenment* (Cambridge, 1983), 235–252; Knud Haakonssen, "Natural Jurisprudence in the Scottish Enlightenment: Summary of an Interpretation," in Neil MacCormick and Zenon Bankowski, eds., *Enlightenment, Rights, and Revolution: Essays in Legal and Social Philosophy* (Aberdeen, U.K., 1989), 36. On the move toward an anthropocentric definition of natural law reasoning in Scottish moral philosophy, see Haakonssen, *Natural Law and Moral Philosophy: From Grotius to the Scottish Enlightenment* (New York, 1996), 1–10. Some scholars have referred to the collective Moderate stance as akin to "the Scottish Enlightenment at prayer"; see Colin Kidd, "Subscription, the Scottish Enlightenment, and the Moderate Interpretation of History," *Journal of Ecclesiastical History,* LV (2004), 503.

litical allegiance. Throughout the British Atlantic world, the public display of passionate emotionalism had defined the culture of evangelical revivalism since the 1730s. Individuals acknowledged their unregenerate stance with a boldly emotional response—demonstrating the visible signs of sin and saving grace and enabling ministers and onlookers to discern the truth of their salvation experience. The culture of evangelical performance contributed to developing rhetorical methods in the patriot movement. Revolutionaries such as Patrick Henry and James Otis were inspired by evangelical revivals in the content, style, and structure of their passionate orations against British corruption. Witherspoon's most famous Revolutionary-era sermon focused on the "the Passions of Men" on all sides of the imperial crisis. The sermon's bleak vision of mutual butchery seemed irreconcilable with an enlightened notion of common sensibility, claiming that a "good form of government may hold the rotten materials together for some time, but beyond a certain pitch, even the best constitution will be ineffectual." It suggested that human sociability and political coherence could not always be guaranteed by the natural law of unregenerate man.[7]

Yet historians have often depicted Witherspoon, generally in passing reference, as a conduit in America for the Scottish Enlightenment appraisal of an innate moral capability common to all men—a relatively sunny vision of ethical sensibility that belied the evangelical emphasis on unregenerate sin. Scholars have often explained the acceptance of Scottish moral sense philosophy on the western side of the Atlantic, including during Witherspoon's later career, by highlighting the shared cultural provinciality of Enlightenment Scotland and eighteenth-century America. Theologians and educators, according to such an interpretation, used the notion of a common moral sense to justify colonial America's provincial connection to London, just as it had been employed to validate Scotland's diminished political authority in the new British state after the 1707 Act of Union. They followed their Moderate Scottish counterparts in claiming that civic stability need not derive from direct political representation, but rather from a common and pre-rational "sensory" understanding of social goodwill. Those who proposed the positive aspects of cultural provinciality did not seek to undermine the political mandate that had created the moral community of the British Empire. Their

7. "Wednesday, December 11, 1776," in Worthington Chauncey Ford et al., eds., *Journals of the Continental Congress, 1774–1789,* 34 vols. (Washington, D.C., 1904–1937), VI, 1022; Witherspoon, *Dominion of Providence,* in [Green, ed.], *Works of Witherspoon,* III, 41. On evangelical rhetorical culture, see Harry S. Stout, "Religion, Communications, and the Ideological Origins of the American Revolution," *William and Mary Quarterly,* 3d Ser., XXXIV (1977), 519–541.

philosophical vision, rather, represented a pragmatic intellectual response to the expanding imperial frontier. In Edinburgh, Philadelphia, Aberdeen, and Princeton, educated teachers and ministers realized their greater relative distance from Westminster governance than English towns and cities. Thus they used moral sense theory to describe their personal contribution to social cohesion, giving them a greater sense of civic purpose in their local realm.[8]

Through the second half of the eighteenth century, American colonists borrowed Scottish moral sensory terminology to describe their shared attachment to the British Empire. Yet the same terminology came to assume a rather different political connotation in American circles during the 1760s and 1770s. It influenced those who sought to justify their separation from imperial jurisdiction. Using rational arguments, some patriots defined British corruption as contrary to constitutional theories that had developed in the American colonies. They proposed an abstract and often legalistic defense of customary American autonomies in order to counter British policy. Problematically, however, their rational propositions were often met with similarly abstract and legalistic counterarguments from British subjects. Moral sense theory, conversely, allowed American Revolutionaries to describe their response to Britain as an uncontrollable reaction: it derived from innate moral values that were pre-rational, commonsensical, and thus irrepressible. They articulated their supposedly uncontainable sense that British authority after the Stamp Act was somehow ugly in nature.[9]

8. According to political scientist Jeffry H. Morrison's important first work on Witherspoon, Witherspoon came "to conclusions in moral anthropology identical to those drawn by his American colleagues like Jefferson." "Witherspoon had cut his intellectual teeth on the philosophy of the Scottish Enlightenment. That philosophical tradition [including Francis Hutcheson and Thomas Reid] — committed to the methods of natural science as well as to empirical and experiential theories of knowledge, and distrustful of metaphysical speculations — actually helped fit Witherspoon and his students for productive American careers." Morrison includes a cogent analysis of the influence of Lockean theory in Witherspoon's political thought. See Morrison, *John Witherspoon and the Founding of the American Republic* (Notre Dame, Ind., 2005), xv, 51 (quotation), 127–128. Scholarly assessment of the literary, religious, and philosophical culture of colonial British America has often followed Bernard Bailyn and John Clive's seminal and still highly influential analysis of shared cultural provinciality between Enlightenment Scotland and colonial America; see Clive and Bailyn, "England's Cultural Provinces: Scotland and America," *WMQ*, 3d Ser., XI (1954), 200–213, esp. 210–213. See also Alexander Murdoch, *Scotland and America, c. 1600–c. 1800* (Basingstoke, U.K., 2010), 144–155; Richard B. Sher, "Introduction: Scottish-American Cultural Studies, Past and Present," in Sher and Jeffrey R. Smitten, eds., *Scotland and America in the Age of the Enlightenment* (Princeton, N.J., 1990), 1–27, esp. 1–8.

9. Much scholarship on this philosophical transformation has followed Caroline Robbins's succinct analysis, made more than fifty years ago, in an article that complemented Bernard Bailyn

The centrality of Scottish Enlightenment thought in America's "cultural provinces"—including its eventual ability to be deployed in moral arguments against Westminster—has underscored the scholarly narrative of Witherspoon's volte-face in moral philosophy. Historians, philosophers, and economists continue to argue whether the Scottish commercial theorist Adam Smith abandoned his early focus on sympathetic benevolence. In an inversion of Smith's purported change in reasoning, Witherspoon is often said to have wielded moral sense philosophy to justify political rebellion from Britain rather than continued integration into its imperial union. Despite his earlier evangelicalism—and notwithstanding the anxieties of his educated Scottish adversaries during the Revolutionary era—scholars have suggested that Witherspoon made young American statesmen more familiar with moral sense theories inspired by Scottish Enlightenment thinkers such as Hutcheson and that he provided them with the conceptual vocabulary

---

and John Clive's important discussion of Scottish-American philosophy: "For an explicit statement, thirty years before Lexington, of 'when it is that colonies may turn independent,' one must turn to the work of Francis Hutcheson, a Scottish professor of moral philosophy"; see Robbins, "'When It Is That Colonies May Turn Independent': An Analysis of the Environment and Politics of Francis Hutcheson (1694-1746)," *WMQ*, 3d Ser., XI (1954), 214-251. For an overview of this scholarship, relative to any emphasis on Scottish evangelicalism, see Alan Gibson, *Interpreting the Founding: Guide to the Enduring Debates over the Origins and Foundations of the American Republic* (Lawrence, Kans., 2006), 37-53. See also David Fate Norton, "Francis Hutcheson in America," *Transactions of the Fourth International Congress on the Enlightenment,* IV (Oxford, 1976), Studies on Voltaire and the Eighteenth Century, CLIV, 1547-1568; Mark Valeri, *Law and Providence in Joseph Bellamy's New England: The Origins of the New Divinity in Revolutionary America* (New York, 1994), 44-50; Douglas Sloan, *The Scottish Enlightenment and the American College Ideal* ([New York, 1971]), 138. On the ways in which Scottish philosophy and a "rural enlightenment" could influence rustic Presbyterian communities in New Jersey, see John Fea, *The Way of Improvement Leads Home: Philip Vickers Fithian and the Rural Enlightenment in Early America* (Philadelphia, 2008), 83. Historians of patriot sensibility remain indebted to the seminal literary definition of a "sentimental formula" whose "simple equation rest[ed] upon a belief in the spontaneous goodness and benevolence of man's original instincts." Readers sympathized with protagonists without necessarily condoning the actions that led to their fall and "could point to what passed for philosophical justification" in the writings of the Scottish Enlightenment—altering the way in which Revolutionary Americans understood the embodiment of shared political feelings. See Herbert Ross Brown, *The Sentimental Novel in America, 1789-1860* (Durham, N.C., 1940), 176; Jay Fliegelman, *Prodigals and Pilgrims: The American Revolution against Patriarchal Authority, 1750-1800* (New York, 1982), 5; Melvyn Yazawa, *From Colonies to Commonwealth: Familial Ideology and the Beginnings of the American Republic* (Baltimore, 1985), 87-110; Knott, *Sensibility and the American Revolution,* 8-10; Sarah M. S. Pearsall, "'The Power of Feeling?' Emotion, Sensibility, and the American Revolution," *Modern Intellectual History,* VIII (2011), 659-667.

FIGURE 1. John Witherspoon's Signature on the Declaration of Independence, July 4, 1776. Detail from the engraving of the Declaration of Independence by William J. Stone, printed on parchment, with Stone's imprint, Washington, D.C., 1823. Courtesy, The National Archives and Records Administration, Washington, D.C.

to contrast British metropolitan corruption with the innate benevolence of patriots. A sharply defined "Moderate" Enlightenment is said to have influenced and even dominated his American teaching, his Christian apologetics, and his wider civic life and legacy—including his contribution to the dissenting Protestant coalition of the American Revolution.[10]

Yet, during his American career, Witherspoon continued to claim that religious regeneration initially required a personal admission of sin, with the help of the Holy Spirit. The latter assisted individuals as they struggled to acknowledge the necessity of grace in supplying a regenerated moral sensibility. Provided their acknowledgment of iniquity was genuine, individuals would then receive divine mercy and a new moral understanding wrought by the "grace of God" and the "Grace of hope." Societal stability, in such a formulation, required enough individuals to become similarly awakened. Moral sensory philosophy, in Witherspoon's opinion, failed to acknowledge such a requirement. Common sensory perception might allow individuals (and their leaders) to apprehend the difference between right and wrong in some circumstances. But Witherspoon's evangelical hermeneutic tended to differ

10. Ned C. Landsman has discussed Witherspoon's surprisingly enlightened place in American historiography, despite his evangelical Scottish career, in an important article. As Landsman shows, scholars have highlighted a dissonance between Witherspoon's religious proclamations in America and his other educational and philosophical statements. See Landsman, "Witherspoon and the Problem of Provincial Identity in Scottish Evangelical Culture," in Sher and Smitten, eds., *Scotland and America*, 30. L. Gordon Tait has written a "first" account of the clergyman's piety in order to show how he "faced up to some of the issues that the Enlightenment had raised and in the end was even influenced by this intellectual movement, perhaps more than he intended"; see Tait, *The Piety of John Witherspoon: Pew, Pulpit, and Public Forum* (Louisville, Ky., 2001), xi, 8–9, 28. Douglas Sloan observes that "when Witherspoon departed for America, he carried more of the Moderate than he, his moderate adversaries, or his American friends would have dared to suppose." Elsewhere, Sloan does suggest that Witherspoon remained uneasy with the notion of innate morality. See Sloan, *The Scottish Enlightenment and the American College Idea*, 119.

from the notion of *sensus communis* in warning that initial moral conceptions did not imply a predictable ethical *reaction,* benevolent or otherwise. A common ability to perceive qualitative moral distinctions did not suggest that individuals could then *act* righteously without previously received divine grace, nor that they would react in the same way as one another. Were moral self-doubt not a common inclination, the vital and continuing role of faith in divine moral assistance would become redundant.[11]

As a minister, teacher, and civic leader, Witherspoon strongly supported the political cause of American independence. But he also warned that patriots might perceive their moral abilities in unrealistic terms when distinguishing their civic ideology from Westminster authority. In describing their opposition to British corruption as a predictable manifestation of their innate ethical sensibility, they risked eschewing the importance of conversion and faith in redeeming grace. Witherspoon's moral critique of patriot reasoning prefigured a civic and theological tension that several scholars have noted in the era of the early American Republic. Some American theologians became more cautious in using the notion of self-evident truth, notwithstanding its earlier contribution to the repudiation of British imperial prerogative. The idea of "self-evidence" potentially undermined the Christian claim that humankind needed God's revelation to determine a moral life. And, even when a moral awakening seemed to occur through the help of the Holy Spirit, its veracity could not always be determined with exactitude.[12]

John Witherspoon's American Revolution uncovers the broader constitutional and civic contexts that framed Witherspoon's critique of moral sense theory. Westminster's British establishment always encompassed a specific constitutional connection to England's Anglican Church. But it also administered an imperial union in which colonial populations allied themselves with separate dissenting Protestant institutions, including those that were led by evangelical Scottish Calvinists. Evangelical Presbyterian opposition to Moderate patronage unsettled the association between centralized Westminster prerogative and the outlying power of Scottish lairds. Similarly, Presbyterian opposition to Anglican religious establishments in the Middle Colonies,

11. See, for example, John Witherspoon, *A Practical Treatise on Regeneration,* in [Green, ed.], *Works of Witherspoon,* I, 248–249, 255; Witherspoon, "Lectures on Divinity," ibid., IV, 13. On the reception of the classical notion of *sensus communis* in the British Atlantic world, see Sophia Rosenfeld, *Common Sense: A Political History* (Cambridge, Mass., 2011), 18–19, 22, 59.

12. Christopher Grasso, "Deist Monster: On Religious Common Sense in the Wake of the American Revolution," *Journal of American History,* XCV (2008), 67. Mark A. Noll has also attended to these ironies. See, for example, Noll, "The Irony of the Enlightenment for Presbyterians in the Early Republic," *Journal of the Early Republic,* V (1985), 149–178.

Virginia, and elsewhere disturbed the Anglocentric imperial unionism that political elites promoted in London. The incorporation of the autonomous Church of Scotland into the British Empire offered a visible model of jurisdictional pluralism to American colonists, a confederal model of autonomy in distinction to the incorporating Westminster Anglican establishment and its perceived colonial proxies. Such a model undermined the constitutional notion of indivisible sovereignty and the singular imperial role of Anglicanism. Long before the imperial crisis, Presbyterian settlers had defined and guarded the autonomy of their religious and educational institutions in the American colonies—including the College of New Jersey, where Witherspoon came to reside after 1768.[13]

During the Revolutionary era, opposition to the supremacy of the English Anglican Church in British America contributed to patriot identity in dissenting Protestant communities, including in Princeton village. It also helped to generate evangelical Presbyterian support for the American cause in Scotland itself. Pro-American sentiment among mainland Scottish Presbyterians did not usually derive from general hostility to Westminster parliamentary authority. More specifically, it drew its critical language and concepts from eighteenth-century opposition to the association between the Scottish nobility and Westminster, which seemed to guarantee the Moderate Presbyterian inclination to promote human-centered moral sense philosophy from church pulpits and university lecterns. In their opposition to imperial Anglicanism during the Revolutionary era, therefore, mainland Scottish evangelicals derived part of their conceptual vocabulary from earlier constitutional critiques of the Moderate establishment. Witherspoon did the same during his American career, enhancing his general opposition to Westminster legislative prerogative to an even greater extent than his former Popular party colleagues.[14]

Thus, *John Witherspoon's American Revolution* considers the ways in which Witherspoon's Presbyterian evangelicalism could compete with, combine with, or even supersede the civic influence of Scottish Enlightenment thought in the British Atlantic world. It uncovers the association between

13. Ned Landsman, "The Episcopate, the British Union, and the Failure of Religious Settlement in Colonial British America," in Chris Beneke and Christopher S. Grenda, eds., *The First Prejudice: Religious Tolerance and Intolerance in Early America* (Philadelphia, 2010), 84–85.

14. On confederal and incorporating definitions of British imperial union and the unsettling model of Kirk autonomy in the empire, see Alison L. LaCroix, *The Ideological Origins of American Federalism* (Cambridge, Mass., 2010), 14, 27–28, 84, 96; Landsman, "The Episcopate," in Beneke and Grenada, eds., *The First Prejudice,* 84–85.

evangelical Presbyterian religion and Anglo-Scottish unionism and the impact of such an association on social, religious, and political developments in American patriot discourse and in early national America. And it highlights the eventual legacy of Presbyterian political theology, through Witherspoon's students, in nineteenth-century America.

"The Hate of Kings, and Glory of the Kirk"?

The oldest of six children, John Witherspoon was born on February 15, 1723, in Gifford, East Lothian, Scotland. Having moved across the Atlantic to take up the presidency of the College of New Jersey in 1768, Witherspoon assumed a public role as an American patriot and presided over what came to be known as a "seminary of sedition" against Britain. In an institution that would soon become more widely known as Princeton, according to the most accurate recent estimation he would teach one president (James Madison, bachelor of arts, 1771) and one vice president (Aaron Burr, bachelor of arts, 1772), forty-nine U.S. representatives, twenty-eight U.S. senators, three Supreme Court justices, one secretary of state, three attorneys general, and two foreign ministers. More than 11 percent of Witherspoon's graduates would become college presidents, in eight different American states. Many would remain concerned with the expansion of Presbyterian piety in the new American confederation, just as their teacher had once supported its outward movement in Britain's imperial union. Former student Samuel Doak would settle in eastern Tennessee, preach in the backcountry, charter Washington College, and eventually found Tusculum College, named after Witherspoon's home in New Jersey, in 1818. Doak would honor a man who had also been a delegate to the Continental Congress from 1776 to 1782, a member of three standing committees during the Revolutionary War, dozens of congressional committees, and the author of a large number of the religious proclamations issued by Congress during his career.[15]

15. On the "seminary of sedition," see Sheldon S. Cohen and Larry R. Gerlach, "Princeton in the Coming of the American Revolution," *New Jersey History,* XCII (1974), 91; David W. Robson, *Educating Republicans: The College in the Era of the American Revolution, 1750–1800* (Westport, Conn., 1985), 67–70. For the statistical account of Witherspoon students in public office, see Jeffry Hays Morrison, "John Witherspoon and 'The Public Interest of Religion,'" *Journal of Church and State,* XLI (1999), 553. For the proportion of Witherspoon students who went on to found other colleges, see Collins, *President Witherspoon,* II, 223–226. For more biographical information on Witherspoon's pupils and their subsequent careers in public office, see also Edwin Mark Norris, *The Story of Princeton* (Boston, 1917), 73; Kenneth E. Harris and

Ridley & Blood, sculp.

Rev.ᵈ J. Witherspoon, D.D.
President of Princeton College,
New Jersey, America.

FIGURE 2. *Revd. J. Witherspoon, D.D., President of Princeton College, New Jersey.*
Engraved by Ridley and Blood after Charles Willson Peale. 1808. Stipple engraving.
Print Collection, Miriam and Ira D. Wallach Division, The New York Public Library.
The New York Public Library / Art Resource, N.Y.

By the time Witherspoon arrived in New Jersey in 1768, an influential and expanding segment of the colonial American population was affiliated in some way with the Presbyterian Church, particularly in the Middle Colonies and in many southern settlements. In 1706, eight Presbyterian ministers had formed the Presbytery of Philadelphia, the first in the New World. A growing population and increased immigration allowed the Presbytery to expand its jurisdiction according to the system of representation that it inherited from Scottish ecclesiology. The Synod of Philadelphia was formed in 1716. An estimated 250,000 Presbyterian Scots had immigrated to America before 1776, of whom many subsequently raised families and increased their numbers threefold within an overall colonial population of around 3,000,000. In addition to these figures, we must add more than 100,000 men and women, mostly Presbyterian, who journeyed from the Irish province of Ulster to the American colonies between 1718 and 1775, "the single largest movement of any group from the British Isles to British North America during the eighteenth century."[16]

Steven D. Tilley, comps., *Index: Journals of the Continental Congress, 1774–1789* (Washington, D.C., 1976), 421–422; James McLachlan et al., eds., *Princetonians: A Biographical Dictionary*, 5 vols. (Princeton, N.J., 1976–1991). Witherspoon also educated 114 ministers, a number of whom founded Presbyterian academies. See Stuart C. Henry, ed., *A Miscellany of American Christianity: Essays in Honor of H. Shelton Smith* (Durham, N.C., 1963), 190. On Samuel Doak's early ministerial and educational activities in Tennessee, see Earle W. Crawford, *Samuel Doak: Pioneer Missionary in East Tennessee* (Johnson City, Tenn., 1999), 12–39. For Witherspoon's religious proclamations on behalf of the Continental Congress, see the discussions in Chapter 8, below.

16. Patrick Griffin, *The People with No Name: Ireland's Ulster Scots, America's Scots Irish, and the Creation of a British Atlantic World, 1689–1764* (Princeton, N.J., 2001), 1. For these statistics on Presbyterian immigration and settlement in North America, see James H. Smylie, "Introduction," in "Presbyterians and the American Revolution: A Documentary Account," special issue, *Journal of Presbyterian History*, LII, (1974), 303–306, esp. 304; Smylie, *A Brief History of the Presbyterians* (Louiseville, Ky., 1996), 39; Fred J. Hood, *Reformed America: The Middle and Southern States, 1783–1837* (University, Ala., 1980), 2; Roger Finke and Rodney Stark, *The Churching of America, 1776–1990: Winners and Losers in Our Religious Economy* (New Brunswick, N.J., 1992), 25; Edwin Scott Gaustad and Philip L. Barlow, *New Historical Atlas of Religion in America* (New York, 2001), 38. Total immigration of Scots and Scots-Irish in the eighteenth century had reached between two and three hundred thousand by 1776. See Douglas Sloan, *The Scottish Enlightenment and the American College Ideal*, 36; William R. Brock, *Scotus Americanus: A Survey of the Sources for Links between Scotland and America in the Eighteenth Century* (Edinburgh, 1982), 13; David Dobson, *Scottish Emigration to Colonial America, 1607–1785* (Athens, Ga., 1994), 33; T. C. Smout, N. C. Landsman, and T. M. Devine, "Scottish Emigration in the Seventeenth and Eighteenth Centuries," in Nicholas Canny, ed., *Europeans on the Move: Studies on European Migration, 1500–1800* (Oxford, 1994), 76–112, esp. 76–86. See also Leonard J. Trinterud, *The Forming of an American Tradition: A Re-examination of Colonial Presbyterianism*

According to the Reverend Jonathan Odell, Witherspoon, having been "receiv'd" into existing colonial Presbyterian populations, inspired them to "rail at Kings, with venom well-nigh burst." Odell failed to see any poignancy in Witherspoon's turn from British prisoner to American Revolutionary, from anti-Jacobite to American Jacobin. Nor did he see any sign of Witherspoon's abandonment of Presbyterian orthodoxy. In his view, the American rise of "Witherspoon the great" was a story of dirty tricks, treason, vile sedition, and Calvinistic zeal. *"I'd rather be a dog than Witherspoon,"* wrote the poet and chaplain of the First Battalion of Pennsylvania Loyalists in 1780—not a reverential way of referring to the only clergyman to sign the Declaration of Independence:

> Ye priests of Baal . . .
>
> .   .   .   .
>
> Mess-mates of Jezebel's luxurious mess,
> Come in the splendor of pontific dress;
> Haste to attend your chief in solemn state,
> Haste to attend on Witherspoon the great:
>
> .   .   .   .
>
>   Scotland confess'd him sensible and shrewd,
> Austere and rigid; many thought him good;
> But turbulence of temper spoil'd the whole,
> And show'd the movements of his inmost soul:
> Disclos'd machinery loses of its force;
> He felt the fact, and westward bent his course.
>
>   Princeton receiv'd him bright amidst his flaws,
> And saw him labour in the good old cause;
> Saw him promote the meritorious work,
> The hate of Kings, and glory of the Kirk.
>
> .   .   .   .
>
> Mean while unhappy Jersey mourns her thrall,
> Ordain'd by vilest of the vile to fall;

(Philadelphia, 1949), 122–134; Michael Kammen, *Colonial New York: A History* (New York, 1975), 238; James G. Leyburn, "Presbyterian Immigrants and the Revolution," *Journal of Presbyterian History,* LIV (1976), 9–17; Patricia U. Bonomi, *Under the Cope of Heaven: Religion, Society, and Politics in Colonial America* (New York, 1986), 134; Jon Butler, *Religion in Colonial America* (New York, 1999), 54; Rodney Stark and Roger Finke, "American Religion in 1776: A Statistical Portrait," *Sociological Analysis,* XLIX (1988), 47.

To fall by Witherspoon — O name, the curse
Of sound religion, and disgrace of verse.

    Member of Congress we must hail him next;
Come out of Babylon was now his text:
Fierce as the fiercest, foremost of the first,
He'd rail at Kings, with venom well-nigh burst;
Not uniformly grand — for some bye end
To dirtiest acts of treason he'd descend;
I've known him seek the dungeon dark as night,
Imprison'd Tories to convert or fright;
Whilst to myself I've humm'd in dismal tune,
I'd rather be a dog than Witherspoon.
Be patient, reader — for the issue trust,
His day will come — remember Heav'n is just.

Better a dog than a writer of doggerel, Witherspoon might have replied. Aside from his debatable literary talent, as an Anglican minister it is not surprising that Odell underscored the religious continuity that underlay Witherspoon's support for American Revolutionaries: the "old cause" of Witherspoon's Presbyterian faith was apparently rooted in "the hate of Kings, and glory of the Kirk." A Scottish Presbyterian heritage, according to Odell, was bound to have attracted Witherspoon to the American revolt against London.[17]

For an Anglican loyalist who was wary of fractious sentiment, Odell's poetic efforts were far from genteel. But then, those of milder religious hue on both sides of the Atlantic had never been particularly moderate in their reaction to Witherspoon in the decades after his release from the Castle Doune. By 1776, eight years after his move to America, the mere mention of Witherspoon's name was enough to make members of Edinburgh's Moderate literati wince, or even curse. Hugo Arnot, a writer, advocate, and sometime member of the Edinburgh Speculative Society, wrote a pamphlet titled *The XLV. Chapter of the Prophecies of Thomas the Rhymer, in Verse; with Notes and Illustrations; Dedicated to Doctor Silverspoon, Preacher of Sedition in America.* In the introduction, Arnot summarized the motivations of "Doctor Silverspoon" and assumed his voice: "The design of this publication is to arouse my sleeping countrymen, to alarm them with imaginary dangers, to blast and eradicate harmony and loyalty, which at present unhappily flourish among this *deluded people;* to clog the wheels of government, nay, to join hand in hand with our

17. Camillo Querno [Jonathan Odell], *The American Times: A Satire in Three Parts; in Which Are Delineated the Characters of the Leaders of the American Rebellion* (London, 1780), 17–19.

brethren in America, and overturn the system." Arnot then sought to explain "the whole mystery of rebellion," whose "political drunkenness" was "distributed" "above all, by seditious Preachers, who gain an *honest liveliehood* by exerting their respective endeavours, conducive to the same end, namely *the destruction of their country.*" Arnot introduced the poetry that followed in honor of "Silverspoon" and his *"wizard brethren"* of evangelical Scottish ministers:

> In a brazen pulpit boil,
> Of flaming zeal the holy oil;
> Throw the seeds of harsh dissentions,
> Lying tales and false pretensions,
> Tongue of Preacher on damnation,
> To a snoring congregation;
> Cimeter, that, with a blow,
> Laid the tyrant Charles low.

> Double, double, toil and trouble,
> Make our brazen pulpit bubble.

> Sound Rebellion's bloody trumpet,
> 'Gainst the scarlet Roman strumpet;
> Wicked statute at her beck,
> Settled Popery in Quebec:
> O'er Presbytry a mist she threw,
> Rank with baleful Romish dew;
> This Popish mist is presentation,
> Grievance dire to Scottish nation.

> We shall rejoice when good kings bleed;
> When, to change administration,
> We embroil the British nation,
> Holding kings in detestation
>   More firmly than our creed.
> . . . .
> But see, thro' silver moon-light gliding,
> Horrid hags in triumph riding,
> Bringing news of joyful tiding,
>   From Discord's dreary dome.
> Lo they bring from coast Atlantic,
> Where fears ideal, yet gigantic,
> Have render'd a whole nation frantic,
>   The gentle Silverspoon.

As an Episcopalian with Stuart sympathies, it is neither surprising that Arnot derided the Presbyterian contribution to political disorder during the seventeenth century nor that he highlighted a "frantic" similarity with the American Revolutionary era. Like Odell, he underscored the continuity in Witherspoon's Presbyterian zeal on both sides of the Atlantic: in debt to the seventeenth-century *"wizard brethren"* who came before him, Witherspoon transferred a "brazen" contempt for royal authority to American classrooms, pulpits, and Congresses. The diabolical discord that characterized Wither-spoon's contribution to American Revolutionary ideology was apparently associated with the anti-Stuart Scottish covenanting movement. Though Arnot called Charles I a "tyrant," he also clarified his disdain for the preachers who had tainted opposition to the popish king with "flaming zeal."[18]

Presbyterians who descended from Scottish and "Scots-Irish" migrations were certainly one of several "Low Church" Reformed traditions who contributed to American Revolutionary identity. Seeking unity against British corruption, their reference to early modern constitutional and confessional struggles was relatively common. The attempt to exert centralized control over American colonists recalled the Anglo-Scottish context of the Civil Wars in Britain and Ireland between 1638 and 1651 (more commonly known as the English Civil Wars), when Laudian policy inhibited Presbyterians alongside Puritan Congregationalists. A century later in the Middle Colonies, Anglican missionaries such as Thomas Bradbury Chandler, Samuel Seabury, Jr., Charles Inglis, and Myles Cooper acted under the auspices of the Society for the Propagation of the Gospel in Foreign Parts. Presbyterians in the region tended to perceive their activities as a proxy for "Anglican Imperialism" and accused them of campaigning for an American bishop. They reproached the King-in-Parliament for adopting Stuart ways by constraining their rights and by indulging Catholics. The ever-present fear of an American bishopric culminated in the vitriolic condemnation of Westminster "Popery" after the 1774 Quebec Act. Rumors circled of a British decision to deploy brigades of Catholic soldiers among regiments that were already quartered in cities such as New York.[19]

18. Hugo Arnot, *The XLV. Chapter of the Prophecies of Thomas the Rhymer, in Verse; with Notes and Illustrations; Dedicated to Doctor Silverspoon, Preacher of Sedition in America* (Edinburgh, 1776), 3, 13–15. If Arnot was "any thing decidedly in politics" or religion, according to a nineteenth-century assessment, "he was a Jacobite, to which party he belonged by descent and by [his Episcopalian] religion, and also perhaps by virtue of his own peculiar turn of mind." See Robert Chambers, *A Biographical Dictionary of Eminent Scotsmen*, I (Glasgow, 1847), 66.

19. Patriot ideology attracted "Low Church" members such as New England Congregationalists, Chesapeake "anti-bishop" Anglicans, Presbyterians, and colonial Baptists. See John L.

The Presbyterian critique of the Anglican establishment in Westminster added to a general perception of British parliamentary corruption among colonists. It seems less surprising, therefore, that Boston Congregationalists joined Presbyterian settlers in alluding to the Scottish covenanting movement of the English Civil Wars. Loyalists, Anglicans, and crypto-Jacobites were not alone in associating the early modern precedent of Presbyterian evangelicalism with American Revolutionary ideology. In the early summer of 1774, Samuel Adams's radical Boston circle invoked a "Solemn League and Covenant" to unite rural and metropolitan New England against British corruption. Adams believed the analogy with the 1643 alliance between Scottish Presbyterians and English Puritans would be understood by townspeople who had already begun to see themselves as "reformers of a corrupted Britain." From 1748 to 1789, at the behest of evangelical ministers, several editions of an *Act of the Associate Presbytery, for Renewing the National Covenant of Scotland* were also printed in Edinburgh and Glasgow. They all referred to the century-old religious pledge. Unlike Arnot and Odell, American patriots and evangelical Scots were positive in their invocation of the political theology of early modern Presbyterianism.[20]

Brooke, "North Atlantic Culture Wars," *Reviews in American History*, XXVIII (2000), 351–359. For Presbyterian fears of Anglican missionaries, see Joseph S. Tiedemann, "Presbyterianism and the American Revolution in the Middle Colonies," *Church History*, LXXIV (2005), 317–318, 322. On the anti-Catholic dimension of American Revolutionary ideology and its inspiration by New England Puritan culture and history, see Bonomi, *Under the Cope of Heaven*, 199–209; Ruth H. Bloch, *Visionary Republic: Millennial Themes in American Thought, 1756–1800* (New York, 1985), 58–59; Harry S. Stout, *The New England Soul* (New York, 1986), 261; John Fredrick Woolverton, *Colonial Anglicanism in North America* (Detroit, Mich., 1984), 185–186; Nancy L. Rhoden, *Revolutionary Anglicanism: The Colonial Church of England Clergy during the American Revolution* (New York, 1999), 73; Joseph S. Tiedemann, *Reluctant Revolutionaries: New York City and the Road to Independence, 1763–1776* (Ithaca, N.Y., 1997), 208–210. J. C. D. Clark includes a brief reference to the Scottish religious motif in pro-patriot sentiment during the 1770s. See Clark, *The Language of Liberty, 1660–1832: Political Discourse and Social Dynamics in the Anglo-American World* (Cambridge, 1994), 120–124, 214–216, 260–271, 296–400, esp. 329–331. See also Richard L. Greaves, "Radicals, Rights, and Revolution: British Nonconformity and Roots of the American Experience," *Church History*, LXI (1992), 151–168; Richard B. Sher, "Witherspoon's *Dominion of Providence* and the Scottish Jeremiad Tradition," in Sher and Smitten, eds., *Scotland and America in the Age of Enlightenment*, 54.

20. On the American Solemn League, see Richard Brown, *Revolutionary Politics in Massachusetts: The Boston Committee of Correspondence and the Towns, 1772–1774* (Cambridge, Mass., 1970), 185, 191, 198 (quotation). See also Gary B. Nash, *The Urban Crucible: The Northern Seaports and the Origins of the American Revolution* (Cambridge, Mass., 1986), 229–230; Merrill Jensen, *The Founding of a Nation: A History of the American Revolution, 1763–1776* (1968; rpt.

Yet, despite the impressive statistics of Presbyterian immigration during the first half of the eighteenth century, Samuel Adams's allusion to the Scottish Solemn League and Covenant, and Witherspoon's signature on the Declaration of Independence, the historiography of patriot political theology has tended to focus on its special debt to New England Congregational piety, albeit in a wider Atlantic context. A synthesis of Protestant Christianity and Lockean philosophy is often said to have influenced a later generation of American Congregational clergymen in their critique of British misrule. The Reverend Samuel West, for instance, claimed that British politicians threatened long-standing individual privileges—including the right to religious conscience—and had not borne in mind the colonial "Right to Rebel against Governors." Other scholars emphasize the influence of early modern English Harringtonian and civic-humanistic impulses on religious notions of virtue during the Revolutionary era.[21]

Indianapolis, Ind., 2004), 468; Jack N. Rakove, *The Beginnings of National Politics: An Interpretative History of the Continental Congress* (New York, 1979), 24-25; William B. Prescott and Barbara S. Prescott, *Patriots and Taxpayers of Colonial Westford, Massachusetts in 1774* (Bound Brook, N.J., n.d.). The specific model that Anglo-Scottish covenants offered to Americans during the colonial and Revolutionary era has received relatively little attention. See Ned C. Landsman, *Scotland and Its First American Colony, 1683-1765* (Princeton, N.J., 1985), chap. 2; Clark, *The Language of Liberty,* 329-331; Tiedemann, "Presbyterianism and the American Revolution," *Church History,* LXXIV (2005), 306-344. For reprinted editions of Scottish covenant renewals, see, for example, *Act of the Associate Presbytery, for Renewing the National Covenant of Scotland, and the Solemn League and Covenant of the Three Nations . . .* (Edinburgh, 1748). On these renewal publications, see Brock, *Scotus Americanus,* 89-90, 254 n. 7.

21. Mark A. Noll claims: "Puritanism is the only colonial religious system that modern historians take seriously as a major religious influence on the Revolution"; see Noll, *America's God: From Jonathan Edwards to Abraham Lincoln* (Oxford, 2002), 32. On New England covenant theology, "English" Puritanism, and Revolutionary intercolonial identity, see, for example, James H. Hutson, *Religion and the Founding of the American Republic* (Washington, D.C., 1998), 3-49, 53-54; John G. West, Jr., *The Politics of Revelation and Reason: Religion and Civic Life in the New Nation* (Lawrence, Kans., 1996), 1-11; Bonomi, *Under the Cope of Heaven,* 187-209; Edmund S. Morgan, "The Puritan Ethic and the American Revolution," *WMQ,* 3d Ser., XXIV (1967), 3-18; Sacvan Bercovitch, "How the Puritans Won the American Revolution," *Massachusetts Review,* XVII (1976), 597-630; Larzer Ziff, "Revolutionary Rhetoric and Puritanism," *Early American Literature,* XIII (1978), 45-49. On "Christian Lockean" thought during the Revolutionary era, see Michael P. Zuckert, "Natural Rights and Protestant Politics," in Thomas S. Engeman and Zuckert, eds., *Protestantism and the American Founding* (Notre Dame, Ind., 2004), 23, 46, 58-65; Rev. Samuel West, "On the Right to Rebel against Governors" (Boston, [May 29], 1776), in Charles S. Hyneman and Donald S. Lutz, eds., *American Political Writing during the Founding Era, 1760-1805* (Indianapolis, Ind., 1983), 410. On patriots joining "classical republican themes of disinterested public service to late-Puritan themes of God-orientated public duty,"

That Scottish Calvinism has had less impact on our understanding of patriot piety is surprising in light of contiguous scholarly developments in "new British history." Historians have widened our geographical, ethnocultural, and religious perspectives of the early modern conflict between Parliament and royal prerogative beyond "the English state and the provinces of its empire." Changes in English politics and theology have been examined as part of a wider "British problem"—the "problem of multiple kingdoms" in the relationship between England, Scotland, and Ireland during the seventeenth century. Presbyterian Scots were part of that problem, as far as new British historians are concerned. Their political theology has been incorporated into the seventeenth-century narrative of civil and monarchical conflict and into subsequent discussions of national unionism during the eighteenth century. New British history has discussed the confluence—or the tension—between constitutional and confessional pluralism in an "archipelagic" perspective. The Atlantic turn in the history of America has attempted to do the same in a wider oceanic context. Both perspectives have claimed that "provincial" populations could be agents of change rather than passive adherents to London's metropolitan jurisdiction. Thus, it should be possible "to imagine" Presbyterians

> acting and traversing in 'British' and 'Atlantic' history . . . [to] investigate the discontents that led to considerable emigration from Ulster to the Alleghenies and elsewhere . . . a history of this people as a presumed entity—a status some have sought to deny them—and a history of the [British] archipelagic, Atlantic, and American complexes organized around the theaters of their successive actions in it.

Yet scholarly accounts of American Revolutionary political theology continue to be rooted in religious and political thought that was inherited from early modern England, rather than in the Presbyterian cultures of Scotland and the Middle Colonies.[22]

---

see Noll, "The Contingencies of Christian Republicanism: An Alternative Account of Protestantism and the American Founding," in Engeman and Zuckert, eds., *Protestantism and the American Founding*, 243. For the potential synthesis between classical and Lockean paradigms in religious circles, see also Noll, *America's God*, 447–451. According to Jonathan Clark, the "Godly Protestants" of the seventeenth century were akin to the Americans of the Revolutionary crisis: all were opposed to centralized control over outlying populations of dissenters; see Clark, *The Language of Liberty*, 296–400, esp. 304–310; Clark, "The American Revolution: A War of Religion?" *History Today*, XXXIX (1989), 10–16.

22. J. G. A. Pocock, *The Discovery of Islands: Essays in British History* (Cambridge, 2005), 289–290; Pocock, "The New British History in Atlantic Perspective: An Antipodean Commen-

The failure to incorporate Presbyterian political theology is certainly not a sign of sloppy scholarship in existing Scottish-American studies. Rather, most assessments of Scottish-American piety have been bound by the nature of their source material. With much richness and subtlety, they have examined hitherto neglected accounts of Presbyterian revivalism from the 1730s and 1740s. Itinerant preachers distinguished their revivals as otherworldly events, seasoned by the Holy Spirit and separate from the political and commercial corruptions of man. Social and political matters were not entirely ignored in the early stages of revival meetings, but they were often used rhetorically, as a counterpoint to the evangelical regeneration that followed. Ministers tended to describe the reception of divine grace as contingent on the transcendence of petty politics and human intrigue. The narrative of Scottish-American revivalism has thus been less concerned with the Presbyterian response to political unionism from the mid-seventeenth to the mid-eighteenth century or its legacy in America during the imperial crisis. In conversion narratives, at least, civil matters were less likely to combine with Presbyterian devotion as a coherent political theology or as a continu-

---

tary," *American Historical Review,* CIV (1999), 497. For a general definition of the meaning and development of "New British History," see John Morrill, "The British Problem, c. 1534–1707," in Brendan Bradshaw and Morrill, eds., *The British Problem, c. 1534–1707: State Formation in the Atlantic Archipelago* (Basingstoke, U.K., 1996), 1–38; Pocock, "British History: A Plea for a New Subject," *Journal of Modern History,* XLVII (1975), 601–621. On the problem of "multiple kingdoms" in a confessional context (Presbyterians, Anglicans, Puritans, and Catholics) up to and beyond the 1707 Act of Union, see Tim Harris, "Critical Perspectives: The Autonomy of English History?" in Glen Burgess, ed., *New British History: Founding a Modern State, 1603–1715* (London, 1999), 275; Charles W. A. Prior, *Defining the Jacobean Church: The Politics of Religious Controversy, 1603–1625* (Cambridge, 2005), 15; Peter Lake, *Anglicans and Puritans? Presbyterianism and English Conformist Thought from Whitgift to Hooker* (London, 1988); Colin Kidd, "Protestantism, Constitutionalism, and British Identity under the Later Stuarts," in Brendan Bradshaw and Peter Roberts, eds., *British Consciousness and Identity: The Making of Britain, 1533–1707* (Cambridge, 1998), 321–342; David Allan, "Protestantism, Presbyterianism, and National Identity in Eighteenth-Century Scottish History," in Tony Claydon and Ian McBride, eds., *Protestantism and National Identity: Britain and Ireland, c. 1650–c. 1850* (Cambridge, 1998), 182–206. David Armitage and Nicholas Canny have suggested that new British and Atlantic perspectives ought to inform the other of the creative tension between center and periphery. See Armitage, "Greater Britain: A Useful Category of Historical Analysis?" *AHR,* CIV (1999), 427–445; Canny, "Writing Atlantic History; or, Reconfiguring the History of Colonial British America," *JAH,* LXXXVI (1999), 1093–1114. Daniel Walker Howe has asked why historians "have not done better by Witherspoon" and has suggested that the clergyman's ambiguous Scottish-American context has discouraged scholars. See Howe, "John Witherspoon and the Transatlantic Enlightenment," in Manning and Cogliano, eds., *The Atlantic Enlightenment,* 68.

ing religious commentary on political and constitutional change in the British Empire.[23]

The historiography of political culture in the Middle Colonies, conversely, has distinguished the general experience of popular piety from the worldly interactions of Presbyterian settlers in day-to-day governance. It has concentrated on the capricious and varied motivations that obliged Scottish and Ulster-Scottish settlers to engage with civic authorities. By the turn of the eighteenth century, Presbyterians began to vie for local power alongside Anglicans, Congregationalists, Quakers, Lutherans, and Dutch Calvinists in a myriad number of local struggles, factional intrigues, and parochial protests. In the settlement of New Jersey from the mid-seventeenth to the mid-eighteenth century, for example, the ambiguous jurisdiction of proprietary governance predisposed Presbyterian settlers to form into various factions, each of which sought representation and socioeconomic privileges from competing elites. The intersection between confessional identity and political jurisdiction often led to complex and unpredictable rivalries, even while most populations were united in their general reverence for the Hanoverian monarchy.[24]

23. See Leigh Eric Schmidt, *Holy Fairs: Scotland and the Making of American Revivalism,* 2d ed. (Grand Rapids, Mich., 2001). Other studies have similarly highlighted the transatlantic dimension of American evangelicalism and its association with Scottish popular piety. See Mark Noll et al., eds., *Evangelicalism: Comparative Studies of Popular Protestantism in North America, the British Isles, and Beyond, 1700–1990* (New York, 1994), 3–6; Michael J. Crawford, *Seasons of Grace: Colonial New England's Revival Tradition in Its British Context* (New York, 1991); Marilyn J. Westerkamp, *Triumph of the Laity: Scots-Irish Piety and the Great Awakening, 1625–1760* (New York, 1988); Susan O'Brien, "A Transatlantic Community of Saints: The Great Awakening and the First Evangelical Network, 1735–1755," *AHR,* XCI (1986), 811–832; O'Brien, "Eighteenth-Century Publishing Networks in the First Years of Transatlantic Evangelism," in Noll et al., eds., *Evangelism,* 38–57. Cultures of Presbyterian evangelicalism also influenced other denominations in colonial and early national America. See Kimberly Bracken Long, *The Eucharistic Theology of the American Holy Fairs* (Louisville, Ky., 2011), 63–83. For an example of local political motifs in the initial stages of New England revivalism, see Frank Lambert, *Inventing the "Great Awakening"* (Princeton, N.J., 1999), 133–135.

24. See Landsman's pioneering study, *Scotland and Its First American Colony,* 101–130. See also Brendan McConville, *These Daring Disturbers of the Public Peace: The Struggle for Property and Power in Early New Jersey* (Ithaca, N.Y., 1999), 28–46, 48–50, 76–89; Richard R. Beeman, *The Varieties of Political Experience in Eighteenth-Century America* (Philadelphia, 2004), 27–28; Joyce D. Goodfriend, *Before the Melting Pot: Society and Culture in Colonial New York City, 1664–1730* (Princeton, N.J., 1992); Patricia U. Bonomi, "The Middle Colonies: Embryo of the New Political Order," in Alden T. Vaughan and George Athan Billias, eds., *Perspectives on Early American History: Essays in Honor of Richard B. Morris* (New York, 1973), 63–92; Michael

Historians are rightly cautious about reading the unity engendered by the American Revolutionary wars into the earlier factional contexts of colonial Presbyterian life. Though scholarship on local political engagement by Presbyterians in New Jersey, Pennsylvania, and New York is rich, it has tended to avoid any broad associations between Presbyterian piety, ecclesiology, and intercolonial American identity. Moreover, it often comes to an abrupt end in the 1760s. Scholars have eschewed more general links between Presbyterian religious ideology and patriot political engagement. They have focused on either the chaotic factionalism of civic life or the otherworldly context of revivalism—most often during the colonial era. The potential depth of the Presbyterian contribution to the emergence of patriot political ideology is still to be assessed.[25]

"Cousin America Has Run Off with a Presbyterian Parson"

What, then, are we to make of loyalist and Anglican assertions regarding the centrality of Presbyterianism in the patriot movement? How exactly should we contextualize the alleged statement from Horace Walpole, who, upon hearing of the American Revolution's latest "extraordinary proceedings," is said to have risen from his seat in the British House of Commons and to have summarized, coolly: "Cousin America has run off with a Presbyterian parson." If we are to believe secondary accounts of Walpole's lament,

---

Zuckerman, "Introduction: Puritans, Cavaliers, and the Motley Middle," in Zuckerman, ed., *Friends and Neighbors: Group Life in America's First Plural Society* (Philadelphia, 1982); Wayne Bodle, "The 'Myth of the Middle Colonies' Reconsidered: The Process of Regionalization in Early America," *PMHB*, CXIII (1989), 527–548.

    25. Liam Riordan argues that, in the transitional decades after the War of Independence, religion became a social tool to organize and delineate interest groups in and around mid-Atlantic towns; see Riordan, *Many Identities, One Nation: The Revolution and Its Legacy in the Mid-Atlantic* (Philadelphia, 2007). For accounts of the relationship between Presbyterian communities and colonial political culture that continue through 1776 rather than 1760 and that contain some discussion of religious actors, see James A. Henretta, *The Evolution of American Society, 1700–1815: An Interdisciplinary Analysis* (Lexington, Mass., 1973), 115–116; Benjamin H. Newcomb, *Political Partisanship in the American Middle Colonies, 1700–1776* (Baton Rouge, La., 1995); Michael C. Batinski, *The New Jersey Assembly, 1738–1775: The Making of a Legislative Community* (Lanham, Md., 1987); Patricia U. Bonomi, *A Factious People: Politics and Society in Colonial New York* (New York, 1971); Alison G. Olson, "Eighteenth-Century Colonial Legislatures and Their Constituents," *JAH*, LXXIX (1992), 543–567; Brendan McConville, *The King's Three Faces: The Rise and Fall of Royal America, 1688–1776* (Chapel Hill, N.C., 2006), 109–110, 146, 298; Landsman, *Scotland and Its First American Colony*, 4, 147–158, 165, 174–176, 184–185, 250.

he was most likely referring to Witherspoon, whose Revolutionary sermons had recently been published in London. In May 1776, Witherspoon had signaled his support for American independence in his *Dominion of Providence* sermon. Its text was widely circulated in Britain's political and intellectual circles during the following year. Witherspoon had written a separate *Address to the Natives of Scotland Residing in America* as an appendix to the text and had made sure that both were published together on both sides of the Atlantic. He wrote: "As soon as I had consented to the publication of the foregoing sermon, I felt an irresistible desire to accompany it with a few words addressed to you [Scots living in Britain and America] in particular."[26]

But how "in particular" did Witherspoon seek to embody their political theology? We know that Anglicans and various other disgruntled parties specified the Presbyterian contribution to patriot ideology, including Witherspoon's role. We know that New British historians have incorporated Scottish evangelicalism in their discussion of early modern political constitutionalism and eighteenth-century nation building. But, as Britain's imperial union began to disintegrate, was there really a distinctive voice of Presbyterian political theology in American patriot thought?

Clarifying the Presbyterian contribution to the social, intellectual, and political culture of Revolutionary and early national America is not easy, despite the seeming evidence of collective religious and political identity in loyalist critiques of "the hate of Kings, and glory of the Kirk." When Witherspoon sought to address Scots in America, he was well aware that a significant number were still likely to be loyal to the British cause, even after he signed the Declaration of Independence. In a new confederation where the nature of authority was not yet clear, they saw much at stake in losing the customary autonomies that they had previously enjoyed. Some were Episcopalian, or Quaker, or of a sufficiently moderate Presbyterian hue that they feared the ascendant role of evangelicalism in inspiring patriot critiques of British corruption. Even among those who considered themselves partial to the idea of American independence, one Presbyterian mind was not necessarily the same as another. The 1647 Westminster Confession of Faith could be read and interpreted very differently depending on education, context, and Old World

26. On the rumored statement by Walpole, see Egbert Watson Smith, *The Creed of the Presbyterians* (Richmond, Va., 1941), 146. On the circulation of Witherspoon's *Dominion of Providence* sermon in England, see the English review of Witherspoon's May 1776 sermon, "The Dominion of Providence over the Passions of Men," in *Monthly Review,* LVIII (March 1778), 246–247. For Witherspoon's reference to Scots as an audience, see John Witherspoon, *Address to the Natives of Scotland Residing in America,* in [Green, ed.], *Works of Witherspoon,* III, 47.

roots. Scottish and Ulster-Scottish settlers who engaged in warfare against French, native American, and then British forces might well have read the catechisms of the Westminster Confession of Faith distinctly from those who sat politely in their Princeton pews. The distinctions among those settlers were perhaps even greater when it came to interpreting the association between colonial Presbyterian piety and the patriot critique of British misrule.[27]

Conversely, if we do attend to the individual nuances of Presbyterian identity, and their potential reflection or repudiation in Witherspoon's influential voice, our account may then overlook the ecumenical dimension of Revolutionary political theology. That we have not heard the orthodox Presbyterian voice—Witherspoon's or otherwise—may be an accurate reflection of the Revolution's "providential" rather than denominational religious rhetoric. Much scholarship, after all, has pointed to a general form of religious unity in the move toward a confederation of former colonies and provinces. References to the "Protestant" or the "Christian" or simply the "religious" contribution to patriot identity may even correspond to the "millenarian" nature of Revolutionary culture. Opposition to imperial tyranny could unite ministers and congregations in eschatological terms. They believed that new forms of union between varying denominations—and even creeds—might offer a portent of the Second Coming.[28]

27. Camillo Querno [Odell], *The American Times*, 18. On Scottish loyalism, see Matthew P. Dziennik, "Through an Imperial Prism: Land, Liberty, and Highland Loyalism in the War of American Independence," *Journal of British Studies*, L (2011), 332–358; United States, Bureau of the Census, *Historical Statistics of the United States: Colonial Times to 1970*, bicentennial ed., 2 vols. (Washington, D.C., 1975), II, 1168; Francis D. Cogliano, *Revolutionary America, 1763–1815: A Political History*, 2d ed. (New York, 2009), 32; Robert V. Wells, "Population and Family in Early America," in Jack P. Greene and J. R. Pole, eds., *The Blackwell Encyclopaedia of the American Revolution* (Oxford, 1991), 41; Robert M. Calhoon, "Loyalism and Neutrality," ibid., 247; Paul H. Smith, "The American Loyalists: Notes on Their Organization and Numerical Strength," *WMQ*, 3d Ser., XXV (1968), 274; Ian Charles Cargill Graham, *Colonists from Scotland: Emigration to North America, 1707–1783* (1956; rpt. Baltimore, 1997), 20; Ned C. Landsman, *From Colonials to Provincials: American Thought and Culture, 1680–1760* (New York, 1997), chap. 1; J. M. Bumsted, "The Scottish Diaspora: Emigration to British North America, 1763–1815," in Landsman, ed., *Nation and Province in the First British Empire: Scotland and the Americas, 1600–1800* (Lewisburg, Pa., 2001), 127–250, esp. 136–137, 144. See also the excellent discussion of the potential differences of opinion among Presbyterian patriots in Tiedemann, "Presbyterianism and the American Revolution," *Church History*, LXXIV (2005), 317–318.

28. Nicholas Guyatt, *Providence and the Invention of the United States, 1607–1876* (Cambridge, 2007), 95–133; Hutson, *Religion and the Founding of the American Republic*, 3–49, 53–54; West, *Politics of Revelation and Reason*, 1–11; Bonomi, *Under the Cope of Heaven*, 187–209;

When defining the general Protestant unity of patriot political theology, including its millenarian dimension, scholars have often referred to the ironic continuity between anti-French, anti-Jacobite, and anti-British ideology. Each could provide unity between "rationalists" and "revivalists" to diminish doctrinal tensions within and between Protestant sects. Such a phenomenon has led historians to question Alan Heimert's famous attempt to link the "evangelicals" and "anti-evangelicals" of the 1740s to the "revolutionaries" and "loyalists" of the 1770s. It is widely accepted that evangelicalism could disturb social authority in general ways, making later Revolutionary activity at least more acceptable in local American communities. Nonetheless, many historical accounts also endorse the conclusion that colonial revivalism did not "directly" predispose Americans to Revolutionary political action, particularly in light of the ecumenical unity among different Protestants against external forces.[29]

Inferring a strong continuity in the association between evangelicalism and political ideology from the 1750s to the 1770s is therefore problematic.

Gordon S. Wood, *The Creation of the American Republic, 1776–1787* (Chapel Hill, N.C., 1969), 114–118. Richard Connors and Andrew Colin Gow, eds., *Anglo-American Millennialism, from Milton to the Millerites* (Boston, 2004), 115–176. On the ecumenical dimension in millenarian and millennial thought during the Revolutionary era, see also Bloch, *Visionary Republic;* Nathan O. Hatch, *The Sacred Cause of Liberty: Republican Thought and the Millennium in Revolutionary New England* (New Haven, Conn., 1977). For a critique of the millenarian thesis, see Stout, *New England Soul,* 306–309.

29. Before the Revolutionary era, according to Mark A. Noll, "Christian Republican" opposition to French Catholic power added a Protestant inflection to existing "Real Whig" critiques of authoritarian corruption. The colonial "turn against Britain as villain" represented an ironic "extrapolation" of the "religious-republican synthesis" that had united moderates and evangelicals against France in the 1740s and 1750s. Moreover, "theological moderates" shared the millenarian tone that was adopted by many Congregational and Presbyterian revivalists during the Anglo-French wars. Articulating radical Whig and "country" principles, their statements were even replete with anti-popish motifs. See Noll, *America's God,* 8, 62–78, 79, 81. On religious attempts to link the defeat of Jacobites in Scotland to those suffered by the French in Canada, see Clark, *The Language of Liberty,* 364–370. On the coming together of "rationalist" and "revivalist" ministers in these contexts, see also Stout, *New England Soul,* 259; Bonomi, *Under the Cope of Heaven,* 161. For Alan Heimert's thesis and its critics, see Heimert, *Religion and the American Mind from the Great Awakening to the Revolution* (Cambridge, Mass., 1966); Philip Goff, "Revivals and Revolution: Historiographic Turns since Alan Heimert's Religion and the American Mind," *Church History,* LXVII (1998), 695–721. As Christopher Grasso has shown, the meaning and context of American evangelicalism was often very different in 1745 than in 1765, particularly in educational settings. Thomas Clap's Yale presidency (1740–1766), for example, witnessed a continual redefinition of theological principles. See Grasso, *A Speaking Aristocracy: Transforming Public Discourse in Eighteenth-Century Connecticut* (Chapel Hill, N.C., 1999), 106, 144–185.

Such an analysis makes it easier to understand why historians have felt comfortable defining Witherspoon's patriot stance through reference to common sensory theories. Despite his earlier evangelicalism, scholars have suggested his influence by a moderate theological and philosophical consensus as he joined patriots in opposition to Britain. This interpretation at least avoids the awkward notion that the radicalism of evangelicalism somehow united the periods of awakening and Revolution. But does it accurately reflect the nature of Witherspoon's moral reasoning and his political theology? Does it really convey the wider meaning and context of a clergyman, teacher, and political representative who endeavored to understand and then articulate the significance of a "cousins' war" — a war whose common butchery hardly seemed to corroborate the Scottish Enlightenment notion of innate moral sensibility?[30]

From Kirk to Congress

Recovering Witherspoon's Presbyterian evangelical voice raises difficult questions about the cultural context in which he was an important religious, educational, and civic figure. But these questions do provide illuminating answers. Situating Witherspoon's piety in the Revolutionary Atlantic world will widen our understanding of the religious, philosophical, and political context of American independence in two important and broadly related ways.

Reintegrating Witherspoon's evangelicalism into the narrative of the Revolutionary and early national era should allow us to question received assumptions about the centrality of Scottish moral philosophy on the western side of the Atlantic. Witherspoon's contribution to educational and civic culture during the American founding did not suggest an entirely binary dichotomy between Enlightenment and religious reasoning. Neither, however, did it imply their easy combination, as much historiography of Scottish-American intellectual and religious culture has claimed.

30. On the problematic association between Great Awakening evangelicalism and patriot ideology, see the counterfactual essay by John M. Murrin. If anything, according to Murrin, Revolutionary-era political radicalism "liberated the spirit of the Awakening, which had grown tepid and largely ineffective among all but Baptists by the 1770s," inspiring a later generation of evangelicals in their desire to "reshape the social landscape." See Murrin, "No Awakening, No Revolution? More Counterfactual Speculations," *Reviews in American History*, XI (1983), 161–171, esp. 169. On the Baptist challenge, see Rhys Isaac, "Evangelical Revolt: The Nature of the Baptists' Challenge to the Traditional Order in Virginia, 1765 to 1775," *WMQ*, 3d Ser., XXXI (1974), 345–368. On the concept of a "cousins' war," see Kevin Phillips, *The Cousins' Wars: Religion, Politics, and the Triumph of Anglo-America* (New York, 1999).

As Chapters 1 and 2 will show, Witherspoon's role in the Kirk allowed him to consider the intersections between moral philosophy, religious revivalism, and civic cohesion. After the 1707 Act of Union, when Edinburgh lost its independent Parliament, the Church of Scotland nonetheless retained its institutional autonomy within the wider British realm (and also, potentially, within the British Empire). Thus, the Kirk General Assembly became Scotland's primary institution in which civic, constitutional, and even imperial issues were debated. Unsurprisingly, those issues tended to achieve a religious inflection when they were raised among assembled Scottish churchmen. In a tense rivalry with their Moderate Presbyterian associates, evangelical members of the Kirk cherished their right to promote what they perceived to be the revivalist doctrines of the 1647 Westminster Confession of Faith. That right, they believed, lay separate from the federal prerogative of the new British Parliament after 1707. They focused on promoting the necessity of salvation before moral reasoning, rather than the innateness of ethical sensibility. In doing so, they offered an alternative vision of Presbyterian confessional authority to provincial Britons, separate from Scottish Enlightenment definitions of civic cohesion.[31]

The legacy of the religious and constitutional debates that took place in the Kirk during the 1740s and 1750s should help us to understand Witherspoon's political sermons, writings, and activities during the later American Revolutionary era—and even those of his most prominent students. Reasserting the role of evangelicalism in his American career, including in his influence over future civic leaders, should illuminate the changing constitutional meaning of Presbyterian religious autonomy in the Atlantic world from the colonial to the Revolutionary period, from Scotland to America, and from the General Assembly of the Kirk to the floor of the nascent U.S. Congress.

Before Witherspoon's arrival in the Middle Colonies, constitutional disagreements in the region often highlighted the ambiguous nature of confessional pluralism in the new British Empire. Examining those disagreements, Chapter 3 will question the notion that Presbyterian civic engagement in New Jersey, New York, and Pennsylvania amounted to byzantine factionalism. Historians are beginning to focus on several important legal arguments in which colonial American Presbyterians referenced the general principle of Kirk autonomy after 1707. They addressed their protests toward royal gov-

31. Colin Kidd, "Religious Realignment between the Restoration and Union," in John Robertson, ed., *A Union for Empire: Political Thought and the British Union of 1707* (Cambridge, 1995), 145–168, esp. 168; Jeffrey Stephen, "The Kirk and the Union, 1706–7: A Reappraisal," *Records of the Scottish Church History Society*, XXXI (2001), 68–96.

ernors, proprietary rulers, or Anglican ministers who could be accused of supporting measures to curtail local religious powers. Their contribution to provincial struggles, ironically, should reduce the tendency to view colonial American history as a prelude to independence. Distance from metropolitan jurisdiction in London was not necessarily perceived in negative or parochial terms. Presbyterian dissension turned on the relationship between local religious independence and wider imperial authority. It did not yet oppose allegiance to the British Empire itself.[32]

Witherspoon's evangelical predecessors who founded the College of New Jersey were often described by American colonists as New Side Presbyterians. Continuing their legacy, Witherspoon outlined the absolute necessity of individual salvation and regeneration through the 1760s and 1770s. New Side Presbyterians had once accused their Old Side adversaries of forgoing a sustained emphasis on salvation and repentance in favor of an educated, polite, and overly rationalistic form of faith. Yet it would be a mistake to suggest that Witherspoon somehow reignited earlier New Side–Old Side Presbyterian divisions upon his arrival in America. As Chapter 3 will show,

32. In both the commercial and religious sphere, Presbyterians throughout the British Atlantic world "came to identify as a 'liberal' point of view" the "just regard for the interests of all parties, provincial as well as metropolitan, which they contrasted with 'confined' or 'narrow' metropolitan views"; see Ned C. Landsman, "The Provinces and the Empire: Scotland, the American Colonies, and the Development of British Provincial Identity," in Lawrence Stone, ed., *An Imperial State at War: Britain from 1689 to 1815* (London, 1993), 265. Most historians have turned to the seventeenth century and identified the eventual move toward toleration in England with pluralism in America during the following era. Yet the role of Presbyterian religion in the British imperial world after the 1707 Act of Union was deemed relevant to colonial religious and political objections against Anglican attempts to curtail their right to organize and preach. Landsman's work on the significance of the Act of Union in North American ecclesiology is important for this discussion: "North American Anglicans did their best to ignore the [Presbyterian] implications of the union," which had the potential to situate colonists — and colonial American Presbyterians, in particular — "beyond the reach" of England's Act of Uniformity. See Landsman, "The Episcopate," in Beneke and Grenda, eds., *The First Prejudice*, 84–85. See also Landsman, "Presbyterians and Provincial Society: The Evangelical Enlightenment in the West of Scotland, 1740–1775," in John Dwyer and Richard B. Sher, eds., *Sociability and Society in Eighteenth-Century Scotland* (Edinburgh, 1993), 194–195; Landsman, "The Legacy of British Union for the North American Colonies: Provincial Elites and the Problem of Imperial Union," in Robertson, ed., *Union for Empire*, 297–318; Tiedemann, "Presbyterianism and the American Revolution," *Church History*, LXXIV (2005), 310; Tiedemann, *Reluctant Revolutionaries*, 35–37; Mark McGarvie and Elizabeth Mensch, "Law and Religion in Colonial America," in Michael Grossberg and Christopher Tomlins, eds., *The Cambridge History of Law in America*, 3 vols. (Cambridge, 2008), I, 324–364.

his immediate forerunners at the College of New Jersey had gone some way toward reducing the dichotomy between extra-institutional evangelicalism and elite establishmentarianism. They chose to instill evangelical principles within a formal institution of higher education, rather than through itinerant revivalism. The institutionalization of evangelical Presbyterian pedagogy had even appealed to the most famous American theologian of the colonial era, Jonathan Edwards. Though he had once castigated Old Light Congregationalists for their stultifying formalism, Edwards came to espouse ministerial and pedagogical "assurance" of the empirical truth of regeneration. In doing so, he used the methodology and analytical terminology of several moral philosophers, despite continuing to oppose their anthropocentric ethical conclusions. Chapter 3 will highlight the similarity between Edwardsean assurance and the formal emphasis on evangelical instruction during the early history of the College of New Jersey. Such a synthesis between evangelicalism and formalism at the college proved attractive to Witherspoon, who noted the similarities with the evangelical emphasis of his previous Popular party allies in the Kirk.[33]

Notwithstanding the institutional and theological association between the predecessors of Edwards and Witherspoon at the College of New Jersey, it has most often been suggested that Witherspoon's educational output and public sermons were somehow dichotomous; that, unlike Edwards, he was content to eschew discussions of salvation and unregenerate morality when educating future statesmen. Chapter 4 will question such a dichotomy. Through his private reading, Edwards encountered the analytical concern with passions and feelings in Scottish philosophy. Yet such an encounter supplied him with important ideas and terminology, which he used in public evangelical discourse. It enabled him to isolate and describe the role of emotions in the experience of faith, regeneration, and external divine assistance. Similarly, Witherspoon often adopted the vocabulary of philosophical scholarship in order to question anthropocentric moral sensory conclusions. Even if we choose to focus on Witherspoon's American moral philosophy lectures rather than on his public sermons, therefore, it is not as easy to identify their repudiation of evangelical ideals as scholars have suggested.[34]

33. On the issue of ministerial assurance in eighteenth-century America, see Grasso, *A Speaking Aristocracy*, 105–106, 124–128.

34. Norman Fiering and Paul Ramsey have disputed the relative role of moral sense reasoning in Edwardsean theological discourse. Each has argued that the other places too great or too little emphasis on the translation of Hutchesonian theory from Edwards's private scholarship to his public evangelical statements. *Pace* Fiering, Ramsey argues that Edwards did not direct his

Witherspoon did not envision the "moral sense or conscience" as exactly akin to an inborn ethical compass, in distinction to the Hutchesonian notion of "moral sense." Rather, he tended to imply that it enabled the Holy Spirit to provide just enough illumination to understand individual sin and the importance of rebirth before full moral conversion. In some of his American lectures, Witherspoon hinted that external illumination could awaken (but not convert) those who had not yet encountered the gospel. Unregenerate individuals might at least be inspired to acknowledge the existence of an afterlife, despite never having been exposed to Christian teaching in their communities. Nonetheless, Witherspoon usually focused on the question of moral illumination in communities that *had* been exposed to the gospel. In those instances, he claimed, the action of the Holy Spirit allowed the individual moral conscience to acknowledge the necessity of further gracious intervention.[35]

Through the mid-eighteenth century, David Hume also adopted an analytical interest in passions and sentiments while questioning moral sensory conclusions. If perception was grounded in sensory feelings, Scotland's great skeptical philosopher claimed, then all objects and actions outside the mind might simply amount to sentimental impressions — always in flux and unable to correspond to an objective and static external reality. Hume was no orthodox Calvinist. Understandably, Witherspoon (and Edwards before him) did not support his insinuation that events recounted by biblical revelation could not be wholly verified. Throughout his career, Witherspoon warned that skep-

---

ire toward Hutcheson to such a great extent. See Fiering, *Jonathan Edwards's Moral Thought and Its British Context* (Chapel Hill, N.C., 1981); Jonathan Edwards, *Ethical Writings*, ed. Paul Ramsey, in Perry Miller et al., eds., *The Works of Jonathan Edwards*, VIII (New Haven, Conn., 1989), 6–7 n. 5, 18 n. 3, 29 nn. 5–6. As Sarah Rivett has argued, Edwards incorporated scholarly methods from Enlightenment empiricism into his Calvinist framework "in an effort to reduce the condition of uncertainty inherent in the problem of grace"; see Rivett, *The Science of the Soul in Colonial New England* (Chapel Hill, N.C., 2011), 296. See also James A. Harris, *Of Liberty and Necessity: The Free Will Debate in Eighteenth-Century British Philosophy* (New York, 2005), 108–127. Sang Hyun Lee has even suggested that the Northampton minister developed his own "philosophical theology"; see Lee, *The Philosophical Theology of Jonathan Edwards* (Princeton, N.J., 1988).

35. Witherspoon, "Lectures on Moral Philosophy," in [Green, ed.], *Works of Witherspoon*, III, 397. Witherspoon discussed the "apprehension" of an afterlife in much of humanity in his American "Lectures on Moral Philosophy"; see [Green, ed.], *Works of Witherspoon*, III, 382, 390. On Augustine and Scottish Calvinism, see P. G. Ryken, "Scottish Reformed Scholasticism," in Carl R. Trueman and R. Scott Clark, eds., *Protestant Scholasticism: Essays in Reassessment* (Carlisle, U.K., 1999), 200–204.

ticism and "immaterialism" were mischievous in questioning the objective stance of those who had witnessed the sacrifice of Christ. Like Hume, nonetheless, he remained wary of the philosophical claim that individuals could discern the morality of external actions in an easy and verifiable manner and that their sensory understanding was thus objective. As Chapter 5 will show, Witherspoon's perception of language and rhetorical expression in American "promiscuous assemblies" even inspired him to laud Hume's determination that unpredictable emotional sentiments required "the violent passionate eloquence that prevailed in Greece and Rome." His focus on the standardization of public expression in higher education sought to synthesize classical and evangelical forms of persuasion. It departed from several rhetorical assumptions that were associated with Scottish moral sense philosophy and that were popular among the private domestic tutors whom parents often hired to educate their offspring, notwithstanding the general concern for proper expression that Witherspoon shared with those same circles.[36]

The importance that Witherspoon attributed to learning, erudition, and literary studies did not require him to abandon the most salient evangelical principles, most notably the need for external divine assistance and regeneration before achieving a working moral compass. He distinguished himself from those who overemphasized their rhetorical ability to arouse innate ethical sensibilities through polite discourse. Surveying the cultural mores of the American home, for example, he perceived a propensity to abjure the role of religious revival in moral learning.

Of course, the notion of divine moral inspiration always retained an element of theological ambiguity in Witherspoon's American thought, just as it did for Edwards before him. Ever since Augustine, Christian theology had demonstrated a fundamental tension in its discussion of the contingent association between moral action and the reception of divine grace. How were

36. For examples of the Humean discussion of the unsettling role of sensations and impressions in human perception, see David Hume, *A Treatise of Human Nature: Being an Attempt to Introduce the Experimental Method of Reasoning into Moral Subjects*, I, *Of the Understanding* (London, 1739–1740), 24, 45, 167; Udo Thiel, *The Early Modern Subject: Self-Consciousness and Personal Identity from Descartes to Hume* (New York, 2011), 404; Paul Russell, *The Riddle of Hume's Treatise: Skepticism, Naturalism, and Irreligion* (New York, 2008), 85–88. For Witherspoon's statements on skepticism, see, for example, Witherspoon, "Lectures on Moral Philosophy," in [Green, ed.], *Works of Witherspoon*, III, 377, 395. On Witherspoon's description of "promiscuous assemblies" and his surprising account of Humean eloquence, see Witherspoon, "Lectures on Eloquence," ibid., 561, 574. But he did not translate this ethical disjuncture into a broader Humean discussion that questioned the general existence of objects and actions outside the mind (the ethical meaning of their interaction was a matter for debate).

individuals even able to understand the necessity of regeneration before its occurrence? Was a qualitative judgment still essential to acknowledge the future requirement of salvation? As a work of intellectual history, therefore, *John Witherspoon's American Revolution* will not eschew the remaining tensions in Witherspoon's moral and political philosophy. In the same sentence, occasionally, Witherspoon discussed and even commended philosophical accounts of natural moral perception only then to return to an evangelical depiction of unregenerate discernment. At times he demonstrated opacity, tentativeness, and even contradiction in accounting for the first origins of moral volition. When alluding to the chaos and violence of the Revolutionary wars, Witherspoon often described the natural disorder of unregenerate humanity and the resulting need for divine assistance. Yet even in these instances his attempted distinction between individual will and divine illumination remained slightly ambiguous. Like many evangelical theologians, Witherspoon often failed to account for the exact provenance of the "sense" that human chaos required external intervention from God.[37]

Ned C. Landsman has suggested that Witherspoon and other evangelical Scots were eventually able to transfer their allegiance to independent America because "Presbyterian orthodoxy" had moved away from the "strictly national and sectarian conception" of previous decades. Building on this insight, Chapter 6 will assess Witherspoon's growing perception that Westminster threatened the loose constitutional framework that underlay Presbyterian evangelical freedom. Scottish moral sense philosophy influenced intellectual circles on both sides of the Atlantic through the eighteenth century. But Presbyterian evangelicalism had also moved fluidly between the different provinces of the new British Empire, often in conjunction with the expansion of Scottish commercial enterprise.[38]

A generation before the imperial crisis, Witherspoon had opposed France in support of the British Empire. During the same period, nonetheless, he had also derided the moral reasoning of a number of his fellow Scotsmen— particularly those Moderates who promoted the notion of inborn morality and who could be found at the nexus between religion, politics, and higher education. Similarly, tensions between moral sensory reasoning and evangelical philosophy were displayed in Witherspoon's patriot political theology, notwithstanding the relative growth of dissenting Protestant unity against

37. Witherspoon, "Lectures on Moral Philosophy," in [Green, ed.], *Works of Witherspoon*, III, 369–370, 374.

38. Landsman, "Witherspoon and the Problem of Provincial Identity," in Sher and Smitten, eds., *Scotland and America*, 30, 37.

British corruption. Witherspoon joined other American Presbyterians in opposition to Britain. He castigated Westminster for constraining provincial forms of freedom—both religious and commercial—that had once developed under the Hanoverian monarchy. But, unlike other educated Revolutionaries, including a number of American Presbyterians, he remained unconvinced by Francis Hutcheson's moral sensory prescription about "when it is that colonies may turn independent"—a prescription shared by many Scottish Enlightenment thinkers during the half a century following Hutcheson's death. He warned patriots against privileging their ethical sensibility alongside their political independence. Uneasy when they denoted their developing ethical stance, he would not permit a breezy connection between their supposed moral sensibility and the legitimacy of their political statesmanship. Reflecting his evangelical Presbyterian origins, he refuted the claim that patriots enjoyed an innate moral understanding of British misrule or that independent Americans would cohere as a result of their inborn benevolence.[39]

Thus, *John Witherspoon's American Revolution* will question Witherspoon's role as a simple conduit for enlightened sensibility in America. It will highlight the constitutional framework in which he offered an evangelical Presbyterian critique of moral sense theory, both in Scotland and in Revolutionary America. It will unsettle the easy synthesis between Enlightenment reasoning and religious philosophy, reasserting the subjective understanding of morality at the heart of Calvinist evangelicalism. According to Witherspoon, the external action of the Holy Spirit on the moral conscience allowed individuals to recognize sin and their need for regeneration—whether they were British subjects or American patriots. Americans, in the aggregate, were morally distinguished from British subjects not because their sensibili-

---

39. Jon Butler has suggested that American "Presbyterians exhibited a particularly mixed record on the Revolution" given that "most members of the Synod of Philadelphia refrained from public comment on the impending conflict." Butler perhaps overemphasizes the unpredictable nature of Presbyterian political theology, particularly in the Middle Colonies. Nonetheless, Butler's observation should remind us that unambiguous public support for the patriot cause was not guaranteed from all Presbyterians. See Butler, *Religion in Colonial America*, 125; Butler, *Awash in a Sea of Faith: Christianizing the American People* (Cambridge, Mass., 1992), 203. See also Larry R. Gerlach, *Prologue to Independence: New Jersey in the Coming of the American Revolution* (New Brunswick, N.J., 1976), 214. On the use of Hutcheson's moral sensory theory to justify American independence, see Caroline Robbins, "'When It Is That Colonies May Turn Independent': An Analysis of the Environment and Politics of Francis Hutcheson (1694–1746)," *WMQ*, 3d Ser., XI (1954), 214–251.

ties were somehow more cultivated, nor because they possessed a special covenant with God. Rather, a greater proportion had been awakened to the sin that they shared with all men. This fact, ironically, legitimized their independence in Witherspoon's political theology: more were likely to follow the action of the Holy Spirit with full conversion, allowing concerted moral action as an external gift of grace. But any decline in humility would threaten the health, stability, and even the legitimacy of their new union.

Presbyterianism divided nations, states, and colonies into multiple layers of religious representation, each in counterpoise to the other, each according to different geographical catchments. Having spent his career in such an ecclesiastical system, Witherspoon became an American political representative at a time when the balance between local, regional, and national power was not fully settled. In a speech to Congress on July 30, 1776, he approved of the common agreement "that there must and shall be a confederacy for the purposes of [unity]." Chapter 7 will examine Witherspoon's understanding of the relationship between disestablishment, piety, and civic representation under the Articles of Confederation. He refrained from supporting political delegates who lobbied the nascent American Congress on behalf of their state religious establishments. Given his earlier experiences in Scotland and New Jersey, his stance was unsurprising. Yet it still remained a tricky task to encourage pious governance without promoting the civil establishment of religion.[40]

On the one hand, Witherspoon desired moral leadership on the state and national level. On the other hand, he also feared a monopoly of civil governance from any one religious group. He would suggest that the political establishment of religion undermined the grassroots power of religious revivalism. But his actual role in Congress, particularly as an author of national Fast Day declarations, came close to implying an association between his political and evangelical vocations. Even as he and other Presbyterians used their political position to negotiate on behalf of disestablished religious institutions, they did so as political representatives in political assemblies. Thus, Chapter 7 will consider whether the medium of Witherspoon's political negotiation ever undermined the nascent message of disestablishment. He resisted any charge that his congressional office set out to secure the interests of his or any other ministerial vocation. But he did wish for religion to contribute to civic order in more general terms. Whether they related to commercial strategy, foreign

40. John Witherspoon, "Part of a Speech in Congress upon the Confederation," in [Green, ed.], *Works of Witherspoon*, IV, 347.

treaties, or moral affairs, Witherspoon's political activities and public statements sought to redefine prevailing associations between innate ethical perception and the representative authority of civic leaders.

As a moral educator of statesmen and a new congressional delegate, Witherspoon sought to reconcile an inchoate understanding of disestablished religion with the need to inculcate piety among future civic representatives—many of them Presbyterian. Chapter 8 will examine the legacy of his attempted reconciliation in the moral and constitutional deliberations of his most famous student, James Madison. The Virginian spearheaded the disestablishment of religion in his home state and defended the new American Constitution by asserting that the "latent causes of faction" were "sown in the nature of man." Madison's understanding of the relationship between piety, factionalism, and federalism was influenced by debates that had taken place in evangelical Presbyterian circles during the previous few decades, if not the entire previous century.[41]

Yet *John Witherspoon's American Revolution* will also note the remaining questions and apprehensions in the intersection between Witherspoon's civic and moral thought and in its legacy. His use of philosophical terminology would lead some former students to extrapolate conceptual conclusions from the intellectual systems that he had mined for descriptive vocabulary. Conversely, his public evangelicalism would lead others to forget his debt to erudition and scholarly terminology. As the memory of his moral education grew more distant and crude, students often found it easier to define their influence either by revivalism or by moral sense theory, rather than suggesting ways in which sensory terminology expressed fundamental evangelical conclusions. By the early 1800s, moreover, some would advocate disestablishment in order to promote a free marketplace of religion—a realm in which different strands of Protestant revivalism could compete and flourish, not least their own. Yet others would support a stronger connection between Presbyterian religious institutions and civic governance on the local and state level. Many journeyed south and west to found educational, religious, and civic institutions. There were those who espoused public evangelicalism and questioned the notion of innate moral sensibility. Others legitimized their new authority in frontier regions by referring to their innate common sense.

41. For James Madison's famous statement and the arguments that framed it, see Madison, *"The Federalist Number 10,"* Nov. 22, 1787, in William T. Hutchinson et al., eds., *The Papers of James Madison,* 34 vols. to date (Chicago, 1962–1977; Charlottesville, Va., 1977–), X, 263–270.

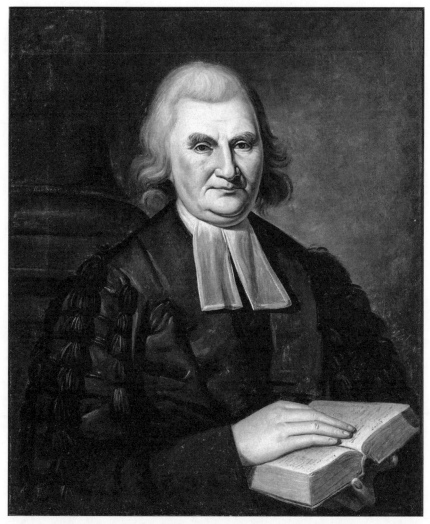

FIGURE 3. *Portrait of John Witherspoon (1723–1794), American Clergyman and Revolutionary Statesman.* By Rembrandt Peale, after Charles Willson Peale's portrait. 1794. Oil on canvas. National Portrait Gallery, Smithsonian Institution, Washington, D.C. / Art Resource, N.Y.

We will thus gain greater understanding of the ambiguity in Witherspoon's eventual American legacy: how he might be considered as both a conduit for moral sense philosophy and for evangelical reasoning and how he came to be conceived as both a progenitor of religious disestablishment and a promoter of pious governance. Even where we find consistency in Witherspoon's

American thought, it will remain important to locate the unintended consequences of its religious, political, and pedagogical influence. The complex
genealogy of Witherspoon's ideas — evangelical or otherwise — will highlight
the tricky relationship between cause and effect in the history of political theology from the Revolutionary period through the antebellum era.[42]

42. On the origins of the "Second Great Awakening" in this interpretation, see Nathan O. Hatch, *The Democratization of American Christianity* (New Haven, Conn., 1989), 35, 96–98, 220; Jonathan D. Sassi, *A Republic of Righteousness: The Public Christianity of the Post-Revolutionary New England Clergy* (Oxford, 2001), 109. On the free marketplace metaphor and disestablish-ment, see Chris Beneke, "The Free Market and the Founders' Approach to Church-State Re-lations," *Journal of Church and State,* LII (2010), 323–352; Philip Hamburger, *Separation of Church and State* (Cambridge, Mass., 2002), 21–65; Robert Calhoon, "Religion, Moderation, and Regime-Building in Post-Revolutionary America," in Eliga H. Gould and Peter S. Onuf, eds., *Empire and Nation: The American Revolution in the Atlantic World* (Baltimore, 2005), 216–220.

{ PART I }

From Scotland to America

"A ROAD TO DISTINCTION VERY DIFFERENT FROM THAT OF HIS MORE SUCCESSFUL COMPANIONS"

Augustinian Piety in Witherspoon's Scotland

In December 1776, at the height of the American Revolutionary crisis, the Scottish Presbyterian minister Alexander Carlyle delivered a pro-British sermon titled *The Justice and Necessity of the War with Our American Colonies Examined.* Preaching to his Edinburgh audience, he defended the moral philosophy of his fellow Moderate churchmen as well as Anglicans in "South Britain" and claimed that misguided American patriots lacked similar ethical and philosophical guidance. Their "treatment of the episcopal clergy," indeed, was "remarkably barbarous" and showed no concern for those from South Britain who were "indisputably the firmest barrier against fanaticism, either in religion or politics." American Revolutionaries were prone to "intangle the many in the mazes of sophistry" as they eschewed their debt to mainland British culture. Under "this government," Carlyle claimed, "we have lived with more security and happiness than any nation ever did. . . . Far superior to the republics of antiquity, the government of Britain has maintained the rights of human nature, with a happy equality." Thus it is "just and necessary to shed our blood now, in reducing our ungrateful children to a sense of their duty. . . . Nor is it *our* interest alone that obliges us to reject their demands, but *their* interest also." Only with British metropolitan support could Americans continue to enjoy religious, cultural, and commercial liberty: "Under this government against which they revolt, they have been free and happy, and have grown to that height of wealth and population which, we say, has made them forget or despise all obligation, and aspire at independency."[1]

By the early nineteenth century, Carlyle's view of the cultural context of

---

1. Alexander Carlyle, *The Justice and Necessity of the War with Our American Colonies Examined; a Sermon, Preached at Inveresk, December 12, 1776, Being the Fast-Day Appointed by the King, on Account of the American Rebellion* (Edinburgh, 1777), 13, 14, 16, 18–20.

Revolutionary America had not changed. In his memoirs, he recalled the journey of his former friend John Witherspoon from the Kirk to the American Congress. The "future life and public character of Dr Witherspoon" was, according to Carlyle, "perfectly known" to all educated men. But his earlier trajectory was less well understood. Witherspoon, who had died a few years earlier in 1794, had once been Carlyle's classmate at the University of Edinburgh during the late 1730s and early 1740s. Carlyle recalled the development of Witherspoon's evangelicalism in America and claimed that it departed from the sunnier view of human capability that they both had encountered during their earlier joint education. He remembered a time when his classmate Witherspoon "was a good scholar, far advanced for his age, very sensible and shrewd, but of a disagreeable temper, which was irritated by a flat voice and awkward manner, which prevented his making an impression on his companions of either sex that was at all adequate to his ability." In Carlyle's assessment, this "defect, when he was a lad, stuck to [Witherspoon] when he grew up to manhood [after his University of Edinburgh education], and so much roused his envy and jealousy, and made him take a road to distinction" in America that was "very different from that of his more successful companions" in Scotland.[2]

Carlyle associated Witherspoon's soberly religious manner, and his inability to match Scotland's developing standards of form and style, with his overweight and overbearing father, who lived on past his son's graduation from university. Carlyle assumed such a correlation in light of the happier persona that he witnessed on fishing trips with the young Witherspoon:

> I used sometimes to go with him for a day or two to his father's house at Gifford Hall, where we passed the day in fishing, to be out of reach of his father, who was very sulky and tyrannical, but who, being much given to gluttony, fell asleep early, and went always to bed at nine, and, being as fat as a porpoise, was not to be awaked, so that we had three or four hours of liberty every night to amuse ourselves with the daughters of the family, and their cousins who resorted to us from the village, when the old man was gone to rest. This John loved of all things; and

2. Alexander Carlyle, *Autobiography of the Rev. Dr. Alexander Carlyle, Minister of Inveresk: Containing Memorials of the Men and Events of His Time* (Edinburgh, 1860), 29–30. The memoirs were penned toward the end of Carlyle's life, probably in the early 1800s, and published posthumously nearly sixty years later. On Witherspoon's early schooling before his time at the University of Edinburgh, including Christian plays in Latin alongside the usual curriculum, see Varnum Lansing Collins, *President Witherspoon: A Biography*, 2 vols. (Princeton, N.J., 1925), I, 3–14.

this sort of company he enjoyed in greater perfection when he returned my visits, when we had still more companions of the fair sex, and no restraint from an austere father; so that I always considered the austerity of manners and aversion to social joy which he affected afterwards, as the arts of hypocrisy and ambition; for he had a strong and enlightened understanding, far above enthusiasm, and a tempter that did not seem liable to it.

Witherspoon's evangelical career in Scotland, and his rise to prominence in America as a leading religious conscience, was apparently an exercise in "hypocrisy and ambition." A life well lived would have been the ultimate response to a puritanical, "sulky and tyrannical" father. Summers with Carlyle offered such a life and demonstrated Witherspoon's true, moderate self. But when autumn came, Witherspoon became his father. He railed against the "social joy" of Scotland's advancing civil and religious culture despite the cheerful self he had shown alongside Carlyle and their "companions of the fair sex." To become an American founder, Witherspoon supplicated himself to the "austere" manner of a father he should have escaped long ago in Scotland. Witherspoon's rise to prominence was hypocritical because the evangelical niche he found for himself in America promoted an ascetic brand of moralism that he had once taken pleasure in escaping. His journey to distinction owed much to the art of "ambition" because it meandered from Scotland to America, where a public evangelical was better able to find a paymaster.[3]

Witherspoon apparently became "close, and suspicious, and jealous, and always aspiring at a superiority that he was not able to maintain" on account of his deficient temperament. According to Carlyle, therefore, he was forced to resort to artless forms of religious expression. His rise to prominence in America, moreover, was an indictment of the underdeveloped cultural context of his new home. Carlyle adopted the structure and tone of a historical inquiry in order to attribute Witherspoon's public success after his 1768 arrival in New Jersey to a dour form of religion. His new environment had allowed his "defect[s]" to provide cultural and clerical cachet. Where else but in the colonies, he insinuated, could Witherspoon's faulty temperament have achieved such public respect? A crude evangelical demeanor was unsuited to Scotland's increasingly sophisticated religious and intellectual culture but was somehow preferred by American colonists, who later became dangerous Revolutionaries.[4]

3. Carlyle, *Autobiography*, 64–65.
4. Ibid., 29–30, 65–66.

Carlyle reflected earlier assumptions about the relationship between Presbyterian evangelicalism and American Revolutionary fervor. But, unlike
American loyalists such as the Reverend Jonathan Odell and Scottish Episcopalians such as Hugo Arnot, he saw no revolutionary or antimonarchical
inevitabilities in the general ideology of Scottish Presbyterianism. Carlyle
was also a Presbyterian, but a moderate one. Looking back to the imperial
crisis, his pejorative reference to Witherspoon's "distinction" drew a clear
and unflattering contrast between the clergyman's American evangelicalism
and Carlyle's own Scottish moral vision. In the decades before formulating his early-nineteenth-century memoirs, Carlyle had become a writer of
belles lettres, an amateur historian, and an esteemed member of the Church
of Scotland's dominant faction of Presbyterian ministers, which some scholars have described as "the Scottish Enlightenment at prayer." He had risen
through the ranks of the Kirk, where Witherspoon's scholarly potential had
not been rewarded.[5]

Carlyle's *Autobiography* was teleological in its depiction of the moral learning that he and Witherspoon had been able to receive in their early years. It
judged Witherspoon's educational development according to Scottish moral
sense theories that had not in fact been normative during the Augustan era. A
greater emphasis on inborn ethical agency certainly became apparent in Scotland's intellectual and religious culture during the first decades of the eighteenth century. Despite Carlyle's later recollection, however, such an emphasis was not yet able to supersede the notion that unregenerate beings lacked
the capacity for innate benevolence. Depending on which minister or teacher
they encountered, Carlyle and Witherspoon could be taught about the innateness of human moral understanding, the necessity of salvation for ethical
sensibility, and many gradations between the two viewpoints.[6]

5. Camillo Querno [Jonathan Odell], *The American Times: A Satire, in Three Parts in Which
Are Delineated . . . the Leaders of the American Rebellion* (London, 1780), 97; Hugo Arnot, *The
XLV Chapter of the Prophecies of Thomas the Rhymer, in Verse; with Notes and Illustrations; Dedicated to Doctor Silverspoon, Preacher of Sedition in America* (Edinburgh, 1776). On the "Scottish
Enlightenment at prayer," see Colin Kidd, "Subscription, the Scottish Enlightenment, and the
Moderate Interpretation of History," *Journal of Ecclesiastical History,* LV (2004), 503. According to Richard B. Sher, Carlyle "articulated his belief that the Church of Scotland could and
should compensate for its lack of wealth with excellence in other areas, including above all polite
learning." See Sher, "Carlyle, Alexander (1722–1805)," in David Cannadine, gen. ed., *Oxford Dictionary of National Biography,* online ed. (Oxford, 2004–).

6. On the Westminster Confession's emphasis on unregenerate sin, see Philip Benedict,
Christ's Churches Purely Reformed: A Social History of Calvinism (New Haven, Conn., 2002),
401. On the range of differences in Scottish moral philosophy, see James A. Harris, "Answering

Modern historiography has followed Carlyle in overlooking the diverse context of the early education that he shared with Witherspoon, but in support of a very different conclusion. Relying on a binary division between an "Arminian" religious enlightenment and evangelical orthodoxy, scholars have suggested that Witherspoon's American career encompassed a turn toward human-centered ethical ideals. Responding to Augustine's defense of original sin, the influential Dutch Reformed theologian Jacobus Arminius (1560–1609) had asserted that freedom of the will derived from a rational approach to faith that gave agency to individuals in their decision to receive God's grace. Aligning Witherspoon with similar reasoning ignores the possibility that aspects of moral sensory terminology could in fact support orthodox evangelical assumptions in both Scotland and America. Before examining the fissures that had opened up in Scotland's church and university establishment by the 1760s, then, it is important to identify and understand Witherspoon's earlier educational upbringing, his developing theological viewpoint as a young minister, and their roots in early modern Scottish piety. Prefiguring his later contribution to American moral philosophy, Witherspoon's Scottish theology often adopted the vocabulary of sensory perception without implying the innateness of human ethical volition.[7]

"The Famous St. Augustine" Comes to Scotland

European Calvinists, including Scottish Presbyterians, often translated the word *covenant* from the Hebrew *berith* and the Greek *diatheke*. Both

---

Bayle's Question: Religious Belief in the Moral Philosophy of the Scottish Enlightenment," in Daniel Garber and Steven Nadler, eds., *Oxford Studies in Early Modern Philosophy*, I (Oxford, 2003), 229–253.

7. On rational faith in Arminian reasoning, see Mark Somos, *Secularisation and the Leiden Circle* (Leiden, Neth., 2011), 10. Arminus's historic followers were known as the Remonstrants. During the eighteenth century, Calvinist theologians—including Witherspoon—were uncomfortable with Arminianism's perceived attempt to eschew the contribution of the external moral will to human choice. See, for example, John Witherspoon, "Lectures on Divinity," in [Ashbel Green, ed.], *The Works of the Rev. John Witherspoon, D.D.L.L.D. Late President of the College at Princeton, New-Jersey* . . . , 2d ed., rev., 4 vols. (Philadelphia, 1802), IV, 14. For a critique of Jonathan Israel's suggestion that secular and Arminian Enlightenment thought dominated Anglo-European ideas, creating a binary between reason and revelation, see Darrin M. McMahon, "What Are Enlightenments?" *Modern Intellectual History*, IV (2007), 601–616. For a general discussion of the dialectical relationship between religious passions and philosophical notions of reason and common sensibility during the eighteenth century, see Isabel Rivers, *Reason, Grace, and Sentiment: A Study of the Language of Religion and Ethics in England, 1660–1780*, II, *Shaftesbury to Hume* (Cambridge, 2000), 188–195.

terms were understood to denote confederal "leagues" or "treaties" that joined separate states and peoples into more singular units. Each component shared faith that God's "covenant of grace" transcended their various constituent parts, allowing their otherwise difficult alliance. The term *federal* derived from the Latin root of the word *covenant,* which was *foedus.* Thus, the "federal theology" of international Calvinism was thought to transcend local boundaries without threatening more specific local identities among its constituent peoples, towns, and nations.[8]

Since the sixteenth century, Scotland's Calvinist establishment had translated its experience of federal theology into Presbyterian ecclesiology. Many believed that a "universal church" transcended its individual congregations in broad association under "one body of Christ." The term *Presbyterian* derived from the structure of ecclesiology rather than from any theological abstraction in regard to doctrine or spirituality. Presbyters, often known as elders, supplied the base for a primary form of church governance in the local church session. The presbytery provided the next tier of oversight, corresponding to a wider geographical region in which several sessions could be found. The same principle applied to the wider regional synod and, finally, to the General Assembly at the national level. Each geographical tier of government, whether local, regional, or national, acted as a check to the other while still remaining part of a wider whole. Setting out these key ecclesiastical issues was the manifesto, *The Form of Presbyterial Church-Government,* drawn up by Westminster divines in alliance with Scottish Presbyterian theologians during the mid-1640s and soon adopted by the Church of Scotland. Over the ensuing decades, the Presbyterian vision incorporated a deliberate tension between center and periphery, dividing nations into multiple layers of religious representation, each in counterpoise to the other, each according to their different geographical catchments but also offering mutual support.[9]

8. For a definition of confederal and federal reasoning in these religious contexts, see Glenn A. Moots, *Politics Reformed: The Anglo-American Legacy of Covenant Theology* (Columbia, Mo., 2010), 178; Daniel J. Elazar, *Constitutionalizing Globalization: The Postmodern Revival of Confederal Arrangements* (Lanham, Md., 1998), 8–10; Rogan Kersh, *Dreams of a More Perfect Union* (Ithaca, N.Y., 2001), 23–58; Allan I. Macinnes, *Union and Empire: The Making of the United Kingdom in 1707* (Cambridge, 2007), 5, 70–72, 102–201, 316–326.

9. See "The Form of Presbyterial Church-Government . . . ," in *The Confession of Faith, the Larger and Shorter Catechisms, with the Scripture-Proofs at Large; Together with the Sum of Saving Knowledge . . .* (1646) (Glasgow, 1765), chap. 9, 553–588. On defining Presbyterian ecclesiology in relation to a "universal church," see the discussions in Bryan F. Le Beau, *Jonathan Dickinson and the Formative Years of American Presbyterianism* (Lexington, Ky., 1997), 15. On

By the seventeenth century, then, Scottish Calvinists had become familiar with the negotiation of shifting layers of representation in a large and
loosely bound union. Their ecclesiastical model, indeed, influenced their
negotiation with English Protestants during the English Civil Wars. As a
condition for entering into alliance with Puritan forces against Stuart corruption, Samuel Rutherford and other influential members of the Kirk were
inspired to formulate a 1643 Solemn League and Covenant with the Westminster Parliament—a covenant that Witherspoon's great-grandfather had
signed. It sought to preserve Presbyterian ecclesiology in any wider association between the Kirk and Westminster. In exchange for Scottish covenanting support against the king, Rutherford and his compatriots demanded the
Church of England's abandonment of episcopalianism and its willingness to
adhere to certain Calvinistic standards. Those standards were subsequently
enshrined in the Westminster Confession of Faith, adopted by the Church of
Scotland without amendment in 1647. The Confession made the encouragement of immediate salvation through grace the central duty of all Presbyterians because scriptural authority derived from divine revelation rather than
the human church. It suggested that the mysterious intermediary role of the
Holy Spirit aided individuals in their encounter with divine revelation in
order to convince them of the need for saving grace. Pious Scots proclaimed
their theoretical support for any British royal line, with an important condition: full autonomy for the continuation and promotion of the theology
and ecclesiology of Presbyterianism as it had developed in the Scottish body
politic up to and including the formulation of the Westminster Confession
of Faith.[10]

------

multilayered dimensions in Presbyterian ecclesiology, see James H. Smylie, *A Brief History of the
Presbyterians* (Louisville, Ky., 1996), 1–28; Leonard J. Trinterud, *The Forming of an American
Tradition: A Re-examination of Colonial Presbyterianism* (New York, 1970), 15–16, 19; S. Rufus
Davis, *The Federal Principle: A Journey through Time in Quest of a Meaning* (Berkeley, Calif.,
1978), 2–3, 216; Lefferts A. Loetscher, *A Brief History of the Presbyterians,* rev. ed. (Philadel-
phia, 1958), 113.

10. On the legacy of Solemn League negotiations, see Colin Kidd, *British Identities before
Nationalism: Ethnicity and Nationhood in the Atlantic World, 1600–1800* (Cambridge, 1999),
128–132. On the negotiation of standards in the Westminster Confession, see Philip Benedict, *Christ's Churches Purely Reformed: A Social History of Calvinism* (New Haven, Conn.,
2004), 401; A. T. B. McGowan, "Evangelicalism in Scotland from Knox to Cunningham," in
Michael A. G. Haykin and Kenneth J. Stewart, eds., *The Emergence of Evangelicalism: Exploring
Historical Continuities* (Nottingham, U.K., 2008), 68–70. In England, the Confession was partly
adopted as the Articles of Christian Religion in 1648, with several sections and chapters omit-

Rutherford was the University of Edinburgh's "regent of humanity" from 1623, and later he became the most distinguished theologian in the Scottish covenanting movement. He was deeply influenced by the account of faith provided by Augustine, the Latin-speaking philosopher, theologian, and church father, who lived from 345 to 430. Rutherford defended an Augustinian theology in scholarly works such as *Lex, Rex*, published in 1644, to counter the notion of innate moral volition, and he helped to ensure the inclusion of Augustinian reasoning in the Westminster Confession of Faith. In a sermon that he delivered late in his life on the "Religious Education of Children," Witherspoon highlighted the theologian's lifelong influence on him when he reminded his American congregation that "the famous St. Augustine" was "one of the most eminent champions for evangelical truth." Thus, in order to understand the system of theology that Witherspoon inherited, it is worth assessing the nature of the relationship between Augustinian ideas and early Scottish piety more closely.[11]

Augustine had confronted the theological movement inspired by Pelagius, a monk thought to have lived in the British Isles. Pelagius's "moral perfectionist" vision suggested that humans could attain virtue through their own efforts. The principle of *"ought* implies *can"* governed his assumption that God would not command humans to improve themselves if it were not possible to do so. Augustine, conversely, sought to show how good works could only follow God's gracious assistance. His treatise on "Grace and Free Choice" described the relationship between divine grace and personal

ted. See *Articles of Christian Religion: Approved and Passed by Both Houses of Parliament, after Advice Had with the Assembly of Divines by Authority of Parliament Sitting at Westminster* (London, 1648). On Witherspoon's mother, Ann Walker, and her maternal grandfather's signing the Solemn League and Covenant, see H[enry] Woods, *The History of the Presbyterian Controversy, with Early Sketches of Presbyterianism* (Louisville, Ky., 1843), 16. On the "subordinate standard" of the Westminster Confession of Faith, see James Moore, "The Two Systems of Francis Hutcheson: On the Origins of the Scottish Enlightenment," in M. A. Stewart, ed., *Studies in the Philosophy of the Scottish Enlightenment* (Oxford, 1990), 39. According to Allan Macinnes, supporters of the Westminster Confession were "not rejecting but adapting the Stuarts' British agenda" — the "organic discourse of imperial monarchy was replaced contractually, not so much by aristocratic republicanism as by covenanted confederalism." See Macinnes, "Regal Union for Britain, 1603-38," in Glenn Burgess, ed., *The New British History: Founding a Modern State, 1603-1715* (New York, 1999), 53, 64.

11. John Coffey, *Politics, Religion, and the British Revolutions: The Mind of Samuel Rutherford* (Cambridge, 1997), 73; Crawford Gibben, "Robert Leighton, Edinburgh Theology, and the Collapse of the Presbyterian Consensus," in Elizabethanne Boran and Gribben, eds., *Enforcing Reformation in Ireland and Scotland, 1550-1700* (Aldershot, U.K., 2006), 163; John Witherspoon, *On the Religious Education of Children*, in [Green, ed.], *Works of Witherspoon*, II, 259.

morality and argued that the direct action of God in converting sinful men allowed their reception of external grace, freeing them from their own iniquities and providing an extra-human means to act on their otherwise unpredictable moral will.[12]

In Rutherford's view, the Presbyterian system was most likely to encourage an Augustinian approach to faith and regeneration. This was made clear in the opening chapter of the Westminster Confession of Faith, which he helped to formulate, "Of the Holy Scripture." God was revealed through " 'the light of nature' " and the "works of creation and providence"—both of which demonstrated the moral chasm between unregenerate men and God's ethical perfection. But human perception of nature was "not sufficient to give that Knowledge of God, and of his will, which is necessary unto salvation." Instead, the authors of the Confession moved on to emphasize the personal interventionism of God in human affairs and the "one only . . . living and true God . . . working all things according to the counsel of his own immutable and most righteous will." They declared that "God from all eternity did, by the most wise and holy counsel of his own will, freely and unchangeably ordain whatsoever comes to pass."[13]

The Reformation leader John Calvin had instructed: "Those whom the Holy Spirit has inwardly taught truly rest upon Scripture . . . [demonstrating how] . . . Scripture indeed is self-authenticated; hence it is not right to subject it to proof and reasoning. And the certainty it deserves with us, it attains by the testimony of the Spirit. For even if it wins reverence for itself by its own majesty, it seriously affects us only when it is sealed upon our hearts through the Spirit." His faithful theology sought no "marks of genuineness upon which our judgment may lean" from natural proofs. The divines who later composed the Westminster Confession of Faith looked to Calvin's reasoning when they delineated the Holy Spirit's role as a conduit between scripture and God's will on earth. The Confession claimed that only after conversion would the word and spirit of God, thanks "to grace and salvation by Jesus Christ *c;* [enlightening] their minds, spiritually and savingly to

12. Peter King, "Introduction," in Augustine, *On the Free Choice of the Will, on Grace and Free Choice, and Other Writings,* ed. King (Cambridge, 2010), xv, xvi; Augustine, "On Grace and Free Choice," ibid., 141–185. See also Ronald H. Nash, *The Light of the Mind: St. Augustine's Theory of Knowledge* (Louisville, Ky., 1969), 94–124.

13. *The Confession of Faith,* 21, 28, 30, 33. On the centrality of Augustinian reasoning in the opening part of the Confession, see also Jack Rogers, *Presbyterian Creeds: A Guide to the Book of Confessions* (Louisville, Ky., 1991), 161–162; Donald K. McKim, ed., *The Westminster Handbook to Reformed Theology* (Louisville, Ky., 2001), 153, 233.

understand the things of God *d;* taking away their heart of stone . . . determining them to that which is good . . . [all] being made willing by his grace."[14]

Rutherford and his colleagues demonstrated traditional scholastic concerns when they suggested that, despite their being some things "concerning the worship of God, and government of the church, common to human
actions and societies, which are to be ordered by the light of nature. . . . All
things in scripture are not alike plain in themselves, nor alike clear unto all."
Using Augustinian reasoning, however, their Confession immediately added
that those things in scripture "which are necessary to be known, believed,
and observed, for salvation, are so clearly propounded and opened in some
place of scripture or other, that not only the learned, but the unlearned, in a
due use of the ordinary means, may attain unto a sufficient understanding of
them." Higher layers of scriptural meaning were accessed through scholastic
analysis, or biblicism, but the most fundamental elements of understanding
required for salvation were provided through divine illumination. The latter
was available to all beings, provided they demonstrated the humility required
to receive grace following inner persuasion by the Holy Spirit.[15]

The Westminster Confession of Faith heralded a unifying role in Scotland's developing religious identity over the following decades. Rutherford
and many of his heirs referred to the notion of a Scottish covenant in order to
describe the explicit and formal acknowledgement of the Confession by the
Scottish body politic. With the official addition of the Westminster Confession of Faith into the Scottish Church in 1690, thus defined as Presbyterian
orthodoxy, covenant theology had become Scotland's normative theological
position governing the appointment of ministers and professors of divinity
at Scottish educational institutions by the end of the seventeenth century.[16]

Despite its increasing acceptance as the standard of Scottish Presbyteri-

14. John Calvin, *Institutes of the Christian Religion,* ed. John T. McNeill, trans. Ford Lewis
Battles, 2 vols. (1960; rpt. Louisville, Ky., 2006), I, 80; *The Confession of Faith,* chap. 10, 69–71.
On the Confession's vision of the role of conversion as vital—and even protoevangelical—see
Gary J. Dorrien, *The Remaking of Evangelical Theology* (Louisville, Ky., 1998), 24.

15. *The Confession of Faith,* chap. 1, 22, 26. On the role of higher layers of analysis and biblicism and their distinction from more fundamental readings, see McGowan, "Evangelicalism in
Scotland," in Haykin and Stewart, eds., *The Emergence of Evangelicalism,* 69–70.

16. On the centralizing role of the Westminster Confession in Scottish civic and religious
culture, see Arthur H. Williamson, *Scottish National Consciousness in the Age of James VI*
(Edinburgh, 1979), 79. For an excellent discussion of Williamson's thesis, see Richard B. Sher,
"Witherspoon's Dominion of Providence and the Scottish Jeremiad Tradition," in Sher and
Jeffrey R. Smitten, eds., *Scotland and America in the Age of the Enlightenment* (Princeton, N.J.,
1990), 53.

anism, however, the Augustinian ideas of the Westminster Confession were conceived in differing ways by ministers and theologians. Augustine himself had often declared the state of theological uncertainty to be an appropriate response to the mystery of predestination. He suggested that faith, mystery, and an uncertain account of individual moral agency were part of man's religious struggle. Unsurprisingly, then, distinctions could be found in Scottish theological discussions of individual moral volition through the second half of the seventeenth century. At the University of Edinburgh during the 1650s, for example, the moderate Robert Leighton taught alongside the "high Calvinist" David Dickson. Leighton suggested that educated men could continue to examine biblical texts to extract and uncover their meaning, faithful to what he saw to be the close biblical scholarship of the Knoxian Reformation. Dickson, conversely, advocated a far more passive and deferential encounter with scripture alongside received Presbyterian confessions. As distinct from Leighton, he believed that individuals were hubristic to suggest that biblical study could extract moral meanings beyond those that were clearly outlined in the Westminster Confession. Leighton suggested that Dickson needlessly rejected an account of innate human moral perception, as described in the Bible itself.[17]

The associated tensions and ambiguities above continued during Witherspoon's and Carlyle's education in Augustan Scotland. They could encounter anthropocentric as well as God-centered accounts of moral volition, with many nuances between the two. Even the Westminster Confession of Faith could be interpreted in different ways in the century after its formulation. The

---

17. On the multifaceted relationship between Augustine and Reformed Christianity, see King, "Introduction," in Augustine, *On the Free Choice of the Will*, ed. King, ix, xxxiii; and Arnoud S. Q. Visser, *Reading Augustine in the Reformation: The Flexibility of Intellectual Authority in Europe, 1500–1620* (Oxford, 2011). On the mystery of predestination, see Augustine, "On the Gift of Perseverance," in *On the Free Choice of the Will*, ed. King, 232–233. On Leighton and Dixon, see Thomas F. Torrance, *Scottish Theology: From John Knox to John McLeod Campbell* (Edinburgh, 1996), 111–122; Crawford Gribben, "Robert Leighton, Edinburgh Theology, and the Collapse of the Presbyterian Consensus," in Boran and Gribben, eds., *Enforcing Reformation*, 163; Michael Sudduth, *The Reformed Objection to Natural Theology* (Farnham, U.K., 2009), 48. On the last years of the influence of Reformed scholasticism at Edinburgh, see P. G. Ryken, "Scottish Reformed Scholasticism," in Carl R. Trueman and R. Scott Clark, eds., *Protestant Scholasticism: Essays in Reassessment* (Carlisle, U.K., 1999), 200; Richard B. Sher, *Church and University in the Scottish Enlightenment: The Moderate Literati of Edinburgh* (Princeton, N.J., 1985), 50–52; Alexander Broadie, *A History of Scottish Philosophy* (Edinburgh, 2009), 105. See also Richard A. Muller, *After Calvin: Studies in the Development of a Theological Tradition* (Oxford, 2003), 10.

standards of Presbyterianism were understood more opaquely than Witherspoon and Carlyle would later recall.[18]

Conflict and Consensus in Augustan Scottish Piety

An emphasis on divine moral inspiration, which countered anthropocentric
currents in Scottish theology, reached its apogee in the University of Glasgow
during the Augustan era. Its chief proponent was Gershom Carmichael, a regent at Glasgow from 1694 and, for his final two years from 1727 to 1729, the
university's first professor of moral philosophy. Carmichael placed a stoical
emphasis on the duty to understand God's central role in the universe, including in ethical interactions between humans. He distinguished his understanding from human-centered accounts of moral perception in natural law
theory. He criticized earlier European thinkers such as Samuel von Pufendorf and Jean Barbeyrac for failing to develop a God-centered account of
moral volition. Through the 1720s, therefore, Carmichael sought to deempha-
size the innate moral capacity of man.[19]

At the University of Glasgow, Francis Hutcheson took note of Carmichael's preoccupation with the natural law tradition but distanced himself
from Carmichael's moral teachings — including his opposition to Pufendorf.
Having matriculated at the University of Glasgow just three years after the
Act of Union, the man lauded by some scholars as the father of the Scottish Enlightenment rebelled against the Augustinian pedantry of Reformed
scholasticism in Scottish higher education. Hutcheson received his degree
from Glasgow in 1712 and obtained his license to preach in the Kirk in 1716.
Many existing ministers associated him with the perceived latitudinarianism
of Glasgow theologian John Simson (circa 1668–1740) rather than with Car-

---

18. On the reassertion of Augustinian theology in the British isles during the early modern
period, see William Poole, *Milton and the Idea of the Fall* (Cambridge, 2005), 21–40; Ryken,
"Scottish Reformed Scholasticism," in Trueman and Clark, eds., *Protestant Scholasticism,* 200–
204.

19. On Carmichael's theological emphasis, see Broadie, *History of Scottish Philosophy,* 107–
108. For Carmichael, according to Brodie, the "precept that we worship God is not traceable
back to the duty to cultivate sociability" (108). Robertson highlights Carmichael's distinct "synthesis of Cartesian Augustinianism and Protestant or reformed scholasticism." See John Robertson, *The Case for the Enlightenment: Scotland and Naples, 1680–1760* (Cambridge, 2005), 143.
On pietism and even an early form of evangelicalism in Augustan Edinburgh and Glasgow, see
A. Ian Dunlop, *William Carstares and the Kirk by Law Established* (Edinburgh, 1967), 100–121;
D. B. Horn, *A Short History of the University of Edinburgh, 1556–1889* (Edinburgh, 1967), 37–47.

michael. He retreated to an academic life in Ireland in order to escape the re-sulting ministerial hostility. During his decade in a Dublin private academy, he increasingly questioned the pessimistic dualism that associated commu-nal sociability with individual egoism. He interrogated the notion that pub-lic benevolence was merely a convenient cover for benefits accrued to indi-viduals in a community, using his 1725 *Inquiry into the Original of Our Ideas of Beauty and Virtue* to "shew, 'That *Human Nature* was not left quite in-different in the affair of *Virtue* . . . ' [and that] [t]he *AUTHOR* of *Nature* has much better furnish'd us for a virtuous Conduct, than our *Moralists* seem to imagine, by almost as quick and powerful Instructions, as we have for the preservation of our Bodys. He has made *Virtue* a *lovely Form,* to excite our pursuit of it; and has given us *strong Affections* to be the Springs of each vir-tuous Action."[20]

Enlightenment thought is often defined in relation to the harnessing of innate reason, the flourishing of an abstract mental capacity to describe logi-cal—rational—inferences. But care is needed with such terminology in any discussion of Scottish Enlightenment philosophy, particularly that which Witherspoon encountered among those such as Carlyle who appropriated Hutchesonian reasoning from the 1730s. Aristotle referred to a common sense that was charged with amalgamating the evidence provided by the five other senses. Scholars have described it as akin to a separate rational faculty. Cicero, following Stoic thinkers, emphasized the overarching coordination of sensory perceptions through a separate perceptual channel. In his view, it defined values and beliefs that humans held in common. Yet Hutcheson often suggested that moral sensibility was contingent on a pre-rational emotional response. Using aesthetic terminology, he defined the ways in which good deeds were sensed in the same way that attractive objects or pleasing literary creations were appreciated immediately and before rational explanation. It

---

20. Broadie, *History of Scottish Philosophy,* 124; T. D. Campbell, "Francis Hutcheson: 'Father' of the Scottish Enlightenment," in R. H. Campbell and Andrew S. Skinner, eds., *The Origins and Nature of the Scottish Enlightenment* (Edinburgh, 1982), 167–185; Moore, "The Two Systems of Francis Hutcheson," in Stewart, ed., *Studies in the Philosophy of the Scottish En-lightenment,* 43; Ryken, "Scottish Reformed Scholasticism," in Trueman and Clark, eds., *Prot-estant Scholasticism,* 200–203; [Francis Hutcheson], *An Inquiry into the Original of Our Ideas of Beauty and Virtue* . . . (1725), 2d ed. (London, 1726), xii, xiv–xv. See also David Fate Norton and Manfred Kuehn, "The Foundations of Morality," in Knud Haakonssen, ed., *The Cambridge History of Eighteenth-Century Philosophy* (Cambridge, 2006), 954–958; Peter Kivy, "The Per-ception of Beauty in Hutcheson's First *Inquiry:* A Response to James Shelley," *British Journal of Aesthetics,* XLVII (2007), 416–431.

appropriated the classical notion of *sensus communis* in order to suggest that an inborn, predictable, and benevolent response would follow any conception of ethical ideals.[21]

In his *Inquiry* and in his *Illustrations on the Moral Sense* (1728), Hutcheson attempted to reconcile innate moral sensibility with biblical precepts. If external divine inspiration were the sole basis of morality, he claimed, there would be no independent faculty of moral judgment to enable the recognition of scriptural authority as morally valuable. He never denied that the similarity between artistic and ethical perception was understood analogously rather than as an identical epistemic reaction. Nonetheless, a focus on pre-rational and innate sensory perception underlay his confidence in the common moral response, separate from that which could be learned from revealed scripture. His common basis for ethical perception was less temporary than Augustinian illumination and less reliant on individual regeneration and the reception of grace. He envisioned sociability as natural to most human beings, who gravitated toward living in societies rather than in isolated environments.[22]

Resisting the charge of indulgent egoism, Hutcheson pointed out that the innate sensory response was necessarily open to hurtful as well as positive stimuli. Faith in the future state outlined by scripture offered important solace for those distressed by the potential melancholy of public sympathy, even if the inborn ethical response that aroused sadness could precede knowledge of Christian revelation. Thus, although Hutcheson was steeped in the tradition of the Presbyterian Church and maintained the importance of Protestant belief, he placed less emphasis on the need for repentance, regeneration, and revival in order to engage individual moral sensibility.[23]

---

21. See Sophia Rosenfeld, *Common Sense: A Political History* (Cambridge, Mass., 2011), 18–19, 22, 59.

22. On these Hutchesonian ethical ideas, see James A. Harris, "Religion in Hutcheson's Moral Philosophy," *Journal of the History of Philosophy*, XLVI (2008), 206; Harris, "Answering Bayle's Question," in Garber and Nadler, eds., *Oxford Studies in Early Modern Philosophy*, I, 229–253; Daniel Carey, *Locke, Shaftesbury, and Hutcheson: Contesting Diversity in the Enlightenment and Beyond* (Cambridge, 2005), 156–158; James Moore, "Hutcheson's Theodicy: The Argument and the Contexts of *A System of Moral Philosophy*," in Paul Wood, ed., *The Scottish Enlightenment: Essays in Reinterpretation* (Rochester, N.Y., 2000), 239–260; Michael B. Gill, *The British Moralists on Human Nature and the Birth of Secular Ethics* (Cambridge, 2006), chap. 14; Kenneth P. Winkler, "Hutcheson and Hume on the Color of Virtue," *Hume Studies*, XXII (1996), 3–22; P. J. E. Kail, "Hutcheson's Moral Sense: Skepticism, Realism, and Secondary Qualities," *History of Philosophy Quarterly*, XVIII (2001), 57–77.

23. On the necessary faith in a future state to prevent present melancholy, see the discussion in Harris, "Religion in Hutcheson," *Journal of the History of Philosophy*, XLVI (2008), 206, 218.

In the decades after the reign of William and Mary, several moral philosophers and theologians at the University of Edinburgh sided with Hutcheson.
Yet it is less well known that a number of Edinburgh professors remained
open to a critique of natural law reasoning. In many cases, they were influenced by Augustinian impulses in the Netherlands. A growing Scottish
intellectual and religious association with Dutch higher education had developed since William of Orange assumed the British throne in the late 1680s.
The Dutch monarch's trusted adviser had been William Carstares, the son
of a Scottish covenanter who was born outside Glasgow and educated at the
University of Edinburgh as well as the University of Utrecht. After William's
death in 1702, Carstares returned to Scotland and became principal of the
University of Edinburgh. He phased out the university's regent system, in
which, for example, a professor of Hebrew might also teach the entire curriculum as well as Hebrew to a particular small cohort of students. He imposed a new lecture scheme that gave each Scottish professor the opportunity to teach his particular field of expertise. Scholars link this development
to the enduring growth and depth of Scottish Enlightenment thought during the following decades. But it is also important to note that a strain of
Calvinistic pietism took its place in the heterogeneous educational culture
that was inspired by Carstares's new system. During the Augustan era, students such as Witherspoon and Carlyle would not necessarily have encountered the same vision of human moral capability in all the new components
of their educational program. That they were not confined to one regent for
all their subjects allowed their potential appropriation of varying definitions
of Presbyterian piety.[24]

On the place of Calvinistic providence in Hutcheson's work, see also David Fate Norton, *David
Hume: Common-Sense Moralist, Sceptical Metaphysician* (Princeton, N.J., 1982), 87–92; Thomas
Ahnert, "Francis Hutcheson and the Heathen Moralists," *Journal of Scottish Philosophy*, VIII
(2010), 51–62; Moore, "Hutcheson's Theodicy," in Wood, ed., *The Scottish Enlightenment*, 206.
On Hutcheson's conception of a future state and redemption in a providential scheme, see also
Knud Haakonssen, *Natural Law and Moral Philosophy: From Grotius to the Scottish Enlighten-
ment* (Cambridge, 1996), 71, 77. For further evidence that Hutcheson placed less emphasis on
regeneration and salvation than many theologians, see Moore, "The Two Systems of Francis
Hutcheson," in Stewart, ed., *Studies in the Philosophy of the Scottish Enlightenment*, 39.

24. On the abolition of the regent system under Carstares, see Dunlop, *William Carstares*,
100–121; Horn, *A Short History of Edinburgh University*, 37–47. On the growth of Scottish Enlightenment culture after Carstares, see, for example, M. A. Stewart, "The Curriculum in Britain, Ireland, and the Colonies," in Haakonssen, ed., *Cambridge History of Eighteenth-Century
Philosophy*, 104; Norbert Waszek, *Man's Social Nature: A Topic of the Scottish Enlightenment in
Its Historical Setting* (Frankfurt, 1988), 315.

Witherspoon's master's thesis from the University of Edinburgh provides evidence that he was influenced by God-centered accounts of moral reasoning, but it also shows his interest in the sensory terminology (rather than necessarily the ethical conclusions) that he had encountered in lectures by John Stevenson. The latter's lectures had immediately appealed to Alexander Carlyle during the 1730s. Yet, depending on which class they happened to attend, Witherspoon and Carlyle were able to encounter different interpretations of human moral agency within the same university system during the late 1730s and early 1740s. This heterogeneous influence can be detected in Witherspoon's thesis. On February 23, 1739, he defended the document, which was written in Latin and titled *Disputatio Philosophical: De Mentis Immortalitae.* The twelve-page text set out to support the notion that the mind and soul were connected and therefore mutually immortal. Skeptics suggested that neither biblical events nor contemporary displays of salvation could have been commonly witnessed or verified. Witherspoon used his thesis to define the common sense of external entities in order to refute such a claim. But he refrained from attaching a notion of innate ethical judgment to his discussion of common sensibility. As far as discerning the moral nature of objective interactions, he defined the mind's immortal distinction from bodies in the world. The work of the mind was associated with the soul through its illumination by divine grace. Witherspoon's logic here was clearly Augustinian, even while he used simple aspects of common sense reasoning to define the mental perception of objects.[25]

In Witherspoon's view, original sin had flawed the human ability to grasp the moral interaction between objects, even while their external form could be perceived accurately. Objective moral reasoning could only be accessed through duty to God and his revealed laws. Because such an obligation was immaterial, it could not die. Moreover, the unpredictable and seemingly unjust dispersal of good and evil in the world proved that there must be a future existence in which good was rewarded more clearly. God had placed a strong yearning in men for a heavenly "future state." Although the mind could perceive "itself and other finite minds," it was also given the gift of duty to "that

25. Witherspoon's master's thesis has been translated from Latin into English by Roger Jerome Fechner, who highlights the argument that, "even though original sin had flawed man's ability to grasp the true nature of things, man could still distinguish the qualities of things" through empirical means. See Fechner, "The Moral Philosophy of John Witherspoon and the Scottish-American Enlightenment" (Ph.D. diss., University of Iowa, 1974), 79–80. On Stevenson, see also Broadie, *A History of Scottish Philosophy,* 108–112. For Carlyle's description of these educational offerings, see Carlyle, *Autobiography,* 36, 54–55.

highest mind, God Almighty." Without offering much elucidation or conceptual analysis on the matter, the sixteen-year-old Witherspoon argued that the knowledge of a future moral universe proved the immortal and atemporal nature of the mind. Its obligation to God's higher faculty, furthermore, underlined the importance of conversion and diminished the notion of innate moral perception.[26]

The Augustinian reasoning demonstrated in Witherspoon's 1739 thesis was shared by many of his new theology professors as he entered the institution's divinity school. Since the late seventeenth century, Swiss theologians such as Francis Turretin, and several other members of the Turretin family, had been absorbed into the Edinburgh theological curriculum. As a pastor and professor of theology after 1653, Turretin had asked whether individuals retained any agency in bringing about the initial stages of religious conversion or whether they could only respond passively to the preceding grace of God. He tended to support the former monergistic account. He affirmed with Calvin, Martin Luther, and Augustine that, after the initial step of regeneration, in the second stage of conversion individuals maintained an active role in their salvation experience. But, following Augustine, he also suggested that in the next stages before regeneration, individuals could not innately orient themselves to enhance their possibility of cooperating with the external grace that was necessary for conversion.[27]

Patrick Cuming, Witherspoon's professor of ecclesiastical history during this period, used as his primary textbook the *Compendium Historiae Ecclesiasticae* by Jean Turretin. Though Jean was the son of Francis, his theology was more liberal in its account of human moral volition. Nonetheless, during this early point in his career, to a greater extent than later, Cuming often claimed that accurate moral judgment was not truly innate. In a 1727 sermon, for example, he had responded to what he described as "the irregular and vitious Practices of some false Professors of Religion, and factious Teachers, who pretended to the only true Knowledge of God." Highlighting the role of external grace in defining individual moral volition, as under-

26. Fechner, "Moral Philosophy of Witherspoon," 78–84 (quotations on 82).

27. On the early interest in Francis Turretin at the University of Edinburgh, alongside seventeenth-century Dutch theologians, see Moore, "The Two Systems of Francis Hutcheson," in Stewart, ed., *Studies in the Philosophy of the Scottish Enlightenment*, 38; Sher, *Church and University*, 30, 50–52. On the distinction between active and passive reception of grace in Turretin's writings and his statements on the moment of conversion, see Martin Bac, *Perfect Will Theology: Divine Agency in Reformed Scholasticism as against Suarez, Episcopius, Descartes, and Spinoza* (Leiden, Neth., 2010), 12–14; R. C. Sproul, *Willing to Believe: The Controversy over Free Will* (Grand Rapids, Mich., 1997), 118–119; Dorrien, *The Remaking of Evangelical Theology*, 22.

stood from scripture, Cuming claimed that *"the Wisdom that is from above, our holy Christian Religion, that Religion which is revealed by God, and descends from Heaven, is first pure . . . [and] restores the Harmony of the Mind, regulates the Passions, and raises the Affections."* At a later point in his sermon, to be sure, Cuming sounded rather closer to Hutcheson when he stated that members of society ought "to consult the Good of the whole . . . [and that by] doing Good, we most effectually consult our own Happiness." But he then went on to describe the ways in which societies were often made up of unregenerate individuals who had failed to act on the duty to receive grace as made known to them by the Holy Spirit. Distinguishing the notion of duty from the idea of moral sensibility, Cuming suggested that unregenerate individual perception remained obscured and capricious, despite the laudable desire for goodness and happiness in society that some maintained. Even the capacity to recognize the need for divine assistance was described as a manifestation of an externally imposed obligation, understood with assistance from the Holy Spirit, and not wholly an innate decision. These ideas were distinguished from Cuming's statements during his later career, when he became more closely aligned with the Moderate Church of Scotland.[28]

Many of Francis Turretin's theological successors were incorporated in Witherspoon's ministerial education as well. John Gowdie, Edinburgh professor of divinity, taught the theological system of Benedict Pictet to Witherspoon and his classmates. Pictet was the Genevan nephew of Francis Turretin, whom he greatly admired. His *Theologia Christiana* was used as a textbook in the University of Edinburgh during Witherspoon's time. It emphasized the double covenant that became more central to the federal theology of Scottish Calvinism during the eighteenth century. A first covenant of works was made by God with Adam, the federal head of the entire human race. It remained binding even after the Fall. Another covenant of grace was apparently drawn through Jesus Christ, who was the second and last federal head of humanity, having assumed the fallen sin of Adam. Pictet suggested, in dense prose since translated into English, that

> the *will of commandment* is, properly speaking, the execution of a part
> of the other will, namely, that part which hath determined what shall
> be revealed to, or enjoined upon, men in due time. For example: God

28. Patrick Cuming, *A Sermon Preach'd at the Opening of the Synod of Dumfreis, April 12th, 1726* (London, 1727), 15–16. On Cuming's use of Jean Turretin, and the orthodox Calvinism of his early career, see Mark G. Spencer, ed., *David Hume: Historical Thinker, Historical Writer* (University Park, Pa., 2013), 21–23; Fechner, "Moral Philosophy of Witherspoon," 84–85 (Fechner refers to Turrentini).

hath required of men faith and obedience, but he had decreed thus to require; in requiring, therefore, he only executes what he had decreed.

Here Pictet avoided defining faith or obedience as an innate moral act. Rather, the willingness to manifest had already been decreed by God. Witherspoon would often refer to Pictet and Francis Turretin with approval during his subsequent career in both Scotland and America. Their works appeared in his library in New Jersey thirty years later, and Pictet was on Witherspoon's recommended list for American ministerial candidates. Unsurprisingly, their theological ideas were also incorporated in his earlier Scottish ministry.[29]

In his later memoirs, conversely, Alexander Carlyle would not recall Gowdie's teaching with fondness. Reflecting his desire to impose later standards onto his earlier experience in divinity school in Edinburgh, Carlyle claimed that there "was one advantage attending the lectures of a dull professor, — viz., that he could form no school, and the students were left entirely to themselves, and naturally formed opinions far more liberal than those they got from the Professor." According to Carlyle, those "liberal" young students would go on to assume prominent positions in Scotland's religious and educational establishment — in contrast to men like Witherspoon.[30]

*"A Subject the Most Wonderful and Mysterious That
Ever Was Offered to the Mind of Man"*

After he finished his ministerial studies in 1743, at the age of twenty, Witherspoon was licensed to preach by the Haddington presbytery, in the synod of Lothian and Tweeddale, around twenty miles east of Edinburgh. He spent a twelve-month probationary period as a licensed minister in his home presbytery while waiting for a full-time parish vacancy to open up. He was eventually ordained in Beith, in the presbytery of Irvine, on April 11, 1745, only

29. Benedict Pictet, *Christian Theology,* trans. Frederick Reyroux (London, 1834), 83–84. On Pictet's federal theology, including the "double covenant," see Moots, *Politics Reformed,* 178; L. Gordon Tait, *The Piety of John Witherspoon: Pew, Pulpit, and Public Forum* (Louisville, Ky., 2001), 6. On Pictet's theological works in Witherspoon's classes under John Gowdie at Edinburgh, see the account in Alexander Grant, *The Story of the University of Edinburgh during Its First Three Hundred Years,* 2 vols. (London, 1884), I, 334. On Pictet in Witherspoon's continued reading in Scotland and America, including at the College of New Jersey, see John Fea, *The Way of Improvement Leads Home: Philip Vickers Fithian and the Rural Enlightenment in Early America* (Philadelphia, 2008), 88; Tait, *Piety of John Witherspoon,* 207 n. 30; Howe, "John Witherspoon," in Manning and Cogliano, eds., *The Atlantic Enlightenment,* 69.

30. Carlyle, *Autobiography,* 48.

to become preoccupied with circumstances that went far beyond the frustrations of probation. Through June and July 1745, Scottish Presbyterian congregations began to hear rumors of "Jacobite" forces that were traveling from coastal France toward Scotland. In what has subsequently been described as the "45" Jacobite rising, Charles Edward Stuart attempted to recover the British crown for the House of Stuart, which had been exiled since the ousting of James II during the 1688 Glorious Revolution.[31]

Often known as Bonnie Prince Charlie or the Young Pretender, Charles arrived by boat in the Outer Hebrides of northeastern Scotland in late July. On August 16, 1745, his supporters engaged in the first official skirmish with British forces in the town of Highbridge. On August 19, Charles claimed the Highland town of Glenfinnan, supported by a number of Catholic clansmen. On September 15, Jacobite forces entered Edinburgh. Edinburgh Castle maintained its defense, though some Jacobites received support from local subjects. For five weeks, Charles held court at Holyrood Palace, the official residence of the British crown in Scotland. Through late September he led a movement south from Edinburgh. During September and October, William Robertson met with members of the presbytery of Haddington, which had only recently licensed Witherspoon as a minister. Robertson, who would become an influential leader and historian in the Kirk, spent time praying together with the community, many of whose members would come to oppose his ethical stance in years to come.[32]

After British forces received Hanoverian reinforcements, groups of Jacobites lost several battles and skirmishes as they moved south toward the English border. At this point in the crisis, Witherspoon responded to resolutions passed by the General Assembly of the Church of Scotland, which recommended that presbyteries and their parishes contribute to the raising of funds and soldiers to defend Scottish towns. Under the behest of the barony of Broadstone in his parish, Witherspoon formulated a "subscription paper" to cover the expenses of a militia from Beith. He proposed to join the militia, which would march to Stirling to join royal commanders, "for the support of our religion and liberty, and in defence of our only rightful, and lawful Soveraign, KING GEORGE, against his enemy engaged in the present rebellion."

---

31. For this part of Witherspoon's early career, see Collins, *President Witherspoon*, I, 20–21.

32. On Robertson's visit to the presbtery, see Jeffrey Smitten, "William Robertson: The Minister as Historian," in Sophie Bourgault and Robert Sparling, eds., *A Companion to Enlightenment Historiography* (Leiden, Neth., 2013), 114. On these Jacobite movements, see Christopher Duffy, *The '45: Bonnie Prince Charlie and the Untold Story of the Jacobite Rising* (London, 2003), 167–171; Robert Chambers, *History of the Rebellion of 1745–6* (London, 1869), 20–26.

Having collected enough money to accompany around 150 Beith militiamen, Witherspoon set off in the second week of January 1746 on what he thought would entail a month-long engagement in and around Stirling. After arriving in Glasgow, however, British military commanders informed Witherspoon and his men that their support was not yet required and that they ought to return home.[33]

After a number of his Beith associates returned to their homes, Witherspoon remained in Glasgow, having heard that British forces were streaming out of Edinburgh toward Falkirk. He decided to make his way to the town as a spectator in any battle. Since the first week of January, six Highland Jacobite battalions had been moving toward Falkirk. They had tried to fool British forces into believing they were heading toward Edinburgh. But, during the second week of January, they turned north before reaching the outskirts of Falkirk and initiating a battle that would see the last Jacobite victory in the rising — a turning point that would lead startled British forces to increase their efforts against Charles Edward Stuart, allowing them a more decisive victory in the following months. The main Battle of Falkirk took place on January 17, 1746, witnessed by Witherspoon on the edge of the field of engagement. The British forces were surprised by an unexpected Jacobite movement from the northwest of Falkirk ridge. As both sides met, heavy rain and storms rendered many British powder cartridges useless. In the darkness and rain, neither side truly perceived the tactics of the other, nor any certain victory or loss. Only by the following morning, when deceased British soldiers were noticed on the battlefield, did Jacobite forces claim victory. Many more British forces had been captured during the battle. Witherspoon, along with ten other spectators and five members of an "Edinburgh company of volunteers," joined them as imprisoned supporters of the British regiment in Falkirk.[34]

There is not much more existing source material detailing Witherspoon's exact movements before and during his imprisonment in Doune Castle, just outside Stirling, where he was taken from Falkirk on January 25, 1746. John Home, in his *History of the Rebellion in the Year 1745,* published half a century later in 1802, recalled his month-long captivity alongside "Mr. John Witherspoon" in support of the Hanoverian union against Jacobites:

33. For Witherspoon's statement to collect money on behalf of a Beith regiment, see Collins, *President Witherspoon,* I, 22.

34. On Witherspoon's role and the Edinburgh Company of Volunteers, see John Home, *The History of the Rebellion in the Year 1745* (London, 1802), 114–124, 133–136, 187. For the details leading up to the Battle of Falkirk, see Duffy, *The '45,* 167–171; Gregory Fremont-Barnes, *The Jacobite Rebellion, 1745–46* (Oxford, 2011), 57–60.

The Castle of Downe, built by Murdoch Duke of Albany, Regent of Scotland, during the captivity of James the First, was in a most ruinous condition when the volunteers came there. The place of their abode was a large ghastly room, the highest part of the Castle, and next the battlements. In one end of this room there were two small vaults or cells, in one of which the volunteers passed the night, with three other persons, one of whom was Mr. John Witherspoon, then a clergyman of the church of Scotland, afterwards President of the College of Jersey in America.

During this period in the "ghastly room," Jacobite forces lost any advantage they had gained on January 17 in Falkirk. Charles Edward Stuart remained in Bannockburn House with flu-like symptoms. British leaders took the opportunity to reinforce their army in Edinburgh, and the Battle of Falkirk would prove to be the final major victory for the Jacobite forces, whose fortunes rapidly waned.[35]

On his eventual release from Doune prison in early 1746, Witherspoon returned to Beith. There, in 1748, he married Elizabeth Montgomery, from Craighouse, in Ayrshire. She was the daughter of Robert Montgomery, and very little is known about her. She was quietly devoted to her piety, and eventually became uneasy about leaving Scotland for North America, where she perceived religious institutions to be underdeveloped. In the two decades before she made known her opposition to leaving Scotland, her husband continued to serve as a minister in Beith until 1757 and then in Paisley's Kirk until 1768. During this period, he wrote two theological treatises and preached sermons to his own and other Scottish congregations. As he would later recall, he also maintained numerous religious contacts with evangelical members of the faculty of the University of Glasgow. Witherspoon eventually published his theological treatises under two titles: *An Essay on the Connection between the Doctrine of Justification by the Imputed Righteousness of Christ, and Holiness of Life* (1756) and *A Practical Treatise on Regeneration* (1764). His motivation derived in part from his perception that ministers had neglected the importance of individual rebirth and regeneration during the previous two decades. Thirteen of Witherspoon's sermons from his early

35. Home, *History of the Rebellion*, 187–188. On Home, see also Henry Grey Graham, *Scottish Men of Letters in the Eighteenth Century* (London, 1908), 72. For an account of Witherspoon's role as a spectator in the Battle of Falkirk and his imprisonment, based on the little evidence that remains, see James McCosh, *The Scottish Philosophy* . . . (New York, 1875), 185–190; Collins, *President Witherspoon*, I, 22–23.

FIGURE 4. *The Battle of Falkirk, January 18, 1746.* Engraving by Thomas Jeffreys.
National Army Museum / The Art Archive at Art Resource, N.Y.

ministry were also later published in 1768 as his *Practical Discourses on the Leading Truths of the Gospel* in Edinburgh, Philadelphia, and London.[36]

Witherspoon used his 1764 *Practical Treatise on Regeneration* to survey the fundamental theological tenets that he had developed over his previous two decades as a minister. Reflecting his revivalist conception of the Westminster Confession of Faith, he referred back to what he thought to be "the most extensive and universal range" of sin's manifestation in the human condition and concluded that there was "scarce any state" in which pride "is not able to exert itself, scarce any circumstance in which it is not able to convert into the means of its own gratification." All people were defined as "originally of one character, unfit for the kingdom of God; unless a change has pas[ed] upon them they continue so; and unless a change do pass upon them hereafter, they must be for ever excluded." Witherspoon's emphasis on the necessary impetus for change in the human moral state was a key characteristic of evangelical doctrine during the mid-eighteenth century, defined through common reference to John 3:3: "Except a man be born again, he cannot see the kingdom of God." Thus, Witherspoon called on God to "enlighten" the mind of all people with this "most salutary of all truths." A conversion experience was imperative as a means to make good the right that all people apparently enjoyed, "a right to the spiritual privileges of the gospel, and the promise of eternal life . . . the only thing that could make the profession [of conversion] valuable or desirable." With a dig at those who did not subscribe to the tenets of evangelical revivalism, Witherspoon admitted to realizing that

> regeneration or the new-birth is a subject, at present, very unfashionable . . . [but is] however, a subject of unspeakable moment, or, rather, it is the one subject in which all others meet as in a centre. The grand enquiry, in comparison of which everything else, how excellent foever, is but specious trifling. What doth it dignify, though you have food to eat in plenty, and variety of raiment to put on, if you are not born again: if after a few mornings and evenings spent in unthinking mirth, sensuality and riot, you die in your sins, and lie down in sorrow?"

36. See John Witherspoon, *A Practical Treatise on Regeneration,* in [Green, ed.], *Works of Witherspoon,* I, 93–265; Witherspoon, "Seeking a Competency in the Wisdom of Providence," ibid., II, 219–227; Witherspoon, *An Essay on Justification,* ibid., I, 45–92. On Elizabeth's eventual objection to coming to America, see the account in L. H. Butterfield, ed., *John Witherspoon Comes to America: A Documentary Account Based Largely on New Materials* (Princeton, N.J., 1953), xii, 23–24, 27, 29–33, 39, 44. For the most important theological sermons Witherspoon published in the two decades before his arrival in America, see the first thirteen works in the first volume of the second edition of his *Works.*

To underline his evangelical insistence on the mechanisms by which the Holy Spirit enabled spiritual change and rebirth to occur among individuals, Witherspoon went on to elucidate: "Regeneration, repentance, conversion, or call it what you will, is a very great change from the state in which every man comes into the world. This appears from our Saviour's assertion, that we must be 'born again.' It appears from a great variety of other scripture phrases, and is the certain consequence of some of the most essential doctrines of the gospel." Witherspoon associated the "fashionable schemes of irreligious, pretended morality" with those who were at liberty to "treat the doctrine of free grace, and of Christ's righteousness and merit, with contempt and scorn." His insistence on distilling "central" doctrines of conversion and rebirth and his desire to distinguish such an approach from other, more "fashionable" theological approaches further underlined his evangelicalism. Witherspoon stressed that humans could only truly understand God's moral vision after acknowledging their sin and their need for divine mercy through Christ.[37]

In another earlier sermon, "The Object of a Christian's Desire," Witherspoon distinguished further his evangelical approach from those such as Hutcheson whom he accused of seeking to "think, and speak, and reason on the perfections of God, as an object of science" rather than endeavoring to "glorify him as God, or to have a deep and awful impression of him upon our hearts." Emphasizing the practical role of conversion, rather than philosophical speculation, Witherspoon suggested that "real believers will know . . . [that a] discovery of the glory of God, is not to inform them of a truth which they never heard before, but to give lively penetrating views of the meaning and importance of those truths of which they had, perhaps, heard and spoken times without number." The "glory" of God lay not merely in majesty but also in the "divine mercy" shown to all people who did not deserve it, through the death and then the love of Christ. Thus, the power of mercy, which was

---

37. Witherspoon, *Practical Treatise on Regeneration*, in [Green, ed.], *Works of Witherspoon*, I, 96–97, 101–103, 154, 262. For a definition of evangelicalism in these Scottish contexts, see David Bebbington, "Scottish Cultural Influences on Evangelicalism," *Scottish Bulletin of Evangelical Theology*, XIV (1996), 23; D. W. Bebbington, "Evangelical Christianity and the Enlightenment," in John R. W. Stott et al., eds., *The Gospel in the Modern World: A Tribute to John Stott* (Leicester, U.K., 1991), 29–30; Bebbington, *Evangelicalism in Modern Britain: A History from the 1730s to the 1980s* (London, 1989), 12, 40–42. See also the general historical definition in Mark A. Noll, Bebbington, and George A. Rawlyk, eds., *Evangelicalism: Comparative Studies of Popular Protestantism in North America, the British Isles, and Beyond, 1700–1990* (New York, 1994), 4–12. For a discussion of Witherspoon's theological stance in his Scottish sermons before 1768, see also Tait, *Piety of John Witherspoon*, 35–118.

central to the conversion experience, was a vital addition to any perception of the "power, wisdom, holiness and justice of God." An acknowledgement of mercy—as directly related to the individual experience of sin—was central to Witherspoon's Presbyterian revivalist theology. Its continued requirement also exposed that which individuals lacked in their innate moral volition.[38]

Witherspoon's evangelical distinction from establishment-minded theologians appeared in some sermons with even greater descriptive vitriol. In "All Mankind by Nature under Sin," Witherspoon recognized that it might be "pleasing and gratifying to human pride, to talk of the dignity of human nature, and the beauty of moral virtue." But such a moral philosophical stance, Witherspoon concluded, risked being applied toward a vision of "man as he now is without regenerating grace," thus forgoing the "power of restraining providence" in defining moral volition. Here, in opposing those who seemed to promote a notion of human-centered ethical capability, Witherspoon is likely to have had in mind ministers and professors who were thought to follow Hutcheson. Indeed, he pointed out that the "most truly excellent characters which are to be found in history, and the most illustrious deeds which those heroes have performed, have for their very foundation the corruption of the human race."[39]

Witherspoon was Augustinian in his claim that Christ was a "Mediator" between divine and human time thanks to the covenant of grace that his resurrection heralded: "Our access to God, and our communion with him, is, and can only be, through the Mediator of the new covenant, in whom we have access, by faith, unto God." Jesus was humiliated while incarnate as a human, and, Witherspoon suggested, "the afflictions of our Lord not only continued but increased, through his life, till they, at last, issued in an extraordinary conflict with the powers of darkness, and an immediate subjection to the wrath of a sin avenging God"—a "cup" that was put to the mouth of Jesus, in order to account for the "dishonor done to God" by Adam, "so soon as he assumed our nature [as a human]." Thus, "the waves of divine wrath went over him; and he waded still deeper and deeper in this troubled ocean, till he was well nigh over-whelmed." Mediating the divine, yet also human, the incarnation of Jesus was, according to Witherspoon, "a subject the most wonderful and mysterious that ever was offered to the mind of man."[40]

38. John Witherspoon, "The Object of a Christian's Desire in Religious Worship," in [Green, ed.], *Works of Witherspoon,* II, 12, 13-14.

39. John Witherspoon, "All Mankind by Nature under Sin," ibid., I, 277.

40. Witherspoon, "Object of a Christian's Desire," ibid., II, 18; John Witherspoon, "The Glory of Christ in His Humiliation," ibid., 31; Witherspoon, "Glorying in the Cross," ibid., I,

Witherspoon's evangelical understanding of the communion ritual centered on the experiential procedures of the *"Lord's Supper,"* where we have a sensible representation of Christ crucified, the great mean of our access to God, that we may serve him." Here, as elsewhere, his account of "sensible" piety used descriptive vocabulary that could also be found in Scottish moral sense philosophy. Yet the descriptions allowed him to underline the necessity of conversion for moral perception, rather than any notion of moral innateness.[41]

On the one hand, Witherspoon understood the specific duties and laws of Presbyterian parish life according to the pious works that all men struggled and strove to carry out in their particular realm. On the other hand, too great an emphasis on local works always threatened to undermine the importance of faith and the universal primacy of grace in the Second Covenant emphasized by the Westminster Confession of Faith. Thus, the vexing tension between religious works and the abstraction of faith, which had been described since Augustine, was tacitly present in some of Witherspoon's Scottish sermons. If good works were a necessary sign of faith before regeneration, it was not always clear whether some sort of innate moral volition was required to gain such humility and whether a conception of good works in relation to providence was a hubristic forethought.[42]

---

387. See also the discussion of Witherspoon's conception of Christ as Mediator, linked to theological assumptions from Calvin onward, in Tait, *Piety of John Witherspoon,* 60–62.

41. Witherspoon, "Object of a Christian's Desire," in [Green, ed.], *Works of Witherspoon,* II, 10. Witherspoon's emphasis on the importance of the sacrament corroborates what scholars have suggested was a central component of Presbyterian revivalism in the Atlantic world during the 1740s: the Augustinian desire to transcend place and time through the reception of atemporal grace. See Noll, Bebbington, and Rawlyk, eds., *Evangelicalism,* 3–6; Michael J. Crawford, *Seasons of Grace: Colonial New England's Revival Tradition in Its British Context* (New York, 1991); Marilyn J. Westerkamp, *Triumph of the Laity: Scots-Irish Piety and the Great Awakening, 1625–1760* (New York, 1988); Susan O'Brien, "A Transatlantic Community of Saints: The Great Awakening and the First Evangelical Network, 1735–1755," *American Historical Review,* XCI (1986), 811–832.

42. See, for example, Witherspoon's sermons, *The Charge of Sedition and Faction against Good Men . . . ,"* in [Green, ed.], *Works of Witherspoon,* II, 415–420, and "All Mankind by Nature under Sin," I, 267–285. A tension between the covenant of works and the covenant of grace was apparent among many Congregational as well as Presbyterian theologians on both sides of the Atlantic during the middle decades of the eighteenth century. Among the former, according to Christopher Grasso, the idea of "two covenants—or two branches of the one Covenant of Grace" amounted to an "unstable combination of Jehovah's Old Testament tribal compact with the chosen people Israel and the New Testament's promise of salvation through Christ";

Like many of his former teachers, Witherspoon tended to respond to the conundrum of moral agency with the settling (if also predictable) suggestion that divine providence predetermined individual humility. In his sermon, "Hope of Forgiveness with God," he claimed that providence underlay the faith that preceded the reception of grace. The "more the sinner looks into his own state," Witherspoon warned, "the more real and thorough his acquaintance with his own heart is, the more he finds, that not the least ray of hope can arise from that quarter." But all was not bleak, as the word "hope" carried another meaning in Witherspoon's sermon. It suggested a yearning and faith that was to be distinguished from empirical perception. The humility required to receive grace represented an unverified but nonetheless powerful desire for a future moral state. Tentative and unverifiable, "hope" comforted individuals without suggesting their innate certainty of any moral outcome. Its evocation provided few easy answers for those who were unsure about the role of individual works in the acknowledgement of sin. "Hope" implied the possibility of future mercy, but also a "trembling" religious struggle.[43]

In order to reduce the likelihood of feigned humility, Witherspoon claimed that only biblical precepts could be trusted to inspire individual self-effacement before regeneration. His 1756 *Essay on Justification* used an empirical account of human experience to describe how individuals might come to understand their need for external religious intervention: It was "vain for any to expect an effectual change of life, but by an acquaintance with Christ, and him crucified. We have indeed the clearest evidence from experience, that no human reason, no argument whatever, drawn from worldly conveniency, is at all sufficient to contend with violent and sinful habits." The passions of human nature negated any attempt to reconcile innate individual perception with societal benevolence.[44]

Augustine's doctrine of illumination suggested that God played an active role in human cognition by somehow clarifying the individual mind, allowing it to perceive that which God concurrently presented to it. Witherspoon similarly preached on the Holy Spirit granting an "inward and spiritual illumination" that was preferable to mere knowledge about divine precepts. Here Witherspoon's description of moral illumination relied on sensory terminology that had also been apparent in Francis Hutcheson's writings. But

---

see Grasso, *A Speaking Aristocracy: Transforming Public Discourse in Eighteenth-Century Connecticut* (Chapel Hill, N.C., 1999), 28.

43. John Witherspoon, "Hope of Forgiveness with God," in [Green, ed.], *Works of Witherspoon*, I, 299; Witherspoon, *Practical Treatise on Regeneration*, ibid., 141.

44. Witherspoon, *Essay on Justification*, ibid., 87.

ethical reasoning, in his account, could only be wrought by grace following conversion — or at least it could be illuminated by the Holy Spirit during the initial stages of regeneration.[45]

Yet Witherspoon's account of regeneration still faced the problem of moral intransigence and its relationship to divine providence. His former teachers had always been aware that knowledge of the necessity of salvation was not always perceived as a gift from the Holy Spirit and that it was often simply ignored. If the first principles of divine illumination led to further regenerative action, did those who remained unregenerate display their own darker agency, separate from the externally imposed moral duties provided by God? If the rejection of moral illumination before salvation did not demonstrate an individual choice, but a providential scheme, then the problematic theological doctrine of divine election was likely to be raised. But rather than examining the validity of such a doctrine, Witherspoon most often avoided the scholastic details that had once been associated with the debate on moral agency in the system of predestination. Instead, as he pointed out in his sermon "The Object of a Christian's Desire," the life of regenerate Christians was a constant struggle, which included trying to understand complex theological questions. Thus, the mystery of grace and "divine all-sufficiency" was to "be considered, as regarding our sanctification as well as comfort." With such a consideration, Witherspoon asked: "What distress does not the Christian often suffer from the treachery of his own heart, and from the power of surrounding temptations? . . . And what courage does he derive from the fulness of divine perfection, the greatness of divine power, and the faithfulness of the divine promise?" Witherspoon likely used the word "Christian" to describe those who had undergone a true form of regeneration. Yet, even in their case, courage was necessary to sustain a Christian life against the likelihood of partial moral regression.[46]

Indeed, the struggle of regenerate life also made missionary work important for Witherspoon. As he pointed out in his sermon *The Absolute Necessity*

45. Michael Mendelson, "Saint Augustine," in Edward N. Zalta, ed., *The Stanford Encyclopedia of Philosophy* (Fall 2008 ed.), http://plato.stanford.edu/archives/fall2008/entries/augustine/; Nash, *Light of the Mind,* 94–124; Witherspoon, "Object of a Christian's Desire," in [Green, ed.], *Works of Witherspoon,* II, 12.

46. Witherspoon, "Object of a Christian's Desire," in [Green, ed.], *Works of Witherspoon,* II, 17–18. For more on the notion of a constant struggle among regenerate evangelicals in the Anglo-American world during the eighteenth century, see Knud Haakonssen, "From Natural Law to the Rights of Man: A European Perspective on American Debates," in Michael J. Lacey and Haakonssen, eds., *A Culture of Rights: The Bill of Rights in Philosophy, Politics, and Law — 1791 to 1991* (Cambridge, 1991), 22–26.

of Salvation through Christ, "the real, the unspeakable moment of propagating Christian knowledge . . . so far as it is cordially embraced" lay in "turning men 'from darkness to light,' and from the 'power of Satan unto God.'" Missionary work also provided a means to propagate an evangelical approach to faith, lest more moderate churchmen take it upon themselves to engage with non-Christian populations. As Witherspoon thus continued: "Let us only suppose those who deny or call in question the absolute necessity of salvation through Christ, employed as missionaries in converting the Heathens: how cold, how ambiguous and inconclusive the arguments with which they would endeavor to press the change!" Missionary activity was even more vital, as Witherspoon argued in another sermon, because "werever they [tenets of the Gospel] are maintained and inculcated, strictness and purity of life and manners will be their natural effect." "On the contrary, where they are neglected, and a pretended theory of moral virtue substituted in their room, it will immediately and certainly introduce a deluge of profanity and immorality in practice." Of this "the present state of our own church and nation, compared with that of former periods," Witherspoon wrote in 1764, "is a strong and melancholy proof." Even here, in an account of the way that evangelism might help others in their natural struggle toward faith through grace, Witherspoon nudged those whom he believed followed Hutcheson in describing the essential moral virtue of common sociability.[47]

Alexander Carlyle's memoirs distinguished Witherspoon's developing evangelicalism, including his focus on missionary activity, from what he saw to be the natural advancement of moral sense theory in metropolitan Scottish culture. Yet it was perfectly possible for Witherspoon to advance an evangelical account of moral reasoning using aspects of the earlier education that he had shared with Carlyle, just as Carlyle could draw different ethical ideas from the writings of Hutcheson, which had been disseminated during the same heterogeneous period. By the 1760s, Carlyle and Witherspoon would define their distinct understandings of morality with increasing vehemence because they came to be associated with different visions of British unionism — including the mission of Scottish piety in the American colonies.[48]

47. John Witherspoon, *The Absolute Necessity of Salvation through Christ* . . . , in [Green, ed.], *Works of Witherspoon,* II, 361; Witherspoon, *A Serious Apology for the Ecclesiastical Characteristics,* ibid., III, 294.

48. According to Haakonssen, a "dividing line lay between [Witherspoon's] own [later] evangelical notions of man's duty and those of mainstream natural-law moralists, of whom his former compatriot and opponent, Francis Hutcheson, was the archetype"; see Haakonssen, "From Natural Law to the Rights of Man," in Lacey and Haakonssen, eds., *A Culture of Rights,* 54.

CHAPTER 2

"OF LOCAL AND TEMPORARY REFORMATION, LOCAL AND OCCASIONAL DEPRAVATION"

Kirk Divisions and American Prospects at Midcentury

Alexander Carlyle and John Witherspoon were both Presbyterian. They went to the same Edinburgh university classes. They once flirted with the same "companions of the fair sex." They studied for the same theological qualifications. Yet, by the 1760s, they had become personally estranged, theological and philosophical rivals in the same Kirk and in the same new British state. During the era of the American Revolution, moreover, they would support separate warring unions using very different theological and philosophical justifications. Their conflict highlighted the perceived divergence between moral philosophy and evangelicalism in Scotland and the wider Atlantic world during the second half of the eighteenth century. They came to define their civil theologies in common opposition, using increasingly vitriolic justifications, as a consequence of their differing perception of the Church of Scotland's continued autonomy in Britain after the 1707 Act of Union.[1]

Like Witherspoon, Carlyle supported the Hanoverian order against Jacobite threats during the 1730s and 1740s. But, in contrast to the evangelical minister, he believed that proper university learning would allow graduating students to harness their common moral sensibility toward civic cohesion in Britain. In the decades following the 1707 Act of Union, the idea of prerational moral perception became more popular as educated Scots sought to moderate their loss of political sovereignty. Following the dissolution of the Edinburgh Parliament, they were no longer in proximity to political governance. They suggested instead that a common ethical sensibility supplied societal cohesion, irrespective of any legislative mandate from political representatives. Educated Scottish elites—including those such as Carlyle whom Witherspoon came to oppose—assumed an ironic degree of paternalism and social stratification in describing what ought to be verified by the

1. Alexander Carlyle, *Autobiography of the Rev. Dr. Alexander Carlyle, Minister of Inveresk: Containing Memorials of the Men and Events of His Time* (Edinburgh, 1860), 65.

common moral response. Conveniently, they suggested that their communitarian leadership reflected the benevolent ethical sense of all their constituents. Thus, they could define their rise to societal prominence as a legitimate manifestation of the popular will. Though they in fact benefited from the private patronage of wealthy landlords and their Westminster representatives, they claimed to embody the benevolent actions and reactions that all men were capable of displaying in their response to moral conceptions.[2]

Through the 1750s, Witherspoon criticized clergymen and professors who claimed to reflect the benevolent stance of their constituents. Such an assertion, in his opinion, buttressed their authority and social status by eschewing their continuing need for external divine assistance. He and other evangelical Presbyterians perceived the promotion of revivalist tenets in the Westminster Confession of Faith as central to the continuing institutional autonomy that the Kirk enjoyed after 1707. This perception was evident in the religious and constitutional reasoning that Witherspoon employed during the midcentury period of heightened conflict between Britain and France. He used a 1758 evangelical sermon on "the charge of sedition" to highlight the perceived persecution of Scottish Covenanters during the 1660s, including their movement from Scotland to North America and elsewhere. In Scotland, "after the restoration," he pointed out:

> Though there was no struggle for civil liberty, all who chose to obey God rather than man, either in the substance or circumstances of religious duties, were charged with treason, and suffered as rebels. They were expelled from the church; yet censured as schismatic. They were harassed, fined and imprisoned, when living in peace, without any fault but "concerning the law of their God"; and yet complained of as troublesome. They were banished, excommunicated, and denied the common benefits of life.

Here Witherspoon incorporated Scottish Covenanters into a story of piety, dissent, and persecution that is more familiarly linked to the struggle of English Puritanism during the second half of the seventeenth century, including on the western side of the Atlantic. Witherspoon used their example to

2. On the link between Scottish enlightened culture and the diminishment of Scottish political authority, see Nicholas Phillipson, "Politics, Politeness, and the Anglicisation of Early Eighteenth-Century Scottish Culture," in Roger A. Mason, ed., *Scotland and England, 1286–1815* (Edinburgh, 1987), 226–246. On the potentially elitist trajectory of the notion of *sensus communis* in the British Atlantic world, including in Scotland, see Sophia Rosenfeld, *Common Sense: A Political History* (Cambridge, Mass., 2011), 144–145.

define the contrast with the present Protestant liberties of British unionism, as distinct from imperial powers such as France. But more explicitly, his example also offered a warning that was addressed to the dominant faction of the Church of Scotland: the freedoms of Protestant dissent, Witherspoon suggested, were likely threatened by overly narrow religious establishments in alliance with government. Witherspoon and others like him attributed the freedom of pietistic religion to the constitutional context of Hanoverian Britain, while also warning of its potential constraint.[3]

Words such as "freedom" and "liberty" were often used by evangelical ministers to describe the expansion of Presbyterian piety in the British Atlantic world. Yet we should be careful to avoid assuming a Whiggish association between constitutional freedom and the extension of Protestant revivalism, Presbyterian or otherwise. Accounts of the development of Anglo-American liberty often claim that dissenters enjoyed increasing toleration for their expression of individual conscience. But, as scholars of religious rights during the later seventeenth century have pointed out, it is problematic to assume a libertarian account of the right of conscience in those cases when it was conceived as "a matter at best of licence rather than liberty," when the individual "conscience" was "free in order that men might grasp the more clearly their ineluctable confinement in the harness in which, ever since the delinquencies of their first ancestor, God had set human beings in the world."[4]

A similar association between rights and duties had governed the Presbyterian drafters of the 1647 Westminster Confession of Faith. In dialogue with English dissenters, they grounded the notion of individual conscience in particular moral obligations because they were aware of the curtailed ethical capability of all unregenerate men. Like the earlier drafters of the Westminster Confession of Faith, the younger Witherspoon avoided defining personal conscience as an innate ethical sensibility during his Scottish ministry. He continued to focus on the imperative of conversion before clear and awakened moral perception. His attachment to the expanding British

3. John Witherspoon, *The Charge of Sedition and Faction against Good Men* . . . , in [Ashbel Green, ed.], *The Works of the Rev. John Witherspoon, D.D.L.L.D. Late President of the College at Princeton, New-Jersey* . . . , 2d ed., rev., 4 vols. (Philadelphia, 1802), II, 422–423.

4. John Dunn, *The Political Thought of John Locke: An Historical Account of the Argument of the "Two Treatises of Government"* (Cambridge, 1982), 264. For discussions and critiques of these Whiggish definitions of Protestant toleration in the British Atlantic world, see Chris Beneke, "America's Whiggish Religious Revolution: An Instance in the Progress of History," *Historically Speaking*, X, no. 3 (June 2009), 31–35; Chris Beneke and Christopher S. Grenda, eds., *The First Prejudice: Religious Tolerance and Intolerance in Early America* (Philadelphia, 2010); Beneke, *Beyond Toleration: The Religious Origins of American Pluralism* (New York, 2006).

state was founded on a constitutional and religious ideal that differed from
the enlightened notion of cultural provinciality that led other Presbyterians
such as Carlyle to define the civic importance of inborn moral sensibility. Instead, Witherspoon continued to argue that religious rights merely allowed
individuals to work out their duty to God, with the help of the Holy Spirit.
After his graduation and ministerial training, he rooted his support for Britain in the religious potential of its imperial union. He hoped that an enlarged
association between Edinburgh and London would enable the expansion of
Presbyterian pietism south of Scotland and farther west into the new British
Empire.[5]

Carlyle eventually suggested that Witherspoon had betrayed their shared
educational heritage by promoting a base form of evangelicalism among
disgruntled Scots and rebellious Americans. He was correct to recall that
Witherspoon's Scottish evangelicalism ultimately developed a political inflection in its association with the fate of the American colonies. But, during
the 1750s and 1760s, support for Presbyterian revivalism in America represented more than a convenient means for sidelined evangelicals to reassert
their influence. It became essential to their identity because it expressed a
fundamental and deeply rooted aspect of their moral epistemology. By the
1740s, Witherspoon and other evangelical Scots no longer felt threatened by
royal authority, and so the legitimacy of the Protestant Hanoverian line became central to their conditional support for British jurisdiction. They continued to allude to the mid-seventeenth-century covenants that had temporarily allied Scottish Presbyterianism with English parliamentarian culture,
finding a model for their own political incorporation into the British Empire.
But the notion of a specifically national Scottish covenant became less pertinent to them. Increasingly, the power and importance of the Westminster
Confession of Faith was conceived according to its description of the universal requirement for salvation. They suggested that all men were required
to acknowledge and partake in God's covenant of grace — irrespective of the
local regional contexts in which they had been born. They continued to main-

5. For Witherspoon on awakening and conversion, see, for example, John Witherspoon,
"Lectures on Moral Philosophy," in [Green, ed.], *Works of Witherspoon*, III, 382. As Knud
Haakonssen has shown, evangelicals in the British Atlantic world often believed that "rights"
were "not simply powers granted, but powers granted for a purpose . . . never granted as open-
ended powers, but always in conjunction with matching duties" to God; see Haakonssen, "From
Natural Law to the Rights of Man: A European Perspective on American Debates," in Michael J.
Lacey and Haakonssen, eds., *A Culture of Rights: The Bill of Rights in Philosophy, Politics, and
Law — 1791 and 1991* (Cambridge, 1991), 36.

tain important aspects of their ethnoreligious Scottish identity. Nonetheless, they also hoped that the retention of the Kirk's confessional independence would expose what they saw to be the revivalist standards of the Westminster Confession to provincial populations outside Scotland, including in North America.[6]

According to Witherspoon, Carlyle and his Moderate associates were too parochial in their reliance on theories that favored the moral development of mainland Britain, particularly as they often benefited from connections through their Scottish patrons. For those who believed that innate ethical volition was unlikely—irrespective of social and cultural advancement—the promotion of conversion was an imperative that was not confined to local populations. The Moderate focus on local civic cohesion, according to Witherspoon, blinded its adherents to the attendant importance of evangelism within and without the British Isles—including in America. He sought to renew an alternative vision of Anglo-Scottish unionism during his later Scottish career. His polemical statements and publications outside the pulpit sought to connect religious, civic, and imperial concerns in order to counter opponents of evangelicalism. They came to focus on the movement of Presbyterian revivalism in Scotland and out into the Atlantic world.[7]

6. For the declining fear of royal authority among revivalist Presbyterians after the Act of Union, see Allan I. Macinnes, *Union and Empire: The Making of the United Kingdom in 1707* (Cambridge, 2007), 137–171. Influential Scots viewed the political integration of the British peoples in light of a "long-term ideological goal to which they were pledged by the Solemn League and Covenant of 1643"; see Colin Kidd, "Conditional Britons: The Scots Covenanting Tradition and the Eighteenth-Century British State," *English Historical Review*, CXVII (2002), 1154. In addition to Kidd's discussion of continued covenanting sentiment during the eighteenth century, including its potential expansion into imperial spheres, see also Richard J. Finlay, "Keeping the Covenant: Scottish National Identity," in T. M. Devine and J. R. Young, eds., *Eighteenth Century Scotland: New Perspectives* (East Lothian, U.K., 1999), 121–133; Philip Benedict, *Christ's Churches Purely Reformed: A Social History of Calvinism* (New Haven, Conn., 2002), 401; David Allan, "Protestantism, Presbyterianism, and National Identity in Eighteenth-Century Scottish History," in Tony Claydon and Ian McBride, eds., *Protestantism and National Identity: Britain and Ireland, c. 1650–c. 1850* (Cambridge, 1998), 182–205. This common conception was akin to Jewish diasporic identity. On the similarity between Scottish and Jewish diasporic identity, see Colin Kidd, *British Identities before Nationalism: Ethnicity and Nationhood in the Atlantic World, 1600–1800* (Cambridge, 1999), 128–132; David George Mullan, *Scottish Puritanism, 1590–1638* (Oxford, 2000), 271–273.

7. See, for example, John Witherspoon, *The Absolute Necessity of Salvation through Christ . . .*, in [Green, ed.], *Works of Witherspoon*, II, 364.

"A Land of Civil Liberty and Yet of Ecclesiastical Tyranny"

The nature of the Kirk's relationship with Westminster — and the Kirk's wider imperial jurisdiction — was contested from the earliest moment of British political integration. During the debate on Edinburgh's political union with London in 1707, some Presbyterian ministers and civic leaders perceived the political incorporation of the British peoples according to earlier standards. They looked back to the Solemn League and Covenant and the Westminster Confession of Faith. Their endorsement of the Act of Union was conditional on the retention of the Church of Scotland's independence and its continued ability to promote Presbyterian piety in the new British Empire, including in North America. The demand that the Act of Union be complemented by An Act for Securing the Protestant Religion and Presbyterian Church Government appealed to officeholders in the "Court Party," such as Patrick Hume, first earl of Seafield, who sought to maintain their position in the Presbyterian establishment against any potential threat from Anglican authorities in Britain and its expanding Empire. Hugh Campbell, third earl of Loudoun, and William Johnson, first marquess of Annandale, also shared this motivation, including its imperial dimension.[8]

Campbell's and Hume's support for Kirk autonomy against the perceived Anglican supremacy of the Westminster political establishment was expressed in protracted negotiations with other members of the Scottish Court Party, who thought slightly differently. Many either equivocated over the issue or believed that the English Parliament was the sufficient guarantor of civil and religious liberties gained during the Glorious Revolution. They suggested that the Kirk was more likely to sustain its relevance and importance through its incorporation in the ecclesiastical establishment of Westminster rather than via its continued institutional independence. Four years

8. Macinnes, *Union and Empire,* 97–98, 286, 302–303, 322. Following the Act of Union, the new British polity incorporated two national churches into a wider imperial union, one that was connected to the imperial state and its Westminster Parliament and one that ostensibly was not. On the Act for the Security of the Kirk, designed to preserve the independence of the Presbyterian establishment in Scotland despite political incorporation into Britain, see also Colin Kidd, "Religious Realignment between the Restoration and Union," in John Robertson, ed., *A Union for Empire: Political Thought and the British Union of 1707* (Cambridge, 1995), 145–168, esp. 168; Jeffrey Stephen, "The Kirk and the Union, 1706–7: A Reappraisal," *Records of the Scottish Church History Society,* XXXI (2001), 68–96; Derek J. Patrick, "The Kirk, Parliament, and the Union, 1706–7," in Stewart J. Brown and Christopher A. Whatley, eds., *The Union of 1707: New Dimensions* (Edinburgh, 2008), 94–115.

later, in 1711, unsurprisingly, a number of their associates supported the Act to Restore the Patrons to Their Ancient Rights of Presenting Ministers to the Churches Vacant in That Part of Great Britain Called Scotland. The act, which came to be known less formally as the Patronage Act, restored lay patronage to Scottish landowners, or lairds. Their wealth and status made them more likely to gain the ear of political representatives in Westminster. Those representatives, in turn, reinforced their ability to control the appointment of Presbyterian ministers and even Scottish university professors. The 1732 General Assembly Act confirmed the statute underlying the 1711 Patronage Act, further cementing the right of lairds to make the final choice for ministers in their parish. Patrons included men such as Alexander Gordon, fourth duke of Gordon (1743-1827), described by the Moderate Lord Kames as the "greatest subject in Britain" owing to the number of Scots who depended on his patronage from the late 1760s. Thus, the scholarly link between moral philosophy and depoliticized identity overlooks the continued association between Moderate Presbyterianism and Westminster governance.[9]

Witherspoon's religious identity assumed a political inflection in opposition to patronage when he became leader and spokesman for the minority evangelical faction of the Church of Scotland in the late 1740s. There is no existing evidence of a formal appointment to leadership of the faction. Rather, from 1747 Witherspoon increasingly assumed a representative function in debates over patronage. No fewer than fifty cases opposed to patronage were brought to the General Assembly of the Scottish Kirk in the period 1740-1750. As the head of the Popular party, Witherspoon castigated Moderate churchmen for preventing lay involvement in the election of Presbyterian ministers. He believed that ministerial choice lay in the hands of the congregation rather than patrons. Along with other Popular party members, he suggested that Moderate churchmen had used their position in the new British union to create their own ecclesiastical establishment rather than an

---

9. Macinnes, *Union and Empire,* 98. On the various acts and statutes for patronage through the 1730s, see Stewart J. Brown, ed., *William Robertson and the Expansion of Empire* (Cambridge, 1997), 11. On the link between Walpole's Whig oligarchy and Scottish land managers such as John Campbell, the second duke of Argyll, see Allan, "Protestantism," in Claydon and McBride, eds., *Protestantism and National Identity,* 182-206; Alexander Murdoch and Richard B. Sher, "Literary and Learned Culture," in T. M. Devine and Rosalind Mitchison, eds., *People and Society in Scotland, 1760–1830* (Edinburgh, 1988), I, 127-138; Sher, *Church and University in the Scottish Enlightenment: The Moderate Literati of Edinburgh* (Princeton, N.J., 1985), 213-261. On the influence of Alexander Gordon, see H. M. Chichester, "Gordon, Alexander, fourth duke of Gordon (1743-1827)," rev. Michael Fry, in David Cannadine, gen. ed., *Oxford Dictionary of National Biography,* online ed. (Oxford, 2004-) (hereafter cited as *DNB*).

FIGURE 5. *Alexander Gordon, 4th Duke of Gordon (1743–1827)*.
By Pompeo Batoni. 1764. Oil on canvas. National Galleries of Scotland, Edinburgh,
Scotland, Great Britain, Dist. RMN–Grand Palais / Art Resource, N.Y.

independent forum to promote evangelism. The division over patronage was explicitly demonstrated by the case of Thomas Gillespie, an evangelical minister from Carnock. In 1752, he refused to participate in the ordination of Andrew Richardson, a Moderate. As a result, he was removed from his position by prominent patrons. He immediately challenged his dismissal in various Presbyterian assemblies. William Robertson, a Moderate, collaborated with other like-minded ministers to write a manifesto opposing his cause, titled "Reasons of Dissent." It was soon followed by a Popular party pamphlet, written primarily by Witherspoon, titled "Answers to the Reasons of Dissent." The Moderates eventually won their case, much to the consternation of the Popular party. Witherspoon protested in 1753 to the Synod of Glasgow: "Is it not, and do we not glory in its being a land of liberty?" He then questioned whether postunion Scotland seemed to have become "a land of civil liberty and yet of ecclesiastical tyranny? Must not a man have equity and justice in the church, as well as the state?" In formulating the "Reasons for Dissent" pamphlet, Witherspoon became even more widely known as the representative head of the Popular party.[10]

Through the 1740s, hitherto separate disputes over the autonomy of Presbyterian ecclesiology became bound up with theological distinctions regarding the nature of moral agency. They were increasingly difficult to distinguish

10. John Witherspoon, "Speech in the Synod of Glasgow . . . ," in [Green, ed.], *Works of Witherspoon,* IV, 252. On the Gillespie patronage affair and Witherspoon's distinction from Robertson over "Reasons of Dissent," see [William Robertson], "Reasons of Dissent from the Judgment and Resolution of the Commission, March 11, 1752," *Scots Magazine,* XIV (April 1752), 191–197; [John Witherspoon], "An Abstract of the Answers to the Reasons of Dissent from the Sentence of the Commission, March 11, 1752 . . . Drawn Up by the Committee Appointed for That Purpose . . . and Dated May 16," ibid., 229–238; John R. McIntosh, *Church and Theology in Enlightenment Scotland: The Popular Party, 1740–1800* (East Lothian, U.K., 1998), 117; Varnum Lansing Collins, *President Witherspoon: A Biography,* 2 vols. (Princeton, N.J., 1925), I, 33–34. According to James A. Harris, Francis Hutcheson's moral philosophy "was [eventually] taken by the Orthodox [in the Popular party] to provide the theoretical foundation for the all-too-worldly sermons of [ministers] such as Hugh Blair, John Home, and William Robertson"; see Harris, "Answering Bayle's Question: Religious Belief in the Moral Philosophy of the Scottish Enlightenment," in Daniel Garber and Steven Nadler, eds., *Oxford Studies in Early Modern Philosophy,* I (Oxford, 2003), 235. On the widening of divisions between Orthodox or Popular Kirk members and Moderates at this point, see also Jonathan M. Yeager, *Enlightened Evangelicalism: The Life and Thought of John Erskine* (New York, 2011), 5–6; Ian D. L. Clark, "From Protest to Reaction: The Moderate Regime in the Church of Scotland, 1752–1805," in N. T. Phillipson and Rosalind Mitchison, eds., *Scotland in the Age of Improvement: Essays in Scottish History in the Eighteenth Century* (Edinburgh, 1970), 200–224. On the critique of Moderate parochialism, see Allan, "Protestantism," in Claydon and McBride, eds., *Protestantism and National Identity,* 182–206.

in the debate on civil theology that was sparked by evangelical opposition
to patronage. A majority of Moderate clergymen and university professors
claimed that patronage was legitimate because it secured their ability to represent the common ethical values of all Scots. In advanced unions, they suggested, educated leaders could corroborate biblical morality by harnessing
their God-given moral sensibility. According to evangelical Presbyterians,
conversely, Moderates privileged stylish and elegant discourse in order to
avoid bothering their patrons with unpleasant notions of universal depravity.
Having secured their clerical standing, in the view of Popular party members,
they undermined the central Presbyterian standards of revival, regeneration,
and salvation in the Westminster Confession of Faith.[11]

Witherspoon distilled his opposition to the Moderate ascendancy in his
publication of 1753 titled *Ecclesiastical Characteristics; or, The Arcana of
Church Policy; Being an Humble Attempt to Open the Mystery of Moderation;
Wherein Is Shewn, a Plain and Easy Way of Attaining to the Character of a
Moderate Man, as at Present in Repute in the Church of Scotland.* First published in Glasgow, it was subsequently printed many times in England as
well as in Scotland. In Maxim I, Witherspoon wrote: "All ecclesiastical persons, of whatever rank, whether principals of colleges, professors of divinity,
ministers, or even probationers, that are suspected of heresy, are to be esteemed men of great genius, vast learning, and uncommon worth; and are,
by all means, to be supported and protected." Thus, protection and support
was to be supplied by patronage in "church-settlements, which are the principal causes that come before ministers for judgement, the only thing to be
regarded is, who the patron and the great and noble heritors are for; the inclinations of the common people are to be utterly despised." Moderation,
according to Witherspoon's satirical account, served a "very noble end" by

11. Colin Kidd, "Constructing a Civil Religion: Scots Presbyterians and the Eighteenth-
Century British State," in James Kirk, ed., *The Scottish Churches and the Union Parliament,
1707–1999* (Edinburgh, 2001), 1–21. On patronage systems that exasperated evangelicals,
see Sher, *Church and University,* 213–261; Ronald M. Sunter, *Patronage and Politics in Scotland, 1707–1832* (Edinburgh, 1986), 199–210; McIntosh, *Church and Theology,* 19–40; Ned C.
Landsman, "Liberty, Piety, and Patronage: The Social Context of Contested Clerical Calls in
Eighteenth-Century Glasgow," in Andrew Hook and Richard B. Sher, eds., *The Glasgow Enlightenment* (East Lothian, U.K., 1995), 214–226. Sher and Alexander Murdoch have questioned
the accuracy of the label "popular" for the evangelical opponents of patronage. The latter did not
support truly popular or congregational calls to the ministry but rather promoted the rights of
representative heritors and elders. See Sher and Murdoch, "Patronage and Party in the Church
of Scotland, 1750–1800," in Norman Macdougall, ed., *Church, Politics, and Society: Scotland,
1408–1929* (Edinburgh, 1983), 197–220.

vindicating "the Christian religion from the objection of some infidels, who affirm that it does not recommend private friendship; now moderate men having all a very great regard to private friendship, and personal connexions ... confute this slander." Moderate theology, then, was bound up with private connections, as Witherspoon began to allude to the chief role of patronage.[12]

Lampooning Moderate theology even further, Witherspoon defined its purported approach to the Westminster Confession of Faith in Maxim III: "Nothing is more easy than for them to keep themselves wholly ignorant of what it [the Confession] contains; and then they may, with a good conscience, subscribe it as true, because it ought to be so." Witherspoon was aware that members of his own evangelical party drew an experiential approach to passionate arousal from their reading of the Confession, particularly its account of the working of the Holy Spirit. For Witherspoon's adversaries, on the other hand, "there is something immoderate in the very idea of raising the passions; and therefore it is contrary to our character: nor was it ever known that a truly moderate man raised or moved any affection in his hearers." And so Moderate clergymen avoided "all the high flights of evangelic enthusiasm, and the mysteries of grace" in order "to substitute the 'moral virtues'" for "'graces of the Spirit.'" They believed "in the beauty and comely proportions of Dame Nature," all moving in a "progressive motion towards the zenith of perfection, and meridian of glory" and driven by individuals who self-conceived as "a little glorious piece of clockwork." "It is well known," Witherspoon continued, that those with a Moderate inclination often "reckon Socrates and Plato to have been much greater men than any of the apostles" — even going as far as claiming that "the apostle Paul had an university-education, and was instructed in logic." Among other writers and philosophers who had inspired Moderates in such an approach, Witherspoon referred in particular to Anthony Ashley Cooper, third earl of Shaftesbury, "so clear-sighted an author, and in all respects so agreeable to our sentiments." The moral theories of the English politician, philosopher, and writer influenced Hutcheson and a later generation of Moderate theologians. Had Shaftesbury "lived to our times, and been an heritor in Scotland," Witherspoon observed, "I can hardly allow myself to think, that ever he would have appeared on the side of the Christian people; though, without all question, he would have been chosen an elder, and sent up, 'duly attested,' to the General Assembly." Here Witherspoon returned to his focus on the

---

12. John Witherspoon, *Ecclesiastical Characteristics* ... , in [Green, ed.], *Works of Witherspoon*, III, 211, 212–213, 237.

link between aesthetic moral theory and the cultivation of private connections within the Kirk.[13]

Shaftesbury had connected individual human affections with communal welfare. In contrast, Witherspoon addressed moral sense philosophers with a very different analysis. Enamored by human-centered moral philosophy, which was popular in elite cultural and political circles, Moderates had apparently lost sight of the singular importance of repentance, which primed unregenerate individuals for the action of the Holy Spirit. The presence of the Holy Spirit, in Witherspoon's evangelical vision, assisted individuals as they struggled to acknowledge the necessity of grace in supplying a regenerated moral sensibility. In a 1757 statement, Witherspoon thus expanded his critique of contemporary moral philosophy even further and asked polemically, "What a melancholy view then does it give us of the state of religion among us at present, that when piety towards God has been excluded from many moral systems, and the whole of virtue confined to the duties of social life, the better half of these also should be cut off, and all regard to the souls of others forgotten or derided?" Once again, Witherspoon depicted a flawed ideal of virtue, in which sensory beauty and affected manners took the place of moral traits.[14]

In May 1757, Witherspoon's move to an official position ministering the town of Paisley, near Glasgow, was delayed by Moderates who dominated the local presbytery and who were not willing to overlook his suspected authorship of *Ecclesiastical Characteristics.* Ironically, they used their association with local landed patrons to prevent him from settling into the presbytery until June 1757. His opposition to Moderate culture only increased as a result of what came to be known as the Paisley affair. His ire was raised to such an extent that his continued evangelical polemics perhaps overemphasized the deistic views of Hutcheson and the Moderate theologians who followed him.[15]

Despite the divisive rhetoric during the 1750s and 1760s, it would be inaccurate to highlight two entirely unified and fully separate parties in the Church of Scotland. There remained much nuance and unorthodox distinction within as well as between these ranks. Never a deist, Hutcheson had

13. Ibid., 219, 221, 223, 233–234, 238.

14. John Witherspoon, *A Serious Inquiry into the Nature and Effects of the Stage* . . . , ibid., 177.

15. For evidence of Witherspoon's move after the delay, see James Baine, *A Sermon Preached at the Translation of the Rev. Mr. Wotherspoon, from Beith to the Laigh Church at Paisley, June 16, 1757* (Glasgow, 1757 [misprinted as 1707]), 1–18; Collins, *President Witherspoon,* I, 49–51.

always suggested that man's innate ethical sense corroborated rather than superseded biblical revelation. Similarly, those such as Carlyle who later appropriated Hutcheson were not simply irreligious philosophers who were unconcerned with a divine role in the universe. Rather than ignoring God's role in the universe, they replaced Stoic conceptions of fate with the notion that God's benevolence had placed a similar sensibility in humans. As such, according to some Moderates, individuals were able to attain a good degree of happiness by exercising benevolent thoughts and deeds, safe in the knowledge that God had enabled their capacity to commit sociable acts.[16]

There is also danger in lumping Hutcheson together with a later generation of Scottish philosophers, particularly Thomas Reid, as well as overlooking differences within that more recent cohort. To do so would incorporate assumptions from Witherspoon and other Presbyterian evangelicals who bundled Moderates and common sense theorists such as Reid alongside Hutcheson as little more than secular dilettantes. Yet Hutcheson's career largely avoided the controversy over ecclesiastical patronage and preceded the fissure that opened up between different factions of Presbyterian churchmen during the 1750s. Furthermore, it was only by the 1760s that James Beattie and Reid integrated the facility of reason more fully into Scottish moral philosophy, focusing on the role of rational moral judgment at the top of a perceptual pyramid. Whether or not they were directly indebted to Hutcheson, moreover, it is not clear whether all later Scottish moral sense philosophers can accurately be allied with the Moderate section of the Kirk. Despite incorporating moral sense reasoning in their writings from the 1760s, figures such as Beattie and James Oswald demonstrated personal distaste for the term "Moderate" — particularly its institutional association with the so-called liberal wing of the Church of Scotland.[17]

16. Historians tend to "lump," "split," or "synthesize" the ideas of loosely related thinkers under their examination. See J. H. Hexter, *On Historians: Reappraisals of Some of the Makers of Modern History* (Cambridge, Mass., 1979), 241–245. On the teleological caricature of Moderate moral philosophy by evangelicals, see Allan, "Protestantism," in Claydon and McBride, eds., *Protestantism and National Identity,* 188–189. On Hutchesonian and Moderate use of stoic philosophy, see Sher, *Church and University,* 176–179; Christian Maurer, "Hutcheson's Relation to Stoicism in the Light of His Moral Psychology," *Journal of Scottish Philosophy,* VIII (2010), 33–49.

17. On the development of Hutcheson's moral philosophy irrespective of the subsequent patronage controversy, see Harris, "Answering Bayle's Question," in Garber and Nadler, eds., *Oxford Studies in Early Modern Philosophy,* I, 235. According to Knud Haakonssen, even Thomas Reid's later "first principles" of "Common Sense philosophy" were partially derived from a Hutchesonian focus on instinctive sensory perception. A combination of innate sensory

Yet, notwithstanding what we now know about the differences between and the ambiguities within the writings of various Scottish moral philosophers during the eighteenth century, it still remains appropriate to highlight certain important similarities in their epistemological ideas over a relatively long historical period. Hutchesonian moral philosophy did offer later Moderate clergymen a more human-centered account of morality than evangelical ministers would have liked. It claimed that moral discernment was not necessarily contingent on the prior knowledge of biblically revealed laws, nor the state that followed the reception of divine grace after personal conversion. Moreover, the faculty psychology of Reid's common sense philosophy continued to rely on the notion of a primary sensory response, as first outlined by Hutcheson. The faculty of reason ordered and discerned pre-rational moral perceptions, which sat at the foundation of the pyramid. Thus, a degree of continuity was evident between Reid's first principles of common sensory perception and those suggested by Moderate writers following Hutcheson. Hutcheson's ethical world consisted of qualities that were perceived innately by the moral sense and which then led to predictable modes of discernment. From the 1760s, Reid claimed that individual ethical identity encompassed relations between people that were judged ethically by each party in light of the first sensory principles that Hutcheson had earlier elucidated. His argument from design was grounded in the necessary first principle "that [God's] design and intelligence in the cause, may, with certainty, be inferred from marks or signs of it in the effect." The second faculty in Reid's deductive philosophy defined the mind's rational moral judgment of primary sensory perceptions.[18]

---

perception, followed by considered rational judgment, allowed individuals to analyze the world outside the mind as evidence of a divine maker. Beattie, a poet and essayist, became professor of moral philosophy at Aberdeen University in 1760. Oswald was a Presbyterian clergyman who published *An Appeal to Common Sense in Behalf of Religion* (Edinburgh, 1766-1772). See Haakonssen, *Natural Law and Moral Philosophy: From Grotius to the Scottish Enlightenment* (Cambridge, 1996), 188. On Oswald and Beattie's problem with the "liberal" wing of the Church of Scotland, see Richard B. Sher and M. A. Stewart, "Oswald, James (1703-1793)," and Roger J. Robinson, "Beattie, James (1735-1803)," both in *DNB*.

18. William Hamilton, ed., *The Works of Thomas Reid . . .* , 7th ed. (Edinburgh, 1872), I, 457, 460. Reid's common sense reasoning ostensibly differed from Hutcheson when it portrayed the moral sense as a matter of judgment, rather than a pre-rational sensory response. But, as Haakonssen has suggested, this difference "may be more limited than Reid thought and rather less dramatic than most scholars would have it. . . . For Reid, as for so many of similar moral and theological outlook, such as the 'Moderate Literati' and the moderate clergy in general, it was of the utmost importance to establish the reality of free human agency." See Haakonssen, *Natural*

To be sure, Reid was wary of admitting that a fundamental part of his own system relied on Hutcheson's account of sensory reasoning. He knew that the philosopher David Hume had extrapolated skeptical conclusions from sensory terminology in order to undermine Hutcheson's moral epistemology. Thus, Reid felt precluded from acknowledging his debt to Hutcheson, lest he suffer the same treatment from skeptics. But, although his Aberdeen and Glasgow education (as well as his initial interest in mathematics rather than moral philosophy) distanced him from Edinburgh ministers and thinkers, his views on religion and the role of the Kirk were largely consistent with those of the Moderate party.[19]

Through the 1760s, as Moderate thinkers such as Carlyle, Adam Ferguson, and Robertson grafted common sensory reasoning onto their Hutchesonian philosophical framework, they avoided the controversial implications of their focus on innate human morality by conceiving of theological development as a natural historical phenomenon. By its very nature, in their eyes, this advancement was Protestant, naturally reforming through time. It was not difficult for Moderate Kirk members to suggest that reforms within their church—including their changing philosophical emphasis—were in the spirit of God's Word. Thus, they came to subscribe to a "historical soci-

---

Law and Moral Philosophy, 188, 197. Peter Kivy claims that "the path that Hutcheson's sense of beauty had to travel in Britain in the waning years of the eighteenth century lay in two directions: [one being] an attempt at epistemological reconciliation with rationalism in the work of Thomas Reid." As Ronald E. Beanblossom has shown, "Reid is willing to offer proof for the belief in finite intelligent beings [using the notion of common sense], because he needs to *prove* the existence of God—an intelligent being; for that proof he needs the necessary first principle, which permits the inference of intelligence in the cause on the basis of signs of intelligence in the effect. Likewise, Reid wants to infer from these signs of intelligence that God has the power or moral liberty to create those things that serve as signs of his intelligence." See Kivy, *The Seventh Sense: Francis Hutcheson and Eighteenth-Century British Aesthetics* (New York, 2003), 158; Beanblossom, "Introduction," in Beanblossom and Keith Lehrer, eds., *Thomas Reid's Inquiry and Essays* (Indianapolis, Ind., 1983), xxxvi.

19. On Reid's wariness of being linked to Hume, thereby eschewing his debt to Hutcheson, see Alexander Broadie, "Reid in Context," in Terence Cuneo and René van Woudenberg, eds., *The Cambridge Companion to Thomas Reid* (Cambridge, 2004), 31. Haakonssen suggests: "Reid was precluded from an adequate appreciation of the relationship between his own Common Sense theory and the classical formulation of the Moral Sense theory by his reading of Hume." See Haakonssen, ed., *Thomas Reid on Practical Ethics Lectures and Papers on Natural Religion, Self-Government, Natural Jurisprudence, and the Law of Nations* (Edinburgh, 2007), li. According to Roy Sorensen, "Reid's common sense looks like an impression left by Hume; concave where Hume is convex, convex where Hume is concave." See Sorensen, *A Brief History of the Paradox: Philosophy and the Labyrinths of the Mind* (New York, 2005), 369.

ology" of religion that did not deny the important role of the Westminster Confession of Faith. Rather, they believed that Britain's advanced cultural context allowed the Confession to be reconceived in light of naturally evolved religious sensibilities. Those sensibilities, they claimed, had developed in tandem with social and political advancements in mainland Britain. In their view, moral sensibility could only flourish in advanced unions that maintained the required balance between agriculture and commerce, between learning and religion, and between elite politics and parochial organization.[20]

According to the conception of history held by many Moderates, including those who became influenced by common sense philosophy, all man-made religious statements—whether the doctrines of John Calvin or the drafters of the Westminster Confession of Faith in the 1640s—were inevitably contingent on their time and context. Moderates were even prone to suggest that historical distance from the Scottish Reformation made the eighteenth-century Kirk comparatively more orthodox and less tainted by Catholicism. Despite all the good that John Knox had done for the reformed cause in the sixteenth century, his actions were still closer in time to a Scottish church that was *not* reformed. Evangelical attempts to return to the Knoxian principles of revival and regeneration were thus circumvented by the Moderate definition of progress. Most Moderate churchmen felt comfortably reformed in their claim that an instinctive moral sense preceded any first reading of scripture but could still be used to support the essential reasonableness of biblical assertions. Some even suggested that the global mission of evangelicalism risked diminishing the special national context in which Scottish churchmen had developed their advanced sensibility.[21]

20. Defining the "historical sociology" of Moderate thinking, Kidd has pointed out that a "faultline runs through the historiography of Moderatism, dividing those historians who believe the Moderates remained committed Calvinists from those who endorse the view of contemporary critics within the Kirk that the Moderates favoured Arminianism, or worse. . . . Although the Moderates continued to uphold subscription to the Westminster Confession of Faith, their writings indicate that an historical sensitivity to theological change replaced what they perceived to be an inevitably time-bound commitment to dogma." See Kidd, "Subscription, the Scottish Enlightenment, and the Moderate Interpretation of History," *Journal of Ecclesiastical History*, LV (2004), 502 (quotation), 503–512. On the notion of historical theological development, see also Alexander Murdoch, *Scotland and America, c. 1600–c. 1800* (Basingstoke, U.K., 2010), 141–152; Haakonssen, *Natural Law and Moral Philosophy*, 155–156; Christopher J. Berry, *Social Theory of the Scottish Enlightenment* (Edinburgh, 1997), 93–99, 109, 151, 184.

21. Kidd, "Subscription, the Scottish Enlightenment," *Journal of Ecclesiastical History*, LV (2004), 502–519. According to Stewart J. Brown, "while Moderates did not directly challenge the Calvinism of the Westminster Confession of Faith, they did tend to ignore the doctrine of

Subscribing to a notion of developmental progress, therefore, Carlyle saw justice in the failure of evangelicals to achieve institutional influence in the Kirk. He believed that pure scholarly intellect was not enough to justify leadership. Sociability, geniality, and elegant speech were also necessary to reflect and harness the common sensibility of students and laymen. In his view, the most competent religious leaders rewarded their congregations with aesthetically pleasing discourse. Their attention to form and style was the most appropriate means to instill religious morality, rather than merely an example of shallow performance. In a later section of his memoirs, Carlyle recalled having attended "Hutcheson's class," where he explained "moral virtues" with "great satisfaction and improvement." Despite having questioned Hutcheson's focus on innate moral sensibility earlier in his narrative, he pointed out that it was thanks to Hutcheson, "Professor of Moral Philosophy, that a better taste and greater liberality of sentiment were introduced among the clergy in the western provinces of Scotland." In the decades following Hutcheson's death, Carlyle joined Scots such as Lord Kames, Adam Ferguson, John Millar, William Robertson, and William Smellie in developing an aesthetic definition of moral sensibility. They suggested that form and style were important components in moral suasion because the laity was primed for a sensory response to well-composed sermons. Both aesthetic form and moral content could be sensed as beautiful.[22]

Witherspoon, conversely, continued to claim that the legacy of the Scottish Reformation was neglected by Moderates. In his "Speech in the Synod of Glasgow," which was written after he was accused of being the author of *Ecclesiastical Characteristics,* he wrote: "Where then is the Church of Scotland's charter of security that none shall ever arise in her deserving such reprimand? . . . And must the man be condemned without hearing and without mercy who is but suspected of hinting that there may be such in her sister

---

predestination and emphasize . . . the harmonies of nature and the capacity of human reason." See Brown, "Religion in Scotland," in H. T. Dickinson, ed., *A Companion to Eighteenth-Century Britain* (Malden, Mass., 2002), 267. On the global mission of evangelicalism as a threat to Moderate parochial culture, see Sher, *Church and University,* 52–54.

22. Carlyle, *Autobiography,* vii, viii, 68–72. Carlyle also enjoyed "Travelling adventures" with "[later Moderates] John Home and Robertson the historian" and contributed to "London society" alongside "Smollett and John Blair." In London he enjoyed "Suppers at the Golden Ball" alongside "theatres and theatrical celebrities" among the city's "Literary society." On Moderate theology and the aesthetic context in which Carlyle developed his understanding of correct discourse, see James Moore, "Hutcheson's Theodicy: The Argument and the Contexts of *A System of Moral Philosophy,*" in Paul Wood, ed., *The Scottish Enlightenment: Essays in Reinterpretation* (Rochester, N.Y., 2000), 239–266.

church?" Witherspoon blamed Moderates for allowing the Scottish Church to regress to its hierarchical past, thanks to patronage and elite definitions of style, taste, and sensibility.[23]

"The Farce after the Play"

Alexander Carlyle had in mind one particular instance when he contrasted Witherspoon's evangelical turn with the natural development of Scottish piety. In his memoirs, he recalled the "zeal and violence" that Witherspoon and other evangelical clergymen had once displayed in their public attack on a play written by John Home. During the late 1750s, Witherspoon had publicly chastised Home for his poetry and theatrical productions, highlighting an "imperfection of the human mind" that his art eschewed. Home's *Tragedy of Douglas,* which was first performed in Edinburgh on December 14, 1756, aroused particular controversy. Home had attended the University of Edinburgh alongside Witherspoon and Carlyle. Since then, he had become a close associate of Carlyle and other Moderate churchmen as well as the skeptical philosopher David Hume. The protagonist of the play was Young Norval, and, as was common in early romantic plays, many characters were drawn into its events, losing their lives. According to most positive reviews, the play aroused the moral sensibility of all who saw it and who surely sympathized with Young Norval.[24]

Home had written the *Tragedy of Douglas* only to have it snubbed by London producers, who claimed that theatrical productions were too tightly controlled by Whig politicians to support their performance. In protest, Scottish literary luminaries, such as Lord Kames, Hugh Blair, Adam Ferguson, and Alexander Carlyle, sponsored a performance in Edinburgh, prompting a fierce evangelical reaction. Carlyle perceived Witherspoon's "grave and soberminded" response to theater as a further example of his departure from natural developments in Scottish literary and moral sensibility.[25]

Witherspoon, in his *Serious Inquiry into the Nature and Effects of the Stage,* which he wrote and published in 1757, reminded his former prison mate John Home that "all men are by nature under the power of sin." But he

---

23. Witherspoon, "Synod of Glasgow," in [Green, ed.], *Works of Witherspoon,* IV, 250.

24. Carlyle, *Autobiography,* 312–313; Witherspoon, *Serious Inquiry,* in [Green, ed.], *Works of Witherspoon,* III, 157n.

25. Carlyle, *Autobiography,* 312–313. For opposition to Home's plays and the various legal acts against theater, see Matthew J. Kinservik, *Disciplining Satire: The Censorship of Satiric Comedy on the Eighteenth-Century London Stage* (London, 2002), 95–134.

did not oppose theater because of its light frivolity, as those who painted him as a colorless evangelical liked to suggest. In fact, Witherspoon claimed that light diversions allowed the mind to rest and refresh before its more serious emotional arousal in the religious context. Rather, Witherspoon's primary objection to theatrical performance related to the claim that its excitement of the passions could evoke a common moral response, irrespective of the state of regeneration in any audience. Theater became problematic when it was justified in moral ways, as *more* than just a recreational diversion. Here it has been suggested that Witherspoon adopted Augustinian reasoning in questioning the play. In his *Confessions*, Augustine had noted the problematic ethical association between pleasure and pain in depictions of tragedy. Though humans were saddened by the plight of tragic protagonists, Augustine stated that they were often also gratified to think that they shared their moral displeasure with other like-minded men. Yet true compassion, Augustine argued, demanded that individuals acknowledge their mutual *inability* to sympathize with one another without external grace. Compassion, like humility, reminds individuals of their duty to God. Similarly, Witherspoon's *Serious Inquiry* argued that innate artistic and intellectual ability remain separate from the human ethical faculty: "Natural talents in the human mind" are "quite distinct from moral dispositions." The "imagination of thoughts of man" masquerade as moral sympathy but are in fact governed by the continued "evil from his youth." Supporters of *The Tragedy of Douglas* supposed that its players were able to arouse the inner moral compass of those who watched them. They failed to restrict the role of theater to mere light entertainment and deployed a language of passion and emotionalism that ought to have been reserved for purely religious contexts.[26]

A desire to display and arouse passions outside the religious sphere, Witherspoon suggested, would only blunt one's necessary moral power: "The seeing of sin frequently committed, must gradually abate that horror which we ought to have of it upon our minds, and which serves to keep us from yielding to its solicitations. . . . It will be difficult to assign any other reason, why wickedness is always carried to a far greater height in large and populous cities, than in the country." The repetition and display of simulated tragedy, according to Witherspoon, made sin a less horrifying prospect. In

26. Witherspoon, *Serious Inquiry*, in [Green, ed.,] *Works of Witherspoon*, III, 156–157. Witherspoon delivered sermons with variations on the title "Mankind under Sin"; for example, see Witherspoon, "All Mankind by Nature under Sin," ibid., I, 267–285. On the link between the Augustinian discussion of pleasure and pain and Witherspoons's theatrical examples, see Jennifer A. Herdt, *Religion and Faction in Hume's Moral Philosophy* (Cambridge, 1997), 89–90.

his estimation, it was no wonder that Moderate theatergoers enjoyed such a sunny vision of moral capability. They were so inured to the display of sin that its central role in human cognition became less terrifying and arresting.[27]

Witherspoon's *Serious Inquiry* broadened its discussion to suggest that seemingly parallel advancements in intellectual and moral knowledge often masked a cyclical return to degeneracy: "With respect to learning, men rise from ignorance to application; from application to knowledge; this ripens into taste and judgment; then, from a desire of distinguishing themselves, they superadd affected ornaments, become more fanciful than solid; their taste corrupts with their manners, and they fall back into the gulph of ignorance." According to Carlyle and Robertson, the moral and aesthetic power of theater derived from the context in which it flourished. Literary Edinburgh, in their perception, encouraged the expression of moral sensibility because of its civic advancement in Britain. An appreciation for theater accompanied the positive evolution of human moral sensibility among educated Scots. In Witherspoon's opinion, conversely, advanced societies would inevitably return to ignorance.[28]

Adam Ferguson, another of Carlyle's and Witherspoon's Edinburgh classmates, also wrote a pamphlet in response to the *Douglas* controversy. Defending "the morality of stage-plays," he lauded theater as a means to display and define the common moral sensibility that all men enjoyed. The universal reaction of theatergoers, Ferguson argued, could only validate the Christian doctrines of humility, neighborliness, and compassion. To underline his argument, he inverted the evangelical claim to religious orthodoxy by alluding to the history of the European Reformation. A "great part of the superstition of the Church of *Rome*," Ferguson argued, had been "derived from . . . inventions" that Protestants rightly rejected. The "Oral Traditions" of the Catholic Church apparently included stern opposition to "Stage-Plays," for "it is well known, that Plays were acted at the Reformation, which very much helped on that work, by exposing the vices and absurdities of the Popish Clergy." Some Presbyterians, according to Ferguson, had inherited this unfortunate oppositional tradition, which was not necessarily aligned with the development of Protestant orthodoxy. According to Ferguson and Carlyle, theatergoing in Edinburgh demonstrated the cultural advancement of Scotland since the Act of Union. The sociability that it engendered among Presbyterians was a natural reflection of their religious evolution and reformation.[29]

27. Witherspoon, *Serious Inquiry,* in [Green, ed.], *Works of Witherspoon,* III, 164.
28. Ibid., 187.
29. Adam Ferguson, *The Morality of Stage-Plays Seriously Considered* (Edinburgh, 1757),

The Douglas controversy demonstrated how far Scottish churchmen had come to differ in their perception of the relationship between moral sensibility and civic cohesion. It highlighted a tension between particularism and universalism. Moderates lauded the specific Scottish context in which moral sensibility could be harnessed. Popular party members recalled the universality of sin, which transcended borders and quashed any hope of an innate ethical stance. The furor highlighted the binary division that had developed between evangelical and Moderate theology during the previous decade. Just as Witherspoon could have been accused of crudeness in his depiction of Moderate irreligion, Carlyle and his allies failed to acknowledge the scholarly depth and *longue durée* of Scottish evangelicalism. Witherspoon and his Popular party colleagues were all too easily dismissed as dour Puritans who were unable to appreciate the beauty of theatrical production. The Moderate critique failed to acknowledge the complexity in their Augustinian discussion of the relationship between passions and performance. As the public debate over the *Douglas* affair waned, distinctions between Moderates and evangelicals did not diminish. Increasingly, they were displayed when Presbyterian ministers discussed the role of America in the British Empire, widening further the emerging fissure in the Kirk. Witherspoon would even begin to wonder whether the American colonies, rather than mainland Britain, might provide a more favorable arena for the expression of the Westminster Confession of Faith.[30]

"The Disputed Limits of Our Territories in America"

Having recalled Witherspoon's "zeal" in response to Scottish theater, Alexander Carlyle's memoirs turned once more to the American crisis. In an aside, Carlyle noted: "It was discovered early in this period [the late 1790s] that the revolt and final disjunction of our American colonies [in the 1770s] was no loss to Great Britain." Carlyle had privileged Scotland's cultural development in mainland Britain over other outlying provinces, including the Ameri-

---

12–15 (quotations on 13, 14). See also Ernest Campbell Mossner, *The Life of David Hume* (New York, 1954), 368. On the friendship between Carlyle and Ferguson, see Carlyle, *Autobiography*, 541. On Ferguson's later opposition to the patriot cause, see Yasuo Amoh, "Ferguson's Views on the American and French Revolutions," in Eugene Heath and Vincenzo Merolle, eds., *Adam Ferguson: History, Progress, and Human Nature* (London, 2007), 73–87.

30. According to Jennifer A. Herdt, "What is striking about attitudes towards theatre in Scotland at this time is that radically divergent views coexisted with utter complacency in each camp about the soundness of their own views"; see Herdt, *Religion and Faction*, 88.

FIGURE 6. *Meeting of the General Assembly of the Kirk of Scotland in the Old Kirk,*
St. Giles's Cathedral. Engraved by R. Scott, after a drawing by David Allan. 1787.
Private Collection. The Bridgeman Art Library

can colonies. William Robertson, the chief moderator of the General Assembly of the Kirk from 1763 and a friend of Carlyle, similarly suggested that the American colonies had failed to advance to the fourth stage of human development—polite commercialism and the harnessing of innate sociability. The history of human progress had not run its true course in the colonies, where British liberties had led both to extravagant and uncouth manners and to religious fervor. They had failed to match mainland Britain in the advancement of their ethical sensibility through the eighteenth century and thus continued to require metropolitan British support. After the imperial crisis, therefore, Carlyle suggested that an independent America was "no loss" because it had only ever derived its prosperity and cultural development through its association with metropolitan Britain.[31]

31. Carlyle, *Autobiography*, 532. On Robertson's Moderate disparagement of the notion of American developmental progress at this point in history, see Jeffrey R. Smitten, "Moderatism and History: William Robertson's Unfinished History of British America," in Richard B. Sher

Popular party opponents of Carlyle and Robertson had always been wary of favoring the moral development of Anglo-Scottish culture in relation to the American colonies. From the late 1740s to the 1760s, they preferred to focus on America as an equal arena for the expansion of Protestant revivalism. Whether they lived in Edinburgh or Philadelphia, Glasgow or Trenton, all subjects of the British Empire were required to acknowledge their need for personal salvation. More particularly, Popular party ministers suggested that it was incumbent on the Kirk to provide ministries and missions to support the growing number of Scottish migrants to North America—an expanding population that risked losing touch with the revivalist tenets of the Westminster Confession of Faith. Immediately after its formation during the late 1740s, therefore, the Popular party began to promote the importance of international missionary activity, which it distinguished from the perceived parochialism of Moderate churchmanship.[32]

Although evangelicalism did not formally emerge until the mid-eighteenth century, a number of early modern Presbyterians had been distinctly concerned with extraterritorial pietism since at least the 1660s. As we have seen, Samuel Rutherford and his Scottish colleagues supported new forms of association between England and Scotland during the formation of the Solemn League and Covenant and the Westminster Confession of Faith. It is less well known that a key motivation for their Anglo-Scottish alliance lay in its potential to enhance the protection of other Protestant communities through diplomacy or even external military intervention. Indeed, Rutherford had been invited to London by Puritan divines in part because his 1644 *Peaceable Plea for the Government of the Church of Scotland* had demonstrated his familiarity with the doctrines and culture of New England Congregationalism. That the Westminster divines incorporated a global outlook highlights a degree of continuity between their seventeenth-century activities and the international evangelical networks that grew during the 1740s.[33]

---

and Smitten, eds., *Scotland and America in the Age of the Enlightenment* (Princeton, N.J., 1990), 164–169; Murdoch, *Scotland and America,* 141–152.

32. On the growth of Scottish missionary activity, see Frederick V. Mills, Sr., "The Society in Scotland for Propagating Christian Knowledge in British North America, 1730–1775," *Church History,* LXIII (1994), 15–30.

33. That the institutional growth and the missionary platform of the Popular party coincided during the late 1740s supports D. W. Bebbington's analysis of the emergence of evangelicalism in the British Atlantic world. See Bebbington, *Evangelicalism in Modern Britain: A History from the 1730s to the 1980s* (London, 1989), 43, 51. Mark A. Noll supports Bebbington's general claim while also showing that pockets of "aggressive heart religion" and "experiential Calvinism" could be found during the seventeenth century, particularly in Scottish, Continental, and

In an important sermon on the relationship between Scottish missionary activity and British military engagements in Europe and North America,
Witherspoon alluded once again to the movement of Presbyterian piety across
the Atlantic during the seventeenth century. In an address delivered in Edinburgh on January 2, 1758, before the Scottish Society for the Promotion of
Christian Knowledge, he offered a complaint against the Moderate character
of Anglo-Scottish union through reference to America. Responding to recent
British setbacks against France in the Seven Years' War, he began by describing the colonies as a refuge for "pious forefathers" fleeing from ecclesiastical
tyranny. Since Witherspoon was addressing a separate Scottish offshoot of
the English Society for the Promotion of Christian Knowledge, rather than
alluding to the English Puritan cousins of Scottish Presbyterianism it is most
likely that he referred to the emigration of Scots into New England, New
York, and New Jersey during the second half of the seventeenth century.[34]

Referring once more to Scotland's pre-Union religious history, Witherspoon stated: "We have been a nation early and long favored with the light of
divine truth, and are therefore bound to communicate it to others." Witherspoon spoke in the present perfect tense ("We have been") to outline the
special nature and context of Scotland's early modern reformation. But he
changed to the present imperative ("and are therefore bound to") when he
highlighted the necessary role of Scottish evangelicalism in the new British

---

New England centers of Reformed Christianity. See Noll, *The Rise of Evangelicalism: The Age
of Edwards, Whitefield, and the Wesleys* (Downers Grove, Ill., 2003), 56, 59. On the perceived
relationship between Anglo-Scottish alliances and "global reordering" before the eighteenth
century, and early Scottish piety and evangelicalism, see Allan I. Macinnes, "Preface," in Steve
Murdoch, ed., *Scotland and the Thirty Years' War, 1618–1648* (Leiden, 2001), x; Roger A. Mason,
"The Scottish Reformation and the Origins of Anglo-British Imperialism," in Mason, ed., *Scots
and Britons: Scottish Political Thought and the Union of 1603* (Cambridge, 1994), 161–186. On
Scottish-English alliances to intervene on behalf of other international Protestants during the
1640s, see John R. Young, "The Scottish Parliament and European Diplomacy, 1641–1647: The
Palatine, the Dutch Republic, and Sweden," in Murdoch, ed., *Scotland and the Thirty Years'
War*, 19, 77–106. On Rutherford's knowledge of New England, see Samuel Rutherford, *The Due
Right of Presbyteries; or, A Peaceable Plea for the Government of the Church of Scotland . . .* (Lon-
don, 1644), 256–323; John Coffey, *Politics, Religion, and the British Revolutions: The Mind of
Samuel Rutherford* (Cambridge, 1997), 52. For Rutherford and other Scots, according to Coffey,
New England Congregationalism "seemed like the most obvious alternative to the Scottish Presbyterian model available to the English" (52). On the links between eighteenth-century evangelicalism and seventeenth-century pietism, see W. R. Ward, *Early Evangelicalism: A Global Intellectual History, 1670–1789* (Cambridge, 2006).

34. Witherspoon, *The Absolute Necessity of Salvation through Christ*, in [Green, ed.], *Works
of Witherspoon*, II, 364.

union. Scotland had been "favored" in its understanding of divinity. But, during the eighteenth century, the "light of divine truth" could be communicated to others outside Scotland, rather than necessarily restricted to any notion of a public covenant.[35]

The imperative of evangelism provided a contrast with the disappointment that Witherspoon outlined as he continued his sermon. He pointed out that the Kirk's independent role in promoting piety had been squandered since the 1707 Act of Union. Discussing the Scottish Society for the Promotion of Christian Knowledge, Witherspoon continued: "There is another part of their design, to spread the knowledge of Christ, the only Saviour of sinners, among the unenlightened Heathen nations. . . . But, except the very restricted efforts of the society, little or nothing has ever been attempted by the British nation." The evangelization of "Indians" had been neglected thanks to the parochial turn in Anglo-Scottish unionism: "Such a particular interpretation of the language of Providence may be thought bold; but there are many circumstances which, in a manner, constrain us to confess its propriety. . . . That distant country [America] was a refuge to many of our pious forefathers, when flying from the rage of ecclesiastic tyranny; and the territory either taken from, or ceded to us by these people [Native Americans], has been the great source of wealth and power to this nation." Witherspoon lamented that further missionary activities had been avoided by "the British nation" since the Act of Union despite all the "wealth and power" that settlers and indigenous Americans had ceded to the Empire.[36]

Witherspoon segued more specifically into a longer discussion of Britain's actions in America in the years after 1707:

> And is not God, in his righteous Providence towards us at present, manifestly and severely punishing us for this neglect? Are we not engaged in war with a potent and formidable neighbor, in which the supreme Disposer of all events hath visibly written disappointment on every one of our attempts? Did not this war take its rise from the dis-

35. Ibid.

36. Ibid., 363–364. On the movement of Scottish missionary organizations to the American frontier during the first half of the eighteenth century, see also Richard I. Shelling, "Benjamin Franklin and the Dr. Bray Associates," *Pennsylvania Magazine of History and Biography,* LXIII (1939), 282–293; Henry R. Sefton, "The Scotch Society in the American Colonies in the Eighteenth Century," *Records of the Scottish Church History Society,* XVII (1972), 169–184; Donald E. Meek, "Scottish Highlanders, North American Indians, and the SSPCK: Some Cultural Perspectives," ibid., XXIII (1989), 378–396; Mills, "The Society in Scotland for Propagating Christian Knowledge in British North America, 1730–1775," *Church History,* LXIII (1994), 15–30.

puted limits of our territories in America? And are not our colonies in
that part of the world exposed to the most cruel and merciless depre-
dations? . . . Who then are the instruments of this cruelty? Must we not
answer, Those very Indians, a great part of whose territory we possess,
and whom, with a contempt equally impolitic and unchristian, we suffer to continue in ignorance of the only living and true God, and Jesus
Christ whom he hath sent?

"We" referred to Britain. America had once been an asylum for Scottish Presbyterians. It was now a battlefield within what ought to have been a pacific
part of a new imperial union. Patronage and interests had prevented the Kirk
from assuming its independent role in Britain and the expanding British Empire. Its ability to encourage revivalism had been circumvented, with "cruel
and merciless" results. The American colonies had become the focus of
worldly interests on the British mainland, rather than an arena for the expansion of evangelical piety, especially among Indians. As Witherspoon pointed
out in his 1758 *Prayer for National Prosperity and for the Revival of Religion
Inseparably Connected,* delivered in response to Britain's initial difficulties in
its war with France: "They [the American colonies] are the chief theatre of
war, because, indeed, they are the subject of the contest. . . . If it please God
to suffer our enemies and to continue their progress, it is hard to say how
far the desolation may extend, or how universal it may prove." The failure to
support missionary activities in North America made local indigenous populations more likely to ally with the French enemies of the British Empire.[37]

In the same sermon on "National Prosperity," Witherspoon lamented that
Britain was no longer "the arbitress of the fate" of European nations in their
activities on either side of the Atlantic. He linked recent evidence of the declining power of the British armed forces to domestic irreligion and asked
rhetorically: "How numerous and expensive, but how useless and inactive,
have been our fleets and armies?" Private and worldly interests either made
British soldiers "useless" or prevented their deployment altogether (they

37. Witherspoon, *The Absolute Necessity of Salvation through Christ,* in [Green, ed.], *Works
of Witherspoon,* II, 363–364; John Witherspoon, *Prayer for National Prosperity and for the Revival of Religion Inseparably Connected,* ibid., 471. The movement of covenanting Presbyterians
to America followed persecution by both Cromwellian and royalist forces. See Ned C. Landsman, *Scotland and Its First American Colony, 1683–1765* (Princeton, N.J., 1985), chap. 2; Clare
Jackson, *Restoration Scotland, 1660–1690: Royalist Politics, Religion, and Ideas* (Woodbridge,
U.K., 2003), 154–155; Francis J. Bremer, "The Puritan Experiment in New England, 1630–1660,"
in John Coffey and Paul C. H. Lim, eds., *The Cambridge Companion to Puritanism* (Cambridge,
2008), 127–142, esp. 137.

were "inactive"). Though discussing North American matters, Witherspoon made direct reference to John Home, his former classmate, fellow prisoner, and author of the *Tragedy of Douglas*. That "infidelity" in mainland Britain spread "its poison" in the Empire was demonstrated by "a new thing on the earth" in Scotland's civil and religious culture: "a minister of Christ leaving the pulpit for the stage." Home and other Moderates had departed from their religious duty. Their attempt to define the common sociability and mutual benevolence of their educated audience placed Presbyterian "Religion" in "its oppressed state at present" and required prayer, "revival," "proper duty, and earnestly pleading for the revelation of the arm of the Lord."[38]

By the 1760s, the "revival" that Witherspoon had recommended in 1758 had failed to materialize. In his *Serious Apology for the Ecclesiastical Characteristics,* written in 1763, Witherspoon examined the degradation of the Scottish Church, where there now seemed to be "far less strictness and tenderness of conversation, less of the appearance of piety and devotion, in persons of the spiritual function, than formerly; and less severity, in the exercise of discipline, upon those who offend." Such diminished piety and institutional decay, Witherspoon noted, "is what the natural course of things teaches us to expect . . . what our Saviour himself hath forewarned us of. . . . The present age is a moving example of this, both with respect to the clergy and laity." Witherspoon did not deny that "the degeneracy of their own times has been the constant and uniform complaint of religious and moral writers in every age, and that they may be liable to some deception in this particular: but at the same time, the records of history put it beyond all question, that there have been many instances, among all nations, of local and temporary reformation, of local and occasional depravation." The capacity for moral regeneration, according to Witherspoon, "often changes its residence, and leaves one nation, to settle in another."

> Nay, it seems very reasonable to believe, that as human things are never at a stand, a church and nation, in a quiet and peaceable state, is always growing insensibly worse, till it be either so corrupt as to deserve and procure exterminating judgements, or . . . by some great shock or revolution, is brought back to simplicity and purity, and reduced, as it were, to its first principles.

Having alluded to his disappointment in the nature of Anglo-Scottish unionism, Witherspoon suggested that over time the moral cause of religious refor-

38. Witherspoon, *Prayer for National Prosperity,* in [Green, ed.], *Works of Witherspoon,* II, 471, 476–477.

mation was not necessarily fixed in one land, even if revolutions might bring matters back to first reformed principles.[39]

It is pertinent to note the distinction that Witherspoon drew between Scotland's religious heritage and the disappointment of evangelicalism at midcentury. A religious and political association between Edinburgh and London had heralded the Westminster Confession of Faith during the 1640s. Yet, according to Witherspoon, their formal political union after 1707 had allowed influential Scots to promote a corrupt vision of innate moral sensibility, secured by their connection to Westminster politicians. Their supposed aversion to the expansion of Presbyterian revivalism led to his disappointment in mainland British culture and brought North America more closely into his horizon. Witherspoon's allusion to the outward movement of piety from Scotland, particularly to America, would not be his last.

39. Witherspoon, *A Serious Apology for the Ecclesiastical Characteristics,* in [Green, ed.], *Works of Witherspoon,* III, 296-297.

{ PART II }

Higher Education

{ CHAPTER 3 }

"THE BULWARK OF THE RELIGION

AND LIBERTY OF AMERICA"

Presbyterian Revivalism and American Higher Education

before Witherspoon

In 1767, Benjamin Rush took particular notice of John Witherspoon's tentative references to the geographically shifting nature of reformation and human virtue. A graduate of the College of New Jersey, founded by prominent colonial Presbyterians in 1746 as an institution of higher education, Rush would go on to sign America's Declaration of Independence alongside Witherspoon before becoming a political representative and a medical theorist. In advance of his rise to prominence, while studying medicine at the University of Edinburgh, he sent a letter to the Scottish clergyman. Though marked from Edinburgh, it carried a message from America: "You can have no prospects of rising into a higher sphere of usefulness in the Church of Scotland, as far as I can understand from the present state of your ecclesiastical affairs. The present ruling faction are opposed to men of your character, and (if I am rightly informed) have marked you out as an object of their resentment for those very things which have made you so popular in America and, I may say, have procured your election to the College."[1]

Rush alluded to Witherspoon's struggle with the Moderate Kirk in his attempt to entice the Scotsman to the College of New Jersey. The institution's trustees were searching for a new president after the death of Samuel Finley (1715-1766), an evangelical Presbyterian. In 1768, Rush gushed that the people of Princeton village yearned to "exult and triumph in the prospect of seeing their darling seminary the bulwark of the religion and liberty of America." The college was indeed situated at an ecumenical junction, albeit between various dissenting Protestants rather than other separate creeds. Its

---

1. Benjamin Rush to John Witherspoon, Apr. 23, 1767, in L. H. Butterfield, ed., *Letters of Benjamin Rush,* 2 vols. (Princeton, N.J., 1951), I, 37. On Rush's career, see Alyn Brodsky, *Benjamin Rush: Patriot and Physician* (New York, 2004).

position in the Middle Colonies was conducive to the outward-looking Protestant evangelical vision that had united revivalist Presbyterians on both sides of the Atlantic, as well as evangelical Congregationalists such as Jonathan Edwards, during previous decades. Although the college lacked funds, it generated a cross-colonial appeal to revivalist Protestant communities.[2]

Rush drew a direct distinction between evangelicalism and Scottish Moderate culture in his claim that New Jersey was more conducive to Witherspoon's "Prospects" as a minister during the late 1760s. Ironically, his attractive proposition prefigured the contrast that Alexander Carlyle would draw in his memoirs between the religious and educational cultures of Scotland and America, albeit with more positive connotations. Rush's reference to America's comparative evangelical freedom is partially corroborated by the historiography of Presbyterian revivalism in the colonies. Three decades before Witherspoon's arrival in America, many newly migrated Presbyterian settlers were aware of contiguous revivals in Scotland, having situated themselves in what has been described as a "transatlantic community of saints." They were alert to the constraints that established Presbyterian leaders and their landowning patrons had imposed on mainland Scottish awakenings. Itinerant preachers such as George Whitefield informed them that their new emphasis on "heart religion" reasserted the simple ideals of the Knoxian Reformation on the new American frontier. Many settlers came to believe that they were reviving ancestral sacramental traditions whose "seasons of grace" had since waned or suffered restrictions in the Old World.[3]

2. Rush to Witherspoon, Dec. 29, 1767, in Butterfield, ed., *Letters of Benjamin Rush,* I, 48. On the college's appeal as a junction between different Protestant denominations, each of which would look to the institution for training, see Varnum Lansing Collins, *President Witherspoon: A Biography* (Princeton, N.J., 1925), I, 98–99. For the connections between evangelicals in the Kirk and the College of New Jersey during the colonial period, see Howard Miller, "Evangelical Religion and Colonial Princeton," in Lawrence Stone, ed., *Schooling and Society: Studies in the History of Education* (Baltimore, 1976), 115–145; Thomas S. Kidd, *The Great Awakening: The Roots of Evangelical Christianity in Colonial America* (New Haven, Conn., 2007), 32–33.

3. Susan O'Brien, "A Transatlantic Community of Saints: The Great Awakening and the First Evangelical Network, 1735–1755," *American Historical Review,* XCI (1986), 811–832; Michael J. Crawford, *Seasons of Grace: Colonial New England's Revival Tradition in Its British Context* (New York, 1991), 172–173; Leigh Eric Schmidt, *Holy Fairs: Scotland and the Making of American Revivalism,* 2d ed. (Grand Rapids, Mich., 2001). Ned C. Landsman has discussed evangelical Presbyterian perceptions of both the potential and the constraints of provincial life in the British Atlantic world and that which motivated a number of evangelicals in western Scotland to move to the American colonies. See Landsman, "Presbyterians and Provincial Society: The Evangelical Enlightenment in the West of Scotland, 1740–1775," in John Dwyer and Richard B.

That which revivalist Congregationalists and Presbyterians shared in common also led to similar opposition within their respective denominational
communities. In his initial overtures to Witherspoon, Rush failed to disclose
these earlier conflicts between evangelical and anthropocentric notions of
moral reasoning in New England and the Middle Colonies—including those
between Presbyterians in Princeton village. In 1741, Samuel Finley highlighted the "sure and infallible Proof of a gracious Work of GOD's Spirit,
when the Devil is cast out by Means of true Gospel-Doctrine." Along with
his New Side evangelical colleagues, the future president of the College of
New Jersey emphasized the importance of a passionate religious awakening
and an unmediated salvation experience. Reflecting a similar division that
had formed between "Old Light" and "New Light" Congregational theologians in New England, they often used their sermons and pamphlets to
question the dry intellectuality and elite leadership of Old Side Presbyterian
ministers. They demonstrated a degree of resentment toward their own colonial synod in Philadelphia, accusing its Old Side leaders of maintaining an
intimate association with imperial governors and their political proxies. They
also reproached synod officials for promoting anthropocentric religious ideas
that were popular among colonial Anglican elites. Unlike their synod adversaries, they had often received a broadly pietistic form of religious training
in a network of log cabins that were modeled on a main site, which William
Tennent, Sr., had erected in Neshaminy, Pennsylvania, in 1721. Educated in
revivalist log colleges, they campaigned for their own independent institution
of higher education in the mid-Atlantic region. In doing so, they sought to
buttress their New Side evangelicalism against their establishment-focused
co-religionists. Initially, at least, they defined the pedagogical and religious
culture of the College of New Jersey in distinction to the Philadelphia Presbyterian synod. They highlighted their dissension from fellow Protestants of
the same denomination, despite their shared opposition to French imperial
power during the same period.[4]

Sher, eds., *Sociability and Society in Eighteenth-Century Scotland* (Edinburgh, 1993), 194–209;
Landsman, "The Provinces and the Empire: Scotland, the American Colonies, and the Development of British Provincial Identity," in Lawrence Stone, ed., *An Imperial State at War: Britain
from 1689 to 1815* (London, 1993), 258–288.

4. Samuel Finley, *Christ Triumphing, and Satan Raging* . . . (Philadelphia, 1741), 22–23.
On Finley's sermon, see also Christopher Grasso, *A Speaking Aristocracy: Transforming Public
Discourse in Eighteenth-Century Connecticut* (Chapel Hill, N.C., 1999), 95; Jonathan M. Yeager,
Early Evangelicalism: A Reader (New York, 2013), 60–67; Benjamin T. Lynerd, *Republican The-
ology: The Civil Religion of American Evangelicals* (New York, 2014), 48. On Presbyterian divi-

Historians have tended to focus on the support for ministerial itinerancy among evangelical Presbyterians during the revivals of the 1740s. The freedom of movement across parish boundaries was certainly an important component in the New Side religious identity of Jonathan Dickinson, one of the College of New Jersey's principal founders and an associate of Finley. A fluid interchange between Congregational and Presbyterian revivalism underlay his career and thought. Having moved from New England to New Jersey as a young man, his conversion from Congregationalism to Presbyterianism preceded his central contribution to the founding of the college in 1746. Yet Dickinson sought to transmit evangelicalism from *within* a fixed educational location (initially in Elizabethtown, New Jersey, before moving to the village of Princeton in 1756, several years after his death). Assessing his synthesis between experiential piety and formal instruction disproves the assumption that Presbyterian revivalism heralded an unruly focus on lay-led piety before Witherspoon's arrival in New Jersey. When it came to their support for institutional authority, Old Side and New Side supporters were less distinct than they had initially tended to believe. Dickinson became associated with presbyteries that continued to object to the activities of the mainline American Presbyterian Synod. Yet even their contribution to rival synods inadvertently demonstrated their support for the principle of formal ecclesiology. It should not be surprising, then, that former Old Side Presbyterians became less distinguished from the heirs of New Side evangelicalism by the 1760s. Both agreed on the general importance of official religious and educational institutions, even if more subtle differences over theological doctrine remained.[5]

------

sions, see Marilyn Westerkamp, "Division, Dissension, and Compromise: The Presbyterian Church during the Great Awakening," *Journal of Presbyterian History,* LXXVIII (2000), 14. To be sure, Westerkamp also emphasizes aspects of agreement over the ensuing years. Some evangelical Presbyterians even linked the enlightened sensibility and worldly interests of Philadelphia's religious and educational establishment to early failures against French military forces. See Bryan F. Le Beau, *Jonathan Dickinson and the Formative Years of American Presbyterianism* (Louisville, Ky., 1997), 169-172. On the construction of binary distinctions between "New" and "Old" Lights (similar to distinctions between New and Old Sides) that did not always match more-nuanced identities, see Grasso, *A Speaking Aristocracy,* 105-106. On the depiction of differences within the printed media (which could become entrenched in reality after, rather than necessarily before, their publication), see Frank Lambert, *"Pedlar in Divinity": George Whitefield and the Transatlantic Revivals, 1737-1770* (Princeton, N.J., 2002).

5. On itinerancy and Presbyterian revivalism (as opposed to institutionalism), see Timothy D. Hall, *Contested Boundaries: Itinerancy and the Reshaping of the Colonial American Religious World* (Durham, N.C., 1994), 118-120. On the origins of Dickinson's move toward Presbyterianism, see Le Beau, *Jonathan Dickinson,* 1-26. For the nuanced relationship between Old Side and

From the late 1740s, Scottish evangelicals also adapted a relatively conservative approach to the growth and maintenance of ecclesiastical and educational institutions. Like Jonathan Dickinson, Witherspoon and his Popular party colleagues sought to incorporate and promote a passionate approach to heart religion within existing ecclesiastical and educational establishments (albeit with less success). They were opposed to the specific nature and output of the Moderate establishment, and its connection to Westminster, rather than the general notion of ecclesiastical and educational order. Witherspoon's clerical training had coincided with the 1742 Cambuslang revival, which took place in a rural parish just outside Glasgow. In the largest evangelical awakening of its time, passionate preachers appealed to vast crowds over many months. Many drew an association between the Cambuslang revival and Presbyterian awakenings in North America during the same era. Yet there is no evidence that Witherspoon had attended the events in Cambuslang. Instead, he chose to develop his evangelical sensibility from within the formal ecclesiastical system of the Church of Scotland. He positioned himself as an outspoken opponent of Moderate culture rather than as a proponent of extra-institutional religious preaching (as had been the case among some Cambuslang attendees). Unsurprisingly, therefore, the founding synthesis between evangelicalism and formalism in the College of New Jersey would prove attractive to Witherspoon.[6]

"Experimental Religion" and Formal Instruction

More recent historiography has located the roots of colonial Presbyterian evangelicalism more firmly in Ulster-Scottish religious culture than in the encounter between nascent Presbyterian communities and Congregational New England churches during the seventeenth and early eighteenth centuries. Although this work has added a welcome new perspective to understandings of piety in the Middle Colonies, there is a danger in jettisoning the

New Side Presbyterianism in America through the mid-eighteenth century, see Ned C. Landsman, *Crossroads of Empire: The Middle Colonies in British North America* (Baltimore, 2010), 172–180; John Fea, "In Search of Unity: Presbyterians in the Wake of the First Great Awakening," *Journal of Presbyterian History*, LXXXVI (2008), 53–60.

6. On Popular party ideology, see John R. McIntosh, *Church and Theology in Enlightenment Scotland: The Popular Party, 1740–1800* (East Lothian, U.K., 1998), 33–35. On attendees at Cambuslang, see Roger L. Emerson, "The Scottish Literati and America, 1680–1800," in Ned C. Landsman, ed., *Nation and Province in the First British Empire: Scotland and the Americas, 1600–1800* (Lewisburg, Pa., 2001), 198.

earlier association between American Presbyterianism and Congregational piety, particularly in relation to the intersection between ecclesiological and educational culture. Presbyterian evangelicalism certainly incorporated the manifest piety of Scottish and Ulster-Scottish migrants and itinerant preachers in the Middle Colonies during the 1730s and 1740s. But it also encompassed a good degree of cooperation with New England theologians, reflecting earlier seventeenth-century associations between Presbyterian ecclesiology and Congregationalism. The chartering of the College of New Jersey in 1746 owed much to the association between Presbyterian evangelicalism and Ulster-Scottish immigration in the surrounding region. Nonetheless, the New England roots of the institution are also important to note, not least in order to comprehend why Witherspoon eventually came to express its religious and educational authority in intercolonial terms, rather than simply as a narrow Presbyterian enterprise that was confined to New Jersey and its catchment of Ulster-Scottish migrants.[7]

Congregational families had settled in the Connecticut River valley since the 1660s, often then moving on to communities in New Jersey, Pennsylvania, and New York. The Congregationalists who remained in southern Connecticut witnessed mounting tensions between clergymen and laymen. Reflecting a familiar fault line in New England Congregational theology, they differed over the role of ministers in arbitrating the nature of individual salvation. By the early eighteenth century, local clergymen in the region felt obliged to draw up a confederal plan of religious governance in order to reduce the effects of those tensions. Finally drafted in 1708, their "Saybrook Platform" adopted the Savoy Confession, which was similar to the 1647 Westminster Confession of Faith. Its authors created a middle way between Congregationalism and Presbyterianism.[8]

The authors of the Saybrook Platform sought to constrain disagreement and encourage heterogeneity in Congregational circles. Yet, ironically, the Platform's partial similarity with the Presbyterian system also predisposed its adherents to new associations and interactions with Ulster-Scottish settlers, who came from outside the Congregational realm. Newly arriving preachers

---

7. According to Leonard J. Trinterud, "Scotch-Irish" settlers were influenced by Congregationalist expressions of "experimental divinity" that had begun to appear on the northern frontiers of Pennsylvania, New York, and New Jersey several decades before their migration. See Trinterud, *The Forming of an American Tradition: A Re-examination of Colonial Presbyterianism* (New York, 1970), 58.

8. On the platform's middle way, see Le Beau, *Jonathan Dickinson*, 13–15.

FIGURE 7. *Jonathan Dickinson (1688–1747), President (1747)*. By Edward Ludlow
Mooney. Oil on canvas. Princeton University Art Museum / Art Resource, N.Y.

and ministers from Scotland and Ireland gravitated toward the first official
presbytery in North America, which had been founded in Philadelphia two
years earlier in 1706. John Wise of Ipswich noted the similarity between the
presbytery's ecclesiology and the ideas espoused by Congregational settlers
in southern Connecticut and northern New Jersey. He publicly disdained
the Presbyterian nature of the Saybrook Platform in his 1713 pamphlet, *The*

Churches Quarrel Espoused. According to Wise, the popularity of the Platform as far south as New Jersey demonstrated the developing alliance between Congregationalists and a new wave of revivalist Scottish settlers.[9]

Thanks to the migration of Presbyterians from Scotland and Ireland, the
number of ministers in the Presbytery of Philadelphia reached a significant
proportion over a large geographical area. From 1716, the enlarged presbytery became known more officially as the Synod of Philadelphia. Jonathan
Dickinson, a minister who had moved from Connecticut to Elizabeth, New
Jersey, completed his community's move toward Presbyterianism by joining
the synod. But links between Presbyterians and Congregationalists did not
diminish entirely over the following decades. Their common influence would
provide an important context for religious revivals during the 1740s. It would
also affect the founding of the College of New Jersey, owing in no small part
to Dickinson.[10]

Given his experience under the Saybrook Platform, Dickinson was familiar with later discussions of ecclesiology and confessional subscription that
he encountered during the 1720s and 1730s. Mirroring their counterparts in
Scotland, Presbyterian ministers in New Jersey, New York, and Pennsylvania failed to agree on their definition of clerical authority. Differing perceptions were particularly apparent in their discussion of the use of religious
confessions and tests. Public dissension over the issue of subscription to the
Westminster Confession of Faith was a heated issue in the decade after the
formation of the Synod of Philadelphia in 1716. As the number of potential Presbyterian ministers migrating to the Middle Colonies began to increase, the 1729 synod proposed that it would follow Scottish and Irish ecclesiology in making subscription to the Confession necessary for ministerial
training, quickly finding a majority in support of the Adopting Act. Before
the 1730s, however, Rutherford's catechism was in no way normative among
North American Presbyterians. Although ministers with recent Scottish or
Irish heritage called for subscriptionist candidates, the heirs of New England
Presbyterianism, such as Dickinson, called for antisubscription measures.
Dickinson feared that universal subscription to the Westminster Confession

9. On immigration to the first founded presbytery following the Platform, see George M.
Marsden, *Jonathan Edwards: A Life* (New Haven, Conn., 2003), 22; Le Beau, *Jonathan Dickin-
son*, 16–17. On the disdain of John Wise of Ipswich for the Platform, see Grasso, *A Speaking
Aristocracy*, 41.

10. For these developments in American Presbyterian ecclesiology, see James H. Smylie,
A Brief History of the Presbyterians (Louisville, Ky., 1996), 43; Le Beau, *Jonathan Dickinson*,
16–17.

of Faith would herald a first step toward more centralized ecclesiastical authority among American Presbyterians. He believed that central orders were likely to emanate from either the General Synod of Ulster or the General Assembly of Scotland. He and several other ministers were anxious that subscription would lead colonial American presbyteries to lose their autonomy to centers of Presbyterian governance on either side of the North Irish Sea. They continued to recommend that candidates and ministers work out the nature of salvation from their own reading of the Confession, according to their own terms and local pedagogical practices, rather than as directed by external reviewers and standardized readers.[11]

Opponents of subscription warned that it would encourage a centralized establishment to the detriment of local revivalism. Its proponents claimed that the Westminster Confession of Faith was itself a catalyst for the promotion of individual salvation and regeneration, irrespective of local communal norms. Thus, neither side of the controversy overlooked the central importance of an individual conversion experience. Rather, they differed in their response to the geographic diversity of Ulster-Scottish settlement in the Middle Colonies. Presbyterians with New England roots tended to envision the expansion of their ministerial authority to incorporate new migrants. More recent settlers, however, feared that existing ministries were too distanced from frontier communities. They also worried that newly arriving religious leaders did not retain sufficient religious training. Clerical subscription to the Westminster Confession of Faith would, in their opinion, provide greater assurance of true faith among laymen.

A more passionate depiction of faith became more popular in some colonial Presbyterian circles in the decade after the subscription crisis, culminating in the evangelical awakening of "heart religion" among New Side Presbyterians in the Middle Colonies during the 1740s. In 1729, for example, the Presbyterian John Tennent proclaimed that any consideration of revelation demonstrated that "all men by nature are virtually disposed to every sin; for we are prone to evil, as the sparks fly upward," and "this informs us of the absolute necessity of a universal change" through regeneration and salvation. During the 1730s, led by John's father William Tennent, Sr., the Tennent family promoted a conversionist form of revivalism in Presbyterian churches in New Brunswick, Staten Island, and in several smaller communities. By the early 1740s, New Side ministers began to gravitate toward the Presbytery

11. On the early subscription controversy, see Charles Hodge, *The Constitutional History of the Presbyterian Church in the United States of America* (Philadelphia, 1839), I, 98–100; Trinterud, *The Forming of an American Tradition*, 28–52; Le Beau, *Jonathan Dickinson*, 27–32.

of New Brunswick, which had been established in 1738 by Gilbert Tennent, the pastor in New Brunswick, New Jersey, and another Tennent son. From the late 1730s, they and many other Presbyterians from western Scotland and Ireland cultivated experiential spirituality as a contrast to rational and seemingly unemotional manifestations of Protestant piety, an approach that they brought from outdoor revival meetings in Scotland and Ireland to congregations in, for example, Freehold, New Jersey.[12]

It is tempting to highlight a continuity between the subscription controversy of the late 1720s and tensions that formed between supporters and opponents of Presbyterian evangelicalism during the "Great Awakening" of Protestant piety a decade later. The division between Old Side and New Side Presbyterians that developed during the 1740s was also partially influenced by the unsettling impact of migration on ministerial and confessional authority. Through the 1730s, the Synod of Philadelphia became ever more circumspect about the mass migration of Ulster-Scottish pastors with questionable qualifications. In 1738, it made the decision to standardize ministerial knowledge and output on the "clergy-scarce frontier." It proposed certain qualifying standards for all who had not received formal training in New England or in European colleges. In particular, they were to be subject to synodical examination by an established hierarchy of ministers. Gilbert Tennent led the New Side delegation in opposition to examinations at the 1738 synod meeting.[13]

Representing his newly formed revivalist Presbytery of New Brunswick, Gilbert Tennent crystallized opposition to the synod proposals in what came to be his most famous sermon, *The Danger of the Unconverted Ministry,* which he delivered in Nottingham, on the border between Maryland and Pennsylvania, in March 1740. He accused the "Natural Men" in the Old Side Presbyterian establishment in Philadelphia of "not having true Love to Christ and the Souls of their Fellow-Creatures" and using synodical examination to continue their emotionless discourse in contrast to the revi-

---

12. John Tennent, "Regeneration Opened: A Sermon by the Rev. John Tennent," in S[amuel] D. A[lexander], ed., *Sermons and Essays by the Tennents and Their Contemporaries . . .* (Philadelphia, 1855), 264. On Tennent and the Log College men around the Presbytery of New Brunswick, see Westerkamp, "Division, Dissension, and Compromise," *Journal of Presbyterian History,* LXXVIII (2000), 5–6; Le Beau, *Jonathan Dickinson,* 106; Ned Landsman, "Revivalism and Nativism in the Middle Colonies: The Great Awakening and the Scots Community in East New Jersey," *American Quarterly,* XXXIV (1982), 149–164.

13. Westerkamp, "Division, Dissension, and Compromise," *Journal of Presbyterian History,* LXXVIII (2000), 7, 11.

valism of new Presbyterian migrations to the Middle Colonies. With words that "freeze between their Lips," according to Tennent, Old Side ministers relied on rational rather than experiential understandings of salvation. As "Pharisee-Teachers, having no Experience of a special Work of the Holy Ghost, upon their own Souls," they were "therefore neither inclined to, nor fitted for, Discoursing, frequently, clearly, and pathetically, upon such important Subjects." Their rational pretensions prevented honest emotionalism in their response to divinity. Instead, they imposed dry legalism through official institutional examination. Failing to "distinguish, as they ought, between *Law* and *Gospel,* in their Discourses to others," they spent all their time as "blind Guides [to] fix a deluded World upon the false Foundation of their own Righteousness; and so exclude them from the dear Redeemer." According to Tennent, therefore, established ministers had become overly focused on their duty to religious laws and human works.[14]

Notwithstanding the unsettling confessional impact of continued Ulster-Scottish migration, however, there were fundamental differences between the conflict over subscription to the Westminster Confession of Faith during the 1720s and the subsequent crisis of ministerial authority that contributed to Tennent's fiery sermon. Later tensions between Presbyterians derived from differing readings of the Westminster Confession of Faith, rather than from any conflict over its general subscription. Officially adopted by the Synod of Philadelphia in 1729, the Confession became normative during the late 1730s as the prediction of the first generation of Ulster-Scottish ministers proved to be accurate: existing forms of clerical authority had become insufficient to cope with the inculcation of revivalist tenets of faith among laymen. Evangelical Presbyterians with New England roots had gravitated toward similarly inclined Ulster-Scottish communities because their claim to indigenous colonial American ecclesiology had become less relevant in light of the sheer volume of migration to the Middle Colonies through the 1730s. Thus, they put aside their earlier divisions over subscription in their joint opposition to synodical examinations. Pietistic ministers proposed subscription to the Confession during the 1720s and 1730s to support the promotion of evangelism on the frontier against the threat of centralized ecclesiastical authority from the eastern side of the Atlantic. By the 1740s, however, they tended to oppose attempts to standardize faith through institutional examination from Old Side leaders on the western side of the Atlantic. Thus, they became increasingly

14. Gilbert Tennent, *The Danger of an Unconverted Ministry, Consider'd in a Sermon on Mark VI. 34 . . .* , 2d ed. (Boston, 1742), 6, 7.

unified in their belief that adherence to the fundamental tenets of the Westminster Confession of Faith justified their religious authority, irrespective of newer and more formal institutional examinations.[15]

It is important to note that evangelical clergymen during the early 1740s were not opposed to the general structure of Presbyterian ecclesiology as it had developed in colonial America. Rather, they accused established ministers of abusing their legitimate representative authority. Those who promoted synodical examination, they claimed, sought to distinguish their worldly erudition from the personal salvation experience of laymen. According to the Tennents, Finley, and even Dickinson, established clerics discouraged experimental piety among their congregants in order to distract from their own unconverted status. In a 1741 sermon, Dickinson described the "Act of *Faith* by which we receive the Lord Jesus Christ . . . [as] indeed distinct from the Duties of religious Worship" but suggested also that "as *Faith* must be obtain'd in a Way of Duty, so it is necessarily productive of a Life of Duty, in all that have it." Both Congregationalists and Presbyterians were to look to God and "Commit the whole Concern of your Salvation to him . . . [and to] Look to him in a Way of constant earnest Prayer and active Diligence, for all Supplies of Grace." They could not "trust too little" their selves, "nor too much to him [God], in the Way of Duty." Individuals were to "resolve therefore constantly to come, empty and self-insufficient, to him." They could only understand their duty to God by reducing their trust in personal conscience. In contrast to rational assertions of faith, then, evangelical Presbyterians such as Dickinson viewed Presbyterian religious revivals as the work of the Holy Spirit and emotional physicality as a sincere response to the terrifying realization of sin and the necessity of saving grace. They defined their adversaries as dry legalists who privileged works over a passionate conversion experience and polite eloquence over inspirational evangelism. They warned that official synodical examinations were corrupted by the latitudinarian higher education of their drafters.[16]

By the 1740s, Dickinson and his associates encouraged the personal experience of sin and salvation among a third wave of settlers. Yet they also

15. On these moves toward greater unity, see Mark A. Noll, *America's God: From Jonathan Edwards to Abraham Lincoln* (New York, 2002), 26; Westerkamp, "Division, Dissension, and Compromise," *Journal of Presbyterian History*, LXXVIII (2000), 9–11.

16. Jonathan Dickinson, *The True Scripture-Doctrine concerning Some Important Points of Christian Faith, Particularly Eternal Election, Original Sin, Grace in Conversion, Justification by Faith, and the Saints Perseverence; Represented and Apply'd in Five Discourses* (Boston, 1741), 202–203, 217. Noll describes Dickinson's reasoning in his sermons during the early 1740s as "revivalistic rather than commonsensical"; see Noll, *America's God*, 102.

required a degree of pedagogical authority in order to train ministers to recognize, corroborate, and verify the truth of individual conversion. Problematically, therefore, it always remained ambiguous whether the assurance of salvation was an entirely individual act. In his overture to Witherspoon, Benjamin Rush avoided making any reference to internal tensions among evangelical Presbyterians during previous decades. But, in fact, initial differences regarding the nature of assurance threatened to reduce the unity that they had gained in opposition to the Synod of Philadelphia. Gilbert Tennent, in his 1740 sermon *The Danger of an Unconverted Ministry,* urged laymen to leave churches if their informal evangelicalism was deemed preferable to corrupted ministerial authority. Dickinson, in his May 1740 work *The Witness of the Spirit,* however, reminded listeners and readers that moral volition remained unreliable even when laymen removed themselves from unconverted ministries. They still required some sort of trained authority in order to help them assure that their display of salvation derived from more than a self-serving desire for communal esteem.[17]

According to Dickinson, overemphasizing the power of the laity remained just as problematic as deferring wholly to ministerial authority. In both cases, he criticized those who confused the work of the Holy Spirit with individual actions, perceptions, and the varying rhetorical capabilities of "Sprightliness and Sagacity." Not all men were "Sons of Thunder," and so all were "accordingly to esteem and value all that are carefully discharging the awful Trust committed to them [ministers with powerful rhetorical qualities] of the Lord, as *Ministers of Christ; and Stewards of the Mysteries of the Kingdom.* And not add to their heavy Weight; and weaken their Hands in their difficult Work, by Slights and Contempts, Abuses and Indignities." Committing such abuses would only serve to give moral agency to individuals rather than divine providence. Any community of believers was therefore "instructed to attend upon the Ministry God hath set over us, with a Dependance not upon the Means; but the God of Means, for the saving Efficacy of it."[18]

17. Jonathan Dickinson, *The Witness of the Spirit . . . Wherein Is Distinctly Shown, in What Way and Manner the Spirit Himself Beareth Witness to the Adoption of the Children of God, on Occasion of a Wonderful Progress of Converting Grace in Those Parts* (Boston, 1740). Although Tennent later modified his opinions, *The Danger of an Unconverted Ministry* reveals what Mark A. Noll has described as a flexibility toward ecclesiastical order with only a few parallels in the Scottish or Irish homelands. See Noll, *America's God,* 26. The second wave of Scottish immigrants moved into "farmtouns" where both tenants and their workers maintained an increasing ethnocultural distinction from other groups in the region. See Ned C. Landsman, *Scotland and Its First American Colony, 1683–1785* (Princeton, N.J., 1985), 19, 101–130.

18. Jonathan Dickinson, *The Danger of Schisms and Contentions with respect to the Ministry*

In his 1740 sermon *Witness of the Spirit,* indeed, Dickinson worried that, despite the "Power and Goodness" of the Holy Spirit in awakening the passions of men throughout the colonies, it was apt to "wonder if the Adversary" might "sow Tares among the Wheat" in reviving communities, even as promoted by well-meaning ministers such as Tennent. Dickinson therefore pointed out the potential problem of unverified spiritual enthusiasm.

> No Idea of sensible Objects can possibly be communicated to those that have not the proper Senses to perceive them; so neither can any just Conceptions of this *Fellowship of the Spirit,* this *Joy of the Holy Ghost,* be communicated to any but those that have Experiences of it in themselves; or at least, spiritual Capacities fitted hereto. — Thence it is, that some Persons from enthusiastick Heats, from working up their animal Affections and Passions, or else from diabolical Delusions, have *pretended* to these immediate Influences of the Spirit of God, where the Consequence has evidently shewn, they have been *Strangers, that have never intermedled with these* Divine *Joys.*

Here Dickinson inverted the analogy that moral sense philosophers such as Francis Hutcheson drew between the sensory perception of objects and the ethical discernment of human interactions. Instead of highlighting the predictable veracity of sensory perception, he focused on those moments when it could not be guaranteed. Its fallibility, in his view, was unfortunately analogous with moral perception. Thus, Dickinson even acknowledged that some individuals trusted too readily in their ability to witness their own reception of grace before their adoption of biblical tenets. Others, conversely, were likely to feel their sin so deeply that they felt unworthy of any sort of grace. He suggested that they risked paralysis by melancholy and gloom. Unlike those who assumed their salvation with (problematic) alacrity, they doubted the possibility of regeneration even when the Holy Spirit was ready and present. According to Dickinson, then, some sort of ministerial judgment among laymen was always necessary.[19]

Despite Dickinson's tacit critique of his fiery recommendations, Gilbert Tennent was never entirely opposed to the notion of clerical judgment ac-

---

and Ordinances of the Gospel, Represented in a Sermon Preached at the Meeting of the Presbytery at Woodbridge, October 10th, 1739: and Published at the Desire of Some of the Ministers Present (New York, 1739), 8, 9, 10–11.

19. Dickinson, *Witness of the Spirit,* 4, 5, 20, 23, 25–26. On Dickinson's fear of fatalism, see Westerkamp, "Division, Dissension, and Compromise," *Journal of Presbyterian History,* LXXVIII (2000), 10; Le Beau, *Jonathan Dickinson,* 118–121; Kidd, *The Great Awakening,* 127.

cording to religious education. Even in his radical sermon, there were signs that he could be amenable to the general principle of ministerial guidance and clerical qualification. Having called for concerted action by laymen against unconverted pastors, he claimed that all "Bowels should be moved with the most compassionate Tenderness, over those dear fainting Souls, that are *as Sheep having no Shepherd"* and recommended that Presbyterians in America "stock the Church with a faithful Ministry . . . [by encouraging] private Schools, or Seminaries of Learning, which are under the Care of skilful and experienced Christians . . . [to only admit those] who upon strict Examination, have in the Judgment of a reasonable Charity, the plain Evidences of experimental Religion." Even according to Tennent, then, formal methods could encourage what had hitherto been expressed in popular, extracongregational, and outdoor meetings.[20]

The realization that formal instruction and evangelical ideals were not antithetical helped to reduce internal evangelical tensions regarding the nature of religious assurance. Dickinson, Tennent, and many of their associates even began to look for religious and pedagogical guidance from a fixed presbytery. Through the early 1740s, their revivalist members came to be defined as New Side Presbyterians in distinction to Old Side representatives in the Philadelphia establishment (previously known as the "Old Side Synod"). Old Side ministers such as John Thomson and Francis Alison were uneasy with developing evangelical assumptions about the centrality of conversion narratives in judging the state of grace and regeneration among individuals.[21]

Yet, rather than denying the importance of Presbyterian ecclesiology, formal educational instruction, and fixed centers of religious learning, revivalist New Side Presbyterians sought out their own, rival religious and pedagogical establishment. By 1743, their Presbytery of New Brunswick increasingly sought to synthesize formal instruction with the promotion of evangelical piety. Its activities provided Jonathan Dickinson with further support in his desire to temper Gilbert Tennent's vision of lay moral authority. Tennent demonstrated even greater acceptance of qualified institutional training after Dickinson made him aware of troubling actions carried out by some New Light preachers as well as the problematic consequence of unmediated lay piety in Pennsylvania's Moravian communities. In a note to the readers of his 1743 *Some Account of the Principles of the Moravians,* Tennent began by acknowledging that it "was with no small Expectation,

20. Tennent, *The Danger of an Unconverted Ministry,* 10–11.
21. Bradley J. Longfield, *Presbyterians and American Culture: A History* (Louisville, Ky., 2013), 9–28.

that many among us, who have long been mourning over the dying Circumstances of experimental Religion, heard of some uncommon Appearances of
its Restoration, in some Parts of *Germany.*" Like all pious communities, they
had ostensibly "learned from God's holy Word, that *Satan* could *transform
himself into an Angel of Light* . . . [and] that Men might, under very plausible
Appearances, *craftily* and *privily,* bring in the most dangerous Doctrines,
and delude weak, tho' honest, Minds into Measures, which might have a Tendency to the Subversion of the Gospel of *Christ.*" Tennent's note to readers
then assumed a far more negative tone, highlighting the ways in which Moravians had apparently ignored such a warning by adopting various problematic church doctrines: a "silent Stupidity" and "Neglect of Prayer" in which
the latter was confined "almost wholly, to the Second Person of the Sacred
Trinity, however to the utter Neglect of the Divine Father." Thus, Tennent
began to note the problem of assurance in communities whose loose principles seemed to have exacerbated problematic doctrines and practices. The
Moravian example informed later sermons such as *The Danger of Spiritual
Pride Represented* and *The Necessity of Studying to Be Quiet, and Doing Our
Own Business.* "It is lamentable to think," Tennent argued in the latter sermon, "how ready some ignorant Novices in Religion, are to take the Bench,
and pronounce Sentence against the Spiritual States of others rashly, and
without sufficient Foundation." According to Tennent, quietude and passionate fervor were linked dialectically. Orderly instruction provided a calm
context in which students learned to verify the contrasting passions of experimental piety and conversion.[22]

22. Gilbert Tennent, *Some Account of the Principles of the Moravians: Chiefly Collected from
Several Conversations with Count Zinzendorf; and from Some Sermons Preached by Him at Ber-
lin, and Published in London; Being an Appendix to a Treatise on the Necessity of Holding Fast the
Truth* (London, 1743), iii, vii; Tennent, *The Danger of Spiritual Pride Represented* . . . (Philadel-
phia [1745]); Tennent, *The Necessity of Studying to Be Quiet, and Doing Our Own Business* . . .
(Philadelphia, [1744]), 10. On the problematic New Light preachers and Moravians whom Ten-
nent came to fear, see also Westerkamp, "Division, Dissension, and Compromise," *Journal of
Presbyterian History,* LXXVIII (2000), 11; Harry S. Stout and Peter Onuf, "James Davenport
and the Great Awakening in New London," *Journal of American History,* LXX (1983), 556–578;
David C. Harlan, "The Travail of Religious Moderation: Jonathan Dickinson and the Great
Awakening," *Journal of Presbyterian History,* LXI (1983), 411–426; Le Beau, *Jonathan Dickinson,* 124–143. As Mark A. Noll has pointed out, the intellectual leaders of colonial Presbyterian
revivalism, "though approaching the twin ideals from different directions, tried to advance both
traditional theology and the era's new evangelical piety. . . . No matter how devoted they were to
piety, the Scotch-Irish in America retained substantial interest in formal doctrine and the niceties
of church order." See Noll, *America's God,* 25, 126.

Tensions over the nature of assurance dissipated even further as New Brunswick Presbyterians responded to the case of David Brainerd, an awakened student who had been expelled from Yale College. Through the early 1740s, New Side ministers continued to claim that Synod of Philadelphia members were attracted to latitudinarian ideas in New England colleges. Their accusation became more vitriolic and unified following the expulsion of Brainerd from Yale. Dickinson and Aaron Burr, Sr., joined Congregational ministers such as Jonathan Edwards in expressing their support for Brainerd's conversionist theology. Even more pertinent, Brainerd's plight inspired Presbyterians in New Brunswick and New York to call for the formation of an institution of higher education that aligned more closely with the theological principles that had led them to ally with his cause. In April 1743, Dickinson and Burr hired Brainerd as a missionary to native Americans in the New Jersey backcountry. In June 1744, the Presbytery of New York ordained him at Newark, New Jersey.[23]

Members of the Presbytery of New Brunswick continued to support Brainerd even after the Synod of Philadelphia expelled them for encouraging the ordination of ministers without synodical examination. Despite their expulsion, they developed greater institutional cooperation with evangelical supporters from other presbyteries, including the Presbytery of New York. Finally, in 1745, they formed the Synod of New York as a rival to the Philadelphia establishment. The Old Side became aligned with the Synod of Philadelphia, and the New Side with the Synod of New York. New Side supporters continued to claim that the Synod of Philadelphia disdained the promotion of experiential piety and discriminated against their own ministers. They questioned those who set the educational standards of ordination, rather than the importance of standards per se.[24]

After New Side petitions to the colonial government of New Jersey, the "College of New Jersey" was eventually granted its official status as an institution of higher education by the acting royal governor, Alexander Hamilton,

---

23. In light of the Brainerd case, according to Le Beau, Dickinson and others began a "quest for a college more sympathetic to their needs"; see Le Beau, *Jonathan Dickinson*, 170. See also John Coffey, "Puritanism, Evangelicalism, and the Evangelical Protestant Tradition," in Michael A. G. Haykin and Kenneth J. Stewart, eds., *The Advent of Evangelicalism: Exploring Historical Continuities* (Nashville, Tenn., 2008), 266.

24. On the final expulsion from the synod, see John Fea, *The Way of Improvement Leads Home: Philip Vickers Fithian and the Rural Enlightenment in Early America* (Philadelphia, 2008), 38. On the later realignment of the synods, see Mark A. Noll and Luke E. Harlow, eds., *Religion and American Politics: From the Colonial Period to the Present*, 2d ed. (New York, 2007), 29-30.

in the name of George II. On October 22, 1746, the "Province of New Jersey" agreed on its charter for "the Education of Youth in the Learned Languages and in the Liberal Arts and Sciences." The first trustees of the institution included William Smith, Peter Can Brugh Livingston, William Peartrea Smith, Jonathan Dickinson, John Pierson, Aaron Burr, Sr., and Ebenezer Pemberton. Initially, from May 1747, the college was stationed in Jonathan Dickinson's parsonage at Elizabeth, New Jersey. After his death a few months later, the college moved to Burr's parsonage in Newark, New Jersey, before eventually finding a home in its final location in Princeton village. The founding of the college — particularly its association with the training of Presbyterian ministers — would carry an important meaning outside the Middle Colonies, both in New England and in Scotland.[25]

Jonathan Edwards, the College of New Jersey, and the Scottish-American Connection

In 1758, Jonathan Edwards assumed the presidency of the College of New Jersey, a decade after Dickinson and a decade before Witherspoon. Though he died only a few weeks into his post, the encounter with Presbyterian educational culture that preceded his short presidency was highly meaningful for the trajectory of Presbyterianism and evangelicalism in America. As an evangelical Congregational minister, he was sandwiched between two Presbyterian presidents — one born in New England and the other raised in Scotland. This observation carries wider historical meaning. In the decades before his presidency, Edwards developed a synthesis between formal instruction and personal conversionism, appealing to evangelical Presbyterians on both sides of the Atlantic. It assuaged their residual anxieties regarding the false assurance of salvation at a time when Scotland and America were engaged in periodic but profound movements of transatlantic revivalism. As a result, Edwards was able to form an association with the Presbyterian founders of the College of New Jersey as well as Witherspoon's nascent Popular party in the Church of Scotland.[26]

25. On the official charter's wording, see Alexander Leitch, *A Princeton Companion* (Princeton, N.J., 1978), 89. On the trustees, see Varnum Lansing Collins, *Princeton* (New York, 1914), 14-15; James McLachlan, ed., *Princetonians, 1748-1768: A Biographical Dictionary* (Princeton, N.J., 1976), I, xviii.

26. For a poignant account of Edwards's brief role in Princeton, see Marsden, *Jonathan Edwards*, 490-495. On the links between Scotland and Edwards, see Jonathan M. Yeager, *Enlightened Evangelicalism: The Life and Thought of John Erskine* (New York, 2011), 11-15, 20-26.

Edwards's daughter Esther was married to Aaron Burr, Sr., the Presbyterian minister who preceded him as president of the College of New Jersey. His daughter's marriage was not the first association that Edwards enjoyed with Presbyterians from the Middle Colonies. Historians often begin their account of the "Great Awakening" with Edwards and his 1734 depiction of "spiritual mirth" in Northampton, Massachusetts. It is usually suggested that Edwards went on to note similar instances of heart religion in other Protestant communities during the following decade, encouraging greater ecumenical association with Presbyterians in particular. Yet he had contributed to early links between Presbyterianism and Congregational revivalism long before the 1740s. The Saybrook Platform encouraged Jonathan Dickinson in his ease of movement between Congregational churches in southern New England and revivalist Presbyterian meetings in northern New Jersey. In an often over-looked parallel, a young Jonathan Edwards moved from Connecticut to contribute to the ministry of a Presbyterian congregation. For eight months between 1722 and 1723, he had assumed the temporary role of "supply pastor" to a small church in New York City. In 1727, Edwards was ordained minister at Northampton, Massachusetts, where he assisted his grandfather. Following Stoddard's death in 1729, he continued to maintain an outward-looking religious identity, renewing his interaction with Presbyterians in the Middle Colonies—including converts from Congregationalism such as Dickinson.[27]

It has been suggested that the efforts of Dickinson to reconcile the multiple commitments of New Side and Old Side theology epitomized "the experiences of scores of ministers who tried to steer between the extremes of

27. For Edwards's perception of "spiritual mirth" in New England and a "shower of divine blessing" in New Jersey Presbyterian communities from the mid- to late 1730s, see Jonathan Edwards, *A Faithful Narrative* (circa 1737), in Edwards, *The Great Awakening*, ed. C. C. Goen, in Perry Miller et al., eds., *The Works of Jonathan Edwards*, IV (New Haven, Conn., 1970), 118, 152. On Edwards's early movements between New England and the Middle Colonies, including his role as a "supply" pastor, see Marsden, *Jonathan Edwards*, 46–60. On Edwards's grandfather, Solomon Stoddard, and his link to the implementation of the Saybrook Platform in Connecticut, see Paul R. Lucas, " 'The Death of the Prophet Lamented': The Legacy of Solomon Stoddard," in Stephen J. Stein, ed., *Jonathan Edwards's Writings: Text, Context, Interpretation* (Bloomington, Ind., 1996), 78; Samuel T. Logan, Jr., "Puritans, Presbyterians, and Jonathan Edwards," in S. Donald Fortson III, ed., *Colonial Presbyterianism: Old Faith in a New Land: Commemorating the 300th Anniversary of the First Presbytery in America* (Eugene, Oreg., 2007), 16. Edwards visited or met with members from Scottish and Dutch Reformed settler communities in New Jersey, particularly Gilbert Tennent, his brothers John and William, their father William, and Frederick Frelinghuysen. See Frank Lambert, *Inventing the "Great Awakening"* (Princeton, N.J., 1999), 55–60, 75.

enthusiasm and formalism." Scholars have contrasted Dickinson's "moderate" evangelicalism during the founding of the College of New Jersey with the uncompromising revivalism of Congregational ministers such as Edwards. Such a contrast, however, risks overlooking the similarity between the two ministers regarding their pedagogical approach to the assurance of faith. Edwards's religious and intellectual trajectory displayed much nuance in the relationship between formal instruction and evangelical piety. His *Distinguishing Marks of a Work of the Spirit of God* (1742), *Some Thoughts concerning the Present Revival of Religion* (1743), and *Religious Affections* (1746) all defended revivalism by delineating the true manifestation of pious regeneration against counterfeit interpretations of experimental religion. Edwards never abandoned his critique of rational apologetics and his support for a passionate and communal religious experience. But he also shared Dickinson's support for institutional mechanisms to define and verify the expression of passions in the process of conversion. Having circulated through the Middle Colonies, moreover, Edwards's *Distinguishing Marks* and *Religious Affections* were widely published and almost immediately disseminated in Scotland. The Scottish evangelical minister John Willison noted that Edwards remained firmly attached to his inherited ecclesiological system and that he was not opposed to the verification of experimental piety through ministerial authority.[28]

The publication of Edwards's *Distinguishing Marks* and *Religious Affections* had coincided with the efforts of Dickinson to coordinate the presbyteries of New York and New Brunswick in support of a formal institution of higher education. By this point, Edwards had renewed his association with a number of their members, thanks in large measure to the mediating influence during the previous years of George Whitefield, an evangelical preacher raised in the Anglican Church who moved between New England and the

---

28. David C. Harlan, "The Travail of Religious Moderation: Jonathan Dickinson and the Great Awakening," *Journal of Presbyterian History,* LXI (1983), 411–412; Leigh Eric Schmidt, "Jonathan Dickinson and the Making of the Moderate Awakening," *American Presbyterians,* LXIII (1985), 344. On Edwards's attempts to assure and regulate the nature of revivalism in his works, see Christopher Grasso, "Misrepresentations Corrected: Jonathan Edwards and the Regulation of Religious Discourse," in Stein, ed., *Jonathan Edwards's Writings,* 26–27. On Edwards's dissemination and the views of Rev. Willison, see "Testimony of the Rev. Mr. Willison, to the Churches of Scotland," in Sereno Edwards Dwight, ed., *The Works of President Edwards: With a Memoir of His Life,* 10 vols. (New York, 1830), I, 155; Christopher W. Mitchell, "Jonathan Edwards's Scottish Connection," in David W. Kling and Douglas A. Sweeney, eds., *Jonathan Edwards at Home and Abroad: Historical Memories, Cultural Movements, Global Horizons* (Columbia, S.C., 2003), 223, 231–234.

Middle Colonies during revivals, particularly through October 1740. Before that point, Edwards had heard much about Whitefield's outdoor preaching methods, including his description of religious revivalism as a transatlantic phenomenon. Thus, Edwards invited the itinerant minister to visit Northampton on his planned New England tour. On his way to meet Edwards, Whitefield was met by established Presbyterian communities who were keen to describe their own contiguous awakenings. During Whitefield's first movements through the American colonies, preachers and printers became more comfortable appropriating terminology from the conflict between Old Light and New Light Congregational theologians — including in their description of tensions between Old Side and New Side Presbyterians. Whether he was preaching to Presbyterian or Congregational groups, therefore, Whitefield tended to use the same rhetoric and language in opposition to the dry legalism of traditional colonial ministerial authority. Unsurprisingly, Whitefield developed a strong association with Gilbert Tennent, whom he praised in later discussions with Jonathan Edwards.[29]

When he met Edwards in 1740, Whitefield was able to provide him with contacts in both colonial American and Scottish Presbyterian communities. In doing so, he assumed an important role in facilitating what would become a long-standing relationship between Edwards and evangelical churchmen and professors in Scotland. Those relationships grew exponentially following the Cambuslang revival of August 1742, when Whitefield addressed a crowd of more than twenty thousand souls gathered in outdoor enclosures west of Glasgow, making sure to describe the kindred religious spirit between evangelical Presbyterians on both sides of the Atlantic. After this point, Edwards began conversing in particular with the evangelical Scot John Erskine, who donated dozens of books and pamphlets to his personal library.[30]

29. On Whitefield's movements and new associations with revivalists in New England and the Middle Colonies, see Marsden, *Jonathan Edwards*, 204-216; William V. Davis, ed., *George Whitefield's Journals, 1737-1741* . . . (Gainesville, Fla., 1969), 144, 350-355; Landsman, *Scotland and Its First American Colony*, 180-184.

30. On Whitefield's involvement in the Cambuslang revival, its transatlantic aspect, and Edwards's growing Scottish-American correspondence network, see Yeager, *Enlightened Evangelicalism*, 32-34, 38; W. R. Ward, *The Protestant Evangelical Awakening* (Cambridge, 1992), 336-337; Marsden, *Jonathan Edwards*, 209-210; O'Brien, "A Trans-Atlantic Community of Saints," *AHR*, XCI (1986), 819. Erskine (1721-1803) took a great interest in the cause of foreign Protestantism and, in particular, the religious potential of America. He went to the University of Edinburgh with Witherspoon and was a leading member of the Popular party in the Kirk. On Erskine's transatlantic correspondence and his donation of material to Edwards, see Ward, *Protestant Evangelical Awakening*, 338-339; Yeager, *Enlightened Evangelicalism*, 147, 150-153, 171-

Erskine and other evangelical Scots, including Witherspoon, drew a contrast between religious revivalism and the parochialism that they perceived in the Kirk's Moderate leadership. As we have seen, they accused Moderates of using patronage to buttress their civic authority, their latitudinarian ideals, and the notion that their mainland British establishment was somehow superior in its cultural development. As a result, according to evangelicals, Moderates had become unlikely to contribute to any broader extraterritorial movement of religious revivalism. Edwards's developing transatlantic association with Erskine derived from a similar perception of parochialism in the religious culture of New England. To be sure, the roots of his disappointment in Congregational ecclesiology appeared several decades before his relationship began with the evangelical wing of the Scottish Kirk. Nonetheless, Edwards's developing unease with public covenanting identity was strengthened by his dialogue with Popular party opponents of parochial religion. He increasingly warned that locally or regionally defined moral norms risked obscuring the importance of a personal salvation experience, which applied to all beings.[31]

Edwards never felt the need to abandon or denigrate his specific Congregational identity when he outlined his vision of evangelical revivalism. Rather, he sought a balance between the specific and the universal, as was clearly articulated in his desire for joint religious awakenings between Presbyterians and Congregationalists on both sides of the Atlantic. In his 1747 *Humble Attempt to Promote Explicit Agreement and Visible Union of God's People,* Edwards outlined his vision of a transatlantic "Concert for Prayer" — a confederation of separate denominations that were united by their common focus on salvation and rebirth. In seeking to "promote the *Increase, Concurrency* and *Constancy*" of a union of prayer, several ministers used their pref-

---

173; Mitchell, "Jonathan Edwards's Scottish Connection," in Kling and Sweeney, eds., *Jonathan Edwards at Home and Abroad,* 234.

31. On the evangelical critique of Moderates as parochial, see Ned C. Landsman, "Witherspoon and the Problem of Provincial Identity in Scottish Evangelical Culture," in Richard B. Sher and Jeffrey R. Smitten, eds., *Scotland and America in the Age of the Enlightenment* (Princeton, N.J., 1990), 33–34. For the global evangelical motivations tying Edwards together with Erskine, see Yeager, *Enlightened Evangelicalism,* 11–15, 20–26; O'Brien, "A Trans-Atlantic Community of Saints," *AHR,* XCI (1986), 811–832; G. D. Henderson, "Jonathan Edwards and Scotland," in Henderson, *The Burning Bush: Studies in Scottish Church History* (Edinburgh, 1957), 151–162; Joseph A. Conforti, *Jonathan Edwards, Religious Tradition, and American Culture* (Chapel Hill, N.C., 1995), 67–68; Ned C. Landsman, *From Colonials to Provincials: American Thought and Culture, 1680–1760* (New York, 1997), 110–116. On Edwards's movement beyond public covenanting identity, see Grasso, *A Speaking Aristocracy,* 24–28, 129–135.

ace to the published version of Edwards's *Humble Attempt* to define the intention "both of the pious *Memorial* of our reverend and dear *Brethren* in *Scotland*" and of like-minded figures in North America and elsewhere. In the main text, Edwards went on to argue that for "God's People in distant Places to agree on certain Times for extraordinary Prayer" allowed a "visible" "Outpouring of the Spirit" that made the period for revival more important than the fixed place in which it might occur. Edwards defined the covenant of grace irrespective of the public moral context in any community. Local or even national covenants, conversely, favored birth into a specific community over the universality of sin. Edwards advised New Englanders, as another provincial people in the British Empire, to eschew any notion that they had received a special public blessing. They would be better served promoting visible and reliable manifestations of faith, regeneration, and personal salvation.[32]

Edwards's Scottish correspondent John Erskine reasserted a similar vision of provincial evangelicalism. Sin and the necessity of salvation, he pointed out, transcended local populations and civic contexts. In a letter of October 14, 1748, Edwards wrote to Erskine, lauding those who were "united in the Concert for Prayer . . . in this province, and other provinces in America." He then stated: "I hope, dear Sir, you will continue still to give me particular informations of things that appear, relating to the state of Zion and the interests of religion, in Great Britain or other parts of Europe. In so doing you will not only inform me, but I shall industriously communicate any important informations of that kind, and spread them amongst God's people in this part of the world." Edwards superimposed the constitutional history of Puritan New England onto Scotland's experience after the Act of Union.

32. Edwards, *An Humble Attempt to Promote Explicit Agreement and Visible Union of God's People in Extraordinary Prayer: For the Revival of Religion and the Advancement of Christ's Kingdom on Earth, Pursuant to Scripture-Promises and Prophecies concerning the Last Time* (Boston, 1747), iii (preface), 92. On Edwards's proposed transatlantic meeting, see Landsman, *From Colonials to Provincials,* 110–116; Conforti, *Jonathan Edwards,* 67–68; Crawford, *Seasons of Grace,* 228–231. On Edwards's providential reading of history, see Avihu Zakai, *Jonathan Edwards's Philosophy of History: The Reenchantment of the World in the Age of Enlightenment* (Princeton, N.J., 2003), 1–26. According to Noll, Edwards endeavored to shift his New England community's covenanting ideology "away from the complex nexus of person, church, and society to a simpler bond between the converted individual and the church"; see Noll, *America's God,* 45. Edwards's theological stance during the late 1740s can be described as "Deuteronomic" in its distinction between denominations and geographical contexts without privileging any one over the other. See Grasso, *A Speaking Aristocracy,* 34, 38, 130; Landsman, *From Colonials to Provincials,* 113.

He suggested that the independence given to Scottish evangelicalism in the new British polity had been similar to that granted to Puritanism in the incorporated British Empire. The joint action of dissenting Scots and New Englanders did not negate their own separate denominational cultures. By 1750, Edwards felt comfortable claiming that there was no "such notion of owning the Covenant any where in the Christian world but in this Corner of it here in New England" and that "the Great part of the Country has forgotten the meaning of their forefathers and have gradually brought in a notion of owning the Covenant of Grace without pretending to profess a compliance."[33]

Public covenanting ideology was especially problematic for Edwards because it eschewed what he viewed as the inevitable — and necessary — struggle to assure the truth of regeneration. Tensions and ambiguities regarding the nature of true virtue were always likely to accompany the path toward a true personal salvation experience. As part of their personal struggle, therefore, Edwards challenged individuals to ask themselves whether their piety in fact derived from an egotistical desire for public esteem. In his view, membership in a public covenant contributed to false assurance because it preceded and even negated the importance of moral introspection. It removed the impetus to acknowledge and account for the manifestation of sin individually. Yet Edwards also suggested that trained clergymen in congregations and colleges were required to verify the personal experience of piety. Rather than confirming laymen's accordance to preconceived public norms, Edwards's ideal minister helped them navigate their distinct and personal ethical struggles.[34]

Notwithstanding Edwards's synthesis between clerical authority and lay piety, publicly defined moral privileges continued to remain important to many Congregationalists, perhaps even a majority, by the mid-1750s. Incompatible understandings of covenanting theology became more visibly divergent in Edwards's evangelical sphere. His opponents did not explicitly object to his preaching on the universality of sin and the common necessity of salvation. More prosaically, they were aware that their social and religious standing was grounded in their confirmation of public moral ideals. Poignantly, members of Edwards's own congregation came to resent his assertion that

33. Edwards to John Erskine, Oct. 14, 1748, in Edwards, *Letters and Personal Writings,* ed. George S. Claghorn, in Miller et al., eds., *Works of Jonathan Edwards,* XVI (New Haven, Conn., 1998), 260; Jonathan Edwards, "Sermon on Ezek. 44:9," cited in Grasso, *A Speaking Aristocracy,* 123. On Edwards's reasoning on the "Concert for Prayer," see also Landsman, *From Colonials to Provincials,* 113–114; Landsman, "Presbyterians and Provincial Society," in Dwyer and Sher, eds., *Sociability and Society,* 194–195.

34. On the ambiguity over the issue of ministerial assurance, see Grasso, *A Speaking Aristocracy,* 105–106, 124–128.

individual regeneration required clerical assurance. In their view, it diminished the importance of their public blessing as Massachusetts Congregationalists. The council of the congregation of Northampton parish eventually voted to remove Edwards from his pastoral authority. The church members ratified the council by a vote of more than two hundred to twenty-three. Finally, a town meeting voted to dismiss Edwards from his Northampton pulpit. He continued to live in the town and preach in the church (supported by the congregation until October 1751). Some future New England theologians would understand the wider meaning of Edwards's dismissal. A number continued to confirm parochial forms of public religious identity, thereby reducing tensions within their own parishes.[35]

Soon after his dismissal, Edwards received letters of support from his Scottish Presbyterian friends. He responded to invitations from Scottish clergymen to take up a position in one of their congregations: "As to my subscribing to the substance of the Westminster Confession," Edwards noted, "there would be no difficulty." Though he highlighted the logistical impossibility of moving across the Atlantic with his family, Edwards clarified that, in principle, "as to the Presbyterian government, I have long been perfectly out of conceit with our unsettled, independent, confused way of church government in this land [New England]. And the Presbyterian way has ever appeared to me most agreeable to the Word of God, and the reason and nature of things, though I cannot say that I think that the Presbyterian government of the Church of Scotland is so perfect that it can't, in some respects, be mended." Were it not for familial logistics, Edwards wrote, "My own country is not so dear to me, but that if there were an evident prospect of being more serviceable to Zion's interests elsewhere, I could forsake it." Here Edwards reflected the political theology of his earlier *Humble Attempt:* a fluid vision of the interests of piety and revival, potentially shifting from one province to another.[36]

During this period, Witherspoon and his colleagues continued to complain that Moderate clergymen prevented evangelical ministers from taking up new parishes and teaching positions. Yet the minority status of existing

35. On the dismissal of Edwards, see Marsden, *Jonathan Edwards,* 360–364. On Edwards's covenanting language and his parishioners' failure to grasp its theological meaning, see Noll, *America's God,* 45; E. Brooks Holifield, *The Covenant Sealed: The Development of Puritan Sacramental Theology in Old and New England, 1570–1720* (New Haven, Conn., 1974), 228–229. For a nuanced account of the continuation of public covenanting ideology during and after Edwards's death (it was by no means dominant), see Grasso, *A Speaking Aristocracy,* 67–85, 124–126.

36. Edwards to John Erskine, July 5, 1750, in Edwards, *Letters and Personal Writings,* ed. Claghorn, in Miller et al., eds., *Works of Jonathan Edwards,* XVI, 355.

Popular party ministers was not threatened in the way of Edwards. Though few in number, the congregations they directed tended to support their assertion that regeneration was contingent on faith rather than church membership or regional location. They often encountered laymen (generally in western Scotland) who were unthreatened by the notion that Presbyterian piety could shift and move from place and context. Given the commercial and migratory orientation of their communities, which moved and traded in increasing numbers from Scotland to North America through the mid-eighteenth century, such a phenomenon is unsurprising.[37]

Edwards, conversely, had been unable to count on a vocal minority of evangelical supporters in Northampton. It is probable that these distinctions informed his eventual decision to take up the presidency of the College of New Jersey. He was well aware that many of the students he encountered were likely to be migrants or descendants from the very regions that Erskine and Witherspoon ministered and that the founders of the college had contributed to the movement of transatlantic revivalism during the previous decade. After his son-in-law Aaron Burr, Sr., died in 1757, therefore, Edwards was persuaded to accept the presidency of the institution. Though his perceived ill health made Edwards wary of such a position, he arrived in January and took up his official role on February 16, 1758.[38]

Edwards had proposed his "concert" between Congregationalists and Presbyterians only a few months after the College of New Jersey was granted its official status as an institution of higher education. It seems fitting, therefore, that the college's early founders and associates were intimately connected to the movement of transatlantic evangelicalism between Scotland, Ireland, and America; that a good number were transplanted Presbyterians with roots in Congregational New England (including Dickinson); and that future presidents would include an evangelical Congregational theologian from New England (Edwards, 1758) and an evangelical Presbyterian minis-

37. Through the 1750s and into the 1760s, Witherspoon's fellow Popular party members continued to define the relationship between confederal religious authority and wider political unionism. They contrasted their definition with Moderate parochialism and expanded it to include the constitutional freedom to promote Presbyterian revivalism in the North American provinces. Yet they also continued to claim that covenanting evangelicalism was united *in* time rather than *by* local place or denomination. See McIntosh, *Church and Theology*, 1–125; Landsman, "Witherspoon and the Problem of Provincial Identity," in Sher and Smitten, eds., *Scotland and America*, 29–33.

38. Edwards was elected president of the College of New Jersey on September 29, 1757, five days after the death of his son-in-law, Aaron Burr, Sr., the college's second president. See Marsden, *Jonathan Edwards*, 493–494.

ter from Scotland (Witherspoon, 1768–1794). The charter of the College of New Jersey was unique in the colonies in its specification that "any Person of any religious Denomination whatsoever" might attend—even while the institution catered primarily to Presbyterians and incorporated theological teaching in specifically Presbyterian values. Though Edwards died from the effects of a smallpox inoculation only a few weeks into his post, therefore, the theological and pedagogical associations that led to his appointment tell us much about the nature and influence of the institution before Witherspoon's arrival: how it negotiated connections between Congregationalists and Presbyterians and between Scotland and America; how it connected evangelicals who remained interested in formal ecclesiology and the assurance of faith through higher education; and why Benjamin Rush would soon define its presidency as central to the continuation of religious revivalism among several denominations.[39]

"Alas! How Are the Principles of Liberty Abused!"

By the time of Edwards's death, the founding synthesis between evangelicalism and formal instruction in the College of New Jersey had contributed to a growing rapprochement between Old Side and New Side Presbyterians. During the 1750s, the college had managed to attract students and supporters from evangelical as well as more traditional presbyteries in the Middle Colonies and the South. As a result, a link can be drawn between the growing moral and cultural authority of the institution and the 1758 "Plan of Union" between hitherto divided presbyteries. When it came to their support for institutional authority, Old Side minsters had become slightly less distinct from New Side ministers than they had initially liked to claim.[40]

During the period in which the Plan of Union was enacted, Samuel Davies assumed the presidency of the College of New Jersey. He was the son of Welsh immigrants to Delaware, and his mother is thought to have converted from a Baptist background. He received his early education under the Reverend Samuel Blair in Faggs Manor, Pennsylvania, after which he was licensed to preach by the New Side Presbytery of New Castle in 1746 and the New Side Synod of New York. He was ordained as an evangelist to Vir-

39. *Charters of the College of New Jersey, October 22, 1746 and September 14, 1748*, in Thomas Jefferson Wertenbaker, *Princeton, 1746–1896* (Princeton, N.J., 1946), 402.

40. For such a link, see, for example, Leigh Eric Schmidt, "Jonathan Dickinson and the Making of the Moderate Awakening," *American Presbyterians: Journal of Presbyterian History*, LXIII (1985), 341–353.

FIGURE 8. *Samuel Davies (1723–1761), Hon. A.M. 1753, President (1759–61).* 1874.
By James Massalon. Oil on canvas. Princeton University Art Museum / Art Resource, N.Y.

ginia in early 1747, where he acted as a minister for dissenting Protestants in
Hanover County, including nascent Presbyterian communities. He became
a leader of Virginia's growing Presbyterian community during the late 1740s
and 1750s. As one of the colony's first published poets, he described the central tenets of Presbyterian evangelicalism in stanzas yearning for "Pardon
from an offended God!" Davies came to believe that the expression of "grace
so rich and free" was constrained by the close association between Anglican

ministers and the political establishment of Virginia. Allied with members of Virginia's Governor's Council and House of Burgesses, Anglicans accused dissenters of ignoring the benefits of communal order through the indulgence of personal piety. Evangelical Baptists and Presbyterians, conversely, opposed Anglican civic authority using a similar classical motif. Davies and his associates highlighted the importance of communal identity and public spiritedness. But they linked those ideals to revivalism and the mutual acceptance of grace.[41]

Having accused Virginia's Anglican establishment of feigning morality through educated erudition, Davies noted a similar phenomenon on an extended visit to Scotland in 1753. He had traveled to the British Isles with Gilbert Tennent on a mission to raise funds and preach. Noting the confluence between transatlantic evangelicalism and commercial enterprise, he set out to convince Presbyterian congregations that the fate of the College of New Jersey was a concern for all pious men. He confided in his diary that "'tis but little that so useless a creature can do for God, during the short day of life; but to be instrumental in laying a foundation of extensive benefit to mankind, not only in the present but in future generations, is a most animating prospect." Once again, Davies combined Calvinist evangelicalism with classical accounts of civic utility, making useless creatures of some use to future societal generations.[42]

Nonetheless, Davies, during his English and Scottish meetings, wrote of his disappointment that so many of the Protestant clergymen on either side of Hadrian's Wall had "generally imbibed Arminian or Socinian sentiments, that it is hard to unite prudence and faithfulness in conversation with them." "They deny the proper divinity and satisfaction of Jesus Christ, on which my hopes are founded. They ascribe a dignity and goodness to human nature in its present state, contrary to my daily sensations: and they are not so dependent upon divine influences as I find I must be." His July 28 diary entry offered a contrast between the latter theological approach and his own emotional evangelical method. He recalled having "had a more lively flow of spirits" since visiting the northern English town of Leeds, yet having also

41. On Davies's early education, see Wertenbaker, *Princeton,* 11; William Henry Foote, *Sketches of Virginia: Historical and Biographical,* I (Philadelphia, 1850), 108. Davies's poetic hymns were first printed in 1769. See the stanza extracts in the discussion by Noll, *America's God,* 26. On Davies, see also George William Pilcher, *Samuel Davies: Apostle of Dissent in Colonial Virginia* (Knoxville, Tenn., 1971). For the famous narrative of strife in Virginia, see Rhys Isaac, *The Transformation of Virginia, 1740–1790* (Chapel Hill, N.C., 1999), 161–198.

42. For Davies's diary entries, see Foote, *Sketches of Virginia,* I, 259.

become so "confused in the prayer before sermon" that he had felt "obliged to break off abruptly" lest his discourse become muddled. Eventually he recovered his "senses, and spoke with unexpected freedom . . . . [having] emerge[d] so suddenly out of darkness and confusion . . . body and mind better disposed to act the orator." Here Davies demonstrated the importance of channeling prayer, senses, and emotions in religious discourse, rather than relying on purely rational preparation. Such an example added weight to his "matter of complaint" regarding some of the English and Scottish Presbyterian ministers he had also recently met: "that the deists generally, if not universally, are of the Whig-party, and join station with the gentlemen of the new [Arminian] scheme. . . . My the Low-Churchmen. Alas! how are the principles of liberty abused!"[43]

Six years before he assumed the presidency of the College of New Jersey, therefore, Davies had begun to think more deeply about the association between Presbyterian evangelicalism and higher education. He perceived a problematic relationship between "Arminian" theology and political connections at the same time and in the same place that Witherspoon criticized Moderate churchmen for their debt to patronage. While in Scotland, Davies found "a great number of the clergy and laity" to "have of late carried church-power to an extravagant height, deny to individuals the right of judging for themselves, and insist upon absolute universal obedience to all the determinations of the General Assembly." The "nobility and gentry who are layelders," Davies continued, "are generally high-flyers: and have encroached upon the rights of the people, especially as to the choice of their own ministers. . . . There is a piece published under the title of the Ecclesiastical Characteristics, ascribed to one Mr. Weatherspoon, a young minister. It is a burlesque upon the high-flyers under the ironical name of *moderate men*."[44]

After his return to America, Davies was eventually incorporated into the fixed institutional and pedagogical culture of the College of New Jersey. Though he remained cautious about any direct association between political and religious institutions, he believed that higher education provided each sphere with virtuous and humble men. In 1760, he praised the "college of NEW-JERSEY, [which,] though an infant institution, is of the utmost importance to the interests of religion and learning in several extensive and populous colonies [because from] it both church and state expect to be supplied with persons properly qualified for public stations." He lauded the "publick Spirit" that could be found in classical literature and attempted to define

43. Ibid., 259, 262, 267–268.
44. Ibid., 262

their complementary role alongside revivalist piety. He reminded his graduating class of 1760 that, "if you feel the generous Impulses of a publick Spirit,
you can never be altogether insignificant, you will never be mere Cyphers
in the World" and then implored them: "IMBIBE AND CHERISH A PUBLICK
SPIRIT. Serve your generation. Live not for yourselves, but the Publick. Be
the Servants of the Church; the Servants of your Country; the Servants of
all." Here Davies avoided the assertion that communal benevolence innately
followed the natural law of all men. Adding a further evangelical emphasis,
therefore, he ended his graduating sermon by linking societal worth with
religious rebirth, asking students to "sink deep into" their hearts that "THE
NEW BIRTH IS THE BEGINNING OF ALL GENUINE RELIGION AND VIRTUE;
it is your first Entrance into a new World of Usefulness." Sadly, he died soon
after his appointment as president, in 1761. But having set out his vision of
the association between classical and evangelical virtue, that which led up to
his presidency nonetheless tells us much about the nature of the institution
on the eve of Witherspoon's arrival.[45]

Samuel Finley (1715–1766), a revivalist minister who had come to reside
in Nottingham, Maryland, was named as the new president. That he also
maintained southern associations demonstrated the growing appeal of the
College of New Jersey to communities outside the Middle Colonies. The
college's attempted synthesis between revivalism and formal instruction appealed to New Englanders such as Edwards as well as southern Presbyterians from Davies and Finley's constituencies. Finley was born in County
Armagh, Ireland. He moved to Philadelphia and is thought to have studied
with William Tennent in Neshaminy, before moving to Nottingham, Maryland. Though he often moved from town to town as an evangelical preacher,
he also founded an academy modeled on Tennent's Log College, affiliated
with his local Maryland church. In association with the Presbyterian Society of Milford, Connecticut, moreover, he was prosecuted in August 1743
for supposedly preaching without the consent of the existing pastor and the
majority of the local population. Some local Congregational strictures (many

45. Samuel Davies, "A Farewell Sermon, Addressed to the Presbyterian Congregation in
Hanover, Virginia, July 1, 1759, on the Author's Removal to the College in New Jersey," in *Sermons on Important Subjects*, ed. Albert Barnes (New York, 1849), III, 480; Samuel Davies, *Religion and Public Spirit: A Valedictory Address to the Senior Class, Delivered in Nassau-Hall, September 21, 1760* ... (Portsmouth, N.H., 1762), 6–7, 13. Davies was one of many early Presbyterian
educators who drew from their experience in log colleges and private academies and "assumed
that [only] a converted ear would express itself" in public rather than private works. See Douglas
Sloan, *The Scottish Enlightenment and the American College Ideal* (New York, 1971), 50–51. On
Davies's brief presidency and his final sermons, see also McLachlan, ed., *Princetonians*, I, xxiii.

of which Jonathan Edwards had opposed) thus did curtail Presbyterian revivalism in their realm.[46]

Notwithstanding various constraints on their revivalism during the 1740s and 1750s, Edwards, Davies, and Finley were still able to contribute to the founding of a college without abandoning their evangelical principles. Moreover, they were able to witness a growing rapprochement between Old and New Side Presbyterians. A similar rapprochement between Moderates and evangelicals in the Scottish Kirk was not witnessed by Witherspoon, the college trustees' prime candidate for president after Finley's death in 1766. By the late 1750s, Witherspoon and his evangelical colleagues remained an oppositional faction in an existing ecclesiastical system. Only a small minority of the Popular party taught in Scottish institutions of higher education. The faculty of the University of Glasgow retained several teachers with evangelical associations. But there was no Scottish precedent for the founding of a major educational institution according to revivalist principles. Restrictions on the relationship between higher education and evangelicalism continued to inspire Witherspoon in his critique of Moderate Presbyterian culture during the 1750s and early 1760s. Moderatism, he argued, squandered the impetus that had been provided by transatlantic revivalism. The College of New Jersey, conversely, tied evangelical ideals to its institutional setting at precisely that same moment.[47]

"Wetherspoon's Name Dwelt upon Every Tongue"

Benjamin Rush, in his effort to recruit Witherspoon as the College of New Jersey's new president, highlighted Witherspoon's failure to advance in the church and university establishment of Scotland. He claimed that the college offered a more promising context for Witherspoon's progression as an evangelical Presbyterian, away from Kirk factionalism. Yet most evidence suggests that the trustees of the college looked to a candidate from outside their

46. See the account of Finley's arrest in Samuel W. S. Dutton, *The History of the North Church in New Haven, from Its Formation in May 1742* . . . (New Haven, Conn., 1842), 45–46; Richard Webster, *A History of the Presbyterian Church in America* . . . (Philadelphia, 1857), 489. For the details on Finley's career, see also Leitch, *A Princeton Companion*, 181–182; "Samuel Finley, D.D.," in William B. Sprague, *Annals of the American Pulpit; or, Commemorative Notices of Distinguished American Clergymen of Various Denominations* . . . , 9 vols. (New York, 1859–1869), III, 96–101; Noll, *America's God*, 25.

47. On the Glasgow faculty at this point, see Roger L. Emerson, *Academic Patronage in the Scottish Enlightenment: Glasgow, Edinburgh, and St. Andrews Universities* (Edinburgh, 2008), 95–110.

FIGURE 9. *Nassau Hall, a North West Prospect* (The College of New Jersey, circa 1764). By Jonathan Fisher. 1807, after engraving circa 1764. Oil on canvas. Princeton University Art Museum / Art Resource, N.Y.

realm precisely because they detected a resurgence of faction and rancor in and around the campus. Internal tensions in the College of New Jersey resurfaced during the mid-1760s in a debate among faculty members and trustees about the best means to counter Anglican influences in the region. Some suggested an expedient strategy to reassert the college's appeal to nonrevivalist Presbyterian influences. Doing so, they believed, would counter even more moderate Anglican norms in the civil and religious culture of the Middle Colonies. Before sending Rush on his mission, therefore, college trustees had wondered whether to build upon and increase the Old Side role in their institution.[48]

The college trustees sought to enlist further Old Side Presbyterians as a subtle buffer against any greater threat from the Church of England in New Jersey and in neighboring colonies. They might have been more moderate, but at least they were not Anglican. Some suggested that Francis Alison

48. For the reference to "Wetherspoon's name" upon "every tongue," see Rush to Witherspoon, Apr. 30, 1768, in Butterfield, ed., *Letters of Benjamin Rush*, I, 59 (Rush is quoting Reverend George Duffield to Mr. Beatty). On the reassertion of tensions between New and Old Sides in Princeton, despite the Plan of Union, and the context for Witherspoon's appointment as president, see L. H. Butterfield, ed., *John Witherspoon Comes to America: A Documentary Account Based Largely on New Materials* (Princeton, N.J., 1953), 1–4; Collins, *President Witherspoon*, I, 75–78.

would provide a good fit as president given his role as a moderate professor of moral philosophy in Philadelphia. Yet these requests and exchanges resurrected older Presbyterian divisions. Alison was thought by some to be a step too far away from the New Side ideal, and a number of faculty members came to perceive his potential appointment as a Trojan horse for the entry of latitudinarian religious influences into their institution. In a letter to Jonathan Bayard Smith, indeed, Benjamin Rush thanked him for corroborating his view of the "schemes" that had been enacted by "Governor Franklin . . . [and] Dr. Allison . . . with regard to the College."[49]

Following the death of Samuel Finley, then, internal discussions among college trustees were unlikely to allude to any contrast between colonial tranquillity and Scottish discord. Rather, they decided that a president from outside the colonies would be most appropriate to reassert harmony between traditionalists and revivalists, as had been gained during the Plan of Union. Several college trustees proposed Witherspoon, suggesting that his experience in Scotland would make him an ideal candidate to heal divisions. Witherspoon had never opposed pedagogical guidance for those who grappled with understanding the universal nature of sin, the unregenerate state, and the association between divine grace and an awakened ethical sensibility. He had avoided the radical excesses of evangelicalism during the Cambuslang revival in western Scotland, preferring instead to promote Presbyterian revivalism from within the infrastructure of the Kirk. Thus, college trustees hoped that his role as an evangelical in a fixed ecclesiastical establishment would remind faculty members and trustees of their own founding synthesis between established pedagogical authority and experimental piety.[50]

Nonetheless, it is surprising that Witherspoon was perceived by trustees as their ideal candidate. In their view, a minister from abroad would have an easier time transcending Presbyterian divisions in America. Yet Witherspoon's public reputation hardly centered on the transcendence of divisions. The Boston Unitarian minister Dr. John Lathrop made known his surprise after he heard the rumor that the College of New Jersey desired Witherspoon as president. He recalled Witherspoon's satire of Moderate Presbyte-

---

49. Rush to Jonathan Bayard Smith, Apr. 30, 1767, in Butterfield, ed., *Letters of Benjamin Rush*, I, 42. On the perceived Anglican threat to the institution, Alison's role, and the move toward Witherspoon, see Collins, *President Witherspoon*, I, 76–78; Butterfield, ed., *John Witherspoon Comes to America*, 15–16.

50. On the idea that Witherspoon could heal divisions, see Butterfield, ed., *John Witherspoon Comes to America*, 1–5. On the curriculum at the College of New Jersey at this point, see Collins, *President Witherspoon*, II, 83–90.

rianism in his *Ecclesiastical Characteristics* and remarked that its account of Kirk divisions demonstrated similarities with developments closer to home in colonial America. He wrote to a friend: "I really hope and believe you will prove a warm defender of the Gospel. . . . I am sorry, in these days of delusion, to hear so many plead for moderation. Pray have you read Dr. Witherspoon's Characteristics? If you have, you will find many characters in this part of the world painted out very exactly."[51]

The trustees seem to have ignored or been unaware of the similarities perceived by Lathrop. Witherspoon's use of learning and rhetoric in his sermons and published theological treatises led them to conclude that more traditional Presbyterians would be mollified by his educated style, even if they did not share all aspects of his evangelical stance. The New Jersey trustees elected Witherspoon to the position of president on November 19, 1766. After hearing the news from college representative Richard Stockton, Witherspoon and his wife Elizabeth reacted with hesitancy, even unwillingness. Benjamin Rush attempted his own rhetorical maneuver in a March letter to Witherspoon: "Should you refuse the call they [All America] would look upon the dispensations of Providence towards that college as more gloomy and mysterious than ever they have been."[52]

Only after Witherspoon's initial decline did Rush warn of developing factionalism in American Presbyterian culture, which would worsen in his absence. As a man who saw himself as "pretty well acquainted with the characters of most of our eminent clergymen in America," Rush wrote to Witherspoon in April 1767 in order to warn of the consequences if Francis Alison were elected to the college presidency. Alison, according to Rush, was "an enemy to vital religion." The "grief and vexation" of some trustees following his election would "be proportioned to their former hopes" regarding Witherspoon. In August 1767, Witherspoon wrote to Rush. Despite his "greatest Anxiety," he had set about persuading his wife to make the move to New Jersey. In December 1767, having heard that Witherspoon had decided to accept their initial offer, the trustees reconfirmed their first recommendation. Rush informed Witherspoon that his news had "banished" the

51. John Lathrop to Rev. Ebenezer Baldwin, June 28, 1768, in Sprague, *Annals of the American Pulpit*, VIII, 71.

52. On the election of Witherspoon, see William Peartree Smith to Witherspoon, Nov. 19, 1766, in Butterfield, ed., *John Witherspoon Comes to America*, 7–8. On the hesitancy of Witherspoon and his wife, see Collins, *President Witherspoon*, I, 81–84. For Rush's statements on "All America" awaiting Witherspoon's response, see Rush to Witherspoon, Mar. 25, 1767, in Butterfield, ed., *Letters of Benjamin Rush*, I, 33.

Higher Education

fears of many trustees, who could "once more exult and triumph in the prospect of seeing their darling seminary the bulwark of the religion and liberty of America."[53]

After an unsuccessful trip to attract Dutch ministers for his new college, Witherspoon landed in Philadelphia on August 7, 1768, accompanied by his wife Elizabeth and his five children: Ann, aged twenty; his seventeen-year-old son James, who for the previous four years had been studying at the University of Glasgow; his eleven-year-old son John; his nine-year-old daughter Frances; and his eight-year-old son David. (Five other children had not reached early childhood.) From there, they went to Princeton village, arriving at the end of the month.[54]

In his very first sermon on American soil, delivered in 1768 to a congregation of Presbyterians, Witherspoon pointed out: "Could we but think as we ought, of the great removal, which we are making from time to time, into an eternal state; the removal of our bodies, and the change of our scene of service from Europe to America, would appear altogether unworthy of notice." The movement of an individual body from Scotland to America was nothing compared with the necessary "removal of our bodies" associated by evangelicals with an "eternal state" that transcended bodies, denominations, and even nations. Witherspoon valued the particular history and ecclesiology of his own denomination. But, like Edwards and Dickinson before him, he also outlined a more universal evangelical vision. Rush promised Witherspoon

53. Rush to Witherspoon, Apr. 23, Dec. 29, 1767, in Butterfield, ed., *Letters of Benjamin Rush,* I, 36–37, 48; Witherspoon to Rush, Aug. 4, 1767, in Butterfield, ed., *John Witherspoon Comes to America,* 49. On the initial stages and logistics of Witherspoon's move from Scotland to America, see ibid., 12–17.

54. On Witherspoon's association with churches in the Netherlands, see Collins, *President Witherspoon,* I, 90–91; William Steven, *The History of the Scottish Church, Rotterdam* . . . (Edinburgh, 1832), 192. For reference to Witherspoon's twelve-week voyage and subsequent welcome in Philadelphia, see Collins, *President Witherspoon,* I, 102–103, citing the October 1768 issue of the *Scots Magazine.* According to the parish manuscript records of Beith and Paisley, cited by Collins, there were ten children by Witherspoon's first marriage to Elizabeth: "(1) Anne or Ann, born at Beith, July 23, 1749, died April 1, 1817, at Princeton, N.J.; (2) Christian, a daughter, born at Beith, August 13, baptised August 14, 1750, died at Beith, December 10, 1756; (3) James, born at Beith, November 17, 1751, died at Germantown, Pa., October 4, 1777; (4) Robert, born at Beith, April 3, 1753, died at Beith, July 1754; (5) Barbara, born at Beith, February 18, baptised February 20, 1756, died at Paisley, August 1, 1763; (6) John, born and baptised at Beith, July 29, 1757, died at sea, 1795 (?); (7) Frances, born at Paisley, August 16, baptised August 26, 1759, died December 14, 1784 at Charleston, S.C.; (8) David, born at Paisley, September 22, baptised September 27, 1760, died 1801; (9) George, born at Paisley, March, died at Paisley, July 27, 1762; (10) a son still-born at Paisley, June 16, 1763" (25).

that evangelical ideas would not arouse rancor or opposition in Princeton village. During his American career, however, they would contribute to tensions and dissension in a wider imperial context. Witherspoon's evangelicalism came to be associated with the civic identity of students such as James Madison and Aaron Burr, Jr., as they prepared to graduate amid increasing social and political strife.[55]

55. John Witherspoon, "The Success of the Gospel Entirely of God," in [Ashbel Green, ed.], *Works of The Rev. John Witherspoon, D.D.L.L.D. Late President of the College at Princeton, New-Jersey* . . . , 2d ed., rev., 4 vols. (Philadelphia, 1802), II, 585.

CHAPTER 4

"ALL THE CONCLUSIONS DRAWN FROM

THESE PRINCIPLES MUST BE VAGUE"

American Moral Philosophy after Witherspoon

In 1725, Francis Hutcheson suggested that "strong affections" excited the pursuit of virtuous action and could be understood self-consciously for the first time during youth. This was an impressionable phase, which Hutcheson's student Hugh Blair later described as a stage when "your character is now . . . of your own forming; your fate is, in some measure, put into your own hands. . . . Habits have not established their dominion. Prejudices have not pre-occupied your understanding." In 1741, Blair would become a minister, and in 1762 he would assume the first Regius Chair of Rhetoric and Belles Lettres at the University of Edinburgh, which he would hold until 1783. He learned from his former teacher and mentor that the senses were "every Determination of our Minds to receive Ideas independently on our Will, and to have Perceptions of Pleasure and Pain." Warm attachment between young men was portrayed by Blair in aesthetic terms: good deeds done by one individual to another were pre-rationally sensed as beautiful. He had also become influenced by new strains of Scottish common sense philosophy, which built on work by John Locke and Hutcheson in order to outline the interaction between primary sentiments and secondary reason. His writings would be widely disseminated in America during and after the Revolutionary era.[1]

1. For Hutcheson on the "strong affections" of moral sensibility, see Francis Hutcheson, *An Inquiry into the Original of Our Ideas of Beauty and Virtue* . . . , 2d ed. (London, 1726), xv. On the "Determination of our Minds," see [Hutcheson], *An Essay on the Nature and Conduct of the Passions and Affections; with Illustrations on the Moral Sense* (London, 1728), 4. See also David Fate Norton and Manfred Kuehn, "The Foundations of Morality," in Knud Haakonssen, ed., *The Cambridge History of Eighteenth-Century Philosophy*, 2 vols. (Cambridge, 2006), II, 954–958. For Hugh Blair on youthful sensibility, see Blair, "Sermon XI," in *Sermons by Hugh Blair, D.D.* . . . , new ed. (Dublin, 1784), I, 176; Blair, "On Taste," in *Essays on Rhetoric, Abridged Chiefly from Dr. Blair's Lectures on That Science,* 4th ed. (London, 1801), [1]. On Blair's popularity in the new American Republic, see Warren Alan Guthrie, "The Development of Rhetorical Theory in America, 1635–1850," *Speech Monographs*, XV (1948), 61–71; David Daiches, *"Style*

Many colonial American clergymen and educators, a good number of whom had transplanted from Scotland, saw few problems in highlighting their debt both to Hutchesonian moral philosophy and to newer strands of common sense reasoning. William Smith and Francis Alison, who taught at the College of Philadelphia (founded in 1755), felt comfortable with the proposition that ethical interactions between objects outside the mind could be perceived objectively. Moral sensitivity, they claimed, was as common to individuals as the sense of touch, sound, or smell. Influenced by Thomas Reid's more recent work in common sense philosophy, they also suggested, through the 1760s, that a primary sensory mechanism underlay the secondary rational response, which resided at the top of a pyramid of individual perceptual faculties. Individuals were able to trust the accuracy of their rational ideas because they were preceded and inspired by predictable, objective, and innate sensory reactions. Helping to develop a new program of moral learning at the College of Philadelphia, Alison and Smith proposed that inborn sensibility enabled individuals to understand the eminent reasonableness of revelation.[2]

Périodique and *Style Coupé:* Hugh Blair and the Scottish Rhetoric of American Independence," in Richard B. Sher and Jeffrey R. Smitten, eds., *Scotland and America in the Age of the Enlightenment* (Princeton, N.J., 1990), 209–226.

2. On Smith and Alison's program of moral philosophy, see David W. Robson, *Educating Republicans: The College in the Era of the American Revolution, 1750–1800* (Westport, Conn., 1985), 85–87; J. David Hoeveler, *Creating the American Mind: Intellect and Politics in the Colonial Colleges* (Lanham, Md., 2002), 155–180. Norman Fiering has suggested that Hutcheson was "probably the most influential and respected moral philosopher in eighteenth-century America." Hutchesonian philosophy, according to Henry May, "seemed to answer the questions Americans wanted to ask"—which is to say, they did not inquire too deeply about the ambiguous relationship between innate moral volition and external divinity among unregenerate men. See Norman Fiering, *Moral Philosophy at Seventeenth-Century Harvard: A Discipline in Transition* (Chapel Hill, N.C., 1981), 3, 53, 56, 199; Henry F. May, "The Problem of the American Enlightenment," in May, *Ideas, Faiths, and Feelings: Essays on American Intellectual and Religious History, 1952–1982* (New York, 1983), 19. On Reid and faculty psychology in America, see Daniel Walker Howe, *Making the American Self: Jonathan Edwards to Abraham Lincoln* (Cambridge, Mass., 1997), 65–67; Howe, "Why the Scottish Enlightenment Was Useful to the Framers of the American Constitution," *Comparative Studies in Society and History*, XXXI (1989), 572–587; Bruce Kuklick, *A History of Philosophy in America, 1720–2000* (New York, 2001), 9–15. On the dissemination of moral philosophy by Scottish tutors in colonial America, see Ned C. Landsman, *From Colonials to Provincials: American Thought and Culture, 1680–1760* (New York, 1997), 21–24. On the publication of Scottish philosophy in America, see Richard B. Sher, *The Enlightenment and the Book: Scottish Authors and Their Publishers in Eighteenth-Century Britain, Ireland, and America* (Chicago, 2006), 503–597.

The correspondence between Hutchesonian and Reidean thought makes the inclination to define the American reception of "Scottish philosophy" or even "Scottish Moderate philosophy" appear less crude. Ministers, educators, and writers might well have been erroneous or lacked nuance in their use of such associative indicators. Nonetheless, such descriptions should not be excluded from American intellectual history. The reception of complex and subtly related philosophies certainly led to the simplification and conglomeration of ideas. But as long as that process is examined on its own terms, scholars will accurately depict the intellectual encounter between American religious ministers and Scottish Enlightenment thinkers—including any misperception that it might have encompassed. The greater danger of scholarly imprecision relates to the attributed dominance of moral sensory ideas over other modes of Scottish thought in America, particularly the Presbyterian evangelicalism that Witherspoon brought with him to New Jersey.

An example of misperception in the encounter between colonial American and Scottish moral thinking can be found in a 1768 letter that Charles Chauncy wrote to Ezra Stiles, pastor of the Second Congregational Church in Newport, Rhode Island, and a future president of Yale. Chauncy, a chief proponent of moral sense reasoning in American Congregational circles, reported to Stiles that the new president of the College of New Jersey, John Witherspoon, was "no friend to the grand and distinguished Tenets of Mr. Edwards w[hi]ch have been almost universally imbibed in that part of the Country." Jonathan Edwards had died a decade earlier, shortly after assuming the presidency of the College of New Jersey. He had questioned the account of innate moral sensibility proposed by educated clergymen and educators in other colonies, including Chauncy. Witherspoon's colleagues in the Popular party of the Kirk had engaged in close and complementary dialogue with him, sharing his opposition to anthropocentric ethical claims. Yet, according to Chauncy's unsubstantiated statement, once Witherspoon became ensconced in his American scholarly setting, he sided with those who opposed Edwardsean evangelicalism.[3]

Chauncy was writing to a man whom historians have often portrayed as an educated "trinitarian Congregationalist"—a "gentle Puritan" who used

---

3. Charles Chauncy to Ezra Stiles, Nov. 7, 1768, cited in Varnum Lansing Collins, *President Witherspoon: A Biography*, 2 vols. (Princeton, N.J., 1925), I, 114. On Edwards's Scottish associations, see Christopher W. Mitchell, "Jonathan Edwards's Scottish Connection," in D. Sweeney, ed., *Jonathan Edwards at Home and Abroad: Historical Memories, Cultural Movements, Global Horizons* (Columbia, S.C., 2003), 223; Jonathan M. Yeager, *Enlightened Evangelicalism: The Life and Thought of John Erskine* (New York, 2011), 11–15, 20–26.

his erudition to mount a rational and common sensory defense of biblical authority and who had neither the time nor the inclination to ally with
Edwardsean evangelicals (unlike the ironic trajectory of Thomas Clap, a predecessor as Yale president). Stiles has thus been described as a true product
of the Yale Library, where he studied as a young man, "a child of the Enlightenment" who connected polite religious order to moral sense theory.
Yet Chauncy's friend did not always share his confidence in the innate moral
compass of men. At significant moments in his life, Stiles demonstrated confusion and even anxiety when he noted the tension between human-centered
discussions of ethical perception and the necessity of redemption, regeneration, atonement by Christ, and the role of the Holy Spirit as disclosed
through revelation.[4]

Witherspoon has most often been portrayed in a similarly enlightened
fashion to the Stiles of earlier historiography, a moderate Presbyterian alongside a moderate Congregationalist—even though such a scholarly depiction
no longer holds for Stiles and other ministers in his circle. Chauncy's statement to Stiles about Witherspoon was reproduced in a 1925 biography of the
College of New Jersey president and has since contributed to a degree of in-
accuracy in subsequent discussions of his moral philosophy. He has been defined as a clear conduit of Enlightenment thinking, and it has been suggested
that he promoted moral sense theory once he was settled in the American
academy despite his evident evangelical opposition to similar ideas during
his earlier Scottish career.[5]

4. Edmund Morgan, *The Gentle Puritan: A Life of Ezra Stiles, 1727–1795* (New Haven, Conn.,
1962), vii, 77, 177; Mark A. Noll, *America's God: From Jonathan Edwards to Abraham Lincoln*
(New York, 2002), 133–134. At points in his life, Stiles often used moral sensory language and
motifs without necessarily repudiating commonly held evangelical assumptions. For a nuanced
depiction of Stiles, including his place in historiography, see Christopher Grasso, *A Speaking
Aristocracy: Transforming Public Discourse in Eighteenth-Century Connecticut* (Chapel Hill,
N.C., 1999), 230–235, 237–238, 243, 245, 252–256. The career of Yale's Thomas Clap during the
late 1750s and early 1760s highlights the complex relationship between moral sense reasoning
and evangelicalism in colonial America immediately before Witherspoon's arrival. The Congregational rector of Yale allied with a number of revivalist ministers and teachers despite having once
disdained their evangelicalism. He came to discern a greater threat to his pedagogical authority
from moderate—perhaps "Arminian"—Anglican and Congregational clergymen in Connecticut's educational establishment. See ibid., 152–153.

5. For the connection between Witherspoon and Chauncy in the 1925 biography, see Collins,
President Witherspoon, I, 114. On Witherspoon as a "conduit" for moral sense philosophy, see
for example, Thomas P. Miller, *The Evolution of College English: Literacy Studies from the Puritans to the Postmoderns* (Pittsburg, Pa., 2010), 223; David VanDrunen, *Natural Law and the Two
Kingdoms: A Study in the Development of Reformed Social Thought* (Grand Rapids, Mich., 2010),

FIGURE 10. *Ezra Stiles (1727–1795) B.A. 1746, M.A. 1749.* By Samuel King (1748/49–1819). 1771. Oil on canvas, 34 x 28 x 1¼ in. (86.4 x 71.1 x 3.2 cm.). Bequest of Dr. Charles Jenkins Foote, B.A. 1883, M.D. 1890. 1955.3.1. Yale University Art Gallery, New Haven, Connecticut, U.S.A. Yale University Art Gallery / Art Resource, N.Y.

Focusing in particular on his "Lectures on Moral Philosophy" and his "Lectures on Divinity," which he wrote and delivered to his students from 1769 and which were published posthumously, scholars have posited that Witherspoon "turned Princeton philosophy away from the metaphysical idealism of his predecessor Jonathan Edwards and toward the common sense realism that became characteristic of Scottish and American academic philosophy for generations to come." Such an assertion aligns Witherspoon with the "moderate" and "didactic" aspect of the Enlightenment in America, adding to the notion that the Enlightenment partially derived from the dissemination of Scottish moral sense philosophy on the western side of the Atlantic. The clergyman is said to have moved toward an anthropocentric and apologetic notion of ethical perception, allowing the idea of innate moral sensibility to provide epistemological grounding for the confirmation of biblical ideals. Thus, his lectures have been examined for any allusions to moral sense reasoning or to the similar ethical faculties associated with a later school of Scottish common sense philosophy.[6]

269; Gordon Graham, "Scottish Philosophy Abroad," in Graham, ed., *Scottish Philosophy in the Nineteenth and Twentieth Centuries* (Oxford, 2015), 190. See also Daniel W. Howe, "John Witherspoon and the Transatlantic Enlightenment," in Susan Manning and Francis D. Cogliano, eds., *The Atlantic Enlightenment* (Aldershot, U.K., 2008), 61–80.

6. Howe, "John Witherspoon and the Transatlantic Enlightenment," in Manning and Cogliano, eds., *The Atlantic Enlightenment,* 65; John Witherspoon, "Lectures on Moral Philosophy," in [Ashbel Green, ed.], *The Works of the Rev. John Witherspoon, D.D.L.L.D. Late President of the College at Princeton, New-Jersey* . . . , 2d ed., rev., 4 vols. (Philadelphia, 1802), III, 367–472; Witherspoon "Lectures on Divinity," ibid., IV, 9–123. On the notion of moderate and didactic characteristics of the Enlightenment in America, see Henry F. May, *The Enlightenment in America* (New York, 1976), 12, 26–66, 177–197, 209, 346; Donald H. Meyer, *The Democratic Enlightenment* (New York, 1976), 32. May uses the words "moderate" and "liberal" to mean a measured stance that emphasized a compromise between religious and moral sense theories. For a discussion of the periodization of didactic and moderate aspects in the historiography of the American Enlightenment and its potential religious context (including through Witherspoon), see Mark A. Noll, "The Rise and Long Life of the Protestant Enlightenment in America," in William M. Shea and Peter A. Huff, eds., *Knowledge and Belief in America* (Cambridge, 1995), 92–95. In a number of influential essays and in his magisterial study *America's God,* Noll has outlined the nexus between Protestant apologetics and Scottish Enlightenment reasoning. See, for example, Noll, *America's God,* 8–9, 94–113; Noll, *Princeton and the Republic, 1768–1822: The Search for a Christian Enlightenment in the Era of Samuel Stanhope Smith* (Princeton, N.J., 1989), 43–44, 63–64; Noll, "Common Sense Traditions and American Evangelical Thought," *American Quarterly,* XXXVII (1985), 216–238. Roger L. Emerson and Paul Wood have challenged the centrality of moral philosophy in the Scottish Enlightenment program. In the historiography of American Enlightenment thought, similar challenges are far less common. See Emerson, "Science and the Origins and Concerns of the Scottish Enlightenment," *History of*

Reasserting the place of evangelical moral theory in Witherspoon's American lectures consequently unsettles his purported role as a key conduit of Scottish Enlightenment thought in America. Doing so also confounds assumptions about the inevitability of the association between Scottish moral sense reasoning and the emerging political languages of American patriot identity. Witherspoon wrote and began delivering his "Lectures on Moral Philosophy" and his "Lectures on Divinity" more than seven years before he signed the Declaration of Independence. Before assessing his contribution to patriot thought, then, it is necessary to consider their content more closely, including their comparison with more explicit moral sensory statements from clergymen and teachers in other newly chartered institutions, such as the College of Philadelphia (1754) and King's College, New York (1755).[7]

The nature of the association between Witherspoon's developing moral philosophy and the earlier values of the College of New Jersey founders, Samuel Finley, Samuel Davies, and Jonathan Edwards, needs reassessment as well. In many ways, Witherspoon continued their synthesis of evangelical moral theory and formal instruction, thereby highlighting the depth of his religious, intellectual, and civic influence. It is important to keep in mind that revivalism was not always antithetical to the conceptual terminology of moral sense theory, much like mainline Congregationalists such as Ezra Stiles were not entirely distanced from evangelicalism by the time Witherspoon arrived in America.

Edwards had always sought to remind colonists of a fundamental aspect of Calvinist religion: the moral chasm that remained between all men before the reception of divine grace. Moreover, he had been prone to use the language

Science, XXVI (1988), 333–366; Charles W. J. Withers and Wood, eds., *Science and Medicine in the Scottish Enlightenment* (East Lothian, U.K., 2002); David B. Wilson, *Seeking Nature's Logic: Natural Philosophy in the Scottish Enlightenment* (University Park, Pa., 2009).

7. Douglas Sloan has suggested that Witherspoon "promoted" both Hutcheson and Reid to American students when he claimed that "the old order" of social laws could legitimately "break up" and "recall their obligation, and resettle the whole upon a better footing" if they became destructive to commonly perceived moral norms. According to Sloan, such a statement demonstrated Witherspoon's debt to Hutcheson's *Illustration on the Moral Sense* and Thomas Reid's more recent formulation of a universal "common sense." See Sloan, *The Scottish Enlightenment and the American College Ideal* ([New York], 1971), 138–139; Witherspoon, "Lectures on Moral Philosophy," in [Green, ed.], *Works of Witherspoon,* III, 432. On Witherspoon's "Lectures on Moral Philosophy" and his "Lectures on Divinity," see Thomas Miller's useful introduction to his edited selection of some of Witherspoon's works, *The Selected Writings of John Witherspoon* (Carbondale, Ill., 1990), 36. Miller also notes that Witherspoon rejected Francis Hutcheson's "aesthetic" connection between virtue and morality.

and terminology of moral sense reasoning to describe conversion. During the latter part of his career, there were times when even Ezra Stiles used moral sensory vocabulary to assert revivalist ideals. He incorporated open and seemingly unanswerable questions of moral volition in his religious discussions, rather than portraying a starkly binary division between anthropocentric and evangelical notions of ethical perception. At points, he questioned the easy common sensory conclusions that were drawn by former Scots such as William Smith and Francis Alison at the College of Philadelphia.[8]

Similarly, easy distinctions between Witherspoon's early evangelical writings and his later references to British moral philosophy cannot be drawn. It is by no means clear that Witherspoon was required to abandon evangelicalism in order to engage the sentimental theories of Locke, Hutcheson, and Reid in America. John Rodgers, the 1802 editor of a number of Witherspoon's works, reported a conversation between Witherspoon and "the celebrated Dr. Robertson" of the University of Edinburgh. After a Popular party member had (mischievously) used the language of Moderate philosophy in an attempt to disprove the notion of innate virtue, Robertson is said to have remarked to Witherspoon, "I think you have your men better disciplined than formerly." "Yes," Witherspoon apparently replied, "by urging your politics too far, you have compelled us to beat you with our own weapons." In satirical publications such as *Ecclesiastical Characteristics* (1753), moreover, Witherspoon often deployed the language of Moderates against their own theoretical assumptions. A philosophical language that focused on sentiments and perception helped Witherspoon explain how individuals might come to terms with their sin through a passionate religious conversion and how a new sense of revealed morality could be implanted through grace in the regenerated heart. Yet scholars have disconnected that discursive tradition, which had been shared by Edwards, from Witherspoon's subsequent American lectures.[9]

---

8. Early proponents of the "New Divinity" movement ironically used the analytical motifs—and sometimes even the ethical ideas—of moral sense philosophy, whereas, conversely, Stiles made increasing reference to evangelicalism. See Grasso, *A Speaking Aristocracy*, 232–235; Noll, *America's God*, 131–138.

9. John Rodgers, "The Faithful Servant Rewarded: A Sermon . . . ," in [Green, ed.], *Works of Witherspoon*, I, 34; John Witherspoon, *Ecclesiastical Characteristics* . . . , ibid., III, 199–261. Examining Witherspoon's American moral philosophy alongside that of Edwards should enhance our understanding of an ironic aspect of post-Augustan evangelicalism, as described by David Bebbington. According to Michael A. G. Haykin's summary and assessment of Bebbington's thesis, the "empiricism of the [early] Enlightenment" allowed later theologians to "extend" its methodological terminology "to the spiritual realm" so that "direct experiences of God became

To be sure, many of Witherspoon's lectures attended to analytical concerns in an order that could be found in textbooks and treatises by Scottish moral philosophers such as David Fordyce, William Smellie, and Francis Hutcheson. But, without revelation, he also tended to claim, the human moral sense was "insufficient" to allow innate benevolence or even to understand the necessary human duty to divine precepts. Such a proviso did not require Witherspoon to ignore uncertainties that remained in the evangelical description of moral regeneration. Even among the faithful and the regenerate, human frailties were still likely to threaten objective understandings of scriptural morality. Like Edwards, Witherspoon defined ethics in Augustinian terms, as a continued struggle to verify the truth of faith and salvation. His lectures encompassed exasperating questions of moral will. Neither the use of sentimental terminology nor the expression of evangelical ideals could ever *truly* define an objective account of human ethical perception. These ambiguities have not received enough attention in the historiography of eighteenth-century American moral thought, however.[10]

---

regarded as trustworthy barometers of assurance." See Haykin, "Evangelicalism and the Enlightenment: A Reassessment," in Haykin and Kenneth J. Stewart, eds., *The Advent of Evangelicalism: Exploring Historical Continuities* (Nashville, Tenn., 2008), 51; D. W. Bebbington, *Evangelicalism in Modern Britain: A History from the 1730s to the 1980s* (London, 1989), 47–50.

10. Witherspoon, "Lectures on Divinity," in [Green, ed.], *Works of Witherspoon,* IV, 47. On Witherspoon's reference to Scottish moral philosophers in his lectures, see Sloan, *The Scottish Enlightenment,* 122. Witherspoon's lectures incorporated what Knud Haakonssen has described as "disturbing elements in the theoretical situation surrounding American ideas of rights" during the late colonial and Revolutionary era: "While it cannot be said that [Witherspoon] worked out the implications of his scattered objections to conventional [natural law] theory, these objections are of obvious importance" in questioning his reliance on Scottish Enlightenment theory from figures such as Hutcheson and Reid. See Haakonssen, "From Natural Law to the Rights of Man: A European Perspective on American Debates," in Michael J. Lacey and Haakonssen, eds., *A Culture of Rights: The Bill of Rights in Philosophy, Politics, and Law — 1791 and 1991* (Cambridge, 1991), 54. In addition to Haakonssen's pertinent analysis above, for studies that touch on Witherspoon's desire to maintain a more orthodox Calvinist form of virtue and duty in his moral philosophy, see also Roger J. Fechner, "The Godly and Virtuous Republic of John Witherspoon," in Hamilton Cravens, ed., *Ideas in America's Cultures: From Republic to Mass Society* (Ames, Iowa, 1982), 7–25; Ned C. Landsman, "Witherspoon and the Problem of Provincial Identity in Scottish Evangelical Culture," and Richard B. Sher, "Witherspoon's *Dominion of Providence* and the Scottish Jeremiad Tradition," both in Sher and Smitten, eds., *Scotland and America,* 29–45, 46–64; Knud Haakonssen, *Natural Law and Moral Philosophy: From Grotius to the Scottish Enlightenment* (Cambridge, 1996), 332–335; James McLean Albritton, "John Witherspoon's Moral Philosophy and American Church and State" (Ph.D. diss., University of Alabama, 2003).

Scholars have highlighted a body of Anglo-American and European thought that sought to establish theoretical order from the "contest[ed] diversity" of human experience. Though clerics and teachers might have differed over the details of epistemological understanding, they perceived their intellectual disagreements as part of a necessary dialectic at the heart of their Enlightenment project. Contradictions, tensions, and opposing ideas were not perceived as antithetical to the eventual evolution of a common philosophical sensibility. Witherspoon's account of philosophical diversity—including the contradiction between viewpoints—demonstrated a different motivation. It came closer to Edwards in its Augustinian claim that the human struggle for moral assurance continued through life. When the details of ethical epistemology seemed too difficult to resolve, or even too complex to elucidate, Witherspoon fell back on the basics of Calvinism. In his view, their irresolution demonstrated the common weakness of human understanding. They provided a useful frustration, even, with its own educational message.[11]

Locke, Franklin, and the Moral Powers of American Education

In order to understand the complex legacy of sensational philosophy in Witherspoon's American thought, it is appropriate to begin with the writings of John Locke because they deeply influenced the moral sensory ideas that Witherspoon interrogated in his New Jersey lectures. In his 1689 *Essay concerning Human Understanding,* Locke had offered the rather unsettling assertion that "the Idea of Substance" could not be defined accurately according to "Sensation or Reflection" and that individuals could "signify nothing

11. On "contesting" diversity, see Daniel Carey, *Locke, Shaftesbury, and Hutcheson: Contesting Diversity in the Enlightenment and Beyond* (Cambridge, 2006). Although those who followed Locke and Hutcheson have subsequently become associated with British Enlightenment thought, many did not feel the need to define their subscription to any specific theoretical system. David Daiches highlights the eclecticism in Witherspoon's New Jersey teaching method. See Daiches, "John Witherspoon, James Wilson, and the Influence of Scottish Rhetoric on America," in John Dwyer and Richard B. Sher, eds., *Sociability and Society in Eighteenth-Century Scotland* (Edinburgh, 1993), 170–171; Daiches, "*Style Périodique* and *Style Coupé,*" in Sher and Smitten, eds., *Scotland and America,* 209–226. Ned C. Landsman has outlined the varied philosophical schooling that Princeton students enjoyed. See Landsman, "The Provinces and the Empire: Scotland, the American Colonies, and the Development of British Provincial Identity," in Lawrence Stone, ed., *An Imperial State at War: Britain from 1689 to 1815* (London, 1994), 278. On the relatively broad curriculum at Princeton, see also Francis L. Broderick, "Pulpit, Physics, and Politics: The Curriculum of the College of New Jersey, 1746-1794," *William and Mary Quarterly,* 3d Ser., VI (1949), 42–68.

by the Word 'Substance' but only an uncertain Supposition of we know not what." Such a conjecture was taken "to be the Substratum, or Support of those Ideas, we do know." Defining the mind's tabula rasa, Locke continued: "All Ideas come from Sensation or Reflection"; "Let us then suppose the Mind to be, as we say, white Paper." The sensationalist model of the mind partially rejected the notion of innate ideas and insisted that all knowledge derived from sensory impressions through direct experience of the world. Lest readers fear that individuals were merely the product of their subjective sensations, however, a second aspect of Locke's argument defined the human capacity for reason. With enough learning and experience, he argued, the mind's rational capacity was primed to order sensory perceptions into fixed ideas.[12]

Locke connected his discussion of moral epistemology to repetitious learning more explicitly in *Some Thoughts concerning Education,* which he first published in 1693. Repeated printings and translations appeared throughout the following century, including on the western side of the Atlantic. Its reasoning built upon his earlier conception of the mind as tabula rasa. Learning, according to Locke, risked becoming contingent on the subjective whims of particular educators, potentially unsettling common moral norms. To counter this danger, Locke highlighted the importance of familial education before formal schooling. Offspring were encouraged to emulate parents so that they might find moral actions favorable to their own childish sense of reputation, which could then be channeled into positive social norms through "Reward and Punishment." Thus, Locke advised "parents and Governors always to carry this in their Minds, that they are to be treated as rational Creatures." Reason permitted youth to act morally because their developing egoism allowed them to conceive of the esteem that would follow their actions. Surprisingly, then, underlying Locke's support for the cultivation of reason was quite a bleak—even Calvinistic—vision of childish ego and individualism. Of course, Locke's discussion of the innate rational capacity in children also demonstrated the influence of natural law reasoning. Children could be taught to order, quash, or even repress sensory desires in light of the communal prestige they might then gain.[13]

12. John Locke, *An Essay concerning Human Understanding* . . . , 17th ed. (London, 1775), 60, 67.

13. John Locke, *Some Thoughts concerning Education* (London, 1693), 53–54, 116, 261 (see also 90–91). On Locke's appeal to childish prestige in Anglo-American educational philosophy, see Lorraine Smith Pangle and Thomas L. Pangle, *The Learning of Liberty: The Educational Ideas of the American Founders* (Lawrence, Kans., 1993), 60–64; Gillian Brown, *The Consent of*

During the mid-eighteenth century, the Scottish skeptic David Hume questioned the association between "Sensation or Reflection" and the secondary capacity of reason. He wondered provocatively whether consciousness merely conformed to a bundle of sensory perceptions. The awareness of external activities, he asserted, might derive from capricious feelings that were determined by the individual's directly sentient response to their arousing object. Humean skeptics argued that objective norms and ideas derived from a universal state of constant sensory perception. As a result, the static and inherent reality of those ideas would become impossible to prove. They were merely an approximation of sensory responses to external objects.[14]

Scottish moral sense theorists became increasingly wary of Hume's skeptical reading of Locke. They worried that it undermined the belief in a common understanding of the moral interaction between objects. The skeptical discussion of sensationalism threatened the notion of innate ideas and weakened the rational contractual model that could be drawn from the second part of Locke's philosophical system. Thus, Scottish Moderate philosophers offered a rejoinder to skeptical claims. In their view, a pre-rational and universal sensory response allowed the mind to trust its ethical perception of objective interactions and communal obligations.[15]

In their encounter with Lockean contractual theory, Moderate churchmen

---

the Governed: The Lockean Legacy in Early American Culture (Cambridge, Mass., 2001), 1–15. On the ability of the mind's rational capacity to order sensory perceptions into fixed ideas, and on religious aspects in the Lockean account of praise and blame, see Jeremy Waldron, *God, Locke, and Equality: Christian Foundations of John Locke's Political Thought* (Cambridge, 2002), 75, 112–116. As Geraint Parry has argued, according to Locke, "Merit and blame can be attached to persons because they are capable of rational reflection on their actions, which distinguishes humans from other beings in the order of nature." To "be effective," Lockean learning was to be "made pleasurable." The prospect of future esteem aroused a pleasing sensory response and made the repression of short-term desires less disagreeable. See Geraint Parry, "Education," in Haakonssen, ed., *Cambridge History of Eighteenth-Century Philosophy*, I, 608–612.

14. On Hume's arguments on the problematic association between sensation and reflection, see Udo Thiel, *The Early Modern Subject: Self-Consciousness and Personal Identity from Descartes to Hume* (New York, 2011), 404; Paul Russell, *The Riddle of Hume's Treatise: Skepticism, Naturalism, and Irreligion* (New York, 2008), 85–88; Michael L. Frazer, *The Enlightenment of Sympathy: Justice and the Moral Sentiments in the Eighteenth Century and Today* (New York, 2010), 73–74.

15. On Scottish moral sensory rejoinders to Humean skepticism, as defined by Thomas Reid, see James Fieser, ed., *Early responses to Hume's Moral, Literary, and Political Writings*, rev. ed., I (Bristol, 2005), 198–199; John Dunn, "From Applied Theology to Social Analysis: The Break between John Locke and the Scottish Enlightenment," in Istvan Hont and Michael Ignatieff, eds., *Wealth and Virtue: The Shaping of Political Economy in the Scottish Enlightenment* (Cambridge, 1983), 119–135.

and educators were by no means part of the radical and secular European Enlightenment that scholars have identified. Rather, they suggested that the infringement of certain rights ought to be punished by civic and legal authorities because they were ultimately a gift from God. Social contracts, they asserted, allowed individuals to choose common means to protect divinely sanctioned privileges. Nonetheless, their reasoning implied a degree of innate morality in the ability to discern the nature of those privileges, irrespective of salvation or regeneration. In 1760, the Scottish moral sense theorist James Fordyce suggested that the sensory awakening of youth made it vital that parents encourage their children to "hearken to" their authority, allowing offspring to react "with equal delight and reverence, as at once their friends and their teachers." "And having thus engaged them to love and honour you, it is natural to think you will the more easily and effectually win them to the love and veneration of your master." According to Fordyce, instruction and friendship marked the relationship between parents and children, which was designed to cultivate moral sensibility:

> A form of pleasure must needs be exhibited: something to charm their imaginations, something to captivate their hearts. The worthier and nobler sensibilities of nature must be indulged and cultivated. A feeling of true honour, the love of virtuous praise, the admiration of moral beauty, the amiable reciprocations of a refined and generous friendship, the sweet sympathies of natural affection, and domestic union, all these must be recommended and encouraged.

Referring to the indulgence and cultivation of sentiment, Fordyce sought to channel natural inclinations, such as attraction to the opposite sex, toward social sympathies, friendship, and union.[16]

---

16. On studies of the Enlightenment and religion, particularly in relation to Jonathan Israel's suggestion of a radically secularizing philosophical culture, see Jonathan Sheehan, "Enlightenment, Religion, and the Enigma of Secularization: A Review Essay," *American Historical Review,* CVIII (2003), 1061–1080. On the degree of innateness in Moderate accounts of duty, see Richard B. Sher, *Church and University in the Scottish Enlightenment: The Moderate Literati of Edinburgh* (Princeton, N.J., 1985), 175–177; Colin Kidd, "Subscription, the Scottish Enlightenment, and the Moderate Interpretation of History," *Journal of Ecclesiastical History,* LV (2004), 503–512. For Fordyce on friendship and youthful sensibility, see James Fordyce, *The Folly, Infamy, and Misery of Unlawful Pleasure a Sermon Preached before His Majesty's Commissioner to the General Assembly of the Church of Scotland, May XXV. M.DCC.LX,* 3d ed. (London, 1760), 45, 50; Fordyce, *Addresses to Young Men* (Boston, [1782]), 98–101. On Fordyce's reasoning in the context of Scottish conceptions of civic virtue and moral sensibility, see John Dwyer, *Virtuous Discourse: Sensibility and Community in Late Eighteenth Century Scotland* (Edinburgh, 1987),

Locke's educational ideas, and their mediation by Scottish moral sense theory, deeply influenced colonial American moral philosophy. His *Some Thoughts concerning Education* is often overlooked in favor of his *Essay concerning Human Understanding* or his *Two Treatises of Government* (1689). Locke's *Two Treatises of Government* interrogated the notion of absolute authority and outlined the contractual relationship between individuals and their civic leaders. *Some Thoughts concerning Education* also focused on the construction of civic norms and profoundly informed notions of power, obligation, and identity among educated American leaders during the Revolutionary era. It might even have been the most widely read and instituted pedagogical theory in eighteenth-century Anglo-American culture. As late as the Revolutionary era, for example, colonial American teaching manuals advised children to compare and contrast different representations to define their sensory agency and their developing rational capacity. But, of course, their individual choices were often thought to correspond naturally to fixed categories, thus confirming their consent to preexisting communal norms. Notwithstanding the popularity of civic languages of virtue in political rhetoric, colonial parents tended to attach individualistic meanings to these educational processes. The cultivation of rational consent defined and validated individual interests even while it related them to communal ideals.[17]

The association between personal interests and communal esteem was strengthened by the reception of Scottish moral sensory ideas in American religious and educational circles. Scottish philosophy sought to reconcile liberal and civic humanistic notions of social order, helping young men to

---

74–75. On the discussions of youth by Scottish Moderate educators, see also Henry Hutchison, "An Eighteenth-Century Insight into Religious and Moral Education," *British Journal of Educational Studies,* XXIV (1976), 233–241.

17. John Locke, *Two Treatises of Government* (London, 1689). On Lockean "consent," see John Simmons, *On the Edge of Anarchy: Locke, Consent, and the Limits of Society* (Princeton, N.J., 1993); Carey, *Locke, Shaftesbury, and Hutcheson,* 122–124. On the reception of Lockean notions of consent in American political and social theory, see, for example, Brown, *The Consent of the Governed,* 1–15; Lee Ward, *The Politics of Liberty in England and Revolutionary America* (Cambridge, 2004), 263–264. On Locke's popularity, see Jay Fliegelman, *Prodigals and Pilgrims: The American Revolution against Patriarchal Authority, 1750–1800* (Cambridge, 1982), 1–35; Lawrence A. Cremin, *American Education: The Colonial Experience, 1607–1783* (New York, 1970); Nathan Tarcov, *Locke's Education for Liberty* (Chicago, 1984). Historians have suggested that the cultivation of individual rationality was central to the civic cachet that higher education endowed on colonial leaders. See Mark Garrett Longaker, *Rhetoric and the Republic: Politics, Civic Discourse, and Education in Early America* (Tuscaloosa, Ala., 2007), 1–40, 54–60; Lee T. Pearcy, *The Grammar of Our Civility: Classical Education in America* (Waco, Tex., 2005), 50.

define their individual sentiments and emotions as a reflection of objective collective ideals. From the 1750s, the writings of Hutcheson and those who followed him were disseminated through a network of Scottish publishers, booksellers, and teachers. By the 1760s, Americans who were schooled in moral sense reasoning became more comfortable expressing Locke's claim that united individual affections could promote common interests. The display of emotions became more legitimate as its relationship to public and personal ideals was described in complementary terms. Within the moderate and politely religious realms of cities such as Philadelphia, empirical reasoning was promoted by clergymen and educators (rather than by the deistic Revolutionaries who have traditionally appeared in scholarship on the continental European Enlightenment). Most colonial philosophers of sensibility drew on Locke's sensationalist epistemology even while many were wary of those who used it to formulate skeptical assertions. The Scottish-American printer Robert Bell was a self-described "Provedore to the Sentimentalists." His distribution of texts in moral philosophy (often alongside sentimental novels) demonstrated how transatlantic currents could shape the culture of sentiment before the Revolutionary era.[18]

18. On moral sense philosophy's definition of common sensibility as a means of mediating between individualist and civic humanistic accounts of virtue in polite circles of Philadelphia and other colonial American cities, see Nicole Eustace, *Passion Is the Gale: Emotion, Power, and the Coming of the American Revolution* (Chapel Hill, N.C., 2008), 138–149, 273–274; Sarah Knott, *Sensibility and the American Revolution* (Chapel Hill, N.C., 2009), 2, 7–8, 21–22, 52, 68, 189–190. On Robert Bell as a "Provedore," see the broadside to his catalog of books, *Robert Bell, Bookseller, Provedore to the Sentimentalists, and Professor of Book-Auctioniering in America, Is Just Arrived from Philadelphia; with a Small Collection of Modern, Instructive, and Entertaining Books* . . . (Philadelphia, 1778). See also Knott, *Sensibility and the American Revolution*, 29–32. More generally, see Knud Haakonssen, "Natural Jurisprudence in the Scottish Enlightenment: Summary of an Interpretation," in Neil MacCormick and Zenon Bankowski, eds., *Enlightenment, Rights, and Revolution: Essays in Legal and Social Philosophy* (Aberdeen, U.K., 1989), 36. In Scotland, Witherspoon and his evangelical supporters argued that moral sensory notions of individual virtue were a philosophical front for patronage and avarice. See John R. McIntosh, *Church and Theology in Enlightenment Scotland: The Popular Party, 1740–1800* (East Lothian, U.K., 1998), 23, 32–35, 62, 92–96. More than two decades ago, Richard B. Sher recommended that it was "high time" for historians of Scottish-American intellectual culture "to replace the fruitless dichotomy between Lockean liberalism and Scottish moralism with a more nuanced approach." According to J. G. A. Pocock, the Scottish Enlightenment's discussion of the link between classical civic philosophy and "civil jurisprudence" suggested that individual rights — including property and other economic interests — were not antithetical to the common good and social stability. See Sher, "Introduction: Scottish-American Cultural Studies, Past and

The cultivation of sentimental philosophy in late colonial cities such as Philadelphia became particularly amenable to the synthesis of public and private interests. The Saint Andrews Society of Philadelphia was founded in 1747 by Scottish immigrants, including James Hamilton, lieutenant governor of Pennsylvania. Hamilton subsequently assumed the chair of the American Philosophical Society, which became a focus of "cultural exchange" between Edinburgh and Philadelphia. As the first president of the society, Benjamin Franklin was a frequent associate of Scottish printers, educators, and writers in Hamilton's circle. Unsurprisingly, then, he appropriated Lockean contractual theory alongside more recent contributions in Anglo-Scottish moral sense philosophy. His educational proposals described the private sensory response as naturally sympathetic to communal standards. They incorporated the public and communitarian focus of civic humanism without diminishing the veracity, morality, and reliability of personal perception.[19]

In 1722, in one of his first publications, "Silence Dogood, No. 11," Franklin used sentimental terminology and themes that were shared by Francis Hutcheson and other Scottish moral sense philosophers. Much later, in a 1762 letter to Lord Kames, the Scottish Moderate writer and philosopher, Franklin described his proposed project on *"The Art of Virtue"* for "the Benefit of Youth." "Many People lead bad Lives that would gladly lead good ones," Franklin argued, "but know not how to make the Change." Potentially dichotomous notions of communal virtue and individual liberty were dually incorporated in his educational theory. Thanks to the mediating influence of

Present," in Sher and Smitten, eds., *Scotland and America,* 26; Pocock, "Cambridge Paradigms and Scotch Philosophers: A Study of the Relations between the Civic Humanist and the Civil Jurisprudential Interpretation of Eighteenth-Century Social Thought," in Hont and Ignatieff, eds., *Wealth and Virtue,* 246–252; Pocock, *Barbarism and Religion,* I, *The Enlightenments of Edward Gibbon, 1737–1764* (Cambridge, 1999), 6–9.

19. On the "cultural exchange" in Philadelphia involving the Saint Andrews Society and other proponents of polite letters, see Andrew Hook, "Philadelphia, Edinburgh, and the Scottish Enlightenment," in Sher and Smitten, eds., *Scotland and America,* 240 n. 8; Knott, *Sensibility and the American Revolution,* 68; May, *Enlightenment in America,* 84. Caroline Robbins has demonstrated that, in addition to Lockean contractual theory, Franklin's intellectual system was indebted to Shaftesbury, Hutcheson, George Turnbull, and David Fordyce, all of whose writings were disseminated by printers in Philadelphia. See Robbins, *The Eighteenth-Century Commonwealthman: Studies in the Transmission, Development, and Circumstance of English Liberal Thought from the Restoration of Charles II until the War with the Thirteen Colonies* (Cambridge, Mass., 1959), 100. See also Frederick B. Tolles, *Meeting House and Counting House: The Quaker Merchants of Colonial Philadelphia, 1682–1763* (Chapel Hill, N.C., 1948), 177.

FIGURE 11. Title page from David Fordyce,
Dialogues concerning Education . . . , 3d ed.,
II (London, 1757). Courtesy, the University
of Lausanne, Switzerland

Scottish moral philosophy, Franklin felt comfortable defining the correspondence between individual emotions and collective benefits.[20]

David Fordyce's *Dialogues concerning Education* (1745) provided a particularly useful model for Franklin in his attempt to reconcile the Lockean theory of rational consent with the civic humanist notion of public virtue. Having set out to devise a curriculum of higher education for the Philadelphia Academy, Franklin wrote the *Proposals Relating to the Education of the Youth in Pennsylvania* (1749), which relied on several recommendations made by Fordyce as well as Francis Hutcheson and George Turnbull. Franklin was attracted to Fordyce's emphasis on the ability of education to train the rational capacity to reflect on the prior working of the moral sense.

20. Benjamin Franklin, "Silence Dogood, No. 11," in Leonard W. Labaree et al., eds., *The Papers of Benjamin Franklin,* 41 vols. to date (New Haven, Conn., 1959–), I, 37–38. On the likely influence of Hutchesonian reasoning on Franklin's early publication on Silence Dogood, see Alan Houston, *Benjamin Franklin and the Politics of Improvement* (New Haven, Conn., 2008), 211. For Franklin's letter to Kames, May 3, 1760, see Labaree et al., eds., *Papers of Benjamin Franklin,* IX, 104–106. According to Andrew Hook, Franklin shared a pedagogical "vision" with Scottish theorists (particularly in Aberdeen) of "a liberal university education, dedicated to the promotion of civic virtue and the protection of liberty" through the promotion of moral sensibility. See Hook, *From Goosecreek to Gandercleugh: Studies in Scottish-American Literary and Cultural History* (East Lothian, U.K., 1999), 35.

He suggested that "the good Education of Youth has been esteemed by wise Men in all Ages, as the surest Foundation of the Happiness both of private Families and of Common-wealths." Franklin's use of moral sense reasoning in his *Proposals* offered a useful rejoinder to the skeptical critique of Locke. The mind's secondary capacity of reason formed ideas from the body's primary sensory response. Those rational ideas persuaded individuals to consent to higher civic powers—a "commonwealth"—in order to protect other aspects of their personal interests.[21]

Franklin emphasized the utilitarian importance of education and warned that inherited classical ideas were not to be treated as infallible proscriptions for virtuous action. The jaundiced perception of classical erudition in his discussion of the usefulness of education reflected an earlier determination by Locke. According to the English philosopher, the empirical capability of individual reason should not automatically defer to the received tenets of classical lore. Ancient notions of virtue denied the dependable rational capacity that Franklin sought to harness through his educational philosophy. In his recommendation, canonical classical works might offer a useful medium to exercise the mind, in the way of any other logical or perceptual challenge. But if their message contradicted or diminished the notion of individual self-reliance, he recommended that they hold no overarching authority.[22]

Franklin's discussion of the association between common sensibility and rational power preceded and then continued alongside the developing radicalism of the American Revolutionary era. Whiggish historians have noted a similar phenomenon in England during the 1680s: Locke defined the complementary relationship between the *sensus communis* and the secondary rational capacity before and during the Glorious Revolution against autocratic power. Thus, it is tempting to infer that the philosophical notion of common sense—including its association with rational consent—would have assumed a radical and socially leveling dimension in America by the 1760s.[23]

21. Benjamin Franklin, *Proposals Relating to the Education of Youth in Pennsylvania,* in Labaree et al., eds., *Papers of Benjamin Franklin,* III, 399–400. On Franklin's Lockean understanding of reason and civic order, see Houston, *Benjamin Franklin and the Politics of Improvement,* 32–34, 74–76, 99. On the potential influence of Hutcheson, Turnbull, and Fordyce on Franklin, see Landsman, *From Colonials to Provincials,* 61, 80.

22. On Franklin's disdain for the classics, see Pearcy, *The Grammar of Our Civility,* 50; Longaker, *Rhetoric and the Republic,* 55–64.

23. On the potential radicalism of Franklin's Enlightenment thought in relation to patriot ideology (and its repudiation by more conservative ideas), see Benjamin L. Carp, "Benjamin Franklin and the Coming of the American Revolution," in David Waldstreicher, ed., *A Companion to Benjamin Franklin* (Malden, Mass., 2011), 160. For an excellent discussion of the Whiggish

From the era of Locke to Franklin, however, the ability to represent common inferences frequently buttressed the power of social and political elites. Following the relaxing of English censorship laws in 1695, for example, prominent civic leaders feared that popular disagreements might evolve into a nightmare of unrestrained sentiment. Their "common sense" of community and sociability tended to require the conservation of received political norms, to the benefit of their own social standing. As in Augustan England, moreover, so in mid-eighteenth-century Scotland. Members of the educated establishment in Edinburgh, Glasgow, and Aberdeen were stratified at just the point that they defined the universal notion of common sensibility. Their endorsement of innate human judgment in educated treatises and conduct manuals also raised their voice above the people at large. It became possible to claim that dissent from their civic vision—either from members of the wider populace or from their intellectual or religious rivals—somehow lacked the common sense of reasonable men.[24]

Just as Locke's sensus communis could herald a conservative interpretation among educated Scots, the many dimensions of Benjamin Franklin's moral and rational philosophy encompassed ambiguous or even elitist social meanings. During those moments when his Newtonian metaphors favored social order above unmediated individual liberty, the radical Enlightenment thinker could fast become a proponent of more conservative ideals. In Franklin's Philadelphia, well-connected men, when they defined their sensory perception and secondary rational capacity in relation to common norms, often gained representative authority and prestige.[25]

Scottish Sensibility at the College of Philadelphia and King's College

Like New Jersey, Benjamin Franklin's Pennsylvania incorporated moderate and evangelical Presbyterians, Quakers, Anglicans, and Scottish Episcopalians in its heterogeneous population. But unlike in Princeton village,

---

interpretation of developing sensus communis, see Sophia Rosenfeld, *Common Sense: A Political History* (Cambridge, Mass., 2011), 17–22.

24. Rosenfeld, *Common Sense,* 25–35, 43–45, 147.

25. On Benjamin Franklin's propensity to move from radical Enlightenment theories toward those that defined the divinely ordained stability of existing societal norms, see Kerry S. Walters, *Benjamin Franklin and His Gods* (Urbana, Ill., 1999), 10, 58. Even in Franklin's sphere, the notion of common sensibility could assume an elite definition. See Sheila L. Skemp, "The Making of a Patriot, 1757–1775," in Waldstreicher, ed., *A Companion to Benjamin Franklin,* 48. On the link between moral sensory reasoning and social stratification, see also Knott, *Sensibility and the American Revolution,* 18.

Philadelphia's split between Old Side and New Side Presbyterians created a power vacuum in which other denominations could prosper. In particular, Episcopalians (mostly Scottish) found themselves well placed to exert their authority through new institutions of higher learning. William Smith was perhaps the most prominent example. He studied to become a minister at King's College in Aberdeen from 1743 to 1747 and then migrated to America where he became head of the Philadelphia Academy in 1753 and provost of the College of Philadelphia two years later. Benjamin Franklin was largely responsible for persuading the trustees of the Philadelphia Academy to appoint Smith as its president and to support him in his desire to build the institution into the degree-granting College of Philadelphia.[26]

Smith's *General Idea of the College of Mirania* was similar to David Fordyce's *Dialogues concerning Education* (1745) in its attempt to define the innate moral sensibility of Miranians, a mythical group attending college in a province that bore a resemblance to Pennsylvania. "Every person of genius, learning, and experience" offered " impartial thoughts" on "a plan of education" for the college. They endeavored to keep "always in sight . . . the easiest, simplest, and most natural method of forming youth to the knowledge and exercise of private and public virtue." God appealed to the human senses "in the constitution of our nature" so that Miranians were able to "do always the greatest good in our power whether to ourselves or fellow-creatures, of whatever country, sect, or denomination they may be; to act a just and honest part in our social capacity; and, lastly, as much as possible, to repair the ruins of our nature, by improving and enlarging our faculties, and confirming ourselves in habits of virtue." Smith's ideal college taught the simple tenets of Christianity to show their verification by natural and inborn human sentiments. It refrained from engaging in more nuanced doctrinal and theological instruction, thereby avoiding any discussion of the problem of moral innateness.[27]

26. On the power vacuum in Philadelphia, Smith's intellectual and philosophical influence therein, and Franklin's association, see Andrew Hook, "Philadelphia, Edinburgh, and the Scottish Enlightenment," in Sher and Smitten, eds., *Scotland and America*, 233; Sloan, *The Scottish Enlightenment*, 83. On the influence of Scottish moral sense philosophy among Philadelphia's new Episcopalian elite, see also May, *The Enlightenment in America*, 80; Peter J. Diamond, "Witherspoon, William Smith, and the Scottish Philosophy," in Sher and Smittten, eds., *Scotland and America*, 123–125.

27. William Smith, "A General Idea of the College of Mirania," in *The Works of William Smith, D.D.: Late Provost of the College and Academy of Philadelphia*, 2 vols. (Philadelphia, 1803), I, pt. 2, 176–178. See also Smith, *Some Thoughts on Education* . . . (New York, 1752), viii. According to Diamond, Smith drew upon his Aberdeen education in order to introduce American colo-

Smith advocated classical learning as a means to define the importance of public leadership. But, like Franklin, he was not entirely comfortable with the civic humanistic notion that the individual will was innately flawed or corrupting. He, too, suggested that personal sentiments were in fact germane to the classical idea of communal virtue, provided they were cultivated through higher learning. His Miranians preferred to study literary texts in English rather than in ancient languages because the vernacular was more likely to inspire their sensory moral response, to the eventual benefit of the common good. Even though Miranians could not "write with classic elegance and purity," Smith sought to avoid "hunting after words to convey" ideas in Latin, which made them "continually on the rack," their "sentiments" and "sprightly sallies of fancy" escaping their memory as a result of the need to grapple for phrases from a "dead language." Moral sensibility could be cultivated through the study of tasteful literature—often in English—because students perceived good acts and belles lettres according to the same involuntary sensory response. Miranians read Hutcheson's moral philosophy and were attracted to literature that united pleasing artistic form with attractive ethical content. This combination in a "taste for polite letters" contributed to social cohesion by helping to "enlarge the mind, refine and exalt the understanding, improve the temper, soften the manners, serene the passions, cherish reflection, and lead on that charming pensiveness of soul and philosophic melancholy, which, most of all, dispose us to love, friendship, and every tender emotion." Smith sent a copy of his educational ideals to Franklin, who had become president of the board of trustees of the Academy and Charitable School of Philadelphia. Franklin wrote to Smith, "I know not when I have read a Piece that has more affected me, so noble and just are the Sentiments, so warm and animated the Language." To be sure, Franklin was also aware of Smith's opponents in Philadelphia, and he added: "I wish you had omitted . . . those Expressions of Resentment against your Adversaries . . . [as] [i]n such Cases, the noblest Victory is obtained, by Neglect, and by Shining on."[28]

---

nists to the writings of " 'moral sense' philosophers" such as Fordyce who "met the ideological needs of a provincial society concerned with engendering among its citizens a practical morality that would enable them to cultivate those virtues deemed useful, as Hutcheson put it, 'for every honourable office in life, and quench that manly and laudable thirst . . . after knowledge.' " See Diamond, "Witherspoon, William Smith, and the Scottish Philosophy," in Sher and Smittten, eds., *Scotland and America*, 115–116, 122.

28. Smith, "A General Idea," in *Works of William Smith*, I, pt. 2, 184, 186, 192–193, 201, 205–206; Franklin to Smith, May 3, 1753, in Labaree et al., eds., *Papers of Benjamin Franklin*, IV, 475–476. On the context for the exchange between Smith and Franklin, see Hoeveler, *Cre-*

When Smith assumed his duties as provost of the College of Philadelphia in 1755, he soon delegated the teaching of moral philosophy to Francis
Alison, another of Franklin's Scottish associates, albeit an Old Side Presbyterian rather than an Episcopalian. Alison had briefly studied with Hutcheson at Glasgow University during the early 1740s. He employed his posthumously published *A Shorter Introduction to Moral Philosophy* (1747) at the
College of Philadelphia. Like Franklin and Smith, he believed that innate
moral sensibility prevented any dichotomy between personal liberty and
the public commonwealth. He recommended that his Philadelphia students
study Locke and Harrington alongside Hutcheson because they were all conducive to biblical morality and civic order. He informed his students through
the 1760s that the secondary capacity of human reason required support from
sensory experience and inward feelings and innate responses. Those uncontrollable feelings and sensibilities enabled them to place their trust in more
rational philosophical arguments.[29]

Although the two men maintained a cordial relationship, Alison suspected
Smith of favoring local Anglican political elites in Philadelphia by seeking
their patronage, privileging their offspring in college admissions, and securing the students' livelihoods after graduation. His suspicion was not baseless.
Through the 1760s, Smith's growing association with political factionalism
embroiled the College of Philadelphia in local intrigues that seemed anything
but virtuous. Some portrayed the provost as a cipher of British proprietary
rule under the guise of Anglican educational authority. Others accused him
of favoring certain constituents in local colonial assemblies, even the Quaker
politicians he had earlier opposed. Smith's reputation for political maneu-
vering belies two key assumptions underlying the scholarly notion of shared
cultural provinciality: that Scottish educators in the colonies followed their
Edinburgh counterparts by lauding their provincial distance from crude political culture, and their theories of innate sociability provided an alternative account of human cohesion beyond the shifting obligations of political
mandates. Yet the later part of Smith's educational career was dominated
by his byzantine political, sectarian, and factional alliances, many of which

---

ating the American Mind, 162–163; Diamond, "Witherspoon, William Smith, and the Scottish
Philosophy," in Sher and Smitten, eds., *Scotland and America,* 124. For more on the links to
Scottish moral sensory ideas in Alison's account of rhetoric and learning, see Franklin E. Court,
The Scottish Connection: The Rise of English Literary Study in Early America (Syracuse, N.Y.,
2001), 21–24.

29. On Alison's Old Side Presbyterian identity and his moral philosophy, see Sloan, *The Scottish Enlightenment,* 88–90; Hoeveler, *Creating the American Mind,* 170–172; Robson, *Educating
Republicans,* 86–87.

responded to chaotic Philadelphia election contests between Presbyterians, Quakers, and Anglicans. Witherspoon, we should recall, accused Moderates in Edinburgh's church and university establishment of conducting themselves in a similar way. He described their claim to eschew traditional notions of political authority as hollow and even hypocritical. He suggested that their connection to patronage made them anything but disinterested in their moral sensibility.[30]

When he drafted the *College of Mirania,* Smith was partly motivated by his perception that Anglican educators in nearby New York were losing the upper hand to Presbyterians. In King's College, New York, unlike in the College of Philadelphia, revivalist Presbyterian ministers applied greater pressure on those who spearheaded its institutional growth and its nascent program of moral philosophy. New Side trustees in Princeton village, as we have seen, accused Anglicans and Old Side Presbyterians of emphasizing the trustworthiness of individual sensibility among the unregenerate and for using higher learning to define their personal prestige. Seeking to prevent an Anglican-led provincial college in New York through the 1750s, however, Presbyterians failed to reflect their counterparts in New Jersey. The Anglican trustees of King's College defined their educational authority as a public-spirited alternative to Presbyterian and Congregational evangelicalism. Their Presbyterian opponents—most notably a young lawyer named William Livingston—thus felt obliged to outline the importance of innate sensibility alongside more traditional classical concerns. Livingston published his proposals in a series of essays in the periodical the *Independent Reflector.* He argued for what has been described as "Lockean notions of a state of nature" in order to limit the authority of established Anglican ministers over individual religious conscience. The "design of erecting a College in this Province" was a "Matter of such grand and general Importance" that Livingston devoted "serious Meditation" to the topic. Separating pedagogy from specific Anglican control, he argued in a 1753 entry to the *Reflector,* enabled the

> true Use of Education . . . to qualify Men for the different Employments of Life, to which it may please God to call them. 'Tis to improve their Hearts and Understandings, to infuse a public Spirit and Love of their

30. On Alison's suspicion of Smith and on Smith's scandals, see Hoeveler, *Creating the American Mind,* 163–169, 170–172. Smith sought to position himself between rival Presbyterians and Quakers, claiming to defuse confessional strains between Presbyterians and Quakers in Pennsylvania following the massacre of Indians by the Paxton Boys. See Melvin H. Buxbaum, *Benjamin Franklin and the Zealous Presbyterians* (University Park, Pa., 1975), 155, 196, 199–200, 211; Robson, *Educating Republicans,* 29–35.

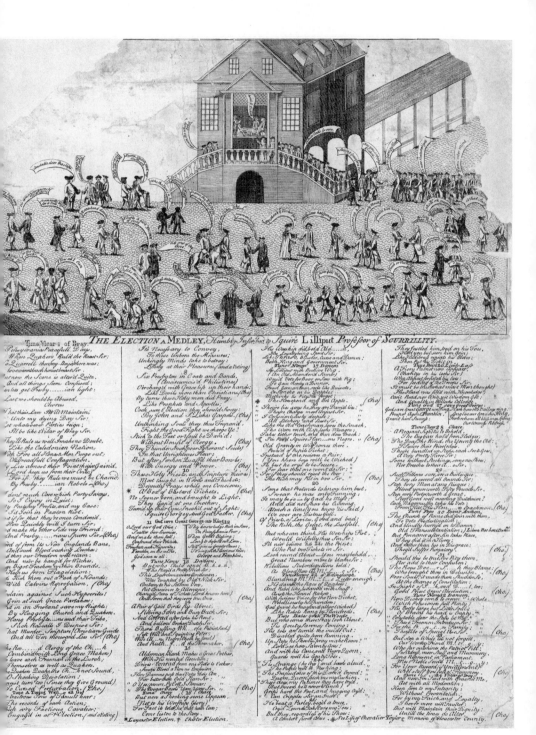

FIGURE 12. *The Election a Medley, Humbly Inscribed to Squire Lilliput Professor of Scurrillity.* By Henry Dawkins. Philadelphia, 1764. Courtesy, Library of Congress Prints and Photographs Division, Washington, D.C.

Country; to inspire them with the Principles of Honour and Probity; with a fervent Zeal for Liberty, and a diffusive Benevolence for Mankind; and in a Word, to make them the more extensively serviceable to the Common-Wealth.

Hence, the "Education of Youth hath been the peculiar Care of all the wise Legislators of Antiquity, who thought it impossible to aggrandize the State, without imbuing the Minds of its Members with Virtue and Knowledge." While referring to civic service, a public spirit, and the importance of a commonwealth, Livingston thus also identified the role of higher education in encouraging liberty and the diffusion of benevolence. In another letter, Livingston observed that, unless the constitution of any proposed college "will admit Persons of all protestant Denominations, upon a perfect Parity as to Privileges, it will itself be greatly prejudiced, and prove a Nursery of Animosity, Dissention and Disorder." He used the language of moral sensibility to show the confluence between individual and communal interests. In doing so, he diminished the evangelical pietism that he and his associates had once displayed. He failed to note any tension between the notion of innate benevolence and the necessity of salvation. Instead, as he sought to counter the Anglican establishment, he focused on the role of dissenters in the encouragement of civil theology and moral behavior.[31]

"There Is No Occasion to Join Mr. Hutchinson or Any Other"

The similar philosophical sensibilities of Livingston, Smith, and Alison belied the prickly assessment of American intellectual culture that Alexander Carlyle included in his discussion of Witherspoon and the imperial crisis. According to Carlyle, the American colonies favored crude evangelicalism over moral sense reasoning because their religious and intellectual values were underdeveloped. Yet educators in Philadelphia and New York clearly incorporated Scottish moral philosophy in their approach to higher learning. Subsequent historiography has taken note of this fact, casting Carlyle's

31. On Smith's perception of Anglican educators in nearby New York, see Charlotte Fletcher, *Cato's Mirania: A Life of Provost Smith* (Lanham, Md., 2002), 8. On "Lockean notions of a state of nature" in Livingston's work, see Robson, *Educating Republicans*, 6–7. For Livingston's statements, see Z. [William Livingston], "Remarks on Our Intended College," Mar. 22, 1753, in William Livingston et al., *The Independent Reflector; or, Weekly Essays on Sundry Important Subjects More Particularly Adapted to the Province of New-York,* ed. Milton M. Klein (Cambridge, Mass., 1963), 172. On the "perfect Parity" of rights among different Protestant denominations, see A. [William Smith], "A Continuation of the Same Subject," Mar. 29, 1753, ibid., 178.

great evangelical opponent alongside Alison and Smith in the promotion of human-centered ethical ideas.

Scholars have most often used Witherspoon's "Lectures on Moral Philosophy" to portray him in a moderate light. In 1769, Witherspoon began delivering his lectures to students in their third and fourth years of study. Influenced by Scottish universities, the College of New Jersey had recently sidelined the regent system of higher education. Tutors were no longer assigned to one particular set of students for all their subjects. Instead, the college had chosen to establish chairs in particular disciplines. Funds prevented the employment of many chaired professors, and thus the president frequently carried out further duties as a professor of moral philosophy and rhetoric, generally delivering lectures to students in their junior and senior years. Ashbel Green, Witherspoon's former student and the editor of his collected works in 1802, wrote the following of Witherspoon's "Lectures on Moral Philosophy":

> In justice to the memory of Dr. Witherspoon, it ought to be stated that he did not intend these lectures for the press, and that he once compelled a printer who, without his knowledge, had undertaken to publish them, to desist from the design. . . . The Doctor's lectures on morals, notwithstanding they assume the form of regular discourses, were in fact, viewed by himself as little more than a syllabus or compend, on which he might enlarge before a class at the times of recitation.

Green pointed out that the lectures were not intended for publication and were only related embryonically to their oral transmission. Despite these caveats, historians have mined them for any references to moral sense philosophy or to the similar ethical faculties associated with a later school of Scottish common sense philosophy.[32]

At first glance, it is easy to understand the tendency to define Witherspoon's lectures as yet another conduit for simple ideas about innate moral perception. In them, his early discussion of "perfect rights" referred to the "duties of justice" and then continued: "A man is said to have a right or power to promote his own happiness only by those means which are not

32. Editorial note by Ashbel Green, in [Green, ed.], *Works of Witherspoon*, III, 366 (see also the advertisement, I, [vi]). Most scholars are indebted to Jack Scott's introduction to the first modern edited collection of Witherspoon's "Lectures on Moral Philosophy"; see Scott, ed., *An Annotated Edition of "Lectures on Moral Philosophy" by John Witherspoon* (Newark, Del., 1982), 1–61. On collegiate developments in which presidents "doubled" as professors of moral philosophy, see Longaker, *Rhetoric and the Republic,* 42; Sloan, *The Scottish Enlightenment,* 23–25.

in themselves criminal or injurious to others." Examined on its own, such a statement could easily have appeared in the writings of Francis Alison or William Smith, as described above, or in any of the major treatises of Scottish moral thought. The same could be said of Witherspoon's brief discussion of Humean skepticism and other forms of philosophical "Immaterialism":

> It is easy to raise metaphysical subtleties, and confound the understanding on such subjects. In opposition to this, some late writers have advanced with great apparent reason, that there are certain first principles or dictates of commonsense, which are either simple perceptions, or seen with intuitive evidence . . . These authors of Scotland have lately produced and supported this opinion, to resolve at once all the refinements and metaphysical objections of some infidel writers.

Here Witherspoon's lectures most explicitly engaged with common sense (rather than simply moral sense) philosophy. They responded to the immaterialist philosophy of the Anglo-Irish thinker George Berkeley (1685–1753), who denied that the material nature of objects could be verified as anything more than ideas in the mind of the receiver. They then simplified and paraphrased the latest arguments proposed by Thomas Reid, who outlined the interaction between primary sentiments and secondary reason in response to his skeptical and immaterialist opponents. In this section, Witherspoon certainly appropriated simple common sense terminology—even principles—regarding the empirical reality of external objects. He did so in order to reduce the claims of immaterialism: "External [sensory perception] arises from the immediate impression of objects from without. . . . In these are observable the impression itself, or the sensation we feel, and the supposition inseparable from it, that it is produced by an external object." Such a straightforward epistemological statement came without any qualifications or hesitations.[33]

Examined without further context, these statements would not contradict Charles Chauncy's insinuation that Witherspoon saw no place for the complicated tenets of Edwardsean reasoning and that he was happy to clarify the association between an innate moral sensibility and biblical ideals. Thus, historians have remained keen to situate Witherspoon within the traditional realm of moral sense reasoning. Many have highlighted a portion of his

33. Witherspoon, "Lectures on Moral Philosophy," in [Green, ed.], *Works of Witherspoon*, III, 370, 376, 377, 395, 407. On Berkeley's discussion of immaterialism, which he publicized in 1711 through *A Treatise concerning the Principles of Human Knowledge*, see P. J. E. Kail, *Berkeley's "A Treatise on the Principles of Human Knowledge": An Introduction* (Cambridge, 2014), 54–69.

"Lectures on Moral Philosophy" in which he suggested: "Mercy is the other great branch of our duty to man, and is the exercise of the benevolent principle in general, and of the several particular kind affections. Its acts, generally speaking, belong to the class of imperfect rights." But Witherspoon's reference to "benevolent principle" and "kind affections" was followed by an important and overlooked clarification: "yet such as cannot be enforced with rigor and precision by human laws." Though he engaged with the arguments of Hutcheson, Locke, and even Reid, it would be a mistake to claim that Witherspoon wholly extrapolated a notion of innate ethical discernment from his précis of common rights. Rather, he distinguished "perfect" from "imperfect rights," such as the right to receive charity or to be treated benevolently by neighbors. The latter were contingent on individual moral choice, which was ultimately fallible. If neglected, there was no political or legal requirement for retribution. Because "all the conclusions drawn from these principles [associated with innate understandings of mercy] must be vague and general, the expectations of the guilty founded upon them, must be very uncertain . . . [so that] the way in which, and the terms on which, he will shew mercy, can be learned from Revelation only." "Perfect" rights, therefore, were protected in light of the knowledge of selfish human nature, as provided by revealed scripture. For a moral decision to avoid caprice, "knowledge of God and a future state" provided important evidence that man was "governed by something else than instinct." The "perfect" morality of God was distinguished from the "imperfect" vision of mercy held by men. It could only be encountered through God's own grace, following conversion and regeneration.[34]

Witherspoon included a similar discussion and distinction in his "Lectures on Divinity." He advised his students to "Pray without ceasing" because "the very spirit and temper of a believer, should be that of dependence upon God, and deriving by faith from him, every necessary supply." In order to "recommend it particularly" to them he observed it to be "peculiarly necessary to be begun in early life; perhaps there are few, if any instances of persons coming to a greater degree of fervour in devotion, or attention to the duty of it, in advanced years, than they had in youth . . . fervour in devotion must be begun early." Here Witherspoon's account of the relationship between individual "temper" and faithful "duty" was at its most Augustinian.

34. Witherspoon, "Lectures on Moral Philosophy," in [Green, ed.], *Works of Witherspoon,* III, 371–379, 399, 400, 407–409. As Douglas Sloan argues, Witherspoon "muted Hutcheson's emphasis upon the close connection between aesthetics and morality"; see Sloan, *The Scottish Enlightenment,* 124.

Their connection was understood to promote "fervour in devotion" rather than modulation by innate and objective perception. Ethical sympathy with other beings was only possible when "Living by faith" in "the whole system of revealed truth" and that which God had "revealed concerning the [flawed] eternal condition of men." Later in his lectures, Witherspoon seemed suddenly to adopt a rational apologetic stance when he claimed to "confess it is agreeable" to show "that the truths of the everlasting gospel are agreeable to sound reason." In the following sentence, however, he asserted: "Yet to begin by making the suggestion of our own reason the standard of what is to be heard or examined as a matter of revelation, I look upon to be highly dangerous, manifestly unjust, and inconsistent with the foundation-stone of all revealed religion, viz. that reason, without it, is insufficient to bring us to the knowledge of God and our duty."[35]

In a brief aside in his "Lectures on Moral Philosophy," Witherspoon did not discount the role of benevolent passions in certain cases of self-sacrifice: "The direct object in view [in more rare cases] is to promote the happiness of others," and "for this" some in history had "been willing to sacrifice every thing, even life itself." But Witherspoon did not elucidate what enabled human passions to be exerted in common favor, bypassing the general "malignity" of human motivation about which he had so much more to say. That these exceptional examples of benevolence were provided by sacrifice and death suggested a moral duty that went beyond normal human behavior, imbuing their actions with a divinely inspired form of heroism.[36]

In the same section that dealt with the case of self-sacrifice, therefore, Witherspoon's "Lectures on Moral Philosophy" referred to "instinct" in Augustinian rather than Hutchesonian terms. It led to a relationship with the Creator himself, rather than to a perception of the world he made. Witherspoon briefly alluded to the specific role of "storge," or "parental tenderness towards offspring," as a potential example of instinctual "moral dispositions." But, given its brief reference, and its association with the maternal protection of progeny, it is unlikely that he sought to provide a general example of Hutchesonian moral benevolence. Indeed, Witherspoon described

35. Witherspoon, "Lectures on Divinity," in [Green, ed.], *Works of Witherspoon*, IV, 13–14, 47. These Augustinian aspects in Witherspoon's reasoning also reflected Calvin's approach to mental perception of external moral norms. See John Calvin, *Institutes of the Christian Religion*, ed. John T. McNeill, trans. Ford Lewis Battles (Philadelphia, 1960), I, 251–252; Paul Kjoss Helseth, "'Right Reason' and the Princeton Mind: The Moral Context," *Journal of Presbyterian History*, LXXVII (1999), 13–28.

36. Witherspoon, "Lectures on Moral Philosophy," in [Green, ed.], *Works of Witherspoon*, III, 373–374, 376.

the importance of that which "governed" man beyond the special relation-ships of blood and familial kinship and then pointed out: "There is no occa-sion to join Mr. Hutchinson or any other, in their opposition to such as make reason the principle of virtuous conduct." Recognizing "the wisdom of the Creator" in the construction of the human body, or in the natural sciences, did not suggest an ability to act with instinctive morality.[37]

Whereas Thomas Reid demonstrated "apparent" reason in his discus-sion of material objects in relation to mental perception in his *Inquiry into the Human Mind on the Principles of Common Sense* (1764), Witherspoon was careful not to engage too closely with the moral dimension of common sense philosophy. Piety was necessary for virtue, which could not "be en-forced with rigor and precision by human laws" or derived from innate in-stinct. Ironically, then, Witherspoon developed his distinction between "per-fect" and "imperfect" sensibilities using moral sensory terminology. As he continued to do so, he came a little closer to the evangelical hermeneutic of Jonathan Edwards and his posthumous followers.[38]

"Duty" and the "Sense of Obligation" from Edwards to Witherspoon

From the late 1740s, Jonathan Edwards sought to understand "the nature of true virtue." He began a systematic critique of Hutchesonian reasoning after detecting a problematic alliance between moral philosophy and Christian apologetics, but he did not entirely eschew philosophical language in the religious sphere. Adopting philosophical terminology and opposing anthro-pocentric moral reasoning were not mutually exclusive, and Edwards used moral sensory terminology in order to examine and assess the provenance and extent of moral understanding in the regenerate.[39]

37. Ibid., III, 371–372, 379. These statements also move Witherspoon further from Reid. As we have seen, Reid appropriated Hutcheson's focus on instinct as a first principle in his own fac-ulty psychology. See also the nuanced discussion of Hutcheson's moral philosophy in relation to New Light theology in Landsman, *From Colonials to Provincials*, 77–80.

38. Witherspoon, "Lectures on Moral Philosophy," in [Green, ed.], *Works of Witherspoon*, III, 377, 395, 409.

39. For Edwards on "the nature of true virtue" in relation to American philosophy, see, for example, Avihu Zakai, *Jonathan Edwards's Philosophy of History: The Re-Enchantment of the World in the Age of Enlightenment* (Princeton, N.J., 2003), 307–324. Norman Fiering has argued that Hutcheson is Edwards's principal target in the dissertation on true virtue. This con-tention is disputed by Paul Ramsey in his edition of Edwards's ethical writings. See Norman Fiering, *Jonathan Edwards's Moral Thought and Its British Context* (Chapel Hill, N.C., 1981), 337–340; Paul Ramsey, "Appendix II: Jonathan Edwards on Moral Sense, and the Sentimen-

Edwards opposed what has since been termed the "rational English Enlightenment" because its perceived emphasis on innate reason threatened to
undermine the role of the emotional senses in faith and regeneration. But he
did not immediately perceive the work of Scottish Enlightenment thinkers in
similarly negative terms. In his early writings, he distinguished Locke's description of sensory perception from his later discussion of innate reason. He
aligned it more approvingly with Scottish thinkers such as Francis Hutcheson. He believed that sentimental terminology was useful in its ability to describe the signs of religious awakening with greater analytical precision. His
Distinguishing Marks of a Work of the Spirit of God (1742), *Some Thoughts concerning the Present Revival of Religion* (1743), and *Religious Affections* (1746)
all set about defining the various emotional stages of regeneration, as distinct
from abstract and rational conceptions of religious experience.[40]

According to Edwards, spiritual discernment could be defined as a new
sense of morality implanted by grace in the regenerated heart. But, although
it was open to all fallen beings, initially through the workings of the Holy
Spirit, not everybody would allow themselves to receive the gift of greater
ethical illumination. In an ironic similarity, the Hutchesonian conception

---

talists," in Jonathan Edwards, *Ethical Writings*, ed. Ramsey, in Perry Miller et al., eds., *The
Works of Jonathan Edwards*, VIII (New Haven, Conn., 1989) 689–705. See also James A. Har-
ris, *Of Liberty and Necessity: The Free Will Debate in Eighteenth-Century British Philosophy* (New
York, 2005), 129; May, *Enlightenment in America*, xii; Avihu Zakai, "Jonathan Edwards, the En-
lightenment, and the Formation of Protestant Tradition in America," in Elizabeth Mancke and
Carole Shammas, eds., *The Creation of the British Atlantic World* (Baltimore, 2005), 188; Eliza-
beth Agnew Cochran, *Receptive Human Virtues: A New Reading of Jonathan Edwards's Ethics*
(University Park, Pa., 2011), 20–24. Sang Hyun Lee has even suggested that Edwards developed
his own "philosophical theology"; see Lee, *The Philosophical Theology of Jonathan Edwards*
(Princeton, N.J., 1988), 163–165.

40. On Edwards's response to the "rational English Enlightenment," see Zakai, "Jonathan
Edwards," in Mancke and Shammas, eds., *Creation of the British Atlantic World*, 188; May,
Enlightenment in America, xii, 49. According to Zakai, Hutcheson's writings initially piqued
Edwards's interest because they isolated the human sensory faculty, distinguished it from mental
reasoning, and seemed to provide a useful philosophical language to reorient individuals toward
an understanding of the centrality of conversion and the reception of grace. Douglas Sloan has
suggested that what "is of special interest in *True Virtue* is that while Edwards worked to undermine Hutcheson's main assumption—the possibility of true benevolence in natural man—he
also adopted and preserved much in Hutcheson that he deemed valuable, including Hutcheson's
terminology and a good portion of his empirical psychology. Experiential religion and empirical
ethics both focused on the emotions as the center of human personality"; see Sloan, *The Scottish
Enlightenment*, 101. For a discussion of the initial use of Hutchesonian motifs in Edwards's writing, see also Harris, *Of Liberty and Necessity*, 128–130.

of innate moral sensibility was not always interpreted in entirely universal terms. Though ostensibly common to all beings, it could be cultivated to a greater extent in some than in others. Although Edwards and Hutcheson differed over the issue of moral innateness, therefore, they both claimed that different gradations of moral insight remained likely in any community.[41]

Notwithstanding the assistance of empirical analysis and sensory termi-nology, assuring the signs of experimental piety and religious affection always remained a tricky endeavor for Edwards. To allow the free illumination of grace, individuals were required to acknowledge their unregenerate moral state, often through a passionate religious experience. But from what, or from where, did such a concession derive? Calvinist theologians had always won-dered whether the human willingness to recognize divine superiority—to re-ceive a new sense of virtue as an external gift of grace—necessarily originated from some sort of internal volition and whether that notion contradicted the doctrine of total human depravity. According to Augustine's ambiguous doc-trine of illumination, as we have seen, God provided unregenerate men with enough insight to acknowledge their fallen state and the resulting impor-tance of salvation. Nonetheless, the exact nature of illumination remained one of faith's mysteries, part of what the church father defined as the neces-sary struggle of Christian experience.[42]

Edwards attempted his own (unfinished) struggle to demonstrate that orthodox theology could reconcile moral responsibility with the idea of divine sovereignty. Grappling with the "controversy, between Calvinists and Arminians," he argued in his *Freedom of the Will*, "depends on the determi-nation of this grand article concerning . . . moral agency . . . [whether] God's moral government over mankind, his treating them as moral agents, making

41. Thus, Edwards initially distinguished between rational and pre-rational sensory lan-guages; the former were problematic because they suggested an innate moral capacity, and the latter were seemingly less threatening to his revivalist vision because they could be used to define the role of passions in evangelical discourse. See Garry J. Williams, "Enlightenment Episte-mology and Eighteenth-Century Evangelical Doctrines of Assurance," in Michael A. G. Haykin and Kenneth J. Stewart, eds., *The Emergence of Evangelicalism: Exploring Historical Conti-nuities* (Nottingham, U.K., 2008), 356–368; Harris, *Of Liberty and Necessity*, 128–130; Grasso, *A Speaking Aristocracy*, 105.

42. See Augustine, *On the Free Choice of the Will, on Grace and Free Choice, and Other Writ-ings*, ed. and trans. Peter King (Cambridge, 2010), 37; Lydia Schumacher, *Divine Illumina-tion: The History and Future of Augustine's Theory of Knowledge* (Chichester, U.K., 2011), 58–66; Ronald H. Nash, *The Light of the Mind: St. Augustine's Theory of Knowledge* ([Louisville, Ky.], 1969), 94–124; Gareth B. Matthews, "Knowledge and Illumination," in Eleonore Stump and Norman Kretzmann, eds., *The Cambridge Companion to Augustine* (Cambridge, 2001), 171–185.

them the objects of his commands, counsels, calls, warnings, expostulations, promises, threatenings, rewards and punishments, is not inconsistent with a determining disposal of all events . . . in his providence; either by positive efficiency, or permission." Such a universal, "determining providence," according to Edwards, inferred "some kind of necessity of all events; such a necessity as implies an infallible previous fixedness of the futurity of the event." Yet, problematically,

> no other necessity of moral events, or volitions of intelligent agents, is needful in order to this, than *moral* necessity; which does as much ascertain the futurity of the event, as any other necessity. But, as has been demonstrated, such a necessity is not at all repugnant to moral agency, and the reasonable use of commands, calls, rewards, punishments.

With these questions and rejoinders ever increasing, Edwards thus became anxious that emotional confessions of faith might mask a degree of insincerity, pointing out that it was "not above the power of Satan to suggest thoughts to men; because otherwise he could not tempt them to sin." And, if Satan "can suggest any thoughts or ideas at all," Edwards continued, "doubtless imaginary ones, or ideas of things external are not above his power." And so Edwards recognized that gracious illumination in the unregenerate could be fleeting, unpredictable, and tricky to verify. In his 1740 sermon *The Witness of the Spirit,* Jonathan Dickinson had made a similar suggestion. Edwards later wrote in *A Treatise concerning Religious Affections* that, if "persons have had great terrors, which really have been from the awakening and convincing influences of the Spirit of God, it don't thence follow that their terrors must needs issue in true comfort." "The unmortified corruption of the heart may quench the Spirit of God (after he has been striving) by leading men to presumptuous, and self-exalting hopes and joys, as well as otherwise."[43]

By the 1750s, Edwards concluded that Scottish moral philosophy had failed to address the vexing question of moral perception with sufficient com-

---

43. Jonathan Edwards, *A Careful and Strict Enquiry into the Modern Prevailing Notion of That Freedom of the Will* . . . , in Edwards, *Freedom of the Will,* ed. Paul Ramsey, in Miller et al., eds., *Works of Jonathan Edwards,* I (New Haven, Conn., 1957), 431; Edwards, *A Treatise concerning Religious Affections, in Three Parts* (1746), in Edwards, *Religious Affections,* ed. John E. Smith, ibid., II (New Haven, Conn., 1959), 157, 215. On the similarity between Dickinson and Edwards on the issue of assurance in these treatises and sermons, see Grasso, *A Speaking Aristocracy,* 91–92. See also the discussion of these continued Augustinian ambiguities in Roger A. Ward, *Conversion in American Philosophy: Exploring the Practice of Transformation* (New York, 2004), xxi; Susan Manning, *The Puritan-Provincial Vision: Scottish and American Literature in the Nineteenth Century* (Cambridge, 1990), 33–35.

plexity, having eschewed the Augustinian struggles of faith. Despite his continued use of sensory terminology, therefore, he became more overtly critical of Hutchesonian ethical conclusions. In his *Nature of True Virtue,* written between 1755 and 1758 and posthumously published in 1765, Edwards responded directly to Hutcheson's *Inquiry into the Original of Our Ideas of Beauty and Virtue* (1725). Hutcheson's "treatise on beauty," he explained, "expresses by uniformity in the midst of variety: which is no other than the consent or agreement of different things, in form, quantity . . . which is no more than to say, the more there are of different mutually agreeing things, the greater is the beauty." In distinction, Edwards asserted that the pre-rational sensory reaction relied on divine volition, with any human-centered account of ethical perception risking self-love rather than true benevolence. As he argued in his 1754 *Freedom of the Will,* individual ethical agency might allow the inference of innate moral sensibility, but its external cause could always choose to change divine will. Thus, Edwards criticized "Arminian" moral philosophers for suggesting that the will had a predictable power of determination before regeneration, despite God's ability to change the nature of the human sensory response at any time.[44]

Scottish moral sense philosophy sought to connect mental perception with external objects, often including their ethical interaction. In 1745, conversely, Edwards suggested that "the mind makes use of signs instead of the ideas themselves." In an undated article in a collection titled "The Mind," written during his youth and consulted through the rest of his life, Edwards responded to a reading of Locke and described the analogy between the mind's perception of color and its conception of ethical ideas:

> Color is only in the mind, and nothing like it can be out of all mind. Hence it is manifest, there can be nothing like those things we call by the name of bodies out of the mind, unless it be in some other mind or minds. And indeed, the secret lies here: that which truly is the substance of all bodies is the infinitely exact and precise and perfectly stable idea in God's mind, together with his stable will that the same shall gradually be communicated to us, and to other minds, according

44. Jonathan Edwards, *The Nature of True Virtue* (1765), in Edwards, *Ethical Writings,* ed. Ramsey, in Miller et al., eds., *Works of Jonathan Edwards,* VIII, 562–563, 575; Edwards, *A Careful and Strict Enquiry,* in Edwards, *Freedom of the Will,* ed. Ramsey, ibid., I, 369–378. See also the discussion in Bruce Kuklick, *A History of Philosophy in America, 1720–2000* (New York, 2003), 5–26. Edwards drew from his earlier critique of natural law reasoning in New England Congregationalism and applied it to his assessment of anthropocentric currents in Scottish Moderate theology. See Harris, *Of Liberty and Necessity,* 112–113, 115.

to certain fixed and exact established methods and laws: or in somewhat different language, the infinitely exact and precise divine idea,
together with an answerable, perfectly exact, precise and stable will
with respect to correspondent communications to created minds, and
effects on their minds.

For Edwards, then, the human moral will was subject to an idea that lay
in God's mind. Those stable ideas—external to the human mind—could
"gradually be communicated" to "created minds." But their slow mental and
sensory "effects" on humans could be altered or transformed at any moment
according to notions hatched in the mind of God. Edwards employed the
language of British moral philosophy in order to counter what he perceived
to be deistic claims and to assure the nature of experimental piety. But, as
he continued to consider the problem of the human will, he increasingly
used the terminology of moral sense philosophy to question the validity of
its own conclusions, which he came to understand more fully by the 1750s.
He adopted the conceptual motifs of sensory moral theory as a means to
describe the role of human passions and sentiments in the steps leading to
salvation, to identify and describe the emotional flurries that preceded the
attendance of grace. He returned to one of the original roots of Scottish ethical philosophy—Lockean sensationalism—in order to query the notion of
objective and innate morality.[45]

Like Edwards, Witherspoon used philosophical terminology to describe
the importance of a new sense of morality as a gift of grace. When he employed
common sensory motifs against the "metaphysical subtleties" of Hume, he

---

45. On the goal of Scottish philosophy, see Theodore Dwight Bozeman, *Protestants in an
Age of Science: The Baconian Ideal and Antebellum American Religious Thought* (Chapel Hill,
N.C., 1977), 9. On Edwards's distinct response, see Jonathan Edwards, "Ideas, Sense of the
Heart, Spiritual Knowledge or Conviction; Faith," quoted in Perry Miller, "Jonathan Edwards
on the Sense of the Heart," *Harvard Theological Review*, XLI (1948), 129; Miller, *Errand into the
Wilderness* (Cambridge, Mass., 1978), 177; Jonathan Edwards, "The Mind," no. 13, in *Scientific
and Philosophical Writings*, ed. Wallace E. Anderson, in Miller et al., eds., *Works of Jonathan
Edwards*, VI (New Haven, Conn., 1980), 344. According to Sloan, Edwards "found in the empirical analysis of the affections an indispensable conceptual tool for spelling out his doctrine of
conversion"; see Sloan, *The Scottish Enlightenment*, 100. According to Grasso, Edwards "tried
to take the middle ground between Stoddardean uncertainty [about the human ability to discern
the signs of regeneration in others] and Separatist certainty"; see Grasso, *A Speaking Aristocracy*, 124, 126. As Elizabeth Cochran has argued, Edwards "theologically modified Hutcheson's
view [of innate moral sense] so that virtuous repentance (as a corollary of true virtue) is limited to those who have received the benefits of spiritual grace"; see Cochran, *Receptive Human
Virtues*, 99–100.

was concerned to verify the simple relationship between the mind and external physical objects — rather than its innate ability to judge their ethical interaction. Similar to Edwards's later writings, Witherspoon's encounter with moral sense philosophy led him to question the innateness of ethical perception in the "present state" of man. In his "Lectures on Moral Philosophy," Witherspoon used Hutchesonian phrasing to describe the "moral sense" as "the law which our Maker has written upon our hearts, and both intimates and enforces duty, previous to all reasoning." The use of the word "hearts" rather than "senses" (from which the moral capacity was always "distinct") was important. According to his evangelical hermeneutic, the "heart" mediated the Holy Spirit through its emotional reaction to grace. Such an association made individuals aware of their "duty" to divine moral precepts, as specified in scripture. Here Witherspoon demonstrated the deep-rooted and complex association between evangelicalism and moral sense reasoning. He was interested in using concepts from philosophical systems that allowed him to isolate passions and sentiments in human behavior. Yet he did so in order to highlight the role of the heart in the experience of faith, rather than to espouse an entirely inborn ethical sensibility. If sheared of its association with "duty" to God, the notion of a "moral sense" risked promoting "the law of nature" rather than revealed divine precepts.[46]

Witherspoon also shared several of the epistemological problems that bedeviled Edwards's system of moral philosophy and that defined the evangelical struggle more generally. He, too, was faced with the problematic task of describing the origins of humility itself. The next section of his lectures asked whether and how individuals could acknowledge the inevitable "errors" of their ethical perception. Doing so, after all, suggested an innate moral understanding of that which was erroneous. Witherspoon's recommendation seemed to belie his earlier insistence on the problematic nature of unregenerate insight. Listing various assumptions that philosophers had used to define the difference between humans and animals, he suggested that "it is by the remaining power of natural conscience that we must endeavor to detect and oppose these errors." Witherspoon implied that men and women were distinguished by an ability to discern their own "errors" and to believe in God and a "future state." Similar apologetic statements were common among Scottish common sense theorists. Here and in a few other instances, therefore, Witherspoon seems to have demonstrated a degree of inconsistency in

46. Witherspoon, "Lectures on Moral Philosophy," in [Green, ed.], *Works of Witherspoon*, III, 370, 376, 379, 395. On the difference between the empirical perception of objects and the human understanding of moral actions, see, for example, ibid., 395–397.

his discussion of moral philosophy. Had he registered the implications of his anthropocentric ethical motif more thoroughly (which he did not), he might well have reconsidered its inclusion in his lectures, or at least the nature of its exposition.[47]

Rather than fully endorsing Thomas Reid's argument from design, to be sure, Witherspoon immediately followed his discussion of "natural conscience" with several qualifiers, all of which reasserted basic evangelical principles. He referred to the disagreements and contradictions that commonly occurred when philosophers sought to define whether reason or prerational "affection" could contribute to moral knowledge. "The connexion between truth and goodness, between the understanding and the heart" was "of great difficulty" and could only truly appear "in the Supreme Being." In humans, unfortunately, "malignity of disposition, even with the greatest natural powers, blinds the understanding, and prevents the perception of truth itself." Humility before regeneration, Witherspoon implied, somehow derived from an external act of grace. Some truths of scripture, moreover, were even likely to remain beyond the power of the regenerate. The axiomatic distinction between human limitation and divinity, he wrote in his "Lectures on Divinity," made it "consonant to reason and the analogy of nature that there should be so many things in the divine nature that we cannot fully comprehend. There are many such things in his providence, and surely much more in his essence." Being "unable to explain [biblical] doctrines" did not "form an objection" against them.[48]

The word "duty"—rather than "benevolence"—appeared most commonly in the qualifications that followed Witherspoon's discussions of moral sense reasoning. Here Witherspoon continued his critique of Hutcheson, which he extended to other moral sense theorists such as Anthony Ashley Cooper, third earl of Shaftesbury (1671–1713). All those who "profess great opposition to the selfish scheme, declare also great aversion to founding the obligation of virtue in any degree on the will of a superior, or looking for any sanction of punishment, to corroborate the moral laws." "This they especially treat with contempt," he wrote, "when it is supposed to be from the deity." Instead, they felt for others in the way that they yearned to be loved, rather than demonstrating the disinterested benevolence of true virtue. Witherspoon thus claimed that Hutchesonian benevolence might only become possible in a heavenly state long after rebirth, before "which is here in a state of

47. Witherspoon, "Lectures on Moral Philosophy," in [Green, ed.], *Works of Witherspoon*, III, 370–371.

48. Ibid., 370, 374, 376; Witherspoon, "Lectures on Divinity," ibid., IV, 67, 91.

imperfection and liable to much opposition." Moral conscience thus represented a process rather than a faculty, the result of what Witherspoon would later describe as "the constant influence and over-ruling power of Divine Providence" that preserved individuals from their own flawed selves. Using the first person point of view, Witherspoon suggested, "I see a higher species of beauty in moral action: but it arises from a sense of obligation." Though using Hutchesonian aesthetic terminology, Witherspoon avoided determining the "moral sense or conscience" to be an innate ethical compass. Rather, it enabled the Holy Spirit to illuminate the nature of individual sin and the importance of rebirth before full moral conversion.[49]

Reflecting a common religious assumption, Witherspoon suggested that "rights and obligations are correlative terms."

> Whatever others have a just right or title to claim from me, that is my duty, or what I am obliged to do to them.
>
> Right in general may be reduced, as to its source, to the supreme law of moral duty; for whatever men are in duty obliged to do, that they have a claim to, and other men are considered as under an obligation to permit them.

Thus, he criticized moral sense philosophy for confusing duty to divine law with an innate ethical stance, drawing a distinction between ethical duty and a form of self-agreement that was masked as a virtuous concern for communal welfare.[50]

Witherspoon's critique was similar to Edwards's earlier discussion of the ways in which sensory reactions were sometimes confused with innately virtuous reactions. Edwards sought a "first foundation and source [for moral perception] in apprehensions of God's supreme dignity and glory, and in answerable esteem and love of him." Witherspoon, similarly, questioned the individual desire to create a society in which they would like to live. Their analogous discussion of the relationship between faith, obligation, and rights affirms that the notion of individual liberty in eighteenth-century American

49. Witherspoon, "Lectures on Moral Philosophy," in [Green, ed.], *Works of Witherspoon*, III, 382, 390, 391; John Witherspoon, "Delivered at a Public Thanksgiving after Peace: Sermon 45," ibid., 64. Anthony Ashley Cooper, third earl of Shaftesbury, created an anthology of his previously published essays, alongside new works, in a collection that he published in 1711. For the most accurate modern edited volume, see Shaftesbury, *Characteristics of Men, Manners, Opinions, Times,* ed. Lawrence E. Klein (Cambridge, 1999).

50. Witherspoon, "Lectures on Moral Philosophy," in [Green, ed.], *Works of Witherspoon*, III, 369, 406.

thought often required the context of divinely established natural law, a context within which individual freedom was constrained by the commands of duty.[51]

At one point in his "Lectures on Moral Philosophy," Witherspoon self-consciously assumed the mantle of a "philosopher" to list Hutchesonian propositions before his New Jersey students. But he did not adopt them himself or speak of them approvingly. He asked, "If I were to lay down a few propositions on the foundation of virtue, as a philosopher, they should be the following?" The language here was both subjunctive and interrogative. His following reference to the "uncorrupted nature" of man, a phrase that even the most moderate Scottish theologian would have avoided, further underlined its hypothetical nature. Witherspoon listed one argument that a "philosopher" might use:

> Private and public interest may be promoted by the same means, but they are distinct views; they should be made to assist, and not destroy each other.
>
> The result of the whole is, that we ought to take the rule of duty from conscience enlightened by reason, experience, and every way by which we can be supposed to learn the will of our Maker, and his intention in creating us such as we are . . . productive of the greatest good.

Witherspoon described these philosophical suppositions immediately after listing an entirely contradictory argument, which seemed closer to the personal asides and clarifications that he included throughout his lectures: "To make the good of the whole our immediate principle of action, is putting ourselves in God's place, and actually superseding the necessity and use of the particular principles of duty which he hath impressed upon the conscience [through the Holy Spirit]." In this passage, Witherspoon indicted those polite moral philosophers like Hutcheson whose natural law reasoning

51. Edwards, *The Nature of True Virtue,* in Edwards, *Ethical Writings,* ed. Ramsey, in Miller et al., eds. *Works of Jonathan Edwards,* VIII, 560–561, 569; Witherspoon, "Lectures on Moral Philosophy," in [Green, ed.], *Works of Witherspoon,* III, 395. On the context of divinely established natural law in the notion of rights and duties, see James T. Kloppenberg, "The Virtues of Liberalism: Christianity, Republicanism, and Ethics in Early American Political Discourse," *Journal of American History,* LXXIV (1987), 9–33, esp. 9, 18. Aspects of Witherspoon's lectures thus corroborate Haakonssen's claim that, in some Anglo-American evangelical circles during the second half of the eighteenth century, notions of "rights" were "not simply powers granted, but powers granted for a purpose . . . never granted as open-ended powers, but always in conjunction with matching duties" to God. See Haakonssen, "From Natural Law to the Rights of Man," in Lacey and Haakonssen, eds., *A Culture of Rights,* 36.

suggested that human ethical sensibilities were accurate, predictable, and benevolent because they had been implanted by [God in order to provide the common good that he sought for mankind. Witherspoon claimed that such philosophy naively pursued "the good of the whole" without attending to the necessity of conversion. He unsettled the association between natural law theory and Scottish Enlightenment reasoning by referring to the necessity of conversion and salvation before moral perception and by pointing out the remaining difficulty even in verifying the ethical state wrought by grace. In doing so, ironically, he incorporated some of the terminology and analytical concerns of moral sense philosophy.[52]

"The Different and Opposite Systems of Philosophers"

According to Charles Chauncy, Witherspoon avoided the metaphysical evangelicalism of Edwards. Witherspoon certainly used his lectures to offer a simple repudiation of skepticism and immaterialism. But, as explained above, his ethical discussions partly diverged from the rational and common sensory defense of Christianity. Scholarship on the New Divinity movement that followed Edwards has suggested that its theology became "Janus-faced" as its ministers inadvertently developed a more human-centered discussion of moral volition. Focusing on Witherspoon's "Lectures on Moral Philosophy," scholars have also described his career as Janus-faced: orthodox and evangelical in Scotland, anthropocentric and philosophical in America. Yet, as we have seen, Witherspoon eschewed any deeper discussion of the trickier aspects of moral volition by pointing out the primacy of revelation and the emotional role of faith in the experience of regeneration. Nonetheless, parts of his lectures also adopted a more subtle Calvinist trope. According to Witherspoon, his lectures' passive description of differing and even contradictory human philosophies taught a wider lesson that could only confirm the specific message of scripture. Having summarized the complex systems of Berkeley, Hume, Hutcheson, Locke, and Reid, among others, Witherspoon suggested early in his lectures:

52. Witherspoon, "Lectures on Moral Philosophy," in [Green, ed.], *Works of Witherspoon*, III, 387–388. According to Haakonssen, Witherspoon tried "to have it a little both ways" in this passage. Although he did not deny that "we should hold fast to the belief that conscience is God's voice speaking through us," he also stressed that we "should not think that we can make God's purpose, the greatest common good, into *our* purpose in our actions." "We simply have to do our duty as we see it by the limited light of our conscience. This is God's law. What it adds up to is God's business, not ours." See Haakonssen, "From Natural Law," in Lacey and Haakonssen, eds., *A Culture of Rights*, 53–56.

The knowledge of human nature . . . is either perplexed and difficult of itself, or hath been made so, by the manner in which writers in all ages have treated it. Perhaps this circumstance itself, is a strong presumption of the truth of the Scripture doctrine of the depravity and corruption of our nature. Supposing this depravity, it must be one great cause of difficulty and confusion in giving an account of human nature as the work of God. This I take to be indeed the case with the greatest part of our moral and theological knowledge.

Referring to natural law theorists who sought to discover "how [man's] Maker formed him," Witherspoon suggested that true knowledge of human nature had always been "perplexed and difficult"—a sign of the "depravity" of the common human state. Variance within and between philosophical systems demonstrated their common inability to define the exact nature of morality. That they could be erudite but also contradictory showed the potential, but also the fallibility, of human moral reasoning.[53]

All philosophical theories, according to Witherspoon, were products of man and were therefore partially tainted. Thus, a curriculum that briefly described the different forms of reasoning underlying various philosophical concepts aptly highlighted the perceptual confusion inherent in the depraved human state. Witherspoon argued that the "connexion between truth and goodness, between the understanding and the heart, is a subject of great moment, but also of great difficulty." He made a different apologetic use of philosophy: he highlighted the divergence of philosophies (plural). A failure to reconcile Thomas Hobbes's focus on "the state of nature being a state of war" with Hutcheson's and Shaftesbury's account of natural benevolence demonstrated that the "inconveniences of the natural state are very many." It "would be more just and useful," Witherspoon proclaimed, "to say that all simple and original discoveries have been the production of Providence, and not the invention of man."[54]

Witherspoon used his "Lectures on Divinity" to stress a similar observation regarding the problematic nature of human moral perception. On the

53. On the "Janus-faced" nature of New Divinity, see Joseph A. Conforti, *Samuel Hopkins and the New Divinity Movement: Calvinism, the Congregational Ministry, and Reform in New England between the Great Awakenings* (Grand Rapids, Mich., 1981), 118; Noll, *America's God*, 136. For Witherspoon's statements on the perplexed nature of moral understanding and "the different and opposite systems of philosophers," see Witherspoon, "Lectures on Moral Philosophy," in [Green, ed.], *Works of Witherspoon*, III, 368–369.

54. Witherspoon, "Lectures on Moral Philosophy," in [Green, ed.], *Works of Witherspoon*, III, 369, 374, 396, 417.

one hand, he reminded his students that "religion is the grand concern to us all, as we are men;—whatever be our calling and profession, the salvation of our souls is the one thing needful." But, of course, doubt and confusion in the realm of theological understanding would always remain a natural—even necessary—part of the evangelical experience. Here Witherspoon distinguished "hope" from empirical certainty about the nature of moral understanding, even after religious awakening: "Every real believer has some degree of hope, which makes him rest and rely on Christ along for salvation . . . so perhaps there are not very many who have such a degree of steady and firm assurance, as to exclude all doubting." Were doubt not an accepted inclination, the vital role of hope and faith (rather than empirical reasoning) would become redundant. Witherspoon's reasoning recalled Edwards's earlier warnings that religious awakenings might not be fully permanent or completely objective in their moral effect. It has been suggested that eighteenth-century Anglo-American evangelicalism was one of the few lines of thought that could unsettle the "Christian-utilitarian foundation for natural law" by reminding people that purportedly common moral ideals in society might not be implanted in men as a predictable sensibility. Witherspoon translated these lines of thought, as he perceived them, from Scotland to America. The subjectivity of human ethics, he asserted, foreshadowed chaotic rivalries between competing egos and varying intellectual propositions. Questioning the notion of an innately benevolent stance, he unsettled the comfortable assertions of moral sense philosophy that continued to be received on the western side of the Atlantic—even while at times he adopted their conceptual terminology.[55]

55. Witherspoon, "Lectures on Divinity," in [Green, ed.], *Works of Witherspoon,* IV, 11, 13, 15. For Edwards's warnings, see the discussion of his *History of the Work of Redemption* (1746), in Grasso, *A Speaking Aristocracy,* 92. On the unsettling "Christian-utilitarian foundation for natural law," see Haakonssen, "From Natural Law to the Rights of Man," in Lacey and Haakonssen, eds., *A Culture of Rights,* 32, 53, 56. Witherspoon thus confirmed Gordon S. Wood's subsequent scholarly observation that the Scottish Enlightenment ideal of innate sociability often seemed unlikely to Calvinist ministers in America. See Wood, *The Creation of the American Republic, 1776–1787* (Chapel Hill, N.C., 1969), 114. Attempting to order or systematize assertions that were only loosely expounded—or even inconsistent—would misrepresent Witherspoon's limited philosophical training. T. J. Hochstrasser has suggested that "continuing tensions between neo-scholastic ethics, and the notions of faith and grace" were "further perpetuated" in the eighteenth-century Atlantic world; see Hochstrasser, *Natural Law Theories in the Early Enlightenment* (Cambridge, 2000), 3.

CHAPTER 5

"WHEN THEIR FATHERS HAVE FALLEN ASLEEP"

Domestic Culture, Public Virtue, and the Power of Language

A few months before arriving in New Jersey, in a February 1768 letter to
Benjamin Rush John Witherspoon had recognized the public importance
of "the present state of things between Brittain and America" — particularly
with regard to "the Direction of the Education of the youth of so considerable
body in the Northern Colonies." Though he was not yet a patriot, Witherspoon realized that rising tensions between Britain and the American colonies called for special attention to the instruction of young men. In a 1768
newspaper advertisement, written on behalf of the College of New Jersey
trustees, he distinguished the institution from other centers of higher education. In particular, he highlighted "Provisions for the Encouragement of
young Gentlemen, who have finished the ordinary Course of Philosophy, to
return and pursue their Studies at College, and fit themselves . . . for serving
their Country in public Stations."[1]

The exact meaning of the word "Country" in such a statement was not
clear. Only three years after the Stamp Act crisis, it is unlikely that Witherspoon referred to his students' fitting themselves for service to Britain. Conversely, only the most radical colonists would have assigned a notion of national independence to the word in 1768. Nonetheless, Witherspoon believed
that educated young men were increasingly likely to assume positions of public prominence in "the present state of things" between Britain and America.
Many of his graduating students were certainly eager to link their educational
development to political concerns. In 1770, the *New-York Gazette* described
a recent College of New Jersey commencement ceremony and felt obliged
to comment on the political activities that accompanied its religious read-

1. John Witherspoon to Benjamin Rush, Feb. 9, 1768, in L. H. Butterfield, ed., *John
Witherspoon Comes to America: A Documentary Account Based Largely on New Materials* (Prince-
ton, N.J., 1953), 69; "For the Information of the Public, by Order of the Trustees of the College of
New-Jersey," *New-York Gazette or, the Weekly Post-Boy*, Oct. 17, 1768, [2]. For more background
on Witherspoon's desire to advertise to "young Gentlemen," see also the introduction in Thomas
Miller, ed., *The Selected Writings of John Witherspoon* (Carbonale, Ill., 1990), 20–21.

ings and sermons: "How happy ought we to esteem ourselves, when we see some of our Youth, who will probably fill some of the highest Stations in their Country, when their Fathers have fallen asleep, so early declaring their Love to their Country." The *Gazette* praised students for incorporating political discussions alongside moral learning. Parents were somnolent and unpatriotic in contrast to their offspring, a new generation of public-minded college students.[2]

The distinction the *Gazette* drew between familial culture and the civic concerns of higher learning was not new. From Socrates to Xenophon, classical theories of higher education often recommended the temporary removal of young men from their domestic context, where ties of blood blurred the boundary between individual and communal identity. Seeking to facilitate public virtue rather than personal sensibility, early modern civic humanist writers revisited classical recommendations and applied them to their own educational thought. By the mid-eighteenth century, a number of colonial American educators read or re-read civic humanist texts, particularly those that had been transmitted through English thinkers such as James Harrington. These educators, including William Smith, Francis Alison, and William Livingston, synthesized moral sense reasoning with civic ideals, determining an association between individual feelings and communal benevolence.[3]

2. See "Extract of a Letter from New-Brunswick, Dated July 24," *New-York Gazette or, the Weekly Post-Boy,* [July 30, 1770], [3]; "Extract of a Letter from Princeton, July 13," *New-York Gazette or, the Weekly Post-Boy,* July 16, 1770, [3]. The "Extract of a Letter from New-Brunswick" in the *New-York Gazette* commented on a previous account stating that "the senior class at Nassau Hall has unanimously agreed to appear at their ensuing commencement, dressed in American Manufactures." See also the discussion in Varnum Lansing Collins, *President Witherspoon: A Biography,* 2 vols. (Princeton, N.J., 1925), I, 133. On continued support for the Hanoverian line despite opposition to parliamentary corruption, see, for example, T. H. Breen, "Ideology and Nationalism on the Eve of the American Revolution: Revisions *Once More* in Need of Revising," *Journal of American History,* LXXXIV (1997), 13–39; Brendan McConville, *The King's Three Faces: The Rise and Fall of Royal America, 1688–1776* (Chapel Hill, N.C., 2006).

3. Classical and then civic humanist theory promoted "horizontal" associations between students outside the home, as distinct from "vertical" relationships between offspring and their parents. See William M. Sullivan, "Making Civil Society Work: Democracy as a Problem of Civic Cooperation," in Robert K. Fullinwider, ed., *Civil Society, Democracy, and Civic Renewal* (Lanham, Md., 1999), 41; Luigino Bruni and Stefano Zamagni, *Civil Economy: Efficiency, Equity, Public Happiness* (Oxford, 2007), 47. On Socrates, Xenophon, and the role of the family in American education during the colonial and Revolutionary era, see Lorraine Smith Pangle and Thomas L. Pangle, *The Learning of Liberty: The Educational Ideas of the American Founders* (Lawrence, Kans., 1993), 39–52. On the synthesis between moral sensory and civic reasoning,

Many colonial American parents correlated the cultivation of individual sensibility with the future prestige of their children. Whether they were Anglican, Congregationalist, Presbyterian, or Quaker, they believed that their sons would gain representative authority if they learned to define personal desires in relation to communal norms. Criticizing (and often caricaturing) these prevailing assumptions during the 1750s and 1760s, Samuel Davies and his fellow Log College men set out their own alternative synthesis of classical and religious learning. As they encouraged youth to leave their domestic environment for higher education, they added a Calvinistic inflection to civic humanism. Both the reception of divine grace, according to their evangelical viewpoint, and the assumption of civic virtue, according to classical reasoning, required the diminution of individual interests and personal sensibilities that had been formed in the home. They accused parents and other educators of using moral sensory and rational ideas to justify personal or sectarian interests. Their religious and civic pronouncements sought to curtail such private concerns and criticized the domestic context for their cultivation. Witherspoon incorporated a similar synthesis between evangelicalism, classicism, and formal instruction during his American career. He defined the importance of higher education away from the domestic environment, especially in relation to the cultivation of new rhetorical and expressive skills.[4]

---

see, for example, Sarah Knott, *Sensibility and the American Revolution* (Chapel Hill, N.C., 2009), 2, 21–22, 189–190. Whether they were alumni of Yale, Harvard, or the College of William and Mary, privileged colonists often encountered classical works as a significant portion of their gentlemanly education, alongside religious studies, mathematics, and natural philosophy. See Mark Garrett Longaker, *Rhetoric and the Republic: Politics, Civic Discourse, and Education in Early America* (Tuscaloosa, Ala., 2007), 177–185.

4. On evangelical critics of moral sensory educational discourse in the Middle Colonies, see Bryan F. Le Beau, *Jonathan Dickinson and the Formative Years of American Presbyterianism* (Lexington, Ky., 1997), 165–186. As Mark A. Noll and others have argued, "classical republican themes of disinterested public service" were frequently co-opted by evangelical clergymen and synthesized with "themes of God-orientated public duty" during the colonial era. See Noll, "The American Revolution and Protestant Evangelicalism," *Journal of Interdisciplinary History,* XXIII (1993), 615–638; Noll, *America's God: From Jonathan Edwards to Abraham Lincoln* (New York, 2002), 447–451; Noll, "The Contingencies of Christian Republicanism: An Alternative Account of Protestantism and the American Founding," in Thomas S. Engeman and Michael P. Zuckert, eds., *Protestantism and the American Founding* (Notre Dame, Ind., 2004), 243. See also Jack P. Greene, "The Concept of Virtue in Late Colonial British America," in Richard K. Matthews, ed., *Virtue, Corruption, and Self-Interest: Political Values in the Eighteenth Century* (Bethlehem, Pa., 1994), 35–42. Scholarship on higher educational enrollment from the 1740s to the 1760s has tended to suggest that its underlying incentive rarely reflected purely classical or religious paradigms of communal virtue. A useful overview of the pragmatic interests governing

Instilling proficiency in public communication without emphasizing the innateness of moral sensory perception was no easy task. Unsurprisingly, the rhetorical theories of Scottish moral philosophy tended to eschew any dichotomy between ethical perception and persuasive expression. Scottish rhetoricians such as James Beattie, Hugh Blair, and George Campbell suggested in the 1770s and 1780s that aesthetic form and moral content in communication evoked a similar sensory response. Both inspired an appraisal of that which was naturally and uncontrollably sensed as beautiful—whether in the nature of good deeds or in their elegant written and oral description. The popularity of Scottish rhetoricians increased markedly in America from the late 1760s. A link between moral philosophy and rhetorical expression could be found in the polite intellectual circles of colonial America and in the didactic pronouncements of books, pamphlets, and primers in the early national era.[5]

The identification of sensory perception as the seat of ethical perception and the pre-rational appeal of elegant writing and oral expression theoretically applied to all people. Yet privileged Americans often claimed that the

---

parental attraction to higher education can be found in Phyllis Vine, "The Social Function of Eighteenth-Century Higher Education," *History of Education Quarterly*, XVI (1976), 409–424. For an example of a sermon linking classical and evangelical accounts of virtue, contrary to theories of innate moral discernment, see Samuel Davies, *Religion and Public Spirit: A Valedictory Address to the Senior Class, Delivered in Nassau Hall, September 21, 1760, the Sunday before the Commencement* ([New York], 1761).

5. On "moderate" enlightened culture, see Henry F. May, *The Enlightenment in America* (New York, 1976), 1, 12. The word rhetoric is used here to describe the ways in which expressive forms could be ordered and deployed through learned patterns or methods in order to gain a desired response from individuals or an audience. Advisory works in Scottish Moderate rhetoric suggested that readers and audience members were primed for a sensory reaction to well-composed statements, whether written or oral. They assured readers that a common sense of aesthetic style was likely to accompany an advanced moral sensibility. On the increasing popularity of Scottish rhetoricians in America from the late 1760s, particularly George Campbell and Hugh Blair, see Warren Alan Guthrie, "The Development of Rhetorical Theory in America, 1635–1850," Speech *Monographs*, XV (1948), 61–71; George M. Marsden, *Fundamentalism and American Culture: The Shaping of Twentieth-Century Evangelicalism, 1870–1925* (Oxford, 1980), 14, 15; David Daiches, *"Style Périodique* and *Style Coupé:* Hugh Blair and the Scottish Rhetoric of American Independence," in Richard B. Sher and Jeffrey R. Smitten, eds., *Scotland and America in the Age of the Enlightenment* (Princeton, N.J., 1990), 209–226; Susan Manning, *Fragments of Union: Making Connections in Scottish and American Writing* (Basingstoke, U.K., 2002), 51, 63, 191; David S. Shields, *Civil Tongues and Polite Letters in British America* (Chapel Hill, N.C., 1997), xvii, 181; Terence Martin, *The Instructed Vision: Scottish Common Sense Philosophy and the Origins of American Fiction* (Bloomington, Ind., 1961).

aesthetic basis of persuasive communication was best harnessed by those whose sensibility had been educated and refined. Hugh Blair's praise for the moral effects of tasteful writing and oral expression allowed American educators to distinguish their rhetorical capacity from simpler public modes of persuasion. The latter became more popular during the early stages of the imperial crisis. Elites worried that the "Grub Street incivility" of Revolutionary-era debate promoted an unorthodox linguistic style and inelegant expression, that public rhetorical expression had become too accessible to those without sufficient education or training. In response, their "civil tongues and polite letters" sought to privatize sentiment in order to distinguish elite expression from popular expressive forms. Scottish rhetoric provided them with a genteel tradition that matched their associates in Britain.[6]

During the colonial and early Revolutionary era, rhetorical cultivation often began within rather than without the home. In the Middle Colonies, but also in parts of Virginia and Maryland, a high proportion of domestic tutors boasted an intellectual background in Scotland's Moderate educational establishment. Drawing an association between moral philosophy and belletristic expression, they demonstrated an acute concern with written and spoken elegance, an interest that had hitherto been more apparent among Moderate literati in Glasgow, Edinburgh, and Aberdeen. Historians have tended to assume that Witherspoon's collegiate educational program was contiguous with these domestic experiences. Examining the "culture of performance" in colonial and Revolutionary language, and the influence of Scottish moral philosophy on that culture, some have even suggested that the College of New Jersey president was "the first important American teacher of rhetoric." But how accurate is it to extrapolate that Witherspoon began a "sea change in American education" that heralded the dominance of rhetoricians such as

6. Shields, *Civil Tongues,* xv, xvii, xviii; Donald H. Meyer, *The Democratic Enlightenment* (New York, 1976), 182–185; May, *Enlightenment in America,* 327–332. The reception of Scottish rhetoric, according to Andrew Hook, even "impeded the development of a native American literary idiom" in the populace at large. See Hook, *Scotland and America: A Study of Cultural Relations, 1750–1835* (Glasgow, 1975), 82. See also David Daiches, "John Witherspoon, James Wilson, and the Influence of Scottish Rhetoric on America," in John Dwyer and Richard B. Sher, eds., *Sociability and Society in Eighteenth-Century Scotland* (Edinburgh, 1993), 170–171; Franklin E. Court, "The Early Impact of Scottish Literary Teaching in North America," in Robert Crawford, ed., *The Scottish Invention of English Literature* (Cambridge, 1998), 134–163. On the elite appropriation of rhetoric, see Thomas Gustafson, *Representative Words: Politics, Literature, and the American Language, 1776–1865* (Cambridge, 1992), 12; Sandra M. Gustafson, *Eloquence Is Power: Oratory and Performance in Early America* (Chapel Hill, N.C., 2000), chap. 4; Longaker, *Rhetoric and the Republic,* 177–185.

Hugh Blair and George Campbell? Such an assumption seems problematic given Witherspoon's partial unease with human-centered ethical assertions, which many of those Scottish theorists promoted in their rhetorical appeal to common sensibility.[7]

While maintaining a number of important facets of Scottish rhetoric and polite discourse, Witherspoon's approach to communication, expression, and "eloquence" was distinct from some of the more anthropocentric theories of Blair and Campbell. He increasingly grew wary of domestic instruction in the American home, including its approach to communication. He perceived its indulgence of youthful sensibility and its propensity to overlook the role of religious revival in moral learning. His focus on the standardization of public expression in higher education instead sought to synthesize classical and evangelical forms of persuasion. In doing so, it departed from several rhetorical assumptions that were associated with Scottish moral philosophy and were popular in other American circles.[8]

7. Jay Fliegelman, *Declaring Independence: Jefferson, Natural Language, and the Culture of Performance* (Stanford, Calif., 1993), 34; Leonard Tennenhouse, *The Importance of Feeling English: American Literature and the British Diaspora, 1750–1850* (Princeton, N.J., 2007), 34–35. Tennenhouse develops Fliegelman's suggestion to portray Witherspoon as precursor to the rise of Scottish Enlightenment rhetoric in English studies in America. On Scottish tutors in America, see Ned Landsman, "The Legacy of British Union for the North American Colonies: Provincial Elites and the Problem of Imperial Union," in John Robertson, ed., *A Union for Empire: Political Thought and the British Union of 1707* (Cambridge, 1995), 303.

8. According to Richard B. Sher, the emphasis on New England religious traditions in the historiography of American political preaching has failed "to take into account the important role played in America by British and European jeremiads"—particularly the concepts and ideas that proliferated in sermons by evangelical Scots. As a supplement to Sher's observation, one must analyze the expressive techniques that were employed by evangelical Presbyterians such as Witherspoon. See Sher, "Witherspoon's *Dominion of Providence* and the Scottish Jeremiad Tradition," in Sher and Smitten, eds., *Scotland and America*, 54; John Witherspoon, "Lectures on Eloquence," in [Ashbel Green, ed.], *The Works of the Rev. John Witherspoon D.D.L.L.D. Late President of the College at Princeton, New-Jersey . . .* , 2d ed., rev., 4 vols. (Philadelphia, 1802), III, 475. In several studies of American rhetorical culture, Witherspoon is said to have moved away from evangelical techniques that were not conducive to the cultivation of aesthetic theories of linguistic expression. See, for example, Daiches, "John Witherspoon," in Dwyer and Sher, eds., *Sociability and Society*, 170–171. On the promotion of evangelical methods of rhetorical expression from the late colonial to the Revolutionary era, see Harry S. Stout, "Religion, Communications, and the Ideological Origins of the American Revolution," *William and Mary Quarterly*, 3d Ser., XXXIV (1977), 519–541; Jerome Dean Mahaffey, *Preaching Politics: The Religious Rhetoric of George Whitefield and the Founding of a New Nation* (Waco, Tex., 2007), 11. To suggest that evangelical methods naturally corresponded to Scottish rhetoric would overlook Hugh Blair's influential claim that moral actions and tasteful expression were dually perceived in aesthetic terms,

Domestic Education and American Moral Sensibility

The Scottish Enlightenment discussion of communal sociability often masked the role of socioeconomic interest among its educated proponents. As Witherspoon declared in his 1757 *Serious Inquiry into the Nature and Effects of the Stage,* wealthy parents encouraged learning in the "taste of this enlightened age" and flattered the sensibility of youth:

> It is to be feared, we may improve it [knowledge] no better than many young men do, who come to the easy possession of wealth of their fathers' getting. They neither know the worth nor the use of it, but squander it idly away, in the most unprofitable or hurtful pursuits. It is doubtless, an easy thing at present, to acquire a superficial knowledge, from magazines, reviews, dictionaries, and other helps to the slothful student. He is now able, at a very small expence, to join the beau and the scholar, and triumphs in the taste of this enlightened age, of which he hath the comfort to reflect, that he himself makes a part. But for our mortification, let us recollect, that as several writers have observed, human things never continue long at a stand. . . . For as states grow up from poverty to industry, wealth and power; so, from these they proceed to luxury and vice; and by them are brought back to poverty and subjection.

The "easy possession" of parental wealth supported the "slothful student" who wished to "acquire a superficial knowledge" in belles lettres. Adopting a Calvinistic tone, Witherspoon criticized the distorting nexus between polite learning and privileged familial culture, which obscured the inevitable "mortification" of worldly endeavors. He repudiated the Moderate association between civic development and advancements in style and expression. In an undated Scottish sermon titled "The Nature and Extent of Visible Religion," most likely delivered around the same time, Witherspoon warned that a "child of a slothful parent, a subject of an unfaithful magistrate, if their profession is such as to make the neglect scandalous, shall despise them in their hearts, and sometimes go so far as to reproach them by their words, even where their own ease and security is wholly owing to that very criminal in-

---

that an innate attraction to pleasing word forms was likely to accompany a positive response to their ethical content. Blair's assumption was not entirely congruent with evangelical methods of persuasion, given its tendency to define inborn moral perception without specifying the role of conversion. See Shields, *Civil Tongues,* xvi–xvii.

dulgence." He highlighted the abrogation of religious responsibility by lazy parents: as "unfaithful magistrate[s]," their pursuit of the worldly "ease and security" of their offspring only leads to "indulgence" and disrespect.[9]

In the American colonies, a number of prominent evangelical clergymen were also wary of parental influences over the moral learning of youth. At times they even suggested that diminishing the primacy of biological kinship would allow a wider fellowship under grace. Jonathan Edwards warned that personal sentiments and sensibilities were too often indulged by familial ties of blood, preventing the necessary realization of universal sin. Edwards's son-in-law, Aaron Burr, Sr., the second president of the College of New Jersey, noted in 1755 that "almost all prevailing Corruptions of the Times" came from a "Want of proper Government, Discipline, and Instruction in families." But, unlike Edwards, Burr was less oriented toward extrafamilial evangelicalism. His solution to impiety still lay within the home: "Parents and Governors of Families" were to "use their Authority and Influence, for the reforming" of their children.[10]

Burr's reorientation of moral suasion toward parental authority fits the model of the family as a corporate moral unit. By the 1750s and 1760s, many prominent households, particularly in New England but also in the Middle Colonies, mediated between their own self-governing morality and that of the wider community. A father might assume the role of an orthodox minister, highlighting the duty that he and his offspring dually owed to God's external mercy and grace. Yet the demand for moral action from his offspring could also be framed in more human-centered terms, according to his own superior conscience. They were to respect him, learn from his example, and develop their ethical sensibility in order to match his own cultivated stance. To re-

9. John Witherspoon, *A Serious Inquiry into the Nature and Effects of the Stage . . .* , in [Green, ed.], *Works of Witherspoon*, III, 187; Witherspoon, "The Nature and Extent of Visible Religion," ibid., I, 540. On the ironic link between the flourishing of moral sensory theories and the elite consolidation of property and patronage, see John Dwyer, *Virtuous Discourse: Sensibility and Community in Late Eighteenth-Century Scotland* (Edinburgh, 1987), 74–75; John Robertson, "The Scottish Enlightenment at the Limits of the Civic Tradition," in Istvan Hont and Michael Ignatieff, eds., *Wealth and Virtue: The Shaping of Political Economy in the Scottish Enlightenment* (Cambridge, 1983), 137–178.

10. On the separation of individuals from the familial context in Edwardsean evangelicalism, see Susan M. Juster, "Patriarchy Reborn: The Gendering of Authority in the Evangelical Church in Revolutionary New England," *Gender and History*, VI (1994), 61–63. For Burr's statements, see Aaron Burr, *A Discourse Delivered at New-Ark, in New-Jersey, January 1, 1755; Being a Day Set Apart for Solemn Fasting and Prayer, on Account of the Late Encroachments of the French, and Their Designs against the British Colonies in America* (New York, 1755), 33.

produce his display of moral conduct, children might surmise, they were to channel their innate but hitherto untapped behavioral faculties.[11]

By the 1760s, moral sensory presumptions were indeed reflected in the program of learning that many young men encountered in and around their domestic environment, including in the Middle Colonies. The College of New Jersey, between its founding and the end of Witherspoon's presidency, drew increasingly large numbers of students from New England and the southern colonies (particularly Maryland) in addition to the mid-Atlantic region. Up until the 1760s, most of the College of William and Mary's students came from Virginia, and more than 90 percent of Harvard's students came from Massachusetts. Yale drew approximately 75 percent of its students from Connecticut. The student body's relative regional diversity was accorded by the College of New Jersey's position as the cheapest institution of stature in the colonies and its special relationship with the evangelical movement throughout the Eastern Seaboard during the previous two decades. Yet the wide catchment area of the college also incorporated students whose earlier learning could not be defined as traditionally evangelical. Before their higher education in Princeton village, a number of young men in New Jersey had sought "the way of improvement" through moral sense reasoning. They had been influenced by Moderate Presbyterian tutors in their homes or in nearby educational academies such as Green Hall.[12]

Many colonial American parents felt inclined to underline the innateness of the moral sense in their children and to support its subsequent cultivation. Implicit in their disposition was a desire to distinguish the moral authority of their children from lower social and vocational orders (mirroring the situation in Enlightenment Scotland). Though moral sensibility was described as

11. Many prominent New England families "had become the self-appointed guardians of liberty, property, and evangelical piety. Conscientious heads of households were now the bulwarks of moral order in an expanded religious marketplace, and the community was encouraged to trust them and the invisible hand of Providence to guide individual moral choices for the good of the whole." See Christopher Grasso, *A Speaking Aristocracy: Transforming Public Discourse in Eighteenth-Century Connecticut* (Chapel Hill, N.C., 1999), 64–65.

12. On figures for the student catchment area, see James McLachlan, *Princetonians, 1748–1768: A Biographical Dictionary* (Princeton, N.J., 1976), xix–xx. See also Lawrence A. Cremin, *American Education: The Colonial Experience, 1607–1783* (New York, 1970), 214; Thomas L. Purvis, *Colonial America to 1763* (New York, 1999), 246. John Fea's account of the early experience of Philip Fithian in rural New Jersey demonstrates his evangelical inspiration but also his increasing encounter with moral sensory ideas in a local academy. See Fea, *The Way of Improvement Leads Home: Philip Vickers Fithian and the Rural Enlightenment in Early America* (Philadelphia, 2008), 64–66, 69.

ostensibly universal and inborn, they wished for their sons to be perceived as upstanding representatives of objective civic norms. A desire for future distinction often underlay their decision to hire private tutors for their sons or to enroll them in small local academies near their homes. Many of those local educators were Scots who had studied in Edinburgh, Aberdeen, and other centers of Moderate education. In search of remuneration and pedagogical respect, they journeyed to plantation dwellings in the southern colonies or to relatively affluent communities in New Jersey, Pennsylvania, and New York. It was through their influence that the formal ideas of moral sense reasoning were often first introduced into American homes, even in isolated rural communities. Their program increasingly focused on an appreciation of literature, conversation, and art—including the ability of those disciplines to transmit moral values through content alongside the aesthetic beauty of their form.[13]

Though he lauded the Calvinist heritage of his new college, Witherspoon soon became anxious about the domestic context from which his students were drawn. Unlike Aaron Burr, Sr., he was not inclined to suggest that the moral reformation of society could be directed primarily by domestic heads of households. In his "Letters on Education," first published in the spring 1775 edition of the *Pennsylvania Magazine,* Witherspoon recalled several observations that he had made during his first few years in America. He complained that too many parents favored the freedom of their children to develop habits of polite conversation and aesthetically pleasing discourse, making them more likely to omit religious worship in the family domain. As "every man's first and great concern," the gift of "religion to know the real connexion between, and the proper mixture of spirit and form" would be lost among offspring in such households. Reflecting his continuing critique of the aesthetic analogy between pleasing form and ethical content, Witherspoon then warned that, even though "the form without the spirit"

13. On the link between rhetorical training and the desire for social prestige in New Jersey, see Longaker, *Rhetoric and the Republic,* 177–185. On academies and private tutors in the Middle Colonies, see Fea, *Way of Improvement,* 60–65; Ned C. Landsman, *From Colonials to Provincials: American Thought and Culture, 1680–1760* (New York, 1997), 22–24. As a tutor in Robert Carter's Virginian plantation home during 1773–1774, the New Jersey Presbyterian Philip Vickers Fithian noted that many schoolmasters from Scotland acted as tutors. See Hunter Dickinson Farish, ed., *Journal and Letters of Phillip Vickers Fithian, 1773–1774: A Plantation Tutor of the Old Dominion* (Williamsburg, Va., 1943), 43; David Dobson, *Scottish Emigration to Colonial America, 1607–1785* (Athens, Ga., 1994), 149; Louis B. Wright, *The Cultural Life of the American Colonies,* ed. Henry Steele Commager and Richard Brandon Morris (Mineola, N.Y., 2002), 70–71, 112.

was "good for nothing . . . the spirit without the form, never yet existed." He noted that, although "severity . . . [and] authority . . . is often decried," off-spring were too often coaxed and indulged, thus eschewing any concern for moral discipline beyond their innate sensibilities.[14]

Witherspoon was particularly concerned that parents in well-to-do American homes had devolved their instructive role to domestic servants. Home helpers, he claimed, were likely to conceal youthful misdeeds because they feared their employers' passionate nature. Too many parents responded to reports of misdeeds with emotional hysteria or tense quietude, sometimes oscillating between the two:

> There are two dispositions in parents, which hinder the servants from making discoveries [about youthful misbehavior]; the first is when they are very passionate, and are apt to storm and rage against their servants, for every real or supposed neglect. . . . The other is, when they are tender-hearted or timorous to excess, which makes them show themselves deeply affected or greatly terrified upon any little accident that befals their children. In this case, the very best servants are unwilling to tell them through fear of making them miserable.

Having given up most of their daily instructive responsibility to servants, parents failed to behave in the "solemn" manner that befitted their humility before God. Servants feared the unpredictable results of parental behavior and kept parents at a distance from daily developments. Children and youth, consequently, failed to receive appropriate chastisement. According to Witherspoon, servants were not to be blamed for their actions: "Granting them [offspring] such indulgences" was the result of parental neglect. "I am," Witherspoon continued, "one of those who think the fault is at least as often in the masters."[15]

Several pages after describing the soft and gentle instructive methods of parents and their devolution of power to servants, Witherspoon claimed:

> It must be a vast advantage that a habit of submission should be brought on so early, that even memory itself shall not be able to reach back to its beginning. Unless this is done . . . the authority will be imperfect; and some in which any thing that deserves that name will be impossible. There are some families, not contemptible either in station or character,

14. Witherspoon, "Letters on Education," in [Green, ed.], *Works of Witherspoon,* IV, 133, 154.

15. Ibid., 130–131.

in which the parents are literally and properly obedient to their children, are forced to do things against their will.

He thus recommended showing that "reproof or correction are the fruit of sanctified love." "Use your authority for God, and he will support it. — Let it always be seen that you are more displeased at sin than at folly." If parents defined their authority according to their innate perceptual skills, rather than by displaying their heightened understanding of religious precepts and duties to God, then they risked losing control of their offspring. Following their lead, their children would seek out their own supposed innate moral values, ultimately diminishing deference to their parents' example.[16]

Francis Hutcheson, in his *System of Moral Philosophy*, which was published nearly a decade after his death in 1755, thought it necessary to point out that children were not merely slaves to their parents. The nature of "parental affection" suggested "the permanent obligation, on parents to preserve their children and consult their happiness to the utmost of their power." But the rights of parents were to be prevented from keeping children "in a miserable state of slavery." Thus, Hutcheson recommended that "parental affection naturally secures to them this emancipation, as the reason God has given them intitles them to it." Guardians were charged with "exerting their own wisdom" wisely. In his American "Letters on Education," Witherspoon used the motif of slavery to make the very different claim that, when "the spirits" too often found themselves "under confinement" by overindulgence and tenderness, they were likely to enter a "dull and languishing state." Hutcheson warned that an involuntary duty to parents was not conducive to the development of a youthful sensibility. Witherspoon, conversely, cautioned that "if parents are too long in beginning to exert their authority" their offspring would become "habituated to indulgence" and "exceedingly impatient of restraint." Witherspoon sought to provide a more serious qualification to "parental tenderness," moving from such moral sensory terminology toward the religious recommendation that a parent should "rejoice in his children, as they are the gift of a gracious God; should put his trust in the care of an indulgent Providence for the preservation of his offspring . . . that they may be, in due time, the heirs of eternal life; and, as he knows the absolute dependance of every creature upon the will of God, should be ready to resign them at what time his Creator shall see proper to demand them."[17]

16. Ibid., 137–138, 141.

17. Francis Hutcheson, *A System of Moral Philosophy: In Three Books*, 2 vols. (London, 1755), II, 188, 190; Witherspoon, "Letters on Education," in [Green, ed.], *Works of Witherspoon*, IV, 127, 129, 134. Christopher Castiglia suggests that Witherspoon's focus on discipline rather than

Though he opposed Hutcheson's formulations, Witherspoon did not suggest that parental authority was automatic. He sought a "middle way" between dialogue and unquestioning power as "recommended by the spirit of God." With that "spirit" in mind, he reminded parents to display their deference to God when in the company of their children. Such a display of meekness, ironically, would inspire greater obedience from offspring: "You cannot easily believe the weight that it gives to family authority, when it appears visibly to proceed from a sense of duty, and to be itself an act of obedience to God. This will produce coolness and composure in the manner, it will direct and enable a parent to mix every expression of heart felt tenderness, with the most severe and needful reproofs." When "visibly" and appropriately exhibited, "duty" and "obedience to God" provided a powerful contrast to the underdeveloped egoism of youth. Sentimentality ("heart felt tenderness") and hierarchical authority ("severe and needful reproofs") both became redundant when parents eschewed their duty to God. The first merely served to flatter and indulge unregenerate sensibility; the second aroused unstable resentment among children.[18]

Deference to God, when prominently displayed, made it appropriate for parents to affirm that "the rod itself is an evidence of love, and that it is true of every pious parent on earth, what is said of our Father in heaven, 'Whom the Lord loveth, he chasteneth, and scourgeth ever son whom he recciveth. If ye endure chastening, God dealeth with you as with sons: for what son is he whom the Father chasteneth not? But if ye are without chastisement, whereof all are partakers, then ye are bastards and not sons.'" Chastisement became legitimate evidence of love when parents adhered to "this maxim in [their] eye." Witherspoon recommended "that solemnity take the place of, and be submitted for severity. . . . To train up a child in the nurture and admonition of the Lord, I know is not impossible." Parents who employed "every [other] soft and gentle" method indulged the limited capacity of youthful insight. Forceful discipline without pious humility was equally problematic, taking the place of divine will. Youthful submission could only be justified when parental authority was shown "to be itself an act of obedience to God."[19]

---

tender indulgence represented a precursor to "Benthamite" forms of surveillance and control during the following century, a legacy of Enlightenment attempts to encourage sensory self-control within the home. In contrast, I read the "Letters on Education" as a response to the Enlightenment's attempt to encourage innate sensory control among youth. See Christopher Castiglia, "Pedagogical Discipline and the Creation of White Citizenship: John Witherspoon, Robert Finley, and the Colonization Society," *Early American Literature*, XXXIII (1998), 196.

18. Witherspoon, "Letters on Education," in [Green, ed.], *Works of Witherspoon*, IV, 141.

19. Ibid., 133–134, 141, 143.

Witherspoon's critique of domestic sentimentality in genteel circles did not prevent him from lauding the association between "ideas of piety and politeness." Both, he claimed, were necessary to prepare youth "for a general intercourse with mankind, or the public duties of an active life." Ostensibly similar statements were often produced by Scottish Enlightenment philosophers. The Moderate literati of Edinburgh used their roles as university professors and ministers to mediate between individual sensibility and civic ideals to propagate polite morality. They suggested that courteous deference between men was a natural means to demonstrate their mutual stake in society.[20]

Notwithstanding the general similarity of their language, however, Witherspoon's American "Letters on Education" were alert to the problem of moral innateness in Moderate accounts of politeness. Having recalled reading several essays on piety and literature by French "Jansenists," Witherspoon suggested that "worldly politeness is no more than an imitation or imperfect copy of christian charity, being the pretence or outward appearance, of that deference to the judgement, and attention to the interest of others, which a true christian has as the rule of his life." The duty of a Christian as well as a citizen was instead defined according to a pedagogical precept, the primary desire to educate children "in the fear of God." Witherspoon argued that it is "a noble support of authority" when education "is really and visibly directed to the most important end . . . the glory of God in the eternal happiness and salvation of children." Polite youth deferred their passions to "think of others just as a christian ought" — perceiving their duty to God rather than relying on their own moral stance.[21]

"Remove the Temptation of Running Home and Lurking in Idleness"

John Locke, in his *Some Thoughts concerning Education* (1693), had claimed that youthful deference was best inculcated through an appeal to rational self-interest in the familial environment. Such educational logic can be distinguished from Witherspoon's warning and reminder in his "Letters on Education." Referencing philosophical theories that linked benevolence with prestige, Witherspoon recommended:

20. Ibid., 144–145. On the Moderate literati's mediation between civic and individualistic ideals, see David Allan, *Virtue, Learning, and the Scottish Enlightenment: Ideas of Scholarship in Early Modern History* (Edinburgh, 1993), 7.

21. Witherspoon, "Letters on Education," in [Green, ed.], *Works of Witherspoon,* IV, 128, 140, 145, 148.

The care of our souls is represented in scripture as the one thing needful. He makes a miserable bargain, who gains the whole world and loses
his own soul. It is not the native beauty of virtue, or the outward credit
of it, or the inward satisfaction arising from it, or even all these combined together, that will be sufficient to change our natures and govern
our conduct; but a deep conviction, that unless we are reconciled to
God, we shall without doubt perish everlastingly.

Witherspoon's reference to the "beauty of virtue" clearly responded to
Hutchesonian educational theories. His discussion of "outward credit" and
"inward satisfaction" also likely alluded to Locke's utilitarian argument that
individual interests were germane to public esteem. Making what he perceived to be a moral distinction, Witherspoon highlighted his recommendation that, as a means to regulate their conduct, offspring should be trained
to pay final "homage" to that "which is due to piety" in order to become
"reconciled to God" and to appreciate their personal obligation to his providential scheme.[22]

In his "Lectures on Eloquence," which he delivered to American students
from 1770 onward, Witherspoon alluded once more to the inculcation of classical and religious notions of virtue. But, in this instance, he described the
importance of a higher education away from the family. He referred in particular to the Greek historian Xenophon (circa 430–354 BCE), who, in his
opinion, was "superior to almost every author in dignity." Admiring Socratic
instructive methods, Xenophon had used his *Education of Cyrus* to suggest
that civic order was strengthened when young men left their familial farms for
Persian cities to be instilled with stoical discipline. The sensory indulgences

22. John Locke, *Some Thoughts concerning Education* (London, 1693), 90–91, 116; Witherspoon, "Letters on Education," in [Green, ed.], *Works of Witherspoon*, IV, 125, 149, 153. On the
distinction between Locke and Witherspoon in his fifth "Letter on Education," see also Pangle
and Pangle, *The Learning of Liberty*, 64. On the wider influence of Locke's *Some Thoughts in
America*, see Jay Fliegelman, *Prodigals and Pilgrims: The American Revolution against Patriarchal Authority, 1750–1800* (Cambridge, 1982), 1–35. This section of Witherspoon's "Letters
on Education" responded even more particularly to a text that he had read in Scotland that he
described as "archbishop Cambray's education of a daughter, an advice to parents to let their
children perceive that they esteem others, not according to their station or outward splendor, but
their virtue and real worth." Witherspoon seems to be referring to François Fénelon (1651–1715),
who was a French Roman Catholic theologian and later the Archbishop of Cambrai, in France.
He was also popular among Moderates in Scotland. See Charles Butler, *The Life of Fenelon,
Archbishop of Cambray* (London, 1810). Witherspoon preferred Cambray's definition of youthful
esteem but ultimately wished for offspring to pay final homage to God. See Witherspoon, "Letters on Education," in [Green, ed.], *Works of Witherspoon*, IV, 149.

of domestic life, according to Witherspoon, could be curtailed through higher education at a distance from the home.[23]

Yet even the disciplined educational practices of classical lore were not sufficient to counter the indulgence of sensibility. Drawing a parallel between the offspring of well-to-do American families and those in ancient Athens, he warned of the platoon-like culture that tended to develop when male youths were removed from their household environment: "I take it for granted, that an assembly of the vulgar in Athens was just like an assembly of common people . . . and that some of them were but mere mobs; and that they were very disorderly in plain from what we read of Plato being pulled down from the desk, when he went up to defend Socrates." Here Witherspoon demonstrated his familiarity with classical accounts in which regimented educational practices sometimes heralded unintended effects.[24]

Scottish moral sense theorists were not unaware of the dangers associated with the extrafamilial education of youth. The editors of the *Scots Magazine* regularly criticized educational handbooks such as *Lord Chesterfield's Letters*, published in 1774, for ignoring the ways in which passionate youth were likely to engage in worldly excess and disorderly behavior when assembled together for an extended period of time. They highlighted the potentially virtuous feelings of susceptible youth and recommended instructive programs to cultivate their natural sensibility and emotionality without descending into passionate disorder. Witherspoon also recommended a strict program of educational training. But, unlike the editors of the *Scots Magazine,* he avoided any strong allusion to sentimental sympathy. Rather, he suggested that the inculcation of duty "as a Christian, or a citizen," would temper the conscience of a young man. Without implanting "the fear of God" into youth, their removal from familial authority would only serve to flatter their unregenerate sensibility and encourage their rambunctiousness. Christian humility, according to Witherspoon, countered youthful excess in the context of higher education to a greater degree than physical punishment in the American home. Though he endorsed the importance of extrafamilial education, he shared the fears of Scottish moral sense theorists that young men might run wild with their passions when removed from paternal authority. Nonetheless, he veered away from their tendency to define the cultivation of inborn moral

23. Witherspoon, "Lectures on Eloquence," in [Green, ed.], *Works of Witherspoon*, III, 484, 511 (see also 515, 530).

24. Ibid., 511. On the perceived link between classical theory and the civic aspect of higher education from the colonial through the Revolutionary era, see Carl J. Richard, *The Founders and the Classics: Greece, Rome, and the American Enlightenment* (Cambridge, Mass., 1994), 17–22.

perception in youth without specifying the necessity of conversion and a new sense of morality wrought by grace.[25]

In order to promote his own particular institution of higher education in New Jersey, Witherspoon wrote a series of public petitions to American parents during the late 1760s and early 1770s. In one petition, he contrasted the discipline of higher learning with the problematic nature of familial life on the western side of the Atlantic. His 1772 *Address to the Inhabitants of Jamaica and Other West India Islands, in Behalf of the College of New-Jersey* was circulated between the mainland American colonies and the British Caribbean. It outlined the merit of moving offspring as far away as they could possibly go from their family homes:

> That places of education on the continent of America are . . . sufficiently distant [from Jamaica and the West Indies] to remove the temptation of running home and lurking in idleness. . . . Those who come from the greatest distance have, in general, behaved with most regularity. Being removed from their relations, it becomes necessary for them to support a character, as they find themselves treated by their companions, teachers, and indeed all other persons, according to their behavior.

In his appeal for prospective students, Witherspoon suggested that "idleness" was an inevitable state of colonial domesticity and that being "removed from their relations" was beneficial to the character of young men. Though he spoke to Caribbean settlers, Witherspoon pointed out that those who came to the College of New Jersey from "the greatest distance [in mainland North America]" demonstrated the most positive behavioral development. They acted "with most regularity" because they were less likely to visit their homes frequently. "The truth is," Witherspoon argued in his "Lectures on Moral Philosophy": "Though man for wise reasons, afterwards to be noticed, continues longer in a family dependance, than other animals, yet in time he becomes *sui juris*." Domestic education was right and necessary up to a point, after which young men were required to address their moral development without the unconditional support of parents.[26]

25. Witherspoon, "Letters on Education," in [Green, ed.], *Works of Witherspoon*, IV, 125, 128, 134. See the discussion of Scottish Moderate concerns over educational handbooks in Dwyer, *Virtuous Discourse*, 74–75.

26. John Witherspoon, *Address to the Inhabitants of Jamaica, and Other West-India Islands, in Behalf of the College of New Jersey*, in [Green, ed.], *Works of Witherspoon*, IV, 186–187 (originally printed in Philadelphia by William and Thomas Bradford and then in the *Pennsylvania Gazette*, Oct. 28, 1772, and the New-York Gazette, Nov. 16, 1772); Witherspoon, "Lectures on Moral Philosophy," in [Green, ed.], *Works of Witherspoon*, III, 418–419.

After the publication of Witherspoon's *Address* in the *Pennsylvania Gazette* and the *New-York Gazette,* it has been suggested that a young Alexander Hamilton made a trip to see the College of New Jersey president. Born and schooled in the West Indies, the future secretary of the U.S. Treasury arrived with his landlord, Hercules Mulligan. On behalf of his parents (both with Scottish ancestry), Hamilton is said to have requested that his proposed study in New Jersey be shortened by avoiding a last term of religious instruction. Hamilton biographers have claimed that the demand was immediately rejected by Witherspoon, leading Hamilton to attend King's College in New York. The desire to truncate studies and reduce religious learning demonstrated that prominent families viewed higher education as a fast means of social connection. Even toward the end of the Revolutionary era, when patriots were less likely to defer to British metropolitan culture, John Jay sought to persuade Robert Morris to send his sons to college in New Jersey rather than Europe because the "connections founded at School and College have much influence, and are to be watched even at that Period—If judiciously formed, they will often endure and be advantageous thro' Life." Alumni connections, rather than the kind of learning that required extended study, was the main order of higher education in these circles.[27]

During the previous decade, in his "Letters on Education," Witherspoon had described his disdain for parents who sought patronage and upward mobility. He noted:

> If they [offspring] perceive you [parents] happy and lifted up with the visit or countenance of persons of high rank, solicitous to entertain them properly, submissive and flattering in your manner of speaking to them, vain and apt to boast of your connexion with them: and if, on the contrary, they perceive you hardly civil to persons of inferior stations, or narrow circumstances . . . will not this naturally lead the young mind to consider riches and high station as the great sources of earthly happiness?

Witherspoon criticized wealthy American parents who "naturally lead the young mind to consider riches and high station as the great sources of earthly happiness." In a letter of 1786, he recalled his experience since arriving in

27. John Jay to Robert Morris, Oct. 13, 1782, in Max M. Mintz, "Robert Morris and John Jay on Education: Two Letters," *Pennsylvania Magazine of History and Biography,* LXXIV (1950), 346. On the supposed meeting between Hamilton and Witherspoon, see Broadus Mitchell, *Alexander Hamilton,* I, *Youth to Maturity, 1755–1788* (New York, 1957), 50–52; Forest McDonald, *Alexander Hamilton: A Biography* (New York, 1979), 12.

America and opposed "the mistaken parents and their desire to precipitate the education of their children" according to their "worldly" concerns. He resolved instead to admit those who would enter one of the lower classes and to graduate only those who had completed a "full course of study" away from home, including moral and religious philosophy.[28]

To be sure, Witherspoon's response to parental authority was never as harsh as that which he had demonstrated during his Scottish career, when he had censured the "slothful student" who used the "easy possession" of parental wealth to "acquire a superficial knowledge" in the "taste of this enlightened age." As the College of New Jersey's latest president, after all, Witherspoon was required to strengthen and widen its potential pool of up-wardly mobile parents. Harvard and Yale awarded 99 percent of all degrees in colonial British America up to 1750. Yet by the 1760s their relative graduation numbers had fallen to a proportion of two-thirds—in part owing to the growth of the College of New Jersey, which recruited from a wider geographical area than the other two institutions.[29]

Parents and their children believed that the combination of learned erudition and representative authority would confirm or enhance their social and economic standing. Yet as an evangelical clergyman Witherspoon continued to oppose the link between the cultivation of innate sensibility and worldly connections. He negotiated this tension in his new vocational duty with a relatively crude and simple portrayal of the usefulness of collegiate education. Deploying classical and religious motifs, Witherspoon appealed to the parental desire for social distinction without explicitly defining the innateness of moral reasoning. In his "Lectures on Eloquence," Witherspoon outlined the "utility" of a pious education away from the home. "True piety" would "direct a man in the choice of his studies." "The object of human

28. Witherspoon, "Letters on Education," in [Green, ed.], *Works of Witherspoon*, IV, 148–149; Witherspoon to Nicholas Van Dyke, May 12, 1786, John Witherspoon Collection, box 1, folder 17, Manuscripts Division, Department of Rare Books and Special Collections, Princeton University Library.

29. Witherspoon, *Serious Inquiry into the Nature and Effects of the Stage,* in [Green, ed.], *Works of Witherspoon,* III, 187. For relative college enrollment and graduation statistics, see Cremin, *American Education,* 214; Purvis, *Colonial America to 1763,* 244-246. On the College of New Jersey's wider catchment area, see McLachlan, *Princetonians,* xx. On the College of New Jersey's graduation numbers from the 1760s through the 1780s, see Collins, *President Witherspoon,* II, 83; Witherspoon, "A Description of the State of New Jersey," in [Green, ed.], *Works of Witherspoon,* IV, 406-407. For the socioeconomic backgrounds of the College of New Jersey's students, see also Longaker, *Rhetoric and the Republic,* 177-185.

knowledge is so extensive, that nobody can go through the whole, but religion will direct the student to what may be most profitable to him, and will also serve to turn into its proper channel all the knowledge he may otherwise acquire." Witherspoon continued, "A man truly pious, has often esteem, influence and success, though his parts may be much inferior to others, who are more capable, but less conscientious." With words such as "profitable," Witherspoon adopted the language of the upwardly mobile, whose sons he sought to educate, in order to portray the value of their education. Witherspoon pointed out in his *Address to the Students of the Senior Class* before their commencement in September 1775 that "great and eminent men have generally, in every nation, appeared in clusters." Once again he portrayed the purpose of higher education in both classical and religious terms. The revival of "piety" among young men allowed them to distinguish themselves above even "those of superior talents" who, "by mere slothfulness and idle habits, or self-indulgence, have lived useless, and died contemptible." It enabled individuals to define their common obligation to God, without which "the advantages" that they had "enjoyed" would become an "aggravation" of their guilt as sinners.[30]

Like Locke (and most subsequent British and American educators), Witherspoon tacitly accepted the relationship between higher education and social stratification. Nonetheless, he also opposed the notion that moral ideas could be cultivated from a blank slate, whether among elites or otherwise. But, although "all mankind, of every rank, denomination and profession" were "sinners by nature," Witherspoon continued in his 1775 address, the "intimacies" of their college education were best kept through adulthood. The watchful eyes of those who shared a vision of humility were of "more value" than "peals of applause from an undiscerning multitude. . . . As it is an important duty of religion, so it is a wise maxim for the conduct of life." Christian humility was grounded in the acknowledgement that ethical guidance could only be gained through the grace of God. But, ironically, the manifestation of Christian humility within a particular educational cohort could distinguish its constituents from the multitude. Even if parents

---

30. Witherspoon, "Lectures on Eloquence," in [Green, ed.], *Works of Witherspoon*, III, 563; John Witherspoon, *An Address to the Students of the Senior Class, on the Lord's Day Preceding Commencement, September 23, 1775,* ibid., 102, 105, 108. For an interesting study of classicism and early Revolutionary higher education, see James McLachlan, "Classical Names, American Identities: Some Notes on College Students and the Classical Tradition in the 1770s," in John W. Eadie, ed., *Classical Traditions in Early America* (Ann Arbor, Mich., 1976), 81–98.

only demonstrated a glib understanding of sin, they were surely pleased that higher education might separate their offspring from the populace at large.[31]

Language and Rhetoric in "Promiscuous Assemblies"

Having introduced the merits of higher education through reference to classical and religious ideas of virtue, Witherspoon's "Lectures on Eloquence" turned to the inculcation of new skills in speech, writing, and rhetoric. Witherspoon asked whether and how young men could learn to communicate theoretical concepts (particularly of a moral nature) when their audience could not be guaranteed to be predictable, homogenous, or objective in their response to ideas. This was an age-old question that skeptical philosophers, moral sense theorists, and evangelical theologians had all encountered during previous decades.

David Hume, in his *Treatise of Human Nature* (1740), had suggested that repeated injunctions—either in written or oral media—affected the "faculty, by which we repeat our impressions" and formed "particular habits" to "keep the mind in a readiness to observe, that no conclusion be form'd contrary to any ideas, which are usually compriz'd under them." Such a process, according to the Scottish skeptic, mirrored a fundamental aspect of human epistemology: repeated "impressions" in the mind were necessary to create "ideas." As these ideas circulated, they allowed an abstract and ultimately imagined sense that the mental universe was able to perceive external objects and their interaction in a common way. Hume continued: "When the impression of one becomes present to us, we immediately form an idea of its usual attendant; and consequently we may establish this as one part of the definition of an opinion or belief, that *'tis an idea related to or associated with a present impression.*" Each and every impression in the mind was inferred from previous impressions, thus providing an imagined sense of coherence. Similarly, repeated statements in the public sphere would assume a semblance of coherence, even if each proclamation in fact was singular, discrete, and subjective. From a very different evangelical standpoint,

---

31. Locke's discussion of the tabula rasa suggested that education could allow the cultivation of rational sensibility in any man. But as Geraint Parry has pointed out, the "radical potential of education in re-shaping and reconstructing all men" was qualified by Locke's decision to draw "back in the face of what he took to be the 'realities' of an inegalitarian society." See Parry, "Education," in Knud Haakonssen, ed., *The Cambridge History of Eighteenth-Century Philosophy* (Cambridge, 2006), I, 614. For Witherspoon's statements to his senior class, see Witherspoon, *An Address to the Students of the Senior Class,* in [Green, ed.], *Works of Witherspoon,* III, 102, 108, 119.

Jonathan Edwards had also wondered if human utterances could ever truly hold a fixed and inherent meaning. His assessment of public expression resembled the discussion of ideational perception in Humean skepticism, even though he opposed Hume's statements on revealed Christianity. Edwards also used skeptical terminology to unsettle the epistemological certainty of common sensibility, particularly when it came to language and public communication.[32]

Witherspoon's general understanding of moral epistemology was similarly germane to aspects of Humean thought, even while he criticized the skeptical approach toward revelation. In particular, Witherspoon tended to affirm Hume directly when he queried the sentimental assumption that orators and writers could arouse innate moral sensibilities. The skeptic found his way into his *Serious Inquiry into the Nature and Effects of the Stage,* which discussed the moral sensory desire to "refine the public ear, and teach them to admire in the right place." In Witherspoon's understanding, English thinkers such as Anthony Ashley Cooper, third earl of Shaftesbury, and a subsequent generation of Scottish Moderates defined a simple and repetitive expressive style as in "bad taste." Yet, according to his *Serious Inquiry,* unpretentious repetition was likely to achieve greater success in "procur[ing] attention" because it did not rely on any "appeal from the judgement of the public or the multitude (as David Hume has said for once according to truth) to the judgement of a wider few."[33]

32. David Hume, *A Treatise of Human Nature: Being an Attempt to Introduce the Experimental Method of Reasoning into Moral Subjects,* I, *Of the Understanding* (London, 1739), 24, 45, 167. On Humean skepticism and the potential conceptual link with Edwardsean philosophy, see Susan Manning, *The Puritan-Provincial Vision: Scottish and American Literature in the Nineteenth Century* (Cambridge, 1990), 20, 37, 44; Manning, *Fragments of Union,* 35–40. Some of Edwards's later critics, such as the Reverend Dr. James Dana, pastor of the first church in New Haven, Connecticut, suggested that his reading of Hume had indeed influenced him more thoroughly than he realized; see Mark G. Spencer, *David Hume and Eighteenth-Century America* (Rochester, N.Y., 2005), 67.

33. Witherspoon, *Serious Inquiry into the Nature and Effects of the Stage,* in [Green, ed.], *Works of Witherspoon,* III, 155. Witherspoon unsurprisingly criticized Hume when he stated that "immaterialism takes away the distinction between truth and falshood"; see Witherspoon, "Lectures on Moral Philosophy," in [Green, ed.], *Works of Witherspoon,* III, 377. Although Hume believed that religion in general was a potentially useful mechanism of social order, he cast doubt on the specific veracity of Christian revelation. According to Hume, theological disagreements between moderates and evangelicals demonstrated the human tendency toward faction and disagreement. See Shane Andre, "Was Hume an Atheist?" *Hume Studies,* XIX (1993), 141–166. Hume's reception in the intellectual culture of Revolutionary and early national America was partially indebted to the continued "expression" of Scottish evangelicalism. Michael O'Brien's

In America, Witherspoon continued to note the vexing relationship between moral epistemology and persuasive expression. He questioned the aesthetic analogy between beautiful ethical ideas and their pleasing style of description. He claimed that a problematic notion of common sensibility underlay the association between form and content. His "Lectures on Eloquence," therefore, lauded Hume for questioning the notion that stylish expression could arouse innate understandings of sociability: "Some very able writers have delivered a contrary opinion, particularly David Hume, who though an infidel in opinion, is of great reach and accuracy of judgement in matters of criticism." Contrary to Scottish stage theories, Witherspoon eschewed the association between cultural evolution and persuasive moral expression. He questioned the suggestion that quieter, more elaborate, and less repetitive persuasive techniques would flourish in particular social contexts, refining the public ear. In his view, the association between societal evolution and advanced expression reintroduced the problem of moral innateness under the guise of rhetorical theory.[34]

In his "Lectures on Moral Philosophy," Witherspoon noted a related paradox: the unchanging similarity of "promiscuous assemblies" through time and place corresponded to their internal variance and their passionate nature. In those assemblies, Witherspoon warned, the "multitude" was "exceeding apt to be deceived by demagogues and ambitious persons." Here the word "promiscuous" assumed a particular sensory meaning. Public assemblies were likely to contain unregenerate men who were unable to judge the qualitative content of rhetorical persuasion. They were prone to change their viewpoint according to the particular whims of orators. Those "ambi-

---

study of the intellectual culture of the antebellum South is one of the few works that discusses the ironic nexus between Humean philosophy and American evangelicalism. See O'Brien, *Conjectures of Order: Intellectual Life and the American South, 1810–1860* (Chapel Hill, N.C., 2004), II, 1020–1045. On skepticism's alternative to *other* forms of Enlightenment reasoning, see John Robertson, *The Case for the Enlightenment: Scotland and Naples, 1680–1760* (Cambridge, 2005), 30.

34. Witherspoon, "Lectures on Eloquence," in [Green, ed.], *Works of Witherspoon,* III, 574. Hume, like Scottish evangelicals, felt sidelined by Scotland's Moderate establishment for questioning anthropocentric accounts of perception. Humean and evangelical Presbyterian moral philosophers were in their own ways influenced by Locke's early discussion of sensationalism, claiming that moral ideas were contingent on the changing nature of sensory observation. While also focusing on the role of sensibility in human perception, they questioned the notion that sentimental reactions verified an objective link between innate conscience and a common understanding of the ethical nature of external interactions.

tious" sorts, according to Witherspoon, used stylish rhetorical forms to portray their quest for power as akin to the common good.[35]

Witherspoon's eloquent rhetorician did not deny, ignore, or seek to sublimate passions in public assemblies. Their occurrence — and their variance — was a universal characteristic of human nature. But did such a diagnosis, which he shared with Hume, simply serve to demonstrate the futility of persuasive expression? Witherspoon sought to counter such an assumption without privileging the role of innate moral sensibility in communication. In his view, Hume offered a refreshing distinction when he "said that human nature is always the same, and that the eloquence which kindles" the "passions" will "always have a great influence in large assemblies, let them be of what station or rank soever." Witherspoon apprehended that his "experience, since his writing the above, has fully justified it." He disapproved of the implication in certain rhetorical theories that advanced expressive techniques became useful when "the circumstances of things" were changed from those that preceded them. He criticized "several writers, [who] in speaking of the ancient and modern eloquence, have taken it for granted" that "the violent passionate eloquence that prevailed in Greece and Rome, would not do in modern times." Witherspoon praised Humean eloquence as a means to kindle the passions and classed it alongside that which had prevailed in the classical world.[36]

Before a public audience, Witherspoon suggested, the orator "of vivacity" and "passion" would be eminent because "fire and impetuosity . . . is of so much importance in speaking to a large and promiscuous assembly." Somehow, the unsettling role of diverse sentimentalism could be mitigated by its very predictability. "Democracy," according to Witherspoon, was likely to encourage "plainness and freedom of speech, and sometimes to a savage and indecent ferocity." The element of democracy in American assemblies — their erratic humanity — could ironically become "the nurse of eloquence, because, when the multitude have the power, persuasion is the only way to govern them." Witherspoon's "Lectures on Eloquence" questioned the notion that a pre-rational aesthetic response could develop through cultural evolution, that modern circumstances no longer required the raising of passions, and that classical and religious methods of communication were less important as a result. "Oratory" enjoyed "its chief power in promiscuous assemblies, and there it reigned of old, and reigns still, by its visible effect." But

35. Witherspoon, "Lectures on Moral Philosophy," in [Green, ed.], *Works of Witherspoon,* III, 434, 511.
36. Witherspoon, "Lectures on Eloquence," ibid., 574.

how, specifically, could this be so? Unsurprisingly, Witherspoon turned to evangelical rhetorical strategies for an answer.[37]

Witherspoon defined the importance of presence and communication in promiscuous American assemblies by adapting his earlier experience of religious expression. His "Lectures on Eloquence" extolled the simple rhetorical technique that he had learned as a revivalist clergyman. Moving on to outline the importance of simple and succinct expression and its relation to the truth it sought to articulate, he began with a discussion of written prose, noting: "David Hume seems to have as happily joined conciseness and perspicuity as most of our English writers. Some pious writers have been as successful this way as most of our nation." Referring to Hume in another part of his lectures, Witherspoon drew an ironic similarity between his expressive style and that which could be found in religious discourse. He examined the aims and methods of those "pious writers" whose eloquence Hume shared and defined their potential application in any public assembly — civic or religious. In particular, he focused on the validity of evangelical methods of persuasion, as pioneered by George Whitefield. Here Witherspoon's "Lectures on Eloquence" offered a rare occurrence. They compared Whitefield and Hume favorably with one another, using similar conceptual terminology.[38]

According to Whitefield, the announcement of universal sin necessarily aroused an emotional response. Intense passions accompanied the realization that an inborn and objective moral compass was unlikely without the grace of God. To appeal to the differing passions in his congregation, Witherspoon noted, he used ministerial rhetoric to communicate the "lively sense of religion upon his own heart." Though Witherspoon used the moral sensory language of feelings in this instance, he avoided any suggestion that the stimulation of sentiments somehow channeled their innate ethical stance. Instead, he focused on the rhetorical importance of encouraging prayer and conversion through emotional feeling in order to provide a new moral sense wrought by grace.[39]

Referring in his "Lectures on Moral Philosophy" to critics of the evangelical method, Witherspoon lambasted "enemies of revealed religion" who questioned preaching and communal prayer for its attempt to graft high emotionalism onto public communication. Disingenuously, according to Witherspoon, they claimed that the exposition of emotions through prayer was "unreasonable, and even dishonorable to the Divine Being" because it

37. Ibid., 438, 479, 511, 574.
38. Ibid., 509, 539.
39. Ibid., 562.

contradicted the notion of divine providence. Yet, in allowing common communication between preachers and their assemblies, the public "worship of
God" was, in Witherspoon's view, "what is due from us to him, in consequence of the relation we stand in to him, [so that] it is proper and necessary
that he should require it." "To honor God is to honor supreme excellence;
for him not to expect and demand it, would be to deny himself." Placing ministerial aims and methods so prominently in his "Lectures on Moral Philosophy" and "Lectures on Eloquence" and in his program of rhetoric and public
speaking, Witherspoon implied that influential communication was contingent on the state of regeneration among audience members — even in ostensibly secular assemblies. Stylish or complex modes of expression reduced
the urgency of communication by inviting and *assuming* a more considered
response and by seeking to harness previously cultivated sensibilities.[40]

In his 1772 *Address to the Inhabitants of Jamaica,* Witherspoon pointed
out that, "in addition" to the regular course at the College of New Jersey,
"the President" taught students to "pronounce orations of their own composition" on a "stage erected for that purpose in the hall, immediately after
prayers." He changed the timetable for lessons in public communication so
that they would take place directly after the students' attendance of sermons
and prayers. In an early college advertisement, Witherspoon announced that,
for the "Purpose" of sound rhetoric, "the Professor of Divinity, besides what
Attention he may give to the Instruction of the Senior Class, will give regular
Lectures upon the System." He made sure to remind parents that training in
classical oratory would be guided by faculty members who had specific religious qualifications and that prayer recitations would take place both before
and after those classes.[41]

"Taste and criticism" — of such great interest to rhetoricians such as Hugh

40. Witherspoon, "Lectures on Moral Philosophy," ibid., 402–403. In his "Lectures on Eloquence," Witherspoon recommended that the "intention of all speech, or writing, which is but
recorded speech, is to persuade [through the arousal of passions], taking the word with lati-
tude"; see Witherspoon, "Lectures on Eloquence," ibid., 555. According to Charles Partee, we
can find an interesting congruence between Calvin's rhetorical practice and Witherspoon's reasoning here in his "Lectures on Eloquence"; see Partee, *The Theology of John Calvin* (Louisville,
Ky., 2008), 45. Witherspoon's desire to exercise "power over the passions" of men added an
evangelical emphasis to what Thomas Miller has suggested were the "pathetic appeals that Aristotle had first defined as essential to the rhetorician's art"; see Miller, ed., *Selected Writings,* 46.

41. Witherspoon, *Address to the Inhabitants of Jamaica,* in [Green, ed.], *Works of Witherspoon,* IV, 193; "For the Information of the Public; by Order of the Trustees of the College of
New-Jersey," *New-York Gazette or, the Weekly Post-Boy,* [Oct. 17, 1768], [3]. On the development
of the institution and curriculum, see Collins, *President Witherspoon,* II, 83–90.

Blair during the following decade—was only discussed in Witherspoon's seventh and final lecture in his "Lectures on Eloquence." The section included a long précis of various British (often Scottish) and French theories of linguistic taste without initially discounting their theoretical force. Witherspoon did not deny that comparing "the best examples" of speech and prose would isolate those that seemed most effective. Asserting his own voice more strongly, however, he warned that "carrying taste to a finical nicety in any one branch, is a thing not only undesirable, but contemptible." Earlier in his career Witherspoon had employed a similar critique in his *Ecclesiastical Characteristics,* accusing Scottish Moderates of favoring style over moral content. In his "Lectures on Eloquence," he continued: "When a person applies his attention so much to a matter of no great moment, it occasions a necessary neglect of other things of much greater value. After you pass a certain point, attachment to a particular pursuit is useless, and then it proceeds to be hurtful, and at last contemptible." According to Witherspoon, stylish rhetorical standards obliged individuals to cultivate their own purported aesthetic sensibility before they even had time to consider the importance of communal virtue.[42]

Some American educators were attracted to Scottish rhetoricians because they sought to define the relationship between uniform language and an education dominated by classical studies. As mentioned above, they did so tacitly (or even explicitly) to distinguish higher-educated men from individuals less well connected. Witherspoon spoke of linguistic consistency in order to express the simplicity of preexisting English standards. He believed that the minimalism and accessibility of classical and evangelical discourse enabled orators and writers to bridge the gap with listeners and readers. He distanced himself from certain English writers such as Samuel Johnson, whom he described as "so stiff and abstracted in his manner and such a lover of hard words, that he is the worst pattern for young persons that can be named." In "common discourse where there is no affectation," he pointed out, "men speak properly."[43]

Several years later, Witherspoon remarked that "we are not by far so much

42. Witherspoon, "Lectures on Eloquence," in [Green, ed.], *Works of Witherspoon,* III, 485, 495, 581, 592.

43. On the link between linguistic uniformity and social stratification, see Stout, "Religion, Communications, and the Ideological Origins of the American Revolution," *WMQ,* 3d Ser., XXXIV (1977), 531. For Witherspoon's statements, see Witherspoon, "Lectures on Eloquence," in [Green, ed.], *Works of Witherspoon,* III, 485, 554. On the relative use of classical methods in collegiate rhetorical curricula, see David W. Robson, *Educating Republicans: The College in the Era of the American Revolution, 1750–1800* (Westport, Conn., 1985), 13–20.

in danger of the charge of affectation for what we omit saying, as for what we do say" because "when a man is fond of introducing hard words, or studies a nice or pompous diction, he brings himself immediately into contempt; but he may easily attain a cautious habit of avoiding low phrases or vulgar terms, without being at all liable to the imputation either of vanity or constraint." Thus, he recommended "a pure, and as it may called, classic simplicity, [which] is the more necessary to guard the reader against the low and grovelling manner which is sometimes mistaken for it." He advised teachers to prepare their students for entry to the College of New Jersey by focusing on English composition. Scholars of rhetoric have noted that as early as 1769 Witherspoon had added formal reading and writing tests in English as a college entry requirement, followed by the compulsory study of the English language in all four years.[44]

In an October 1773 newspaper announcement describing curricular developments at the college, Witherspoon reminded readers that the institution had introduced "a taste for the study of the English Language, not without considerable success," and required entering students to maintain proficiency in "Orthography, Punctuation and Grammar of their own Language" alongside classical languages. In one of his "Druid" essays surveying the nature of language in America, which was published in the May 9, 1781, edition of the *Pennsylvania Journal,* Witherspoon further described the curriculum that had developed in the College of New Jersey over the previous decade. He admitted that linguistic standards were likely to be "very imperfect in any seminary where no care is taken to form the scholars to taste, propriety and accuracy, in that language which they must speak and write all their life," and then concluded: "Our situation in America is now, and in all probability will continue to be such, as to require peculiar attention upon this subject." In a 1787 letter to a friend, he recalled his students' education in classical rhetoric

44. John Witherspoon, "The Druid No. VI," in [Green, ed.], *Works of Witherspoon,* IV, 468. On Witherspoon's "Druid" essays and his broader wish to standardize English language teaching using Robert Lowth's *Short Introduction to English Grammar* . . . (London, 1762), John Holmes's Art of *Rhetoric Made Easy* . . . (London, 1739), Thomas Sheridan's *Rhetorical Grammar of the English Language* . . . (Dublin, 1781), and his own course in rhetoric, see Thomas Jefferson Wertenbaker, *Princeton, 1746–1896* (Princeton, N.J., 1946), 91–92; Miller, ed., *Selected Writings,* 21; John Howe, *Language and Political Meaning in Revolutionary America* (Amherst, Mass., 2004), 31–33. Darrel Guder associates such a focus on English language and composition with a more secular program of belles lettres. See Guder, "The Story of Belles Lettres at Princeton: An Historical Investigation of the Expansion and Secularisation of Curriculum at the College of New Jersey with Special Reference to the Curriculum of English Language and Letters" (Ph.D. diss., University of Hamburg, 1964).

and English grammar, which had been developed and deployed in civic debate over the previous two decades: "It was a pleasure for me to receive your letters because you have Precisely the Idea which I wish were more general respecting education. We are obliged to contend against the Prejudices of the Times which are much against the ancient Language meaning particularly the Latin and Greek." He had endeavored to increase understanding of "not only the ancient Languages but the modern and the Theory of universal Grammar" alongside classical and religious "methods of persuasion" through public speaking.[45]

Witherspoon's desire to promote a "pure" and "classic simplicity" was also motivated by his fear of provincialism in public communication. As he tried to uphold simple standards of English, implementing rhetorical methods from evangelical and classical discourse, he continued to worry about regional irregularities in public expression. In his essay "The Druid Number V," Witherspoon explained the complicated British question by reminding his American audience that "Scotland, or the northern part of Great-Britain, was once a separate independent kingdom, though, except in the Highlands, the people spoke the same language as in England; the inhabitants of the Lowlands, in both countries, having been originally the same." Had they remained separate, Witherspoon continued, the "small differences in dialect and even in pronunciation, would not have been considered as defects; and there would have been no more opprobrium attending the use of them in speech or writing, than there was in the use of the different dialects of the ancient Grecian republics." And so, by losing the Edinburgh Parliament after 1707 and placing the British legislature in London, "the Scottish manner of speaking came to be considered as provincial barbarism; which, therefore, all scholars are now at the utmost pains to avoid." Here Witherspoon sounded surprisingly similar to Scottish Moderates. Yet his resulting recommendations were distinct from their cultivated ideal of rhetorical expression. He did not seek to match or surpass ornamental advancements in the literary establishments of London, Oxford, and Cambridge. He was comparatively more interested in public communication than private spectatorship. Thus, he was concerned that aesthetic and cultural quirks in provincial

45. Announcement in *Pennsylvania Journal; and The Weekly Advertiser,* [Oct. 13, 1773], [3] ; Witherspoon, "The Druid Number V," in [Green, ed.], *Works of Witherspoon,* IV, 458 (originally published in the *Pennsylvania Journal and the Weekly Advertiser,* May 9, 1781); Letter from John Witherspoon to St. George Tucker, May 1, 1787, John Witherspoon Collection, Princeton University Library, box 1, folder 16A, Manuscripts Division, Department of Rare Books and Special Collections, Princeton University Library.

language would only appeal to audience members with specific local or cultural foreknowledge. The passions of the greater multitude risked remaining unaroused.[46]

In the same essay, Witherspoon coined the word "Americanism" and claimed that it was "exactly similar in its formation and significtion to the word Scotticism." Seeking to curtail unwieldy provincialism among his students, he was immediately determined to encourage simple precision in public expression after his arrival in New Jersey. Though English was their vernacular tongue, "Americanisms" were problematic in the same way that "Scotticisms" affected English-speaking Scots north of Hadrian's Wall. Witherspoon warned his readers: "We are at a great distance from the island of Great-Britain, in which the standard of language is as yet supposed to be found. Every state is equal to and independent of every other; and, I believe, none of them will agree, at least immediately, to receive laws from another, in discourse, any more than in action." In his "Lectures on Eloquence," Witherspoon even linked the supposed moral and political immaturity of native American communities with the relative complexity of their "figurative" speech, which was "frequent and very strong." Witherspoon continued: "The Indians in America have a language full of metaphors. They take up the hatchet, for going to war, and they brighten the chain, when they confirm a peace." In and of themselves, such phrases were relatively simple and succinct. But as metaphors they relied on associations whose meanings were subjective, or at least contingent on place or context. Thus, they potentially excluded audience members.[47]

In "The Druid Number V," Witherspoon would avoid distinguishing between the colonial era and his more recent experience of American independence. He would assert that no less a figure than Thomas Paine was often guilty of provincial vulgarism when it came to his language and expression. His use of a particular colloquial term demonstrated that the "renowned author of Common Sense, who is an Englishman born . . . has so happy a tal-

46. Witherspoon, "The Druid, Number V," in [Green, ed.], *Works of Witherspoon*, IV, 447–448, 461, 468.

47. Ibid., 458–459, 460, 462; Witherspoon, "Lectures on Eloquence," ibid., III, 503. On the subject of Scotticisms, see James G. Basker, "Scotticisms and the Problem of Cultural Identity in Eighteenth-Century Britain," *Eighteenth-Century Life*, XV, nos. 1–2 (February and April 1981), 81–95; Pat Rogers, "Boswell and the Scotticism," in Greg Clingham, ed., *New Light on Boswell: Critical and Historical Essays on the Occasion of the Bicentenary of the "The Life of Johnson"* (Cambridge, 1991), 56–71; Richard B. Sher, *Church and University in the Scottish Enlightenment: The Moderate Literati of Edinburgh* (Princeton, N.J., 1985), 108. See also David Walker Woods, Jr., *John Witherspoon* (New York, 1906), 137, 141, 183.

ent of adopting the blunders of others, that nothing decisive can be inferred from his practice." "It is, however, undoubtedly an Americanism, for it is used by authors greatly superior to him in every respect." Even the linguistic benefit Paine enjoyed as "an Englishman born" did not protect him on the western side of the Atlantic, where he strayed from the correct expression of his place of birth. According to Witherspoon, America had not yet reached the capacity to match its previous metropolitan benchmark. It was in an embryonic stage of national development, and older provincial identities risked producing local vulgarisms, just as in the colonial era.[48]

Witherspoon speculated that "time and accident must determine what turn affairs will take" with respect to American linguistic uniformity, "whether we shall continue to consider the language of Great-Britain as the pattern upon which we are to form ours; or whether, in this new empire," other prescriptive centers of language will arise and "shall obtain influence and prescribe the rules of speech and writing to every other part." The phrase "as yet" suggested that linguistic standards might be set closer to home but that such a time had not yet arrived. As further evidence on the matter, Witherspoon even took a little poke at the southern states in his "Druid Number VII": "*Raw Salad* is used in the South for *salad*. N. B. There is no salad boiled." Local vulgarisms were made more likely by America's distance from Britain and were exacerbated by the great space between educated centers within its inchoate political union.[49]

"An Animated Son of Liberty"

John Adams would praise Witherspoon for his expressive style, albeit with a slightly ambiguous qualification. On August 16, 1777, after hearing Witherspoon preach, Adams wrote: "I find that I understand the Doctor better since I have heard him so much in conversation, and in the Senate." Presumably, Adams could only pronounce the excellence of Witherspoon's sermon because he was by now used to hearing his Scottish tone and was better able to decipher his words. Elsewhere Adams would claim: "Dr. Witherspoon

48. Witherspoon, "The Druid Number V," in [Green, ed.], *Works of Witherspoon*, IV, 462. For Witherspoon's coinage of the term "Americanism," see also *Oxford English Dictionary*, 2d ed. (Oxford, 1989), I, 398.

49. Witherspoon, "The Druid Number V," in [Green, ed.], *Works of Witherspoon*, IV, 459; Witherspoon, "The Druid Number VII," ibid., 469. On Witherspoon's continuing provincial understanding of linguistic uniformity after independence, see Landsman, "The Legacy of British Union for the North American Colonies," in Robertson, ed., *A Union for Empire*, 317.

enters with great spirit into the American cause. He seems as hearty a friend as any of the natives, an animated Son of Liberty." The phrase "as any of the natives," nonetheless, still questioned Witherspoon's American identity.[50]

The following discussions will examine the political context that led Witherspoon to associate with Thomas Paine and John Adams. When Witherspoon began delivering his "Lectures on Eloquence" in 1770, there were clear parallels between the growth of public political debate and what has been described as "the rise of English studies." The number of American newspapers rose from twenty-six to forty-four in the decade preceding the Declaration of Independence, and the number of published books in English-language studies quadruped between 1769 and 1789. Witherspoon strengthened the link between standardized English and public political discourse at a time when such an association became ever more pertinent.[51]

During a September 1769 College of New Jersey commencement ceremony, John Hancock and John Dickinson were given honorary degrees. Both had been prominent in their resistance to the Townshend duties imposed by Britain in the previous years. In September 1770, New Jersey governor William Franklin warily listened to students debate and orate on the nonimportation of British goods. In the following weeks, local newspapers provided evidence for nonimportation protests by the student body. The "Grandeur and Decorum with" which a commencement ceremony was conducted included "their united Efforts to appear in Cloth manufactured in America." Over the next two years, newspapers in New Jersey and Pennsylvania often carried letters criticizing the politicized public discourse in College of New Jersey ceremonies. Witherspoon's critics wished for a return to passive education in received myths and stories from the classical world. They were less familiar with instruction in classical composition and rhetoric and feared its deployment in mock-political debate.[52]

50. See the diary of John Adams, Sept. 3, 1774, Aug. 17, 1777, in Charles Francis Adams, ed., *The Works of John Adams, Second President of the United States: With a Life of the Author, Notes, and Illustrations,* 10 vols. (Boston, 1850), II, 363, 434–435.

51. For these figures on English language publications, see Miller, ed., *Selected Writings,* 25.

52. See "Extract of a Letter from a Gentleman in Princetown, to His Friend in Philadelphia," *Pennsylvania Gazette,* Oct. 18, 1770, [3]. On Franklin's attendance at the September 1770 commencement ceremony, see Irving Brant, *James Madison,* I, *The Virginia Revolutionist* (New York, 1941), 94; Collins, *President Witherspoon,* I, 134. For an example of the negative letters sent to newspapers between 1770 and 1773, see A Friend to Impartiality, "To the Printer of the Pennsylvania Chronicle," Oct. 19, 1772, *Pennsylvania Chronicle and Universal Advertiser,* Oct. 31, 1772, [1]. On criticisms of classical public rhetoric in commencement ceremonies, see also Miller, ed., *Selected Writings,* 23; Longaker, *Rhetoric and the Republic,* 188. Students were most

A few years after Witherspoon's arrival at the college, several student societies were founded in which public speaking, debate, and expressive writing skills were honed. So-called Paper Wars were also formulated by society members. In 1771, for example, Whig Society members Hugh Henry Brackenridge and Philip Freneau demonstrated a style and language that was distinct from contemporary poetry and belles lettres and closer to the simpler language employed in satirical works that could be found in newspapers and pamphlets. In one performance, they ridiculed the complex and ornate style of delivery employed by "Tories" during declamation exercises. Those of a more loyalist persuasion in New Jersey thus lamented the abandonment of private and supposedly more neutral forms of expression under Witherspoon.[53]

In the early period of the imperial crisis, it became less clear whether Witherspoon's students would continue to defer their full authority to London. It was certainly apparent that they would graduate in an ambiguous political environment. In that environment, Witherspoon believed, opportunities for public leadership were more abundant—and potentially more important—than in Scotland. The cultivation of public virtue rather than individual sensibility was at a premium. The revival of piety in higher education was thought to be vital. Removed from their parents, students were required to develop a public mode of expression that combined religious and classical rhetorical methods. Witherspoon opposed those who viewed collegiate education as a finishing school in which innate capacities were refined in order to link personal sensibilities to communal esteem. When he first composed his "Lectures on Eloquence," it is unlikely that Witherspoon envisaged the later context for his synthesis between classical and religious rhetorical expression. By the mid-1770s, though, the need for appropriate forms of civic leadership, language, and rhetorical performance had assumed a wider, more overtly political, and eventually revolutionary meaning. Higher education would assume greater importance, even as some American fathers remained fast asleep.

---

likely used to public orations that had been influenced by the rhetorical theories of Peter Ramus (1515–1572), a French Protestant convert, educational theorist, and logician. According to Miller, the "formulaic logic of Aristotelianism" had suited "ambivalent attitudes to the worldliness of classical learning [and] the civic vision of classical rhetoric." Witherspoon's students used the contemporary idiom to address public issues, rather than passively absorbing the "abstractions of scholastic epistemology and ontology" that had been recommended by Ramus. See Miller, ed., *Selected Writings*, 17.

53. On the "Paper Wars" against "Tory" students, see Longaker, *Rhetoric and the Republic*, 189–190.

PART III

American Independence

CHAPTER 6

"EVERY ONE OF THEM FULL OF THE

OLD CAMERONIAN RESISTING SENTIMENTS"

Piety, Anglo-Scottish Union, and American Independence

In a private letter sent to John Witherspoon before his departure to America in 1768, Thomas Randall, a fellow Scottish clergyman, wrote that Witherspoon's call "to the Presidency of N. Jersey College" ought to be "judged" as

> a matter of thankfulness to GOD; as I have long thought it the intention of Providence (after our abuse of our great mercies, and our dreadful degeneracy from real religion) to fix the great seat of truth and righteousness in America; and that N. Jersey seemed to promise fair for being the *nursery* of the most approved instruments, for carrying on that great design, in that wide continent. . . .
>
> As to you, therefore, I esteemed it a distinguished honour, to be called forth from so distant a region to the exercise of your talents in a station so advantageous in the work of the gospel.

Randall sought to transport the "seat of truth and righteousness" from Scotland, where it had been corrupted by enemies, to America. He wrote to a man who, five years earlier, had claimed publicly that piety "often changes its residence, and leaves one nation, to settle in another." Witherspoon changed his residence and supported the formation of a new political union. In 1643, his great-grandfather had signed a Solemn League and Covenant between the two nations of England and Scotland. In 1746, he had offered to fight in battle to continue their political union. Yet, in 1776, three decades after opposing Jacobites on behalf of Britain, he became the only clergyman to sign America's Declaration of Independence.[1]

---

1. Thomas Randall to John Witherspoon, Mar. 4, 1767, in L. H. Butterfield, ed., *John Witherspoon Comes to America: A Documentary Account Based Largely on New Materials* (Princeton, N.J., 1953), 29; John Witherspoon, *A Serious Apology for the Ecclesiastical Characteristics*, in [Ashbel Green, ed.], *The Works of the Rev. John Witherspoon D.D.L.L.D. Late President of the College at Princeton, New-Jersey . . .* , 2d ed., rev., 4 vols. (Philadelphia, 1802), III, 223–224,

Modern historiography has resisted any temptation to connect 1643 and 1776, great-grandfather and grandson, and their two signatures on declarations of union. Witherspoon is said to have turned away from the Calvinist rigors of the Westminster Confession of Faith and the Solemn League to a more optimistic philosophy of individual and social moral potential as he shifted his allegiance from Great Britain to America. The unifying context of the patriot cause—opposition to the indulgence of Catholicism through the Quebec Act, to the forced quartering of soldiers near married women in New York, and to the shooting of Protestant children in the Boston snow— is said to have been enough to bring clergymen such as Witherspoon closer to erstwhile theological foes, even if they promoted a more moderate religious vision. In their resistance to the French imperial monarchy during the 1740s and 1750s, colonial American Congregationalists, Baptists, and Presbyterians demonstrated a surprising degree of religious unity, ranging from evangelical Presbyterians such as Samuel Davies to Congregational moderates such as Charles Chauncy. The extrapolation of "religious-republican" ideology from the Seven Years' War against France to the imperial crisis entailed similar concord in the struggle against Britain—despite philosophical differences between moderate and evangelical dissenters on more specific doctrinal issues. As radical opposition to British policy grew stronger, a relationship developed between classical republican themes of impartial public service and religious notions of public duty. Noting the unity between moderate and evangelical Protestants in opposition to French and then British imperial governance, scholars have tended to look for new examples of consensus in Witherspoon's attempt to define the political context of the American Revolution in religious and philosophical ways.[2]

---

297. Randall was an orthodox Presbyterian minister in Edinburgh and a close friend of Witherspoon in Scotland.

2. On religious unity and the extrapolation of "religious-republican" ideology from the 1750s through the Revolutionary era, see Mark A. Noll, *America's God: From Jonathan Edwards to Abraham Lincoln* (New York, 2002), 59–70, 81, 447–451; Noll, "The Contingencies of Christian Republicanism: An Alternative Account of Protestantism and the American Founding," in Thomas S. Engeman and Michael P. Zuckert, eds., *Protestantism and the American Founding* (Notre Dame, Ind., 2004), 243; Noll, "The American Revolution and Protestant Evangelicalism," *Journal of Interdisciplinary History,* XXIII (1993), 615–638; Jack P. Greene, "The Concept of Virtue in Late Colonial British America," in Richard K. Matthews, ed., *Virtue, Corruption, and Self-Interest: Political Values in the Eighteenth Century* (Bethlehem, Pa., 1994), 35–42. According to David W. Robson, Witherspoon and his evangelical predecessors in the College of New Jersey had all been "awakened" to the "wider significance of government and religion in British North America" as a result of the developing conflict between the British and French empires. They ap-

The depth of scholarly discussion on the relationship between Scottish moral philosophy and the syllogistic reasoning of the American Declaration of Independence makes it even easier to understand the temptation to assert Witherspoon's move toward the ethics of the "Moderate Enlightenment." That a Scot became the only clergyman to sign the Declaration has added further impetus to the contention that Hutchesonian philosophy inspired its authors to elevate communal happiness over individualistic interests. Despite critiques of such an analysis, which reassert the role of Lockean contractualism in the document, Hutchesonian philosophy has retained its general importance in our understanding of the "sensibility" of the Revolutionary era—including in discussions of Witherspoon's contribution to patriot ideology. Human-centered moral sense philosophy, as *the* Scottish intellectual influence in American patriot thought, maintains a central role among the multiple traditions of the American founding. The distinction between classical notions of communal virtue and the Lockean concept of individual liberty was partially reduced thanks to moral sense philosophy's mediating influence. Its emphasis on divinely established natural law enabled patriots to reconcile private rights and the public good, innate personal sensibilities and communitarian ideals. Hutchesonian ideas allowed them to adapt the public focus of civic humanism without diminishing the veracity, morality, and reliability of private emotions. Patriots could describe their individual sentiments—even their personal desire for commercial prosperity—as a reflection of objective communal ideals. By defining their innately benevolent feelings as God-given, they were also shielded from the charge of secularism.[3]

---

parently shared moral convictions against centralizing French political authority with more moderate religious educators in America such as Provost William Smith, Francis Alison, and even Samuel Johnson. Their unity of "political activism" was eventually reoriented against British metropolitan authority. See Robson, *Educating Republicans: The College in the Era of the American Revolution, 1750–1800* (Westport, Conn., 1985), 43. On the declining inclination to examine the political impact of theological differences between moderates and evangelicals from the colonial to the Revolutionary era in scholarship following Alan Heimert, *Religion and the American Mind: From the Great Awakening to the Revolution* (Cambridge, Mass., 1966), see Philip Goff, "Revivals and Revolution: Historiographic Turns since Alan Heimert's *Religion and the American Mind,*" *Church History,* LXVII (1998), 695–721. For a discussion of Witherspoon's incorporation in such a historiographical trend, see Ned C. Landsman, "Witherspoon and the Problem of Provincial Identity in Scottish Evangelical Culture," in Richard B. Sher and Jeffrey R. Smitten, eds., *Scotland and America in the Age of the Enlightenment* (Princeton, N.J., 1990), 30–32.

3. For an influential statement on the potential centrality of Hutcheson to the reasoning of the Declaration of Independence, see Garry Wills, *Inventing America: Jefferson's Declaration of Independence* (Garden City, N.Y., 1978), 205, 211. On Jefferson's potential influence by Lord Kames, see Jean M. Yarbrough, *American Virtues: Thomas Jefferson on the Character of a Free*

Yet, in tracing Witherspoon's orientation toward the new American Congress, one must question whether support for the patriot cause could easily reconcile evangelical and moderate ideas of moral perception. The argument that Witherspoon promoted anthropocentric moral sense reasoning in his lectures on ethics, divinity, and rhetoric as well as in his general philosophy of higher education has been modified. His contribution to public political debate during the Revolutionary era similarly avoided a volte-face in discussions of human ethical capabilities. Many of Witherspoon's students became well-known patriot leaders. Linking his critique of moral sense reasoning in the educational sphere with his developing political theology in the expanding public domain of the Revolutionary era makes it clear that he did not permit an easy contrast between American moral virtue and British corruption, even as he strongly supported the move toward American independence and encouraged his students toward the same goal.

Witherspoon's political deflection from the British Empire, which so

---

People (Lawrence, Kans., 1998), xvii, 3, 22–23, 29–34, 36, 46; Allen Jayne, *Jefferson's Declaration of Independence: Origins, Philosophy, and Theology* (Lexington, Ky., 1998), 44, 62–67. Scholars have noted significant problems in Wills's thesis, which perhaps assumes too much philosophical knowledge on behalf of Jefferson and overlooks what remained (albeit crudely) "Lockean" in his political philosophy. See Ronald Hamowy, "Jefferson and the Scottish Enlightenment: A Critique of Garry Wills's *Inventing America: Jefferson's Declaration of Independence,*" *William and Mary Quarterly,* 3d Ser., XXXVI (1979), 503–523; John Patrick Diggins, *The Lost Soul of American Politics: Virtue, Self-Interest, and the Foundations of Liberalism* (New York, 1984), 33–34; Gary Schmitt, "Sentimental Journey: Garry Wills and the American Founding," *Political Science Reviewer,* XII (1982), 99–128. On both the "Scottish Conversation" and the "Multiple Traditions" in the American founding, see Alan Gibson, *Interpreting the Founding: Guide to the Enduring Debates over the Origins and Foundations of the American Republic* (Lawrence, Kans., 2006), 37–64. On Scottish moral philosophy as a mediator between liberal individualism and civic communitarianism, see James T. Kloppenberg, "The Virtues of Liberalism: Christianity, Republicanism, and Ethics in Early American Political Discourse," *Journal of American History,* LXXIV (1987), 16; J. G. A. Pocock, "Cambridge Paradigms and Scotch Philosophers: A Study of the Relations between the Civic Humanist and the Civil Jurisprudential Interpretation of Eighteenth-Century Social Thought," in Istvan Hont and Michael Ignatieff, eds., *Wealth and Virtue: The Shaping of Political Economy in the Scottish Enlightenment* (Cambridge, 1983), 235–252; Knud Haakonssen, "Natural Jurisprudence in the Scottish Enlightenment: Summary of an Interpretation," in Neil MacCormick and Zenon Bankowski, eds., *Enlightenment, Rights, and Revolution: Essays in Legal and Social Philosophy* (Aberdeen, U.K., 1989), 36. On the ways in which political critiques were framed using a synthesis of clerical and moral sensory languages, see Sarah Knott, *Sensibility and the American Revolution* (Chapel Hill, N.C., 2009), 2, 21–22, 189–190; Nicole Eustace, *Passion Is the Gale: Emotion, Power, and the Coming of the American Revolution* (Chapel Hill, N.C., 2008), 3, 172.

angered Anglican loyalists, Scottish literati, and Moderate Presbyterian churchmen, can only be understood in light of his continuing Presbyterian evangelical beliefs. As Westminster leaders were seen to constrain civic, commercial, and religious freedoms in North America, he turned on London. Only a decade earlier, he had castigated Presbyterians who defined their attachment to Britain according to the evolution of moral sensibilities within the Anglo-Scottish union. Through the imperial crisis, Witherspoon's continuing critique of innate ethical perception highlighted a related and often overlooked aspect of Revolutionary ideology: what he viewed as the moral hubris among fellow patriots. His warning against such hubris was often far louder than his criticism of external British corruption.

Witherspoon arrived in America's mid-Atlantic region during the early period of the imperial crisis. He encountered co-religionists who conceived of their provincial piety in ways that recalled his earlier support for Anglo-Scottish integration. Like their mainland Scottish counterparts, American Presbyterians had often been suspicious of Anglican attempts to link religious and political authority. But their recent history, which had witnessed moments of internal denominational division, also evoked Witherspoon's struggle with the Moderate Kirk. During the American Revolution, to be sure, evangelical Presbyterians allied with a number of their co-religionists who descended from Old Side communities. Yet it would be erroneous to assume that their mutual opposition to Britain required them to define the relationship between piety and political unionism in exactly the same way. Historians have queried the notion of Protestant harmony in eighteenth-century British imperial identity, given the Reformed Christian tendency to fissure over issues such as the innateness of moral agency. The relationship between Witherspoon's ethical philosophy and his American Revolutionary identity raises a similar question. In emphasizing the civic necessity of personal religious conversion, Witherspoon was partially distinguished from other Presbyterian patriots who linked societal coherence to the innate ethical sensibility of all men. During the 1750s and 1760s, Britain's conflict with France did not prevent Witherspoon from opposing Protestants closer to home. Through the Revolutionary era, his opposition to Britain did not inhibit him from censuring fellow Americans for their privileged account of ethical capability.[4]

4. On initial Old Side–New Side divisions (which were by no means always binary by the 1760s), see Marilyn Westerkamp, "Division, Dissension, and Compromise: The Presbyterian Church during the Great Awakening: A Look at the Problems That Tore Presbyterianism in Two at the Time of the Great Awakening in the 1740s," *Journal of Presbyterian History*, LXXVIII

In order to situate Witherspoon's political theology in a wider context, a comparison with other religious educators in the Middle Colonies, particularly Scots in institutions such as the College of Philadelphia, is necessary. Several prominent members of the Philadelphia Presbyterian establishment feared threatening their social and cultural cachet—including their association with Edinburgh's Moderate literati—by supporting the idea of American independence. The ambivalence of William Smith, for example, provides a clear point of comparison to Witherspoon. Somewhat mournfully, the College of Philadelphia provost articulated a vision of cultural unity between Edinburgh and Philadelphia, London and New York, Anglicans and Presbyterians, between mutually enlightened teachers on both sides of the Atlantic.[5]

Distinctions also appeared between Witherspoon and fellow Presbyterian patriots. Francis Alison, for example, was closely associated with the Synod of Philadelphia. During the 1740s, he founded the New London Academy as a seminary for Old Side ministerial candidates. He assumed the status of vice-provost of the College of Philadelphia from the mid-1750s. Alison's pedigree might have led to the same loyalist stance as the Scottish Episcopalian William Smith. Yet, in fact, Alison supported the American struggle. Unlike Witherspoon, however, he did so by outlining the innate moral sensibility of patriots. Its arousal, he suggested, offered a natural critique of British misrule and made the cause of independence legitimate.[6]

Scottish Moderates such as Alexander Carlyle used moral sense reasoning rather differently from Smith or Alison. Though all men enjoyed common moral sensibility, they argued, it could only flourish in specifically advanced regions. In their opinion, the cultural chasm between metropolitan Britain and colonial America was too great for cities such as Philadelphia to survive without British leadership. When Carlyle surveyed the American colonies, he failed to notice Smith's picture of Enlightenment or Alison's moral sensory arguments. Rather, he observed America's preponderance for crude

(2000), 7. On Protestant imperial unity against Catholics, see Linda Colley, *Britons: Forging the Nation, 1707–1837* (New Haven, Conn., 1992). For the critique of Colley from the perspective of the history of British Protestant piety, see Tony Claydon and Ian McBride, "The Trials of the Chosen Peoples: Recent Interpretations of Protestantism and National Identity in Britain and Ireland," in Claydon and McBride, eds., *Protestantism and National Identity: Britain and Ireland, c. 1650–c. 1850* (Cambridge, 1998), 3–29.

5. Jon Butler, *Awash in a Sea of Faith: Christianizing the American People* (Cambridge, Mass., 1992), 20.

6. See J. David Hoeveler, *Creating the American Mind: Intellect and Politics in the Colonial Colleges* (Lanham, Md., 2002), 176; Robson, *Educating Republicans*, 34.

evangelicalism, as manifested by the rise to cultural and political prominence of his old adversary Witherspoon.[7]

Though its reasoning was far from crude, Witherspoon's evangelicalism was indeed transferred from his educational sphere to the public forums of the Revolutionary era. Deriving in part from a Presbyterian jeremiad tradition, his Revolutionary political theology appealed to colonists. A good number of them were more familiar with the ideas of religious revivalism than the moral sensory writings of Francis Hutcheson. These colonists formed an important yet somewhat overlooked audience for Witherspoon's patriot preaching, particularly when examining the content, tone, and reception of his most famous May 1776 sermon, *The Dominion of Providence over the Passions of Men.* The text came to be read by Presbyterians as far south as Georgia and as far north as Maine, before then reaching Witherspoon's former colleagues on the eastern side of the Atlantic. Witherspoon's Revolutionary political theology adds a Scottish inflection to the "post-Puritan" paradigm of Congregational and Baptist patriot discourse. Assessing his Presbyterian voice uncovers aspects of patriot thought that were distinct to the Scottish Calvinist influence.[8]

Yet the *longue durée* of the association between Scottish Calvinism and New England Congregationalism, and its impact on patriot ideology, should not be overlooked. During the 1740s, Edwardsean and Scottish revivalism lauded their specific denominational contexts without privileging the moral stance of their subjects. Similarly, three decades later, Witherspoon was careful to show that the righteousness of the patriot cause did not suggest the innate moral superiority of its adherents. Whether they were colonists or independent citizens, Presbyterian or Congregationalist, they still required re-

7. Alexander Carlyle, *Autobiography of the Rev. Dr. Alexander Carlyle; Minister of Inveresk, Containing Memorials of the Men and Events of His Time* (Boston, 1861), 29–30, 65.

8. On Witherspoon's publisher, Robert Aitken of Philadelphia, and the dissemination of the *Dominion of Providence* sermon in Scotland and America, see Richard B. Sher, *The Enlightenment and the Book: Scottish Authors and Their Publishers in Eighteenth-Century Britain, Ireland, and America* (Chicago, 2006), 532–537. Assessing the Presbyterian influence should respond to Richard Sher's pertinent observation that the emphasis on New England religious traditions in the historiography of American political preaching has failed "to take into account the important role played in America by British and European jeremiads"—particularly the concepts and ideas that proliferated in sermons by evangelical Scots such as Witherspoon. See Sher, "Witherspoon's *Dominion of Providence* and the Scottish Jeremiad Tradition," in Sher and Smitten, eds., *Scotland and America,* 52. On the post-Puritan "paradigm," see Charles L. Cohen, "The Post-Puritan Paradigm of Early American Religious History," *WMQ,* 3d Ser., LIV (1997), 695–772.

generation. In his "Lectures on Moral Philosophy," Witherspoon suggested that the disparity of moral "writers in all ages" served as proof of the "truth of the Scripture doctrine of the depravity and corruption of our nature." It is vital to examine the related political meaning of his salutary observation, delivered a month before signing the American Declaration of Independence: "How deeply affecting is it, that those who are the same in complexion, the same in blood, in language, and in religion, should, notwithstanding, butcher one another with unrelenting rage, and glory in the deed?"[9]

The "Problem of Dominion" in Presbyterian Patriot Thought

In his 1775 *Address to the Students of the Senior Class,* Witherspoon warned his commencing students of their "lost state by nature and practice" and their need to maintain "an unfeigned reliance on the pardoning mercy and sanctifying grace of God" for the greater good of the American colonies. The commencement exercise included rituals similar to owning of the covenant ceremonies that continued to occur in Scottish religious gatherings on the eastern side of the Atlantic. Witherspoon turned toward the college and confirmed the ceremony's religious nature to the more secular wider community. Students were publicly questioned by clergymen and public figures—akin to the queries fielded by new ministers in the Kirk before their public confession of faith.[10]

Students acknowledged the "sanctifying grace of God" before commencing their adult lives in an unstable political context. According to some visitors to the College of New Jersey, the political radicalism of the imperial crisis could be detected in their behavior. In November 1774, a Scottish visitor to the College of New Jersey was startled to hear what he discerned to be "forty boys repeat Orations" at the college "commencement, every one of

9. John Witherspoon, "Lectures on Moral Philosophy," in [Green, ed.], *Works of Witherspoon,* III, 369; Witherspoon, *The Dominion of Providence over the Passions of Men* . . . , ibid., 22. On the fears of New England clergymen, particularly those of Standing Order Congregationalists (the most common New England church establishment, with roots in Puritan congregations), see James B. Bell, *A War of Religion: Dissenters, Anglicans, and the American Revolution* (Basingstoke, U.K., 2008). Bell focuses particularly on Congregational clergyman and patriot Jonathan Mayhew.

10. John Witherspoon, *An Address to the Students of the Senior Class, on the Lord's Day Preceding Commencement, September 23, 1775,* in [Green, ed.], *Works of Witherspoon,* III, 103. On the commencement rituals, see Ashbel Green, *The Life of the Revd John Witherspoon, D.D., L.L.D; with a Brief Review of His Writings: And a Summary Estimate of His Character and Talents,* ed. Henry Lyttleton Savage (Princeton, N.J., 1973), 32–34.

them full of the old Cameronian resisting sentiments." The visitor referred to those who followed Richard Cameron's teachings in the decades after his death. Cameron, who was killed in 1680 by pro-Royal Scottish lairds, had formed the most radical (even secessionist) religious coalition against perceived Stuart attempts to curtail the autonomy of the Church of Scotland. Of course, Witherspoon was no Cameronian. He had never opposed British unionism in principle. Rather, he objected to the nature of Anglo-Scottish unionism in practice, particularly the connection between Westminster political patronage and Scottish Moderate churchmen.[11]

The term "Cameronian" was at least appropriate in its general conjunction of political radicalism with religious revivalism. Both characterized the College of New Jersey campus in the years after Witherspoon's arrival. During the early Revolutionary era, the College of New Jersey drew on an intercolonial religious constituency that had developed in association with the awakening of evangelical revivalism from the late 1730s to the early 1750s. "New Light" Congregationalists, who perceived their marginalization by influential educators and theologians in Harvard and Yale, corresponded with and even publicly supported "New Side" Presbyterians in the Middle and southern colonies, who felt similarly distanced from their own religious and educational establishments. Of course, a problematic teleology links the Great Awakening of American evangelicalism in the mid-eighteenth century to the political origins of the American Revolution. Moreover, those who decided to enroll in the College of New Jersey were not always traditionally evangelical in their inclination. Nor was evangelicalism in 1770 necessarily identical to experimental piety in 1740.[12]

11. James Parker to Charles Steuart, Nov. 3, 1774, in William R. Brock, *Scotus Americanus: A Survey of the Sources for Links between Scotland and America in the Eighteenth Century* (Edinburgh, 1982), 254 n. 8. Cameronian representatives signed the "Sanquhar Declaration" in 1680 and sought to separate their ecclesiastical structures from the mainline Scottish Presbyterian church after the religious settlement of 1690. After 1743, they came to be known as Reformed Presbyterians and often set themselves in opposition to the terms of Anglo-Scottish union. On Cameronian ideology, see Jeffrey Stephen, *Scottish Presbyterians and the Act of Union 1707* (Edinburgh, 2007), 207–217.

12. James McLachlan, *Princetonians, 1748–1768: A Biographical Dictionary* (Princeton, N.J., 1976), xx. For a famous critique of Heimert's thesis linking colonial revivalism to the American Revolution, see John M. Murrin, "No Awakening, No Revolution? More Counterfactual Speculations," *Reviews in American History*, XI (1983), 161–171. On the difference in evangelicalism between the 1740s and 1770s, see the example of Yale in Christopher Grasso, *A Speaking Aristocracy: Transforming Public Discourse in Eighteenth-Century Connecticut* (Chapel Hill, N.C., 1999), 144–185.

Nonetheless, it is clear that religious revivalism at least coincided with the growth of politicized identity on campus following the Stamp Act crisis. In the summer and early fall of 1770, as well as in early 1772, Andrew Hunter, Jr., informed his fellow student Philip Fithian: "We have had a considerable stir of religion in college since you went away, Lewis Willson is thought to have got religion; and the formerly abandoned Glover is seeking the way to heaven. Our orations are put off lest they should do some harm to some under concern." Hunter defined his fellow students' collective religious identity (*"we have had a considerable stir of religion"*) in distinction to the experience of those who went "away" to their homes. They acted to encourage others like Glover, apparently a reformed troublemaker, to seek their "way to heaven." That said, Israel Evans later described Glover's "stealing of Turkies" through winter, which led to his expulsion from the college. Other students, Evans noted, were "fined by the civil magistrate" for similar offences. Although they and Glover seemed "hopelessly converted," he informed Fithian, it now seemed that there was "no knowing who is converted only by their after conduct in life, such things however open the mouths of the enemies of religion." "It is a great work to change the carnal heart and if so many bid fair for the kingdom of heaven and yet come short," he wrote, "what reason for strict and frequent examination in order to know whether we be in the faith of our Lord Jesus Christ." Fithian, Hunter, and Evans came to their Calvinist conclusion on the matter of the stolen turkey within a revived context of piety that pleased those in the college environs, such as Benjamin Rush, who had perceived Witherspoon's arrival as a sign of an imminent religious awakening in the town.[13]

In 1773, Hunter wrote to Fithian to assure him that they went "on pretty well in College" while Witherspoon was on a trip to New England, other than having to contend with a few avowed loyalist students on the campus: "I hope we shall have two or three of the *possessed swine* turned off when the Doctor comes home." A year later, many of his fellow students would place the winter supply of tea in a large bonfire along with an effigy of the Massachusetts governor. There is no evidence that Witherspoon imposed any

13. Andrew Hunter, Jr., to Philip Fithian, Mar. 18, 1772, Israel Evans to Fithian, Jan. 25, 1773, in John Rogers Williams, ed., *Philip Vickers Fithian: Journal and Letters, 1767–1774, Student at Princeton College, 1770–72, Tutor at Nomini Hall in Virginia, 1773–74* (Princeton, N.J., 1900), 22, 30. Fithian graduated from one of Witherspoon's first classes in the College of New Jersey and would eventually suffer a poignant and premature death during the early stages of the American Revolution. On Fithian's last days, see John Fea, *The Way of Improvement Leads Home: Philip Vickers Fithian and the Rural Enlightenment in Early America* (Philadelphia, 2008), 180–207.

discipline on those who took part in these actions. In addition to Fithian, Hunter, and, of course, James Madison, many other students who attended the College of New Jersey during the early period of Witherspoon's tenure as president emerged as prominent members of the Revolutionary struggle. They included John Beatty, Hugh Henry Brackenridge, Gunning Bedford, William Bradford, Aaron Burr, Frederick Frelinghuysen, Philip Freneau, John Henry, Henry Lee, Morgan Lewis, Aaron Ogden, and Caleb Wallace. Brackenridge became a writer of poems, novels, and political polemics, all while qualifying as a lawyer, judge, and justice of the Pennsylvania Supreme Court. Bedford would serve in the Delaware General Assembly, the Continental Congress, and the 1787 Constitutional Convention. Bradford became a lifelong friend of Madison, a lawyer and judge in Philadelphia, and the second United States attorney general (1794–1795). Frelinghuysen became a New Jersey provincial congressman and senator, a U.S. senator during the mid-1790s, and a military officer on the western frontier. Freneau became known for his poetic accounts of the American Revolution. Henry assumed the governorship of Maryland (1797–1798) and became a member of the Senate (1789–1797). Before becoming governor of New York from 1804 to 1807 (defeating college classmate Aaron Burr), Lewis trained as a lawyer and served as an army captain during the Revolutionary War. Ogden became a U.S. senator (1801–1803) and governor of New Jersey (1812–1813). Between 1769 and 1775, 178 men studied under Witherspoon. Of those, 105 went on to assume public office.[14]

Witherspoon was able to serve in the same national Congress as his students because his activities during the Revolutionary era transcended collegiate political culture. Several months before his "Cameronian" university commencement ceremony, he had been elected to the Committee of Correspondence of Somerset County, New Jersey. In September 1774, after traveling to Philadelphia as an observer of the first Continental Congress, Wither-

14. Hunter to Fithian, Sept. 6, 1773, in Williams, ed., *Philip Vickers Fithian*, 42. On the "possessed" loyalists and burning of tea in early 1774, see Thomas Jefferson Wertenbaker, *Princeton: 1746–1896* (Princeton, N.J., 1946), 56–77; L. Gordon Tait, *The Piety of John Witherspoon: Pew, Pulpit, and Public Forum* (Louisville, Ky., 2001), 16. On the college's relative radicalism, see Robson, *Educating Republicans*, 90–93. On the trajectory of the Witherspoon students, see John Maclean, *History of the College of New Jersey: From Its Origin in 1746 to the Commencement of 1854* (Philadelphia, 1877), I, 357–362; Wertenbaker, *Princeton*, 48; McLachlan, *Princetonians*, 663–667; Richard A. Harrison, *Princetonians, 1776–1783: A Biographical Dictionary* (Princeton, N.J., 1981), xxxi, 541–550; Ralph Ketcham, *James Madison: A Biography* (1971; rpt. Charlottesville, Va., 1990), 34–35; Joseph S. Tiedemann, "Presbyterianism and the American Revolution in the Middle Colonies," *Church History*, LXXIV (2005), 339.

spoon prepared an essay for distribution among its members. His "Thoughts on American Liberty" suggested that the "Congress is, properly speaking, the representative of the great body of the people of North America" and recommended that "a plan of union should be laid down for all the colonies."[15]

During the same period, New England delegates to the Continental Congress came through Princeton village on their way to Philadelphia. Among them was John Adams, who described Witherspoon "as high a son of liberty as any Man in America." En route to the Continental Congress some weeks later, Adams spent several days in Princeton village. On Saturday, he noted that the "scholars" in Witherspoon's circle sang "as badly as the Presbyterians at New York." Adams recalled having wine in Witherspoon's house, at which point the college president recommended that "the Congress should raise money and employ a number of writers in the newspapers in England, to explain to the public the American plea, and remove the prejudices of Britons." Adams also recalled Witherspoon's suggestion that "we should recommend it to every Colony to form a society for the encouragement of Protestant emigrants from the Three Kingdoms." The next day, Adams attended church and "heard Dr. Witherspoon all day; a clear, sensible preacher."[16]

Yet, to a greater extent than Adams, Witherspoon still remained loyal to the British crown through 1774. Continuing to perceive royal and political powers as distinct from one another, Witherspoon's "Thoughts on American Liberty" responded to "late acts with respect to Boston, to ruin their capital, destroy their charter, and grant the soldiers a licence to murder them" by declaring: "We esteem the claim of the British parliament to be illegal and unconstitutional [and] that we are firmly determined never to submit to it, and do deliberately prefer war with all its horrors, and even extermination itself to slavery, rivetted on us and our posterity." Yet Witherspoon claimed "to profess as all the provincial and county rulers have done, our loyalty to the king, and our backwardness to break our connexion with Great Britain, if we are not forced by their unjust impositions . . . [and] our detestation of the virulent and insolent abuse of his majesty's person and family."[17]

15. John Witherspoon, "Thoughts on American Liberty," in [Green, ed.], *Works of Witherspoon*, IV, 297, 300.

16. John Adams, Diary, Aug. 27, 28, 1774, in Charles Francis Adams, ed., *The Works of John Adams, Second President of the United States: With a Life of the Author, Notes, and Illustrations* (Boston, 1850), II, 355–356.

17. Witherspoon, "Thoughts on American Liberty," in [Green, ed.], *Works of Witherspoon*, IV, 298–300. On Witherspoon's continued loyalty to the British crown, despite his support for nonimportation measures, see also John Witherspoon, "On the Controversy about Independence," ibid., 301–304. On the Committee of Correspondence of Somerset County, New Jersey,

In early 1775, Witherspoon was reelected to the Somerset County Committee of Correspondence. A few months later, he authored a pastoral letter on behalf of the entire Philadelphia Synod. Circulated between church congregations for several weeks before being read from pulpits on June 29, 1775 (a fast day appointed by the Continental Congress), the letter responded to the first military encounter between Britain and the American colonies in Lexington and Concord. This was likely the first official occasion that Witherspoon's religious writings were publicly connected to political developments. The pastoral letter claimed to support independence from Westminster's political jurisdiction without renouncing any allegiance to the House of Hanover. The inevitable and just colonial reaction to Westminster legislation, according to Witherspoon, portended "the horrors of a civil war throughout the great continent" of North America. But, in contrast to the seventeenth-century English Civil Wars (which incorporated Scottish Presbyterians), Witherspoon advised colonists to oppose Parliament rather than the monarchy. He petitioned Presbyterians to maintain their attachment to George III.[18]

Despite offering public religious support for the continuing critique of British misrule, therefore, aspects of the letter might not have appealed entirely to patriots such as John Adams, who had become more vocal in his opposition to the British monarchy as well as the Parliament after the battles at Lexington and Concord. Having heard from his wife about the bloody conflict in Massachusetts, Adams became weary of those whom he deemed as too moderate in their opposition to the British King-in-Parliament. In his pastoral letter, conversely, Witherspoon described a civil war against the British legislature, rather than full separation from the House of Hanover. He also warned "brethren" in America to "look beyond the immediate authors either of your sufferings or fears [the British Parliament], and to acknowledge the holiness and justice of the Almighty in the present visitation . . . [to] humble themselves before his throne, to confess their sins, by which they have provoked his indignation, and intreat him to pour out upon all ranks a spirit of repentance and of prayer." The colonists required the same salvation as mainland British subjects. On the one hand, Witherspoon deplored

---

see also John E. Pomfret, *Colonial New Jersey: A History* (New York, 1973), 252; Varnum Lansing Collins, *President Witherspoon: A Biography*, 2 vols. (Princeton, N.J., 1925), I, 208–209.

18. Synod of New-York and Philadelphia [John Witherspoon], *A Pastoral Letter from the Synod of New-York and Philadelphia to the Congregations under Their Care; to Be Read from the Pulpits on Thursday, June 29, 1775, Being the Day of the General Fast* (New York, 1775), in [Green, ed.], *Works of Witherspoon*, III, 9.

corrupt British politicians for curtailing provincial freedoms that imperial subjects had enjoyed for decades. On the other hand, he reminded colonists that their own "pride" and "luxury" had ironically been "aggravated" by the freedom granted to them by the very same "inestimable privileges" that they had "hitherto enjoyed without interruption since the first settlement of this country." Every "battle of the warrior," Witherspoon continued, "is with confused noise, and garments rolled in blood." It was "impossible to appeal to the sword without being exposed to many scenes of cruelty and slaughter; but it is often observed that civil wars are carried on with a rancor and spirit of revenge much greater than those between independent states." In the inevitable conflict that faced colonists, Witherspoon advised that "man will fight most bravely, who never fights till it is necessary, and who ceases to fight as soon as the necessity is over."[19]

Despite Witherspoon's continued support for the Hanoverian monarchy, in contrast to patriots such as Adams, loyalists spent much energy decrying the confluence between Presbyterianism and republicanism. During the early 1770s, it was convenient for loyalists and Anglicans to suggest that Presbyterians such as Witherspoon were innately antimonarchical, indebted to their unruly seventeenth-century heritage. Reverend Jonathan Odell attributed Witherspoon's patriot turn to his Presbyterian heritage, in which the "hate of Kings" had always summoned the "glory of the Kirk." Hugo Arnot, a prominent member of the Edinburgh literary and rhetorical debating circle known as the Speculative Society, explained "the whole mystery" of American's "rebellion" through reference to "seditious Preachers" such as "Silverspoon." Their seventeenth-century predecessors had apparently sowed the "seeds of harsh dissentions" in their covenanting "zeal" against monarchical authority. Such crude historical associations prevented loyalists from acknowledging the conservative language of Presbyterian patriotism at that point in the imperial crisis, language that often sought to return to or uphold monarchical unionism while attacking Westminster.[20]

Most loyalist opponents of Presbyterian patriotism overlooked the common support for the Hanoverian monarchy among Presbyterians on both

19. Ibid., 10, 12, 14, 15.

20. Camillo Querno [Jonathan Odell], *The American Times: A Satire in Three Parts in Which Are Delineated the Characters of the Leaders of the American Rebellion* (London, 1780), 18; [Hugo Arnot], *The XLV. Chapter of the Prophecies of Thomas the Rhymer, in Verse; with Notes and Illustrations; Dedicated to Doctor Silverspoon, Preacher of Sedition in America* (Edinburgh, 1776), 3, 5–6, 11. A list of loyalist references to supposed Presbyterian republicanism can be found in Tiedemann, "Presbyterianism and the American Revolution," *Church History*, LXXIV (2005), 313–314.

sides of the Atlantic. The principles of the Westminster Confession of Faith had once galvanized English and Scottish dissenters against Stuart autocracy. But, after the 1707 Act of Union, the same principles rarely accompanied any animosity toward a British monarch. More commonly, they were expressed in tension with Westminster's parliamentary establishment, which was distinguished from the House of Hanover. In 1746, after all, Witherspoon had organized men in battle on behalf of the British crown. In 1774, when a group of evangelical Presbyterians called for a renewal of the 1643 Solemn League and Covenant among Scotland's clerical and educational establishment, they did not express any republican leanings. Instead, they advocated the restoration of piety as a departure from the latitudinarian religious ideas promoted by their Moderate rivals. Rather than addressing their indignation toward monarchical interests, they accused political, pedagogical, and religious leaders of laxity in their opposition to Catholicism and in their support for Protestant settlers in North America. Without singling out the Hanoverian royal house, they used a bodily metaphor to describe the "corrupted" ways of the metropolitan establishment in the British union. Cultural and civic leaders — particularly Scotland's Moderate establishment — had "foresaken the Holy One of Israel. The whole Head is sick, and the whole Heart is faint." During the same year, notwithstanding their English Congregational roots, Boston radicals drew further inspiration from Scotland's early modern covenanting movement. They formed a "Solemn League" against the corruption of British imperial governance, addressing their opposition more clearly against the British Parliament than the British crown.[21]

Even while he opposed Westminster's political and Anglican establishment, therefore, Witherspoon continued a long tradition of provincial evangelical support for the British monarchy. With the entrenchment of a Protestant royal line through the eighteenth century, evangelical Presbyterians on both sides of the Atlantic had become increasingly more likely to criticize the worldly corruption of the British Parliament than the British crown. Sermonizing just as the Seven Years' War drew to a close, College of New Jersey president Samuel Davies had suggested that "the name of George the Second must be dear in these rescued provinces, and particularly in Nassau-Hall [New Jersey]" before speaking "in favour of . . . the succes-

21. "Act of the Associate Presbytery for Renewing the National Covenant of Scotland, and the Solemn League and Covenant of Three Nations, Edinburgh 1774," in Brock, ed., *Scotus Americanus,* 89. On the New England Solemn League, see Richard D. Brown, *Revolutionary Politics in Massachusetts: The Boston Committee of Correspondence and the Towns, 1772–1774* (Cambridge, Mass., 1970), 185, 191, 198.

sion in the Hanover-family: of liberty, the Protestant religion and George the Third, which are inseparably united." Two decades later, Witherspoon made known his disdain for "insolent abuse" against George III on both sides of the Atlantic. As a general Protestant unifier, the Georgian line galvanized the various dominions of the British Empire without demanding their incorporation in more specific legal, political, and ecclesiastical ways. By the 1770s, conversely, most Presbyterian patriots did not assume a similar level of attachment to Westminster governance, particularly in its recent incarnation.[22]

When American Presbyterians distinguished the corruption of the British Parliament from the continued benevolence of the crown, it was not impossible to find precedents in the earlier history of the Civil Wars in Britain and Ireland between 1638 and 1651. As detailed previously, the Presbyterian divines who wrote the Westminster Confession of Faith were not opposed to monarchy in principle. Moreover, the "Malignant Faction Theory" of English Congregational ministers such as John Goodwin had refrained from advocating republicanism even while it opposed the specifics of Stuart autocracy. It sought to purify rather than dismantle Britain's regal constitution, reasserting its perceived association with dissenting freedom. A few menacing factions, it suggested, undermined the civil theology of a state that was especially blessed by God. Though men like Goodwin claimed their natural right to resist corrupt factions, they were not motivated by any general desire to overturn the principle of royal authority. They opposed Stuart autocracy without disclaiming their theoretical support for the civil magistracy of the British crown.[23]

Scholars have suggested that the developing idea of a New England cove-

22. Samuel Davies, "Sermon LX: On the Death of His Late Majesty, King George II; Delivered in Nassau-Hall, Jan. 14, 1761," in *Sermons on Important Subjects* . . . , 5th ed., 3 vols. (New York, 1792), III, 352, 363; Witherspoon, "Thoughts on American Liberty," in [Green, ed.], *Works of Witherspoon*, IV, 298. On continuing loyalism to the Hanoverian system, see also Brendan McConville, *The King's Three Faces: The Rise and Fall of Royal America, 1688–1776* (Chapel Hill, N.C., 2006), 255-272.

23. Goodwin was an independent opponent of Charles I. On "Malignant Faction Theory" from the perspective of Presbyterians during the English Civil Wars and the Revolutionary era, see Keith L. Griffin, *Revolution and Religion: American Revolutionary War and the Reformed Clergy* (New York, 1994), 23-25; Tiedemann, "Presbyterianism and the American Revolution," *Church History*, LXXIV (2005), 322-324. As Allan I. Macinnes has shown, the Presbyterian divines who wrote the Westminster Confession of Faith were not opposed to monarchy in principle: "Resistance to Charles the man was in the long-term interests of monarchy and people, a necessary curative if the kingdom were to be restored to godly rule." See Macinnes, *Union and Empire: The Making of the United Kingdom in 1707* (Cambridge, 2007), 68.

nant formed a bridge between the malignant faction theory of early modern English Congregationalists and the political theology of Presbyterian patriots. During the first generation of New England settlement, Massachusetts ministers such as John Cotton followed their English counterparts in criticizing corrupt members of the Stuart court for negating the special moral ideals of his community. Similar critiques affected patriot Presbyterian ideology, particularly among those in the Middle Colonies who remained influenced by the public covenanting theology of New England Congregational ministers. During the Revolutionary era, according to such a narrative, Presbyterian political theology adopted the Congregational desire to cast out governors who broke communally defined moral norms, even though such a desire had germinated in English dissenting circles.[24]

Assessing the true meaning and importance of public covenanting ideology during the Revolutionary era, despite the examples above, remains a tricky and problematic endeavor. That pro-Hanoverian Presbyterians adopted New England's "elect nation" critique of corrupt magistracy is a particularly awkward notion. John Goodwin's role as a bridge to the political theology of New England Congregationalism and then Middle Colony Presbyterianism is difficult to reconcile since his covenanting identity was formed in specific tension *with* Presbyterians. More generally, the view that elect nation ideology allowed the enlargement of New England public covenants fails to reflect the confessional and constitutional motivations of many Presbyterians during the colonial and Revolutionary era, including Witherspoon. It defines Presbyterian political theology without assigning much agency to Presbyterians themselves. The first principles of their patriot ideology are assumed to lie in Puritan and post-Puritan notions of national election without enough direct evidence to support such an assertion.[25]

In 1765, the Stamp Act Congress suggested that, "from and under the English constitution, we derive all our civil and religious rights and liber-

---

24. On the "bridge" between New England malignant faction theory and Presbyterian patriot sentiment and the idea that a New England covenant widened in order to incorporate Presbyterians in the Middle Colonies, see Griffin, *Revolution and Religion*, 26–27, 73; Noll, *America's God*, 38–39.

25. On Goodwin's disdain for Presbyterianism during the English Civil Wars, see John Coffey, *John Goodwin and the Puritan Revolution: Religion and Intellectual Change in Seventeenth-Century England* (Woodbridge, U.K., 2006), 131. By the American Revolution, according to Grasso, the notion of a public covenant had often "become increasingly awkward as a depiction of corporate identity." "Who was in the covenant? New England? Great Britain, too? The thirteen colonies? It was no longer effectively used to legitimate moral regulations and the union of church and state." See Grasso, *A Speaking Aristocracy*, 30–31, 135.

ties." Such a claim reflected one of many instances during the Revolutionary era when religious rights and liberties were defined in Anglocentric terms, including in association with the common law freedoms accorded to New England Congregationalism. Yet Presbyterian patriots offered an alternative to such an Anglocentric paradigm. In the American colonies, Presbyterians had been prone to challenge restrictions on their authority (whether commercial or religious) through reference to "British" rather than "English" constitutionalism. In particular, they alluded to the jurisdictional autonomy accorded to the Kirk in the British Empire after the 1707 Act of Union. Most Presbyterian patriots traced their American origins to the period during and after the formation of the British state. Thus, they were more inclined to envision colonial rights—and any threats to their autonomous expression—in relation to constitutional developments that had taken place since 1707. Their migrating parents and grandparents had cherished their ability to trade with other provinces in the British Empire, unrestricted by English protectionism. A good number had assumed—or at least hoped—that the liberty to promote Presbyterian revivalism represented another positive aspect of British provincial life. Defining a natural affinity between Presbyterianism and republicanism eschews these legacies of British provincial evangelicalism during the Revolutionary era, as does the argument that Presbyterians simply appropriated Congregational ideas of civil and religious liberty as they joined the patriot movement.[26]

Thus, Witherspoon was not alone among American Presbyterians in describing his allegiance to George III while also criticizing the actions of the British Parliament. Continuing to support the Hanoverian monarchy until as

26. See the Stamp Act statements cited in John Phillip Reid, *Constitutional History of the American Revolution,* II, *The Authority to Tax* (Madison, Wis., 2003), 24. According to Reid, common use of the "English" moniker in patriot discourse against Britain derived from the perception that "there was no British law . . . no British attorney general. . . . It was the English law and only English law that was in contention during the revolutionary era." Yet the differing constitutional conceptions of Scottish migrants in America offered another interpretation, particularly among those whose communities had previously noted the jurisdictional autonomy of the Kirk as a provincial liberty, separate from Westminster's Anglocentric prerogative. See Ned C. Landsman, "Roots, Routes, and Rootedness: Diversity, Migration, and Toleration in Mid-Atlantic Pluralism," *Early American Studies,* II (2004), 267–309; Landsman, "The Legacy of British Union for the North American Colonies: Provincial Elites and the Problem of Imperial Union," in John Robertson, ed., *A Union for Empire: Political Thought and the British Union of 1707* (Cambridge, 1995); Landsman, "The Provinces and the Empire: Scotland, the American Colonies, and the Development of British Provincial Identity," in Lawrence Stone, ed., *An Imperial State at War: Britain from 1689 to 1815* (London, 1994), 258–288.

late as 1776, then, Presbyterian patriots were less prone to evoke Anglocentric ideas of political and religious liberty, at least in comparison to New England ministers such as Jonathan Mayhew and Samuel West. Joseph Montgomery, a Pennsylvania Presbyterian minister and a delegate to the Continental Congress, used a July 20, 1775, sermon to support a recent congressional fast day proclamation. Its wording, he noted, sought to

> avert those desolating judgements with which we are threatned, and to bless our rightful Sovereign, King George the Third, and inspire him with wisdom to discern and pursue the true interest of all his subjects — that a speedy end may be put to the civil discord between Great-Britain and the American Colonies . . . and that [America's] civil and religious privileges may be secured.

Montgomery linked the biblical Exodus story to the "British" context for the seventeenth-century struggle against Stuart tyranny, making sure to avoid any reference to English Puritans at the expense of the Scottish Presbyterian contribution to the struggle. The sermon then described a loose union of colonies, each under separate charters but bound by the same Hanoverian monarchy. In his opinion, Anglocentric government ministers had become envious of the provincial strength of the American dominion in the British Empire. Thus, "unconstitutional statutes" were formed by "the parliament of Great Britain" to denigrate colonial legal autonomy. London's metropolitan government had become so fearful of the strength of the colonies that they wilfully sought to "get them up to an independent state and become a rival empire." Montgomery's American colonists sought only to continue in their prosperity within the *British* Empire. Westminster politicians preferred creating a rival empire rather than allow strong American provinces to retain a confederal role as British subjects within a wider imperial polity.[27]

In 1775, Presbyterian minister and College of New Jersey graduate Robert Cooper reminded his listeners that the events of the imperial crisis demonstrated that "the doctrine of unlimited passive obedience and non-resistance has been exploded by Britons," who had trampled upon "certain rights derived from the God of nature, which no man can transfer to another, even if he were willing." Suggesting that the present tension with Westminster reflected an internecine conflict among provinces of the British Empire, Cooper specified certain "late acts of the British Parliament," such as the 1766 Declara-

27. Joseph Montgomery, *A Sermon, Preached at Christiana Bridge and Newcastle, the 20th of July, 1775; Being the Day Appointed by the Continental Congress, as a Day of Fasting Humiliation, and Prayer* . . . (Philadelphia, 1775), 8, 10-11, 23-24, 26-27.

tory Act, which had "brought on a civil war" owing to its claim that "the Imperial Crown and Parliament of Great-Britain" retained "full power and authority to make laws and statutes of sufficient validity to bind the Colonies and people of America, subjects of the Crown of Great-Britain, in all cases whatsoever." Cooper made sure to define such a constitutional problem in relation to religious as well as political authority, pointing out that the incorporating acts laid "sufficient foundation for a system of tyranny, both civil and ecclesiastic." The "time may come," Cooper envisioned, "when the whole of Great-Britain, may bear no greater proportion to the British Colonies, either with regard to circuit or number of inhabitants, than one of our counties now do to a province." But he also noted that such loose confederalism would break down if the colonies continued to "have no other security against tyranny and oppression, but the complexion of the British Parliament, the evils incident to which we can neither prevent nor remedy." An overly unified definition of British imperialism, according to Cooper, had thus made colonists "not merely the subjects of the Imperial Crown of Great Britain [a legitimate stance], but the slaves of the Parliament of Great-Britain." The British Parliament was problematic in having attempted to incorporate colonists under the indivisible jurisdiction of Westminster. Using similar reasoning to that in Witherspoon's recently published pastoral letter, Cooper described a civil war within the British Empire rather than defining the necessity of total American independence. He placed provincial Americans in a struggle against the British legislature, rather than necessarily advocating full separation from the Hanoverian monarchy.[28]

During the same year, the Presbyterian reverend John Carmichael turned to "the Gentlemen of the *Militia,* Officers and Soldiers," who appeared be-

28. Robert Cooper, *Courage in a Good Cause; or, The Lawful and Courageous Use of the Sword; a Sermon, Preached Near Shippensburgh, in Cumberland County, on the 31st of August, 1775, — to a Large Audience, in Which Were under Arrest Several Companies of Col. Montgomery's Battalion; and Published at Their Request* (Lancaster, Pa., 1775), 9, 12, 20–22. As T. H. Breen has argued, colonists without purely "English" ancestry were more likely to make reference to "British" rights during the Revolutionary era, notwithstanding the Anglocentric statements made at the Stamp Act Congress. See Breen, "Ideology and Nationalism on the Eve of the American Revolution: Revisions Once More in Need of Revising," *Journal of American History,* LXXXIV (1997), 13–39. Those who used the English moniker rarely demonstrated any specific opposition to British constitutionalism. Rather, they were simply more familiar with early modern discussions of English rights, as translated through Congregational ministers and educators. On these problems and ambiguities of description during the Revolutionary era, see also Dror Wahrman, "The English Problem of Identity in the American Revolution," *American Historical Review,* CVI (2001), 1236–1262.

fore him "in Church in their UNIFORM," and referred to their home as a "province" of the British Empire, whose liberties were kept in check by benevolent "gentlemen of the sword." In their province, moreover, Carmichael implored them to

> continue to revere royalty, and observe your allegiance to the King, on the true principles of the constitution. Your drawing the sword now must not be against the person of his Majesty; but the mal-administration of his government, by designing, mischief-making ministers. Your present appearances must then be not of choice, but of necessity. While his Majesty George the third will observe his own coronation oath, and the principles of the revolution, for the support of which against all Jacobite factions, and Tory plots of popery, his ancestors of illustrious line of Brunswick were placed on the throne of Great Britain, do you observe your allegiance.

Carmichael expressed his theoretical support for royal authority when he protested against constraints on colonial freedom. His reference to maladministration and mischief used a vocabulary that was similar to that used in malignant faction theory, yet there is no evidence that he was required to consult the writings of Goodwin when he set about distinguishing corrupt magistracy from the patriot cause. He simply accused parliamentarians of restricting religious, political, and commercial freedoms that had been protected under the Hanoverian system:

> The angry tools of power who mislead government, may call us American "rebels, who would throw off all government, — would be independent and what not." But . . . we desire no such things. . . . We do in America all declare ourselves the subjects of King George the third, but we never swore allegiance to the Parliament of Great-Britain — or else we would have above 500 Kings — they are our fellow-subjects, chosen by the freeholders of that island to legislate for them, as our Assembly doth for Pennsylvania; but if their present claims are admitted, we may give up our Assemblies — and our Charters are cyphers!

Thus, Carmichael made sure to highlight the positive "British" dimension to provincial identity in America: loyalty to the Protestant crown without direct incorporation by the Parliament of Westminster.[29]

29. John Carmichael, *A Self-Defensive War Lawful, Proved in a Sermon, Preached at Lancaster, before Captain Ross's Company of Militia, in the Presbyterian Church, on Sabbath Morning, June 4th, 1775* . . . (Philadelphia, 1775), 18, 22–24, 28–32.

In 1777, Presbyterian Yale graduate Abraham Keteltas followed John Carmichael and Robert Cooper in recalling the effects of the Declaratory Act by defining the encroachment of rights in provincial British America. Having outlined familiar biblical typologies of tyranny and enslavement, Keteltas then described the struggle against Westminster corruption through reference to more recent events in Calvinist Europe, particularly in its Dutch and Swiss states. The "revolt of the seven united provinces of the Netherlands" against "Philip the 2d, king of Spain," demonstrated the power of outlying populations against the corrupt measures of imperial centralization. When the "civil and religious liberties" of the Dutch were "oppressed," they "petitioned for a redress of their grievances . . . and at length, after a long, and arduous struggle, were acknowledged by their tyrants, to be FREE and INDEPENDENT STATES!" Keteltas then moved from the Dutch example to the "Swiss cantons, long oppressed by the mighty house of Austria, [who] at last formed the glorious and magnanimous resolution of throwing off the abhor'd yoke of slavery and vile subjection . . . [becoming] the freest people upon earth." Against this backdrop, Keteltas turned to the American struggle, which he placed within a larger eighteenth-century context of British provincial liberty. Having alluded to the corrupt factions of the English Civil Wars, Keteltas made sure to focus on the Hanoverian context for the development of autonomy in British America: "We cannot therefore doubt, that the cause of liberty, united with that of truth and righteousness, is the cause of God. This is the glorious cause in which Great-Britain herself, has frequently and strenuously contended against tyrants and oppressors." Thus, Keteltas reminded his listeners:

> For the sake of liberty and the protestant religion, during the reign of this glorious and auspicious king, the Pretender was excluded from the throne, and the succession to it, was settled in the royal house of Hanover. Great-Britain cannot in justice blame us, for imitating her in those noble struggles for liberty, which have been her greatest glory — she cannot condemn us, without condemning the conduct of her greatest patriots and heroes, virtually denying her king's right to his crown . . . [in] opposition to the spirit and interest of her own excellent constitution. I am bold to affirm that all the surpassing glory, by which she has eclipsed other nations, has been owing to this admirable form of government.

Framing the struggle for Protestant rights as fundamentally British, Keteltas criticized those in London who had endeavored to define Parliamentary sovereignty "in all cases whatsoever." He reminded his Presbyterian listeners that any constitutional interpretation in which the "parliament of Great Britain, hath power, and of right ought to have power, to make laws and statutes to bind these colonies in all cases whatsoever" was in fact "contrary to the laws of God and man, to the British constitution, Magna-Charta, the bill of rights, the Charters of the Colonies, and the express stipulations of preceeding kings and their representatives" during the Hanoverian era. Keteltas's reference to the Magna Carta certainly alluded to the importance of English common laws in colonial America, some of which had been incorporated in colonial charters before the Act of Union. But their role was to be understood in conjunction with a "British constitution" that had guaranteed institutional autonomies in the American colonies since 1707. In New Jersey and Pennsylvania, for example, local Presbyterian populations had defined the disestablished confessional status of presbyteries and synods through reference to British rights. Royal governors had even sanctioned the founding of Presbyterian-led educational institutions, most prominently the College of New Jersey.[30]

Most Presbyterian patriots did not appropriate Puritan ideas of national election, then; rather, they tended to interrogate the "problem of dominion" in eighteenth-century British constitutionalism. Many Presbyterian patriots believed that it was possible for colonial provinces to maintain local institutional, religious, and commercial autonomies while still remaining part of a wider imperial union. Less concerned with their incorporation in an enlarged public covenant, they reasserted the importance of loose confederalism among provincial populations in the British Empire, all under the same Protestant monarchy. Witherspoon and others were disappointed in British

30. Abraham Keteltas, *God Arising and Pleading His People's Cause; or, The American War in Favor of Liberty, against the Measures and Arms of Great Britain, Shewn to Be the Cause of God: In a Sermon Preached October 5th, 1777 at an Evening Lecture, in the Presbyterian Church in Newbury-Port* (Newburyport, Mass., 1777), 18, 20, 21, 25, 30. For cases involving colonial Presbyterian conceptions of confessional identity in British constitutionalism, see Ned Landsman, "The Episcopate, the British Union, and the Failure of Religious Settlement in Colonial British America," in Chris Beneke and Christopher S. Grenda, eds., *The First Prejudice: Religious Tolerance and Intolerance in Early America* (Philadelphia, 2011), 84–85; Tiedemann, "Presbyterianism and the American Revolution," *Church History*, LXXIV (2005), 325. According to Barry Shain, the word "British" often denoted greater universalism than English liberties that were attached to specific aspects of common law (including the Magna Carta). "British" rights allowed some colonists to describe themselves as "a people [who] derive their Liberty from God, the Author of their Being." See Barry Shain, "Religious Conscience and Original Sin: An Exploration of America's Protestant Foundations," in David Womersley, ed., *Liberty and American Experience in the Eighteenth Century* (Indianapolis, Ind., 2006), 180.

parliamentary policy during the early 1770s because it constrained autonomies that had developed under the Hanoverian system and that they continued to associate with royal benevolence.[31]

The association between Anglo-Scottish constitutionalism and American
patriot thought was also referenced in a posthumously published essay by
Witherspoon, "On Conducting the American Controversy." By April 1776,
when he intended to publish his essay, he was at pains to point out that
the cause of liberty was not limited to English radical critiques of corruption—whether on the eastern or the western side of the Atlantic. He criticized the "many American patriots" who were seen "to countenance, and
to think themselves interested in the prosperity of that most despicable of
all factions that ever existed in the British empire, headed by the celebrated
John Wilkes, esq." Wilkes, a radical English member of Parliament, used
pamphlets, popular meetings, and print journalism to define the rights of
ordinary English voters against the oligarchical interests and old corruption
of the King-in-Parliament. His activities in England had become well known
in America by 1775 because patriots drew clear parallels with their own movement against Westminster. In 1768, protesting against Wilkes's temporary
imprisonment in King's Bench Prison, seven of his supporters were killed
in what came to be known as the St. George's Fields Massacre. After that,
Wilkes had sponsored debates to call for a bill on parliamentary reform in
Westminster and had made known his support for the American rebellion
against unrepresentative parliamentary legislation. Yet, writing in the radical
newspaper the *North Briton*, published in London between 1762 and 1763,
Wilkes had also demonstrated unambiguous disdain for Scots in the British
union in terms that have since been described as radical English "Scottophobia." Witherspoon referred to Wilkes's public denigration of all Scots
as avaricious and venal supporters of Westminster largesse. Ironically, his
former evangelical colleagues in the Popular party were not entirely dissimilar from the English radical in their diagnosis of civil corruption. They never
lost an opportunity to decry the patronage networks that had developed between genteel Scots and the Westminster political establishment. Nonetheless, their critique avoided the English nationalistic rhetoric of Wilkes. Corruption, they argued, united established elites on both sides of Hadrian's
Wall. Wilkes, conversely, made no distinction between Moderates and evangelicals. He failed to acknowledge the role of Popular party members in op-

31. In addition to work by Landsman cited above, see James H. Smylie, "Presbyterian
Clergy and Problems of 'Dominion' in the Revolutionary Generation," *Journal of Presbyterian
History*, XLVIII (1970), 161–175.

posing specific corruptions in British constitutionalism. Instead, as Wither-spoon pointed out in his May 1776 *Address to the Natives of Scotland Residing in America,* Wilkes sought to revive all ancient tensions between Scotland and England, proclaiming a superior moral sense on the part of English radi-calism.[32]

In his *Address,* Witherspoon highlighted the failure of some Scots living in America to oppose the corruptions of Westminster prerogative. He linked their reticence to an association that had developed between patriot ideology and Wilkes's English radicalism. After his arrival in New Jersey, Witherspoon had soon realized that, after the Stamp Act crisis, Wilkes's *North Briton,* no. 45 (Apr. 23, 1763), had become extremely popular among "the friends of lib-erty in many places of America." Colonists believed themselves to be "en-gaged in the same cause with . . . John Wilkes Esq. of London"—whom they had "seemed to consider" as "their patron and friend." As a result, Wilkes's pamphlet, "which was the most offensive number of a worthless paper, was repeated and echoed, by the most silly and ridiculous allusions to it, through every part of the country." In his view, Scottish settlers were likely to think twice before joining patriots who championed Wilkes as their ideological hero without realizing his denigration of "North British" identity. Wilkes had "stir[red] up a national jealousy between the northern and southern parts of the island [of Britain]," and "in these circumstances" it was "to be won-dered at, that many who left Scotland within the last fifteen years, when they

32. John Witherspoon, "On Conducting the American Controversy," in [Green, ed.], *Works of Witherspoon,* IV, 306–307; Witherspoon, *Address to the Natives of Scotland Residing in America,* ibid., III, 48–50. For the most infamous example of Wilkes's disdain for Scotland's role in Britain, see [John Wilkes], *North Briton,* no. 45, Apr. 23, 1763. On Wilkes's English radical-ism and his negative appraisal of Scotland, see Adam Rounce, "'Stuarts without End': Wilkes, Churchill, and Anti-Scottishness," *Eighteenth-Century Life,* XXIX, no. 3 (Fall 2005), 20–43. On Wilkes's negative portrayal of Scots, see John Brewer, "The Misfortunes of Lord Bute: A Case-Study in Eighteenth-Century Political Argument and Public Opinion," *Historical Journal,* XVI (1973), 3–43; Colin Kidd, "North Britishness and the Nature of Eighteenth-Century British Patriotisms," ibid., XXXIX (1996), 361–382, esp. 381–382. According to Linda Colley, Wilkite "Scottophobia" was a paradoxical sign of British integration. It implied that increased Scottish participation in British metropolitan governance led to factional intrigues, patronage, and the central role of venal political placemen. Dustin Griffin has shown that Scottophobia was preva-lent among English Anglican ministers after midcentury. "Like Wilkes," they "usually preferred to use the old term 'England' instead of the politically correct new *Great Britain* (encompass-ing both England and Scotland)." See Colley, *Britons,* 113–117; Griffin, *Patriotism and Poetry in Eighteenth-Century Britain* (Cambridge, 2005), 241. On "Scottophobia," see also Douglas Hamilton, *Scotland, the Caribbean, and the Atlantic World, 1750–1820* (Manchester, U.K., 2005), 20; Bruce Lenman, *Integration and Enlightenment: Scotland, 1746–1832* (Edinburgh, 1981), 39.

heard Wilkes and those who adhered to him [in the patriot coalition], extolled and celebrated by the sons of liberty, should be apt to consider it as an evidence of the same spirit, and that they were engaged in support of the same cause."[33]

Witherspoon, then, was not blind to those Presbyterians whose comfortable experience in the British Empire led them to avoid criticizing the Westminster Parliament in any public way. Neither were other high-ranking Presbyterians as they took steps to remedy the phenomenon by highlighting their opposition to parliamentary corruption, if not yet the Hanoverian king. In 1775, Francis Alison and several other Philadelphia Presbyterian ministers sent an "Address" to Highland Scottish settlers in North Carolina, who were assumed to be pro-British. Although "it is said, that the Parliament of England has supreme power, and that no one ought to resist," the "Address" noted, "this we allow, while they make Acts that are reasonable, and according to the British Constitution; but their power has bounds and limits that they must not exceed." And, "when our oppression becomes intolerable, to whom shall we complain, or who will redress our grievances?" it asked its North Carolina audience, before answering:

> Not the British Parliament, for they will be our oppressors: nay, they do plead that they have a right to be our oppressors; not our King, because he will, probably, be led to ratify all the Acts of Parliament, to tax us; and to resist will be counted rebellion: and what shall we do? Shall we now admit that they have a right thus to tax, and to enslave us? God forbid: and this occasions our present struggle for liberty, which we are fully persuaded you will contend for, as firmly as we do, when you are rightly informed, and will not give up your property to such as have no right to demand it.

Although the "Address" was certain that the "British" Parliament would negate the rights of colonists, its authors adopted a more tentative tone in

---

33. Witherspoon, *Address to the Natives of Scotland Residing in America,* ibid., III, 48–50. Witherspoon also discussed John Wilkes and the imperial crisis in Witherspoon, "On Conducting the American Controversy," ibid., IV, 307–308. On Scottish loyalism during the American Revolutionary era, see Ian Charles Cargill Graham, *Colonists from Scotland: Emigration to North America, 1707–1783* (1956; rpt. Baltimore, 1997), 20; Daniel Blake Smith, *Inside the Great House: Planter Family Life in Eighteenth-Century Chesapeake Society* (Ithaca, N.Y., 1980), 200; Ned C. Landsman, *From Colonials to Provincials: American Thought and Culture, 1680–1760* (New York, 1997), chap. 1; J. M. Bumsted, "The Scottish Diaspora: Emigration to British North America, 1763–1815," in Landsman, *Nation and Province in the First British Empire: Scotland and the Americas, 1600–1800* (Lewisburg, Pa., 2001), 127–150, esp. 136–137, 144.

concluding that the king would "probably" ratify the corrupt legislation of the Parliament. "That we are wronged and injured," the "Address" also noted,

> is believed and insisted on by the greatest and best men of all religious denominations on the Continent of America, who are firmly united in this glorious struggle for liberty: and shall it be said that you, our friends and brethren, shall desert us in the mighty contest, and join with our enemies; will you strengthen the enemies of the British Constitution, and join with them to fasten on our chains, and to enslave us forever? If we are now wrong in our conduct, our forefathers that fought for liberty at Londonderry and Enniskillen in King James' time, were wrong; nay, they were rebels, when they opposed, and set aside that bigotted Prince, and the Stewart family, and set the Brunswick family on the throne of England. But we hope such language will never be heard from the mouth of a Protestant, or from an English subject, and much less from anyone of our denomination, that have ever maintained the Revolution Principles, and are firmly devoted to the present reigning family, as the assertors of the British privileges and English liberty.

Making sure to reference "British" provincial rights alongside more commonly conceived English liberties, Alison and his colleagues alluded to extra-English battles that had taken place in the British Isles and Ireland during the previous century, in Londonderry, Enniskillen, and elsewhere, where Presbyterians had featured prominently. From November 1775 through mid-1776, various New Jersey presbyteries sent representatives to the Carolinas — many of them College of New Jersey graduates — to persuade Presbyterians in the region to become patriots, with only mixed success.[34]

Without the distraction of Wilkes, Witherspoon believed, more Presbyterian colonists would offer a receptive audience for patriotic proclamations. By the time he wrote his April 1776 pamphlet "On Conducting the American Controversy" and his May 1776 *Address to the Natives of Scotland Residing in America,* Presbyterians maintained nearly six hundred congregations

34. Francis Alison et al., "An Address to the Ministers and Presbyterian Congregations in North Carolina," in William L. Saunders, ed., *The Colonial Records of North Carolina . . .* , X (Raleigh, N.C., 1890), 222–226. In North Carolina, the Highlanders typically became loyalists, and the Scots Irish, patriots. See James G. Leyburn, *The Scotch-Irish: A Social History* (Chapel Hill, N.C., 1962), 252–254. On the context for the address, see also Tiedemann, "Presbyterianism and the American Revolution," *Church History,* LXXIV (2005), 315; J. C. D. Clark, *The Language of Liberty, 1660–1832: Political Discourse and Social Dynamics in the Anglo-American World* (Cambridge, 1994), 123.

in America, mostly in the Middle and southern colonies. Total immigration of Scots and Scots-Irish in the eighteenth century had reached between two and three hundred thousand by 1776, around one-tenth of the white colonial American population. Presbyterian congregations also formed a bloc with other denominations, including the Dutch and German Reformed churches and some parts of the Congregational movement. Like all colonists, Witherspoon believed, they could legitimately protest the most egregious aspects of Westminster power. But they were also obliged to define their general attachment to the British monarchy. As late as April 1776, Witherspoon continued to define the British Empire in confederal terms, as a collection of semi-autonomous provinces and institutions united by a single monarchy.[35]

Early patriot discussions of pluralistic representation in the British Empire were at cross purposes with Westminster's definition of metropolitan governance. Since the Stamp Act crisis, the concept of indivisible sovereignty had been conveyed with increasing vehemence in response to American conceptions of confederal authority. As English legal theorist William Blackstone had written in 1765, an empire such as that which Britain controlled required

> a supreme, irresistible, absolute, uncontrolled authority, in which the *jura summi imperii,* or the rights of sovereignty, reside. And this authority is placed in those hands, wherein (according to the opinion of the founders of such respective states, either expressly given, or

35. On the Presbyterian bloc during the Revolutionary era and more general immigration figures, see James H. Smylie, "Introduction," *Presbyterians and the American Revolution: A Documentary Account,* special issue of *Journal of Presbyterian History,* LII (1974), 303–306; Fred J. Hood, *Reformed America: The Middle and Southern States, 1783–1837* (Tuscaloosa, Ala., 1980), 2; Roger Finke and Rodney Stark, *The Churching of America, 1776–1990: Winners and Losers in Our Religious Economy* (New Brunswick, N.J., 1992), 25; Edwin Scott Gaustad and Philip L. Barlow, *New Historical Atlas of Religion in America* (New York, 2001), 38; David Dobson, *Scottish Emigration to Colonial America, 1607–1785* (Athens, Ga., 1994), 33; T. C. Smout, N. C. Landsman, and T. M. Devine, "Scottish Emigration in the Seventeenth and Eighteenth Centuries," in Nicholas Canny, ed., *Europeans on the Move: Studies on European Migration, 1500–1800* (Oxford, 1994), 76–112, esp. 76–86. On Ulster Scots in the Anglo-American Atlantic world, see Patrick Griffin, *The People with No Name: Ireland's Ulster Scots, America's Scots Irish, and the Creation of a British Atlantic World, 1689–1764* (Princeton, N.J., 2001). Witherspoon's stance corroborates scholarship on the nature of American Revolutionary identity before the Declaration of Independence. Alison L. LaCroix, for example, has suggested that federal and confederal political ideology can be traced to early patriot debates about the nature of colonial autonomy within the wider British imperial union, rather than solely looking to discussions that took place in the decades *after* the Declaration of Independence. See LaCroix, *The Ideological Origins of American Federalism* (Cambridge, Mass., 2010), chap. 1.

collected from their tacit approbation) the qualities requisite for supremacy, wisdom, goodness, and power, are the most likely to be found.

Westminster's legal theorists believed that the king and the Privy Council maintained complete authority over colonial affairs. They increasingly rejected confederal definitions of imperial identity, whether expressed through autonomies in local church assemblies, regional law courts, colonial houses of assembly, local trading guilds, or intercolonial congresses.[36]

Benjamin Franklin, like most patriot leaders, opposed the incorporating turn in Westminster governance. But he was notable among non-Presbyterians in his specific reference to the Scottish aspect of British constitutionalism. In 1754, he had contributed to the Albany Congress that met in New York. It responded to demands by the British Board of Trade that the American colonies coordinate their efforts against French and Indian forces. Franklin's (eventually unsuccessful) plans for union drew inspiration from the suggestions of many Scots who worked in colonial American governance and who favored a greater degree of union between the British colonies, in distinction to its association with Westminster. His developing constitutional theory might also have been influenced by Archibald Kennedy's pamphlet, *The Importance of Gaining and Preserving the Friendship of the Indians to the British Interest Considered,* which seems to have incorporated both Scottish and Iroquois confederal theories. In 1759, Franklin would visit Scotland, where he came to note its ambiguous role in Britain. While maintaining representatives in the Parliament of Westminster, he realized, Scotland retained important aspects of its autonomy as an equal province in the British Empire. In 1770, Franklin similarly argued that, within the British Empire, "the Colonies originally were constituted distinct States, and intended to be continued such." This fact was clear to Franklin "from a thorough Consideration of their original Charters . . . [before] the Parliament . . . [in Britain] . . . usurp'd an Authority of making Laws for them, which before it had not." Problematically, recent Westminster policy had tended "to confirm a Claim [of] Subjects in one Part of the King's Dominions [England] to be Sovereigns over their Fellow-Subjects in another Part of his Dominions," but

> in truth they have no such Right, and their Claim is founded only on Usurpation, the several States having equal Rights and Liberties, and being only connected as England and Scotland were before the Union,

36. William Blackstone, *Commentaries on the Laws of England: In Four Books,* 14th ed. (London, 1803), I, 48–49. On Blackstone's reasoning in the context of Revolutionary debate, see Jack P. Greene, *The Constitutional Origins of the American Revolution* (New York, 2011), 98–99.

by having one common Sovereign, the King. . . . England and Scotland were once separate States, under the same King. The Inconvenience found in their being separate States did not prove that the Parliament of England had a Right to govern Scotland. A formal Union was thought necessary, and England was an hundred Years soliciting it, before she could bring it about. If Great Britain now thinks such an Union necessary with us, let her propose her Terms, and we may consider of them.

With the analogy between Scotland and the American colonies at the forefront of his mind, Franklin suggested that one province could not enjoy any special dominion over other provinces in the Empire, notwithstanding their shared British attachments under the Hanoverian crown. Like Scotland, and the American colonies under their separate charters, England was nothing more than a dominion itself.[37]

In 1773, the Massachusetts General Court was noteworthy for referencing Scotland in a similar definition of British imperial identity. Scottish precedents were central to its written response to Governor Thomas Hutchinson, who had rejected the notion of divided imperial sovereignty. The court referred to the case of Anglo-Scottish integration and earlier colonial history in order to offer its alternative viewpoint. Under the charter of 1629, the court argued, the Massachusetts colony had been subject to the king and not the controlling power of the Westminster Parliament. Precedent, customary rights, and "the great case of the union of the realm of Scotland with England" only served to strengthen that fact during the eighteenth century. Though Scotland had lost its Parliament in 1707, the court seemed to imply its retention of important representative autonomies. Just as Scots maintained autonomous legal and religious customs despite their political union with England, "the opinions" of the "greatest Sages and Judges of the law in the Exchequer Chamber, ought not to be considered as decisive or binding, in our present controversy with your Excellency, any further, than they are consonant to natural reason." Thus, the Massachusetts General Court looked to Scotland's role as a semi-autonomous province in the British Empire and

37. On the potential influence of Archibald Kennedy on Franklin, see Alexander Murdoch, *Scotland and America, c. 1600–c. 1800* (Basingstoke, U.K., 2010), 149–150; Landsman, "The Provinces and the Empire," in Stone, ed., *An Imperial State at War,* 267; Ned Landsman, "The Legacy of British Union for the North American Colonies: Provincial Elites and the Problem of Imperial Union," in John Robertson, ed., *A Union for Empire: Political Thought and the British Union of 1707* (Cambridge, 1995), 307–309. For Franklin's statements on Anglo-Scottish union, see Benjamin Franklin to Samuel Cooper, June 8, 1770, in Leonard W. Labaree et al., eds., *The Papers of Benjamin Franklin,* 41 vols. to date (New Haven, Conn., 1959–), XVII, 161–164.

distinguished its jurisdiction from the English legal mechanisms that Blackstone sought to instill in North America.[38]

Westminster politicians were increasingly vehement in their rejection of any federal or confederal vision of the British Empire that defined the semi-autonomy of colonial constitutions within a wider imperial constitution. On July 5, 1775, the Second Continental Congress offered what became infamously known as the Olive Branch Petition to Lord Dartmouth, secretary of state for the colonies. The petition defined the loyalty of American colonists to the British Empire, describing the imperial crisis as a conflict between colonial provincial assemblies and specific corrupt ministers in the Westminster Parliament. It entreated George III to respond to colonial loyalty by intervening in the crisis on behalf of Americans, to the ultimate benefit of all sides in the conflict. Yet, on August 23, 1775, in response to news of the Battle of Bunker Hill, British politicians persuaded the House of Hanover to issue the "king's proclamation for suppressing rebellion and sedition," declaring the North American colonies to be in a state of rebellion and ordering "all our officers . . . and all other our obedient and loyal subjects, to use their utmost endeavours to withstand and suppress such rebellion." Colonists took the proclamation as evidence of the king's rejection of the Olive Branch Petition.[39]

In his July 1775 fast day sermon, the Reverend Joseph Montgomery made sure to point out that the "good old King" during the previous decades had "always [been] willing to extend his parental kindness towards us." But circumstances had recently changed such that "the fatal day, contrary to our ardent wishes, and prayers, is come, when our connection with the parent state must be dissolved." As distinct from those who defined colonial American Presbyterians as innately republican, Montgomery accompanied his newfound opposition to the King-in-Parliament with wistful regret. During the second half of the following year, Witherspoon and other Presbyterian colonists would also find it increasingly difficult to distinguish between monar-

38. "Answer of the Council to the Speech of Governor Hutchinson, of February Sixteenth . . . February 25, 1773," in *Speeches of the Governors of Massachusetts from 1765–1775: And the Answers,* [ed. Alden Bradford] (Boston, Mass., 1818), 355, 386–387. See also the account of the Hutchinson-Massachusetts constitutional debate in LaCroix, *Ideological Origins of American Federalism,* 88–92.

39. "The King's Proclamation for Suppressing Rebellion and Sedition (23 August 1775)," in Merrill Jensen, ed., *English Historical Documents: American Colonial Documents to 1776* (New York, 1969), IX, 850–851. On these final constitutional acts, see also Greene, *Constitutional Origins of the American Revolution,* i.

chical and parliamentary prerogative—despite the subtlety of their earlier dominion theory.[40]

Tories, Whigs, and "Christian Magnanimity"

A few weeks after George III officially rejected the colonial Olive Branch Petition, Witherspoon delivered and published an important sermon titled *Christian Magnanimity.* Though it refrained from specific reference to the imperial crisis, his September 1775 treatise at least considered resistance to royal authority in theoretical terms. It reflected on the proper response to victory against a hitherto powerful king. Witherspoon sought to show that the "nobleness of sentiment, which rendered the ancients so illustrious, and gives so much majesty and dignity to the histories of Greece and Rome," was not dichotomous with "real greatness [as] inseparable from sincere piety; and that any defect in the one, must necessarily be a discernible blemish in the other." Christian magnanimity, according to Witherspoon, required individuals "to attempt, 1. Great and difficult things: 2. To aspire after great and valuable possessions; 3. To encounter dangers with resolution; 4. To struggle against difficulties with perseverance; and 5. To bear sufferings with fortitude and patience." Fundamental to classical heroism, magnanimity enabled newfound independence without overemphasizing the individual moral capability of victors. As is well known, classical authors were paramount in the intellectual ponderings of America's founding generation. Yet it is less well known that future leaders such as James Madison and Aaron Burr thus encountered classical ideals in synthesis with religious reasoning. Witherspoon's sermon was deliberately written to resonate with this wider context. It was delivered during a commencement ceremony to students who were entering a changing political climate that called for their greater participation. Those who now performed in front of visiting civic leaders and who listened to Witherspoon's address had experienced religious revivalism and political radicalization on a twin track.[41]

40. Montgomery, *Sermon, Preached at Christiana Bridge and Newcastle,* 26.

41. John Witherspoon, *Christian Magnanimity, Sermon 46; Preached at Princeton, September 1775, the Sabbath Preceeding the Annual Commencement; and Again with Additions, September 23, 1787; to Which Is Added an Address to the Senior Class, Who Were to Receive the Degree of Bachelor of Arts,* in [Green, ed.], *Works of Witherspoon,* III, 89–90. On classical theory in the Revolutionary account of leadership, see Carl J. Richard, *The Founders and the Classics: Greece, Rome, and the American Enlightenment* (Cambridge, Mass., 1994), 51–52, 124–130, 145–157, 205–206; Gary L. Gregg II, ed., *Vital Remnants: America's Founding and the Western Tradition* (Wilmington, Del., 2006), 72–74, 86–87, 90–95, 144–145.

Seven months after Witherspoon delivered this sermon, as the British King-in-Parliament hardened its stance against American colonists, Witherspoon chaired the Somerset County Committee of Correspondence. After the meeting on April 18, 1776, Elias Boudinot, a New Jersey lawyer and College of New Jersey trustee, reacted with shock and trepidation in his journal, as shown in an entry titled "Rev. John Witherspoon Advocates The Separation Of The Colony Of New Jersey From Great Britain." Boudinot claimed to have been "astonished" by Witherspoon's "great Influence among the People" during his speech on the possible separation between Britain and the American colonies. He had also been mortified that some might think the entire episode had been planned by artful members of a clandestine "Presbyterian Interest":

> The Doctor known to be at the head of the Presbyterian Interest, and Mr. Smith and Myself both Presbyterians, arriving at New Brunswick in the morning, as if intending to go forward and then staying and attending the meeting, altogether looked so like a preconcerted Scheme, to accomplish the End, that I was at my wit's end, to know how to extricate myself from so disagreeable a situation.

Witherspoon contributed to what Boudinot feared was an overtly Presbyterian delegation to the New Jersey Provincial Congress. According to minutes, Witherspoon made a sudden suggestion that New Jersey declare its independence from the British crown. He was opposed by Boudinot and several others members of the meeting. Boudinot feared that Reverend Witherspoon's involvement in politics and his influence over former College of New Jersey students (many of them ministers) threatened to unite civil and ecclesiastical power under a Presbyterian faction. Notwithstanding his misgivings, the April 1776 meeting was perhaps the first occasion in New Jersey when full independence was at least discussed in a formal political meeting.[42]

Boudinot misunderstood Witherspoon, who had been opposed to church patronage before his arrival in America but who also suggested that clerics could become politicians while still maintaining a necessary distinction between the ecclesiastical and legislative realms. Nonetheless, Boudinot was at least accurate in noting the close political association between Witherspoon and a younger generation of minsters at the New Jersey Provincial Congress, each of whom had graduated from the College of New Jersey. Between the

---

42. Elias Boudinot, *Journal or Historical Recollections of American Events during the Revolutionary War* (Philadelphia, 1894), 5–7. On the New Jersey delegation and Boudinot's activities, see Collins, *President Witherspoon*, I, 185–187.

autumn of 1775 and the late spring of 1776, they all came to oppose the British crown alongside the Westminster Parliament. They provide a small snapshot of the developing nature of Presbyterian political theology in Witherspoon's wider circle.

Consider, for example, the case of Enoch Green, a 1760 graduate of the College of New Jersey. Boudinot had suggested Witherspoon's influence on Green in his prickly Provincial Congress statements. Before developing ties with the Somerset Country delegation, Green had made a career educating and preparing prospective students for entry to the College of New Jersey, including Philip Vickers Fithian. In early 1776, he became Presbyterian chaplain of the New Jersey militia. In a sermon upon his appointment, he highlighted the importance of the Protestant succession in the House of Hanover. Like the Reverend Joseph Montgomery, a fellow graduate of the College of New Jersey, he made sure to define his theoretical support for monarchical authority. The entrenchment of Protestantism by the Hanoverian line had coincided with the growth of Presbyterian institutions in the American colonies. "But now" that "George" had "turned Tory," the semi-autonomous rights of colonists could not be guaranteed. As members of the New Jersey militia marched past his Deerfield Presbyterian church, then, Green responded to the perceived rejection of the Olive Branch Petition by George III several months earlier.[43]

Significantly, Green adopted the adjective "Tory" rather than "tyrannous" or "corrupt." When used by dissenting ministers during the Revolutionary era, the term "Tory" often encompassed confessional associations. Tories, of course, were thought to champion the establishment of Anglican religion in Westminster. When George III was a Whig, he acted according to the general Protestant cause of the British Empire. He had supported the rights of all its dissenters, including Presbyterians. Their vision of British imperial unionism contrasted with Tory claims of the sovereignty of the (Anglican) King-in-Parliament in the American colonies. By the 1707 Act of Security, Tories argued, British monarchs were obliged to make a coronation oath to maintain the Church of England in the three kingdoms as well as imperial territories. In the decades following the Act of Union and the Act of Security, conversely, Whig authorities tended to perceive the assertion of imperial Anglicanism as an unnecessary constitutional complication. Ironically, then, the push for a sitting Anglican bishop on the western side of the Atlantic had

43. Fea, *Way of Improvement,* 64–66; Enoch Green, "Upon His Appointment as Chaplain of the New Jersey Militia, 1776," cited in Griffin, *Revolution and Religion,* 57–58. See also Charles Harrison, *Cumberland County, New Jersey: 265 Years of History* (Charleston, S.C., 2013), 25.

FIGURE 13. *An Attempt to Land a Bishop in America.* London, 1768.
Etching and engraving. Courtesy, Library of Congress Prints and
Photographs Division, Washington, D.C.

most often derived from American rather than mainland English Anglicans. The former surmised that an alliance with sitting bishops would give them the upper hand in local power struggles against dissenting communities.[44]

In Enoch Green's New Jersey, therefore, the word "Tory" had often been reserved for Anglican elites in local constitutional conflicts with Presbyterians—including those that had contributed to the founding of the College of New Jersey. Middle Colony Anglicans claimed to reflect Westminster's legislative authority when they defined the Church of England as the appropriate arbiter of civil, religious, and educational disputes—even when their arguments favored a stricter form of civil-religious establishment than many metropolitan legal theorists in London. In the controversy over the founding of King's College in New York, conversely, revivalist Presbyterians such as William Livingston had maintained that the 1707 Act of Union secured two separate ecclesiastical establishments despite its indivisible political incorporation and had allowed colonies such as New York and New Jersey to distinguish the religious aspect of their constitutionalism from that in colonies such as Virginia. In New York and New Jersey, after all, parochial Anglican elites supported colonial episcopacy as a means to oppose the threat of regional Presbyterian ascendancy in chartered educational institutions.[45]

Thus, the debate over the charter and founding of colleges in the Middle Colonies—and their continued growth through the 1760s—had become intertwined with local conflicts over the nature of established religious authority. The implications of Tory magistracy, then, had always retained a particular resonance for evangelical Presbyterians. When their confessional freedom had been challenged, especially in educational controversies, they often invoked their support for the Hanoverian monarchy against contrary measures enacted by local political and Anglican elites. During the early Revolutionary era, Enoch Green translated those distinctions into the imperial context. Until as late as 1775, he had distinguished Hanoverian authority from Westminster's Tory curtailments on religious, commercial, and political au-

44. On the controversy over imperial Anglicanism and its link to identities of loyalism and patriotism, see Landsman, "Failure of Religious Settlement," in Beneke and Grenda, eds., *The First Prejudice,* 77, 88–90; Bell, *A War of Religion,* 196; Noll, *America's God,* 79, 83, 89, 246. It is also worth noting the ironic case of Scottish Episcopalians such as Samuel Blair of Virginia. Blair opposed imperial Anglican episcopacy in order to buttress his own alternative power within the colonial episcopal establishment. See William Henry Foote, *Sketches of Virginia: Historical and Biographical,* I (Philadelphia, 1850), 109–117.

45. On the dispute over Anglicanism within British imperial constitutionalism in these contexts, see Landsman, "Failure of Religious Settlement," in Beneke and Grenda, eds., *The First Prejudice,* 94–95; Robson, *Educating Republicans,* 33–37.

tonomy. By mid-1776, however, Green's distinction between Hanoverian liberty and Tory parliamentary corruption had become too difficult to support. He warned of constraints from episcopacy and excessive tax duties now that George III had turned Tory.[46]

For the majority of Presbyterians in Witherspoon's wider circle, including Montgomery, Carmichael, and Green, issues of unjust commercial regulation, the perceived threat of Anglican episcopacy, and illegitimate political authority came to be associated with the imperial power of the King-in-Parliament. In early 1777, when British forces occupied Nassau Hall and Witherspoon's office at the College of New Jersey, many of Witherspoon's papers and writings went missing or were purposely burned. For this reason, perhaps, there is not much written evidence elucidating Witherspoon's decision to oppose the British crown six months earlier. After the proceedings of the Somerset County delegation, however, Witherspoon did write a brief letter about "the independent controversy in the newspapers" under the pseudonym "Aristides." The letter, printed in the *Pennsylvania Packet* on May 13, 1776, defended the cause of intercolonial union and, for the first time in Witherspoon's public writing, lauded the general reasoning in Thomas Paine's *Common Sense*. Paine's treatise, which had been published in several editions during the previous six months, argued that full separation from the British monarchy was necessary and timely.[47]

To be sure, Witherspoon's approval of Paine was displayed inadvertently as he attempted a separate rhetorical maneuver. As Aristides, Witherspoon criticized corrupt printers such as the "illustrious, and exalted" Robert Bell for publishing writings such as *Plain Truth,* an anonymous loyalist argument against Paine, to profit from the imperial crisis. Whether they printed patriot or loyalist writings, Witherspoon claimed, printers such as Bell made no attempt to maintain the rhetorical quality or written clarity of their published articles. To make his point, Witherspoon turned to Paine's recently published *Common Sense* as a contrast to Bell's output. Paine "did not write his book to shew that we ought to resist the unconstitutional claims of Great Britain, which we had all determined to do long before; he wrote it to shew that we ought not to seek or wait for a reconciliation, which in his opinion, is now become both impracticable and unprofitable, but to establish a fixed regular government, and provide for ourselves." The "question then is," Wither-

46. On Green's activities at this point, see Fea, *Way of Improvement,* 142, 188.

47. For the text of Witherspoon's published letter briefly outlining his support for American independence, see John Witherspoon, *Aristides,* in [Green, ed.], *Works of Witherspoon,* IV, 309–316.

spoon wrote, "shall we make resistance with the greatest force, as rebel subjects of a government which we acknowledge, or as independent states against
an usurped power which we detest and abhor"? Though *Common Sense* was
written with poor grammar and prose style, according to Witherspoon, it
contained valid arguments. In contrast, Bell's *Plain Truth* was "covered over,
from head to foot, with a detestable and stinking varnish." It was "so ridicu-
lously ornamented with vapid, senseless phrases and feeble epithets, that his
meaning could hardly be comprehended . . . . often [putting him] in mind of
the painted windows of some old gothic buildings, which keep out the light."
Describing the "egregious" use of parody in writings published by mercenary
printers such as Bell, Witherspoon pointed out the many ways that he had
heard Hamlet's famous soliloquy used as an unwelcome means to compli-
cate the colonial response to British corruption: "To speak, or not to speak,
that is the question — To fight, or not to fight, that is the question — To wed,
or not to wed, that is the question." Witherspoon now opposed such equivocation and suggested that it was no longer "a time for filling the newspapers
with such egregious trifling." At some point in the previous few months,
likely inspired by his reading of Paine following George III's rejection of the
Olive Branch Petition, Witherspoon became more comfortable supporting
full separation from the British crown as well as the Westminster Parliament.
His letter asked whether it was possible to show "that Great-Britain can be
sufficiently sure of our dependence, and yet we sure of our liberties" and
whether "our efforts for resistance" would be "as effectual, by the present
loose and temporary proceedings, as when the whole are united by a firm
confederacy, and their exertions concentrated like the strength of a single
state?" Witherspoon still implied that "these points" might be "the hinge of
the controversy" in any well-written newspaper treatise (in contrast to Bell's
publications). But his reference to the need for an intercolonial confederacy,
coupled with his approval of Paine's reasoning, suggested his own personal
move toward the republican position in patriot ideology.[48]

During the period when Witherspoon wrote and published his letter, the
Provincial Congress elected the following members to represent New Jersey
at the Continental Congress: Abraham Clark, John Hart, Francis Hopkin-
son, Richard Stockton, and Witherspoon. All but Clark were College of New

48. Ibid., 309–316, esp. 311–312. On Bell and other printers as suspected loyalists and for
an assessment of Witherspoon's response to the commercialization of printing in *Aristides,* see
Philip Gould, "Loyalists Respond to *Common Sense:* The Politics of Authorship in Revolutionary America," in Jerry Bannister and Liam Riordan, eds., *The Loyal Atlantic: Remaking the
British Atlantic in the Revolutionary Era* (Toronto, 2012), 118–122.

Jersey graduates, though they attended before Witherspoon's tenure as presi-dent. The word "Tory" had once been used in intracolonial conflicts between dissenting Protestant settlers and local Anglicans. In the 1760s, it had come to denote the singular metropolitan authority of the Westminster Parliament, including its Anglican establishment. Then, by mid-1776, many more Presby-terians saw fit to apply the term to George III himself. The head of the House of Hanover had finally become defined as the ultimate seal of authority for political, economic, and religious constraints on colonial life—and a threat to previous conceptions of provincial evangelical autonomy.[49]

"In Sacred Bond of Harmony and Public Happiness"?

Unlike Witherspoon's Presbyterian associates from the College of New Jer-sey, Scottish-born William Smith largely avoided redefining local constitu-tional conflicts in relation to British imperial corruption during the 1760s and early 1770s. Instead, the Episcopalian provost of the College of Philadelphia used the language of moral philosophy to denote the natural benevolence of his denomination in the British Empire. As he did so, he defined his own moral and pedagogical authority against rival Presbyterian and Quaker fac-tions. To be sure, Smith criticized specific instances of British corruption during the early period of the Revolutionary era and was even selected to the Philadelphia Committee of Correspondence in 1774. Nonetheless, most patriots came to perceive him as a neutral, or even a tory, as he tended to join Revolutionary committees in order to demonstrate that his empathy with colonial grievances was not dichotomous with his unwavering support for metropolitan British imperial authority and the "sacred bond of harmony and public happiness" that bound Britain to the American colonies.[50]

49. On College of New Jersey graduates at the Continental Congress, see the congressional journal entry for Friday, June 28, 1776, in Worthington Chauncey Ford et al., eds., *Journals of the Continental Congress, 1774–1789*, 34 vols. (Washington, D.C., 1905–1937), V, 489. On the enmeshing between Presbyterianism and politics, see also Mark A. Noll, "Observations on the Reconciliation of Politics and Religion in Revolutionary New Jersey: The Case of Jacob Green," *Journal of Presbyterian History*, LIV (1976), 217–237.

50. On Smith's selection to the Philadelphia Committee of Correspondence in 1774 and his embroilment in factional issues, see Robson, *Educating Republicans*, 33–35. On the "sacred bond of harmony and public happiness," see William Smith, "Sermon XIV; on the Present Situation of American Affairs; Preached in Christ-Church, June 23, 1775; at the Request of the Officers of the Third Battalion of Volunteer Militia of the City of Philadelphia, and District of Southwark," in *The Works of William Smith, D. D.: Late Provost of the College and Academy of Philadelphia* (Philadelphia, 1803), II, 286.

In his sermon "The Present Situation of American Affairs," which he preached on June 23, 1775, Smith used stadial reasoning to describe the cultural and moral development of America. He used the language of sentiment and feeling to highlight what he saw to be a fundamental irony of the imperial crisis: the activities of loyalists and patriots derived from the same common sensory desire to uphold communal norms. He alluded to the Hutchesonian principle that populations could resume self-governance if their common liberties and moral sensibilities were sufficiently threatened. But he immediately suggested that it was "more than time, for a great and enlightened people to make names bend to things," to create a "great and liberal plan of policy to re-unite" the members of the "mighty" British Empire "as the sole bulwark of Liberty and Protestantism." Such an endeavor, according to Smith, would avoid providing an impetus to "encrease the importance of those states that are foes to freedom, truth and humanity." Instead, he advised, Americans ought to return to "the times of ancient virtue and renown" and to the spirit of colonial American forefathers. "Mercies," according to Smith, were likely "held forth" to American colonists in "the shape of sufferings" so that "the vicissitudes of [their] fortune in building up this American fabric of happiness" might well be "various and chequered." But God had "been pleased" to adorn the region "with men of enlightened zeal," whose education in the arts and sciences allowed "the principles that withstood oppression, in the brightest era of the English history" to flourish in America. Smith certainly outlined the legitimacy of specific American grievances. But, unlike Witherspoon during the same period, he avoided distinguishing between a benevolent crown and a nefarious Parliament. Instead, he focused on general threats to the imperial status quo. Enlightened subjects, he argued, could find a "policy to re-unite" as a means to show the congruence between their ethical sensibility and their shared Protestant religion. Smith reminded patriots and those who remained loyal to metropolitan British authority that innate feelings were naturally oriented toward public happiness and thus a continuation of their current political union was required. His neutral stance sought to maintain cultural networks that connected educated cities such as Philadelphia and Edinburgh. Any political interruption of their philosophical exchange threatened to undermine the common sensibility that he so cherished.[51]

51. Smith, "Present Situation of American Affairs," in *The Works of William Smith,* II, 262, 277, 280, 282–283, 286. On Smith's vision of mutual cultural discourse between Philadelphia and Edinburgh, see Andrew Hook, "Philadelphia, Edinburgh, and the Scottish Enlightenment," in Sher and Smitten, eds., *Scotland and America,* 233–236.

Francis Alison shared the moral sensory language of Smith, whom he worked under as vice president of the College of Philadelphia. Through his lectures, as previously discussed, Alison promoted anthropocentric ethical ideas that were distinct from Witherspoon's moral philosophy. His definition of the relationship between civic representation and religious identity suggested a higher degree of moral innateness than many evangelicals were comfortable supporting. But, unlike Smith, he unambiguously supported the patriot cause. He transformed long-standing tensions with local Anglicans into a broader movement against imperial episcopacy. He used sentimental philosophical terminology to suggest that Americans were sufficiently mature to deserve their independence and that an Anglican imperial establishment was not required to maintain moral and civic order. Drawing a closer association between local and imperial episcopacy, he connected support for a sitting bishop among Philadelphia Anglicans with their failure to oppose the Stamp Act and sought "to shew that, we are alarmed with just fears, lest the introduction of Bishops affect our civil and Religious liberties." At the same time, however, he also sought to buttress the religious, civic, and educational authority of the moderate Presbyterian synod against nonaligned evangelical Presbyterians. Revivalist Presbyterians opposed imperial episcopacy using critiques that were strikingly similar to those that had once been deployed against Old Side establishment Presbyterians such as Alison. Alison, conversely, feared that sitting bishops would restrict the freedom that had enabled his Presbyterian allies to form a colonial synod, to support moderate educational institutions such as the College of Philadelphia, and to engage in civic culture through representation in local political assemblies. The threat of sitting bishops came to be associated with Anglican factions that included William Smith, the president of his own College of Philadelphia.[52]

As the threat of imperial episcopacy came to be understood alongside other aspects of British metropolitan corruption, Alison used moral sensory philosophy to distinguish the American cause even more generally. He venerated the innate ethical sensibility of patriots in order to underline the general validity of their struggle, as he once used similar reasoning to distinguish moderate Presbyterian benevolence from local factional intrigues. According to most scholars of American moral thought, Alison believed that moral benevolence preceded and therefore underlay all civil governance. Individuals

52. See Alison to Stiles, Dec. 4, 1766, cited in Carl Bridenbaugh, *Mitre and Sceptre: Transatlantic Faiths, Ideas, Personalities, and Politics, 1689–1775* (New York, 1967), 274. On Alison's fear of Anglican sitting bishops, see Hoeveler, *Creating the American Mind*, 336; Robson, *Educating Republicans*, 36–38.

enjoyed an innate (albeit God-given) ability to conceive of the public interest over their personal concerns. Thus, Alison used Hutchesonian theory to
define the trustworthiness of American moral perception in contrast to corrupt British magistracy. His Hutchesonian reasoning provides further evidence that Old Side–New Side distinctions could not easily predict the Presbyterian political theologies of the Revolutionary era. Scholars once drew an
association between the evangelicals and anti-evangelicals of the 1740s and
the Revolutionaries and loyalists of the 1770s. Yet Alison's stance as a patriot challenges the notion that evangelicals (including Presbyterians) became
the more sincere Revolutionaries in the decades after the Great Awakening.
Distinct understandings of moral philosophy—albeit less stark than those
that divided Old and New Side Presbyterians during the 1740s and early
1750s—were not always correlated with the relative sincerity of patriot ideology. Alison and other moderate Presbyterians shared an affinity for the Revolutionary cause with the heirs of New Side evangelicalism. They only differed
in the moral sensory reasoning that they used to describe their support for
American independence.[53]

On some occasions, indeed, Alison even incorporated a darker Calvinistic vision in his developing political theology. In a number of 1768 essays
in the *Pennsylvania Journal,* he linked British authoritarianism with local
Episcopalian efforts to control religious and educational institutions. Writing under the name of "Centinel," he used Hutchesonian ideas to discuss
the importance of good governance. But he also added a more ambiguous—
and less anthropocentric—dimension to his discussion of social and political equilibrium:

> The passions and prejudices of men are constantly leading them into
> one mistake or another; and the remonstrances of reason and duty

53. On Alison and Hutcheson, see David Fate Norton, "Francis Hutcheson in America,"
Transactions of the Fourth International Congress on the Enlightenment, IV (Oxford, 1976),
Studies on Voltaire and the Eighteenth Century, CLIV, 1553–1555. Heimert extrapolates that
evangelicals became more likely than moderate clergymen to oppose British corruption with
a radical public voice. See Alan Heimert, *Religion and the American Mind: From the Great
Awakening to the Revolution* (Cambridge, Mass., 1966). On the debate set off by such a suggestion, see Edmund S. Morgan, review of Heimert in *WMQ,* 3d Ser., XXIV (1967), 454–459;
Sidney E. Mead, "Through and Beyond the Lines: A Review of Alan Heimert, *Religion and
the American Mind from the Great Awakening to the Revolution,*" *Journal of Religion,* XLVIII
(1968), 274–288; William G. McLoughlin, "Essay Review: The American Revolution as a Religious Revival: 'The Millennium in One Country,'" *New England Quarterly,* XL (1967), 99–110;
John M. Murrin, "No Awakening, No Revolution? More Counterfactual Speculations," *Reviews
in American History,* XI (1983), 161–171.

alone, are but feeble restraints. In order therefore to curb the licentiousness of leading men, it hath been found expedient to distribute the powers of government among the different sorts and orders of which the community is composed, so as to excite, and employ those of one rank and interest, to correct the irregularities of another.

Alison responded to intrigues that threatened to sideline his moderate Presbyterian allies with an argument that in fact undermined the notion of innate moral sensibility. Elsewhere he suggested that an inborn ethical compass, if correctly cultivated, could enable men to champion the importance of civic order and benevolence. Contrary to William Smith, he tended to claim that British misrule had aroused the innate ethical stance of patriots to make the cause of independence legitimate. But, in this instance, he pointed out that natural factionalism required passions to check other passions, rather than simply relying on any transcendent common sensibility.[54]

"The Same in Complexion, the Same in Blood, in Language, and in Religion"

That even Francis Alison could be moved to describe the role of passions and factionalism during the early Revolutionary era adds further context to Witherspoon's most famous sermon, *The Dominion of Providence over the Passions of Men*. Delivered in Princeton village on Congress's recommended fast day of May 17, 1776, six weeks before Witherspoon signed the Declaration of Independence, it provides the next surviving evidence of his turn against the British crown. Like Alison, Witherspoon supported the republican cause of American independence from mid-1776. But, to a far greater degree than Alison's 1768 aside in the *Pennsylvania Journal* or any of his later statements, Witherspoon's sermon highlighted the inevitable role of pride and passionate disorder among those who sought to create new forms of civil union and political representation. Its title signaled his intention to examine the role of divine providence in the Revolutionary struggle. It also alluded to the impact of subjective human passions in the disintegration of the British Empire—including among patriots themselves. The sermon expounded on the biblical refrain, "Surely the Wrath of Man shall praise thee; the remainder of Wrath shalt tho restrain," in order to show that God's providence would grant American victory in the struggle for independence but would also re-

54. The Centinel No. IX [Francis Alison], *Pennsylvania Journal*, May 19, 1768, [1]. See also Elizabeth I. Nybakken, ed., *The Centinel: Warnings of a Revolution* (Newark, N.J., 1980), 20–23.

quire the humility of Americans during and after the crisis. In creating a new union of people, American independence was providentially necessary to shock British subjects into repentance. But the chaos of the Revolutionary war, Witherspoon portended, would also remind Americans of their own mortality as subjective and passionate men and their own continuing need for salvation through grace, notwithstanding the legitimacy of their newfound political independence.[55]

Witherspoon began the sermon by defining the context for North American liberty in what seemed to be traditional Anglocentric religious terms. He pointed out that the violent persecution of "many eminent Christians" in England led them to New England, "where the light of the gospel and true religion were [previously] unknown." Witherspoon—a former Scot—began his most famous patriot sermon with a reference to the flourishing of Puritan piety in seventeenth-century America. As Witherspoon continued, however, it became clear that he did not intend to restrict his discussion to the precedent of New England piety. Before broadening his assessment of the relationship between piety and political independence, he inserted a rare footnote below his reference to Congregational religion, which can be found in the sermon's published version. To counter the charge that his religious support for American independence should offer "a temporising compliment to the people of New-England," he thought "it proper to observe that the whole paragraph is copied from a sermon on Psal. lxxiv. 22. prepared and preached in Scotland, in the month of August, 1758." Witherspoon clearly and self-consciously defined the moral parity between separate provinces of the British Empire before the imperial crisis. That his observation was first delivered in a Scottish church made it less likely that "the people of New-England" could claim a monopoly on religious liberty. That the culture of Scottish evangelicalism had permitted him to preach about the virtues of Congregational piety implied their equal correspondence. Witherspoon sought to avoid emphasizing the public nature of New England revivalism, just as he had remained uneasy when Scottish Moderates had focused on the development of moral sensibility in their own realm. With his first footnote, therefore, it was evident that his political theology would not offer an easy distinction between colonial morality and British corruption.[56]

Witherspoon's Scottish footnote against New England superiority was, ironically, congruent with certain strains of Congregational evangelicalism.

---

55. Witherspoon, *Dominion of Providence,* in [Green, ed.], *Works of Witherspoon,* III, 17.
56. Ibid., 30–31 (note on 31).

T. M. Harris

The Dominion of Providence over the Paf-
fions of Men.

A

S E R M O N

PREACHED

AT PRINCETON,

On the 17th of MAY, 1776.

BEING

The GENERAL FAST appointed by the CONGRESS
through the UNITED COLONIES.

TO WHICH IS ADDED,

An ADDRESS to the NATIVES of SCOTLAND refiding in
AMERICA.

By *JOHN WITHERSPOON*, D. D.

PRESIDENT OF THE COLLEGE OF NEW-JERSEY.

PHILADELPHIA:

PRINTED AND SOLD BY R. AITKEN, PRINTER AND
BOOKSELLER, OPPOSITE THE LONDON COFFEE-
HOUSE, FRONT-STREET.
M.DCC.LXXVI.

As noted previously, Jonathan Edwards's famous "Concert of Prayer" endeavored to galvanize the joint action of Scots, Americans, and the entire British Reformed community. He perceived the growth of Congregational governance in New England as a positive manifestation of provincial life in the British imperial world. The last years of his life coincided with the early period of the Seven Years' War, when Britain and the American colonists suffered several defeats at the hands of the French. But, although Edwards could be vitriolic in his condemnation of the French, he did not abandon his attention to the universality of sin, nor his unease with public covenanting civil theology. Were he alive in 1776, then, it is unlikely that he would have disapproved of Witherspoon's footnote disclaiming New England moral superiority.[57]

Like Edwards, Witherspoon's condemnation of imperial France during the 1750s had not been accompanied by any moral flattery toward his own provincial population (Scotland). Two decades later, his essay "On the Controversy about Independence" used similar reasoning to highlight the "common deception of little minds," irrespective of their national context. Written in early 1776, it developed ideas from his treatise *Christian Magnanimity*, questioning the dichotomy between American morality and corrupt British magistracy: "It has been my opinion from the beginning," Witherspoon argued, "that we did not carry our reasoning fully home, when we complained of an arbitrary prince, or of the insolence, cruelty and obstinacy of Lord North, Lord Bute, or Lord Mansfield." Focusing too greatly on the dishonest machinations of particular British politicians risked obscuring the wider importance of American independence. Providence, rather than the comparative morality of Americans, made the imperial crisis inevitable. "What we have to fear, and what we have now to grapple with, is the ignorance, prejudice, partiality and injustice of human nature." The true corruption of West-

---

57. On Edwards's positive view of provincial evangelicalism, see Ned C. Landsman, *From Colonials to Provincials: American Thought and Culture, 1680–1760* (Ithaca, N.Y., 1997), 110–116; Joseph A. Conforti, *Jonathan Edwards, Religious Tradition, and American Culture* (Chapel Hill, N.C., 1995), 67–68; Michael J. Crawford, *Seasons of Grace: Colonial New England's Revival Tradition in Its British Context* (New York, 1991), 228–231. New Englanders who fought against the French were described by Edwards as "God's people" because "they fought *for* Christ's church (though many of them might not have been fully *in* Christ's church) against its openly professed enemies," and not because of any automatic regional covenant. See Grasso, *A Speaking Aristocracy*, 30–31, 72–76, 135. Of course, as we have seen, Edwards's suggestion that regeneration required further assurance beyond public context struck fear into those who vested their moral authority in the attachment of covenant to place.

minster politicians lay in their humanity, regardless of their behavior toward American colonists.[58]

Providence had manifested in an unequal relationship between Britain and the American colonies. But the resulting move toward American independence did not denote the innate ethical superiority of patriots, who remained mere men. In his essay "On Conducting the American Controversy," posthumously published in his collected works, Witherspoon claimed that the imperial crisis would determine "the state of the human race through a great part of the globe, for ages to come" — rather than simply enshrining the public blessing of America alone.[59]

Witherspoon expanded ideas from his essays on the controversy of American independence when he moved into the main body of his *Dominion of Providence* sermon. He claimed that "there are few surer marks of the reality of religion, than when a man feels himself more joined in spirit to a true holy person of a different denomination, than to an irregular liver of his own" — the inverse to his earlier claim that "little minds" eschewed the universal need for salvation and were united by their "common deception." Such an ecumenical aspect in Witherspoon's political theology reflected his upbringing during an earlier period of transatlantic revivalism, when ministers had extended their religious purview beyond their particular provinces in the British Empire, even while they revered the particular denominational values that had developed in their own realms.[60]

58. Witherspoon, "On the Controversy about Independence," in [Green, ed.], *Works of Witherspoon*, IV, 302, 304.

59. Witherspoon, "On Conducting the American Controversy," in [Green, ed.], *Works of Witherspoon*, IV, 306, 308. Similarly, in Congregational circles "providential" thought often provided a better fit than public covenanting ideology for ministers who remained influenced by Edwards's legacy and who wished to support the American cause by the 1770s. It enabled them to support patriot ideology without flattering the moral agency of individual Americans. See Nicholas Guyatt, *Providence and the Invention of the United States, 1607–1876* (New York, 2007), 95–133; Grasso, *A Speaking Aristocracy*, 30–31. As Harry S. Stout has pointed out, "regular preaching" by evangelical Congregational ministers often "retained its subject matter of salvation, self-examination, and godly living." However much "themes of civil liberty and resistance to tyranny dominated the occasional pulpit, they did not come at the expense of personal salvation." They rarely signaled "a new 'civil religion' replacing the old otherworldly religion" through public covenanting ideology. See Stout, *The New England Soul: Preaching and Religious Culture in Colonial New England* (New York, 1986), 268, 271. Witherspoon's essays "On the Controversy about Independence" and "On Conducting the American Controversy" were intended for the press but were published posthumously after they were found in Witherspoon's papers by Ashbel Green.

60. Witherspoon, *Dominion of Providence*, in [Green, ed.], *Works of Witherspoon*, III, 42.

Jonathan Edwards had once warned of the problematic notion that inner morality derived from individual incorporation within an external public covenant. He had questioned the validity of the common contrast between a public New England covenant and imperial French power during the 1740s and 1750s. Two decades later, Witherspoon highlighted the humility that pious people shared in common, irrespective of region or province. Just as Edwards had criticized triumphalist Congregational distinctions from imperial France, Witherspoon suggested that he who was "the best friend to American liberty" was "most sincere and active in promoting true and undefiled religion" and set "himself with the greatest firmness to bear down profanity and immorality of every kind" within his *own* nation. Witherspoon opposed British governors, not "because they are corrupt or profligate, although probably many of them are so, but because they are men, and therefore liable to all the selfish bias inseparable from human nature." These statements exposed Witherspoon's continuing definition of providentialism in his sermon. He sought to downplay any distinction between heightened American ethics and corrupt British magistracy. An overly specific focus on the corrupt particularities of British governors risked concealing the religious meaning of American independence. Providence, rather than the relative morality of Americans, made the struggle against Britain legitimate. Providence had transformed common human corruption—the sin and pride of all men—into a political melee. It legitimized the cause of American independence, according to Witherspoon, because successful independence would necessarily shock British subjects into moral rumination. The providential manifestation of bloody chaos, moreover, would remind victorious Americans that they were nonetheless men, with all the biases that were inseparable from human nature—men that would require continued introspection and humility as independent citizens.[61]

Witherspoon used moral sensory language and terminology to define the unsettling implications of unregenerate humanity. Despite evidence of "unrelenting rage" on all sides, Witherspoon called for a "cool and candid attention" to history and current events. Such an appeal might seem, on first glance, to reference Francis Hutcheson's work on the relationship between human sociability and the study of past societies, or even Thomas Reid's dispassionate philosophy of common sense. But Witherspoon revealed human disorder wherever one looked: "Men of lax and corrupt principles, take great delight in speaking to the praise of human nature, and extolling its dignity, without distinguishing what it was, at its first creation, from what it is in its

61. Ibid., 34, 36, 37, 42.

present fallen state." Yet "a cool and candid attention, either to the past history, or present state of the world, but above all, to the ravages of lawless power, ought to humble us in the dust." Witherspoon's appeal for political action contained a further warning: "Have you assembled together willingly to hear what shall be said on public affairs, and to join in imploring the blessing of God on the counsels and arms of the united colonies, and can you be unconcerned, what shall become of you for ever, when all the monuments of human greatness shall be laid in ashes, for 'the earth *itself* and all the works that are therein shall be burnt up.'" Witherspoon continued: "Unless you are united to him by a lively faith, not the resentment of a haughty monarch, but the sword of divine justice hangs over you, and the fulness of divine vengeance shall speedily overtake you." Preaching to a Scottish congregation outside Glasgow during the same year, Witherspoon's evangelical Presbyterian correspondent William Thom applied similar reasoning before his own audience. In a sermon discussing the American crisis and the righteous struggle of the colonists, he described the "woeful war" on behalf of a "ministerial party" intent on "revenue squeezed from America." Yet he also implored both the British and American people to think of the eternal world rather than their power over particular dominions.[62]

Because Americans were affected by the realization that the "lust of domination should be so violent and universal," Witherspoon generalized in *The Dominion of Providence*, they possessed greater humility than British leaders. But he also warned of any "criminal inattention" to "the singular interposition of Providence" on "behalf of the American colonies" in their conflict with Britain. Their political struggle coincides with a time when those who are "the same in complexion, the same in blood, in language, and in religion . . . butcher one another with unrelenting rage" and glory in the deed. As humans, their superior ethical will was an unlikely prospect when success in conflict derived from providence rather than inborn capabilities or a special covenant with God. "Nothing can be more absolutely necessary to true religion, than a clear and full conviction of the sinfulness of our nature and state," Witherspoon continued; although even a "good form of government

---

62. Ibid., 22–23, 32–33; William Thom, *Sermon V: From Whence Come Wars? Preached in the Church of Govan on the Public Fast, 1779*, in *The Works of the Rev. William Thom, Late Minister of Govan, Consisting of Sermons, Tracts, Letters* . . . (Glasgow, 1799), 150, 154. Richard Kent Donovan describes Thom's ideology as akin to "evangelical civic humanism." See Donovan, "Evangelical Civic Humanism in Glasgow: The American War Sermons of William Thom," in Andrew Hook and Richard B. Sher, eds., *The Glasgow Enlightenment* (East Lothian, U.K., 1995), 227–245. See also Stephen Conway, *The British Isles and the War of American Independence* (New York, 2002), 89.

may hold the rotten materials together for some time," he warned, "beyond a certain pitch, even the best constitution will be ineffectual." Only "when true religion and internal principles" maintained "their vigour" would "the attempts of the most powerful enemies to oppress them" become "commonly baffled and disappointed."[63]

In the passage above, Witherspoon did not mean to define religious virtue as a convenient civil theology, a way of maintaining moral order against those who tried to disrupt any political constitution. Such a definition risked reducing the motivation for piety to the human-centered realm of good governance. Rather, Witherspoon repeated the phrase "true religion," which he had only a few sentences earlier defined as "a full conviction of the sinfulness of our nature and state." Personal salvation followed such a conviction, allowing a new sense of objective morality through God's grace in the regenerated heart. According to Witherspoon's evangelical reasoning, a regenerated sensibility could go some way toward galvanizing society, provided enough individuals were similarly awakened. Witherspoon made sure to remind his listeners that American patriots and British subjects were equally sinful, whatever the outcome of their conflict. Nonetheless, his description of American humility through "true religion" implied that a greater number in their realm were (or at least could become) regenerate. Their understanding of sin provided them with a new moral sense, wrought by grace, which too many British subjects lacked. Of course, the desire for personal salvation was required to precede any wish for national stability, lest the former became disassociated from the universal immediacy of individual iniquity. In communities that had encountered the gospel, the external action of the Holy Spirit on the moral conscience allowed individuals to recognize sin and their need for regeneration irrespective of their nationality or political ideology. Collectively, Americans were not morally distinguished from British subjects because of their cultivated moral sensibility. Nor, according to Witherspoon, did they possess a special covenant with God. Rather, a greater proportion of their population had been awakened to the universal nature of sin and the requirement for regeneration. More were likely to follow the action of the Holy Spirit with full conversion, allowing concerted moral action as an external gift of grace. But any diminishment in their relative humility would threaten the strength and even the legitimacy of their new political union.[64]

Here, as elsewhere, Witherspoon avoided describing the events of the

63. Witherspoon, *Dominion of Providence,* in [Green, ed.], *Works of Witherspoon,* III, 20, 21, 22, 30, 33, 37, 41.

64. Ibid., 41.

American Revolution according to a millennialist account of societal progress. After the Seven Years' War, some New England ministers had begun to
define the "sacred cause of liberty" as a political conflict between good and
evil, rather than one that took place in the ecclesiastical realm. Corrupt politicians—rather than the pope or corrupt religious establishments—were often
described as the primary agents who stood against God's plan for history.
Witherspoon rarely if ever displayed such an eschatological focus. Instead
of linking the necessity of American independence to the second coming of
Christ, his *Dominion of Providence* sermon emphasized the dialectical relationship between cyclical backsliding and forward momentum. His evangelical conception of historical development was similar to that which Jonathan
Edwards had once employed in his *History of the Work of Redemption,* begun
in 1739 and published in 1746. The move toward American independence,
according to Witherspoon, offered a step forward in secular history because
enough Americans had been awakened to their sin. They could form a stable
civic entity because their greater humility allowed their experience of God's
grace. But the structure of their political union, in and of itself, was no more
moral than any other. Should its constituents regress and gain an inflated
sense of their own ethical abilities, it would crumble just as easily as the
British Empire. That there remained room for moral backsliding on the western side of the Atlantic made Witherspoon unlikely to define the American
Revolution as a special event in sacred history. To be sure, singular acts of
divine providence had allowed Americans to demand their independence.
But their political actions and reactions could not be directly linked to the
imminence of Christ's return to earth.[65]

As well as eschewing millennialism, therefore, Witherspoon's providentialism questioned the Scottish Enlightenment conception of stadial historical progress. Moderates, most notably William Robertson, claimed that advanced cultural contexts allowed the natural evolution of ethical sensibilities.
The ability to harness an innately benevolent response, according to such a
conception, developed in tandem with social and political advancements in
particular historical circumstances. According to Witherspoon's sermon, in
contrast, a free and stable society was bound by its members' primary duty

65. On millennialism and the American Revolution, see Nathan O. Hatch, *The Sacred Cause
of Liberty: Republican Thought and the Millennium in Revolutionary New England* (Binghamton,
N.Y., 1977), 17, 36, 59–60, 88; Melvin B. Endy, Jr., "Just War, Holy War, and Millennialism in
Revolutionary America," *WMQ*, 3d Ser., XLII (1985), 3–25. For Edwards's earlier conception of
providential history, see Jonathan Edwards, *A History of the Work of Redemption,* ed. John F. Wilson, in Perry Miller et al., eds., *The Works of Jonathan Edwards,* IX (New Haven, Conn., 1989).

to God, followed by all other obligations. Only God could "grant that in America true religion and civil liberty may be inseparable, and that the unjust attempts to destroy the one, may in the issue tend to the support and establishment of both." The unencumbered relationship between individuals and God enabled them to acknowledge the necessity of his external moral assistance, before the development of any civil association. When political tyranny prevented individuals from working out their duty to God, resistance became legitimate. Confrontation — even national independence — simply reasserted those obligations. Humility expressed the importance of obedience over innate sensibility and was the only legitimate response to national independence. It clarified the obligations that all humans shared, irrespective of time and place.[66]

"*Too Much Scoticism! He Wants to Save His Countrymen*"

According to one contemporary observation, Witherspoon's *Dominion of Providence* was less concerned with the synthesis between religious and patriot identity than with the commercial livelihood of Scots, irrespective of their national context. Ezra Stiles, who would become president of Yale in 1778, wrote in his August 1776 diary entry: "Dr. Witherspoon . . . published a Sermon preached at Continental Fast in May last: and subjoyned an Address to his Countrymen the Scotch in America to reconcile them to Independency. This he says will be best for G. Britain; and that at the Peace we shall trade with G. Britain as formerly. I doubt. Too much Scoticism! He wants to save his Countrymen, who have behaved most cruelly in this American conflict." Stiles noted Witherspoon's decision to attach the *Address to the Natives of Scotland* to the *Dominion of Providence* during its publication and circulation in the months after May 1776. In addition to denigrating John Wilkes, Witherspoon's *Address to the Natives* suggested that Atlantic commerce ought to be free, open, and distinct from the protectionist philosophy of Westminster politics. It claimed that Scottish support for American independence would not preclude — and would even enhance — America's eventual trading relationship with Britain. Yet Stiles perceived Witherspoon's motivation in cynical terms. In his view, Witherspoon wished to "save his [Scottish] Countrymen" by redefining the nature of American independence in their commercial favor, irrespective of where they lived on either side of the Atlantic.[67]

66. Witherspoon, *Dominion of Providence,* in [Green, ed.], *Works of Witherspoon,* III, 30, 46.

67. Ezra Stiles, *The Literary Diary of Ezra Stiles, D.D., LL.D., President of Yale College,* ed. Franklin Bowditch Dexter (New York, 1901), II, 41.

Stiles's prickly depiction of Scottish-American identity might well have contributed to (or even derived from) his desire to buttress Congregational religious authority during the Revolutionary era. His 1761 *Discourse on the Christian Union* had called for unity between Presbyterians and Congregationalists against the threat of colonial episcopacy. During the later 1770s, however, he was slightly more reticent about the prominent role of Presbyterians in the Revolutionary struggle. It is possible that he had Witherspoon in mind when he warned against ministers who were more prone to "intermeddle" with "Politics" than to promote "evangelical Truth and spiritual Liberty."[68]

Contrary to Stiles, Witherspoon's desire to address Scots was far from a sentimental appeal to his former countrymen. Neither did it represent a cynical attempt to eschew their position as mainland British subjects in order to protect them commercially from patriot ire. Rather, as demonstrated in the discussion above, Witherspoon's note to Scotland showed the link between his patriot identity and his evangelical piety, and thus a key aspect of his Revolutionary political theology. The piety that supplied a greater connection between Americans and would secure victory against redcoats might also provide the means to reach out to Britain—and Scots, in particular—after the war. To underscore Stiles's misunderstanding even further, it is worth recalling the migratory nature of Witherspoon's former constituency in Scotland. The resulting association between Scottish provincial evangelicalism and commercialism led to a strong Scottish attachment to the British Empire. But it could also very quickly translate into a patriot critique of London's metropolitan rule, as in Witherspoon's case.

Puritan theology in colonial America was able to accommodate the pursuit of commercial prosperity. In the eighteenth century, a similar adjustment had taken place among pious Presbyterian traders on both sides of the Atlantic Ocean, particularly on the route between western Scotland and the Middle and southern colonies. During the 1750s, Popular party clergymen happily published sermons with titles such as a *Prayer for National Prosperity and for the Revival of Religion Inseparably Connected* and *The Influence of Religion on National Happiness*. According to many Scottish traders, the addi-

68. At a time of cultural and institutional flux, Stiles went as far as adopting a revivalist religious style in order to appeal to a broader Congregational audience against rival Anglican influences. He might well have feared inroads from Presbyterians as well as Anglicans, particularly as the former gained a stronger voice as part of the Revolutionary coalition. See the discussion of Stiles's *Discourse on the Christian Union* in Grasso, *A Speaking Aristocracy*, 238. For Stiles's reference to intermeddling ministers, see Noll, *America's God*, 134.

tion of new European commercial networks to British America also provided fresh havens for Protestant religious freedom. The movement of Protestants between provincial boundaries supported the prosperity and piety of communities on both sides of the Atlantic Ocean. Trade opened up emigration networks, and emigration networks opened up trade. Their reciprocal relationship provided greater support for the settlement of merchants, many of whom were from evangelical constituencies.[69]

Beginning with the transatlantic religious awakenings of the 1730s and 1740s, commercial connections had helped to launch parallel correspondence networks with both Presbyterian and Congregationalist ministers across the Atlantic. Revivalist Presbyterians from towns west of Glasgow believed that they had been shut out of local economic prosperity by well-connected lairds and their Moderate allies. Thus, those who departed for North America were often evangelical merchants who sought to reassert their disappointed provincial freedoms away from Moderate patronage and commercial protectionism.[70]

Long before the American crisis, however, the ease with which provincial commercialism could turn into grievance with British governance was apparent. During the 1730s and 1740s, as a further example, a debate took place about whether linen or woolen manufacture offered the best platform for Scottish development. Woolen manufacturers employed rhetoric that foreshadowed Anglo-Irish and American grievances, questioning whether they enjoyed the same privileges as all British subjects and the same rights to

69. John Erskine, *The Influence of Religion on National Happiness* . . . (Edinburgh, 1756); J. Witherspoon, *Prayer for National Prosperity and for the Revival of Religion Inseparably Connected* . . . (London, 1758). On the Puritan accommodation of commercialism, see, for example, Mark A. Peterson, *The Price of Redemption: The Spiritual Economy of Puritan New England* (Stanford, Calif., 1997). For the potential dichotomy between commerce and virtue in the Scottish-American intellectual context, see Pocock, "Cambridge Paradigms and Scotch Philosophers," in Hont and Ignatieff, eds., *Wealth and Virtue*, 253-274, Istvan Hont, "The 'Rich Country-Poor Country' Debate in Scottish Classical Political Economy," 271-316. On the adjustment to transnational trade among evangelical Presbyterian traders (particularly descending from western Scotland), see Landsman, "Provinces and the Empire," in Stone, ed., *An Imperial State at War*, 265; Ned C. Landsman, "Presbyterians and Provincial Society: The Evangelical Enlightenment in the West of Scotland, 1740-1775," in John Dwyer and Richard B. Sher, eds., *Sociability and Society in Eighteenth-Century Scotland* (Edinburgh, 1993), 194-209; Landsman, "The Legacy of British Union for the North American Colonies," in Robertson, ed., *Union for Empire*, 297-318; Landsman, "Liberty, Piety and Patronage," in Hook and Sher, eds., *The Glasgow Enlightenment*, 214-227.

70. Landsman, "Provinces and the Empire," in Stone, ed., *An Imperial State at War*, 260, 268.

manufacture. Many Scots who contributed to religious revivalism were members of the wool camp. Thus, the scope of international commerce and migration appealed to them because it opened up new markets as well as new means of achieving religious autonomy. By the 1760s, Popular ministers such as John Erskine continued to accuse Scottish placemen of circumventing the international trading system—and their links to the western Atlantic—through managed domestic interests. Erskine and others eventually adopted the language of American radicals in their opposition to restrictions on commerce, migration, and missionary work between Scotland and America. Popular party spokesmen perceived London's encroachment on American freedom according to their own local struggle against patronage.[71]

Through the 1760s and early 1770s, Witherspoon continued to encourage migration and commerce between Scotland and America. Indeed, contrary to Ezra Stiles's perception, some Scots accused Witherspoon of betraying his brethren by encouraging their emigration to the western side of the Atlantic. In a 1773 letter to Edinburgh, Witherspoon reduced such an "accusation" to "the following argument—Migrations from Britain to America, are not only hurtful, but tend to the ruin of that kingdom; therefore, J.W. by inviting people to leave Scotland, and settle in America, is an enemy to his country." He countered the charge by stating that it was "impossible for them to do any thing for the improvement of America that will not in the end redound to the advantage of Great Britain." To make his point, Witherspoon claimed that the emigration of Protestants from Europe alongside Presbyterians from the "north of Ireland" coincided with increasing metropolitan wealth in

71. Kidd, "North Britishness," *Historical Journal,* XXXIX (1996), 377; Ned C. Landsman, *Scotland and Its First American Colony, 1683–1765* (Princeton, N.J., 1985), 72–99; Landsman, "The Legacy of British Union," in Robertson, ed., *Union for Empire,* 297–318; Robert Kent Donovan, *No Popery and Radicalism: Opposition to Roman Catholic Relief in Scotland, 1778–1782* (New York, 1987), 72–73, 158–162, 239; Dalphy L. Fagerstrom, "Scottish Opinion and the American Revolution," *WMQ,* 3d Ser., XI, (1954), 268. According to David Armitage, "Scottish colonial ventures were indebted to English models, but in pursuit of their Scottish investors' and settlers' interests." See Armitage, "Making the Empire British: Scotland in the Atlantic World, 1542–1707," *Past and Present,* no. 155 (May 1997), 7. On Scottish evangelical disappointment in the treatment of Americans, see also John R. McIntosh, *Church and Theology in Enlightenment Scotland: The Popular Party, 1740–1800* (East Lothian, U.K., 1998), 155–160. Toward the end of 1776, James Boswell, the lawyer, diarist, commentator, and author, "grew so angry with Hugh Blair for praying against the Americans on a fast day appointed by the King for that very purpose that he began to 'shun' the New Kirk whenever Blair preached." See Richard B. Sher, "Scottish Divine and Legal Lairds: Boswell's Scots Presbyterian Identity," in Greg Clingham, ed., *New Light on Boswell: Critical and Historical Essays on the Occasion of the Bicentenary of "The Life of Johnson"* (Cambridge, 1991), 39.

mainland Britain. Witherspoon, like many other Presbyterians, believed that movement within and between Protestant regions was nothing more than the fulfilment of providential history.[72]

By the 1770s, therefore, Witherspoon had become particularly sensitive to the idea that the spiritual and commercial freedoms of British provincial life were dually threatened. By appending his *Address to the Natives of Scotland Residing in America* to his sermon on the *Dominion of Providence,* and by making sure that they were circulated on both sides of the Atlantic, Witherspoon clarified his attention to economic aspects of liberty alongside his spiritual discussion of American independence. In his *Address,* he pointed out that British taxation of the colonies reflected insular corruption. It fed "the insatiable desire of wealth in placemen and pensioners, to increase the influence of the crown, and the corruption of the people." In the *Dominion of Providence,* he noted that, if "we yield up our temporal property, we at the same time deliver the conscience into bondage."[73]

Evidence of the popularity of Witherspoon's *Dominion of Providence* and *Address* in Scotland is provided by the large number of reprints in the region. Members of Witherspoon's former Popular party constituency certainly found it difficult to resist identifying the American struggle—as he had defined it in religious and economic terms—with their own stand against patronage. Members of the Moderate Kirk, they claimed, received patronage from a regime that threatened to subjugate Americans with episcopacy and commercial regulation. Thus, Popular party theologians deployed what has been described as "evangelical civic humanism" in their support for American patriots. According to the Reverend William Thom of Govan, a friend

72. John Witherspoon, "Letter Sent to Scotland for the Scots Magazine," in [Green, ed.], *Works of Witherspoon,* IV, 281–282, 287.

73. Witherspoon, *Address to the Natives of Scotland Residing in America,* in [Green, ed.], *Works of Witherspoon,* III, 55; Witherspoon, *Dominion of Providence,* ibid., 37. The first edition of Witherspoon's *Address to the Natives of Scotland Residing in America* was printed in 1776 by Robert Aitken of Philadelphia. Second and third editions were reprinted in 1777 in Glasgow. A fourth edition was reprinted in Philadelphia and London in 1777, and a fifth copy was published in London in 1779. All were attached to Witherspoon's *Dominion of Providence.* By 1759, Aitken was operating as a "bookseller, bookbinder, and proprietor of a circulating library in Paisley" and "belonged to the radical denomination of Presbyterian seceders from the Church of Scotland known as the anti-burghers." He also maintained close relations with Witherspoon and other evangelicals who remained in Scotland, and he eventually moved to Philadelphia. See Sher, *The Enlightenment and the Book,* 535–537. For the Scottish edition of the *Dominion of Providence,* see Witherspoon, *The Dominion of Providence over the Passions of Men . . . to Which Is Added, "An Address to the Natives of Scotland Residing in America" . . . ,* 2d ed. (Glasgow, 1777), 2–3.

and correspondent of Witherspoon, elites in England and Scotland laid all their "hope" in "fine gold" rather than helping the poor and disconnected. Thom did not axiomatically link corruption to the pursuit of individual interests per se. He believed instead that corruption was the result of the monopoly of interests by a small number of elites, which prevented the outward growth of commercial and religious liberties.[74]

British corruption was, according to Thom, the partial result of England's protectionist involvement in Scottish markets, which inspired venal Scottish landlords to raise the rents of tenants and control the production and trade of goods in their narrow favor. If a "British Achan [the biblical motif of his sermon] is half-detected," Thom pointed out, "his friends, as guilty perhaps as himself, will plead strongly in his behalf. He is of noble extraction, will they say; his family was always loyal; himself hath long been a faithful servant to the crown . . . [and if] public monies . . . will be found in his hand, they will obtain a mandate from the sovereign, to stop all further inquiry." The imperial crisis, according to Thom, had inevitably followed the mounting greed of British elites, disrupting the honest trade of middling merchants who suffered boycotts and embargoes on both sides of the Atlantic. In 1778, he situated American Protestants alongside the Dutch in a wider history of

74. Donovan, "Evangelical Civic Humanism," in Hook and Sher, eds., *The Glasgow Enlightenment*, 227–245; William Thom, *The Revolt of the Ten Tribes*, in *Works of the Rev. William Thom*, 82–83. See also Robert Kent Donovan, "The Popular Party of the Church of Scotland and the American Revolution," in Sher and Smitten, eds., *Scotland and America*, 87. On continued reactions to the patriot cause in Scotland, particularly through Thom, see McIntosh, *Church and Theology*, 117–118, 128–131, 158–160. By the end of the war, some British subjects also predicted that American independence would lead to the expansion of Britain's informal empire, "partly because a substantially provincial political economy emphasizing the determining power of population and commerce was prevailing in the metropolis as well." See Ned C. Landsman, "Nation, Migration, and the Province in the First British Empire: Scotland and the Americas, 1600–1800," *American Historical Review*, CIV (1999), 474. See also Eliga H. Gould, "A Virtual Nation: Greater Britain and the Imperial Legacy of the American Revolution," ibid., 476–489; Landsman, "Witherspoon and the Problem of Provincial Identity," in Sher and Smitten, eds., *Scotland and America*, 29–45. The commercial identity of Scottish evangelicals further underscores why only the Kirk's Popular party faction came out publicly in support of the American cause. See Fagerstrom, "Scottish Opinion and the American Revolution," *WMQ*, 3d Ser., XI (1954), 268; Richard B. Sher, *Church and University in the Scottish Enlightenment: The Moderate Literati of Edinburgh* (Princeton, N.J., 1985), 269–270. Katherine Carté Engel has suggested that the English Society for Promoting Christian Knowledge, conversely, avoided defining the Revolution as an event that turned on the fracturing of British Protestant unity. See Engel, "The SPCK and the American Revolution: The Limits of International Protestantism," *Church History*, LXXXI (2012), 77–103.

suffering: their abandonment in the 1760s was akin to the war that a corrupt monarch such as Charles II, allied with Louis XIV, had waged against Calvinists in the Netherlands. Americans followed the same trajectory as the Dutch. Both were allies of Scottish Presbyterianism, heavily involved in international trade, and eventually abandoned by Westminster.[75]

"As Was the Case with the British Themselves in the Scotch Rebellion of 1745"

In the month that followed Witherspoon's May 1776 *Dominion of Providence* sermon, he played an active role in removing the royal governor of New Jersey, William Franklin. The New Jersey Provincial Congress castigated Franklin for his defiance of an order to support patriot assemblies. Having written to the Continental Congress during the previous week about their intentions, representatives of the New Jersey Congress, along with several soldiers, arrested Franklin on June 21. At the official interrogation of Franklin, Witherspoon criticized his supposedly pretentious manner and lack of loyalty. During the same period, Witherspoon joined the Continental Congress. On June 28, 1776, shortly after a debate between John Adams and John Dickinson on the question of independence, Witherspoon entered the chamber. Some in the Continental Congress suggested at this point that more deliberation was needed between colonies that were not "ripe" for independence. According to accounts by other delegates, Witherspoon is said to have responded that the country was "not only ripe for the measure, but in danger of becoming rotten for the want of it."[76]

During these early congressional sessions, what has been described as "the Scottish distinction between a federal and an incorporating union" continued to influence debates—particularly when Benjamin Franklin was

---

75. William Thom, "Sermon IV: Achan's Trespass in the Accursed Thing Considered; Preached in the Church of Govan, on the Public Fast, 1778," in *Works of the Rev. William Thom*, 111–112, Thom, "Sermon V: From Whence Come Wars?" 132–138. On Thom's wider reasoning, see also Landsman, "Witherspoon and the Problem of Provincial Identity," in Sher and Smitten, eds., *Scotland and America*, 39.

76. Sheila L. Skemp, *William Franklin: Son of a Patriot, Servant of a King* (New York, 1990), 210–212. On the background to the Provincial Congress delegation turning on Governor Franklin, see also Collins, *President Witherspoon*, I, 208–211. The account of Witherspoon's reaction to the "ripeness" of the colonies appears in Ashbel Green's work on Witherspoon's life, which he wrote after 1812. See Green, *Life of the Revd John Witherspoon*, ed. Savage, 159–160, 162. For the events surrounding Witherspoon in Congress up to the Declaration, see also Collins, *President Witherspoon*, I, 218–221.

present. In the July 1, 1776, congressional debate on the Articles of Confederation, Witherspoon listened to Franklin draw an analogy between the demand for equal representation among American states and Scotland's desire to maintain its voice in union with England. According to Thomas Jefferson's account of the debate, it was argued that "at the time of the Union between England and Scotland, the latter had made the objection which the smaller states now do; but experience had proved that no unfairness had ever been shewn them: that their advocates had prognosticated that it would again happen, as in times of old, that the whale would swallow Jonas." But Franklin pointed out that in fact "Jonas had swallowed the whale; for the Scotch had in fact got possession of the government, and gave laws to the English." Franklin offered this interpretation of the 1707 Act of Union to oppose the proposed Article XVII of America's new binding document, which suggested that each state maintain one vote, regardless of population differences.[77]

Witherspoon, who had begun his own term in Congress ten days earlier, was able to respond to Franklin's statement. Unlike the new American confederation, he claimed, Anglo-Scottish union had increasingly taken on an incorporating character. It failed to offer confederal equality to Scots, dashing their earlier hopes for British integration. In the present political context, moreover, the institutional autonomy of American colonists had been similarly disappointed by Westminster. The time was ripe for equal representation among American states because common danger gave a common basis for political association. As Witherspoon claimed in "Part of a Speech in Congress, upon the Confederation," delivered during the same week as Franklin's statement:

> If therefore, at present, when the danger is yet imminent, when it is so far from being over, that it is but coming to its height, we shall find it impossible to agree upon the terms of this confederacy, what madness is it to suppose that there ever will be a time, or that circumstances will so change, as to make it even probable, that it will be done at an after season? Will not the very same difficulties that are in our way, be in the way of those who shall come after us? Is it possible that they should be ignorant of them, or inattentive to them? Will they not have the same

77. LaCroix, *Ideological Origins of American Federalism*, 121–123. Benjamin Franklin's words were cited by Thomas Jefferson and James Madison in their accounts of the congressional meetings. See Thomas Jefferson Randolph, ed., *Memoir, Correspondence, and Miscellanies, from the Papers of Thomas Jefferson* (Charlottesville, Va., 1829), I, 26–27 (quotation); Henry D. Gilpin, ed., *The Papers of James Madison . . .* (Washington, D.C., 1840), I, 34.

jealousies of each other, the same attachment to local prejudices, and particular interest?

Thus, Witherspoon made the case for concerted action using a providential account of universal prejudice.[78]

There is a legend that Witherspoon delivered a speech in Congress a few days after Franklin, providing the final impetus for the passing of the Declaration of Independence on July 4, 1776. The secondhand account of this speech is inscribed on the monuments to Witherspoon in Philadelphia and Washington, with the phrase: "There is a tide in the affairs of men — a nick of time. We perceive it now before us. To hesitate, is to consent to slavery." Though there is no evidence for such a speech or statement, Witherspoon did sign the Declaration, becoming the only minister to do so.[79]

We do not have an exact account of Witherspoon's actions on the Fourth of July. We do know that he signed the Declaration, as evidenced by his signature at the bottom of the document, and there is the suggestion that he prickled at the use of the word "Scotch" in the phrase "Scotch and foreign mercenaries" in Jefferson's original draft. According to Richard Henry Lee's memoir, published in Philadelphia in 1825, "Dr. Witherspoon, the learned president of Nassau Hall College, who was a *Scotchman* by birth, moved to strike out the word '*Scotch,*' which was accordingly done." Lee's assertion assumes more weight in light of Witherspoon's May 1776 *Address to the Natives of Scotland Residing in America,* in which he stated, "It has given me no little uneasiness to hear the word *Scotch* used as a term of reproach in the American controversy." Witherspoon resented patriots who used "Scotch" as a reproach for clannishness, narrow-mindedness, or even mercenary loyalism. He might well have been aware of the claim that British mistreatment of the colonies derived from "Scotch politics" and "Scotch

78. Witherspoon, "Part of a Speech in Congress, upon the Confederation," in [Green, ed.], *Works of Witherspoon,* IV, 349–350. Witherspoon was reelected every year in November, other than in the year from November 1779 to November 1780, when he chose to devote more time to his duties as college president. His last term ended on Nov. 5, 1782. Evidence for these aspects of his career can be gleaned from the *Journals of the Continental Congress* and from statements James Madison and Thomas Jefferson recorded in their congressional diaries. Alison LaCroix claims that, "if the lesson of 1707 demonstrated anything to participants in the American debates of the 1770s, it was that a state with imperial aspirations would not easily consent to a truly federal association with another, less powerful state. Thus, although a federated union might be possible, a federated empire was unlikely to thrive." See LaCroix, *Ideological Origins of American Federalism,* 124.

79. Collins has discounted the legend. See Collins, *President Witherspoon,* I, 218–221.

FIGURE 15. *The Declaration of Independence, July 4, 1776.* By John Trumbull. 1832. Oil on canvas. Wadsworth Atheneum Museum of Art / Art Resource, N.Y.

Butchery" — particularly because of the involvement of Scottish troops and military leaders in the 1775 attack on Boston after Lexington and in skirmishes in Charlestown during the June 17, 1775, Battle of Bunker Hill; the influence of Scots such as the British solicitor-general Alexander Wedderburn, who launched stinging criticisms of Benjamin Franklin and other patriots in Privy Council discussions; and the activities through mid-1776 of the British Seventy-first regiment, led by the Scot Simon Fraser, some of whose members wore Highland garments. Yet, as Witherspoon always sought to make clear, the experience of pious Scots in the British Atlantic world made them fully aware of the importance of American liberty.[80]

Two months after signing the Declaration of Independence, Witherspoon once again interjected in a congressional debate with reference to Scotland

80. Richard H. Lee, *Memoir of the Life of Richard Henry Lee, and His Correspondence with the Most Distinguished Men in America and Europe, Illustrative of Their Characters, and of the Events of the American Revolution* (Philadelphia, 1825), I, 176; Witherspoon, *Address to the Natives of Scotland Residing in America,* in [Green, ed.], *Works of Witherspoon,* III, 47. On the notion of "Scotch Butchery" in the British army in America, see Vincent Carretta, *George III and the Satirists from Hogarth to Byron* (Athens, Ga., 2007), 200–202. On Alexander Wedderburn's castigation of Benjamin Franklin before the British Privy Council in January 1774, see Carla J. Mulford, *Benjamin Franklin and the Ends of Empire* (New York, 2015), 265–271.

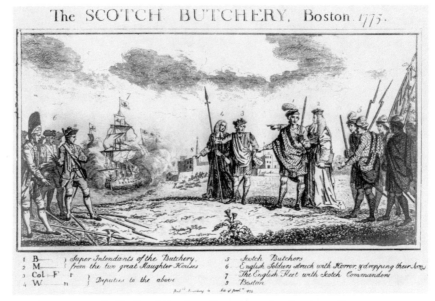

FIGURE 16. *The Scotch Butchery, Boston 1775.* London, 1775. Courtesy,
Library of Congress Prints and Photographs Division, Washington, D.C.

and the nature of its union with England. In his "Part of a Speech in Congress, on the Conference Proposed by Lord Howe," he made an analogy between redcoats and Scottish Jacobites:

> Lord Howe speaks of a decisive blow not being yet struck; as if this
> cause depended upon one battle, which could not be avoided. Sir, this
> is a prodigious mistake. We may fight no battle at all for a long time, or
> we may lose some battles, as was the case with the British themselves
> in the Scotch rebellion of 1745, and the cause notwithstanding be the
> same. I wish it were considered, that neither loss nor disgrace worth
> mentioning, has befallen us in the late engagement, nor comparable to
> what the British troops have often suffered. At the battle of Preston, sir,
> they broke to pieces and ran away like sheep, before a few highlanders.
> I myself saw them do the same thing at Falkirk, with very little differ-
> ence, a small part only of the army making a stand, and in a few hours
> the whole retreating with precipitation before their enemies. Did that
> make any difference in the cause? Not in the least—so long as the body
> of the nation were determined, on principle, against the rebels.

In this instance, Witherspoon was perfectly comfortable using the word
"Scotch." The description referred to those who fought for the cause of

British unionism against Jacobitism — rather than parochial clannishness. Witherspoon had once referred to Britain as "we." Now, speaking before an American Congress, he cast himself as an observer of "the British themselves" — "I myself saw *them*." As a revivalist Scot, he had opposed the Jacobite cause and supported Britain's Hanoverian union. Yet the British were now akin to rebels he had opposed "in the Scotch rebellion of 1745." British victories against patriots would undermine the expansion and stability of their independent Protestant confederation. Jacobites had posed a similar threat to Anglo-Scottish integration at the "battle of Preston." Nonetheless, Britain eventually won its wider war. With a pious union on its side, according to Witherspoon, America would also eventually achieve victory. Once again, he alluded to piety and unionism in the Hanoverian context. Rather than referencing the English Civil Wars or the Glorious Revolution, the battles at Preston and Falkirk were foremost in his mind.[81]

Already anxious that Witherspoon chose to address Scots alongside Americans, Ezra Stiles became aware of Witherspoon's early congressional discussion of Scottish precedent. In a July 1777 diary entry, Stiles wrote:

> There are only two Scotchmen in Congress viz. Dr. Witherspoon Presidt. of Jersey College, and Mr. Wilson of Pensylva,, a Lawyer. Both strongly national, and can't bear any Thing in Congress which reflects on Scotland. The Dr. says that Scotland has manifested the greatest Spirit for Liberty as a nation, in that their History is full of their calling Kings to account and dethroning them when arbitrary and tyrannical.

Stiles denied Witherspoon's (supposed) argument that Scotland's history of "calling Kings to account and dethroning them when arbitrary and tyrannical" was any model for American liberty:

> But Dethronizations and Revolutions are constantly taking place at Constantinople, Ispahann, and Delhi; no one however thinks that this will prove the Policies of Persia, and the Mogul and Turkish Empires friendly to *Liberty*. The Policy of Scotland and all the governmental Ideas of the Body of that People, are abhorrent to all Ideas of civil Liberty and are full of rigorous tyrannical Superiorities and subordinations.

81. John Witherspoon, "Part of a Speech in Congress, on the Conference Proposed by Lord Howe," in [Green, ed.], *Works of Witherspoon*, IV, 319–320. On the influence of the 1745 Jacobite rising on religious perception of the Americas, see Frederick V. Mills, Sr., "The Society in Scotland for Propagating Christian Knowledge in British North America, 1730–1775," *Church History*, LXIII (1994), 15–30; Geoffrey Plank, *Rebellion and Savagery: The Jacobite Rising of 1745 and the British Empire* (Philadelphia, 2006), 77–102.

According to Stiles, nationalistic Scots such as Witherspoon were responsible for prolonging what ought to have been a brief battle between American colonists and Britain: "Dr. With. goes all lengths with the Congress
both in the War, Independy, and foreign Alliances." The separation between
America and Britain was inevitable, but the extended war that ensued was
not. Witherspoon prolonged the conflict because "he had Discernment to
see from the Beginning that America would be inevitably dismembered, and
then acted as all Scotchmen would do under such a conviction, determined
to rise and figure in the Dismemberment and p[er]h[a]ps lay a foundation of
reconciling the Americans to the Scots." Thus, "Scotchmen" in the British
government had provoked the war; "Scotchmen" in America used the ensuing turmoil to facilitate their rise to prominence and then worked to reconcile America's independence with specific interests in Scotland: "The Dr.
is a politician. We may use him as far as he is for America—but scorn to be
awed by him into an ignominious Silence on the subject of Scots Perfidy and
Tyranny and Enmity to America." Stiles continued with even greater vitu-
peration: "Let us boldly say, for History will say it, that the whole of this War
is so far chargeable to the Scotch Councils, and to the Scotch as a Nation (for
they have nationally come into it) as that had it not been for them, this Quarrel had never happened."[82]

Clearly, Witherspoon's continued allusion to Scots and Scottish precedent risked arousing charges of disloyalty to the new American union. Yet
Ezra Stiles misrepresented Witherspoon's political theology. Witherspoon's
support for American independence, as we have seen, did not require him to
eschew moral concern for those who resided outside America. Ironically, an
anonymous Scottish editor of his *Dominion of Providence* accused Witherspoon of having betrayed his previous Anglo-Scottish identity, offering a
further misrepresentation of the clergyman's viewpoint. Simply known as
"S. R.," the editor reproached Witherspoon for his role in unsettling Americans and encouraging them to revolt against Britain, particularly through his
"clerical influence." Though "not credited by many of his favourites in this
country [Scotland]," S. R. suggested that, by publishing Witherspoon's treatise, he would "fully justify the allegation, and silence the doctor's friends"
who denied his role in the "American revolt." He might well have associated
Witherspoon with pleas for American independence from the Kirk's Popular party. According to S. R., the reader "will easily perceive, that the doctor
[Witherspoon] not only exerts his utmost abilities to instigate the deluded

82. Stiles, *Literary Diary*, II, 184–185.

colonists to persevere in their rebellious courses, but labours to inflame their minds against the determinations of the British parliament." Though they came to diametrically opposed conclusions regarding the nature of his national identity, Stiles and S. R. both misconstrued Witherspoon's political theology, which supported American independence without lauding the sensibility of patriots and without abandoning all concern for the social and moral development of Britain.[83]

In his congressional speech on the conference proposed by Lord Howe, Witherspoon pointed out that his support for the formation of a new American confederation did not suggest that he was one "of those who either deny or conceal the depravity of human nature, till it is purified by the light of truth, and renewed by the Spirit of the living God." Thus, he underlined his unease with the claim that any political association could cohere—and progress—according to the innate moral benevolence of its constituents. Yet Witherspoon then contradicted his reasoning, demonstrating a surprising— and unusual—change in his tenor. He began by tempering his tone with a rhetorical question: "Shall we live without government, because every constitution has its old age, and its period?" After such a suggestion, Witherspoon would usually claim that inaction provided no answer to universal human sin—a common evangelical response to the charge of fatalism. In his speech, Witherspoon did indeed offer such a response. But having done so, he then echoed the stadial reasoning of the Moderate Kirk, begging "leave to say something more, though with some risk it will be thought visionary and romantic." Having only just pointed out that total human depravity precluded the notion of steady institutional progress within societies, he suggested that future Americans might witness an "order and perfection of human society, greater than we have yet seen: and why should we be wanting to ourselves in urging it forward"—particularly when "human science and religion" had "greatly assisted each other's progress in the world." As a Calvinist clergyman in the nascent U.S. Congress, Witherspoon likely feared that other delegates would assume his dour assessment of American political progress at a time when they looked for motivation against Britain. In this context, in order to outline a more positive stance, Witherspoon adopted a rare apologetic motif that suggested societal development rather than cyclical backsliding. Witherspoon might have put such progress down to divine providentialism rather than the heightened ethical sensibility of Americans.

83. Editorial comment to Witherspoon, *Dominion of Providence*, 2d ed., ii–iii. See also Sher, *Church and University*, 269–270.

But as he noted in his reference to problematic romanticism, he adopted a positive developmental vocabulary that was not common in his public statements. Still, Ezra Stiles continued to prickle at his references to Scotland.[84]

"Either to Be Roasted in Florida, or Frozen to Death in Canada"

Contrary to those who perceived a hint of betrayal in his appeal to the moral and commercial development of Britain, Witherspoon strongly distinguished his viewpoint from loyalists and neutrals such as William Smith, whether they were Scottish or otherwise. Having outlined the problematic association between innate ethical sensibility and patriot thought, he increasingly turned his attention to those who refrained from supporting American independence. In particular, he concentrated his ire on members of Philadelphia's literary and educational establishment, many of whom were associated with Smith's circle. In his "Humble Representation and Earnest Supplication of James Rivington" (1779), for example, Witherspoon wrote as James Rivington, a printer, "that no danger can arise from me, for I am as great a coward as King James the VIth of Scotland, who could never see a naked sword without trembling; having been, as it is said, frightened in his mother's belly." Rather than castigating Rivington for his pro-British stance, Witherspoon reserved special disdain for his propensity to change sides according to his perception of power relations.[85]

During the early Revolutionary era, Rivington had realized that, if the journal he published offered several political viewpoints, including a prominent loyalist voice, it could rely on British government patronage. Thus, Witherspoon had Rivington underscore his caprice even further:

> All the wisdom that I was ever possessed of is in me still, praised be God, and likely to be so. . . I have heard some people say that dishonor was worse than death, but with the great Sancho Pancha, I was always of a different opinion. I hope, therefore, your honors will consider my sufferings as sufficient to atone for my offences, and allow me to continue in peace and quiet, and according to the North British proverb, *sleep in a whole skin.*

84. Witherspoon, "Part of a Speech in Congress," in [Green, ed.], *Works of Witherspoon,* IV, 350.

85. Witherspoon, [on behalf of James Rivington], "Supplication of J. R********* . . . The Humble Representation and Earnest Supplication of J. R——, Printer and Bookseller in New York" (June 1779), ibid., 390.

Witherspoon compared Rivington with the quixotic character in Miguel de Cervantes's novel, the flighty and opportunistic servant Sancho Panza. As a fawning petitioner, indeed, Rivington had no desire "either to be roasted in Florida, or frozen to death in Canada or Nova Scotia." He implied that his printing profited from the continuing imperial crisis, rather than from its resolution through American independence. Thus, Rivington became more likely to support the British status quo, lest any new American government end the crisis and reduce his capacity to enjoy commercial gains and luxury.[86]

Witherspoon's satirical pamphlets were written and published in the months after the death of his son James at the Battle of Germantown. James died in a conflict that his father had described as mutual butchery a year earlier. Witherspoon continued to criticize those who privileged their common sensibility after the Declaration of Independence, whether patriots who sought to define the legitimacy of their cause through their innate morality or neutral printers who claimed to speak for common ideals that were shared by all conflicting parties. Incongruously, during the same year, London editors and reviewers of Witherspoon's *Dominion of Providence* provided the most accurate contemporary representation of his political theology. Attaching his own preface, the editor explained that Witherspoon's sermon, "first printed at *Philadelphia,* was, some time since, reprinted in *Scotland,* with *notes,* intended to guard the author's country-men against his political principles." He suggested that he, instead, sought to show "the great moral and religious instructions" that the sermon contained. Whatever "be the truth with regard to the present unhappy contest between Great Britain and America," the editor continued, "the discourse contains many admirable hints of advice, which, if properly regarded, will tend to the prosperity of both countries." Though the editor's portrayal of Witherspoon may seem rather too irenic for a clergyman who endeavored to motivate Americans on the battlefield, it touched on the underlying message of magnanimity in his early Revolutionary sermons and proclamations.[87]

In their role as British subjects, Scottish Presbyterian ministers affirmed their conditional support for the formation of an Anglo-Scottish union after 1707.

86. Ibid., 393, 388. On Rivington's capricious career as a printer, see Catherine Snell Crary, "The Tory and the Spy: The Double Life of James Rivington," *WMQ,* 3d Ser., XVI (1959), 61–72.

87. "Advertisement" (anonymous editorial comment), in John Witherspoon, *The Dominion of Providence over the Passions of Men; a Sermon, Preached at Princeton, May 17, 1775, Being the General Fast Appointed by the Congress through the United Colonies* (London, 1778), iii–iv. On various advertisements and reviews of the sermon in Britain, see also Collins, *President Witherspoon,* I, 227–230.

They were aware that their forebearers had confederated Scottish religious assemblies with English councils in order to expand the revivalist doctrines of the Westminster Confession of Faith. Under a Hanoverian monarchy, Witherspoon had contributed to the development of provincial evangelical identity in mainland Britain and in the American colonies. When the provincial freedoms that underlay that identity were threatened, he joined other American Presbyterians in opposition to Britain. Trying at first to maintain a confederal vision of the British Empire, with allegiance to the monarchy rather than Westminster, he eventually came to support the republican ideology of the most radical patriots. But, unlike a number of his co-religionists in the Middle Colonies, Witherspoon warned Revolutionaries against emphasizing their innate ethical sensibility as a means to justify their opposition to Britain and their eventual political coherence as independent citizens. Americans, he suggested, were justified in their struggle against Britain, not because their innate ethical stance was somehow more cultivated, nor because they enjoyed a public covenant with God. Rather, more Americans shared an awakened understanding of the sin that they shared with all individuals. Providentially, a greater proportion were predisposed to follow the action of the Holy Spirit with full conversion, allowing greater ethical humility as an external gift of grace and a means to create a more stable union of people. Thus, the former leader of the Popular party of the Kirk transferred the focus of his political theology to the moral character of the American Congress. Though deserving political autonomy, its constituents required the same humility as all other people—including British subjects. Any decline in their magnanimity would diminish the stability and even the political legitimacy of the new union whose independence he had helped to declare.[88]

88. On conditional Presbyterian support for Anglo-Scottish unionism after 1797, see Colin Kidd, "Conditional Britons: The Scots Covenanting Tradition and the Eighteenth-Century British State," *English Historical Review*, CXVII (2002), 1147–1176; Richard J. Finlay, "Keeping the Covenant: Scottish National Identity," in T. M. Devine and J. R. Young, eds., *Eighteenth Century Scotland: New Perspectives* (East Lothian, U.K., 1999), 122–134.

CHAPTER 7

"HOW FAR THE MAGISTRATE OUGHT TO INTERFERE IN MATTERS OF RELIGION"

Public Faith and the Ambiguity of Political

Representation after 1776

John Witherspoon's contribution to the developing American political land-scape as a congressional delegate raises the question of the relationship be-tween Presbyterian ecclesiology and political federalism. Yet it remains diffi-cult to find specific evidence of Scots or former Scots, including Witherspoon, who articulated their direct conceptual association. It is certainly possible to highlight theoretical parallels that might have allowed their greater under-standing of layered governance under the Articles of Confederation. The fed-eral theology of international Calvinism had always transcended local bound-aries without threatening the specific institutional identities of its constituent peoples, towns, and nations. Scottish Presbyterians, more particularly, incor-porated local congregational concerns in a wider ecclesiastical confederation. All degrees of authority corresponded to expanding geographical areas, each of which acted as a check to the other while still remaining part of a wider whole. Contrary to episcopacy, higher layers of Presbyterian governance did not correspond to a separate bishopric that exerted central authority from the top down. Rather, they were composed by representatives and figureheads whose power was vested in lay elders—and the laity itself.[1]

1. The general structure of Presbyterian ecclesiology conformed to the political institutions that had first shaped Reformed Protestantism in German, Swiss, and Dutch confederations. See Glenn A. Moots, *Politics Reformed: The Anglo-American Legacy of Covenant Theology* (Columbia, Mo., 2010), 178. The structure of Presbyterian representation incorporated a degree of federal authority through the General Assembly. But, whether they lived in Scotland or North America, Presbyterians had envisioned most aspects of their ecclesiology in looser confederal terms. They perceived a balance of representative power between laymen in specific congregations and the General Assembly. They generally refrained from defining the central authority of the assembly as innately superior in jurisdictional terms. Rather, it contributed to a balanced relationship be-

Some scholars argue that American politicians were directly influenced by Presbyterian notions of jurisdictional pluralism as they sought to reconcile the independence of various political, economic, and religious institutions with the need for a wider national union between states. Though this view on the American founding era is contentious, it is certain that different visions of governance were incorporated in numerous new state constitutions, each of which then had to cohere in a wider confederal union. In the Continental Congress, delegates argued whether a national body of government should have a role in the patronage of local religious institutions. Through the early 1780s, the Articles of Confederation expanded the constitutional and representative authority of the Continental Congress in order to provide military alliance and greater coordination in conflict with Britain. But its politicians and legal theorists remained uncertain about the precise nature of the relationship between state and central authority, or, indeed, the role of autonomous civil and religious institutions in either sphere. The impact of these debates on Witherspoon's role in the American Congress is thus pertinent but also problematic to assess.[2]

---

tween local and regional authority. See James H. Smylie, *A Brief History of the Presbyterians* (Louisville, Ky., 1996), 39–68.

2. On possible connections with Presbyterian theology, see Daniel J. Elazar and John Kincaid, eds., *The Covenant Connection: From Federal Theology to Modern Federalism* (Lanham, Md., 2000), 66–67; Donald S. Lutz, "From Covenant to Constitution in American Political Thought," *Publius: The Journal of Federalism,* X, no. 4 (Fall 1980), 102; Glenn A. Moots, "The Covenant Tradition of Federalism: The Pioneering Studies of Daniel J. Elazar," in Ann Ward and Lee Ward, eds., *The Ashgate Research Companion to Federalism* (Surrey, U.K., 2009), 391–412; Daniel J. Elazar, *Covenant and Commonwealth: From Christian Separation through the Protestant Reformation* (New Brunswick, N.J., 1996), II, 255–305. During the early modern era, European political thought loosely defined the confederal representative model as delegating a few jurisdictional powers to a central authority while devolving other forms of autonomy to semi-independent entities. For a general account of the continuation of confederal ideology during this period, see Alison L. LaCroix, *The Ideological Origins of American Federalism* (Cambridge, Mass., 2010), 126–136. On congressional debates and uncertainties over the role of national government in local and state religious institutions during the 1770s and 1780s, see Gordon S. Wood, *The Creation of the American Republic, 1776–1787* (Chapel Hill, N.C., 1969), 50–64; Donald S. Lutz, "The Articles of Confederation as the Background to the Federal Republic," *Publius: The Journal of Federalism,* XX, no. 1 (Winter 1990), 57; Daniel J. Elazar, "The Principles and Traditions Underlying State Constitutions," ibid., XII, no. 1 (Winter 1982), 12–14; John F. Wilson, "The Founding Era (1774–1797) and the Constitutional Provision for Religion," in Derek H. Davis, ed., *The Oxford Handbook of Church and State in the United States* (New York, 2010), 21–41; Robert M. Calhoon, "Religion, Moderation, and Regime-Building in Post-Revolutionary America," in Eliga H. Gould and Peter S. Onuf, eds., *Empire and Nation: The American Revolu-*

Evangelical Presbyterians had always been uncomfortable with Anglican (or any other denominational) establishments in the British Empire. Witherspoon believed that churches and universities were duty-bound to encourage religious regeneration among young men before they entered into civic assemblies—whether in Scotland, London, or farther afield in the British imperial world. Their ability to do so, he had always argued, was contingent on ecclesiastical independence from the political establishment of Westminster—including its patronage. Witherspoon had spent his Scottish career in opposition to the close association between Moderate churchmen and political representatives. In his 1758 sermon *The Charge of Sedition and Faction against Good Men,* he had warned that ministers should "take care to avoid officiously intermeddling in civil matters [and] . . . should be separated and set apart for his own work . . . consecrated to his office." Thus, it was "sinful and dangerous" for ordained ministers "to desire or claim the direction of such matters as fall within the province of the civil magistrate . . . [because] When our blessed Saviour says, 'My kingdom is not of this "world,"'" he plainly intimates to his disciples that they have no title to intermeddle with state affairs. Nay, he expressly warns them against a lordly and arbitrary dominion, even in their own proper sphere." Witherspoon could not "help mentioning here, that this is one of the things, for which our worthy ancestors of the church of Scotland (now despised by many) deserve the highest commendation." "It was an invariable principle with them," he wrote, "to be against the civil power and places of kirkmen."[3]

In 1785, Witherspoon's "Description of the State of New-Jersey" outlined the Protestant denominational freedom of his new state. Yet it also noted the domination of government by Presbyterians—English, Scottish, and Dutch—at the expense of Quakers and Episcopalians:

> There is no profession of religion which has an exclusive legal establishment. . . . All protestants are capable of electing and being elected, and indeed have every privilege belonging to citizens. There are in New Jersey, English presbyterians, Low Dutch presbyterians, episcopalians, baptists, quakers. The two first [Presbyterians], except the difference of

tion in the Atlantic World (Baltimore, 2005), 217–236; Barry Shain, "Religious Conscience and Original Sin: An Exploration of America's Protestant Foundations," in David Womersley, ed., *Liberty and American Experience in the Eighteenth Century* (Indianapolis, Ind., 2006), 161–186; Philip Hamburger, *Separation of Church and State* (Cambridge, Mass., 2002), 21–65.

3. John Witherspoon, *The Charge of Sedition and Faction against Good Men* . . . , in [Ashbel Green, ed.], *The Works of the Rev. John Witherspoon, D.D.L.L.D. Late President of the College at Princeton, New-Jersey* . . . , 2d ed., rev., 4 vols. (Philadelphia, 1802), II, 438–439.

the national connexion of the one with the church of Scotland, and the other with the church of Holland, and the language, are of the same principles as to doctrine. They have the same worship and government, and they are by far the most numerous.

Given his earlier experiences in Scotland and his subsequent assessment that New Jersey lacked an "exclusive legal establishment," it thus seems unlikely that Witherspoon would have supported the formal establishment of religion in the new American confederation. Yet he became the only clergyman to sign a national political declaration and then assume membership of several political assemblies. On the state and national level, he contributed to the growth and consolidation of America's political independence by opposing loyalists and neutrals, by continuing to educate statesmen, by writing about politics, commerce, and diplomacy, and by formulating religious declarations on behalf of the nascent American Congress. The previous discussion recounted Elias Boudinot's disdainful response to Witherspoon in the New Jersey provincial congress. According to the College of New Jersey trustee, Witherspoon's dual political and religious role alongside his students threatened to impose a new form of episcopacy—with a Presbyterian tinge—on independent Americans. Indeed, as Witherspoon himself noted in his "Description of the State of New-Jersey":

> There is a great majority of the present legislature of these two denominations [English, Scottish, and "Dutch" Presbyterians]. Formerly the quakers, though not the majority, had considerable influence; but since the late contest with Great-Britain, they are fewer in number, and altogether without power. The episcopalians are few. The baptists are presbyterians in all other respects, only differing in the point of infant baptism; their political weight goes the same way as the Presbyterians; [though] their number is small.

How, then, could Witherspoon define his duty as a clergyman in the worldly affairs of political governance?[4]

In the decade after the Declaration of Independence, the call for humility in Witherspoon's civic and fast day proclamations informed his congressional activities and political writings in many forums, including those that concerned America's nascent economic and diplomatic policy. Whether they

---

4. John Witherspoon, "A Description of the State of New-Jersey," ibid., IV, 406; Elias Boudinot, *Journal or Historical Recollections of American Events during the Revolutionary War* (Philadelphia, 1894), 5.

related to commercial strategy, foreign treaties, or moral affairs, his political activities and public statements questioned and redefined certain prevailing associations between innate ethical perception and representative authority in America. Notwithstanding the communal nature of congressional representation, Witherspoon challenged those politicians who claimed to embody the common moral sensibility of all citizens.

"I Believe He Would Send Them to the Devil If He Could"

On September 25, 1776, a commencement ceremony was held privately for the first time under John Witherspoon's tenure as president of the College of New Jersey. The college board of trustees decided on closing the doors to the public owing to the difficult circumstances of the imperial crisis. Witherspoon presided at the ceremony after traveling from Philadelphia, where he had been in Congress since late June. He remained in Princeton village during October and the beginning of November, leaving as news of advancing British troops made it to campus. Witherspoon recalled carrying few possessions as he fled the town on his "sorrel mare." On December 7, 1776, a British brigade in Princeton placed Nassau Hall, the College of New Jersey's administrative center, under occupation as a barracks and stable. Several weeks later, they were joined by Hessian soldiers. All forces remained in the village until January 3, 1777, when the Battle of Princeton took place. The previous night, George Washington led a successful counteroffensive against the British in Trenton, New Jersey. The British soldiers in Princeton remained in place and did not join in the nearby skirmish. On January 3, Washington moved several of his brigades on his way to free the garrison at Princeton from British control. Brigadier General Hugh Mercer led a relatively small group of men against two regiments under British command. In a desperate situation, Mercer and his men were overrun, requiring further assistance from patriot militia. Noting the dire situation of Mercer's fleeing forces, much of the militia made a bid to turn in their tracks. While doing so, however, Washington arrived with further assistance and galvanized them to remain in an advancing battle against the British regiments. In Princeton village, despite the retreat of many British soldiers into the backcountry and beyond, a number of redcoats continued sheltering in Nassau Hall until they were forced to surrender. After yet another defeat in the region, the British moved out of southern New Jersey.[5]

5. On the trustees' decision to hold a private ceremony, see [William Armstrong Dod], *History of the College of New Jersey, from Its Commencement, A.D., 1746, to 1783* (Princeton, N.J.,

Sergeant Thomas Sullivan of the British Forty-ninth regiment of Foot described the activities that had taken place in the college as the war had moved from Trenton, toward the outskirts of the village, and eventually to its administrative headquarters: "Our army when we lay there spoiled and plundered a good Library that was in it." Indeed, many of Witherspoon's works were burned during the last hours of the battle. Several histories of the Battle of Princeton suggest that British forces vandalized the college buildings deliberately, including Witherspoon's library and papers. In a letter to Thomas Jefferson, Thomas Nelson wrote:

> There is Scarcely a Virgin to be found in the part of the Country that they have pass'd thro' and yet the Jersies will not turn out. Rapes, Rapine, and Murder are not sufficient to rouse the resentment of these People. If they be not sufficient provocations I dispair of any thing working them up to opposition. . . . Old Weatherspoon has not escap'd their fury. They have burnt his Library. It grieves him much that he has lost his controversial Tracts. He would lay aside the Cloth to take revenge of them. I believe he would send them to the Devil if he could, I am sure I would.[6]

Those who had remained in the village during late December and early January faced great peril. Two students, Guy and Paul Rupert, would even lose their lives. Witherspoon had avoided the bloody aftermath of Princeton's occupation and had chosen not to return to a semideserted Princeton village, but he visited the College of New Jersey on his way from Baltimore to Philadelphia in May 1777. Despite his proposing its reopening, the college buildings remained a military post under the control of the American army until June 1777. The college did reopen the following month, and Witherspoon visited again in August, temporarily pausing his congressional attendance. He soon heard of the death of his son James, killed at the Battle of Germantown on October 4, 1777. We have no evidence of his private or public reaction to that loss.[7]

1844), 47. On Witherspoon's abrupt departure, see Varnum Lansing Collins, *President Witherspoon: A Biography,* 2 vols. (Princeton, N.J., 1925), II, 89–92. On Witherspoon's use of a "sorrel mare" to move away, see John Witherspoon to David Witherspoon, Jan. 8, 1777, in Paul H. Smith et al., eds., *Letters of Delegates to Congress, 1774–1789,* 26 vols. (Washington, D.C., 1976–2000), VI, 63.

6. Thomas Sullivan, "The Battle of Princeton" (January 1777), *Pennsylvania Magazine of History and Biography,* XXXII (1908), 54; Thomas Nelson to Thomas Jefferson, Jan. 2, 1777, in Julian P. Boyd et al., eds., *The Papers of Thomas Jefferson,* II (Princeton, N.J., 1950), 3–4.

7. On the death of the students and the college's eventual reopening, see Harrison, *Prince-*

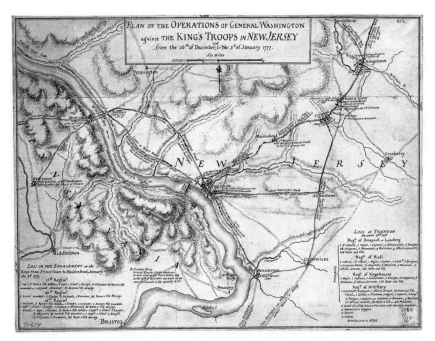

FIGURE 17. *Plan of the Operations of General Washington against the King's Troops in New Jersey from the 26th of December 1776 to the 3d of January 1777.* Courtesy, Library of Congress Geography and Map Division, Washington, D.C.

From winter 1777 to 1779, as the college was rebuilt, never more than ten undergraduates were in attendance. They often used Witherspoon's private home as a classroom. In a September 1778 letter to Scotland, which was never sent, Witherspoon surveyed the sudden disintegration of the British Empire, which had brought the destruction of his library, the death of Guy and Paul Rupert, and the loss of his son: "I look upon the separation of America from Britain to be the visible intention of Providence . . . perhaps to the advantage of both." Witherspoon had lost a son in battle, killed by a British cannon ball. Yet he continued to seek the "advantage of both" nations.[8]

---

tonians, xiii; Collins, *President Witherspoon,* II, 91–99. For the events in the college during the aftermath, see also Witherspoon, "A Description of the State of New-Jersey," in [Green, ed.], *Works of Witherspoon,* IV, 403–412. For the little we know about the death of Witherspoon's son James, see Collins, *President Witherspoon,* II, 31.

8. John Witherspoon, "On the Contest between Great Britain and America" (Sept. 2, 1778), in [Green, ed.], *Works of Witherspoon,* IV, 376. For events in the college through 1779, see Collins, *President Witherspoon,* II, 99–100.

FIGURE 18. *The Death of General Mercer at the Battle of Princeton, January 3, 1777.* By John Trumbull. Circa 1789–circa 1831. Oil on canvas, 51.1 x 75.9 cm. (20⅛ x 29⅞ in.). Trumbull Collection, 1832.6.1. Yale University Art Gallery, New Haven, Connecticut, U.S.A. Yale University Art Gallery / Art Resource, N.Y.

From his New England vantage point, Ezra Stiles detected an element of political ambiguity in Witherspoon's desire to address and seek the advantage of British subjects on both sides of the Atlantic. Presbyterian civic engagement in the former Middle Colonies was certainly complex, particularly in Pennsylvania and New Jersey. Witherspoon lived close to men who switched political affiliations on multiple occasions, including his former congressional associate Richard Stockton.[9]

But, rather than noting the caprice of Presbyterian politicians, or even their potential loyalism, it is more likely that Stiles and other non-Presbyterians

9. Ezra Stiles, *The Literary Diary of Ezra Stiles,* ed. Franklin Bowditch Dexter, 3 vols. (New York, 1901), II, 185. For an account of defections and the relations of Middle Colonists with the British forces at this time, see Ira D. Gruber, "Lord Howe and Lord George Germain, British Politics and the Winning of American Independence," *William and Mary Quarterly,* 3d Ser., XXII (1965), 225–243. On Presbyterian loyalism in the Middle Colonies, see Joseph S. Tiedemann, "Presbyterianism and the American Revolution in the Middle Colonies," *Church History,* LXXIV (2005), 339–343; Timothy M. Barnes and Robert M. Calhoon, "Moral Allegiance: John Witherspoon and Loyalist Recantation," *American Presbyterians,* LXIII (1985), 277–278.

FIGURE 19. *Battle of Germantown. Attack on Judge Chew's House.*
Circa 1783–circa 1870. Print Collection, Miriam and Ira D. Wallach Division,
the New York Public Library. The New York Public Library / Art Resource, N.Y.

tacitly feared their growing civic engagement. In neighboring Pennsylvania,
for example, patriot circles were often dominated by Presbyterians. By 1779,
they made up close to 44 percent of the Philadelphia legislature. Most, if
not all, openly supported the patriot cause. Looking back over the previous
decade, Benjamin Franklin wrote to a friend in 1784: "It is a fact, that the
Irish emigrants and their children are now in possession of the government
of Pennsylvania, by their majority in the assembly, as well as of a great part
of the territory; and I remember well the first ship that brought any of them
over." More cynical Quakers, Anglicans, and even Congregationalists feared
that Presbyterian opposition to British policy was a mere pretext to asserting and strengthening the public voice of Presbyterians relative to other dissenters. Indeed, Professor James Cannon, an evangelical Presbyterian born

in Edinburgh, assisted by George Bryan, another prominent Presbyterian, provided much material for the phrasing of the Pennsylvania Constitution.[10]

Scholars have suggested that Cannon and many of the framers of the Pennsylvania Constitution emphasized corporate identity over individual rights in matters not involving conscience. They have traditionally described the right to religious conscience in the Pennsylvania Constitution (and in other state constitutions) as one of several inalienable privileges, including freedom of movement, ownership of property and habeas corpus. Yet, of all the various natural rights that were defined during the founding era, the sanctity of religious conscience came to be perceived as the only implicitly guaranteed individual right with respect to the communal norms of any state. It enjoyed an incomparable status in Pennsylvania because it was the only individual right that could not be surrendered or transferred as an individual moved from a state of nature to one of civil society. All other individual rights were viewed as negotiable and potentially subject to corporate oversight and restrictions. A similar distinction between religious and corporate authority could be found in the state constitutions of New Jersey, Delaware, Maryland, New Hampshire, and several other new states.[11]

In light of the strong Presbyterian involvement in the Pennsylvania Constitution, it is worth considering the possible correspondence between the Westminster Confession of Faith and the privileged status of individual religious conscience over other corporate prerogatives. Though the Westminster Confession that was distributed among Americans at this time included some corporate oversight for the church, it was at least relatively radical in suggest-

10. Benjamin Franklin to William Strahan, Aug. 19, 1784, in *Memoirs of Benjamin Franklin . . .* (Philadelphia, 1840), I, 582. On Presbyterian civic statistics and Franklin's statement, see Howard Miller, "The Grammar of Liberty: Presbyterians and the First American Constitutions," *Journal of Presbyterian History*, LIV (1976), 151–152. On the Presbyterian contribution to the framing of the Pennsylvania Constitution, see Burton Alva Konkle, *George Bryan and the Constitution of Pennsylvania, 1731–1791* (Philadelphia, 1922), 136; Alexander Graydon, *Memoirs of His Own Time, with Reminiscences of the Men and Events of the Revolution*, ed. John S. Littell (Philadelphia, 1846), 285–286. For more on Presbyterian tensions and alliances with other denominations, see Tiedemann, "Presbyterianism and the American Revolution," *Church History*, LXXIV (2005), 331; Melvin H. Buxbaum, *Benjamin Franklin and the Zealous Presbyterians* (University Park, Pa., 1975), 160–163, 211; Joseph S. Foster, *In Pursuit of Equal Liberty: George Bryan and the Revolution in Pennsylvania* (University Park, Pa., 1994), 35–57; Patricia U. Bonomi, *Under the Cope of Heaven: Religion, Society, and Politics in Colonial America* (New York, 1986), 168–171.

11. Shain, "Religious Conscience and Original Sin," in Womersley, ed., *Liberty and American Experience*, 171–172.

ing that the "civil magistrate may not assume to himself the administration of the word and sacraments, or the power of the keys of the kingdom of heaven." We can compare this statement with the religious clauses of the 1776 Pennsylvania Constitution, which read that "no authority can or ought to be vested in, or assumed by any power whatever, that shall in any case interfere with, or in any manner controul, the right of conscience in the free exercise of religious worship." The authors of both statements opposed any communal civic institution that might interfere with voluntary religious associations and described personal religious conscience as vital. According to both documents, any communal establishment of religion risked undermining the primacy of the personal duty to God, reducing its sanctity as an individual right. To be sure, the Pennsylvania Constitution was at this point still rather more radical than the Confession, which, as we shall see, would only achieve greater parity following its revision in a Pennsylvania Presbyterian meeting more than a decade later, when most remaining corporate oversight clauses were removed.[12]

Witherspoon, though he became a politician representing New Jersey rather than Pennsylvania, subscribed to the same version of the Westminster Confession of Faith that was at least wary of corporate oversight of religious conscience. The comparisons above are therefore pertinent for assessing his contribution to political and constitutional deliberations on the state and congressional level. Given his evangelicalism and his experience opposing the Moderate establishment in the Kirk, it would be reasonable to assume that Witherspoon followed his Philadelphia counterparts in asserting the supremacy of individual religious conscience over worldly civic authority. During the same period, however, he began to issue religious statements and civic proclamations on behalf of the new American Congress in a political career that ran parallel to his continuing duties as college president. Unsurprisingly, as the only clergyman to sign the Declaration of Independence,

12. For the civil magistrate clause in the Westminster Confession of Faith in use during the 1770s, see *The Confession of Faith; the Larger and Shorter Catechisms, with the Scripture-Proofs at Large; Together with the Sum of Saving Knowledge* . . . (Glasgow, 1765), 135. For the religion clause in the Pennsylvania Constitution, see Conrad Henry Moehlman, ed., *The American Constitutions and Religion: Religious References in the Charters of the Thirteen Colonies and the Constitutions of the Forty-Eight States: A Source-Book on Church and State in the United States* (Clark, N.J., 2007), 51. For a comparison between the inherited 1647 version and the later revised American version of the Westminster Confession, see Nicholas P. Miller, *The Religious Roots of the First Amendment: Dissenting Protestants and the Separation of Church and State* (New York, 2012), 149–151. See also Shain, "Religious Conscience and Original Sin," in Womersley, ed., *Liberty and American Experience*, 172 n. 51.

he was often asked to draft the text of congressional fast day proclamations. Most followed victory—or perceived victory—in battle against Britain. In them, he sought to encourage individual Christian humility. Yet he was required to do so from a public civic platform.[13]

Witherspoon negotiated a delicate constitutional balance between the notion of corporate piety and the primacy of personal religious conscience during his five years in Congress, which he served between June 21, 1776, and November 5, 1782. He was reelected every year in November, except for the year between November 1779 and November 1780, when he chose to devote more time to his duties as college president. After 1783, he continued to engage in political debate from outside Congress.

Despite the prevalence of religious acts and religious language in the early Congress, clergymen such as Witherspoon were not unanimously thought to have a legitimate role in political service. From as early as 1775, founders such as John Adams complained that clergymen in political life mixed the sacred and secular worlds in problematic ways and that their experience of civil affairs made them likely to seek the benefit of their churches rather than the wider community. Ironically, their reasoning was similar to that which Witherspoon had once used against educated Moderate churchmen. In the decade after the Declaration of Independence, moreover, seven states disqualified ministers from serving in public office, often with support from prominent figures such as Thomas Jefferson—even as they passed laws securing the rights of independent religious denominations.[14]

In such a context, Witherspoon was understandably wary of the implication that he was part of a civic religious establishment or that he generated moral edicts from the top downward. Interestingly, founders in his close circle, such as Benjamin Rush and James Madison, were less keen to bar ministers from sitting as political representatives, even though they, too, advocated the disestablishment of religion. In any case, Witherspoon sought to define his entry into Congress as service from a private citizen, rather than as a means to benefit his ministerial vocation. More broadly, he used his various public fast day proclamations between 1776 and 1786 to outline the complex association between representative leadership and universal sin. In

13. On the origins and background of these first declarations, see Derek H. Davis, *Religion and the Continental Congress, 1774–1789: Contributions to Original Intent* (New York, 2000), 76–80.

14. On the discussion of John Adams's reservations regarding ministers in Congress, and on the disqualification of ministers in several new states, see Davis, *Religion and the Continental Congress,* 69.

doing so, moreover, he attempted to define the constitutional importance of independent and disestablished religious societies for civic virtue.[15]

The first recorded fast days of the imperial crisis had appeared in the Massachusetts towns of Boston, Braintree, Charleston, and Lexington in September 1768. In 1774, under pressure from Virginian Presbyterians and Baptists, Thomas Jefferson recorded that he shared the desire of Virginians such as Patrick Henry and Richard Henry Lee to "take an unequivocal stand in the line with Massachusetts, determined to meet and consult on the proper measures, in the council chamber, for the benefit of the library in that room" in order to appoint a day of fasting and prayer. Thus, having "rummaged over for the revolutionary precedents and forms of the Puritans of that day [the era of the French and Indian War in 1755]," Jefferson recalled having "cooked up a resolution, somewhat modernizing their phrases, for appointing the 1st day of June . . . for a day of fasting." Jefferson described the fasts as necessary to rouse the minds of the people of the colony into concerted action. Inspired by their perceived success, Jefferson and other political delegates subsequently agreed that the Confederate Congress should issue similar national fast day proclamations.[16]

Jefferson's observations gave credence to the anthropocentric assumption that moral actions could somehow preempt political or military success, that religious fasts were a means to affect the minds of a newly independent people and to unify them in civic and martial terms. Notwithstanding Jefferson's desire to shock Americans into action, Witherspoon defined the civic importance of fast day proclamations in rather different terms. As an evangelical minister, he was less likely to describe religious edicts as a convenient means to spur communities toward successful political activity. According to Witherspoon, conversely, fast day declarations became disadvantageous if used solely to alarm people during times of national suffering or jeopardy. If their primary goal were to inspire united political activity, they would lead to "such distraction of mind [away from Scripture] as is little favourable to the practice of piety." The "public service" of war and national unity had too "many times" been used "to justify what would otherwise have been highly improper."[17]

15. On Rush's disdain for barring ministers from office, see ibid., 69–70.

16. Thomas Jefferson Randolph, ed., *Memoir, Correspondence, and Miscellanies from the Papers of Thomas Jefferson* (Charlottesville, Va., 1829), I, 5–6. On the background to Jefferson's statements and the previous New England fast days, see Davis, *Religion and the Continental Congress*, 84; Samuel A. Bates, ed., *Records of the Town of Braintree, 1640–1793* (Randolph, Mass., 1886), 421.

17. John Witherspoon, "Delivered at a Public Thanksgiving after Peace: Sermon 45" (Nov.

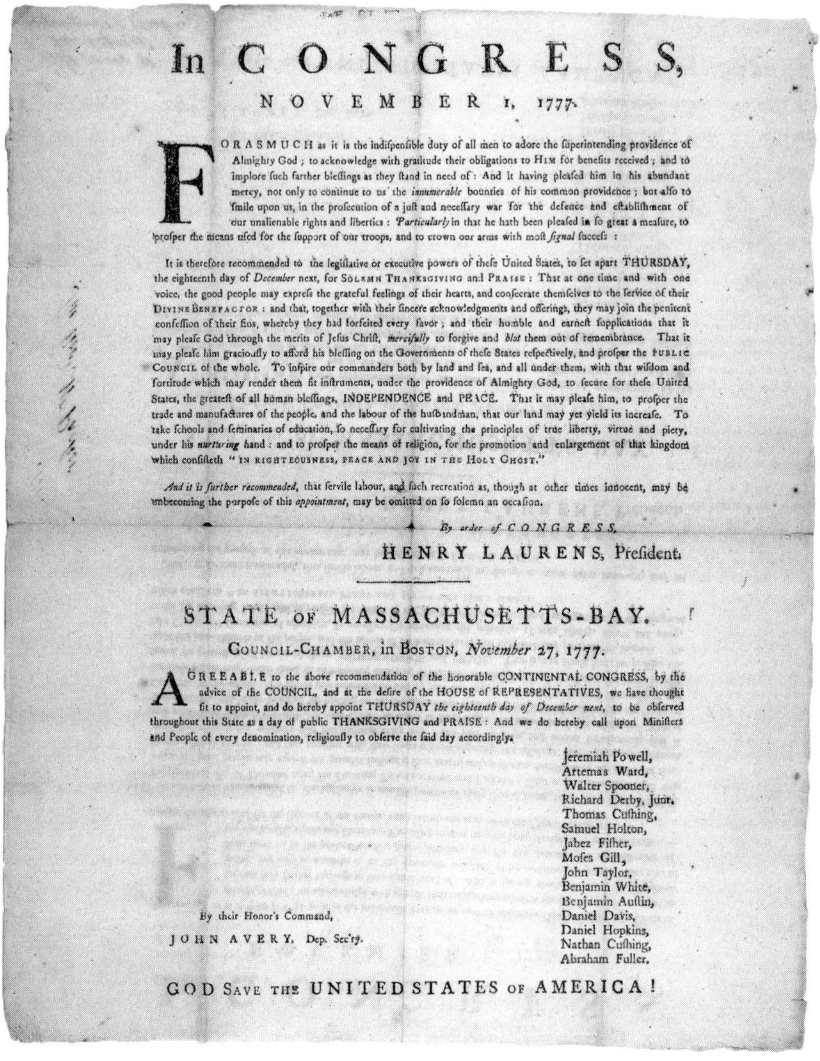

In CONGRESS,

NOVEMBER 1, 1777.

FORASMUCH as it is the indispensible duty of all men to adore the superintending providence of Almighty God; to acknowledge with gratitude their obligations to HIM for benefits received; and to implore such farther blessings as they stand in need of: And it having pleased him in his abundant mercy, not only to continue to us the *innumerable* bounties of his common providence; but also to smile upon us, in the prosecution of a just and necessary war for the defence and establishment of our unalienable rights and liberties: *Particularly* in that he hath been pleased in so great a measure, to prosper the means used for the support of our troops, and to crown our arms with most *signal* success:

It is therefore recommended to the legislative or executive powers of these United States, to set apart THURSDAY, the eighteenth day of *December* next, for SOLEMN THANKSGIVING and PRAISE: That at one time and with one voice, the good people may express the grateful feelings of their hearts, and consecrate themselves to the service of their DIVINE BENEFACTOR: and that, together with their sincere acknowledgments and offerings, they may join the penitent confession of their sins, whereby they had forfeited every favor; and their humble and earnest supplications that it may please God through the merits of Jesus Christ, *mercifully* to forgive and *blot* them out of remembrance. That it may please him graciously to afford his blessing on the Governments of these States respectively, and prosper the PUBLIC COUNCIL of the whole. To inspire our commanders both by land and sea, and all under them, with that wisdom and fortitude which may render them fit instruments, under the providence of Almighty God, to secure for these United States, the greatest of all human blessings, INDEPENDENCE and PEACE. That it may please him, to prosper the trade and manufactures of the people, and the labour of the husbandman, that our land may yet yield its increase. To take schools and seminaries of education, so necessary for cultivating the principles of true liberty, virtue and piety, under his *nurturing* hand: and to prosper the means of religion, for the promotion and enlargement of that kingdom which consisteth "IN RIGHTEOUSNESS, PEACE AND JOY IN THE HOLY GHOST."

And it is further recommended, that servile labour, and such recreation as, though at other times innocent, may be unbecoming the purpose of this *appointment,* may be omitted on so solemn an occasion.

By order of CONGRESS,

HENRY LAURENS, President.

STATE OF MASSACHUSETTS-BAY.

COUNCIL-CHAMBER, in BOSTON, *November* 27, 1777.

AGREEABLE to the above recommendation of the honorable CONTINENTAL CONGRESS, by the advice of the COUNCIL, and at the desire of the HOUSE of REPRESENTATIVES, we have thought fit to appoint, and do hereby appoint THURSDAY *the eighteenth day of December next,* to be observed throughout this State as a day of public THANKSGIVING and PRAISE: And we do hereby call upon Ministers and People of every denomination, religiously to observe the said day accordingly.

Jeremiah Powell,
Artemas Ward,
Walter Spooner,
Richard Derby, Junr.
Thomas Cushing,
Samuel Holton,
Jabez Fisher,
Moses Gill,
John Taylor,
Benjamin White,
Benjamin Austin,
Daniel Davis,
Daniel Hopkins,
Nathan Cushing,
Abraham Fuller.

By their Honor's Command,

JOHN AVERY, Dep. Sec'ry.

GOD SAVE THE UNITED STATES OF AMERICA!

FIGURE 20. "In Congress, November 1, 1777. Forasmuch as it is the indispensible duty of all men to adore the superintending providence of Almighty God, to acknowledge with gratitude their obligations to Him for benefits received . . ." (Boston, 1777). Ephemera Collection, portfolio 40, folder 14, Library of Congress, Washington, D.C.

Witherspoon's fast day statements tended to focus on the role of the heart in moral regeneration, rather than the cultivation of political identity in rational minds. This inclination was demonstrated in an early congressional proclamation that was released on March 16, 1776, the sole authorship of which has often been linked, possibly erroneously, to William Livingstone. Before he became the governor of New Jersey in October, Livingstone had worked alongside Witherspoon as a New Jersey member of the Continental Congress and on the New Jersey Committee of Correspondence. It is not unlikely that Witherspoon had a role in drafting the text with Livingstone. The proclamation urged colonists, "with united hearts," to "confess and bewail" their "manifold sins and transgressions . . . and by inclining their hearts to justice and benevolence, prevent the further effusion of kindred blood." The meaning of the phrase "kindred blood" was ambiguous. It might have referred solely to the health and safety of American patriots. Yet it is more likely that it referred to patriots and redcoats alike. This part of the proclamation was similar in language and tone to Witherspoon's *Dominion of Providence*, which he authored two months later. In this sermon, Witherspoon called for peaceful independence after making the arresting observation that those who were "the same in blood" nonetheless butchered one another. As distinct from the rational language that Jefferson deployed, the fast day congressional proclamation described unity between confessing "hearts."[18]

The religious tone of the 1776 proclamation differed from the allusion to divine blessing in statements by several other early congressional delegates. In the same year, for example, colonial governor Jonathan Trumbull wrote to George Washington and incorporated Old Testament imagery to suggest that the American army enjoyed a special relationship with God, providing its leaders with moral distinction. Some Protestant ministers, such as Cyprian Strong and John Murray, used similar reasoning in the decade following the Declaration of Independence, expanding the corporate covenants of New England to envision America as a new nation with a special blessing. Yet other clergymen, including those associated with the New Divinity movement, questioned the moral veracity of regional and public covenants while maintaining their support for American independence. Though most New Divinity theologians, such as Samuel Hopkins and Joseph Bellamy, were

28, 1782) (hereafter cited as "Thanksgiving Sermon"), in [Green, ed.], *Works of Witherspoon*, III, 80.

18. See "Congressional Declaration, March 16, 1776," in Worthington Chauncey Ford et al., eds., *Journals of the Continental Congress, 1774–1789*, 34 vols. (Washington, D.C., 1904–1937), IV, 209 (hereafter cited as *JCC*).

Congregationalists rather than Presbyterians, Witherspoon shared important aspects of their political theology. In all the congressional proclamations and sermons he delivered between 1776 and 1783, he avoided specifying a particular public or corporate covenant between God and the American people. Instead, he used them to remind citizens of the inborn sin that they shared with those within and without their political union. In doing so, he reflected his still-prevailing evangelical identity. His December 11, 1776, fast day proclamation, for example, asked new states "to implore of Almighty God the forgiveness of the many sins prevailing among all ranks" even while they fought a "just and necessary war." It "recommend[ed] to all the members of the United States, and particularly the officers civil and military under them, the exercise of repentance and reformation."[19]

The dominance of moral introspection over religious triumphalism was germane to the unsettled political context in which Witherspoon drafted his first proclamations. The notion of a corporate blessing risked being perceived as hollow and hubristic at a time when Americans were not seen to enjoy any particular divine favor in their conflict with Britain. In the month following Witherspoon's December 1776 proclamation, after all, Americans were engaged in bloody military battles across New York and New Jersey. Notwithstanding his support for the war effort, on July 15, 1777, Witherspoon petitioned a "Memorial" to the Congressional Board of War requesting that American troops refrain from using the campus as barracks, thereby allowing teaching to resume in the college.[20]

Witherspoon continued to move between Philadelphia and the College of New Jersey, balancing his collegiate and congressional duties. By the time he joined the Congressional Board of War in late 1777, the British general John Burgoyne had surrendered near Saratoga Springs. In a January 8, 1778, congressional speech, addressing "the Convention with General Burgoyne," Witherspoon implored Congress to "detest the thoughts of embracing any measure which shall but appear to be mean, captious, or insidious, whatever

19. Fast day proclamation of Dec. 11, 1776, *JCC*, VI, 1022. On Trumbull's reasoning, see Davis, *Religion and the Continental Congress*, 88. On the questioning of public covenanting discourse by New Divinity theologians, see, for example, Christopher Grasso, *A Speaking Aristocracy: Transforming Public Discourse in Eighteenth-Century Connecticut* (Chapel Hill, N.C., 1999), 71–73; Jonathan D. Sassi, *A Republic of Righteousness: The Public Christianity of the Post-Revolutionary New England Clergy* (New York, 2001), 41–42. Sassi does note certain instances of public covenanting discourse that also remained.

20. For Witherspoon's July 1777 Memorial, see Collins, *President Witherspoon*, II, 84, 97–98.

advantage may seem to arise from it" while also making sure that the American "public suffer no injury by deception, or abuse and insult" from enemies who feigned surrender. During the same year, Witherspoon assumed the chairmanship of a committee on suspected British mistreatment of American prisoners. The closing paragraph of the committee's manifesto might have been drafted by Witherspoon in his capacity as chairman of the commission and its only clerical member. The statement claimed that, "while the shadow of hope remained that our enemies could be taught by our example . . . to comply with the dictates of a religion which they pretend in common with us to believe and revere," it had become unfortunately clear that further armed response was necessary.[21]

Thus, Witherspoon tended to avoid vituperative condemnation or words of revenge even as he contributed to a congressional investigation on British misbehavior during the war. While trawling through congressional accounts of British and Hessian misdemeanors in Germantown, Pennsylvania, he might well have been forced to audit his own son's death. Yet, after the intense battles of 1776 and 1777, it is difficult to discern any change in tone in Witherspoon's public voice. Uneasy defining an innate moral distinction between warring parties, yet strongly supporting American independence, Witherspoon avoided much editorial judgment in his account of British war atrocities, particularly any notion that British misdemeanors reflected the greater intrinsic immorality of redcoats. One partial exception can be found in a section of the congressional manifesto he helped to draft, which was sent to Scotland and printed in the *Scots Magazine,* ostensibly under the name of Congressional Secretary Charles Thomson. According to the manifesto:

> The Congress considering themselves bound to love their enemies, as children of that Being who is equally the Father of All; and desirous, since they could not prevent, at least to alleviate the calamities of war, have studied to spare those who were in arms against them, and to lighten the chains of captivity.
>
> The conduct of those serving under the king of Great Britain hath, with some few exceptions, been diametrically opposite. They have laid waste the open country, burned the defenceless villages, and butchered the citizens of America.
>
> Their prisons have been the slaughter-houses of her soldiers, their

21. John Witherspoon, "Speech in Congress, on the Convention with General Burgoyne," in [Green, ed.], *Works of Witherspoon,* IV, 325, 329; Congressional Manifesto, Oct. 30, 1778, *JCC,* XII, 1082.

ships of her seamen; the severest injuries have been aggravated by the grossest insults.

The manifesto even suggested that the British had "made a mock of religion by impious appeals to God, whilst in the violation of his sacred commands." At the end of 1779, after completing his reports for the Board of War, Witherspoon left Congress, not expecting to return, in order to devote his attention more fully to his educational duties. But, despite retirement, as the war continued and as Congress called for public fast days to demonstrate the humility of American forces, Witherspoon would return to Philadelphia in just under a year, in November 1780.[22]

Witherspoon continued his presidential and teaching duties in the College of New Jersey as best he could, composing fast day proclamations in Princeton village and sending them to Philadelphia. By this time, proclamations were often followed by thanksgiving declarations. On October 26, 1781, for example, the day after the British surrender at Yorktown, Witherspoon asked for "all ranks to observe and thankfully acknowledge the interpositions of his Providence in their behalf." His proclamation continued:

> Through the whole of the contest, from its first rise to this time, the influence of divine Providence may be clearly perceived in many signal instances, of which we mention but a few.
>
> In revealing the councils of our enemies, when the discoveries were seasonable and important, and the means seemingly inadequate or fortuitous; in preserving and even improving the union of the several states, on the breach of which our enemies placed their greatest dependence; in increasing the number, and adding to the zeal and attachment of the friends of Liberty.

The proclamation further recommended that December 13 "be religiously observed as a Day of Thanksgiving and Prayer."[23]

Without further elucidation, Witherspoon's reference to the interposition of providence on behalf of Americans might have suggested their special relationship with the merciful hand of God, even their special covenant. Yet, a year later, Witherspoon clarified his understanding of the role of provi-

22. Congressional Manifesto, Oct. 30, 1778, *JCC*, XII, 1081; "America: By the Congress of the United States, Manifesto," *Scots Magazine* (Edinburgh), XL (December 1778), 654. On Witherspoon's decision to leave Congress in 1778, see John Witherspoon, "On the Affairs of the United States" (Mar. 20, 1780), in [Green, ed.], *Works of Witherspoon*, IV, 380.

23. Thanksgiving proclamation, Oct. 26, 1781, *JCC*, XXI, 1074–1076.

dentialism in the Revolutionary War, demonstrating its congruence with the statements on magnanimity and universal sin that he had delivered before signing the Declaration of Independence. On October 11, 1782, at Witherspoon's behest, Congress published a proclamation to suggest that a fast day of thanksgiving be observed on Thursday, November 28, 1782, to underline "the practice of true and undefiled religion, which is the great foundation of public prosperity and national happiness." In the sermon he gave to accompany the occasion, Witherspoon outlined instances of chaos, near defeat, and capricious success in order to demonstrate that external providence, rather than the relative morality or superior sensibility of Americans, had brought about victory against Britain. Witherspoon acknowledged that, although he usually did not wish to "intermix politics with the ordinary service of the sanctuary, on the weekly returns of the christian sabbath, further than fervent supplications to the Throne of Grace for divine direction to the public counsels, and assistance to those who are employed in the public service," on days "of this kind" it became "part of a minister's duty to direct the attention of the hearers to events of a public nature." "This you know I did with great concern and at considerable length six years ago on a public Fast Day. I would therefore willingly in this more advanced period, take a view of what is past, and endeavor to direct you in what remains, of your duty to God, to your country, and to yourselves." [24]

Witherspoon organized the structure of his 1782 thanksgiving statement as a response to the scriptural precept that "Salvation belongeth unto the Lord," which was found in Psalms 3:8. He directed Americans to their "duty to God" through "the assistance of divine grace" in order to "lay before" them a "succinct view of what the United States of America owe to Divine Providence in the course of the present war." The events that had presaged peace and political independence, Witherspoon claimed, could be understood only according to the role of providence, as outlined in biblical writings such as the Psalm that he presently discussed. American successes during the American Revolutionary War could not be attributed to concerted human action nor innate moral understanding. Rather, they were to be "distinguished from human or created help, and therefore all confidence in man stands opposed to the sentiment expressed by the holy Psalmist in the text." "It is not op-

24. Thanksgiving proclamation, Oct. 11, 1782, *JCC*, XXIII, 647; Witherspoon, "Thanksgiving Sermon," in [Green, ed.], *Works of John Witherspoon*, III, 62. Some scholars argue that the sermon was delivered only on Apr. 19, 1783. Morrison has convincingly discounted that claim. See Jeffry H. Morrison, *John Witherspoon and the Founding of the American Republic* (Notre Dame, Ind., 2005), 184.

posed to the use or application of, but to an excessive or undue reliance on human means, or second causes of any kind."[25]

The continued success of American political independence could be understood only "by adhering strictly to what appears to be the mind of the spirit of God, in the passage before us" because continuity of divine law through revealed scripture made "religion . . . the same in substance in every age." Thus, "the reflections of pious persons in the course of providence" in events that led to the consolidation of American independence arose "from the same examples, and lead to the same end." In light of the continued revelation of scripture, "success in any attempt" was "to be ultimately attributed to God." "That it is he who by his providence provides outward means, who raises up friends to his people, or causes *their enemies to be at peace with them. That it is he who in cases of difficulty and danger, directs their hands to war and their fingers to fight.*" If anything, Witherspoon argued, the unpredictable events of the previous decade had served only to "confound" the common perceptions of men (whether British or American) at any one point in time:

> If any person desires to have his faith in this truth, confirmed or improved, let him read the history of mankind. . . . He will then perceive that every page will add to his conviction. He will find that the most important events have seemed to turn upon circumstances the most trivial and the most out of the reach of the human direction. A blast of wind, a shower of rain, a random shot, a private quarrel, the neglect of a servant, a motion without intention, or a word spoken by accident or misunderstood, has been the cause of a victory or defeat which has decided the fate of empires.

Here Witherspoon offered an early providential history of the American Revolution. The exposition and meaning of its "most important events" were far removed from the ability of "human direction." Accidents, misunderstandings, trivialities, and "random" shots all demonstrated the unfathomable role of providence in their unfolding occurrence. Only the account of providence in revealed biblical texts could make sense of those events, thus demonstrating that "Salvation" only "belongeth unto the Lord."[26]

As in his *Dominion of Providence,* Witherspoon applied the language and terminology of moral sense reasoning in his thanksgiving sermon as a means to define the limits of unregenerate perception. When past events were con-

25. Witherspoon, "Thanksgiving Sermon," in [Green, ed.], *Works of Witherspoon,* III, 62–63, 65.

26. Ibid., 63–64.

sidered in a "cool and considerate manner," it became clear that they could not have been preempted or enacted through innate volition because their unpredictable occurrence appeared from outside "the human direction." Thus, Witherspoon later continued, "How contrary to human appearance and human conjectures have many circumstances turned out." Appearances and conjectures — the stuff of common human perception — are likely to be faulty and unreliable. After all, Witherspoon continued,

> our most signal successes have generally been when we had the weakest hopes or the greatest fears. What could be more discouraging than our situation at the close of the year 1776? when, after general Howe's arrival with so powerful and well appointed an armament, our army enlisted but for a few months, was almost entirely dispersed? Yet then did the surprise of the Hessians at Trenton, and the subsequent victory at Princeton. . . . The great victory over general Burgoyne and his army . . . opened the eyes of Europe in general, and in some degree even of Britain, happened at a time when many were discouraged. It happened when after the losses of Brandy-Wine and Germantown, the British were in possession of Philadelphia, and the Congress of the United States were obliged to fly to a distant part of the country. It happened not long after our disgraceful flight from Ticonderoga, and the scandalous loss of that post, which was every where said and thought to be the key of the continent, and the possession of it essential to our security.

Far from representing the culmination of individual human sensibilities or common strategic perceptions, all the occurrences Witherspoon described owed their "great favor" to "Providence." And so he saw it as his "proper business" to highlight the work of "the providence of God in general, to offer with sincerity and gratitude the sacrifice of praise for his many mercies, and to make a wise and just improvement of the present promising situation of public affairs." American colonies had never planned for independent government, nor separation from the British crown. There had been no "pre-contract" between them, no attempt to gain foreign aid, no military development. Even British corruption was understood as a providential dispensation, its manifestation serving to move the colonies toward independence. Every step the British took to prevent independence had only served to hasten its resolution, "which has generally been the case when men have undertaken to go in opposition to the course of Providence, and to make war with the nature of things."[27]

27. Ibid., 61–62, 66–67, 79; John Witherspoon, *The Dominion of Providence over the Passions of Men . . .* , ibid., 23.

Witherspoon recommended that all Americans "testify our gratitude to God for the many signal interpositions of his providence . . . by living in his fear, and by a conversation such as becometh the gospel" because "their state is little to be envied who are free as citizens, but slaves as sinners." Political freedom was irrelevant if citizens failed to acknowledge their wider debt to divine mercy, as shared by all humans. "All temporal comforts," according to Witherspoon, derived their value from their being the fruits of divine goodness, the evidence of covenant love, and the earnest of everlasting mercy." Rather than suggesting a special contractual relationship with God, Witherspoon's allusion to "covenant love" directly referenced the covenant of grace that was drawn through Christ as the second federal head of humanity. According to his Calvinist theology, Jesus had assumed the fallen sin of Adam, allowing a more universal covenant of love with any human who acknowledged his mercy, irrespective of regional context or national history.[28]

"O the Shortsightedness of Human Wisdom"

Witherspoon's 1782 thanksgiving statement reminded Americans that "it is our duty to testify our gratitude to God, by usefulness in our several stations, or in other words by a concern for the glory of God, the public interest of religion." Although such gratitude was an important duty for "every person, even of the lowest station," it was "especially the duty of those who" were "distinguished" by "office and authority." Witherspoon referenced "two sorts of persons" in particular: "ministers and magistrates, those who have the direction of religious societies, and those who are vested with civil authority." Specifically separating the provinces of civil and religious power, Witherspoon nonetheless placed moral duties on both. He suggested that "minsters" were "under the strongest obligations to holiness and usefulness in their own lives" as "the world expects it from them, and demands it of them." He had "peculiarly in view" their "strictness in religious discipline, or the inspection of the morals of their several societies" because "by our excellent constitution, they [independent church "denominations" and "societies"] are well secured in their religious liberty."[29]

Though he distinguished between civil and confessional authority, Witherspoon did not deny the important role of independent religious societies in generating social and political stability. They would encourage the moral regeneration of individuals at an early stage in their lives, certainly by young

28. Witherspoon, "Thanksgiving Sermon," ibid., 80.
29. Ibid., 80–81.

adulthood. By maintaining their institutional independence from government, Witherspoon asserted, they would supply public institutions with sufficiently pious leaders. The "public interest of religion" required future civic representatives to demonstrate their moral regeneration as individuals before and separate from their entry into public office. Witherspoon used contractual terminology to suggest that the "return" that was expected from religious societies to "the community, is that by the influence of their religious government, their people may be the more regular citizens."[30]

When he outlined the expected return for denominational freedom, Witherspoon contributed to what scholars have described as an implicit bargain between government and religion during this period. In exchange for the free exercise of dissenting denominations, in a disestablished context, a number of evangelical Protestants agreed to impress moral order and discipline upon those who were set to assume positions of political representation. Witherspoon negotiated this constitutional obligation — some might say, tension — in his role as a minister, a religious teacher, and a public representative. He advocated the separation of civil and religious spheres while also emphasizing the important influence that independent confessional institutions would exert on political governance. He was keen to promote the national strength, consolidation, and moral authority of representative institutions, as was desired by those who advocated the establishment of religion. Yet he had spent his Scottish career opposing those whom he accused of maintaining a corrupt connection to the Westminster government. It is less surprising, therefore, that his 1782 thanksgiving statements were sympathetic to dissenting claims to independent religious representation. He recommended "a concern for the glory of God" and suggested that "ministers" were obliged to carry out the "inspection of the morals of their several societies [such as local churches, colleges, and academies]." Their constituents would then become "more useful members of society."[31]

Though the individual duty to God was unencumbered by political directives or ordinances, it was nonetheless essential to the electoral process

30. Ibid., 81. As Fred J. Hood has shown, several other ministers who influenced the formulation and ratification of new state constitutions described the importance of moral education before the assumption of public office. They linked the inculcation of morality, separate from present political interests, with national prosperity. Their reasoning was similar to that used by Witherspoon to correlate public piety with disestablished constitutionalism. See Hood, *Reformed America: The Middle and Southern States, 1783–1837* (University, Ala., 1980), 7.

31. Witherspoon, "Thanksgiving Sermon," in [Green, ed.], *Works of Witherspoon*, III, 80–81. On "implicit bargain" scholarship, see Calhoon, "Religion, Moderation, and Regime-Building," in Gould and Onuf, eds., *Empire and Nation*, 218.

in "free states" with a stable "civil society." When "the body of a people are altogether corrupt in their manners," Witherspoon recalled, "the government is ripe for dissolution." "Good laws may hold the rotten bark some longer together, but in a little time all laws must give way to the tide of popular opinion, and be laid prostrate under universal practice." It "clearly" followed, then, "that the teachers and rulers of every religious denomination, are bound mutually to each other, and to the whole of society, to watch over the [religious] manners of their several members." That inalienable obligation, in fact, allowed the fulfilment of their civic duty to elect public magistrates. As private citizens educated by disestablished ministers, voters were obliged to elect civil "magistrates" who were suitably pious. "The people in general," Witherspoon suggested, "ought to have regard to the moral character of those whom they invest with authority, either in the legislative, executive or judicial branches." Individuals were free to worship God according to their conscience. But they were also duty-bound to make political choices according to the fixed ethical code of biblical revelation. Because "civil liberty" could not "be long preserved without virtue," a "double duty" connected moral citizens to their political government. The "people themselves" had the "appointment of rulers" as an important obligation and "that of their representatives, who are intrusted with the exercise of this delegated authority."[32]

Thus, Witherspoon reasserted the role of ordinary individuals in the implicit (and potentially ambiguous) bargain of political disestablishment. Giving "credit to the holy scriptures," Witherspoon reminded citizens that "he that ruleth must be just, ruling in the fear of God." Such a maxim applied to those chosen for "the legislative, executive or judicial branches, such as are so promoted may perceive what is and will be expected from them." Witherspoon continued, "If you ask me what are the means which civil rulers are bound to use for attaining these ends, further than the impartial support and faithful guardianship of the rights of conscience; I answer that example

32. Witherspoon, "Thanksgiving Sermon," in [Green, ed.], *Works of Witherspoon,* III, 81–84. Witherspoon's proclamation adds further support to the emerging scholarly consensus that, from an orthodox Calvinistic perspective, individual rights were often grounded in duties and obligations. See James T. Kloppenberg, "The Virtues of Liberalism: Christianity, Republicanism, and Ethics in Early American Political Discourse," *Journal of American History,* LXXIV (1987), 9–33, esp. 9, 18; Knud Haakonssen, "From Natural Law to the Rights of Man: A European Perspective on American Debates," in Michael J. Lacey and Haakonssen, eds., *A Culture of Rights: The Bill of Rights in Philosophy, Politics, and Law—1791 and 1991* (Cambridge, 1991), 36. For a slightly different interpretation of Witherspoon's famous thanksgiving sermon, see L. Gordon Tait, *The Piety of John Witherspoon: Pew, Pulpit, and Public Forum* (Louisville, Ky., 2001), 162–165; Morrison, *John Witherspoon and the Founding,* 28–30.

itself is none of the least." Ironically, then, protecting the action of faith from the constraints of established religion was vital for the growth of moral government. Witherspoon added, "I hope it will be no offence in speaking to a Christian assembly, if I say that reverence for the name of God, a punctual attendance on the public and private duties of religion, as well as sobriety and purity of conversation, are especially incumbent on those who are honored with places of power." "Those therefore who pay no regard to religion and sobriety, in the persons whom they send to the legislature of any state are guilty of the greatest absurdity, and will soon pay dear for their folly." Government, according to Witherspoon, remained separate from the province of personal religious regeneration. Yet the freedom afforded to individuals imposed its own moral obligation in their capacity as voters and, more generally, in the independent ways in which they and their voluntary religious societies prepared men to enter office as pious citizens.[33]

Benjamin Rush, who had first attracted Witherspoon to the College of New Jersey, demonstrated a similar understanding of the republican role of independent religious institutions. In his famous *Thoughts upon the Mode of Education, Proper in a Republic*, which he published in 1786, he commented:

> The only foundation for a useful education in a republic is to be laid in RELIGION. Without this, there can be no virtue, and without virtue there can be no liberty, and liberty is the object and life of all republican governments. Such is my veneration for every religion that reveals the attributes of the Deity. . . . But the religion I mean to recommend in this place is the religion of JESUS CHRIST.

During the period when Rush composed his statement, the legal enforcement of disestablishment stymied the ability of clergymen to contribute to the development of civic institutions and republican ideology. Yet, in their recommendations at least, Witherspoon and Rush did not draw any dichotomy between disestablishment and the civic role of independent religious institutions.[34]

---

33. Witherspoon, "Thanksgiving Sermon," in [Green, ed.], *Works of Witherspoon*, III, 82–83.

34. Benjamin Rush, *A Plan for the Establishment of Public Schools and the Diffusion of Knowledge in Pennsylvania; to Which Are Added, Thoughts upon the Mode of Education, Proper in a Republic*, in Charles S. Hyneman and Donald S. Lutz., eds., *American Political Writing during the Founding Era, 1760–1805* (Indianapolis, Ind., 1983), I, 681. For the claim that the disestablishment of religion in various states during the 1780s "cost ministers dearly" by "eliminating state support, leaving them to their congregations on fixed salaries that dwindled during inflationary cycles," see Robert A. Ferguson, "The Dialectic of Liberty: Law and Religion in Anglo-American Culture," in Womersley, ed., *Liberty and American Experience*, 108–109. See also Leonard W.

There were, of course, residual ironies, and possibly even contradic-tions, in Witherspoon's attempt to describe the association between popu-lar morality, disestablishment, and elite political authority. John Knox had described the paradoxical social importance of a natural aristocracy during the Scottish Reformation. His aristocrats were those whom "the people" had deemed most proficient in their ability to articulate the universal state of human sin. Similarly, Witherspoon set about educating future leaders to dis-play the "piety and virtue" that underlay "the standard of public honor." As he suggested in his 1782 proclamation, the need to testify gratitude to God was "especially the duty of those" that were distinguished by "office and au-thority." In his 1775 treatise *Christian Magnanimity,* which he repeated as a sermon in 1787, Witherspoon pointed out that "one of the best and hap-piest effects of serious reflection" was "to bring us, in a great measure, all upon a level; as, indeed, in one most important respect, the magistrate with his robes, the scholar with his learning, and the day-laborer that stands un-noticed, are all upon the same footing—for we must all appear before the judgement-seat of Christ." Civic leaders were required to demonstrate their continued humility—through fast day proclamations, for example—because they required regeneration in just the same way as those they represented. Yet it could not be denied that Witherspoon's robed magistrate remained visibly stratified in social and political terms, even if he was thought to be equally accountable in his duty and humility before God.[35]

Classical accounts of virtue defined elite representation according to its accomplished display of humility. Witherspoon incorporated a similar para-dox in his account of civic and moral distinction. Whether they were leaders or laymen, citizens were unable to rely on an innate moral sense to guide

Levy, *The Establishment Clause: Religion and the First Amendment* (Chapel Hill, N.C., 1994), 15, 62; Michael W. McConnell, "The Origins and Historical Understanding of Free Exercise of Religion," *Harvard Law Review,* CIII (1990), 1436-1437.

35. Witherspoon, "Thanksgiving Sermon," in [Green, ed.], *Works of Witherspoon,* III, 81, 85; John Witherspoon, *Christian Magnanimity, Sermon 46; Preached at Princeton, September 1775, the Sabbath Preceeding the Annual Commencement; and Again with Additions, September 23, 1787; to Which Is Added an Address to the Senior Class, Who Were to Receive the Degree of Bachelor of Arts,* in [Green, ed.], *Works of Witherspoon,* III, 99. For Knox's account of natural aristocracy, see John Knox, *On Rebellion,* ed. Roger A. Mason (New York, 1993), xxiii, xxiv, 78, 87; David Stevenson, *Revolution and Counter-Revolution in Scotland, 1644-1651* (London, 1977), 135. On Knox's desire to use fast days to define the humility of civic and religious leaders in the century following the Scottish Reformation, see W. Ian P. Hazlett, "Playing God's Card: Knox and Fasting, 1565-66," in Roger A. Mason, ed., *John Knox and the British Reformations* (Alder-shot, U.K., 1998), 176-198.

them toward a common civic good. But, because scripture was a continuous and objective moral code, deference to its fundamental tenets could provide a distinguished public platform for civic leaders. In his 1782 proclamation, therefore, Witherspoon suggested that "civil liberty cannot be long preserved without virtue." He recommended that citizens "check every disposition to luxury, effeminacy, and the pleasures of a dissipated life" and to "put honor upon modesty and self-denial, which is the index of real merit." His classical allusions quickly assumed a specifically Christian basis: "We are one of the body of confederated states. For many reasons, I shall avoid making any comparisons at present, but may venture to predict, that whatsoever state among us shall continue to make piety and virtue the standard of public honor, will enjoy the greatest inward peace, the greatest national happiness, and in every outward conflict will discover the greatest constitutional strength." Here Witherspoon urged leaders to restrain their passions as a means to justify their representative authority.[36]

That political distinction or representative authority followed the display of humility raises a further irony. The slippery notion of common sensibility retained the potential to exclude and stratify during the early national era. The democratic potential of the concept of common sense could veer toward a populist rather than a purely egalitarian agenda, allowing political figures to distinguish their voice and standing through their purported representation of universal ideals. A similar phenomenon took place when educated religious ministers appropriated common sense reasoning. Witherspoon's evangelicalism was removed from prevailing notions of common sensibility during the 1780s. As explained above, his virtuous civic leaders acknowledged their subjective moral stance and defined their duty to external religious guidance. But, in doing so, ironically, their political distinction mirrored that which was gained by elite proponents of common sensibility.[37]

The exact relationship between actual and representative morality had famously vexed the civil theology of New England a century earlier, when leaders and laymen had differed in their interpretation of "visible sainthood." Witherspoon's 1782 proclamation certainly did not suggest that civic repre-

36. Witherspoon, "Thanksgiving Sermon," in [Green, ed.], *Works of Witherspoon*, III, 61, 63, 82, 85.

37. Sophia Rosenfeld, *Common Sense: A Political History* (Cambridge, Mass., 2011), 169–170, 179–180. According to Robert A. Ferguson, for moderate colonial clergymen such as Jonathan Mayhew, "common sense clarified scripture *and* liberty; both came directly from heaven and reached down to the people's earthly capacity, enabling them to act as proper judges when a ruler oppressed them." See Ferguson, "Dialectic of Liberty," in Womersley, ed., *Liberty and American Experience*, 121.

sentatives were regenerate simply as a result of their election by pious citizens or that they were somehow the refined moral products at the top of a political pyramid. Nonetheless, through their distinct authority civic leaders were provided with certain jurisdictional prerogatives that did not always imply an entirely disestablished constitutional framework. Notwithstanding his general support for a disestablished political context, therefore, Witherspoon confirmed a continuing tension in early national constitutionalism. Religious conscience was perceived to be the only truly inalienable individual right, grounded in personal duty to divine law. Yet those who claimed to uphold and protect that right assumed powerful jurisdictional privileges. As Witherspoon had already noted in a section of his "Lectures on Moral Philosophy," "how far the magistrate ought to interfere in matters of religion" was always a matter of interpretation. It is less surprising, then, that the discussion of the relationship between disestablished piety and civil magistracy in the last section of Witherspoon's 1782 sermon ended abruptly with the following qualifier: "But I cannot content myself with this." Magistrates, Witherspoon argued, were to be "a terror to evil doers" because

> that society will suffer greatly, in which there is no care taken to restrain open vice by exemplary punishment. . . . Those magistrates who would have their authority both respected and useful, should begin at the source, and reform or restrain that impiety towards God, which is the true and proper cause of every disorder among men. O the shortsightedness of human wisdom, to hope to prevent the effect, and yet nourish the cause!

Witherspoon had suggested earlier that the separation between government and personal religious conscience obliged the people as voters and guardians to ensure the moral rectitude of those who might then become civil magistrates. Yet, in this final part of his sermon, to a degree, he passed the privilege of moral enforcement back to those magistrates. They were given the ability to reform and restrain from the top downward, notwithstanding Witherspoon's earlier suggestion that disestablishment was vital to allow independent religious societies to effect change from the bottom upward. Further explaining his sudden reassertion of intervention by magistrates, Witherspoon warned Americans to "guard against using our liberty as a cloak for licentiousness; and thus poisoning the blessing after we have attained it." On the last page of his sermon, Witherspoon further clarified his suggestion that magistrates were entitled to impose punishments for moral impropriety, despite their disestablishment from churches and religious institutions. "Whence come dishonesty and petty thefts? I say, from idleness, sabbath-breaking, and uninstructed families. . . . Whence come violence, hatred, and strife? From drunkenness, rioting, lewdness, and blasphemy." He continued, "Drunk-ards, swearers, profane and lascivious jesters, and the whole tribe of those who do harm to none but themselves, are the pests of society, the corruptors of the youth, and in my opinion, for the risk of infection, thieves and robbers are less dangerous companions."[38]

Similar ambiguities can be seen in the developing political theology of Congregational New England from the early national era into the nineteenth century. Oliver Ellsworth, a future Connecticut senator and strong supporter of the Federal Constitution, used language and reasoning that was compa-rable to the final caveats that had appeared in Witherspoon's 1782 thanks-giving sermon. Ellsworth, a 1765 College of New Jersey graduate, included a slight dig at Presbyterianism in his 1787 sermon, suggesting that public reli-gious edicts had often proved problematic with regard to the curtailment of civil liberties: "In the time of the civil wars . . . the presbyterians got the upper hand, and inflicted legal penalties upon all who differed from them in their sentiments respecting religious doctrines and discipline." But he then went on to explain why some sort of civil oversight in moral matters was necessary:

> While I assert the rights of religious liberty, I would not deny that the civil power has a right, in some cases, to interfere in matters of religion. It has a right to prohibit and punish gross immoralities and impieties; because the open practice of these is of evil example and detriment. For this reason, I heartily approve of our laws against drunkenness, profane swearing, blasphemy, and professed atheism.

Thus, Ellsworth inserted a caveat that regrafted moral oversight onto corpo-rate authority.[39]

The Irony of Early American Diplomatic History

On April 19, 1783, after the formal end of military hostilities between Ameri-can and British forces, Witherspoon delivered a thanksgiving day sermon at the

38. Witherspoon, "Thanksgiving Sermon," in [Green, ed.], *Works of Witherspoon*, III, 83–84; John Witherspoon, "Lectures on Moral Philosophy," ibid., 448–449.

39. Oliver Ellsworth, "Letters of a Landholder," in Paul Leicester Ford, ed., *Essays on the Constitution of the United States, Published during Its Discussion by the People, 1787–1788* (New York, 1892), 168, 171. On the tension between individual conscience and corporate constraints among ministers such as Ellsworth, see Shain, "Religious Conscience and Original Sin," in Womersley, ed., *Liberty and American Experience*, 193–194; Hamburger, *Separation of Church and State*, 76–77.

College of New Jersey. Princeton residents met at the village flagstaff and then moved to the college hall to listen to Witherspoon deliver the sermon on salvation and providence. By August, the national Congress of the United States had begun to sit in the small college town. George Washington had arrived in America's fleeting capital after reading extracts from Witherspoon's various thanksgiving sermons and proclamations. In his welcome address to Washington, Witherspoon spoke of the course of "Providence" that lay behind "the unanimous appointment" of his "Excellency to the command of the army."[40]

As the peripatetic Congress moved through various towns, including Princeton village, Witherspoon assumed several political responsibilities alongside his religious statements. Having opposed civil interference in the work of religious societies, he turned to the sphere of economic and diplomatic policy in order to question other forms of government protectionism. He opposed restrictions on the free trade and movement of individual American citizens and questioned constraints on immigration to America. In several congressional speeches from the late 1770s, Witherspoon began by suggesting that Protestant peoples and Protestant confederations (such as the Dutch and Swiss unions) offered the most natural commercial and political models for the new American union. Their confederal forms of governance were thought to reduce the potential for internal conflict among their heterogeneous economic and religious institutions, making them ideal partners in the eyes of a number of American congressmen during the early 1780s. In his "Part of a Speech in Congress, upon the Confederation," he looked to the Netherlands as an ideal model for the new union of American states, just as his forebearers had once sought to strengthen Anglo-Scottish unionism through Dutch commercial and religious alliances. In the same congressional speech, he stressed that man could be moral only if "purified by the light of truth, and renewed by the Spirit of the living God."[41]

Notwithstanding his admiration for Dutch and Swiss confederations,

40. For Witherspoon's statements on Washington, see John Witherspoon, "Address to General Washington," in [Green, ed.], *Works of Witherspoon,* IV, 363. On Washington's visit to Princeton with the Congress, see Varnum Lansing Collins, *The Continental Congress at Princeton . . .* (Princeton, N.J., 1908), 100–104; Henry Carrington Alexander, *Life of Joseph Addison Alexander, D.D., Professor in the Theological Seminary at Princeton, New Jersey,* 2 vols. (New York, 1908), I, 16.

41. John Witherspoon, "Part of a Speech in Congress, upon the Confederation," in [Green, ed.], *Works of Witherspoon,* IV, 347, 350. On the American desire for Dutch alliance at this point, see LaCroix, *Ideological Origins of American Federalism,* 123; Wood, *Creation of the American Republic,* 114–118.

Witherspoon's congressional declarations also contained increasingly positive references to Catholic France. On October 11, 1776, Witherspoon had been appointed to the congressional Committee on Secret Correspondence, which was absorbed into the Committee on Foreign Affairs in 1777. On the committee Witherspoon advocated for greater centralization and a diplomatic executive in order to facilitate America's growing alliance with France. Most obviously, their coalition would strengthen America's military capability in its war with Britain. Louis XVI of France signed the February 8, 1778, Treaty of Amity and Commerce that guaranteed military support for America.[42]

Presbyterians, including Witherspoon, described these surprising diplomatic developments in distinctly providential terms. Having joined a new political union, separate from Britain, Witherspoon's continuing providential piety also heralded a change in the geopolitical dimension of his political theology. As a provincial subject in imperial Britain, he had once led a Scottish presbytery that called for the humility of its constituents without making any positive reference to Catholic political powers. Three decades earlier, only a few years after licensing Witherspoon to preach, the Presbytery at Haddington had recommended a fast day to give thanks for British victory against Jacobite forces that it suspected of gaining support from Catholic France. By May 1778, the context for Witherspoon's political theology had changed dramatically. God's providential hand, he claimed, provided legitimacy for the independence of American citizens. But the external force of providence still required them to acknowledge their unregenerate ethical stance, their continued need for humility, and their attendant desire for salvation. Yet such a providential context had been facilitated in part by God's role in creating a French alliance. Thus, Witherspoon and other Presbyterians in his circle became less likely to define the civil liberty of Americans, including its association with continued humility, in direct contrast to French Catholic corruption.[43]

Evangelical Scots on the eastern side of the Atlantic formed an association between anti-Catholicism and domestic support for the American cause. On

42. On the February 1778 Treaty of Amity and Commerce, see Franklin and Silas Deane to the President of Congress, Feb. 8, 1778, in Leonard W. Labaree et al., eds., *The Papers of Benjamin Franklin,* 41 vols. to date (New Haven, Conn., 1959-), XXV, 634-635. For Witherspoon's early congressional dealings with France, see Collins, *President Witherspoon,* II, 13-15, 38-41, 51-63.

43. On the Haddington Presbytery's response in 1745-1746, see Jeffrey Smitten, "William Robertson: The Minister as Historian," in Sophie Bourgault and Robert Sparling, eds., *A Companion to Enlightenment Historiography* (Leiden, Neth., 2013), 114.

FIGURE 21. *Alliance de la France avec L'Amerique en 1778.* Anonymous,
Eighteenth century. Etching. CFA c 293, Musee de la cooperation franco-americaine,
Blerancourt, France. © RMN–Grand Palais / Art Resource, N.Y.

the western side of the Atlantic, however, Witherspoon's discussion of the
benefit of free commerce during the 1780s required him to reconcile even
greater support for an alliance between Protestant America and Catholic
France. Witherspoon's 1782 thanksgiving sermon even suggested that French
support for America was "surely" the result of

a great favor of Providence to raise up for us so great and illustrious an ally in Europe. This Prince has assisted us, as you all know, in a very powerful and effectual manner, and has granted that assistance upon a footing so generous as well as just, that our enemies will not yet believe, but there must be some secret and partial stipulations in favor of himself and his subjects, although no such thing exists.

Britain had made "use of every topic, which they apprehended, would be inflammatory and popular, to produce jealousies between us and our allies. Yet is has been wholly in vain. Not only, have the officers and soldiers of the American and French armies, acted together, with perfect cordiality, but the troops of our allies have met with a hearty welcome wherever they have been." These statements confirm the diplomatic context for the partial degree of toleration for Catholicism in America during the Revolutionary and early national eras.[44]

In his writings and proclamations as a congressman during the 1780s, Witherspoon broadened his discussion of the association between divine providence and the Franco-American alliance. As America consolidated its independent standing in the world, he suggested, its diplomatic and trading ties with France would also provide a check to British protectionism— benefiting British traders in the long run. France would gain strength through its providential alliance with America, reducing Britain's relative military dominance in mainland Europe. Britain's reduced strategic dominance would no longer allow its ministers to maintain a policy of economic protectionism. Starting with their Protestant brethren in various European

44. Witherspoon, "Thanksgiving Sermon," in [Green, ed.], *Works of Witherspoon*, III, 68, 70–71. On Catholicism and Revolutionary identity, see Davis, *Religion and the Continental Congress*, 152–157; Chris Beneke, "The 'Catholic Spirit Prevailing in Our Country': America's Moderate Religious Revolution," in Beneke and Christopher S. Grenda, eds., *The First Prejudice: Religious Tolerance and Intolerance in Early America* (Philadelphia, 2011), 268–286. By the late 1770s, support for America among evangelical Scots living in Britain was often a primary means of opposing Catholic relief domestically. They connected Britain's indulgence of Catholicism at home to its persecution of Protestant Americans on the western side of the Atlantic. See Robert K. Donovan, "Evangelical Civic Humanism in Glasgow: The American War Sermons of William Thom," in Andrew Hook and Richard B. Sher, eds., *The Glasgow Enlightenment* (East Lothian, U.K., 1995), 227–245; Donovan, "The Popular Party of the Church of Scotland and the American Revolution," in Sher and Jeffrey R. Smitten, eds., *Scotland and America in the Age of the Enlightenment* (Princeton, N.J., 1990), 87; Donovan, *No Popery and Radicalism: Opposition to Roman Catholic Relief in Scotland, 1778–1782* (New York, 1987), 72–73, 158–162, 239; Donovan, "The Military Origins of the Roman Catholic Relief Programme of 1778," *Historical Journal*, XXVIII (1985), 79–102.

nations, they would be forced to expand British trade in freer and more fluid terms. This providential (if perhaps byzantine) reasoning was most apparent in Witherspoon's published writings on behalf of the congressional standing committee, the Board of War, particularly his 1781 *Memorial and Manifesto of the United States of North-America, to the Mediating Powers in the Conferences for Peace, to the Other Powers in Europe, and in General to All Who Shall See the Same.* Having defined the events of the imperial crisis as "the purpose of God Almighty," Witherspoon went on to conclude that, "since the American colonies were, from their extent and situation, ripe for a separation from Great-Britain," the "nature of things seemed to demand" the reduction of British power in relation to France. Thus, "it pleased God to incline the heart of the king of France to give relief to the oppressed" through a treaty with the United States.[45]

During the 1750s, Witherspoon had lamented British losses against France in North America because they threatened Britain's position as the "arbitress of the fate" of Europe. By 1781, conversely, he supported an American alliance with French forces. Witherspoon hoped that "the revolution which they [American states] have effected, will meet with universal approbation [among Europeans]." Thus, he used his congressional status to propose a greater rapprochement with Catholic France, never describing any contradiction with his dissenting Protestant identity.[46]

By the late 1790s, Witherspoon's pro-French stance would have allied him with opponents of Hamiltonian finance. The association he drew between Franco-American cooperation and commercial prosperity could be distinguished from later Federalist attempts to maneuver America as Britain's primary economic partner. Moreover, his opposition to centrally managed economic processes would also have raised tensions with Hamiltonian Federalists. His December 1779 open letter, "On the Proposed Market in George Washington's Camp," suggested that free trade between states would flow according to supply and demand in their various local markets, without protectionist constraints imposed from any central directive. Witherspoon

45. John Witherspoon, *Memorial and Manifesto of the United States of North-America, to the Mediating Powers in the Conferences for Peace, to the Other Powers in Europe, and in General to All Who Shall See the Same,* in [Green, ed.], *Works of Witherspoon,* IV, 370, 372–373.

46. John Witherspoon, *Prayer for National Prosperity and for the Revival of Religion Inseparably Connected,* in [Green, ed.], *Works of Witherspoon,* II, 471; Witherspoon, *Memorial and Manifesto,* ibid., IV, 373. On Franco-American congressional relations, see Benjamin H. Irvin, *Clothed in Robes of Sovereignty: The Continental Congress and the People out of Doors* (New York, 2011), 263–265.

highlighted problems that were associated with the plan to set fixed prices in Washington's camp and its surrounding regions: "Such laws, when they only say men shall be punished if they sell at any higher prices than the legal, and that if any will not sell at these prices, their goods shall be taken by force, have some meaning in them, though little wisdom: but to publish a list of fixed prices, as an encouragement to a weekly market, is a new strain of policy indeed." Supply and demand, Witherspoon pointed out with slightly simplistic reasoning, determined fair prices better than any civic statute ever could.[47]

Other aspects of Witherspoon's economic writings, however, seem more contiguous with later developments in Hamiltonian commercial theory. Underlying his opposition to government protectionism lay a belief that free trade would increase general prosperity, thereby enabling the national government to extract greater revenue from the people through taxation and bonds. Thus, in his role on a congressional "committee of three" to "devise ways and means for defraying the expences," Witherspoon described the general importance of centralized American finance in relation to the assumption of state debts and the payment of foreign creditors.[48]

Witherspoon's September 1782 congressional speech, "On a Motion for Paying the Interest of Loan-Office Certificates," suggested that European lenders were already so "sufficiently exasperated" with the failure of America to pay its debts that they had begun "looking with an evil eye upon some new men coming into play [in the U.S. Congress], and thinking themselves unjustly and ungratefully used." Thus, Witherspoon recommended that Congress pass measures to pay the interest on international loans, notwithstanding any public backlash. He considered "the effect upon our credit at home" of "making some payment to the public creditors immediately, and

47. John Witherspoon, "On the Proposed Market in General Washington's Camp: To His Excellency General Washington, and the Officers of the American Army," in [Green, ed.], *Works of Witherspoon*, IV, 359, 361.

48. For Witherspoon's role on the financial committee, see the congressional entry of minutes for Thursday, May 15, 1777, *JCC*, VII, 362. For the debate on the assumption of state debts at this point and for Witherspoon's depiction of Washington's camp, see Keith L. Dougherty, *Collective Action under the Articles of Confederation* (Cambridge, 2001), 99–101. Peter S. Onuf has described the ambiguous relationship between early federal and economic identities. In a discussion of the varying meanings of Adam Smith's free trade theories in early national America, Onuf asks: "Did Americans constitute a single people or nation? If the United States was, in the words of James Madison, 'partly federal, and partly national,' how would the distinction be applied and sustained in [economic] practice?" See Onuf, "Adam Smith and the Crisis of the American Union," in Susan Manning and Francis D. Cogliano, eds., *The Atlantic Enlightenment* (Aldershot, U.K., 2008), 150.

prosecuting the measures already begun for further security." If the security of independent America "were good, and our credit entire, so that obligations by the public would be turned into money at any time, at par or at little less, we should find no considerable number of lenders." And so Witherspoon supported the federal assumption of state debt as a primary means to facilitate the commercial trading power of Americans. Like many Scots, he had once lauded the benefit of commercial trade between equal provinces in the British Empire. Taking his place in a new American confederation, he feared that each state might be tempted into parochial protectionism (as had been the accusation leveled against English commercial theorists during the early Revolutionary era). Advocating a coherent and centralized economic strategy, therefore, Witherspoon sought to prevent the American confederation from splintering into protectionist constituents. He suggested that a sound national credit rating would allow Americans to trade freely with other nations and provinces.[49]

Notwithstanding his support for a Franco-America alliance, Witherspoon traveled to London and Scotland to garner funds for the College of New Jersey. This was a strange proposition given current geopolitical circumstances, more so given the seditious reputation of the college. He arrived in London in late January 1784 and made contact with his evangelical Scottish friend the Reverend John Erskine, who had always lauded the freedom offered to Protestant revivalism on the western side of the Atlantic. Erksine had conversed with Jonathan Edwards through the 1740s, as we have seen, and he had also maintained contact with Witherspoon during the later Revolutionary era. Holding out little hope for Witherspoon's trip, Erskine contacted Charles Nisbet, who later wrote to Witherspoon that Erksine had given him "the first notice" of Witherspoon's arrival in Scotland. Nisbet described having "a thousand questions to put to you on the state of religion, morals and politics in America, which must be delayed till meeting." He hoped that Witherspoon would visit Scotland to understand how "the deadness of trade and manufactures and the rise of rents and public burdens [had] brought the lower ranks to a state of the most abject servitude and poverty."[50]

49. John Witherspoon, "Speech in Congress, on a Motion for Paying the Interest of Loan-Office Certificates" (Sept. 9, 1782), in [Green, ed.], *Works of Witherspoon,* IV, 333, 335–337.

50. Charles Nisbet to John Witherspoon, Mar. 16, 1784, in Whitfield J. Bell, Jr., "Scottish Emigration to America: A Letter of Dr. Charles Nisbet to Dr. John Witherspoon, 1784," *WMQ,* 3d Ser., XI (1954), 283, 285–287, 289. On the wish to appropriate state funds for the college and on the events surrounding Witherspoon's visit to Scotland and his letters to Erskine, see Collins, *President Witherspoon,* II, 110, 137–142.

Nisbet thus viewed Scottish socioeconomic development after the American War of Independence in bleak terms. He did not share Witherspoon's confidence that American independence from Britain would be beneficial to both nations. Immigration to America seemed his only "disconsolate" concern as a "persecuted . . . friend of America during the war." Nisbet viewed immigration to North America as particularly amenable to a certain kind of man: a "sincere and primitive Christian, of competent knowledge and an honest zeal for serving the interests of immortal souls." Amid outlining the economic problems of Scotland in relation to America, therefore, Nisbet highlighted their variance in relation to the growth of "evangelical" piety. Reminding Witherspoon of his former religious context, he suggested: "You may be sure I shall not be able to send you many Orthodox clergymen, for a reason that will readily occur." After his brief visit to Scotland, during which he left few records of his movements, Witherspoon returned to the United States in September.[51]

Witherspoon continued to reconcile private commercial concerns with piety and communal stability. A similar synthesis had earlier appeared in Puritan New England, where sound commercial governance was deemed to denote God's blessing of the region. Witherspoon, however, was less likely to favor one region or province over another. Having seen the ways in which Scotland's commercial culture had suffered after it lost access to American markets, his simple vision of free trade and economic migration continued to suggest that American independence would benefit all states and confederations, both without and within the new American union. Arguing that irregular fluctuations in supply and demand were inevitable, he demonstrated a subtle understanding of the chaotic marketplace during the early national era. Witherspoon believed that trade was fluid, unpredictable, and could not be confined to internally managed systems. He opposed the assumption that trading systems could be managed by trained commercial theorists, or even that particular nations (such as France) should be shut out of international commerce.[52]

51. Nisbet to Witherspoon, Mar. 16, 1784, in Bell, "Scottish Emigration to America," *WMQ*, 3d Ser., XI (1954), 284, 285, 287.

52. Mark Valeri has distinguished between the merchant guilds that idealized trade as a source of civic and national improvement and those Puritans who "interpreted" and denigrated "the market" using "a different conceptual framework" that focused on "avarice" and selfishness. A number of Puritans responded to these tensions by adopting a regional understanding of providentialism. The notion of "economic reform" even came to rest "in the responsibility of civil leaders to rule according to their social expertise" so that, as long as merchants avoided "gross

Witherspoon crystallized many of his economic ideas in his *Essay on Money*, which was published in Philadelphia in 1786. Furthering his case against mercantile protection over paper money, Witherspoon claimed that there was

> sometimes a fluctuation in the comparative value of gold and silver, and in these cases, though no doubt a debtor, till the error that has crept in be rectified by authority, has a right to pay in any lawful money; yet if I were selling goods, and gold had fallen in its value, I might safely say to the customer, in what coin are you to pay me?

Such a rhetorical question led Witherspoon to conclude that people ought to value paper money in relation to more objective commodities, without necessarily giving up on paper altogether. In his view, individuals could not predict, manage, or direct fluctuating commercial ideals. Yet, ironically, it would be a mistake to assume that such a predicament required a different medium of exchange, governed by an expert few. Here Witherspoon's commercial theory continued its alliance with his moral philosophy. The excitable sensory response, he warned, was too personal to allow economic management from afar. As a human artifice without inherent value (unlike gold), paper money would be malleable enough to match changing opinions of worth.[53]

During the same period in which Witherspoon wrote his commercial essays, George Washington seemed to be aware of his moral duties as a relatively prosperous individual. In 1784, he wrote a long letter to Witherspoon regarding the settlement of his western lands with religious societies and their ministers. Through Witherspoon's congressional activities on commercial, political, and diplomatic committees, and following his fast day and Thanksgiving declarations, he had become known to Washington and other founders for questioning and redefining prevailing associations between inborn moral perception and representative authority. When it came to economic affairs, for example, his influence could be found in the alliance between his moral philosophy and his simple version of free market theory: differing and subjective human perceptions, he argued before other con-

---

excesses" and "downright avarice," their pursuit of profit was not subject to church censure. See Valeri, *Heavenly Merchandize: How Religion Shaped Commerce in Puritan America* (Princeton, N.J., 2010), 26, 31, 103–105.

53. John Witherspoon, *An Essay on Money, as a Medium of Commerce; with Remarks on the Advantages and Disadvantages of Paper Admitted into General Circulation* (Philadelphia, 1786), in [Green, ed.], *Works of Witherspoon*, IV, 227–228, 241.

gressmen, were likely to reduce the efficacy of centralized protectionism and instead encourage the natural oscillation of commercial value.[54]

Washington's reference to religious societies, moreover, complemented Witherspoon's stated desire to promote moral ideals among future civic leaders in independent religious institutions. Witherspoon offered important support for the implicit bargain between autonomous religious groups and civil magistrates. Thus, he can be situated as an important figure in America's historical trajectory toward state and federal disestablishment, with a few caveats: Witherspoon navigated his constitutional bargain while never fully conquering the tension between his role as a minister, a religious educator, and a political representative. At points, he even encouraged corporate oversight of certain moral issues. As a result of his new prominence in the American Congress, he became wary of discouraging *all* forms of corporate religious power, in the way of his earlier Scottish opposition to Moderate patronage, even while making general overtures to disestablishment. A more marked distinction between Witherspoon's career in the Kirk and his position in the American Congress appeared in his response to Catholic France. From the late 1770s, he and other American Presbyterians decided that divine providence did not discount an alliance with the old enemy of Anglo-Scottish unionism — another sign of the ways in which novel political contexts and exigencies could be drafted into providential thought, demonstrating both the change and the continuity in Witherspoon's evangelicalism.

54. "From George Washington to John Witherspoon, 10 March 1784," in W. W. Abbot, ed., *The Papers of George Washington:* Confederation Series, I, *January–July 1784* (Charlottesville, Va., 1992), 197–201.

{ PART IV }

Legacies

CHAPTER 8

"THE LATENT CAUSES OF FACTION ARE THUS SOWN IN THE NATURE OF MAN"

John Witherspoon, James Madison, and the American Founding

> *"I take it for granted that an assembly of the vulgar in Athens*
> *was just like an assembly of common people among us. . . . that they were*
> *very disorderly is plain from what we read of Plato being pulled down*
> *from the desk, when he went up to defend Socrates."*
> John Witherspoon, "Lectures on Eloquence" (1772)

> *"Had every Athenian citizen been a Socrates, every Athenian*
> *assembly would still have been a mob."*
> James Madison, *"The Federalist* Number 55" (1787)

Evangelical Presbyterians—and Witherspoon, in particular—unsettled the imperial notion of indivisible unionism. Whether in Scotland or in colonial North America, they believed that British political incorporation did not require the diminishment of institutional religious independence. They were aware that cooperation between Scottish and English parliamentarians had heralded the formulation of the Westminster Confession of Faith, a standard for Presbyterianism that allowed its institutional and theological distinction from Anglicanism, Congregationalism, and other Protestant denominations. Their strong attachment to the British Empire was contingent on the retention of the Church of Scotland's autonomy after the 1707 Act of Union. From then on, the Kirk represented an alternative religious establishment alongside the Anglican Church. Its parallel religious jurisdiction empowered colonial American Presbyterians to oppose the claims of political and confessional establishments on their religious and institutional autonomy.

Evangelical Presbyterians on both sides of the Atlantic accused their moderate counterparts of matching Anglican corruption through their association with elite politics. Popular party churchmen in Scotland opposed Moderate patronage from Westminster and claimed that British constitutionalism ought to guarantee the disestablished power of its various Protestant churches. Similarly, Log college men in the Middle Colonies censured Old Side elites in the Philadelphia Presbyterian Synod for making private alliances with local political assemblies. Reflecting Scottish evangelicals on the eastern side of the Atlantic, they questioned the privileged relationship between religious assemblies and political governance—whether local or imperial. Thus, the debate over the establishment of religion among Presbyterians had turned on the nature of religious independence in a pluralistic, rather than indivisible, British Empire.

The historical impact of Presbyterian pluralism on American constitutionalism is evident in the developing political and religious identity of Witherspoon's most famous student, James Madison. Less than two decades after graduating from the College of New Jersey in 1771, the future fourth American president became a father of the U.S. Constitution. His understanding of the relationship between religious disestablishment and American federalism was influenced by debates that had taken place in Presbyterian circles during the previous few decades, if not the entire previous century. By the mid-1790s, religious statements became conspicuous by their absence in Madison's public and private declarations. The historiography of his later career suggests tensions and contradictions regarding the nexus between faith, religion, and political establishments. But, before that period, Madison maintained close contact with his primarily Presbyterian college classmates as well as his former teacher and often proclaimed the necessity of personal piety and religious regeneration. He frequently referred to Witherspoon in letters to friends and even served alongside him in the Continental Congress in 1781–1782. Witherspoon, having spent his Scottish career in opposition to religious assessments and political patronage, used his congressional platform to promote the continued institutional freedom of religious societies—including local churches, regional ecclesiastical bodies, and colleges of higher education. When he returned to his home state of Virginia after graduation, Madison outlined his own theoretical opposition to civil-religious establishments. Though he was not Presbyterian, he approved of his friends who came from the "Northern Colonies" to preach in the Chesapeake. He shared their belief that "Ecclesiastical Establishments" created "ignorance and Corruption."[1]

---

1. On Madison's continued association with, and reference to, Witherspoon in the decade after his graduation, see James Madison to William Bradford, Apr. 28, 1773, Madison to James Monroe, Aug. 11, 1786, in William T. Hutchinson et al., eds., *The Papers of James Madison*, 34 vols. to date (Chicago, 1962–1977; Charlottesville, Va., 1977–), I, 83–85, IX, 90–91; Ralph Ketcham, *James Madison: A Biography* (1971; rpt. Charlottesville, Va., 1990), 30–42. For Madi-

The historiography of religious toleration in early national America has often focused on the important role played by southern Baptists such as Samuel Stillman and Elijah Craig, comparing their impact on Thomas Jefferson with that of Madison. Craig was arrested in the winter of 1773 for preaching and for undermining the authority of licensed Anglican ministers. In 1776, he worked with Madison and other Virginian lawyers on the issue of religious establishment in their state's new constitution. As many scholars have shown, evangelical Baptists in Virginia favored state disestablishment in order to distance themselves from the perceived deism of governing classes. They envisioned the growth of piety through independent institutions, rather than from the top downward, thus allowing a "one-way permeable membrane" in which grassroots religion would eventually have an impact on the moral quality of those who entered public office. They were indeed a strong part of Madison's political constituency in Virginia from the 1770s through the late 1780s. Yet historians have only rarely assessed the equally unsettling role of Presbyterian evangelicalism during the same period (and often in the same state). Madison, thanks in part to his education and continuing association with his teacher, was alert to Presbyterian claims in the conflict with Anglican episcopacy and in relation to the civil establishment of religion more generally. It was in association with a number of Presbyterians that he became central to efforts that ultimately blocked Patrick Henry's 1784 plan to require Virginians to pay for their particular Christian congregation. Madison's vocal participation in the Virginia state legislature between 1776 and 1786 prefigured his contribution to the First Amendment of the U.S. Constitution by setting out his argument that civil magistrates should avoid any legal oversight in matters of personal religious conscience. In the Virginia debates, as in those regarding religion amendments to the Federal Constitu-

---

son's reasoning on "ignorance and corruption," see Madison to Bradford, Jan. 24, 1774, in Hutchinson et al., eds., *Papers of James Madison*, I, 104–105. For Witherspoon on religious "societies," see John Witherspoon, "Delivered at a Public Thanksgiving after Peace: Sermon 45" (hereafter cited as "Thanksgiving Sermon"), in [Ashbel Green, ed.], *The Works of the Rev. John Witherspoon, D.D.L.L.D. Late President of the College at Princeton, New-Jersey . . .* , 2d ed., rev., 4 vols. (Philadelphia, 1802), III, 82. On the "many Madisons" of his later career and in the historiography of religion during the early national era, see Jack N. Rakove et al., "Forum: The Madisonian Moment," *William and Mary Quarterly,* 3d Ser., LIX (2002), 865–956; Rodney A. Grunes, "James Madison and Religious Freedom," in John R. Vile, William D. Pederson, and Frank J. Williams, eds., *James Madison: Philosopher, Founder, and Statesman* (Athens, Ohio, 2008), 127; Gary Rosen, *American Compact: James Madison and the Problem of Founding* (Lawrence, Kans., 1999), 1–9.

tion, Madison warned that established religion risked promoting public ethical norms at the expense of personal moral reflection.[2]

Witherspoon described the importance of separating the religious and civil spheres. He always highlighted the natural degeneracy of the human state. But religious regeneration still retained an essential civic function in his eyes. Future civic leaders, he hoped, would experience conversion in their independent religious institutions before assuming office. Thus, he insisted that no civil constitution would last long unless religious societies remained free to inculcate piety among future citizens. Madison espoused similar ideals in his religious statements immediately after graduation. These ideals also governed his contribution to the debate on the establishment of religion in Virginia, particularly his 1785 *Memorial and Remonstrance,* written to oppose religious assessments. Though supporting the separation between civil and religious spheres, he described the important role of pious institutions in encouraging the regeneration of future public magistrates.[3]

In mid-August 1786, Madison wrote to James Monroe, a Virginian member of the Continental Congress, that he "had some conversation at Princeton with Docr. Witherspoon on the subject which agitates you so much in Congs [western land claims]. He sees it in its proper light, and when an opportunity offers will not withhold his ideas from those to whom they may be useful." A year later, after contributing to the formulation of the U.S. Constitution, he was awarded an honorary doctorate of laws from the College of New Jersey. These were also Witherspoon's last years at the college. Madison's teacher informed him:

2. On the "one-way permeable membrane," see Barry Shain, "Religious Conscience and Original Sin: An Exploration of America's Protestant Foundations," in David Womersley, ed., *Liberty and American Experience in the Eighteenth Century* (Indianapolis, Ind., 2006), 174. On Craig's arrest, see Ketcham, *James Madison,* 57. On Madison's early work on these issues in Virginia, see Irving Brant, *James Madison,* I, *The Virginia Revolutionist* (Indianapolis, Ind., 1941), 128; Lance Banning, "James Madison, the Statute for Religious Freedom, and the Crisis of Republican Convictions," in Merrill D. Peterson and Robert C. Vaughan, eds., *The Virginia Statute for Religious Freedom: Its Evolution and Consequences in American History* (Cambridge, 1988), 109–138; John A. Ragosta, *Wellspring of Liberty: How Virginia's Religious Dissenters Helped Win the American Revolution and Secured Religious Liberty* (New York, 2010), 166–167; Jewell L. Spangler, *Virginians Reborn: Anglican Monopoly, Evangelical Dissent, and the Rise of the Baptists in the Late Eighteenth Century* (Charlottesville, Va., 2008), chap. 2; Thomas E. Buckley, "Evangelicals Triumphant: The Baptists' Assault on the Virginia Glebes, 1786–1801," *WMQ,* 3d Ser., XLV (1988), 68–69.

3. Witherspoon, "Thanksgiving Sermon," in [Green, ed.], *Works of Witherspoon,* III, 82; James Madison, *Memorial and Remonstrance against Religious Assessments* (circa June 20, 1785), in Hutchinson et al., eds., *Papers of James Madison,* VIII, 295–306.

I hope you will have no Difficulty in beleiving *[sic]* that all concerned in this College were not barely willing but proud of the Opportunity of paying Some Attention to and giving a Testimony of their Approbation of one of their own Sons who has done them so much honour by his publick Conduct. And as it has been my peculiar Happiness to know perhaps more than any of them your Usefulness in an important Station on that and some other Accounts there was none to whom it gave more Satisfaction than to Sir.

From his station, Madison had earlier observed in his letter to Monroe that Witherspoon would not withhold his ideas. Those ideas influenced his evolving political philosophy in more general terms, aside from the issue of the establishment of religion on the state and federal level. A broader association developed between Madison's Calvinistic education under Witherspoon and his emerging constitutional theory.[4]

During their year-long joint congressional career, Madison and Witherspoon collaborated on a committee to choose suitable books for the new Congress. Their selections included several works by the Scottish skeptical philosopher and political theorist David Hume but also various theological recommendations. Witherspoon approved of Hume's approach to "eloquence" because it acknowledged the subjective and factional nature of human perception in promiscuous assemblies. This tempered approval has not yet found its way into American intellectual history, and it is certainly not a part of the common understanding of the "Madisonian Moment" during the late 1780s. Yet, as strange as it might sound, Madison's education by a Scottish evangelical likely contributed to his growing attraction to Humean political ideas before and during the Constitutional Convention. Unsurprisingly, Madison and Witherspoon opposed Hume's skeptical approach to the Christian doctrine of revelation. But, like Hume, they questioned political systems whose sound function was contingent on the innate moral sense of their constituents.[5]

Of course, the similarities between Witherspoon and Madison in their

4. Madison to Monroe, Aug. 11, 1786, John Witherspoon to Madison, Aug. 11, 1788, in Hutchinson et al., eds. *Papers of James Madison,* IX, 90–91, XI, 230–231. On Madison's honorary doctorate of laws from the College of New Jersey, see also Ketcham, *James Madison,* 231.

5. Ketcham, *James Madison,* 652–653; James Madison, "Report on Books for Congress," in Hutchinson et al., eds., *Papers of James Madison,* VI, 62–115; Rakove et al., "The Madisonian Moment," *WMQ,* 3d Ser., LIX (2002), 865–956. Congress acquired more than thirteen hundred volumes and pamphlets. On the book committee, see William Dawson Johnston, *History of the Library of Congress,* I, *1800–1864* (Washington, D.C., 1904), 535.

approach to the relationship between piety and political unionism must also be balanced by a discussion of their differences. When Madison eventually articulated a national understanding of federalism, he was less hopeful than Witherspoon regarding the disestablished civic role of religious societies. He came to realize that the machinery of central government might be required to function without the prior occurrence of moral regeneration. Madison certainly asserted that people were free to worship God according to the dictates of their own conscience. Yet he also suspected that a significant number of national politicians would not assume public magistracy as regenerate men. National representatives were likely to originate from different states, each with varying confessional contexts. Not all were likely to supply civic leaders with sufficient humility to grapple with their naturally selfish desires. The seeds of factionalism were sown in the nature of human representatives. As a result, Madison sought to provide constitutional balance through the institutionalization of schismatic rivalry, irrespective of the state of regeneration among political actors. Whether Madison's skepticism could be described as Humean, Augustinian, or both, Madison turned to systems that checked and balanced different human interests and inclinations, each against the other in continuous tension. Even in these instances, it is worth considering whether his reasoning could ever be described as Calvinistic.

"The Convincing Argument of Actual Disappointment"

Madison's religious identity during his early career continues to be something of a puzzle. Although his father was a vestryman who acculturated his son within the established Anglican Church of Virginia, Madison never identified as an Anglican or Episcopalian. He never participated in full communion, although he attended church regularly through his youth and past his teenage years. He was educated, from age eleven, by several tutors who had been reared in the moral philosophy of the Scottish Enlightenment. Yet, in July 1769, concerned about the rumored spread of deism through worldly Anglican teachers at the College of William and Mary, the Madisons sent their son to the College of New Jersey, known as an institution with Presbyterian affiliations and a more orthodox approach to the primacy of Christian revelation. Madison graduated in 1771 but remained on campus for "miscellaneous studies," including some Hebrew, in Witherspoon's circle. According to Bishop William Meade of the Virginia Anglican Church, during this period "a great revival took place, and it was believed that he partook of its spirit. On his return home he conducted family worship in his father's house." Madison might well have chosen to study farther away from the tide-water region because a more northerly climate was less problematic for his continual breathing problems. Yet, confirming statements by Madison and his family, Meade suggested that the young man had been "sent to Princeton College,—perhaps through fear of the skeptical principles then so prevalent at William and Mary." After his graduation, itinerant Presbyterian ministers and former College of New Jersey classmates Caleb Wallace, Nathaniel Irwin, George Luckey, and Moses Allen all preached at Madison's home, Montpelier, and in the Anglican parishes of surrounding Orange County. But, despite these statements, and the qualitative distinction he and his parents made between the College of William and Mary and the College of New Jersey, scholars often define Madison broadly as a deist. Focusing on private and public statements during his middle years, it is usually claimed that Madison sought to verify the existence of God through empirical observation of the natural world rather than through any more intangible faith in the tenets of revealed religion.[6]

Yet, at least in the years following his graduation, Madison demonstrated a distinctly Calvinist rather than deistic worldview, particularly as shown in a voluminous correspondence with his former classmate William Bradford. In the course of the three years after their graduation, they recalled the education that they had received under Witherspoon, which they distinguished from their present cultural context. In 1774, Madison used religious terminology to describe to Bradford his orientation away from belles lettres toward public rhetoric:

6. On the "puzzle" of Madison's religiosity, see Banning, "James Madison," in Peterson and Vaughan, eds., *Virginia Statute for Religious Freedom*, 109; Grunes, "James Madison and Religious Freedom," in Vile, Pederson, and Williams, eds., *James Madison*, 106. On Meade's comments regarding Madison's attendance and the "great revival," Madison's move to the College of New Jersey for health and religious reasons, and his "miscellaneous studies" after graduation, including Hebrew, see Brant, *James Madison*, I, 20, 110, 113. On Madison's regular church attendance yet his failure to take full communion, see Ralph L. Ketcham, "James Madison and Religion—A New Hypothesis," *Journal of the Presbyterian Historical Society*, XXXVIII (1960), 76–77. On Madison's Presbyterian classmates visiting him and preaching in his town through 1773, including a visit by his friend Erwin, see Madison to Bradford, Sept. 5–6, 1773, in Hutchinson et al., eds., *Papers of James Madison*, I, 93; Mark A. Beliles, "The Christian Communities, Religious Revivals, and Political Culture of the Central Virginia Piedmont, 1737–1813," in Garrett Ward Sheldon and Daniel L. Dreisbach, eds., *Religion and Political Culture in Jefferson's Virginia* (Lanham, Md., 2000), 7. On Madison as a deist, largely through reference to his middle and later years, see David L. Holmes, *The Faiths of the Founding Fathers* (New York, 2006), 96–98.

I was afraid you [Bradford] would not easily have loosened your Affections from the Belles Lettres. . . . I myself use to have too great a han-
kering after those amusing Studies. Poetry wit and Criticism Romances
Plays etc captivated me much: but I begin [to] discover that they deserve but a moderate portion of a *mortal's* Time, and that something
more substantial more durable more profitable befits a riper Age. It
would be exceeding improper for a labouring man to have nothing but
flowers in his Garden or to determine to eat nothing but sweet-meats
and Confections.

Before this sanctimonious reorientation, between 1762 and 1767 Madison
had studied privately under the Scottish tutor Donald Robertson, whose
father had been suspected of Jacobitism. Robertson received his Edinburgh
theological education when moral sensory theories had begun to become
more popular, and he seems to have influenced Madison's earlier orientation
toward belles lettres that linked aesthetic and moral concerns. From a French
author, Cardinal de Retz, Madison noted, for example: "I knew a Man who
had but small defects, and every one of these defects was either the product
or the cause of some good Qualities in him." Here, as in many of his other
notations on magazines and excerpts, he viewed the benevolence and moral
potential of men and relished annotating such a vision through epigrammatic
statements.[7]

Yet, only a few years later, in a 1773 letter to Bradford, Madison criticized "encourage[r]s of free enquiry" who engaged in literary criticism. What
amounted to their own opinion was disguised in a critical language of neutrality and taste. They were "loose in their principals [and] encourage[r]s
of free enquiry even such as destroys the most essential Truths, Enemies to
serious religion." In his 1774 letter on "Poetry wit and Criticism," Madison
claimed that belles lettres deserved only a "moderate portion" of a *"mortal's* Time." Referring to mortality in his anxious desire to fill "Time" with

7. Madison to Bradford, Jan. 24, 1774, in Hutchinson et al., eds., *Papers of James Madison*,
I, 105–108. On Madison's early tutoring and course material, see William Hutchinson's introduc-
tory essay, ibid., 6. On Madison's excerpt from Cardinal de Retz, see ibid., 7. For the little background that scholars have on Donald Robertson, see Ketcham, *James Madison*, 19–21, 25, 48,
59. On Madison's reorientation away from polite letters in conversation with Bradford, see also
Louis C. Schaedler, "James Madison, Literary Craftsman," *WMQ*, 3d Ser., III (1946), 517–519;
J. David Hoeveler, *Creating the American Mind: Intellect and Politics in the Colonial Colleges*
(Lanham, Md., 2002), 302–303. On the religious relationship of Bradford and Madison after
their schooling under Witherspoon, see also Garrett Ward Sheldon, *The Political Philosophy of
James Madison* (Baltimore, 2001), 23–26.

"durable" rather than "amusing" studies, Madison resembled a sober minister. He criticized the "Luscious performances" of belletristic expression using the metaphor of a garden with too many flowers. A similar metaphor appeared in an anecdote about Witherspoon, which often circulated during Madison's time in the College of New Jersey. A visitor had observed that Witherspoon solely grew vegetables in his garden: "Doctor . . . I see you have no flowers in your garden!" Witherspoon had replied: "No . . . nor in my discourses either." Madison had heard Witherspoon state in his "Lectures on Eloquence":

> Carrying taste to a finical nicety in any one branch, is a thing not only undesirable, but contemptible; the reason of which may be easily seen: when a person applies his attention so much to a matter of no great moment, it occasions a necessary neglect of other things of much greater value. After you pass a certain point, attachment to a particular pursuit is useless, and then it proceeds to be hurtful, and at last contemptible.

Recall also Witherspoon's statement in his "Lectures on Divinity":

> I have often thought that great natural abilities, and great acquired knowledge, operate as a temptation, in a way similar to great wealth or external property—they are apt to intoxicate the mind—to produce self sufficiency and contempt of others, and to take away from that humility which is the greatest beauty, or if the expression be proper, the real glory of a Christian. I would therefore begin, by earnestly beseeching you to keep clear views of the importance both of piety and literature, and never suffer them to be divided.

According to Witherspoon, Scottish Moderate Presbyterians promoted an aesthetic analogy between attractive ethical ideas and their pleasing style of description. Such an analogy, he believed, eschewed the subjective nature of unregenerate perception. In his letters to Bradford, similarly, Madison suggested that the faith in "free enquiry" among literary critics unrealistically emphasized their innate moral stance and made them "Enemies to serious religion."[8]

Like Witherspoon, Madison adopted a synthesis between religious and

8. Madison to Bradford, Dec. 1, 1773, Jan. 24, 1774, in Hutchinson et al., eds., *Papers of James Madison*, I, 101, 105-106. On the flower anecdote, see Varnum Lansing Collins, *President Witherspoon: A Biography*, 2 vols. (Princeton, N.J., 1925), I, 147-148. For Witherspoon's statements on taste and beauty, see John Witherspoon, "Lectures on Eloquence," in [Green, ed.], *Works of Witherspoon*, III, 592; Witherspoon, "Lectures on Divinity," ibid., IV, 11.

classical rhetoric. But Madison also acknowledged the problems — even the corruptions — of classical expression. In his "Brief System of Logick," which he compiled between 1770 and 1772, he criticized the "very captitious and insiduous Method" of Socratic teaching. Witherspoon had often reminded his students that Plato was "pulled down from the desk, when he went up to defend Socrates," providing further evidence that individuals were prone to passionate disorder. According to Madison, Socratic persuasion might provoke such problematic behavior because it disguised the contingent opinion of an individual (an amalgamation of varying perceptions) with universal sensory claims. The deft use of a "sudden conviction or an absurdity" provided a rhetorical counterpoint to the teacher's supposedly true vision. Such sleight of hand fooled students into believing that their innate perception suddenly corresponded to that of their instructor; all the while his "manner was, when he intended to confute or convince any one, to introduce some Topick suitable to his Design, never to declare his own opinion but to ask Questions as if he desir'd instruction, having his mainpart in view, and wheeling the Stream of the Discourse Slyly to his Purpose." But many students would eventually come to notice his rhetorical artifice. According to Madison, their resulting hatred and disorder would diminish its effectiveness in defining objective ideas.[9]

The discussion of subjective opinion in Madison's "Brief System of Logick" and in the letters he received from Bradford during the early 1770s recalled David Hume's unsettling response to Scottish moral philosophy. In a letter to Madison discussing piety, human nature, and perception, Bradford paraphrased Hume. "Human nature" was "the same in every age" — a study of "opinions and passions." Such a statement takes on greater meaning in light of the education Madison and Bradford had experienced under Witherspoon. Their teacher had lauded Hume for acknowledging the subjective role of passions in human perception, even while he had criticized the skeptic for his comments on organized religion. He had also called for attention to the divergence of human sentiments, claiming that the study of varying philosophical views highlighted the "truth of the Scripture doctrine of the depravity and corruption of our nature." In his early letters to Madison, Bradford also questioned the notion of innate moral reasoning, making reference to the superior role of revealed ethical laws. In an October 17, 1774, letter, he assured his friend that another of their classmates had maintained

9. James Madison, "A Brief System of Logick," in Hutchinson et al., eds., *Papers of James Madison*, I, 39; Witherspoon, "Lectures on Eloquence," in [Green, ed.], *Works of Witherspoon*, III, 511.

an "orthodox" Christian understanding of unregenerate perception, much to his approval: "I went yesterday to hear our classmate McCorkle predicate: and I assure you his sermon was very orthodox: The point he chiefly Laboured to prove was 'that the Laws of God were superior in wisdom to the Laws of men'; and I think his arguments on this part were in a gr[e]at measure unanswerable." The "Laws of men" attempted to draft moral edicts to the benefit of civic order. But, as human artifacts, their ethical "wisdom" would always defer to the moral reasoning of revelation.[10]

References to "serious religion" and even to revivalism could be found in other parts of the correspondence of Madison and Bradford, revealing their budding understanding of human sociology. In one letter, Madison outlined his belief in an afterlife. The notion of a "future State," in his view, necessarily distanced worldly achievements from their present benefits. Thus, Madison proposed that a "watchful eye must be kept on ourselves." He wrote as if the future celestial Madison were observing his present worldly actions, as if the meaning and objective morality of these actions could not be known without reference to their future heavenly judgment. Without knowledge of future death, "ideal monuments of Renown and Bliss" would be temporary, contingent, and prone to disintegration. Their construction would not guarantee enrollment "in the Annals of Heaven." According to Madison, "Wisdom and Religion" only cohered in light of the "convincing argument of actual disappointment." Though the inevitable frustration of actual events was depressing, it also inspired "latent expectation of obtaining more than ordinary Happiness" on earth. Here Madison's discussion can be compared to an important assertion that Witherspoon delivered in his "Lectures on Moral Philosophy." According to Madison's former professor, only an "apprehension or belief that reward or punishment will follow [our conduct]" could truly motivate ethical activity. Witherspoon validated the "belief or apprehension of a future state of rewards or punishment" outside human time.[11]

Upon learning that Bradford had chosen not to become a religious minister, Madison revealed that, in 1773, at least, he felt comfortable enough to proclaim to his friend that "even the most rational and manly" individuals

10. Bradford to Madison, Oct. 13, 1772, Oct. 17, 1774, in Hutchinson et al., eds., *Papers of James Madison,* I, 73, 127 (on Madison's reference to portions of Hume's *Enquiry concerning Human Understanding,* see 74 n. 7); Witherspoon, "Lectures on Eloquence," in [Green, ed.], *Works of Witherspoon,* III, 539, 574; Witherspoon, "Lectures on Moral Philosophy," ibid., 369.

11. Madison to Bradford, Nov. 9, 1772, in Hutchinson et al., eds., *Papers of James Madison,* I, 74–75; Witherspoon, "Lectures on Moral Philosophy," in [Green, ed.], *Works of Witherspoon,* III, 382, 390.

were bound to "declare their unsatisfactoriness by becoming fervent Advocates in the cause of Christ." Having studied under Witherspoon, Madison
sought to convince Bradford that, whatever his chosen profession, religious
concerns ought to remain central in his mind. He also advised Bradford
against the hubristic assumption that college graduates were equipped to
study history and moral philosophy without scriptural precedent: "I doubt
not but you design to season them [your scholarly and vocational works]
with a little divinity" in order to "make them more precious than fine gold."
The "specious Arguments of Infidels," Madison pointed out in another letter,
were ironically necessary to establish "the faith of Enquiring Christians."[12]

In 1774, Madison expanded upon his belief that "the frequent Assaults
that have been made on America . . . Boston especially . . . will in the end
prove of real advantage" in uniting colonists. He suggested that, if "the
Church of England had been the established and general Religion in all the
Northern Colonies as it has been among us here and uninterrupted tranquillity had prevailed throughout the Continent," then "slavery and Subjection might and would have been gradually insinuated among us." Any
union of "Religious Sentiments," Madison argued, "begets a surprising confidence and Ecclesiastical Establishments tend to great ignorance and Corruption, all of which facilitate the Execution of mischievous Projects." If the
Anglican establishment of England had been implemented more coherently
in the northern colonies, Madison implied, the colonies would have experienced a decline in their political liberty long before the current crisis. Established religious authorities in the colonies would have prevented grassroots
moral forces from influencing local magistrates, many of whom then would
not have opposed further mischief from Westminster. Writing several years
before the American Declaration of Independence, Madison foreshadowed
the "implicit bargain" that would take place between disestablished revivalist
ministers and civic authorities during the 1780s. In opposing the notion of a
religious establishment in another letter, he did not deny the "good effects"
of "religious as well as Civil Liberty" on the moral health of society. Witherspoon had made a similar claim in his lectures, a claim that, as we have seen,
he expanded in his civic proclamations during the early 1780s.[13]

12. Madison to Bradford, Nov. 9, 1772, Sept. 25, 1773, July 1, 1774, in Hutchinson et al., eds.,
Papers of James Madison, I, 75, 96, 115.

13. Madison to Bradford, Jan. 24, Apr. 1, 1774, ibid., I, 105–106, 112. On the idea of an "im-
plicit bargain," see Robert M. Calhoon, "Religion, Moderation, and Regime-Building in Post-
Revolutionary America," in Eliga H. Gould and Peter S. Onuf, eds., *Empire and Nation: The
American Revolution in the Atlantic World* (Baltimore, 2005), 217–218. Many scholars of reli-

In an April 1774 letter, Madison considered whether "something will be done in behalf of the dissenters [in Virginia]: Petitions I hear are already forming among the Persecuted Baptists and I fancy it is in the thoughts of the Presbyterians also to intercede for greater liberty in matters of Religion." Lamenting the influence of Virginia's Anglican religious establishment, Madison admitted to being "very doubtful of" Presbyterians "succeeding in the Attempt" to gain greater autonomy for their denomination given that

> such incredible and extravagant stories were told in the [Virginia] House of the monstrous effects of the Enthusiasm prevalent among the Sectaries and so greedily swallowed by their Enemies that I believe they lost footing by it and the bad name they still have with those who pretend too much contempt to examine into their principles and Conduct and are too much devoted to the ecclesiastical establishment to hear of the Toleration of Dissentients . . . [all becoming] a pretext for rejecting their requests.

Bradford, according to Madison, ought to consider the treatment of dissenting Protestants in distinguishing between different colonial settings. As Madison began to contribute to constitutional and confessional debates in Virginia's nascent political assemblies, he would not jettison his Calvinistic mode of description and analysis.[14]

Madison bemoaned the dominance of corrupting ecclesiastical establishments in Virginia. Yet his home state would in fact become the center of early national opposition to religious privileges. By the late 1770s, political representatives such as Patrick Henry and Luther Martin attempted to buttress the institutional sovereignty of their local churches through political patronage, religious tests, or special taxes. A group of dissenters, however, petitioned state congressional assemblies to permit the independence of their religious institutions from civil directives. In particular, evangelical Presbyterians and Baptists pressured Anglican elites to allow a distinction between civil and religious authority. Only with disestablishment, they argued, would

---

gious toleration and disestablishment have noted Madison's perceived distinction between the Virginian establishment and religious contexts farther north in his hypothetical statement on the Church of England. See, for example, Nicholas P. Miller, *The Religious Roots of the First Amendment: Dissenting Protestants and the Separation of Church and State* (New York, 2012), 142; Thomas S. Kidd, *God of Liberty: A Religious History of the American Revolution* (New York, 2010), 39; Lance Banning, *The Sacred Fire of Liberty: James Madison and the Founding of the Federal Republic* (Ithaca, N.Y., 1995), 81–82.

14. Madison to Bradford, Apr. 1, 1774, in Hutchinson et al., eds., *Papers of James Madison*, I, 112–113.

dissenting churches remain free to flourish as autonomous institutions in a wider political confederation. Several petitioners were former College of New Jersey students who had joined Presbyterian communities in the state. Not being officially Presbyterian, Madison avoided signing documents that originated in specific churches and presbyteries. Nonetheless, with his tacit support, the Presbyterian petitioners set about securing the institutional autonomy of Presbyterian churches alongside other religious groups on the state level.[15]

"A Religion Not Invented by Human Policy"

The issue of ecclesiastical establishments in Virginia provided further impetus for Madison's developing constitutional understanding of the relationship between public piety and political unionism. It delivered a conceptual bridge between his correspondence with Bradford and his eventual contribution to the national architecture of American federalism. As a young delegate to the Virginia convention in May and June 1776, Madison modified George Mason's original draft of an article on religion. Madison and Mason met in a Revolutionary political body that served as a provisional governing institution even before the Declaration of Independence. In mid-May 1776, Mason wrote that "all men should enjoy the fullest toleration in the exercise of religion." Madison's modification sought to strengthen the principle of the "free exercise of religion" because he was wary that the reference to "toleration" described that which could be extended by magistrates according to their own contingent will and thus did not defend what he understood to be an immutable right of conscience. Many ministers, including Witherspoon, perceived an unencumbered duty to God as perhaps the only truly individual right without deference to corporate moral authority. Several historians of the First Amendment have pointed to a similar understanding of rights in their assessment of its conceptual roots in the Virginia convention. As early as 1776, then, Madison had suggested that conscience was grounded in a God-given and inborn duty to divine law rather than a corporate responsibility.[16]

15. On the growth of Presbyterian petitioning movements in Virginia at this point, see Ragosta, *Wellspring of Liberty*, 127–130; Banning, "James Madison," in Peterson and Vaughan, eds., *Virginia Statute for Religious Freedom*, 115–116.

16. For these citations from James Madison, including George Mason's first draft in italics, see "Committee's Proposed Article on Religion, 27–28 May 1776," in Hutchinson et al., eds., *Papers of James Madison*, I, 173, and "Madison's Amendments to the Declaration of Rights," 174–175. On this famous exchange over the meaning of toleration, see also Ragosta, *Wellspring of Liberty*, 154; Miller, *The Religious Roots of the First Amendment*, 143–144; Banning, "James

Madison's opposition to the state establishment of religion was shared by the rank and file of Virginia's Presbyterians in the weeks and months after the Declaration of Independence. Like Madison, they highlighted the distinction between equal religious entitlement and mere toleration by civil magistrates. John Todd, from the Hanover Presbytery, presented his "Memorial" to the Virginia state legislature on October 24, 1776, alongside Madison's friend and College of New Jersey classmate, the minister Caleb Wallace. Adopting a historical analysis to make a point of political theology, their petition suggested that, before and during the Revolutionary era, some had

> either remained in the place of their nativity, or preferred worse civil government, and a more barren soil [unlike Virginia], where they might enjoy the rights of conscience more fully than they had a prospect of doing it, in this. From which we infer, that Virginia might have now been the capital of America, and a match for the British arms . . . had it not been prevented by her religious establishment.

Having linked civil prosperity to the freedom of religious conscience, despite otherwise unfavorable contexts, the petition came to its central point: that it cannot "be made appear that the Gospel needs any such civil aid" — and thus is required a "quiet possession" of "unalienable rights and privileges." Wallace complained that church members in their presbytery were still being forced to support the institutional establishment of the Episcopal clergy, even after American independence.[17]

As Madison sought to appeal to Virginia's growing constituency of anti-establishment Presbyterians, and as he carried on his correspondence with Bradford and other former college classmates, it is unlikely that he defined the individual conscience according to its inborn moral compass. Further

---

Madison," in Peterson and Vaughan, eds., *Virginia Statute for Religious Freedom,* 112; Ketcham, *James Madison,* 73; Sheldon, *The Political Philosophy of James Madison,* 31; Daniel L. Dreisbach, "Church-State Debate in the Virginia Legislature: From the Declaration of Rights to the Statute for Religious Freedom," in Garret Ward Sheldon and Daniel L. Dreisbach, eds., *Religion and Political Culture in Jefferson's Virginia* (Lanham, Md., 2000), 138–139. On the notion that unencumbered rights related only to duty to God, see Shain, "Religious Conscience and Original Sin," in Womersley, ed., *Liberty and American Experience,* 171–172.

17. "Memorial," in William Henry Foote, *Sketches of Virginia: Historical and Biographical,* I (Philadelphia, 1850), 323–324. According to Leonard W. Levy, Presbyterian "clergy during 1785 returned to the principles of the Hanover Presbytery of 1776"; see Levy, *The Establishment Clause: Religion and the First Amendment* (Chapel Hill, N.C., 1994), 67. On Todd and Wallace's petition, see Beliles, "Christian Communities," in Sheldon and Dreisbach, eds., *Religion and Political Culture,* 21.

evidence for Madison's belief in the circumscribed nature of innate ethics can be found in his correspondence with former classmate Samuel Stanhope Smith. In September 1778, Smith responded to a letter from Madison that had discussed the nature of unregenerate moral volition. In January of that year, Madison had become a member of the Virginia Council of State. But he had not eschewed his concern with ethical epistemology during the interim period. Madison had forwarded summaries of theological writings by Jonathan Edwards and other evangelical theologians. Most of the writings implied that any moral choice between conflicting impulses was in fact predetermined by a chain of preceding forces that only God could foresee and control. Good actions, according to Madison, were determined by the preceding actions of all other beings, in contexts that overlapped in time and space. That only God could understand such a chain of causation reduced the role of individual agency in moral choice. In response, Smith wrote that he had "read over" Madison's "*theoretical* objections against the doctrine of moral liberty." Using Hutchesonian reasoning, he claimed that all beings retained a predictable moral response that was akin to a pre-rational sense; a clear "sentiment of nature to appeal to, as in the case of colour." According to Smith, Madison remained far more reticent in his account of individual moral ability. In contrast, Smith tried to show that moral sentiments were trustworthy in and of themselves.[18]

Madison further elucidated his Calvinistic understanding of ethical insight while a Virginia delegate to the Continental Congress (1780–1783) and as an Orange County representative to the Virginia General Assembly (1784–1786). Contrary to Francis Hutcheson's attempt to verify immutable moral sensibilities from seemingly diverse human nature, Witherspoon had exposed Madison and his classmates to divergent and contradictory philosophies as a sign of "the fruit and evidence" of humanity's "departure from its original purity." Witherspoon did not believe that it was possible to historicize the developing evolution of innate moral sensibility. Through the early 1780s, Madison's compilation of data on ancient and modern republics similarly catalogued past historical errors — whether in philosophical theory or political strategy. In doing so, he derived a rather bleak assessment of the universal weaknesses and vices that those errors implied. By the middle of the decade,

18. Samuel Stanhope Smith to Madison, Sept. 15, 1778, in Hutchinson et al., eds., *Papers of James Madison*, I, 253–254, 256. See also Make A. Noll and Ralph Ketcham's discussion of this exchange between Smith and Madison in Noll, *Princeton and the Republic, 1768–1822: The Search for a Christian Enlightenment in the Era of Samuel Stanhope Smith* (Princeton, N.J., 1989), 70–72; Ketcham, *James Madison*, 83–84.

he had consulted hundreds of books from the Library Company of Philadelphia, the catalog of William Byrd's library, and lists obtained through
a growing friendship and association with Thomas Jefferson and had compiled a list of more than three hundred works on law, politics, social theory,
treaties, and historical narratives. As is evidenced by his letters to Jefferson
and others during the period, his cataloguing and reading led him to assume
a kind of universality in the precarious and fallible nature of humanity and
the civil societies it sought to create. This bleak taxonomy, Madison suggested to many of his friends, was discoverable through a careful analysis of
past experiences, mistakes, and foibles. Its unsettling truths, moreover, required acknowledgment by living generations of aspiring nation makers.[19]

In his capacity as a Virginia delegate to the Continental Congress and as
an Orange County representative to the Virginia General Assembly, Madison
continued to oppose the payment of religious teachers using public funds.
He responded in particular to the Virginia General Assembly's attempt to
define the notion of a "general assessment" to benefit all religious societies in
the state—a seemingly ecumenical definition that was nonetheless thought of
as the best means to fund the dominant Anglican institutions. In the decade
after the Declaration of Independence, Virginian politicians such as John
Tyler and Wilson Miles Cary became fearful that dissenters were growing
stronger in their demand for full disestablishment, which would in their view
reduce morality in the civic sphere. They objected in particular to the proposed Virginia Statute for Religious Freedom, which Thomas Jefferson had
drafted in 1777 and which was introduced for debate in the Virginia General
Assembly in 1779. The statute had endeavored to remove established privileges that the Church of England enjoyed in Virginia. On October 25, 1779,
a general assessment bill was proposed by Anglican opponents of Jefferson's
Virginia Statute for Religious Freedom. Though defined as a means to provide tax revenue to any Protestant church in the state, Anglicans hoped that
such a bill would appease dissenters while also providing funds to maintain
their own position as the dominant clerical denomination. Their proposed
bill, however, was delayed as predominantly Anglican assembly members
came to the conclusion that it was not in their wider interest to raise the ire

19. Witherspoon, "Lectures on Moral Philosophy," in [Green, ed.], *Works of Witherspoon*, II,
369–370, 374. On Madison's use of various libraries and his developing bibliographic relationship with Jefferson, see Ketcham, *James Madison*, 39–40. For Madison's bleak reading of past
historical errors during this period, see his long series of assessments of problematic confederacies and political unions in James Madison, "Notes on Ancient and Modern Confederacies,"
circa April–June 1786, in Hutchinson et al., eds., *Papers of James Madison*, IX, 3–24.

of dissenters any further. Many Presbyterians and Baptists, after all, were engaged in the ongoing battle with British redcoats on behalf of Virginia and the wider American union. Yet, as was evidenced by assembly proceedings through December and the following year, Anglican politicians still believed that some sort of religious establishment would eventually be reasserted and strengthened through taxes and general assessments if and when the war with Britain subsided.[20]

As Anglican politicians continued to seek support for general assessment rather than full disestablishment in Virginia, their cause was increasingly championed by Patrick Henry, whose response to the Statute for Religious Freedom brought him into direct conflict with Madison. During 1784, Henry became known for spearheading Anglican support for a state assessment bill. The bill required Virginians to choose any particular denomination to support via central taxation measures or to contribute to a general fund. As an ironic consequence, Madison supported the election of Henry from the Virginia legislature to the governorship of the state in an uncontested election. With Henry outside the legislative sphere, Madison calculated, the strongest advocate for religious assessment would be neutralized.[21]

It is important to note that sensitivity to Presbyterian political theology provided a catalyst for Madison's continued opposition to the assessment bill, which came to be known more formally as A Bill Establishing a Provision for Teachers of the Christian Religion after being drafted under Patrick Henry and presented by Middlesex County delegate Francis Corbin in a December 2, 1784, session of the Virginia legislature. Before mid-1784, Madison had been tempted to focus on other constitutional matters, thinking that the bill was unlikely to pass. But, through spring 1784, a seeming volte-face by influential Presbyterians in the state reignited his anti-assessment drive. During the previous years, Presbyterian clergymen had continually proposed

20. On Jefferson's proposal, see "A Bill for Establishing Religious Freedom," June 18, 1779, in Julian P. Boyd et al., eds., *The Papers of Thomas Jefferson*, II (Princeton, N.J., 1950), 545–553. On the events leading up to Jefferson's proposal and on Anglican-led "general assessment" schemes in response, see Calhoon, "Religion, Moderation, and Regime-Building," in Gould and Onuf, eds., *Empire and Nation*, 222, 224–225; Ragosta, *Wellspring of Liberty*, 65–68; Beliles, "Christian Communities," and Dreisbach, "Church-State Debate in the Virginia Legislature," both in Sheldon and Dreisbach, eds., *Religion and Political Culture*, 22, 150–152; Chris Beneke, *Beyond Toleration: The Religious Origins of American Pluralism* (New York, 2006), 163–166.

21. On the election of Patrick Henry and Madison's calculated support for him, see Calhoon, "Religion, Moderation, and Regime-Building," in Gould and Onuf, eds., *Empire and Nation*, 222, 224–225; Dreisbach, "Church-State Debate in the Virginia Legislature," in Sheldon and Dreisbach, eds., *Religion and Political Culture*, 150.

FIGURE 22. *James Madison.* Bust portrait miniature, facing slightly right.
By Charles Willson Peale. 1783. Courtesy, Rare Book and Special Collections
Division (LC-USZ62-5310), Library of Congress, Washington, D.C.

written memorials against civil interference in religious affairs. Yet, as Madison noted with disappointment, several ministers offered sudden and contradictory support for the assessment bill. Presbyterian ministers such as John Blair Smith, the new president of Hampden-Sydney College, had calculated that Episcopalians would always maintain a tacit connection to the state's legislative procedures, given the deep roots of their social and commercial networks. He and other Presbyterian leaders surmised that supporting general assessment for clergy of all denominations would at least allow Presbyterians some part in the state legislative process, particularly when taking into account their growing number in relation to Episcopalians. In order to compete with the Anglican Church, Smith had concluded, they would have to funnel their own way into the establishment. Fearful of these and similar mercenary calculations by Presbyterian ministers, Madison sought to remind them of the religious liberties they would lose with *any* sort of assessment, however ecumenical its terms might have seemed.[22]

As rhetorical support, Madison wrote to Smith and his associates to remind them that Episcopalians in the region were continually seeking to incorporate their church more officially into the civic establishment. Madison seems to have realized that such reference to incorporation provided an opportunity to undercut the problematic coalition that threatened to develop between Presbyterians and Episcopalians in favor of general assessment. Madison implied in a series of private letters that general assessment was likely a Trojan horse for the incorporation of only the Episcopalian Church. Presbyterian clergymen who suddenly supported general assessment, Madison implied, were naive in their presumption that the Virginia assembly would use its powers to include them in a broader religious establishment that enabled them to gain greater civic authority as well financial support from state taxes. With the general push for Episcopalian incorporation at the forefront of his analysis, Madison suggested that the general regulation of spiritual concerns by the state portended privileges granted to its most influential churches, rather than to all denominations equally. This argument was successful in gaining back the support of most Presbyterian ministers in Virginia as well as their political representatives in the General Assembly. Thus, on December 24, 1784, Madison and his dissenting allies succeeded in persuading the assembly to postpone the final reading of the bill until nearly a year later, in the next house legislative session in November 1785.[23]

22. On Madison's other constitutional interests in 1784 and 1785, which he eventually put aside in order to concentrate on the issue of religious assessments in Virginia, see Ketcham, *James Madison,* 154–160. On the Presbyterian reversal of opinion, which shocked Madison, see Banning, "James Madison," in Peterson and Vaughan, eds., *Virginia Statute for Religious Freedom,* 116. On Francis Corbin's bill for Christian teachers and Madison's successful attempt to postpone further discussion of the assessment bill to November 1785, see Dreisbach, "Church-State Debate in the Virginia Legislature," in Sheldon and Dreisbach, eds., *Religion and Political Culture,* 150–151.

23. On Madison's desire to reduce the likelihood of a link between Presbyterians and Episcopalians and his petitions to various Presbyterian communities on the issue, see John Blair Smith to Madison, June 21, 1784, in Hutchinson et al., eds., *Papers of James Madison,* VIII, 81–82; Ragosta, *Wellspring of Liberty,* 126–130. According to Ragosta, Madison "may have seen

With time to galvanize further grassroots support against religious assessment, Madison was encouraged by fraternal Virginia congressmen Wilson Cary Nicholas and George Nicholas to formulate a coherent argument against Henry's bill that would be attached to circulating petitions throughout Virginia. By summer 1785, Madison drew together his various arguments against Henry's bill in his *Memorial and Remonstrance.* Distributed among Presbyterian and Baptist circles, it helped to mobilize more than eleven thousand Virginians—many Presbyterian—to sign anti-assessment petitions.[24]

As Jefferson made clear in the opening statement of his 1779 Statute for Religious Freedom, he opposed Patrick Henry's bill because he believed that the "evidence proposed" to individual minds underlay their free conscience. Innate benevolence, according to Jefferson, did not require government directives or religious assessments. Ironically, then, moral sensory views enabled him to support the claims of evangelical Baptists, many of whom defined the nature of their religious conscience in less anthropocentric terms. Madison's account of duty in his *Memorial and Remonstrance* distinguished his opposition to the assessment bill from several of its other challengers, including Jefferson. He proposed that religion lay outside the authority of civil governance because it was concerned with future salvation rather than worldly political matters. When defined as a "duty," religious conscience was "unalienable, because the opinions of men, depending only on the evidence contemplated by their own minds cannot follow the dictates of other men." Religious conscience was unalienable also because human laws—"right towards men"—were grounded in personal duties "towards the Creator" as defined by scripture.[25]

---

in the language used on [Episcopal] incorporation an opportunity to undermine what he saw as a dangerous alliance between the Presbyterians and Episcopalians on the question of general assessment" (127).

24. On the estimated eleven thousand signatories, see Calhoon, "Religion, Moderation, and Regime-Building," in Gould and Onuf, eds., *Empire and Nation,* 225. Many scholars of the disestablishment of religion have analyzed Jefferson's 1802 "Wall of Separation" letter to the Danbury Baptists of Connecticut, yet Madison's *Memorial* deserves equal, if not more, attention. On the overlooked nature of the *Memorial* in contrast to the Jefferson letter, see Miller, *The Religious Roots of the First Amendment,* 143.

25. "A Bill for Establishing Religious Freedom," June 18, 1779, in Boyd et al., eds., *Papers of Thomas Jefferson,* II, 545. On Jefferson's reasoning, as distinct from Madison, see J. G. A. Pocock, "Religious Freedom and the Desacralization of Politics: From the English Civil Wars to the Virginia Statute," in Peterson and Vaughan, eds., *Virginia Statute for Religious Freedom,* 60–70. For Madison's statements, see Madison, *Memorial and Remonstrance,* in Hutchinson et al., eds., *Papers of James Madison,* VIII, 299.

Madison emphasized "conscience" as that which enshrined the personal obligation to God, irrespective of corporate civil authority: "This duty is precedent, both in order of time and degree of obligation, to the claims of Civil Society. . . . [so that,] in matters of Religion, no mans right is abridged by the institution of Civil Society and that Religion is wholly exempt from its cognizance." Several scholars have suggested Madison's reading of John Locke in these and other passages of his *Memorial,* noting potential similarities with Locke's *Letter concerning Toleration,* written around 1685. Both sought to distinguish the province of civil affairs from that of personal religious conscience and salvation. Both detached contractual civic associations from a more transcendent human duty to God. In defining the immutable duty to God that individuals used their conscience to acknowledge, and that preceded the ethical pronouncements of any civil magistrate, Madison avoided a libertarian reading of the right of conscience in Locke's letter. Paradoxically, according to many scholars, Locke implied that individuals were free to come to terms with their individual moral confinement as fallen men. Grasping such a conception, Madison recommended a distinction between government and the province of religion, claiming:

> A member of Civil Society, who enters into any subordinate Association, must always do it with a reservation of his duty to the General Authority; much more must every man who becomes a member of any particular Civil Society, do it with a saving of his allegiance to the Universal Sovereign. We maintain therefore that in matters of Religion, no mans right is abridged by the institution of Civil Society and that Religion is wholly exempt from its cognizance.

Although civil society retained its own legal institutions, the corporate authority of those institutions did not encompass religious conscience, given the grounding of conscience in presocietal duties to God.[26]

Madison's reasoning in *Memorial and Remonstrance* galvanized evangelical Presbyterian opponents of the general assessment bill, many of whom sought to return to the principles of the Hanover Presbytery of 1776, which had suggested that all spiritual institutions ought to remain wholly separate

26. Madison, *Memorial and Remonstrance,* in Hutchinson et al., eds., *Papers of James Madison,* VIII, 299. On the potential link between John Locke and Madison, see ibid., 297, 305; Banning, *Sacred Fire of Liberty,* 92–93; Calhoon, "Religion, Moderation, and Regime-Building," in Gould and Onuf, eds., *Empire and Nation,* 225. For a suggestion of Locke's relatively Calvinistic conception of conscience as duty to God, see John Dunn, *The Political Thought of John Locke: An Historical Account of the Argument of the "Two Treatises of Government"* (Cambridge, 1969), 264.

from worldly governance. He argued: "The establishment proposed by the Bill is not requisite for the support of the Christian Religion. To say that it is, is a contradiction to the Christian Religion itself, for every page of it disavows a dependence on the powers of this world: it is a contradiction to fact." Using a Roman allusion, Madison proposed an early reading of religious history. He suggested that early Christianity grew popular despite — and not because of — Roman attempts to incorporate its power within an imperial political establishment: "Religion both existed and flourished, not only without the support of human laws, but in spite of every opposition from them; and not only during the period of miraculous aid, but long after it had been left to its own evidence and the ordinary care of Providence." During the period of miracles (the life of Jesus), Roman politicians had famously persecuted Christian followers. Their later co-optation of Christianity, according to Madison, rang hollow — a fact demonstrated by residual constraints that Roman rulers continued to impose upon Christians. For "a Religion not invented by human policy," Madison argued,

> must have pre-existed and been supported, before it was established by human policy. It is moreover to weaken in those who profess this Religion a pious confidence in its innate excellence and the patronage of its Author; and to foster in those who still reject it, a suspicion that its friends are too conscious of its fallacies to trust it to its own merits.

Since the classical era, establishments detrimentally weakened the pre-societal claims of religion. They simply served to arouse further suspicion among naysayers who denied the immutable laws of revelation and who could suggest instead that they were imposed by fallible human authorities.[27]

Madison concluded his *Memorial* by discussing the necessary promotion of evangelicalism, referencing the Incorporation Bill that had been proposed by Episcopalians. It threatened to stunt religious revivalism because

> the policy of the Bill is adverse to the diffusion of the light of Christianity. The first wish of those who enjoy this precious gift ought to be that it may be imparted to the whole race of mankind. Compare the number of those who have as yet received it with the number still remaining under the dominion of false Religions; and how small is the former! Does the policy of the Bill tend to lessen the disproportion? No; it at once discourages those who are strangers to the light of reve-

27. Madison, *Memorial and Remonstrance,* in Hutchinson et al., eds., *Papers of James Madison,* VIII, 301.

lation from coming into the Region of it; and countenances by example
the nations who continue in darkness, in shutting out those who might
convey it to them. Instead of Levelling as far as possible, every obstacle
to the victorious progress of Truth, the Bill with an ignoble and unchristian timidity would circumscribe it with a wall of defence against
the encroachments of error.

In referencing the Incorporation Bill here, Madison continued to use an example that he hoped could be related to general assessment more broadly.
Among other motivations, he sought to arouse Presbyterian fears in a way
that led their ministers and laity to conflate the two legislative propositions.
Once again, he was successful in appealing to the rank and file of Presbyterian
petitioners, and there was to be no further volte-face on the issue of general
assessment from their dissenting quarters. After only brief considerations in
fall 1785, the sheer volume of anti-assessment petitions discouraged assem-
blymen from any further debate over the Bill Establishing a Provision for
Teachers of the Christian Religion. Along with many other less well-known
petitions, Madison's *Memorial and Remonstrance* had been decisive.[28]

In a May 1785 letter to James Monroe, Madison wrote of his opposition
to recent congressional measures to distinguish public land in various states
"for supporting the Religion of the Majority of inhabitants." Such a policy,
in his view, recalled "an antiquated Bigotry." Thus reminded of the issue
of religious establishments, he then outlined his pleasure that "the Presbyterian Clergy" in the state, unlike many other Virginian representatives,
were no longer "general friends to the scheme" and had adopted "another
tone" on the matter. His rhetorical sleight of hand in using the Incorporation
Bill to undermine unity between Presbyterians and Episcopalians, enhancing "opposition to the general assessment" bill, was described in private in
a letter to Thomas Jefferson in August 1785. At *"the instance of some* of *its*
[the Bill] *adversaries,"* Madison referenced his *Memorial and Remonstrance,*
which had been *"sent* thro' the *medium of confidential persons"* in a number

---

28. Ibid., 303. On the success of Madison's *Memorial,* including resulting petitioning movements, and its influence on the assembly, see Dreisbach, "Church-State Debate in the Virginia
Legislature," in Sheldon and Dreisbach, eds., *Religion and Political Culture in Jefferson's Virginia,* 153; Marvin K. Singleton, "Colonial Virginia as First Amendment Matrix: Henry, Madison, and Assessment Establishment," in Robert S. Alley, ed., *James Madison on Religious Liberty*
(New York, 1985), 164–167. On the success of petitioning in the context of Madison's strategic
and "Chameleon-like" use of the Episcopalian incorporation issue, see Ragosta, *Wellspring of
Liberty,* 123, 126–129 (esp. 127), 143.

of the upper counties of Virginia, and which he had been "told will be pretty extensively signed." Thus, Madison was fully aware of that which he owed to his Presbyterian constituencies in the region.[29]

Madison believed that the defeat of the general assessment measure provided an appropriate context to reestablish support for Jefferson's Statute for Religious Freedom. On October 31, 1785, therefore, he did so through the Virginia House of Delegates Bill 82, newly titled A Bill for Establishing Religious Freedom. It was debated on December 15, and it became law on January 19, 1786.[30]

As Madison stated in a 1786 letter to Jefferson, Presbyterian politicians had offered vital support in the eventual passage of the Statute for Religious Freedom. Describing the popular role of dissenters in opposition to religious assessment, the Presbyterian Church was the only religious denomination that he specifically referenced. To be sure, Madison also remained close to Baptist challengers to religious establishment. His *Memorial and Remonstrance,* after all, aligned him more closely with their definition of conscience, which also highlighted the unencumbered duty to God. But his desire to separate the "victorious progress of Truth" and the "light of revelation" from government "encroachments" also specifically appealed to Presbyterians who gave up their initial equivocation over general assessment, particularly in light of the Episcopalian Incorporation Bill.[31]

Notwithstanding his opposition to the general assessment of religion, Madison did not deny the role of government in the assertion of certain moral activities. While helping to spearhead the Statute for Establishing Religious Freedom, he also stood behind a November 21, 1786, Bill for Punishing Disturbers of Religious Worship and Sabbath Breakers. He thus revealed a constitutional tension that was also evident in Witherspoon's congressional proclamations during the same period. Witherspoon advocated the institutional freedom of religious societies. But he also continued to suggest that certain moral activities could be imposed by civil government. Such activities tended to concern laws such as keeping the Sabbath rather than abstract issues re-

29. Madison to James Monroe, May 29, 1785, Madison to Thomas Jefferson, Aug. 20, 1785, in Hutchinson et al., eds., *Papers of James Madison,* VIII, 286, 345.

30. On the passing of A Bill for Establishing Religious Freedom, see Beliles, "Christian Communities," and Dreisbach, "Church-State Debate in the Virginia Legislature," in Sheldon and Dreisbach, eds., *Religion and Political Culture,* 23–24, 163–164 n. 140.

31. Madison to Jefferson, Jan. 22, 1786, in Hutchinson et al., eds., *Papers of James Madison,* VIII, 473–474. On the "victorious progress of Truth," see Madison, *Memorial and Remonstrance,* ibid., 303.

lating to faith and salvation. This constitutional ambiguity regarding Sunday laws and other moral activities would only be (partially) resolved during the nineteenth century in a second disestablishment.[32]

"Even the Best Constitution Will Be Ineffectual"

In May 1787, the same month that James Madison entered the U.S. Constitutional Convention in Philadephia to draw up a new national framework for the government of the United States, John Witherspoon contributed to a constitution that removed references to the association between civil and religious jurisdiction. Witherspoon took his seat in Philadelphia on May 18, 1787, in the synod of the Second Presbyterian Church to create a new "Draught of the Form of the Government" for the "Presbyterian Church in the United States." The two meetings brought Witherspoon and Madison to the same city during the same month in order to deliberate on two constitutions. Though Witherspoon might well have been able to join the New Jersey delegation to Madison's convention, his religious meeting took precedence. Witherspoon and his associates met to discuss the relationship between the federal structure of Presbyterianism and the new political union in which it was encompassed. They also set about producing an updated version of the Westminster Confession of Faith.[33]

In most of the written material produced at the Presbyterian convention, the synod drafters defined the confessional importance of separation between civil and religious jurisdiction. In both the writings on Presbyterian governance and in the new Confession, civil leaders were now largely limited to protecting the free exercise of religion and independent religious societ-

---

32. See "A Bill for Punishing Disturbers of Religious Worship and Sabbath Breakers," in Boyd et al., eds., *Papers of Thomas Jefferson,* II, 555–556. As William Lee Miller points out, the "same Assembly that passed Jefferson's religious liberty bill also passed a statute requiring the observance of Sunday as a day of rest [on Nov. 27, 1785]." See Miller, *The First Liberty: America's Foundation in Religious Freedom,* rev. ed. (Washington, D.C., 2003), 48. See also Robert L. Cord, "Mr. Jefferson's 'Nonabsolute' Wall of Separation between Church and State," in Sheldon and Dreisbach, eds., *Religion and Political Culture,* 171–172. On the continued constitutional tension during later decades, see Steven K. Green, *The Second Disestablishment: Church and State in Nineteenth-Century America* (New York, 2010), 231–247.

33. See *A Draught of the Form of the Government and Discipline of the Presbyterian Church in the United States of America* (New York, 1787). On Witherspoon's potential contribution to the introduction of the *Draught* and the amended Confession, see David Walker Woods, *John Witherspoon* (London, 1906), 173–177.

ies — a radical shift in political theology. Yet there were also aspects of the Presbyterian meeting that recalled the constitutional ambiguities of Witherspoon's previous civic proclamations during the early 1780s. The introduction to the new Confession offered ostensible support for the state's role in securing and protecting the free exercise of religious groups (as long as it did not favor any one group over the other). Paradoxically, such a support mechanism still offered a slight role for government in religious affairs, albeit as a means to protect free exercise.[34]

In his writings on the disestablishment of religion, Madison supplied comparatively few caveats that could be interpreted in favor of state intervention in private religious affairs. His *Memorial* had simply suggested that:

> Whilst we assert for ourselves a freedom to embrace, to profess and to observe the Religion which we believe to be of divine origin, we cannot deny an equal freedom to those whose minds have not yet yielded to the evidence which has convinced us. If this freedom be abused, it is an offence against God, not against man: To God, therefore, not to man, must an account of it be rendered. . . . Government will be best supported by protecting every Citizen in the enjoyment of his Religion with the same equal hand which protects his person and his property; by neither invading the equal rights of any Sect, nor suffering any Sect to invade those of another.

Madison upheld an equal freedom not just among Christian sects but also in relation to non-Christians. Of course, his use of the word "yet" suggested that, in his opinion, those nonbelievers would likely "yield" to the evidence of the gospel in due time. Denying their right to conscience was an "offence

34. For the section highlighting the limited religious jurisdiction of civil magistrates, see *Draught of the Form of the Government*, [iii]. On the limitation of civil leaders to the protection of the free exercise of religion and the independence of religious societies in the *Draught of the Form of the Government* and the updated version of the Westminster Confession of Faith, see Miller, *The Religious Roots of the First Amendment*, 149–151; Leonard J. Trinterud, *The Forming of an American Tradition: A Re-examination of Colonial Presbyterianism* (Philadelphia, 1949), 292–293; Bradley J. Longfield, *Presbyterians and American Culture: A History* (Louisville, Ky., 2013), 47–50; Frank A. Beattie, *Companion to the Constitution of the Presbyterian Church (U.S.A.): Polity for the Local Church* (Louisville, Ky., 1999), 4. On the stipulation that civil magistrates might still retain some control to secure and protect the free exercise of religion, see Miller, *The Religious Roots of the First Amendment*, 151. Here I differ slightly with Miller, arguing that such a caveat somewhat reduced the radicalism of the synod drafters, at least in comparison to Madison's *Memorial*.

against God, not against man," because it prevented God's eventual role in their personal salvation.[35]

Two years later, in 1787, at the Constitutional Convention, Madison continued to define his position regarding the disestablishment of religion using reasoning that he had begun to display as a young man following graduation. In 1789, having given up his opposition to the notion of a Bill of Rights, Madison spoke in favor of the First Amendment to the U.S. Constitution. He used reasoning similar to that in his *Memorial and Remonstrance,* as shown in the discussion of the first clause of the Bill of Rights, "No religion shall be established by law, nor shall the equal rights of conscience be infringed." Mr. Madison "said, he apprehended the meaning of the words to be, that Congress should not establish a religion, and enforce the legal observation of it by law, nor compel men to worship God in any manner contrary to their conscience." Although the First Amendment restricted any national religious establishment, it was also written, without Madison's full support, to allow a degree of autonomy within each constituent state in matters of corporate religious oversight. Later, in *"The Federalist* Number 51," looking back on events since the 1787 Constitutional Convention, Madison concluded: "The security for civil rights must be the same as that for religious rights. It consists in the one case in the multiplicity of interests, and in the other, in the multiplicity of sects."[36]

Aside from the specific issue of constitutional religious establishment, other more general religious influences in Madison's constitutionalism before ratification can also be detected in his writings. In his *Memorial and Remonstrance,* Madison warned that the subjective conclusions of civic actors ought to remain separate from the province of faith, religious duty, regeneration, and salvation. Opposing civic intervention in matters of religious conscience, he had claimed that moral opinion depended on evidence contemplated by the human mind. The subjective nature of ethical contemplation made it problematic to assume that individuals could commonly follow moral dictates from other people in civic positions. Such a statement could easily have appeared in the writings of Jonathan Edwards or, indeed, Witherspoon.

35. Madison, *Memorial and Remonstrance,* in Hutchinson et al., eds., *Papers of James Madison,* VIII, 300, 302.

36. For Madison's arguments on the First Amendment, see statement by James Madison in "Amendments to the Constitution," Aug. 15, 1789, in United States, Congress, *The Debates and Proceedings . . . ,* I (Washington, D.C., 1834), 758; Ralph Ketcham, *Framed for Posterity: The Enduring Philosophy of the Constitution* (Lawrence, Kans., 1993), 103. For Madison's statement on the "multiplicity of sects," see Publius [James Madison], *"The Federalist* Number 51," Feb. 6, 1788, in Hutchinson et al., eds., *Papers of James Madison,* X, 478–479.

Yet, two years later, the debates at the Constitutional Convention generally omitted reference to Christian doctrine even though the framers believed that republican government required a virtuous populace. And, according to the established historiography, it was David Hume, as political theorist—rather than Calvin, Edwards, or Witherspoon—who most influenced Madison during the 1787 Constitutional Convention.[37]

It is true that Madison reflected several Humean concerns regarding the structure of governance. Most notable was his suggestion that factions were inevitable but that an extended republic would allow a sufficient number to neutralize any one particular interest group. The argument for centralized constitutional government was amenable to Hume's political philosophy because both systems of thought sought to maintain a coherent connection between individuals in a community, despite the inherent difficulty in proving their common perception of the public good. Madison and his Federalist allies were Humean in their understanding that individual sentiments cohered in communal identity through the repetition of civic messages (rather than from any innate common sense). Anti-Federalists were more Hutchesonian in their support for personal and specific ties of benevolence, which they argued were best asserted on the local, rather than national, level. Precise sensory reactions to personal associates were necessary to maintain social coherence, rather than abstractions such as "opinion"—particularly when formed through repeated civic mandates.[38]

---

37. Madison, *Memorial and Remonstrance*, in Hutchinson et al., eds., *Papers of James Madison*, VIII, 299. On the omission of reference to Christian doctrine, see Rodney Grunes, "James Madison and Religious Freedom," in Vile, Pederson, and Williams, eds., *James Madison*, 110. There is no doubt that Hume's political theory influenced Madison in his understanding of the role of factions in society, particularly Hume's 1752 "Idea of a Perfect Commonwealth." See Douglass Adair, " 'That Politics May be Reduced to a Science': David Hume, James Madison, and the Tenth *Federalist*," *Huntington Library Quarterly*, XX (1957), 348–349; Roy Branson, "James Madison and the Scottish Enlightenment," *Journal of the History of Ideas*, XL (1979), 244; Marc M. Arkin, "The Intractable Principle: David Hume, James Madison, Religion, and the Tenth Federalist," *American Journal of Legal History*, XXXIX (1995), 148–157; Banning, *Sacred Fire of Liberty*, 204; Ralph L. Ketcham, "Notes on James Madison's Sources for the Tenth Federalist Paper," *Midwest Journal of Political Science*, I (1957), 20, 23; Mark G. Spencer, *David Hume and Eighteenth-Century America* (Rochester, N.Y., 2005), 240–246; Spencer, "Hume and Madison on Faction," *WMQ*, 3d Ser., LIX (2002), 869–896; Robert A. Manzer, "A Science of Politics: Hume, *The Federalist*, and the Politics of Constitutional Attachment," *American Journal of Political Science*, XLV (2001), 508–518.

38. On the role of "opinion" and sentiments of allegiance through repetition (rather than innate sensibility), see Colleen A. Sheehan, "Madison v. Hamilton: The Battle over Republicanism and the Role of Public Opinion," *American Political Science Review*, XCVIII (2004),

In an ironic parallel with evangelical thinking, Hume's distinction between shifting public opinion and objective communal ideas had often unsettled the notion of a common moral sensibility. Madison's association of
contingent mental evidence and changing opinion in his *Memorial and Remonstrance* could in fact have appeared in Hume's writings—as well as in
those of Witherspoon or Edwards. Indeed, the Humean influence on Madisonian federalism could very well have been related to the education Madison received from Witherspoon. Scholars have not yet made this connection, and certainly not in terms of its religious basis, which is unsurprising
given Hume's famous skepticism of revealed religion. Much later in Madison's life, when Jefferson requested that he prepare a catalog of books on
religion for the library at the University of Virginia, Madison included a collection of writings and sermons by John Calvin as well as Jonathan Edwards.
Translated works by Calvin had been included on the College of New Jersey reading lists that were circulated to Madison and his classmates. Many
of Witherspoon's sermons, following Calvin, were framed as a response to
Paul's Epistle to the Galatians, showing the centrality of sin and the necessity of faith in saving grace. Witherspoon's "Lectures on Moral Philosophy"
and "Lectures on Divinity" included positive references and allusions to the
reasoning in Calvin's *Sermons on Galatians.* To date, to be sure, there is no
evidence that Witherspoon somehow met with Madison in Philadelphia during the summer of 1787 or that he implored his student to apply Calvinist
doctrines on human depravity to his political deliberations in general or to
his reading of Hume in particular. Nonetheless, it is possible to highlight certain analogues in their discussion of the relationship between human nature
and political government and certain ironies in their similarity to those employed by Hume.[39]

405–424. Sheehan discusses Madison's understanding of the need to channel naturally differing
public sentiments into a form of public opinion, allowing some semblance of political stability.
Richard C. Sinopoli, discussing the relative Humean and Hutchesonian influences on Federalists and Anti-Federalists, suggests that both groups conceived of virtue as a *"sentiment* of allegiance from which a disposition to undertake civic duties would emerge," but they differed in
their understanding of the nature of that sentiment. See Sinopoli, *The Foundations of American
Citizenship: Liberalism, the Constitution, and Civic Virtue* (New York, 1992), 6, 8, 20.

39. Ralph Ketcham points out that Hume was also on Witherspoon's reading list, but he does
not follow up this observation. In a 1961 article for the *Princeton University Library Chronicle,*
James H. Smylie suggested that Princeton religiosity might have influenced Madison's political
thought. Although he did not point to any epistemological similarity between Humean skepticism and Witherspoon's brand of Calvinism, Smylie made a pertinent link between Witherspoon and Madison that has often been overlooked in subsequent decades. As an exception,

Four years after Madison's graduation, we should recall, Witherspoon had pointed out in his *Dominion of Providence* that a "good form of government may hold the rotten materials together for some time, but beyond a certain pitch, even the best constitution will be ineffectual." In his essay "On the Origin of Government," written around 1774, Hume had claimed that humanity's perverse propensity for faction required men to "palliate what they cannot cure" by instituting a government. Witherspoon's "good form of government" allowed rotten individuals to cohere for longer than normal, but not interminably. Hume's use of the term "palliate" had suggested a similar process: individual corruptions could be managed despite their overall inability to cohere. Witherspoon had offered a similar argument in his 1776 "Speech in Congress upon the Confederation":

> Shall we establish nothing good, because we know it cannot be eternal?
> Shall we live without government, because every constitution has its old
> age, and its period? Because we know that we shall die, shall we take no
> pains to preserve or lengthen out life? Far from it, sir: it only requires
> the more watchful attention to settle government . . . that it may last as
> long as the nature of things will admit.

Witherspoon had hoped to "to settle government" so that "it may last as long as the nature of things will admit"—never in perpetuity, but for as long as possible before the inevitable disintegration of human artifice.[40]

In *Dominion of Providence,* however, Witherspoon also suggested that "true religion and internal principles" could provide greater coherence in society, despite the rotten nature of the unregenerate state. His definition

---

Garrett Ward Sheldon and Mary Elaine Swanson have followed Smylie and Ketcham in noting Witherspoon's influence over Madison, albeit without regard to the Humean association. See Ketcham, *James Madison,* 32-45, 652; Smylie, "Madison and Witherspoon: Theological Roots of American Political Thought," *Princeton University Library Chronicle,* XXII (1961), 118-132; Sheldon, *The Political Philosophy of James Madison* (Baltimore, 2001), 13-15; Mary-Elaine Swanson, "James Madison and the Presbyterian Idea of Man and Government," in Sheldon and Dreisbach, eds., *Religion and Political Culture,* 119-132. For the works by John Calvin, see Calvin, *Sermons on Galatians,* trans. Kathy Childress (Edinburgh, 1997). For examples of Witherspoon's response to the Epistle to the Galatians, see Witherspoon, "Lectures on Divinity," in [Green, ed.], *Works of Witherspoon,* IV, 118; John Witherspoon, "The World Crucified by the Cross of Christ," ibid., I, 407-446; Witherspoon, "Glorying in the Cross," ibid., 387.

40. John Witherspoon, *The Dominion of Providence over the Passions of Men* . . . , in [Green, ed.], *Works of Witherspoon,* III, 41; David Hume, "On the Origin of Government," in Hume, *Political Essays,* ed. Knud Haakonssen (Cambridge, 1994), 35; Witherspoon, *Part of a Speech in Congress, upon the Confederation,* in [Green, ed.], *Works of Witherspoon,* IV, 350.

of true religion centered on a "full conviction of the sinfulness of our nature and state." Supplied as a gift of grace in the regenerated heart and then vigorously proclaimed throughout society, a new moral sense of revealed law could provide greater civic stability, as long as personal sin, rather than social coherence, was the primary motivation for the conversion of individuals. This aspect of Witherspoon's political theology contributed to his inchoate support for the disestablishment of religion. In order to govern according to the moral light of revelation, future magistrates were required to work out their salvation independently, or at least within independent churches, before any thought of governance or civic leadership.[41]

Madison, in comparison, enjoyed less leeway to define the civic importance of regeneration at the Constitutional Convention. He was no clergyman describing the ideal republic. Rather, he was faced with the actual task of crafting a new system of government. Its constituents could not be guaranteed to be faithful. Thus, he could not rely solely on the role of disestablished piety in supplying leaders with humility, as defined by their ability to acknowledge the fallible nature of their innate moral stance. Madison assumed greater realism regarding the ability of government to cohere. Like Witherspoon, his description of the propensity for faction was both Humean and Calvinistic. But his remedy required the machinery of central government to function *even if* its constituents were corrupt or unregenerate.

In his "Lectures on Eloquence," Witherspoon had reminded his students, including Madison, that any "assembly" of men, whether in present-day America or in the classical period, would be disorderly and without any moderating common sense. In *The Federalist,* Madison's Humean arguments similarly described the inherent difficulty in galvanizing common sentiments through human government. In his letters to William Bradford after graduation, he had pronounced his unease with Socratic rhetoric. In *"The Federalist* Number 55," he warned that, "had every Athenian citizen been a Socrates, every Athenian assembly would still have been a mob." In his famous discussion of factions in *"The Federalist* Number 10," Madison's depiction of "the numerous advantages promised by a well constructed union" claimed that it was "impracticable" to give "every citizen the same opinions, the same passions, and the same interests" because the "latent causes of faction are thus sown in the nature of man." In outlining his "republican remedy for the diseases most incident to republican government," Madison highlighted the human propensity for corruption and the human susceptibility to self-

---

41. Witherspoon, *Dominion of Providence,* in [Green, ed.], *Works of Witherspoon,* III, 20, 41. On disestablishment and independent societies, see the discussion in Chapter 7, above.

love, separate from virtuous action toward the public good. Governance was required to harness rather than deny the subjective nature of human perception:

> Extend the sphere, and you take in a greater variety of parties and inter-ests; you make it less probable that a majority of the whole will have a common motive to invade the rights of other citizens; or if such a com-mon motive exists, it will be more difficult for all who feel it to discover their own strength, and to act in unison with each other.

Thus, Madison's account of human nature isolated the defects of representa-tive government in order to reduce the potential of factions by checking one against the other.[42]

Madison's desire to check natural human defects in a subordinate political system reflected Hume's palliative recommendations for political confedera-tions. That Madison used a religious motif to do so offers a little more sup-port for the comparison that several scholars have made between his famous reference to humans, angels, and governance in *"The Federalist Number 51"* and a similar statement by John Calvin in his *Sermons on Galatians.* Madison considered what "devices should be necessary to control the abuses of gov-ernment" before asking: "But what is government itself but the greatest of all reflections on human nature? If men were angels, no government would be necessary. If angels were to govern men, neither external nor internal controls on government would be necessary." Calvin asserted, in the same subjunctive mood: "If we were all like angels, blameless and freely able to exercise perfect self-control, we would not need rules or regulations. Why, then, do we have so many laws and statutes? Because of man's wickedness, for he is constantly overflowing with evil; this is why a remedy is required." Madison demon-strated a similarity with Calvin's syllogistic argument. Both began with a similar question (what if men were angels?) that was followed by an answer (they were not) and a remedy (a realistic form of governance). There are cer-tainly some Madison scholars who have not eschewed the potential link be-tween a Calvinist doctrine of factional egoism and the Virginian's desire to check potential corruptions within a political system. But they have not made the ironic link to Hume through Madison's exposure to a Scottish evangeli-cal teacher. Witherspoon outlined the common variation between individual

---

42. Witherspoon, "Lectures on Eloquence," in [Green, ed.], *Works of Witherspoon,* III, 511; Publius [James Madison], *"The Federalist* Number 10," Nov. 22, 1787, and *"The Federalist* Num-ber 55," Feb. 13, 1788, both in Hutchinson et al., eds., *Papers of James Madison,* X, 263, 264, 265, 268–270, 505.

interests and their necessary counterbalance. Similar to Madison in his later writings, he highlighted the folly in trusting directly elected representatives of the people to act like angels, or even with a modicum of integrity. In promiscuous assemblies, factionalism was likely to develop as a result of the divergence between subjective sensibilities, particularly when the moral regeneration of their constituents could not be guaranteed. Instead, a nexus and counterpoise was a more realistic option, deriving from each subjective interest checking the other. All these ideas, from a Calvinist standpoint, sound oddly similar to Humean skepticism as it came to be refracted through Hume's political writings. Hume's "Idea of a Perfect Commonwealth," for example, focused on balancing those factions that were unable to perceive the world through objectively predictable ideas.[43]

But, of course, elsewhere Witherspoon went on to recommend religious regeneration before governance. Within a disestablished realm, true conversion would allow a new sense of revealed morality among future magistrates, inspired by the Holy Spirit and then wrought by the divine grace of God. Madison, conversely, returned to the notion of counterpoise among subjective factions. Perhaps realizing that not all national representatives were likely to be regenerate, he described a different vision of the "genius of the people." No one faction could dominate American political life if enough varying interests and perceptions were included at its heart—a calculated model of chaos at the center of government.[44]

43. [Madison], "*The Federalist* Number 51," Feb. 6, 1788, in Hutchinson et al., eds., *Papers of James Madison*, X, 477; Calvin, *Sermons on Galatians*, 313, 435; Calvin, *Sermons on Galatians*, cited in David W. Hall, *The Genevan Reformation and the American Founding* (Lanham, Md., 2003), 6; Witherspoon, "Lectures on Moral Philosophy," in [Green, ed.], *Works of Witherspoon*, III, 435. For rare references to the broad link between Madison's reasoning in *The Federalist* and Witherspoon's Calvinist sensibility, see Sheldon, *The Political Philosophy of James Madison*, 17, 62–88; Smylie, "Madison and Witherspoon," *Princeton University Library Chronicle*, XXII (1961), 123. For Madison and Scottish Enlightenment ideas (often incorporating Hume), see Ralph L. Ketcham, "James Madison and the Nature of Man," *Journal of the History of Ideas*, XIX (1958), 62–76; Branson, "James Madison and the Scottish Enlightenment," ibid., XL (1979), 235–250. Samuel Fleischacker has suggested that Madison's understanding of religious faction and disestablishment derived from his reading of Adam Smith on the same issue, notwithstanding scholarly misreadings of Smith on the "invisible hand" in social, economic, and religious relationships. See Fleischacker, "Adam Smith's Reception among the American Founders, 1776–1790," *WMQ*, 3d Ser., LIX (2002), 897–924. For Hume on faction, including in his "Idea of a Perfect Commonwealth," see Note 37, above.

44. On Madison's conception of a "genius of the people," see Madison to Jefferson, May 9, 1789, in Hutchinson et al., eds., *Papers of James Madison*, XII, 143; Gordon S. Wood, *The Creation of the American Republic, 1776–1787* (Chapel Hill, N.C., 1969), 93–97.

Hutcheson, Hume, and Witherspoon: What would each have made of Madison's famous statement that "the latent causes of faction are thus sown in the nature of man"? Moderate Scots read Hutcheson and became a faction, despite believing themselves to be above party. Evangelical Scots became ever more fractious — perhaps even uncharitable — in their opposition to Moderates. Hume observed both, noted the irony, and formulated his own skeptical philosophy. It is the irony of American history that all three might have claimed Madison's phrase as their own, using it as a signifier of depraved humanity, a spur for skepticism, or an emblem of that which advanced sociability, with its discovery of the common sense, had quashed.

"The Finiteness of the Human Understanding Betrays Itself on All Subjects"

In December 1787, while Madison publicized his thoughts on faction in *The Federalist,* Witherspoon took his place as a representative at the New Jersey state ratification proceedings for the U.S. Constitution, held in Trenton. Opposing the Anti-Federalist writings of "Brutus," which were likely the work of Robert Yates in resistance to the notion of a strong national government, Witherspoon spoke in favor of a "rotating center" for the administrative capital in his new nation. He questioned Congress's desire to create a fixed location to house the representatives of the citizens of the new United States — "a federal city, in a central place, yet thinly inhabited." The "Swiss Cantons," Witherspoon pointed out, enjoyed "no federal city" and instead "held their Diets in different places" with great success. Thus, he argued that, "if the particular states are to be preserved and supported in their constitutional government, it seems of very little consequence where the Congress, consisting of representatives from these states, shall hold their sessions." Conversely, he continued, several "advantages might arise from their being unfixed and ambulatory." Witherspoon, whose evangelicalism had always been unfixed and ambulatory, did not wish for the seat of social and political control to be located permanently in any particular city or region. Perhaps he had in mind the corrupt benefits that, in his view, Moderate ministers had accrued in their dealings with Westminster.[45]

Madison, late in his own life, after serving as U.S. secretary of state and president of the United States, responded to a request from Frederick Bea-

---

45. John Witherspoon, "A Few Reflections Humbly Submitted to the Consideration of the Public in General, and in Particular to the Congress of the United States," in [Green, ed.], *Works of Witherspoon,* IV, 415–416.

sley. An educator, moral philosopher, and College of New Jersey graduate, Beasley asked for Madison's opinion regarding a pamphlet he had written, which discussed God's existence and attributes. Madison, at the age of
seventy-five, wrote: "The belief in a God All Powerful wise and good, is so
essential to the moral order of the World and to the happiness of man, that
arguments which enforce it cannot be drawn from too many sources nor
adapted with too much solicitude to the different characters and capacities
to be impressed with it." Further in the letter, he concluded:

> The finiteness of the human understanding betrays itself on all sub-
> jects, but more especially when it contemplates such as involve infinity.
> What may safely be said seems to be, that the infinity of time and space
> forces itself on our conception, a limitation of either being inconceiv-
> able; that the mind prefers at once the idea of a self-existing cause . . .
> and that it finds more facility in assenting to the self-existence of an in-
> visible cause possessing infinite power, wisdom and goodness, than to
> the self-existence of the universe, visibly destitute of those attributes,
> and which may be the effect of them. In this comparative facility of
> conception and belief, all philosophical Reasoning on the subject must
> perhaps terminate.

In his letter, Madison claimed that moral norms could not be determined
solely through innate sense, or reason: the "finiteness of the human understanding betrays itself on all subjects." To support his assertion, Madison
referred to works of theology "which [he] read 50 years ago"—during and
immediately after his period studying divinity and Hebrew under Witherspoon.[46]

Judging by his statement in old age, at least, the religious education
Madison had received under Witherspoon resonated for decades, though,
of course, he had become far more reticent when defining his faith in public forums or in discussing his beliefs on the exact nature of the connection
between church and state. But, before the nineteenth century, Madison's approach to disestablishment and his general understanding of political factionalism was influenced by his learning at Witherspoon's Princeton. Madison's
parents sent him from Anglican Virginia to a primarily Presbyterian college.
The "great revival" of religion that took place among the student body predisposed his later readings of history and politics, as did his continuing re-

46. For Madison's late statements on religion, see James Madison to Frederick Beasley, Nov.
20, 1825, in Gaillard Hunt, ed., *The Writings of James Madison* (New York, 1910), IX, 229–231.

lationship with his teacher in and out of Congress. Had Madison attended the College of William and Mary, and had he not gravitated toward evangelical Presbyterians in New Jersey and Virginia, he would have been less likely to question political systems that required innate benevolence among their leaders and constituents. He also would have found it more difficult to gain such a broad constituency of support for his movement toward disestablishment in Virginia.

By the late 1780s, to be sure, Madison demonstrated greater realism when estimating the power of local religious institutions to provide pious civic officers ready to grapple with their sin and to channel the external moral will of God. In designing the Federal Constitution, he was required to consider the sectional contingencies of an entire union of people. The difficulties he faced—including opposition from slaveholders who feared losing authority to nonslaveholding representatives—confirmed his Calvinistic assumption that the latent causes of faction were sown in the nature of man. But those complications also required him to construct a representative system in which interests and egos were checked against one another, without relying on all citizens achieving moral regeneration before voting or officeholding.[47]

As Madison forged compromises on the enslavement of people and the representation of slaveholders—what he referred to as "the great division of interests"—his mentor also briefly considered the role of slavery in the union. As a member of a New Jersey legislative committee from late 1789, Witherspoon shared the vision of gradualists who favored the eventual diminishment of slavery in America without setting out any immediate program of abolition. Like many in the northern states, he often defined the evolution of universal liberty in the narrow legal sense, rather than suggesting an evolving freedom of the ethical will in more general philosophical terms. Yet, according to tax records, he had owned one or two enslaved people who worked on his farm at Tusculum. Like many founders, including Madison, clues from Witherspoon's estate inventory were not entirely congruent with the few statements in which he queried the validity and morality of slavery

47. On Madison and the debate over slavery during the drafting and ratification of the Constitution, see Jeff Broadwater, *James Madison: A Son of Virginia and a Founder of the Nation* (Chapel Hill, N.C., 2012), 190, 200; Jan Lewis, "The Three-Fifths Clause and the Origins of Sectionalism," in Paul Finkelman and Donald R. Kennon, eds., *Congress and the Emergence of Sectionalism: From the Missouri Compromise to the Age of Jackson* (Athens, Ohio, 2008), 19–46; John P. Kaminski, ed., *A Necessary Evil? Slavery and the Debate over the Constitution* (Madison, Wis., 1995), 42–44.

in America. Following the relative silence of the founding generation on the ethics of American slavery, constitutional compromises perpetuated the institution through the nineteenth century. Madison, and those who followed him into government, would witness conflicts over the expansion of the institution that transcended mere factionalism.[48]

48. For Madison's conception of the "great division of interests," see Lewis, "The Three-Fifths Clause," in Finkelman and Kennon, eds., *Congress and the Emergence of Sectionalism*, 19; Max Ferrand, ed., *The Records of the Federal Convention of 1787*, 4 vols. (1911; rpt. New Haven, Conn., 1966), I, 486. For Witherspoon's few words on the New Jersey Committee that considered the role of slavery, see L. Gordon Tait, *The Piety of John Witherspoon: Pew, Pulpit, and Public Forum* (Louisville, Ky., 2001), 46–47.

CHAPTER 9

"GREAT THINGS HATH GOD DONE

FOR HIS AMERICAN ZION"

Presbyterian Moral Philosophy and Educational

Conflict during the Nineteenth Century

On Monday, May 30, 1791, John Witherspoon married a twenty-four-year-old widow, Ann Dill, the wife of his former pupil, Dr. Armstrong Dill. Witherspoon was sixty-nine years old, and his courtship with a twenty-four-year-old woman might have raised eyebrows. But, when he returned to his college after his marriage ceremony, students pushed the cannon that lay near Nassau Hall and fired in honor of the college president's recent nuptials. The hall was then lit up by six hundred candles, with students singing in Witherspoon's honor, all before a gathering crowd. Just over two decades earlier, on the night of Witherspoon's arrival to the College of New Jersey, every window in the main college building had been similarly illuminated. Between those two candlelit moments, the building had been surrounded by fire in the midst of Revolutionary battle.[1]

In May 1791, Witherspoon was appointed by the General Assembly of the American Presbyterian Church as a delegate to the General Association of Connecticut, which sought greater cooperation between Congregational and Presbyterian churches in regional pastoral activities. By this point, he was steadily going blind, a condition that had worsened since his trip back to Britain several years earlier. On November, 15, 1794, after a brief illness, he died at his home in Tusculum, just outside Princeton village. Writing from Nassau Hall around two weeks later, Joseph Warren Scott, who would graduate in 1796, described the sad news to John Henry Hobart, and he included a message from his friend Joseph Caldwell. Caldwell inquired whether Hobart

---

1. See "Marriages," *Scots Magazine,* LIII (August 1791), 413. On local gossip regarding Witherspoon's new marriage, see the account by Ashbel Green in Varnum Lansing Collins, *President Witherspoon: A Biography,* 2 vols. (Princeton, N.J., 1925), II, 169. On the college candle ceremony for Witherspoon on his arrival and after his later wedding, see ibid., I, 104, II, 170.

would come to visit Princeton in the aftermath of Witherspoon's death and advised Hobart to "be expeditious, or otherwise we will not have a sufficient barrier against infidelity [in the college]." Caldwell's message to Hobart was described as a "stroke" against Scott for having chosen to read some works by David Hume, the author Witherspoon had once described as an infidel while also lauding certain aspects of his style.[2]

Witherspoon's final public composition, "A Letter respecting Play Actors," had criticized theater for arousing moral sympathy through the false display of emotions. He had dictated the letter in late 1793 or early 1794, hoping that it would be published in the Philadelphia *National Gazette*. It offered a strong critique of previously published comments by his former student, Philip Freneau, who had lauded the moral capacity of American theater in the new Republic. "Players," according to Witherspoon, "appearing continually in an assumed character, or being employed in preparing to assume it, must lose all sense of sincerity and truth." "Truth is so sacred a thing, that even the least violation of it, is not without its degree of guilt and danger." Witherspoon's final composition recalled the argument from his *Serious Inquiry into the Nature and Effects of the Stage*, which he had written and published in 1757. Witherspoon had reminded his former classmate—and later prison mate— John Home, the author of a popular play, that "all men are by nature under the power of sin." He objected to theatrical performance because it claimed to arouse the innate moral sensibilities of audience members, irrespective of their state of regeneration. Witherspoon warned that feigned emotional displays would inure individuals to the true feelings experienced before religious conversion. Notwithstanding their shared education at Edinburgh University, Witherspoon's *Serious Inquiry* demonstrated their subsequent disagreement over moral philosophy. Witherspoon and former friends such as Home and Alexander Carlyle came to attach different meanings to their moral philosophies, despite their common education at Edinburgh University. Witherspoon chose to use moral sensory descriptions in order to explain the nature of salvation through grace. Home and Carlyle used sensory terminology to denote innate ethical perception, paying less attention to the necessity of conversion.[3]

2. Joseph Warren Scott to John Henry Hobart, Nov. 27, 1794, in Arthur Lowndes, ed., *The Correspondence of John Henry Hobart*, 6 vols. (New York, 1911), I, 106–107. For Witherspoon's statement on Hume, see John Witherspoon, "Lectures on Eloquence," in [Ashbel Green, ed.], *The Works of the Rev. John Witherspoon, D.D.L.L.D. Late President of the College at Princeton, New-Jersey . . .*, 2d ed., rev., 4 vols. (Philadelphia, 1802), III, 574. See the account of the last years of Witherspoon's life in Collins, *President Witherspoon*, II, 174–179.

3. John Witherspoon, "A Letter respecting Play Actors," in [Green, ed.], *Works of Wither-*

As for Witherspoon's legacy in the decades that followed his "Letter respecting Play Actors," from the early national era through the mid-nineteenth century, his students' views came to reflect similar disagreements, distinctions, and divergences. The Scottish moral philosophy of Home, Carlyle, and their Moderate associates became increasingly prominent among educated Americans. Its proponents included a number of Witherspoon's former students, most conspicuously Samuel Stanhope Smith. Yet other graduates, notably Ashbel Green, opposed Smith's stance. The era also witnessed resurgent movements of evangelical revivalism, some of which were led by Presbyterians who had studied under Witherspoon. These seemingly contradictory occurrences conformed to historical patterns that had earlier appeared in Hanoverian Scotland. In early national America, moral sensory reasoning and evangelical revivalism were once again positioned in mutually reinforcing counterpoise, each defining their moral epistemology against the other yet also sharing conceptual languages.

The contested nature of Witherspoon's wider legacy can be detected in what has been described as an age of "intense strife between 'elite' and 'democratic' interests, between 'formalist' and 'antiformalist' Protestants." During his College of New Jersey presidency, Witherspoon demonstrated important continuities with the evangelicalism of previous college leaders such as Jonathan Dickinson, Samuel Davies, and even Jonathan Edwards. But, through his teaching, he also incorporated the terminology of moral sense philosophy to a greater extent than his predecessors—even if often only to describe familiar concepts such as the sensory awakening to the Holy Spirit and moral regeneration. In doing so, he opened the door for future students who would deduce anthropocentric conceptual inferences from the systems of moral philosophy that he used to provide a richer descriptive vocabulary.[4]

Witherspoon's Conflicted Legacy:
Samuel Stanhope Smith and Ashbel Green

The legacy of eighteenth-century evangelicalism followed a volatile and even ironic pattern. During the 1740s and 1750s, Jonathan Edwards had carefully distinguished between sentimental epistemology and anthropocentric ethical

---

spoon, III, 195–196; Witherspoon, *A Serious Inquiry into the Nature and Effects of the Stage . . .* , ibid., 156.

4. Mark A. Noll, *America's God: From Jonathan Edwards to Abraham Lincoln* (New York, 2002), 131.

assumptions. He sought to delineate the new sense of morality wrought by grace, using philosophical vocabulary to do so. During the early nineteenth century, Congregational theologians became more familiar with the terminology of moral sense philosophy thanks in part to the renewed dissemination of Edwards's writings. Yet a number of the same theologians gravitated toward ethical conclusions that Edwards would not necessarily have supported. New Divinity ministers such as Samuel Hopkins and Joseph Bellamy became less likely to describe the importance of divine grace according to its association with the undeserving individual moral state. Rather than saving undeserving sinners, gracious assistance somehow restored the moral basis of the natural order, including a common sense of benevolent ethical ideals among all people.[5]

The growing popularity of works by Thomas Reid and James Beattie supports the contention that a new moral philosophy in educated Congregational and Presbyterian circles promoted common sense reasoning as a means to ground ethics in universal human instincts. Beattie's *Essay on the Nature and Immutability of Truth* (1770) and his two-volume work the *Elements of Moral Science* (1790–1793) were increasingly referenced in American political and intellectual spheres during Witherspoon's later years and in the half a century after his death. Even more influential were reprints of Thomas Reid's *Inquiry into the Human Mind on the Principles of Common Sense* (1764) along with various essays that he subsequently published. Their work suggested that man's innate understanding—in both its rational and sentimental capacity—naturally confirmed moral precepts that could be found in biblical revelation.[6]

Reid's argument from design was grounded in the necessary first principle that "intelligence, wisdom, and other mental qualities in the cause, may

5. See Noll, *America's God*, 132, 136. For more on the New Divinity theologians in this respect, see Mark A. Noll, "The Enlightenment and Evangelical Intellectual Life," in Peter A. Coclanis and Stuart Bruchey, eds., *Ideas, Ideologies, and Social Movements: The United States Experience since 1800* (Columbia, S.C., 1999), 49–50; Joseph A. Conforti, *Samuel Hopkins and the New Divinity Movement: Calvinism, the Congregational Ministry, and Reform in New England between the Great Awakenings* (Grand Rapids, Mich., 1981), 118; Theodore Dwight Bozeman, *Protestants in an Age of Science: The Baconian Ideal and Antebellum American Religious Thought* (Chapel Hill, N.C., 1977), 6–12; Donald H. Meyer, *The Democratic Enlightenment* (New York, 1976), 30–33.

6. David Lundberg and Henry F. May highlight "a sharp growth in the popularity of the Scots" during the years 1777–1790, especially Beattie, Blair, Ferguson, Kames, Reid, and Smith. See Lundberg and May, "The Enlightened Reader in America," *American Quarterly*, XXVIII (1976), 269. See also May, *The Enlightenment in America* (New York, 1976), xvi, 12, 327–332.

be inferred from their marks or signs in the effect." The notion of an inborn common sense, before any encounter with biblical revelation, represented a departure from Calvinist orthodoxy. Yet a new generation of American ministers and civic leaders found the idea of universal moral intuition rather amenable to their authority. It usefully described the correspondence between ethical sensibility and scriptural morality. Though such an association was evident to all men, the ability to describe its role inevitably distinguished ministers' representative power. Opportunely, they suggested that their communitarian leadership reflected the benevolent ethical sense of all their constituents, students, and laymen. Thus, they could define their rise to societal prominence as a legitimate manifestation of the popular will. Though they found themselves in respected positions of authority as professors, clergymen, and local civic leaders, they claimed to embody the compassionate actions and reactions that all men were capable of displaying in their response to moral conceptions. By defining the innate ethical response as God-given, they avoided the charge that they were advocating secularism or denigrating biblical morality. Rather, they argued that inborn ethical interpretations would surely confirm biblical ideals in scripture—ideals that they were well positioned to elucidate as public leaders.[7]

Such an analysis supports scholarly assessments of the ironic relationship between common sense philosophy and elite authority in the decades following the Declaration of Independence. An "indisputable, plainspoken, popular common sense" was often described as a natural component in the democratic egalitarianism that took root in Philadelphia and elsewhere in early national America. Yet such a populist message enabled representative elites to define the meaning of "common sense" in order to outmaneuver those who were less adept at evoking the plain-speaking sensibility of the wider population. They incorporated scholarly philosophical ideas in a way that strengthened their elite standing without explicitly denigrating the notion

---

7. Thomas Reid, "Essay VI," *Essays on the Intellectual Powers of Man* (Edinburgh, 1785), 622; Noll, *America's God*, 94; Sophia Rosenfeld, *Common Sense: A Political History* (Cambridge, Mass., 2011), 147–148. Educated young men gravitated toward Scottish philosophy because "they were now out in the open without a theological canopy" that had previously emphasized the unregenerate nature of moral perception. See Noll, *America's God*, 93–113, 136, 253–268; Mark A. Noll, *Princeton and the Republic, 1768–1822: The Search for a Christian Enlightenment in the Era of Samuel Stanhope Smith* (Princeton, N.J., 1989), 185–243; Noll, ed., *The Princeton Theology, 1812–1921: Scripture, Science, and Theological Method from Archibald Alexander to Benjamin Breckinridge Warfield* (Grand Rapids, Mich., 1983), 30–33; E. Brooks Holifield, *Theology in America: Christian Thought from the Age of the Puritans to the Civil War* (New Haven, Conn., 2005), 173–196; May, *The Enlightenment in America*, 337–357.

of democratic expansion. On the one hand, Thomas Paine's famous treatise *Common Sense* applied the first principles of Reid's epistemological system to support a political cause rather than an abstract ideal in ethical philosophy. It reminded ordinary people that their common sense had been obscured by familiar prejudices and customs—including those that buttressed existing forms of hierarchical authority. On the other hand, new constitutional debates also hinted at the surprising congruence between Scottish common sense philosophy and more radical understandings of popular will. A vision of common sense supplied a basis for government by the will of the people, according to their communally held beliefs and experiences. But it also provided the means for leaders to justify their stratified authority *over* the people, persuading them that it had been their will to create the systems of government that allowed executive judgment and power by elites. Thus, the democratic potential of common sense could veer toward a "populist" rather than a purely egalitarian agenda. It allowed political and religious leaders to define the legitimacy of their own representative authority, often against rival leaders. Rather than turning toward the Painite definition of common sense, some early national politicians looked to the relatively conservative context in the Scottish philosophical tradition. They claimed to represent self-evident norms on behalf of the people, highlighting the distinction between power derived from the people as an abstract norm and power more pointedly seated in the people.[8]

Witherspoon, other than in a few specific sections of his "Lectures on Moral Philosophy" (many of which focused on parental love), often opposed the Hutchesonian notion of innate ethical perception, both as a philosophical ideal in its own right and as a component in a pyramid of perceptual faculties, as outlined by Thomas Reid. Unlike Paine, moreover, he had avoided any notion that individuals instinctively perceived the general interest and the common good. But his evangelical qualifications at least shared the Painite tendency to unsettle the association between common sensibility and public leadership. By the turn to the nineteenth century, however, some of his former students paid less attention to the distinction their teacher had drawn between the common perception of external objects and an innate judgment of their ethical interaction. They translated their familiarity with the terminology of Scottish philosophy into a broader confirmation of its anthropocentric moral claims. As ministers and civic leaders, they distinguished their moral authority from more egalitarian accounts of common sensibility, as

8. See Rosenfeld, *Common Sense,* 134, 138, 144–145, 147, 163, 168, 171, 175–180 (quotation on 178).

implied by Paine, as well as from the populist characteristic of evangelical enthusiasm, which had begun to appear in a new wave of religious revivalism. The conservative aspect of Scottish philosophy thus proved convenient to their assumption of social authority. They were able to claim that dissenters from their civic vision — either members of the wider populace or their intellectual and religious rivals — somehow lacked the common sense of reasonable men.[9]

The career of Samuel Stanhope Smith provides the clearest example of such a divergent legacy. He had graduated from Witherspoon's College of New Jersey in 1769 and so had heard Witherspoon's earliest "Lectures on Moral Philosophy." He underwent further training to become a Presbyterian minister and professor, beginning at Hampden-Sydney College. Eventually, he assumed the role of president of the College of New Jersey (increasingly known as Princeton University) between 1795 and 1812. Smith was not exposed to Witherspoon's teaching to the extent of Madison and other students who arrived later in his tenure. Nonetheless, he returned to Princeton to undergo further theological training, including under Witherspoon, before taking his position at Hampden-Sydney College. In 1775, Smith married Witherspoon's daughter Ann. He reencountered Witherspoon's lectures when he returned to Princeton in 1779 as a professor of moral philosophy. He often taught while Witherspoon was away in Philadelphia and elsewhere, and he also acted as an administrator. During his subsequent career as Princeton president, Smith attempted to highlight continuities between his anthropocentric ethical philosophy and that which could be found during Witherspoon's earlier presidency.[10]

Smith's attraction to innate moral sensibility was evident from as early as the late 1770s, when he corresponded with James Madison on the subject

9. On the new channels for Scottish common sense philosophy during the early nineteenth century, see Daniel Walker Howe, *Making the American Self: Jonathan Edwards to Abraham Lincoln* (Cambridge, Mass., 1997), 65–67. The post-Revolutionary era offered former College of New Jersey students such as Samuel Blair, Jr. (1741–1818), "the chance to modify inherited faith along lines pursued by liberals in the old country and the advanced Congregationalists of Boston." Though they were "descendants" of "midcentury" evangelical communities, men such as Blair chose to avoid the experimental piety of earlier generations. See Noll, *America's God*, 127–128.

10. Noll, *America's God*, 129; Noll, *Princeton and the Republic*, 54; Bradley J. Longfield, *Presbyterians and American Culture: A History* (Louisville, Ky., 2013), 62–64; Charles Bradford Bow, "Reforming Witherspoon's Legacy at Princeton: John Witherspoon, Samuel Stanhope Smith, and James McCosh on Didactic Enlightenment, 1768–1888," *History of European Ideas*, XXXIX (2013), 657–663.

FIGURE 23. *Samuel Stanhope Smith (1750–1819), Class of 1769, President (1795–1812).* By Charles B. Lawrence. 1813–1825. Princeton University Art Museum / Art Resource, N.Y.

of free will. Madison and his friend William Bradford looked back to their earlier moral education under Witherspoon and asserted the importance of conversion and "experimental," or experiential, piety before moral reasoning. Smith, as we saw previously, argued for the less orthodox principle of the will's ability to determine ethical choices. He used sensory terminology, which he had encountered under Witherspoon. But, in doing so, he asserted anthropocentric ethical claims that Witherspoon had once questioned or qualified with what he considered to be more orthodox religious assertions. Alluding to the theory of Francis Hutcheson and Thomas Reid, Smith suggested to Madison that "in every common phenomenon of nature we must be contented with some inexplicable circumstance," and he asked, rhetorically: "Can we explain how the colour of green is formed? can we even explain what green is, unless by appealing to a common sensation of mankind?" Smith then linked his question analogously to his discussion of morals, supporting the claim that an innate mental understanding could explain ethical freedom just as individuals were intuitively able to discern colors.[11]

During the same period, Smith contributed to the founding and establishment of Hampden-Sydney College in Virginia. The institution was formally established in late 1775 under the auspices of the Hanover Presbytery in Prince Edward County. The board of trustees retained four College of New Jersey graduates: Smith, John Todd, Caleb Wallace, and the Reverend Samuel Leake. Todd, as we have seen, signed many petitions on religious freedom as a moderator of the Hanover Presbytery, and he was also a colonel in the Louisa County militia. Smith, during Hampden-Sydney's initial years in operation and before his assumption of the presidency of Princeton, was assisted by other former College of New Jersey men, including his brother, John Blair Smith, Samuel Doak, John Springer (a college preacher), and David Witherspoon (another of John Witherspoon's sons).[12]

Hampden-Sydney College, founded during the critical months before the Declaration of Independence, experienced continual tensions with local Anglican interests in Virginia. Through the early national era, Anglicans feared their loss of representative authority as state disestablishment seemed more likely. Yet, in seeking a measured reaction to Anglican criticisms of his Presbyterian authority, ironically, Smith encouraged new opposition from members of his own denomination. The resulting conflict provided further evidence of the tension between his developing moral philosophy and the

11. Samuel Stanhope Smith to James Madison, Sept. 15, 1778, in William T. Hutchinson et al., eds., *The Papers of James Madison*, 34 vols. to date (Chicago, 1962-1977; Charlottesville, Va., 1977-), I, 253, 256. See also the discussions in Noll, *America's God*, 129; Noll, *Princeton and the Republic*, 69-71.

12. On Smith and his associates at Hampden-Sydney, see Donald Robert Come, "The Influence of Princeton on Higher Education in the South before 1825," *William and Mary Quarterly*, 3d Ser., II (1945), 371-372; William Henry Foote, *Sketches of Virginia: Historical and Biographical*, I (Philadelphia, 1850), 393-394, 400; Henry Alexander White, *Southern Presbyterian Leaders* (New York, 1911), 141.

ethical ideas of revivalist Presbyterianism. Rev. John Blair Smith, who graduated from Witherspoon's College of New Jersey in 1773, increasingly accused his elder brother of adopting Arminian ideas in order to appease Anglicans. He is alleged to have made the infamous suggestion: "Brother Sam, you don't preach Jesus Christ and Him crucified, but Sam Smith and him dignified." Smith resigned from his position in 1779, taking up a teaching position at Princeton instead.[13]

Through the 1780s, Smith's brother John Blair delivered sermons and lectures on moral philosophy at Hampden-Sydney, having succeeded him as president. As scholars have shown, John Blair Smith and other Presbyterians in his circle differed from evangelical Baptists in the same region because they defined uncertainty in religious belief as initially natural and even necessary in dialectical terms; it encouraged soul-searching and the eventual acknowledgment of divine authority. Baptists, conversely, tended to define ignorance or doubt as a form of apostasy. Presbyterian young men were discouraged from glibly assuming their innate ethical abilities and, in addition, their teachers and ministers reminded them to avoid excess certainty following their conversion. Indeed, following Samuel Stanhope Smith's departure in 1779, John Blair Smith used his presidency to reemphasize the moral importance of conversion and continual public prayer. According to the revised Calendar of Laws and Ordinances for the college under his tenure, "publick prayers" were to "be held every morning," and "all the students" were "required to attend publick worship on the Lord's-day whenever it shall be convenient." His desire to reassert the importance of religious revivalism — often through specific reference to the Westminster Confession of Faith — eventually led to accusations of sectarianism from non-Presbyterians in the county, prompting his resignation in 1789. The conflict between Rev. John Blair Smith and his brother demonstrated the divergent ways that Witherspoon's students came to define the public importance of personal piety. John Blair Smith's views on the centrality of religious regeneration before moral perception were more in line with those of Witherspoon than of Samuel Stanhope Smith. Yet the two men had studied under the same minister and became instructors in the same educational institution.[14]

13. On the alleged statement to "Brother Sam" and Samuel Stanhope Smith's move away from the institution, see Noll, *Princeton and the Republic*, 134.

14. On John Blair Smith's pedagogy, the difference with Baptist theology in the region, and his disdain for previous ecumenical approaches at Hampden-Sydney, see Philip N. Mulder, *A Controversial Spirit: Evangelical Awakenings in the South* (New York, 2002), 23, 26, 46, 48, 105; David W. Robson, *Educating Republicans: The College in the Era of the American Revolu-*

Through the 1780s, Samuel Stanhope Smith continued to demonstrate the divergent legacy of his earlier educational context when he supported the account of moral innateness that was promoted by his friend and uncle, Samuel Blair, Jr. By the time he assumed his role as president of Princeton in 1795, Smith had become a chief American proponent of moral sense philosophy, reviving the pedagogical legacy of colonial American professors such as Francis Alison to a far greater extent than Witherspoon. He also incorporated the insights of Thomas Reid into his own work, which he taught more systematically than any previous American professor. In his moral philosophy lectures, eventually published in 1812, he informed students that "by distinguishing accurately the objects" of the "faculty" of the human sense, "we shall arrive at more precise apprehensions of its nature" — including a natural propensity to believe in God. Such an apologetic statement avoided discussing the importance of conversion before understanding divine truths. Instead, Smith contributed even further to the didactic religious aspect of American Enlightenment reasoning. He used the notions of self-evidence and reliable moral perception to confirm received religious ideas, underscoring his authority as an educated moral leader. He asserted that human moral volition was only infallible when guided by divine revelations. But, in doing so, he implied some innate agency in at least enabling people to confirm and conform to the self-evidence of God's design through their own innate moral capacity.[15]

In his lectures on moral philosophy, Smith referenced those "theories, which were leading the mind to universal scepticism," before suggesting with satisfaction that their "charm of novelty" had begun to subside: thinkers were returning "in a retrograde direction to the calm and rational dictates of the common feelings of mankind." Even more happily, according to Smith, a "number of ingenious writers, especially in Scotland," had "appeared against these novel doctrines, who studiously labored to set this part of philosophy

tion, 1750–1800 (Westport, Conn., 1985), 198–200. For the Hampden-Sydney Ordinances under Rev. John Blair Smith, see "Laws and Ordinances for the Regulation of the College of Hampden-Sydney," in Alfred J. Morrison, ed., *The College of Hampden-Sidney: Calendar of Board Minutes, 1776–1876* (Richmond., Va., 1912), 30. On the accusation of sectarianism against Rev. John Blair Smith, see Come, "The Influence of Princeton," *WMQ*, 3d Ser., II (1945), 373.

15. Samuel Stanhope Smith, *The Lectures, Corrected and Improved, Which Have Been Delivered for a Series of Years, in the College of New Jersey; on the Subjects of Moral and Political Philosophy*, 2 vols. (Trenton, N.J., 1812), I, 139, 302, 303–304. On Smith's developing apologetic philosophy, see Noll, *America's God*, 124, 128–130; Noll, *Princeton and the Republic*, 185–213; James H. Moorhead, *Princeton Seminary in American Religion and Culture* (Grand Rapids, Mich., 2012), 1–28.

on its proper foundation—that common sense which it had deserted." Demonstrating a distinctly positive view of human moral capability in his explanation of Thomas Reid's "science" of moral philosophy, Smith later defined the "end for which the Creator has implanted in man this high relish for the sublime in the works both of nature and of art" with the claim that the mind "becomes more conscious of the dignity of its being, and more inclined to cultivate the pure and noble affections of virtue." The moral faculty apparently allowed an intrinsic understanding of ethics through the pre-rational and uncontrollable reactions that it produced. Its response mechanism was akin to the sense of touch or smell. Directly alluding to Reid early in his lectures, Smith claimed that the "wisdom of modern science has justly excluded from philosophy all hypotheses, by which the operations of nature are attempted to be conjecturally explained. . . . Experience, therefore, and a diligent and attentive observation of the course of nature, and of the actions of mankind in every variety of situation in which they may be placed, is the only legitimate means of attaining a competent knowledge of the laws of either the material, or the moral world."[16]

Elite learning distanced Smith's moral system from the potential disorder of both religious enthusiasm and democratic populism: the "seeds of moral discernment" required cultivation during the period of youth because the "moral principle, like reason, or like taste in the liberal arts, has its infancy when it is yet feeble in its perceptions, and liable to error in its decisions." The various disciplines of a well-rounded education, according to Smith, allowed young men to draw out and clarify inborn ethical capacities.[17]

Scottish Moderates had once claimed that the cultural framework of colo-

16. Smith, *Lectures*, I, 10–12, 138–139, 193–194. On Smith's developing moral philosophy, see also Noll, *Princeton and the Republic*, 185–204. According to Bow, Smith's suggestion of a well-rounded education with a strong core of belles lettres and moral philosophy was designed to "shed light on God's intention for humanity, independent of revealed religion." See Bow, "Samuel Stanhope Smith and James McCosh," *History of European Ideas*, XXXIX (2013), 659.

17. Smith, *Lectures*, I, 304, 311–313. In some respects, Smith's focus on the didactic importance of cultivation reflected a number of his contemporaries in post-Revolutionary France. There, as Rosenfeld shows, the primary job of common sensibility was to bolster "a self-conscious defence of the pre-revolutionary status quo, the very world that revolutionaries [had been] eager to leave behind." The German dramatist and poet Friedrich Schiller later explained this irony even more clearly. The notion of innate individual sensibility has the potential to render a "harmony and equality to society as a whole and produces the triumph of common sense" but is in actuality only applicable to a "tiny, rarified portion of the population" who believe that their training and education allow them to channel the common aesthetic sensibility. See Rosenfeld, *Common Sense*, 181, 225, 226.

nial America was insufficiently advanced to harness the common sensibility of its settlers. Several decades later, however, Smith employed developmental reasoning toward a different end. Although "nature" had "given to man the powers of action, it is education which directs their operation:—the soil is prepared by nature, but the harvest it shall produce depends upon its culture." In the "idea of education," Smith continued before his American students,

> I include . . . intercourse with mankind, which contributes to form the character . . . [so that] [o]ne of the first of parental duties is to have children initiated in some useful arts. . . . And in the middling and superior classes it is perhaps still more necessary to awaken a generous ambition of becoming useful, or of rising to distinction in it by their virtues and their talents.

Outlining the importance of educated leadership in galvanizing independent American society, Smith's lectures on moral philosophy made few explicit references to the necessity of religious conversion before the assumption of moral leadership. Rather, they demonstrated a positive association between individual ethical volition and civic benevolence. Witherspoon had warned against emphasizing the moral nature of public governance over the imperative to undergo personal salvation. Without conversion, the "rotten materials" of society would fail to respond to positive leadership. Smith, conversely, followed Benjamin Franklin and the College of Philadelphia's provost William Smith in opposing the classical constraints of antiquity in favor of the moral capacity of educated young men. Learning to define their personal ideals in relation to civic norms, they would become legitimate public representatives.[18]

In Smith's discussion of the innate moral faculty in his moral philosophy lectures, he distinguished between natural law and biblical precepts of marriage, and so he did not entirely dismiss polygamy. In Smith's view, moral philosophers were obliged to consider whether the practice was shunned as a result of contingent cultural mores or according to natural laws that could be distinguished by moral sensory perception. The question of legal polygamy,

18. Smith, *Lectures*, II, 145–146; John Witherspoon, *The Dominion of Providence over the Passions of Men* . . . , in [Green, ed.], *Works of Witherspoon*, III, 41. On Franklin's similar approach, see Alan Houston, *Benjamin Franklin and the Politics of Improvement* (New Haven, Conn., 2008), 74–76. On Smith's common sensory approach to cultivation, see also Charles Bradford Bow, "Samuel Stanhope Smith and Common Sense Philosophy at Princeton," *Journal of Scottish Philosophy*, VIII (2010), 189–209.

as stated in the second volume of Smith's lectures, "relates chiefly to the age anterior to the christian dispensation, and to those nations who do not enjoy the light of the gospel." Thus, the professor warned his students to "be very cautious in pronouncing those, who did not enjoy the illumination of that [Christian] law, to have been guilty of any crime in not conforming themselves to its dictates." In a neutral societal context, polygamy was unlikely to arouse an innate negative reaction. "It should be remembered," Smith pointed out, "that, if the eastern nations are, at present, and for a long time have been, inferior in the energies both of body and mind to the people of Europe, this ought not to be ascribed to any single institution [such as monogamy], but to the combination of an infinite variety of causes which equally affect all nations in their decline." Smith deferred to the Judeo-Christian tradition only by stating his personal preference for monogamy. He noted monogamy's positive effects on social stability in Christian realms, having previously claimed that polygamy was not congruent with natural moral values. His support for Christian precepts thus assumed a relativistic aspect.[19]

Smith's moral philosophy met increasing opposition from several former students of Witherspoon, most notably Ashbel Green. Soon after graduating from the College of New Jersey in 1783, Green was ordained at Philadelphia's Second Presbyterian Church, where he then served as a minister. What began as private criticism of Smith during the early 1790s developed into a public attack by Green on Smith's ethical approach through the late 1790s and early 1800s. The attack was just as vituperative as Witherspoon's earlier Scottish campaign against Moderate professors. Most infamously, tensions were manifested in the growing controversy sparked by Smith's purported approval of polygamy, which developed between 1804 and 1812. Green concluded that Smith had in fact tacitly endorsed polygamy. In his opinion, Smith's support for the Christian faith was not so easily congruent with his discussion of natural law reasoning. Smith's argument seemed to incorporate a dangerous form of moral contingency, undermining the objective superiority of monogamy. Even more problematic, individuals were obliged to assess whether ethical assertions were governed by cultural mores or an innate form of moral perception. Such a distinction, according to Green, avoided acknowledging the importance of conversion as a precursor to ethical reasoning. Two decades later, Green made clear reference to Smith's arguments in his *Lectures on the Shorter Catechism of the Presbyterian Church* (published in 1829): the "existence of polygamy among the ancient patriarchs is no evidence of its lawfulness. It is no where warranted in scripture, but only

19. Smith, *Lectures*, II, 120–121, 123.

FIGURE 24. *Ashbel Green (1762–1848), Class of 1783, President (1812–22)*.
Oil on canvas. Princeton University Art Museum / Art Resource, N.Y.

tolerated as an inveterate evil, which was permitted to remain during an imperfect dispensation."[20]

20. Ashbel Green, *Lectures on the Shorter Catechism of the Presbyterian Church, in the United States of America: Addressed to Youth* (Philadelphia, 1829), 184. On Green's early rivalry with Smith and his public attacks over the polygamy affair, see Noll, *Princeton and the Republic*, 182–184; Bow, "Samuel Stanhope Smith and James McCosh," *History of European Ideas*, XXXIX (2013), 660–662; Moorhead, *Princeton Seminary in American Religion and Culture*, 21.

Through the first decade of the nineteenth century, Green petitioned Princeton college trustees to curtail what he perceived to be Smith's relativism. He consciously described his campaign as a means to reassert evangelical principles that had been espoused by Witherspoon, his early mentor. Over the ensuing period, he delivered evangelically inflected sermons, such as *The Efficacy of Divine Truth* (1828), which defined the necessity of "revealed truth on the human mind . . . [giving] light and understanding even to the simple" and pointed out that "men of inferior natural powers, or of little learning, are frequently seen to obtain, by a diligent perusal of the Sacred Scriptures, a far better knowledge of God, of true religion, and of sound morality, than is ever acquired by the ablest philosopher, or the most erudite scholar, who rejects revelation." During the same period, he assumed the role of chief editor of Witherspoon's works. Yet, looking back on his life in a partially finished autobiography begun in his "eighty-second year," Green demonstrated a kinder view of Smith, "the son-in-law of Dr. Witherspoon, and his successor in the presidentship"—at least insofar as Smith was responsible for introducing Green to Witherspoon, when they took "tea and spen[t] a part of [an] evening" together. On this first encounter, Green recalled asking Witherspoon's advice about entering the ministry on a "walk back to the town," to which Witherspoon replied:

> Do you not make a mistake in this matter? Is it really a question in regard to your *duty?* Is it not rather a question which produces a conflict between your *inclination* and your *duty?* . . . Theology . . . is not the road either to fame or wealth. The law, in this country, leads to those objects. But if you wish to do good, and prefer an approving conscience before all other considerations, I have no hesitation in saying that you ought to preach the gospel.

Green recalled being so "roused" by these statements that shortly after he "hastened" to his study and "there, in a very solemn and decisive manner," made his "election in the vocation" in which he spent his "long life—having never, for a single moment, regretted" his choice. Of Witherspoon's works, Green wrote: "But there is, I fear, little prospect that his works and life, which I wished should accompany each other, will be published before my death; as all my endeavours to bring them before the public have hitherto proved abortive."[21]

21. Ashbel Green, "Sermon XXXIX: Delivered at the Opening of the Synod of Philadelphia, Oct. 25, 1826," in Austin Dickinson, ed., *The American National Preacher; or, Original Monthly Sermons from Living Ministers of the United States* (New York, 1828–1829), III, 17;

Notwithstanding his later warm recollections, in the medium term Green's campaign contributed to Smith's eventual resignation in 1812 and his own election as the eighth president of the college. Smith suggested that the evangelical orthodoxy of Green and his allies required doctrinal submission to received religious catechisms, rather than any faith in personal moral volition. Having jettisoned Smith's lectures, Green used Witherspoon's "Lectures on Moral Philosophy," which he had recently edited, as course material — suggesting that he perceived the relative distinction between Witherspoon's writings and Smith's anthropocentric ethical system, which he had opposed so publicly in previous years. Like his former professor, Green never claimed to be a philosopher. Rather, he simply introduced students to various systems of ethical thinking. He often made sure to insert religious caveats and qualifications following their passive description. He used his presidency to reassert what has aptly been described as "moderately enthusiastic revivalism."[22]

The divergence between Smith and Green reveals much about the ambiguous nature of Witherspoon's legacy. Witherspoon's use of philosophical terminology led Smith to extrapolate conceptual assumptions from the intellectual systems that his teacher had mined for descriptive vocabulary. Conversely, Witherspoon's reputation for public evangelicalism led Green to fear the degree of erudition and scholarly terminology that Smith displayed during his college presidency. There was much continuity between Witherspoon's evangelical statements and his private American lectures. Nonetheless, there were times when both displayed a certain degree of ambiguity regarding the association between moral action and the reception of grace. Neither entirely avoided theological and philosophical tensions over the question of moral innateness: whether individuals were ever able to understand the necessity of regeneration before its occurrence and whether some sort of qualitative judgment was required to acknowledge the future requirement of salvation. In some instances, Witherspoon inserted caveats that were

---

Green, *The Life of Ashbel Green, V.D.M., Begun to Be Written by Himself in His Eighty-Second Year and Continued to His Eighty-Fourth,* ed. Joseph H. Jones (New York, 1849), 145–147. On Green's letters and campaigns against Smith, see Noll, *Princeton and the Republic,* 182–183. On Green's subsequent relationship with Witherspoon's works, see Mark A. Noll, "The Princeton Trustees of 1807: New Men and New Directions," *Princeton University Library Chronicles,* XLI (1980), 208.

22. On Smith's eventual resignation, which coincided with the formation of Princeton Theological Seminary, see Noll, *Princeton and the Republic,* 211. On the rejection of Smith's lectures by Green and the use of Witherspoon's lectures, see Bow, "Samuel Stanhope Smith and James McCosh," *History of European Ideas,* XXXIX (2013), 662. On Green's "moderately enthusiastic revivalism," see Noll, *America's God,* 300.

designed to reassert fundamental evangelical tenets, yet he failed to modify previous statements that seemed more ambiguous. These inconsistencies surely added to the complexity of his legacy. Green and Smith could each find inspiration for their differing outlooks in their respective institutional contexts. It is possible to detect similar ambiguities in the legacy of Witherspoon's political theology among other former students, both with regard to their differing moral philosophies and in their accounts of the role of religion in civic life.

Presbyterian Revivalism and the New Educational Frontier

A generation of historians have adopted a "free marketplace" metaphor to describe the denominational rivalries that followed the removal of Anglican establishments and religious tests throughout the new United States. Aware of the need to compete for the salvation of souls in a disestablished context, evangelism became more prevalent after the separation of religious and civic spheres. Because of the opposition to cultivated forms of moral sensibility, a "Second Great Awakening" of evangelical piety drew from (and contributed to) the nascent political ideology of Jeffersonian republicanism. By the turn to the nineteenth century, "Federalist ministers" used common sensory ideas to describe the benevolent nature of their clerical power and the civic importance of their stable religious governance. A new generation of itinerant preachers, conversely, censured elite religious leaders for eschewing the importance of religious conversion by privileging the refinement of innate ethical faculties.[23]

From the mid-1790s to the second decade of the nineteenth century, a resurgence of Presbyterian evangelicalism swept backcountry Virginia and Pennsylvania, rural regions of North Carolina, and the new frontiers of Kentucky and Tennessee. In 1804, a report from the General Assembly of

---

23. On the free marketplace metaphor and public religion during the early national era, see Chris Beneke, "The Free Market and the Founders' Approach to Church-State Relations," *Journal of Church and State*, LII (2010), 323–352; Philip Hamburger, *Separation of Church and State* (Cambridge, Mass., 2002), 21–65; Robert M. Calhoon, "Religion, Moderation, and Regime-Building in Post-Revolutionary America," in Eliga H. Gould and Peter S. Onuf, eds., *Empire and Nation: The American Revolution in the Atlantic World* (Baltimore, 2005), 216–220. On the notion of a Second Great Awakening, see Nathan O. Hatch, *The Democratization of American Christianity* (New Haven, Conn., 1989), 35, 96–98, 220. On Federalist ministers, see Jonathan D. Sassi, *A Republic of Righteousness: The Public Christianity of the Post-Revolutionary New England Clergy* (New York, 2001), 109.

FIGURE 25. *Sacramental Scene in a Western Forest.* Lithograph by P. S. Duval and Co.,
circa 1801. From Joseph Smith, *Old Redstone; or, Historical Sketches of Western
Presbyterianism: Its Early Ministers, Its Perilous Times, and Its First Records*
(Philadelphia, 1854). Courtesy, General Collections, Library of Congress,
Washington, D.C.

the Presbyterian Church in America noted that, within the "wide districts,
towards the south and west" of the United States, "the power of religion appears still to prevail, with little abatement." Referring to those who criticized
Presbyterian evangelicalism as unruly and even violent, the missionaries admitted that, although some instances of "human frailty, some errors, extrava-
gancies, and instances of reproachful behaviour, have taken place," they did
not match the "malignity with which the enemies of religion" had "studied
to misrepresent, and rejoiced to exaggerate." In a following report, the Synod
of Pittsburgh wrote to the *Western Missionary Magazine* to explain that "great
things hath God done for his American Zion" following revivals and con-
certs of prayer in new frontier communities. Newspapers and pamphlets referred to widespread religious revivalism in the well-known Gasper River and
Cane Ridge meetings. Thousands of participants engaged in a passionate religious experience. Itinerant ministers lauded physical and emotional manifestations of the Holy Spirit during conversion and specifically distinguished

these experiences from rationalistic and common sensory accounts of inborn morality. The Appalachian backcountry and other regions witnessed a re-assertion of sacramental seasoning in popular outdoor religious meetings.[24]

Trained to become ministers, many of Witherspoon's former students contributed to the expansion of higher education in the same frontier com-munities that experienced Presbyterian revivalism. From the Revolutionary era to the third decade of the nineteenth century, according to one estima-tion, more than 11 percent of Witherspoon's graduates became (mostly Pres-byterian) presidents of colleges of higher education in eight different Ameri-can states. As one of many examples from throughout the South and West, a number of students from the early 1770s eventually settled in small Presbyte-rian churches along the borders of Kentucky and Tennessee. In Tennessee, Washington College, Greenville College, Tusculum College, Cumberland College, and the University of Nashville were all founded by former students. Tusculum, of course, was the name that Witherspoon had given to the home in which he lived just outside the Princeton campus. Founded in the 1820s, the institution was named in his honor.[25]

24. General Assembly Report, May 1804, *Assembly's Missionary Magazine; or, Evangelical Intelligencer* (February 1805), 59, "Thoughts on the Missionary Spirit," 64. On western Presby-terian missionaries during the early nineteenth century, see James R. Rohrer, *Keepers of the Cove-nant: Frontier Missions and the Decline of Congregationalism, 1774–1818* (New York, 1995), 47, 72. On the sacramental "season," see Leigh Eric Schmidt, *Holy Fairs: Scotland and the Making of American Revivalism*, 2d ed. (Grand Rapids, Mich., 2001), 59–68, 93–97.

25. On the revivals in Kentucky and Tennessee, see John B. Boles, *The Great Revival, 1787–1805: The Origins of the Southern Evangelical Mind* (Lexington, Ky., 1972), 36–89; Catharine C. Cleveland, *The Great Revival in the West, 1797–1805* (Chicago, 1916); Paul K. Conkin, *Cane Ridge: America's Pentecost* (Madison, Wis., 1990); William Warren Sweet, *Revivalism in America: Its Origins, Growth, and Decline* (New York, 1944), 122–125. Witherspoon's graduates became the first presidents of "Union College, New York; Washington College and Hampden-Sidney Col-lege in Virginia; Mount Zion College in South Carolina; Queen's College and the University of North Carolina in that State, and of Washington, Greenville, Tusculum and Cumberland Col-leges and the University of Nashville in Tennessee." They were also college founders, such as Thaddeus Dod (1773) of Washington College, Pennsylvania; John McMillan (1772) of Jefferson College, Pennsylvania; and Caleb Wallace (1770) of Transylvania College in Kentucky. Finally, the second presidents of Hampden-Sidney, Jefferson College, Franklin College, and Oglethorpe University in Georgia had also been Witherspoon's students. See Collins, *President Witherspoon*, II, 223–226; Come, "The Influence of Princeton," *WMQ*, 3d Ser., II (1945), 387–393; Samuel Davies Alexander, *Princeton College during the Eighteenth Century* (New York, 1872), xii, xiv; William Henry Foote, *Sketches of North Carolina, Historical and Biographical, Illustrative of the Principles of a Portion of Her Early Settlers* (New York, 1846), 516–517; Charles L. Coon, *North Carolina Schools and Academies, 1790–1840: A Documentary History* (Raleigh, N.C., 1915), 574;

Yet the dual occurrence of Presbyterian-founded institutions of learning and evangelical revivalism did not necessarily imply their direct causal association. In southern and western territories, the possibility remained that new institutional leaders might follow the path of Samuel Stanhope Smith, translating their recollection of moral sensory terminology into support for anthropocentric ethical claims. Other former students of Witherspoon might well have followed Ashbel Green in opposing Arminian reasoning, dry religious speculation, and ministerial patronage. But, although many of Witherspoon's students aligned themselves more closely with the evangelical discourse of popular revivalism, the exact nature of their role as higher educators still remained ambiguous. Green used his Princeton presidency to reassert the centrality of prayer and conversion over rational and common sensory accounts of innate morality. Nonetheless, his activities did not correspond with the tradition of extra-institutional evangelicalism, at least as it has been described by scholars of the Second Great Awakening. Contrary to the notion of unruly revivalism during the early 1800s, Green promoted his moral system from within a formal collegiate setting.

As they moved into the new American frontier, other former students pursued a model similar to that of Green. In taking the time to institute their own educational establishments, they demonstrated that formal pedagogical practice and evangelical piety were not necessarily perceived as antithetical. Ministers and teachers from frontier academies were often present at camp revivals. Their desire to assure the nature and truth of awakenings was not generally observed as a hierarchical imposition. Their didactic contribution to revivalism was described by Congregational missionaries who witnessed several large-scale Presbyterian meetings during the early 1800s. Joseph Badger, for example, published an 1803 report on a Cross Creek communion in western Pennsylvania in which he criticized those who claimed that revivalism amounted to disorder and unbridled enthusiasm. Emphasizing the role of order and even clerical instruction, he stressed that "ministers, Elders, and pious experienced Christians do watch and strictly guard against every appearance of wildness and disorder." Badger was particularly impressed that two of the ministers at Cross Creek, James Hughes and George Scott, were

---

Donald G. Tewksbury, *The Founding of American Colleges and Universities before the Civil War, with Particular Reference to the Religious Influences Bearing upon the College Movement* (New York, 1932), 17, 34, 36; Clinton B. Allison, "Doak, Samuel," in John F. Ohles, ed., *Biographical Dictionary of American Educators*, 3 vols. (Westport, Conn.., 1978), I, 381–382; Robson, *Educating Republicans*, 199–203; Frank T. Wheeler, *Tusculum College, Tennessee* (Charleston, S.C., 2000), 7–10.

College of New Jersey graduates and local teachers. The sacrament of Holy Communion remained important even among revivalist Presbyterian communities on the early-nineteenth-century frontier. Here it was not uncommon to witness their "fencing the table," permitting members to take Communion only after being examined by a minister who corroborated the truth of their spiritual awakening and who issued them a "token" that admitted them to the sacrament ceremony.[26]

A stark dichotomy between the movement of popular evangelicalism and the founding of local colleges was thus unlikely to develop. Their contiguous occurrence in new western and southern frontiers offered an alternative means of binding local society, beyond traditional forms of political authority. New colleges took advantage of their independence from government just as revivals responded to the formal disestablishment of religion.[27]

Though religiously founded colleges and voluntary organizations asserted their institutional independence from the civic realm, they did not deny the importance of political governance altogether. Rather, they tried to sanction an implicit bargain between government and disestablished piety. Through the early nineteenth century, therefore, Presbyterian college founders faced the same delicate task that Witherspoon had encountered during the 1780s: encouraging moral governance without promoting the civil establishment of religion. There had been a few inconsistencies in Witherspoon's inchoate support for the disestablishment of American religion. The clergyman had recommended strong moral leadership in all forms of civic representation. But he also feared a monopoly of political authority from any one religious group and claimed that the political establishment of religion undermined the grassroots power of Protestant revivalism. Though he and other prominent Presbyterians made a public call for disestablishment, they often did so as political representatives in civic forums. Moreover, Witherspoon did, in some instances, recommended biblically mandated interventions from political government. Similar tensions and ambiguities were reflected among his former students as they negotiated the civic role of religiously founded colleges. Alongside traditional forms of learning in classics, rhetoric, mathemat-

26. Joseph Badger to Abel Flint, July 19, 1803, cited in Rohrer, *Keepers of the Covenant,* 93–94, 173 n. 68. On fencing the table and token rituals, see Schmidt, *Holy Fairs,* 88, 96, 109.

27. As Noll has suggested, "with almost none of the uneasiness which their Old School party would later display, Presbyterians in the early nineteenth century began to advocate" forming educational "societies like Princeton College" alongside "voluntary societies and evangelistic campaigns rather than the new nation's political structures as the religiously inspired means to preserve American society." See Mark A. Noll, "The Irony of the Enlightenment for Presbyterians in the Early Republic," *Journal of the Early Republic,* V (1985), 167.

ics, and divinity, the formal inculcation of revivalist principles was thought to support the separate civic realm. In exchange for institutional independence, Presbyterian college presidents perceived it to be their duty to encourage true piety—and further moral education—among those who were set to assume positions of public authority. Assuring the authenticity of conversion through formal instruction and guidance was therefore conceived as a civic obligation.[28]

In his contribution to the formation of the University of North Carolina at Chapel Hill, for example, Witherspoon's former student Samuel McCorkle sought to channel evangelical moral ideas into a fixed and formal system of higher education. His birth in 1746 coincided with the official charter of the College of New Jersey. Before that point, revivalist Presbyterians had perceived an Arminian influence in the Philadelphia Synod. But, rather than resting on their association with itinerant preaching, they set about instilling evangelical precepts through formal pedagogical instruction. Half a century later, McCorkle attempted to do the same in North Carolina. Like Ashbel Green, he encountered Presbyterian ministers and teachers who did not always subscribe to his evangelical moral philosophy. He was wary of abandoning a focus on religious revival in favor of greater moderation and polite sensibility. Nonetheless, he also perceived the importance of assuring conversion and faithful piety through ministerial and professorial means. His career as a minister and college founder in new southern communities provides another pertinent example of the legacy of evangelical education from the Revolutionary era through the Second Great Awakening.[29]

McCorkle kept a diary of his final year of study at the College of New Jersey, describing his religious conversion and rebirth throughout 1772. He raised several observations and themes that would govern his understanding of the relationship between moral regeneration, higher learning, and civic virtue from the 1790s to 1819, most notably the surprising degree of congru-

28. On the implicit bargain between religious institutions and civic authorities at this point, see Calhoon, "Religion, Moderation, and Regime-Building," in Gould and Onuf, eds., *Empire and Nation*, 218. According to Mulder, although "Presbyterians adjusted to the new nation's religious freedom and acknowledged the legitimacy of other religions, they did not abandon their own goals. Instead of pursuing ascendancy as the true state church, Presbyterians defaulted to their other favorite tactic for spreading their truth—education . . . [keeping] them a step above their religious competitors, the Baptists and Methodists." See Mulder, *A Controversial Spirit*, 104–105.

29. On the coincidence between McCorkle's birth and the charter, see Robert Calhoon, "Ordered Liberty in the Southern Backcountry and the Middle-West," *Journal of Backcountry Studies*, I, no. 1 (Fall 2006), 4.

ence between passionate piety and formal moral learning. McCorkle adopted a traditional evangelical emphasis in his desire to harness emotionalism and fervent religious feeling during his personal awakening. He approved of theological works that historians have subsequently described as Edwardsean and lauded them for bringing him to an understanding of the requirement of saving grace. He recalled having run "into frequent cavils against the dispositions of Providence in the creation of man, and His justice in condemning him . . . [and] found a secret disposition to clear myself by the doctrine of man's inability, till I read Mr. Smalley's Sermons on that subject, which seemed to give me considerable light in vindicating the justice of God." He also claimed to have "received considerable light by Mr. Green's Sermon, which showed me that sinners only desire a partial Saviour—a Saviour from misery, but not a Saviour from sin." Thus, McCorkle perceived a distinction between God's moral volition and the alternative "doctrine of man's inability."[30]

Like many evangelical Presbyterians, McCorkle highlighted the chasm between unregenerate moral perception and God's ethical standing outside human time: "Also in viewing the dreadfulness and misery of man's estate, and the horrid nature of sin . . . my sins seemed to be so aggravated, that they made me sometimes almost despond of God's mercy; and what seemed most of all terrible to me, was, that I had in that state been admitted to the table of the Lord." In his struggle to describe the exact nature of moral volition, he implied his own awareness of an element of personal hubris. Though he acknowledged his inability to match divine moral volition, he tried to contemplate such a state before full regeneration. Thus, he wrestled with age-old questions: From where did the desire to acknowledge sin originate in the first place? Did it represent some sort of internal decision? And did such a notion contradict the doctrine of total human depravity? Inspired by his complex moral learning at the College of New Jersey and his own extracurricular reading, he admitted the incapacity of his own reason to understand God's way, using logical terminology to underline that divine revelation transcended human rationality.[31]

---

30. Diary of Samuel Eusebius McCorkle, Apr. 11, 1772, in Foote, *Sketches of North Carolina,* 352–353. On McCorkle's early encounter with Edwardsean religious materials, see Mulder, *A Controversial Spirit,* 24–25.

31. Diary of McCorkle, Apr. 11, 1772, in Foote, *Sketches of North Carolina,* 353. For more background on McCorkle's desire "to understand the complicated process of conversion in order to undergo it, even if that understanding forced him to comprehend something beyond intellectual processes in salvation," see Mulder, *A Controversial Spirit,* 25–26.

Concerned with the vexing problem of unregenerate ethical agency, McCorkle eventually settled on the mediating role of God, including through the Holy Spirit, before salvation. His account of conversion and regeneration implied that the acknowledgment of sin was necessarily personal and distinct from hierarchical human authority. Yet Witherspoon had pointed out to McCorkle and his fellow class of 1772 that there were "not very many who have such a degree of steady and firm assurance, as to exclude all doubting" after conversion. With the help of his teachers and ministers, therefore, McCorkle was required to understand many theological concepts, without eschewing the inevitable crises that developed when they could not immediately be reconciled. What have been described as "puzzlements" in McCorkle's thinking reflected similar ambiguities in Witherspoon's "Lectures on Moral Philosophy." When the details of ethical epistemology had seemed too difficult to comprehend, Witherspoon suggested that their irresolution demonstrated the common weakness of human understanding. Their opacity simply provided further evidence for the necessity of conversion and moral regeneration. Similarly, uncertainties in McCorkle's moral system were eventually reconciled as necessary in dialectical terms, a personal perceptual struggle that highlighted the transcendent mystery of divine revelation. Complexity and moral confusion delineated what McCorkle described as the distinction between the human and divine condition. When William Bradford heard McCorkle deliver a sermon two years after his graduation, he assured his friend James Madison that the reasoning "was very orthodox" in its attempt to "prove" that "the Laws of God were superior in wisdom to the Laws of men."[32]

McCorkle's conversion while enrolled in formal higher education provided an important paradigm for his later career as a minister and college founder. After he moved to North Carolina to minister local Presbyterian congregations, he found a catchment of young men whom he believed would benefit from higher learning, provided they were contiguously exposed to the importance of religious revivalism. He personally witnessed revivals in Kentucky and North Carolina at several points between 1784 and 1791, well over a decade before the period that has come to be known as the Second Great Awakening. He viewed passionate outdoor meetings on the eastern frontier of North Carolina with some approval but also noted the importance of the attending ministers and divinity professors. He believed that the few mistakes

32. John Witherspoon, "Lectures on Divinity," in [Green, ed.], *Works of Witherspoon*, IV, 13. On "puzzlements" in McCorkle's vision, see Mulder, *A Controversial Spirit*, 25. See also Bradford to Madison, Oct. 17, 1774, in Hutchinson et al., eds., *Papers of James Madison*, I, 127.

that occurred in the eastern revivals were the fault of poor leadership, high-lighting the continued need for a properly educated clergy. Thus, in 1785, McCorkle constructed a school in his house, where the distinction between formal pedagogy and church worship was often blurred. He also served as a trustee of Liberty Hall Academy in Charlotte and helped to relocate the institution to Salisbury, where it came to be known as Salisbury Academy in 1784. He remained as president of the institution until its closing in 1791. In notes to a 1792 sermon, McCorkle described the mixture of teaching and prayer in his classes and services as a "plan of catechising from the Scriptures, as the platform or ground of a Catechism . . . [proceeding] from Genesis to Job, and through part of the four Evangelists . . . asking questions that lead to reading and reflection." McCorkle continued these methods in 1794, when, with the help of his Presbyterian congregation, he founded Zion-Parnassus Academy, west of Salisbury. The academy combined classical and theological studies until it closed in 1798, at which point McCorkle helped to form a new charter for the hitherto defunct Salisbury Academy under new trustees. In his various schools and colleges during the 1790s, McCorkle taught several judges and state officers as well as many future Presbyterian ministers.[33]

Drawing impetus and inspiration from the religious and educational endeavors above, McCorkle spearheaded the founding of the University of North Carolina through the 1790s. Many years earlier, at the 1776 North Carolina constitutional convention, largely Presbyterian delegates from Mecklenburg County had promoted the establishment of a statewide institution of higher education without much success. In 1784, then, McCorkle redrafted a proposal to found a university in North Carolina, taking into account the earlier recommendations of the 1776 constitutional framers. The legislature rejected the proposal, fearing that it did not yet have the means to support such an endeavor. William R. Davie, a 1776 College of New Jersey graduate, reintroduced the bill in 1789. On that occasion, the plan to establish the university was successful. After the cornerstone for the university was laid on October, 12, 1793, McCorkle delivered a celebratory address to the assembly of governors. He proclaimed his pride "not only as a minister

---

33. McCorkle's 1792 sermon notes can be found in Foote, *Sketches of North Carolina*, 360. On these events in McCorkle's mid-career, see "McCorkle, Samuel Eusebius," in William S. Powell, ed., *Dictionary of North Carolina Biography*, 6 vols. (Chapel Hill, N.C., 1991), IV, 129; James F. Hurley and Julia Goode Eagan, *The Prophet of Zion-Parnassus, Samuel Eusebius McCorkle* (Richmond, Va., 1934), 83; Mulder, *A Controversial Spirit*, 23, 129. On McCorkle's subsequent legacy among students and future ministers, see Come, "The Influence of Princeton," *WMQ*, 3d Ser., II (1945), 380; Foote, *Sketches of North Carolina*, 513–515.

of religion, but also as a citizen of the State, as a member of civil as well as religious society," before then imploring, "May this hill be for religion as the ancient hill of Zion." Continuing to preside over Zion-Parnassus Academy, he nonetheless assumed the chairmanship of a curriculum committee to organize scholarly teaching at the University of North Carolina. As a trustee, he also recommended compulsory student attendance at religious services as well as examinations and tests on religious and moral affairs. Given the dominance of Presbyterian ministers and professors in a state institution of higher education, McCorkle risked being accused of sectarianism (particularly when the religious examinations he proposed seemed to be modeled on specific edicts laid out in the Westminster Confession of Faith). While maintaining his focus on the assurance of Christian faith, therefore, he made sure to define prohibitions against showing disrespect to any particular religious denomination in relation to another.[34]

In 1782, as a congressional representative, Witherspoon had outlined the role of independent religious and educational societies in a disestablished civic system. A decade later, McCorkle used a 1793 sermon and treatise to frame a similar argument, "with a design to solicit Benefactions for the University of North-Carolina." First delivered in Salisbury, North Carolina, McCorkle's discourse suggested that the encouragement of conversion and regeneration among young men would fit them for future public stations. He consciously "extended" his sermon "to religious and political" themes in order to appeal to "the candour of the Legislators and other officers of the state—the Trustees of the University—and the Clergy and people of all denominations." In the realm of religious education, which remained "distinct" from civic governance, the "minister of mercy, or of religion," stepped "forth into the other circle" and "persuade[d] men to love God." McCorkle's account of religious persuasion was evangelical in its focus on the necessary immediacy of conversion. But it was certainly not opposed to pedagogical authority and formal guidance through regeneration. McCorkle qualified the notion that "some denominations of christians" seemed to "exist *without* a regular educated ministry" by pointing out:

34. On the Mecklenburg County delegation and the proposal for a university, McCorkle's reference to the ancient hill of Zion, and the later charge of sectarianism, see Come, "The Influence of Princeton," *WMQ*, 3d Ser., II (1945), 382–383; Mulder, *A Controversial Spirit*, 105; J. G. de Roulhac Hamilton, *William Richardson Davie: A Memoir* (Chapel Hill, N.C., 1907), 16–17; Kemp P. Battle, *Sketches of the History of the University of North Carolina, Together with a Catalogue of Officers and Students, 1789–1889* (Chapel Hill, N.C., 1889), 3–15. For McCorkle's address on laying the cornerstone, see Foote, *Sketches of North Carolina*, 531–533.

It has been well observed, that they exist *among* such a ministry, and avail themselves of their labours: Just as a few individuals, who refuse to take arms, may be defended by those who take them. To state the matter fairly, we should suppose that both were separated from the rest of men, and were left to form a nation or a church by themselves. In that situation we would see how they would exist without education and without arms.

McCorkle opposed proponents of natural religion who dismissed the role of pedagogical direction in understanding the world revealed by scripture. But he also criticized those evangelicals who claimed that formal instruction in educational institutions would diminish the emotionalism and truth of the personal salvation experience.[35]

McCorkle suggested that "some men" were "called forth by their God" into "the public offices of society" in order to execute "righteous laws." Through "distinct" churches and colleges, he claimed, individuals would receive the necessary assistance to assure the nature of their salvation. Such support would allow a true understanding of scripture to inform their governance in future public office. Thus, McCorkle added,

> the national wealth and glory which christianity requires and promotes, the religious assemblies and worship it introduces . . . together with teachers in such seats [of higher education], all demand liberty and good laws; otherwise the seats of literature shall be demolished, the ministers of the gospel persecuted, the wealth of the church and nation wasted, and their glory tarnished by the despotism of a tyrant, and the servility of slaves.

Here McCorkle outlined the ironic association between disestablished religious institutions and public magistrates, using reasoning similar to that of Witherspoon and other earlier evangelical Presbyterian ministers: "These relations and offices, though distinct," required "each-other's assistance." Revivalist denominations relied on the political realm to protect their liberty of religion, allowing them to concentrate on the conversion of individuals rather than the vagaries of civic patronage. Political government depended on the harnessing of individuals' autonomy by religious institutions to encourage

---

35. John Witherspoon, "Delivered at a Public Thanksgiving after Peace: Sermon 45," in [Green, ed.], *Works of Witherspoon,* III, 81; Samuel E. McCorkle, *A Charity Sermon; First Delivered in Salisbury, July 28* . . . (Halifax, N.C., 1795), 3, 5, 53, *Documenting the American South,* University Library, The University of North Carolina at Chapel Hill, 2005, http://docsouth.unc .edu/unc/mccorkle/mccorkle.html.

the conversion of future civic leaders. McCorkle continued: "Not more than a fifth part of the duties of society are enforced by civil laws. Hence the necessity of religion, and of the ministers of religion, in order to persuade men to obedience for conscience sake." Men's sense of moral duty should not merely arise from a fear of worldly authority. In his opinion, the role of religious revival in a "well conducted . . . university education" was central to "raising up regular well educated ministers of state, who shall protect and favour religion, and form and execute righteous laws." McCorkle asked rhetorically whether public magistrates could

> make laws and execute them without the assistance of religion? . . . What hold can you take of each other, or of your constituents, without the *religion* of an oath? Without this, what can all your courts of justice do? Perjury they may punish, but cannot *prevent.* How can the principles of religion be explained and inculcated without ministers of religion? You may as well make laws without law-makers, and hold courts without judges.

Thus, McCorkle continued to outline the quid pro quo between religious education and political institutions, "not as a *minister* of religion, but as a *member* of the state—as a member of civil society." "If the ministers of religion be necessary or useful to the nation, enough has been said to show that they cannot be properly qualified but at seats of public education. If you [wish] your teachers to be more *useful,* take the proper means to qualify them for *usefulness"*—as religion was "necessary to the nation, so are its ministers." With a flourish, McCorkle concluded: "My hearers of all classes, ages and characters! View yourselves as citizens, and as christians by profession. And adore the King of saints and nations for the privileges you have both in prospect and possession."[36]

In 1795, McCorkle joined William Davie as one of the chief founders of the University of North Carolina on "the Chappel Hill." As a principal trustee during the following years, he continued to draft and modify the curriculum and institutional laws, with religion and piety at the forefront of his efforts. Yet, as he consolidated his role as a trustee and curriculum coordinator, familiar tensions arose at the university. Mirroring the distinction that had previously developed between Samuel Stanhope Smith and John Blair Smith at Hampden-Sydney College, as well as the emerging division between Smith and Green at the College of New Jersey, Davie and McCorkle differed in their vision of the role of moral learning. Their developing conflict pro-

36. McCorkle, *Charity Sermon,* 5-7, 54, 58.

vides further evidence of the continuing tension between anthropocentric and God-centered moral epistemology in Presbyterian educational circles. In order to prepare students for public leadership, Davie adopted a similar stance to Samuel Stanhope Smith, advocating the cultivation of moral faculties that were innate in all young men. His alternative curricular emphasis made far less reference to the centrality of prayer and conversion during the formative period of higher education. By the late 1790s, he had managed to persuade other trustees to modify and even supplant McCorkle's curriculum with one emphasizing moral sense philosophy and belles lettres.[37]

As Davie continued to question his system of moral education, McCorkle offered a countercritique of moral sensory reasoning in a number of pamphlets, most notably in his *Four Discourses on the General First Principles of Deism and Revelation Contrasted: Discourse I* (1797). Reflecting Witherspoon's similar distinction between "perfect and imperfect rights," he claimed that true moral decisions — such as the ability to show mercy — only derived from a new sense of revelation following conversion. Despite his efforts, however, McCorkle failed to become acting president at the University of North Carolina, which he put down to Davie's maneuverings. After December 1799, he resigned from the institution altogether, lamenting deistic philosophical influences and a lack of student examinations on divinity carried out by the new faculty. In a letter of 1799, he condemned "the Jacobine Morality which judges the virtue or vice of an action by its utility alone and its utility by our limited and often erroneous conceptions, or that Morality which teaches that Motives sanctify measures, and measures sanctify the end." More specifically, he criticized "the discarding or banishing of examinations on Divinity every Sabbath evening. . . . as if religion . . . had . . . abandoned the University." He alleged that students were being taught problematic precepts of human-centered moral philosophy that undermined the ethical primacy of revelation, which was necessary for moral action.[38]

---

37. For McCorkle's structure of curricular life at the university and the origins of the "Chappel Hill" moniker, see Calhoon, "Ordered Liberty in the Southern Backcountry," *Journal of Backcountry Studies,* I, no. 2 (Fall 2006), 5, 11.

38. Samuel E. McCorkle, *Four Discourses on the General First Principles of Deism and Revelation Contrasted: Delivered in Salisbury and Thyatira on Different Days in April and May 1797: Discourse I* (Salisbury, N.C., 1797). On McCorkle's *Four Discourses,* see Thomas T. Taylor, "Samuel E. McCorkle and a Christian Republic, 1792–1802," *American Presbyterians: The Journal of Presbyterian History,* LXIII (1985), 375–376. On Witherspoon's distinction between perfect and imperfect rights, see John Witherspoon, "Lectures on Moral Philosophy," in [Green, ed.], *Works of Witherspoon,* III, 371–379, 399–409, 417. For McCorkle's statements on Jacobin-

Witherspoon's former student Samuel Doak tried to prevent similar theological and philosophical dissension in the educational institutions that he founded on the Tennessee frontier. He arrived as the first registered minister in the territory several years after his 1775 graduation from the College of New Jersey and a brief role as tutor at Hampden-Sydney College in Virginia. As a preacher, he was described as a "rigid opposer of innovation in religious tenets . . . uncompromising in his love of the truth," and a "John Knox in his character, fearless, firm, nearly dogmatical." He settled in eastern Tennessee and established a "log college" in the Mississippi Valley that from 1788 came under civic control of the state of North Carolina. By 1795, the institution was incorporated under the territorial jurisdiction of the legislature of Tennessee, coming to be known as Washington College. Doak was president of the college until 1818, when he passed on the position to his son, the Reverend John M. Doak. During the same year, the elder Doak moved to the town of Bethel along with another son, Samuel Witherspoon Doak, whose middle name was inspired by the former president of the College of New Jersey. Doak Senior soon founded Tusculum Academy, named after Witherspoon's home in New Jersey. There he taught until his death in 1829.[39]

Like McCorkle and Green, Doak positioned himself against those who increasingly came to be described as New School theologians. He adopted aspects of common sense reasoning without appropriating the notion of an innate ethical faculty, as was the earlier charge against Smith and his associates. He was careful to acknowledge the role of doubt and uncertainty during moral awakening. Doak, McCorkle, and Green all spearheaded the foundation of higher educational institutions, rather than relying on the spread of evangelicalism through informal outdoor meetings. In those institutions, the empirical terminology of common sense philosophy proved useful in training students to examine the ways in which their moral sensory state was potentially capricious. By the antebellum era, both Old School and New School Presbyterians perceived the institutional independence of their churches and colleges as contingent on the separation between religious and civic spheres. They differed in their view of the role of moral learning in those autonomous

---

ism and deism, see Samuel E. McCorkle to John Haywood, Dec. 20, 1799, Ernest Haywood Collection of Haywood Family Papers, Southern Historical Collection, University of North Carolina at Chapel Hill, 3, *Documenting the American South,* http://docsouth.unc.edu/unc/unc04-39/unc04-39.html.

39. On Doak's career and his assessment as "a rigid opposer of innovation in religious tenets," see the citations and discussion in Donald Robert Come, "The Influence of Princeton," *WMQ,* 3d Ser., II (1945), 389-390; Foote, *Sketches of North Carolina,* 311.

realms and in the nature of the relationship between ethical sensibility and the cultivation of sound civic leadership.[40]

Charles Hodge, Moral Philosophy, and the Legacy of Faction

During his early Princeton presidency, Ashbel Green was central to the founding of Princeton Theological Seminary in 1812. The institution he envisioned would promote the central importance of scripture, prayer, and ministerial training. Those religious ideals, in his view, would remain ring-fenced, guarded against any changes and developments in the adjacent university. Yet, in spearheading the founding of a separate theological institution, Green might have inadvertently distanced his legacy from that of his former mentor at the College of New Jersey.[41]

Toward the end of his life, Witherspoon came to perceive the institutional autonomy of religious societies in relation to their inculcation of piety among future public leaders. He sought to frame a rigorous approach to collegiate learning with an equally important focus on religion and prayer. Conversely, the formation of a separate theological institution risked delineating the province of higher education—classics, rhetoric, natural science, English language, oratory—from the realm of religion. The concentration of religious studies in a discrete institution potentially eschewed what Witherspoon had always defined as the practical correspondence between conversion and other civic and intellectual activities, whether or not students were destined to enter clerical life. The creation of a separate institutional context for religious education implied a narrower correspondence between piety and learning: as a specific means toward ministerial training, a speculative and specialized form of scholarship, or, most worryingly for some evangelicals, a combination of the two.

The development of "Princeton Theology" in the seminary did indeed open up religious education to treatment as an abstract philosophical system. Witherspoon and Green had queried Hutchesonian accounts of innate moral sensibility. Conversely, influential Princeton theologians developed Hutcheson's axioms in light of more recent writings by Thomas Reid. Subsequently,

40. On the growing distinction between Old School and New School Presbyterians, despite their shared attachment to formal pedagogy, see Noll, *America's God,* 129–130.

41. On the founding and success of the Princeton Theological Seminary but also its potential theological distance from the college in Princeton, see James D. Bratt, "America: Confessional Theologies," *The Blackwell Companion to Nineteenth-Century Theology* (Chichester, U.K., 2010), 320–323.

an increasing number of theologians in the seminary suggested the coherence between immutable ethical perceptions and a benevolently created divine cosmos that those perceptions seemed to corroborate.[42]

Even in Princeton Theological Seminary, however, the reincorporation of Hutchesonian ideas alongside more recent common sensory theories heralded tensions, ambiguities, and opposing moral assertions. Many middle-ranking professors and tutors in the seminary justified their anthropocentric philosophy through reference to the alternative dangers of deism and enthusiasm. But several leading ministers were more reticent in incorporating philosophical concepts into their theological system. Archibald Alexander (1772-1851), for example, continually noted his desire to promote a passionate form of piety that had governed his conversion as a younger man in Virginia. The former president of Hampden-Sydney College and the first official president of Princeton Theological Seminary, Alexander matched Ashbel Green in highlighting the congruence between passionate revivalism and formal religious instruction. Recalling Witherspoon's earlier distinction between philosophical medium and ethical message, the empirical language of common sense philosophy provided a means to examine and describe the emotional workings of faith and to prevent or diagnose the false assurance of regeneration. On other occasions, however, Alexander adopted what has been described as a "Baconian Enlightenment model" in order to outline the common sense of scripture alongside the Westminster Confession of Faith. It remained ambiguous whether individuals were passively guided by the Confession as a divinely inspired document (perhaps in association with the Holy Spirit) or by their own instinctive perception of its convincing arguments in favor of revelation.[43]

Charles Hodge (1797-1878), who followed Alexander, demonstrated similar ambiguities in his ethical system during his fifty years as president (1829-1878). He sought to reconcile Baconian and common sensory empirical methods without giving up a Calvinistic account of the necessity of conversion. In doing so, he did more than any other intellectual figure to systemize what has come to be known as Princeton Theology by formulating and managing output in the *Biblical Repertory and Theological Review* and in his three-volume *Systematic Theology* (1871-1873). In all these theological activities, Hodge at times employed moral sense reasoning to provide an apologetic account of the natural divinely sanctioned order. But he also tended to

---

42. On the development of Princeton Theology in these ways, see ibid., 322-323.

43. On Alexander's movement between passionate piety and his sometime "Baconian" model, see ibid., 322.

avoid discussing the anthropocentric implications of common sense philosophy too deeply, and certainly did not defend it wholeheartedly. He gave much
attention to the overarching importance of revealed scripture, like Alexander
before him. He realized that his systematic attention to philosophy and epistemology threatened to overlook the role of moral doubt before conversion.
While seeking to develop a coherent system of religious philosophy, he was
periodically reminded that such a program risked rationalizing passionate
religious experience, abjuring the role of faith in the counteraction of uncertainty. As he sought to reconcile tensions within his own theological system,
Hodge eventually tried to situate himself on a religious trajectory that began
with the president of the College of New Jersey during the Revolutionary era
and that had been reasserted by Ashbel Green.[44]

As the sectional crisis over the nature and expansion of American slavery
grew through the 1830s and 1840s, Hodge seemed perturbed by the tendency of northern abolitionists to describe the evolution of their moral sensibility. In an 1836 essay for the *Biblical Repertory and Princeton Review*,
Hodge wrote that abolitionist "confusion" over the role of slavery in biblical accounts matched its imprecision in defining the contemporary nature
of the institution; its adherents were thus brought "into conflict with the
scriptures" while also failing to gain the "confidence of the north." If "every
man who regards slavery as an evil, and wishes to see it abolished, were
an abolitionist," he wrote in an 1844 essay in the same publication, "then
nine tenths of the people in this country would be abolitionists." Yet many
formal abolitionists, in his opinion, used their title to denote their greater
moral sensibility in political terms, even though "religious truth has a more
direct and powerful influence on the character of men than mere political
opinions." Notwithstanding the overall illegitimacy — and immorality — of
slavery, Hodge pointed out that moralistic judgments of slaveholders by self-
titled abolitionists perverted "the moral sense of the man who holds it" by
assuming too much innate capability. He was by no means a supporter of
enslaved labor. Nonetheless, he was concerned that white Protestants used
the antislavery movement to define their inner moral authority, irrespective

44. Ibid. On Hodge's attempt to adopt Baconian empirical methods without giving up a
Calvinistic account of the necessity of conversion, see Bozeman, *Protestants in an Age of Science*,
151–170. During his later years, Hodge wrote a history of the *Princeton Review*, making sure to
point out how he and other "Old School" theologians had conformed to a different Calvinist ac-
count of human sin, despite their use of common sense philosophy. On his early association with
Green and this later attempt to reconcile the trajectory of orthodox Calvinism in his theology, see
Noll, *America's God,* 266, 300, 332–333. On Hodge's developing theological critiques, see also
Bratt, "America," *Blackwell Companion to Nineteenth-Century Theology,* 323–324.

of their state of regeneration. Thus, he often deprecated northern abolition-ism for assuming moral perfection in its advocates. He also pointed out that the Bible did not condemn slavery unambiguously. In order to question the inherent accuracy of abolitionist moral sensibility, he sought to untie the bib-lical proofs against slavery on scriptural grounds.[45]

Hodges's unease with abolitionist discourse recalled earlier Presbyte-rian discussions of antislavery ideology, particularly those of Rev. William Graham. A graduate of Witherspoon's class of 1773, Graham had assumed leadership of Liberty Hall Academy in May 1776. Archibald Alexander, who would later evoke the legacy of Witherspoon in his presidency of Hampden-Sydney College, described his education under Graham as "precisely the same as that pursued at Princeton while Mr. Graham was a student in that college; even the manuscript lectures of Dr. Witherspoon were copied, and studied by the students." Graham taught most of the men who entered the Presbyterian ministry in the district, and he promoted the standard ortho-doxy of the Westminster Confession of Faith in opposition to the perceived growth of deism in intellectual circles. But, in opposing deism and anthropo-centric moral reasoning, he also developed a tortuous critique of antislavery ideology. The reverend opposed critics of slavery in Virginia by referring to the inevitable restrictions of unregenerate moral sensibility. Emancipa-tory rhetoric, according to Graham, used the religious language of regenera-tion to describe worldly notions of freedom. Rather disingenuously, he sug-gested that individuals should remain focused on the role of grace and their association with the love of God, rather than ascribe religious changes in moral sensibility to more prosaic alterations in the political or civil status of people. Through the turn to the nineteenth century, Graham used his educa-tional lectures to describe the relationship between religious revivalism and popular civic engagement. But he also used them to restrict rights to white men. Hodge was less likely than Graham to translate his unease with aboli-tionism into proslavery discourse. But his critique of the abolitionist use of the Bible has made historians less likely to note what in actuality underlay a more ambiguous account of gradual emancipation (as opposed to immedi-ate abolition).[46]

45. [Charles Hodge,] review of *Slavery,* by William Ellery Channing (Boston, 1845), *Bibli-cal Repertory and Theological Review,* VIII (1836), 279; [Hodge], review essay on abolitionism, *Biblical Repertory and Princeton Review ...,* XVI (1844), 546–547. On Hodge's critique of abo-litionism, see Moorhead, *Princeton Seminary in American Religion and Culture,* 157–161; Bratt, "America," *Blackwell Companion to Nineteenth-Century Theology,* 324.

46. For the assessment of Graham, see Archibald Alexander, "Address before the Alumni

On the eve of the Civil War, some of the late Witherspoon's family had spread to the American South. Many had become Confederates. A number of his former students worked in educational institutions that tacitly or explicitly supported the continuation of slavery. From his Princeton vantage point, Hodge opposed the paternalistic ideology of southern slaveholders using the same reasoning that he had once employed against northern abolitionists. In his view, paternalism privileged the ethical sensibility of slaveholders, just as abolitionists had delineated the superiority of their own moral capacity. He focused on the role of independent churches and voluntary societies in spearheading the gradual contraction of slavery as an institution. Moral judgments of civic procedure, according to Hodge, belonged to local church courts. Eventually, in his opinion, they would link the amelioration of slavery to its gradual eradication. Ultimately, like many in the northern states, Hodge justified the Civil War as a means to maintain the union of the United States.[47]

Association of Washington College," *Washington and Lee Historical Papers,* II (1890), 131, cited in Come, "The Influence of Princeton," *WMQ,* 3d Ser., II (1945), 370. For William Graham's proslavery reasoning, see Graham, "Lecture 30th: An Important Question Answered, 1796," in Jeffrey Robert Young, ed., *Proslavery and Sectional Thought in the Early South, 1740–1829: An Anthology* (Columbia, S.C., 2006), 168–169; Calhoon, "Ordered Liberty in the Southern Backcountry," *Journal of Backcountry Studies,* I, no. 2 (Fall 2006), 12; Douglas Ambrose, "Of Stations and Relations: Proslavery Christianity in Early National Virginia," in John R. McKivigan and Mitchell Snay, eds., *Religion and the Antebellum Debate over Slavery* (Athens, Ga., 1998), 47–48; David W. Robson, "'An Important Question Answered': William Graham's Defence of Slavery in Post-Revolutionary Virginia," *WMQ,* 3d Ser., XXXVII (1980), 644–652. According to Mark A. Noll, in "a series of learned works," Hodge "conceded the biblical grounding for slavery as an institution but argued that a proper understanding of Scripture, as well as a right judgment on American circumstances, should move toward the amelioration of slavery and then its effacement." See Noll, *America's God,* 414–415.

47. On Hodge's critique of southern justifications for slavery, which were congruent philosophically with his earlier criticisms of abolitionism, see Allen C. Guelzo, "Charles Hodge's Antislavery Moment," in John W. Stewart and James H. Moorhead, eds., *Charles Hodge Revisited: A Critical Appraisal of His Life and Work* (Grand Rapids, Mich., 2002), 299–326; Bratt, "America," *Blackwell Companion to Nineteenth-Century Theology,* 324. Paternalism suggested that white slaveholders somehow retained a common moral sensibility, enabling their protection of slave welfare. This argument, of course, had been used by Thomas Jefferson, who often committed himself to the moral sensory reasoning of Francis Hutcheson while presiding over his Monticello plantation. See Charles L. Griswold, "Rights and Wrongs: Jefferson, Slavery, and Philosophical Quandries," in Michael J. Lacey and Knud Haakonssen, eds., *A Culture of Rights: The Bill of Rights in Philosophy, Politics, and Law—1791 and 1991* (Cambridge, 1991), 179 n. 88. On the spread of Witherspoon's family into the American South during the antebellum era, including his son David, see Joseph Bailey Witherspoon, *The History and Genealogy*

Despite sharing ironic similarities in their philosophical critiques, the sectional crisis over slavery divided Hodge from James Henley Thornwell, the South Carolina college professor who would help to found the Presbyterian Columbia Theological Seminary (1812-1862). Witherspoon had once justified his emerging support for disestablishment by suggesting that churches, voluntary organizations, and colleges could encourage the moral conversion of citizens. Thornwell, however, became suspicious of independent moral institutions and pressure groups in antebellum America. He criticized their assumption of general ethical benevolence without attending to the regeneration of their members.[48]

Thornwell's critique was not dissimilar to that which had motivated Hodge to question the ideologies of abolitionism and southern paternalism. Like many dissenting Protestants during the final stages of the sectional crisis, they were blinded to that which, in religious philosophy, they might have shared in common. Hodge often stressed the importance of an unmediated salvation experience, the necessity of moral conversion, and the primacy of the Westminster Confession of Faith. But, as a minister who was born and raised in the plantation South, Thornwell could not see past Hodge's civic context. He focused intensely on those instances where Hodge used common sensory or Baconian terminology. He assumed that Hodge was an advocate of moral innateness and that he placed too much trust in church boards that were constituted by fallible humans. He accused the Princeton minister of theological mistakes that Hodge had ironically once used as evidence in his critique of abolitionism.[49]

After 1860, the Southern Presbyterian Church duly splintered from its nationwide denomination—a confessional union whose constitution Witherspoon had once helped to write. Thornwell and his Southern Presbyterian colleagues gave their official blessing to the Confederate cause. As war broke out, Americans of differing denominations began to slaughter one another.

———
of the Witherspoon Family (1400–1972) (Fort Worth, Tex., 1973), 18–109. On former College of New Jersey students in southern educational institutions that profited from slavery, see Craig Steven Wilder, *Ebony and Ivy: Race, Slavery, and the Troubled History of America's Universities* (New York, 2013), 118–110.

48. James Oscar Farmer, *The Metaphysical Confederacy: James Henley Thornwell and the Synthesis of Southern Values* (Mercer, Ga., 1986), 92, 127–130, 186, 266, 275; Bratt, "America," *Blackwell Companion to Nineteenth-Century Theology,* 325.

49. On the growing division between the two figures and Thornwell's accusation that Hodge had eschewed the spiritual dimension of the church in favor of a human-centered account of its role in civic affairs, including slavery, see Longfield, *Presbyterians and American Culture,* 103–104.

Fire burned on the horizon of Southern frontiers. The steeples of Presbyterian churches and colleges were often silhouetted against the smoke. Many had been founded and erected by Witherspoon's former students, each of whom had graduated during the infancy of the United States.[50]

Through the tumult of the Civil War, Hodge and several other ministers in Princeton Theological Seminary looked back on the history of Presbyterian piety in the College of New Jersey. Naturally, they turned to Witherspoon. In 1863, responding to New School Presbyterians who tried to claim Witherspoon as a moderate, Lyman Atwater wrote a long treatise for the *Biblical Repertory and Princeton Review*. He suggested that Witherspoon had promoted clear evangelical edicts, outlining the subjective morality of all unregenerate men and the immediate requirement of saving grace. Witherspoon, according to Atwater, defined the "universal corruption and degradation of our race, inasmuch as it is the penalty and effect of Adam's first sin." As the essay began to circulate, the infrastructure of many American states lay in ruins, just as the buildings of the College of New Jersey had once crumbled and burned following the Battle of Princeton.[51]

50. On the final decision of the Southern Presbyterian Church to secede, see Noll, *America's God*, 399–400, 420–421.

51. [Lyman Atwater], "Witherspoon's Theology," *Biblical Repertory and Princeton Review*, XXV (1863), 596–610 (esp. 598). On the disputed legacy of Witherspoon in this affair, see Noll, *America's God*, 125.

CONCLUSION

"Unrelenting Rage"

From the 1760s, the developing provincial autonomies of colonial America diverged from metropolitan constitutional ideology in Westminster. Colonists were predisposed to conflict with the King-in-Parliament and the King-in-Council because their pluralistic legal customs did not conform to the incorporating system of British governance, which increasingly defined the indivisibility of sovereignty in the imperial realm. Historians of religion have assimilated the legacy of Puritan and post-Puritan piety into such a narrative of constitutional cross-purposes. They have distinguished between the customary religious autonomy of New England Congregationalism and the incorporating nature of British unionism during the imperial crisis, which threatened to curtail the independence of Congregational institutions through the promotion of established Anglican interests. Acknowledging the importance of Presbyterian critiques of centralizing authority, which were rooted in the ambiguous context of British imperial jurisdiction during the first half of the eighteenth century, broadens the confessional dimension of such an analysis.[1]

1. See the incorporating system enshrined in William Blackstone's midcentury vision of "indivisible sovereignty" and its analysis in Jack P. Greene, *Negotiated Authorities: Essays in Colonial Political and Constitutional History* (Charlottesville, Va., 1994); and Greene, *The Constitutional Origins of the American Revolution* (Cambridge, 2011), 30–42. On New England Congregationalism and imperial unionism, see Philip Goff, "Revivals and Revolution: Historiographic Turns since Alan Heimert's *Religion and the American Mind*," *Church History*, LXVII (1998), 695–672; James H. Hutson, *Religion and the Founding of the American Republic* (Washington, D.C., 1998), 3–49, 53–54; John G. West, Jr., *The Politics of Revelation and Reason: Religion and Civic Life in the New Nation* (Lawrence, Kans., 1996), 1–11; Patricia U. Bonomi, *Under the Cope of Heaven: Religion, Society, and Politics in Colonial America* (New York, 1986), 187–209; Gordon S. Wood, *The Creation of the American Republic, 1776–1787* (Chapel Hill, N.C., 1969), 114–118. On the important role of the "Glorious Revolution" in developing American conceptions of "natural rights"—including freedom for dissenting Protestantism—see Richard S. Dunn, "The Glorious Revolution and America," in Nicolas Canny, ed., *The Oxford History of the British Empire*, I, *The Origins of Empire: British Overseas Enterprise to the Close of the Seventeenth Century* (Oxford, 1998), 445–466, esp. 446; Greene, *Negotiated Authorities*, 78–92; David S. Lovejoy, *The Glorious Revolution in America* (New York, 1972); Lee Ward, *The Politics of Liberty in England and Revolutionary America* (Cambridge, 2004).

During the 1640s, the Scottish Presbyterian authors of the Westminster Confession of Faith allied with English dissenters in order to reform the Stuart line. When Edinburgh lost its independent Parliament following the 1707 Act of Union, the Kirk retained its institutional autonomy in Britain. By the 1740s, Popular party ministers recalled the 1643 Solemn League and Covenant and found a model for their incorporation into Britain under a Hanoverian crown with their confessional independence intact. As they traded, preached, and settled across the provincial boundaries of the British Atlantic world, evangelical Presbyterians perceived their freedom to define the universal importance of salvation through grace. They promoted what they understood to be the revivalist doctrines of the Westminster Confession. Their right to do so, they believed, was unaffected by the federal prerogative of the new British Parliament and also applied in the North American colonies. Thus, the standards of Presbyterian revivalism became less nationally oriented than Samuel Rutherford might have anticipated during the 1640s, when he drafted his Confession to secure the religious ideals of the Scottish Reformation in negotiation with English dissenting Protestants.[2]

Like mainland evangelical Scots, many American Presbyterians perceived the distance between center and periphery in the British Empire as a positive aspect of their constitutional experience. Revivalist communities in New Jersey, Pennsylvania, New York, and even in the southern colonies believed that distance from Westminster underlay their local religious autonomy. The Kirk's autonomous incorporation into the British Empire offered them a visible model of jurisdictional pluralism. They thus cherished the independence of their religious and educational institutions — including the College of New Jersey, where John Witherspoon came to reside.

Yet, on both sides of the Atlantic, evangelical Presbyterians were also alert to constraints on their provincial freedoms, whether from members of their own denomination, rival confessional communities, or imperial establishments. The varying contexts for Presbyterian dissension in the British Atlantic world eventually influenced Witherspoon's contribution to the ideology

2. The Hanoverian line seemed to guarantee Presbyterian religious freedoms alongside other institutional autonomies (such as trade guilds, educational foundations, and local legal statutes). See Colin Kidd, "Conditional Britons: The Scots Covenanting Tradition and the Eighteenth-Century British State," *English Historical Review,* CXVII (2002), 1147–1176; Richard J. Finlay, "Keeping the Covenant: Scottish National Identity," in T. M. Devine and J. R. Young, eds., *Eighteenth Century Scotland: New Perspectives* (East Lothian, U.K., 1999), 121–133; David Allan, "Protestantism, Presbyterianism, and National Identity in Eighteenth-Century Scottish History," in Tony Claydon and Ian McBride, eds., *Protestantism and National Identity: Britain and Ireland, c. 1650–c. 1850* (Cambridge, 1998), 182–205.

of the American founding. Before his arrival in New Jersey, Witherspoon had accused Moderate Presbyterians of colluding with British parliamentary placemen in order to guarantee their personal interests. Noting a problematic relationship between ecclesiology, Enlightenment philosophy, and political patronage, he accused Moderate churchmen and professors of using political connections to buttress what he claimed were unorthodox Presbyterian ideas. He reproached them for ignoring the impetus to promote religious revivalism in the British Atlantic world, thereby squandering the autonomy of the Kirk.

During the same period, colonial American Presbyterians addressed protests toward royal governors, proprietary rulers, Anglican ministers, or even members of their own synod, provided any of the above could be accused of supporting measures to curtail local religious powers. Through the 1740s, the College of New Jersey founder Jonathan Dickinson found himself in conflict with the Old Side Presbyterian establishment in the Philadelphia Synod. Aaron Burr, College of New Jersey president from 1748 to 1757, engaged in continual confrontations with well-to-do New Jersey Anglicans, East Jersey Anglican proprietors, and a series of royal governors. He defended the specific reference to Presbyterian identity in the College of New Jersey charter. Samuel Davies, college president from 1759 to 1761, spent much of his earlier career founding revivalist Presbyterian academies and churches in Virginia and was often in conflict with local Anglican statutes and established authorities. Samuel Finley, college president from 1761 to 1766, suffered under Connecticut's restrictions on foreign ministers who preached without the consent of their local Congregational hosts. Witherspoon, using similar language and motifs in his most famous American Revolutionary sermon, criticized Westminster for developing a new stranglehold over provincial autonomy, both commercial and religious. He warned that, if "we yield up our temporal property, we at the same time deliver the conscience into bondage." Like many Presbyterians in America, he reincorporated critical language from earlier constitutional tussles. In Scotland, moreover, his former Popular party associates found it difficult to resist identifying the American struggle with their own stand against patronage, which he had once spearheaded.[3]

---

3. John Witherspoon, *The Dominion of Providence over the Passions of Men* . . . , in [Ashbel Green, ed.], *The Works of the Rev. John Witherspoon, D.D.L.L.D. Late President of the College at Princeton, New-Jersey* . . . , 2d ed., rev., 4 vols. (Philadelphia, 1802), III, 37. For the various struggles of Witherspoon's Presbyterian predecessors in New Jersey, see Alison B. Olson, "The Founding of Princeton University: Religion and Politics in Eighteenth-Century New Jersey," *New Jersey History*, LXXXVII (1969), 133–150; David C. Humphrey, "The Struggle for Sectar-

Samuel Adams, a descendent of New England Congregationalists, invoked the 1643 Solemn League and Covenant in order to define the unity of American radicalism against the British King-in-Parliament. During the period that he composed his *Dominion of Providence* sermon, Witherspoon joined Adams and other patriots in conceding that George III was inseparable from the corruption of the Westminster establishment. According to the Reverend Jonathan Odell, Witherspoon's Anglican loyalist opponent, "Princeton receiv'd" the Presbyterian clergyman,

> bright amidst his flaws,
> And saw him labour in the good old cause;
> Saw him promote the meritorious work,
> The hate of Kings, and glory of the Kirk.

But there had been nothing inevitable about the association between Presbyterian evangelicalism and antimonarchical identity. After all, in 1746 Witherspoon had led a militia against Jacobites in support of a Protestant kingdom. In 1775, even as an American patriot, he had questioned "insolent abuse of his majesty's person." Only a year before he signed the Declaration of Independence, Witherspoon opposed specific corruptions in Anglo-Scottish constitutionalism while remaining loyal to the British crown. He had believed that the Hanoverian line guaranteed important principles of provincial freedom in the British Empire, commercial, legal, and, above all, religious.[4]

The outward-looking nature of Scottish evangelicalism during the Hanoverian era makes it easier to understand the ease with which Witherspoon addressed Scottish Presbyterians specifically while also appealing to the broader Protestant coalition of the American Revolution. Witherspoon had attached an *Address to the Natives of Scotland Residing in America* to his

-----

ian Control of Princeton, 1745–1760," ibid., XCI (1973), 77–90; John E. Pomfret, *Colonial New Jersey: A History* (New York, 1973), 158–159, 161–163; and Nicholas Murray, *Notes, Historical and Biographical, concerning Elizabeth-town, Its Eminent Men, Churches, and Ministers* (1844; rpt. New York, 1941), 1–12; George William Pilcher, *Samuel Davies: Apostle of Dissent in Colonial Virginia* (Knoxville, Tenn., 1971), 159–169; Samuel Davies, *The State of Religion among the Protestant Dissenters in Virginia . . .* (Boston, 1751), 19, 41–42; See Edwin Scott Gaustad, *The Great Awakening in New England* (New York, 1957), 74–75, 123. On reactions in Scotland, see John R. McIntosh, *Church and Theology in Enlightenment Scotland: The Popular Party, 1740–1800* (East Lothian, U.K., 1998), 117–118, 128–131, 158–160.

4. Camillo Querno [Jonathan Odell], *The American Times: A Satire in Three Parts in Which Are Delineated the Characters of the Leaders of the American Rebellion* (London, 1780), 17–19;

John Witherspoon, "Thoughts on American Liberty," in [Green, ed.], *Works of Witherspoon,* IV, 298–300.

most famous Revolutionary sermon, the *Dominion of Providence*, in which he claimed that there were "few surer marks of the reality of religion, than when a man feels himself more joined in spirit to a true holy person of a different denomination." He suggested that American independence would ultimately benefit the religious and commercial interests of mainland Britain as well as America to "the advantage of both." He educated future statesmen at an institution that had been founded by evangelical Presbyterians, many of whom were descended from Scotland. Yet, as the only clergyman to sign the Declaration of Independence and as an author of religious proclamations on behalf of the new American union, Witherspoon also addressed patriots from differing Protestant denominations.[5]

The ecumenical aspect in Witherspoon's political theology reflected an earlier period of transatlantic revivalism. Whether they resided in New England, New Jersey, or Scotland, many ministers extended their theological identity beyond their particular provinces in the British Empire, even while they cherished specific religious values that had developed in their own realms. Jonathan Dickinson moved from New England to New Jersey and from Congregationalism to Presbyterianism between 1710 and 1740. He looked outward to dissenting academies in Europe yet also supported Presbyterian institutional concerns closer to home. Jonathan Edwards warned of prevailing associations between inner morality and the notion of an external public covenant. During the late 1740s, he endeavored to create a concert of prayer between different dominions and denominations in the British Empire, attending to his Congregational ministry while also maintaining alliances with evangelical Presbyterians. Witherspoon delivered Scottish sermons in which he lauded piety in New England as well as the Presbyterianism of the Middle Colonies. All three men came to be associated with the formative years of the College of New Jersey.

It has been suggested that British Protestant unity developed when imperial subjects faced external Catholic powers from the 1740s to the 1760s. Yet Dickinson, Edwards, and Witherspoon formed evangelical alliances following tensions with Moderate or Old Side members of their own denominations. There were certainly important theological dimensions in their

5. Witherspoon, *Dominion of Providence*, in [Green, ed.], *Works of Witherspoon*, III, 34; John Witherspoon, "On the Contest between Great-Britain and America" (Sept. 3, 1778), ibid., IV, 376; Richard D. Brown, *Revolutionary Politics in Massachusetts: The Boston Committee of Correspondence and the Towns, 1772–1774* (Cambridge, Mass., 1970), 185, 191, 198; J. C. D. Clark, *The Language of Liberty, 1660–1832: Political Discourse and Social Dynamics in the Anglo-American World* (Cambridge, 1994), 329–331.

ecumenical desire for a communion of regenerated souls. More prosaically, however, cooperation between evangelical Presbyterians and Congregationalists was partially motivated by the similar nature of discord in their respective communities. Britain's battle with France did not prevent Witherspoon from censuring Protestants within his own community. Nor did it stop Edwards from questioning Congregational thinkers in his own sphere. Through the Revolutionary era, similarly, Witherspoon's opposition to Britain did not inhibit him from reproaching fellow Americans for privileging their innate ethical capability over the capacities of imperial forces.[6]

Those who distinguished their innate ethical stance from British subjects risked eschewing the continuing importance of conversion. Witherspoon was wary that ostensible Protestant unity against British corruption risked masking the varying state of regeneration among Americans. This aspect of his political theology had been honed in constitutional and confessional conflicts with fellow Protestants when he had opposed the tendency to associate Anglo-Scottish unionism with the societal development of innate ethical sensibilities. Americans, Witherspoon suggested, did not enjoy a more cultivated ethical stance, nor any special covenant with God. Rather, providentially, the imperial crisis channeled common human corruption into a political standoff. Such an impasse, according to Witherspoon, necessarily required American independence. In allowing the formation of a new American union, God supplied British subjects with a necessary shock, which might then facilitate their greater awareness of sin and their heightened propensity for repentance. But the chaos of the Revolutionary war, Witherspoon reminded patriots, should also remind them of their own fallibility as men and their own continuing need for salvation through grace. If a significant proportion of Americans remained predisposed to follow the action of the Holy Spirit with full conversion, allowing greater ethical humility as an external gift of grace, they would maintain the stability of their inchoate union. Though deserving political autonomy, Witherspoon believed, Americans required the same humility as all other people, including the British. They were no less in need of salvation, no less influenced by passions in the process of regeneration.

Ironically, Scottish moral philosophy supplied Witherspoon with a means to describe the role of emotions in the experience of faith and conversion and to pronounce the state of sensory awareness that followed regeneration.

6. Linda Colley, *Britons: Forging the Nation, 1707–1837* (New Haven, Conn., 1992), 1–43. For a discussion of the potential unity between moderate and evangelical Protestants in colonial British America during the Anglo-French wars, see Mark A. Noll, *America's God: From Jonathan Edwards to Abraham Lincoln* (New York, 2002), 80–82.

He often adopted its language and motifs in order to question one of its central tenets: the existence of innate ethical sensibility. In some of his lectures, Witherspoon undoubtedly simplified and paraphrased the latest arguments proposed by philosophers such as Thomas Reid on the empirical reality of external objects. Skeptics suggested that neither biblical events nor contemporary displays of salvation could be commonly witnessed. Witherspoon used simple common sense epistemology to refute such a claim. He was most often concerned to verify the simple relationship between the mind and external physical phenomena (such as the outward signs of a conversion experience) rather than any innate ability to judge the qualitative nature of ethical interactions. In his 1776 *Dominion of Providence*, Witherspoon recommended "cool and candid attention" to the events of the imperial crisis. But their common observance, he concluded, only raised awareness of "the ravages" of human power in the unregenerate state—a fact that "ought to humble us in the dust." To be sure, Witherspoon often implied that a greater number of Americans had become awakened to the necessity of conversion and that their new union would persist more cohesively as a result. Yet he warned that the desire for personal salvation should precede any aspiration for national stability. Even when citizens demonstrated their ostensible humility, moreover, an unsettling doubt in the truth of their regeneration would always remain.

The civic importance of conversion underlay Witherspoon's emerging understanding of the role of disestablishment during the 1780s. He contributed to what historians have begun to describe as an implicit bargain between government and religion. In exchange for the institutional independence of Presbyterian institutions, he saw the need to inculcate social discipline and moral virtue among those who might assume positions of political representation. Witherspoon desired moral leadership on the state and national level. He also feared a monopoly of civil power from any one religious group. It was always a delicate task to encourage pious governance without promoting the civil establishment of religion. After all, he negotiated on behalf of disestablished religious institutions while also a political representative in civic assemblies.[7]

7. Robert M. Calhoon, "Religion, Moderation, and Regime-Building in Post-Revolutionary America," in Eliga H. Gould and Peter S. Onuf, eds., *Empire and Nation: The American Revolution in the Atlantic World* (Baltimore, 2005), 218; Marc W. Kruman, *Between Authority and Liberty: State Constitution Making in Revolutionary America* (Chapel Hill, N.C., 1997), 45–46; Thomas J. Curry, *The First Freedoms: Church and State in America to the Passage of the First Amendment* (New York, 1986), 218–222. For a critique of this interpretation, see Frank Lambert, *The Founding Fathers and the Place of Religion in America* (Princeton, N.J., 2003), 246–253.

As Witherspoon's student James Madison made his way in Virginia politics during the 1780s, the struggle over the political assessment of religion in Presbyterian circles influenced his developing constitutional thinking. His emerging argument for disestablishment recommended that independent religious institutions encourage the moral regeneration of future political leaders. In his *Memorial and Remonstrance,* he devolved moral power to individuals and their independent societies, hoping to provide the new nation with more ethical civic leaders. Early in his career, at least, he suggested that the religious conversion of individuals would facilitate greater civic coherence. Like his mentor, he questioned the viability of political systems that relied on the innate ethical sensibility of their constituents. Even during the 1780s, Witherspoon had highlighted the bleak context for the formation of the United States: the disintegration of a familial empire in death and war. Witherspoon's former student, now a legislator, reminded himself that men were unlikely to be angels, whether or not they had supported the cause of American independence.

When Madison eventually articulated his vision of federalism at the Constitutional Convention in 1787, he realized that national representatives would originate from different states, each with varying confessional contexts. Not all were likely to supply civic leaders with sufficient humility to grapple with their naturally selfish desires, as Witherspoon's thanksgiving sermons had once hoped. Notwithstanding the retention of his personal faith, therefore, Madison was required to incorporate many different representatives in government, irrespective of their exact state of regeneration. Thus, he sought to balance faction against faction, subjective interest against subjective interest. His greater realism did not deny the role of factionalism—even moral discrepancy—in human association. In this respect, at least, he did not contradict the Calvinistic emphasis of his earlier learning. He would construct a national constitution with the human propensity for factionalism, egoism, and disorder at the forefront of his mind.

Madison hoped that factional competition would become multifaceted and complex so that the desires of any particular interest group would be balanced and neutralized by other competing actors. Yet sectional arguments required a constitutional compromise that denied the full humanity of enslaved people, each of whom were defined as three-fifths of one person, thereby imbuing political representation with a specific factional cause. Seventy years later, with an absence of sound political leadership in many spheres, Americans went to war again. As James Henley Thornwell, Charles Hodge, and other Presbyterian leaders debated whether Witherspoon's legacy could be claimed as moderate or evangelical, their inchoate continental empire threatened to disintegrate less than a century after the American Revolution. To use Witherspoon's earlier words in the *Dominion of Providence over the Passions of Men,* they watched as men butchered one another with unrelenting rage and gloried in the deed—seeming, again, to mock the idea of a commonly benevolent moral sensibility.[8]

8. Witherspoon, *Dominion of Providence,* in [Green, ed.], *Works of Witherspoon,* III, 37. On Madison and the Three-Fifths Compromise, see Jeff Broadwater, *James Madison: A Son of Virginia and a Founder of the Nation* (Chapel Hill, N.C., 2012), 190, 200.

INDEX

❦

Page numbers in italic refer to illustrations.

Index